joseph lowery & eric ott

macromedia®

Dreamweaver®
MX 2004
web Application
Recipes

asp javascript
asp vb script
coldfusion
php

CODE BY

800 E. 96th Street Indianapolis, IN 46240
An imprint of Pearson Education
Boston • Indianapolis • London • Munich • New York • San Francisco

Macromedia Dreamweaver MX 2004 Web Application Recipes

International Standard Book Number: 0-7357-1320-0

Library of Congress Catalog Card Number: 2002111050

Printed in the United States of America

First edition: November 2003

07 06 05 04   7 6 5 4 3 2

Interpretation of the printing code: The rightmost double-digit number is the year of the book's printing; the rightmost single-digit number is the number of the book's printing. For example, the printing code 04-1 shows that the first printing of the book occurred in 2004.

Trademarks

Warning and Disclaimer

Publisher
Stephanie Wall

Production Manager
Gina Kanouse

Senior Acquisitions Editor
Linda Anne Bump

Senior Development Editor
Jennifer Eberhardt

Senior Project Editor
Lori Lyons

Copy Editors
Karen Gill
Ben Lawson
Amy Lepore

Indexer
Lisa Stumpf

Proofreader
Linda Seifert

Composition
Gloria Schurick

Manufacturing Coordinator
Dan Uhrig

Interior and Cover Designer
Alan Clements

Media Developer
Jay Payne

Marketing
Scott Cowlin
Tammy Detrich
Hannah Onstad Latham

Publicity Manager
Susan Nixon

To my good friend Massimo Foti, whose inspiration combines the sweetness of Swiss chocolate with the crusty exterior of a loaf of good Italian bread.

—Joseph Lowery

For my wife, Monique—thanks for your vision, expression, and strength.

—Eric Ott

Contents at a Glance

Table of Contents

About the Authors

Joseph Lowery's books on the Web and Web-building tools are international bestsellers, having sold more than 300,000 copies worldwide in 9 different languages. He is the author of *Beyond Dreamweaver* (New Riders) and *From FrontPage to Dreamweaver* (Que) as well as the *Dreamweaver MX 2004 Bible* and the *Fireworks MX Bible* series (Wiley). He also co-authored the *Dreamweaver MX Killer Tips* series (New Riders) with Angela Buraglia. As a programmer, Joseph contributed two extensions to the latest release of Fireworks and has many, many extensions available for Dreamweaver. He is also a consultant and trainer and has presented at Seybold in both Boston and San Francisco, Macromedia conferences in the U.S. and Europe, ThunderLizard's Web World, and Fawcette Publication's WebBuilder. As a partner in Deva Associates, Ltd., Joseph developed the Deva Tools for the Dreamweaver set of navigational extensions. With Edoardo Zubler, Joseph created FlashBang!, Flash navigation for Dreamweaver users.

Eric Ott has more than 10 years of experience as a pioneer in the Web industry. His position at Macromedia as the product manager for Dreamweaver enabled him to define the direction of this highly regarded Web-development platform from its early days. His knowledge and experience in Web design and development have given him strong insight into ways to achieve success on the Web. Eric is currently the President at WebAssist.

About WebAssist

What is your Dream? Code Less. Play More.

You've got a life. Who wants to spend it behind a computer? WebAssist products give you all the functionality, flexibility, and good looks you dream of from Macromedia Dreamweaver tools—without the hassle.

WebAssist.com Corporation is the leading provider of extensions (software add-ons) for Macromedia MX. These products transform complex tasks and coding requirements into a powerful and easy-to-use visual process—proven to save time, effort, and money. WebAssist also offers a complete set of expertise-via-professional services. Dreamweaver integration (extension creation) enables native support for third-party technology and allows businesses to reach a new and expanding market. Custom Web application development combines years of experience with an established methodology to deliver robust, dynamic solutions. WebAssist.com hosts a self-service developer community with more than 100,000 members registered. WebAssist's partners include Macromedia, PayPal, PayDirect, YAHOO!, WorldPay, Interwoven, and Vitria.

About the Technical Reviewers

These reviewers contributed their considerable hands-on expertise to the entire development process for *Macromedia Dreamweaver MX 2004 Web Application Recipes*. As the book was being written, these dedicated professionals provided code suggestions and reviewed all the material for technical content, organization, and flow. Their feedback was critical to ensuring that *Macromedia Dreamweaver MX 2004 Web Application Recipes* fits our reader's need for the highest-quality technical information.

Matt Brown is a consultant based in the Bay Area. He has edited more than 20 Dreamweaver and Photoshop books over the years. He has taught at Foothill College and in the Multimedia Studies Program at San Francisco State University. He was on the Dreamweaver team for 5 years in a number of capacities, finally as Community Manager. Matt is married to a magnificent woman, Marcella, keeps chickens, loves to cook, and creates all sorts of art.

Gareth Downes-Powell is a partner in Buzz inet (http://www.buzzinet.co.uk), an Internet company specializing in Web design and hosting, and a member of Team Macromedia Dreamweaver. He has written a number of PHP books for various publishers and worked as a technical editor on many more. Gareth regularly writes for a number of Web sites, including DMX Zone at http://www.dmxzone.com/.

Massimo Foti began using Dreamweaver on the very day the first beta was available, and he has used it ever since. Massimo has been a prolific extension developer since the pioneering days of Dreamweaver 1. He is the creator of www.massimocorner.com and is a winner of the Macromedia Best Extension Developer award. His extensions are featured on the Macromedia Exchange for Dreamweaver and have been included in many books and magazines. Massimo works at www.amila.ch developing database-driven Web sites using ColdFusion, PHP, and different kinds of databases.

Nancy Gill is an eight-year veteran to Web development and the owner of Web Wish Productions in Central California. She is currently serving her 4th term as a Team Macromedia Volunteer for Dreamweaver MX. She has served as technical editor and reviewer for many Dreamweaver MX and Contribute books and most recently, co-authored her first book, *Dreamweaver MX: Instant Troubleshooter*. She has also written articles for the Macromedia Web site.

Tim Green is an author, a full-time IT Consultant, eBusiness/B2B Advisor, and CEO of The Rawveg Consultancy (www.rawveg.org). Beginning his working life as a COBOL and Assembly Language programmer, he moved into Web application development in 1996, after dabbling in numerous other careers, from acting to being a chef. A contributing developer to PHAkT, an implementation of PHP for UltraDev 4, Tim now concentrates on the development of PHP utilities for Dreamweaver MX, and has released a shopping cart management system, IntelliCART MX, to critical acclaim. He has also been a contributing author to a number of sites, books, and magazines, including *Dreamweaver MX: PHP Web Development* (Wrox), and has given public demonstrations and lectures at Macromedia events in Europe.

Sean R. Nicholson is the network administrator and Web developer for the Career Services Center at the University of Missouri, Kansas City. He and his development teams architect, develop, and manage foundation and backend execution for programs such as the CareerExec Employment Database (careerexec), UMKC Career Services Website (career.umkc), and UMKC's Virtual Career Fair (umkc/virtualfair). Sean also does private contract work and consulting on database and Web development with organizations and individuals. Sean's technical publications include *Inside UltraDev 4*, *Discover Excel 97*, and *Teach Yourself Outlook 98 in 24 Hours*, and he has written several legal articles ranging in topics from Canadian water rights to the protection of historic artifacts lost at sea.

Acknowledgments

Thanks to my fellow team members, Eric Ott and Ray Bourdin, for bringing this dream a long, arduous way to reality. It's been a high-energy project right from the very beginning. I'm grateful that I had two partners who, simultaneously, stoked the engine and hung on for dear life, all the way to the end.

I owe a special thank you to Tim Green, who took on the Herculean task of translating our existing recipes for PHP.

We've been unbelievably blessed to have a full slate of technical editors—Massimo Foti, Sean Nicholson, Gareth Downes-Powell, Matt Brown, and Nancy Gill—who have gone beyond the call of duty time and again to help shape this project. Thanks to Monique for helping to manage such an unwieldy beast and to Julie Ott for giving it such a pretty face.

I really appreciate all the hard work put in by everyone at New Riders: David, Chris, Linda, Jennifer, Lisa, Alan, Lori, Gloria, and all the others. Thanks again to my agent, Laura Belt, for watching out for me.

One last special thanks to Debra and Margot, who had the good grace to give me a little breathing room during the day and fill my nights with tales of fencing, digital video, and the mysteries and joys of repatterning.

—Joseph Lowery

Joseph Lowery, the team's expert author, spearheaded the effort. He transformed our computer files and code snippets into a book you can hold in your hands. Ray Borduin, VP of Technology at WebAssist, spent countless hours developing the recipe source code for the book. Julie Ott, my sister, volunteered her creative talent to produce the Web designs included with this book. And our team of tech editors provided great support and critical feedback.

I really appreciate the vision and support of New Riders for bringing this product to market. David Dwyer, Chris Nelson, and Linda Bump helped provide the operational direction needed to produce this book. The community of developers appreciates the platform provided by New Riders to share our knowledge and war stories.

Some of the recipes and techniques in this book are based on work and direction outside the core team. Thanks as well to the following individuals: Hieu Bui, Kurt O'Donnell, Tim Sweeney, Dave Hoffman, Matt Eastling, Tom Gade, Neal Hansch, Sho Kuwamoto, Amit Kishnani, George Comninos, Dave DeVisser, Eric Wittman, Rob Christenson, Joe Marini, Eric Lerner, Matt Lerner, Mike Sundermeyer, Ken Sundermeyer, NJ, Heidi Bauer, and Daniel Taborga.

—Eric Ott

Tell Us What You Think

As the reader of this book, you are the most important critic and commentator. We value your opinion and want to know what we're doing right, what we could do better, what areas you'd like to see us publish in, and any other words of wisdom you're willing to pass our way.

As the Senior Acquisitions Editor for New Riders Publishing, I welcome your comments. You can fax, email, or write me directly to let me know what you did or didn't like about this book—as well as what we can do to make our books stronger. When you write, please be sure to include this book's title, ISBN, and author, as well as your name and phone or fax number. I will carefully review your comments and share them with the author and editors who worked on the book.

Please note that I cannot help you with technical problems related to the topic of this book, and that due to the high volume of email I receive, I might not be able to reply to every message.

Fax: 317-428-3280

Email: linda.bump@newriders.com

Mail: Linda Bump
        Senior Acquisitions Editor
        New Riders Publishing
        800 E. 96th Street, 3rd Floor
        Indianapolis, IN 46240 USA

Introduction

The transition from static Web page designer to data-driven Web application developer is a daunting one. Designers in this position might consider themselves strangers in a strange land. Not only are the natives speaking a different language (or worse, languages), but they also appear to have come from an entirely separate culture. Where in this world, designers ask, do I start?

We created *Macromedia Dreamweaver MX 2004 Web Application Recipes*, in part, to answer just that question. Inside this book, you'll find eight full-featured, professional-grade Web applications explained step-by-step. Best of all, we make it possible for you to build the applications as you learn. This feature serves two goals. First, in our experience, people learn best by doing, and they retain the gained knowledge even longer when they're doing something meaningful.

This brings us to our second goal: providing solutions. Beginning developers often find themselves in a sink-or-swim situation where they need to produce workable Web applications in a relatively short time. The Web applications included in this book are rooted in the real world and are suitable for small- to medium-sized organizations. They're real working applications that you can use today; they're not just make-work tutorials.

Another over-arching purpose of this book is to help you get the most out of Dreamweaver. The latest version of Dreamweaver is a powerful professional Web authoring tool that can create the full range of static and dynamic Web sites. Right out of the box, Dreamweaver gives you the tools to fashion a wide range of Web applications without ever looking at, much less enhancing, the code. However, the point-and-click approach will only take you so far and, sooner than later, you'll need to work on the code level to get the desired results. *Macromedia Dreamweaver MX 2004 Web Application Recipes* is—like Web applications themselves—a blend of design and code, with every step along the way explained so that you understand not just what to do, but why you're doing it.

Web Application Recipes Audience

The ideal reader is one who has been designing Web sites with Dreamweaver for a while and wants to create one of the eight supplied Web applications. However, we realize it is far from an ideal world and, hopefully, we've provided enough tools so that even a Web designer new to Dreamweaver can use the book. Nor is the desire for a specific application paramount. This book is written in such a way as to offer general methods and ways of working as well as specific instructions.

Although the applications have uses in many areas, this book will prove especially useful to those working in intranets and small workgroups. We've structured the example applications so that they are flexible and, in server jargon, scalable. Developers take these applications as they are, and, by changing a logo or two, use them immediately—or they can repurpose and extend the substantial base of code, saving time and resources.

Web Application Recipes Structure

Macromedia Dreamweaver MX 2004 Web Application Recipes is divided into two, purposely unbalanced sections. Upfront, you'll find a primer of sorts that is intended to serve as a general introduction to both the world of data-driven Web technology and Dreamweaver's implementations. Read these chapters if you are new to working with data sources on the Web, and especially if you are new to Dreamweaver. The bulk of the book is devoted to the Web application recipes.

The recipes themselves are separated into two sections, or cuisines, if you'll indulge us in the recipe metaphor. First you'll find instructions on building for intranet-oriented applications, including user login, employee lookup, a conference room scheduler, and an online in/out board. Many of these applications have uses that you can apply to general Web applications. User login, for example, contains authentication routines that you can apply to any portion of the Web where you want to display different content to different groups of users.

The second set of applications is based on workgroup needs. With these applications, you can log billable project hours (Time Cards), create an online opinion-gathering system (Survey Builder), facilitate and archive team communication (Journal), and send a personalized email announcement in bulk (Mail Merge). As with the intranet applications, you can extend the workgroup recipes to fit many situations.

Each recipe is structured in a top-down approach. At the beginning of each chapter are diagrams and ingredient listings to provide an overall view of the project so that you can really understand the concept and what's required before going forward into the actual steps. Web applications are composed of a series of intertwining pages, and each application presented is described page-by-page. Each page, in turn, is built up in a series of steps designed to follow the standard developers' workflow and, in the process, teach best practices.

Macromedia Dreamweaver MX 2004 Web Application Recipes offers every recipe in four variations: ASP-VBScript, ASP-JavaScript, ColdFusion, and PHP. The ColdFusion code is designed and tested to be compatible with ColdFusion 5 as well as ColdFusion MX. Each language is clearly marked with an icon, so there's no confusion among the variations. For steps that should be taken by all server models, a separate icon is used:

📖	Steps for all recipe users
(VB)	For ASP-VBScript
(JS)	For ASP-JavaScript
(CF)	For ColdFusion
(PHP)	For PHP

The code is professional quality and targeted to today's Web. Reflecting the state of the Web, Cascading Style Sheets are used for the basis of the design and integrated with structured tables for a degree of backward compatibility. As designers do, we need to make certain choices, such as deciding only to support Internet Explorer 5 and above and Netscape 6 and above.

Note: Code lines that do not fit within the margins of the printed page are continued on the next line and are preceded by a code continuation character: ➥.

Web Application Recipes Resources

A key companion to this book is the Web site (`webassist.com/recipes`). Far more than just a collection of demo programs and clip art, the Web site offers all the data sources, code, and files necessary to create the applications in the book. Moreover, the code is encapsulated in Dreamweaver snippets that, once installed through the Extension Manager, is immediately available for drag-and-drop coding. The Web site also contains links to some superb extensions from WebAssist to make your application building even smoother. More information and resources are also available on the Web site: You'll find FAQs and general support for helping you realize your goals as a Web application developer.

Web Application Recipes Setup

Dreamweaver MX 2004 Web Application Recipes comes complete with everything you need to build eight multi-page, data-driven applications in four different server languages. All the template pages, data sources, and snippets are included in a single Dreamweaver extension—there's even a dedicated online help system to make sure you get started quickly and easily. Follow these steps to transfer and install the Recipe files:

1. Visit `www.webassist.com/recipes`.

   You'll find a full range of support options at the *Dreamweaver MX 2004 Web Application Recipes* home page, hosted by WebAssist.

2. Click the **Get Recipe Files** button.

   If you're shopping while you're at the WebAssist site, you can also choose the Add to Cart button. When you're ready to complete your transaction, select Checkout from any page.

3. In the next page, enter your name and email address so you can receive your confirmation and serial number.

4. Answer the book-related security question.

   The security question references a particular page and word in the book. You'll need your copy of *Dreamweaver MX 2004 Web Application Recipes* handy to answer the security question properly.

5. Download the Dreamweaver extension file and copy your unique serial number.

6. After the extension has completely downloaded, launch Dreamweaver and select **Commands > Manage Extensions** to open the Macromedia Extension Manager.

7. In the Extension Manager, choose **File > Install Extension** and navigate to the extension file just downloaded and click **Install**.

   The Extension Manager will unpack all the needed files to a common folder and also install two menu items: Copy Snippet and the Web Application Recipes help file. The Copy Snippet command is a free extension that enables you to copy and paste complex SQL, JavaScript, and other snippet code into dialog boxes; this command is accessible from the Snippets panel Options menu.

8. Accept the End User License Agreement to continue the installation.

9. Once completed, quit and relaunch Dreamweaver.

10. In Dreamweaver, select **Help > Web Application Recipes**.

    The Web Application Recipes help file will help you to set up your data sources and transfer files to the desired location. You'll need to enter your unique serial number to access the information.

If you need assistance at any point, check the Help file for support options.

Part I

Starters: Fundamental Elements of Web Applications

Chapter 1
Basic Principles of Data Source Design

Chapter 2
Building Applications in Dreamweaver Workspace

Chapter 1

Basic Principles of Data Source Design

So, you've been building static Web sites for a while now and you've decided to take the plunge into data-driven Web work. Your main question probably is, "Where do I start?" The short answer: here. A slightly longer answer—about 600 pages—follows....

Before you begin crafting dynamic Web sites and adding Developer to your designer credentials, it's best to spend some time learning the fundamentals. Whereas the recipes in this book are all hands-on, build-them-today-and-use-them-tomorrow applications, this chapter—and the one that follows it—is more theoretical. To get the most out of this book, you have to understand both theory and practice.

This initial chapter explains the mechanics behind dynamic sites so that you can begin to see the potential of server-side coding. You'll also find an overview of the various application technologies and the different types of data sources. After you have decided on the application server and the data source to work with, you'll need to know how to connect the two; this information is covered in the section on connections, "Connecting to Data Sources."

The final section in this chapter serves to introduce the Structured Query Language (SQL), which is the underlying language of data source communication and an essential component of data-driven sites. Although Macromedia Dreamweaver's interface allows you to create basic applications without knowing—or even seeing—SQL, a basic awareness of the language will help you to create more sophisticated applications.

How Web Applications Work

The same core functionality of the browser that fed the Web's phenomenal growth across platform and operating systems also proved to be an inherent weakness. After downloading the code for an HTML page and all of its parts, browsers render the page on the client side. Client-side rendering gave a universality to Web browsing at the cost of sacrificing server-side power and connectivity to data sources and other server-related functions, such as email. The rise of application server technology combined the universal access of the client-side browser with the far-ranging power of server-side programming.

All application server technology—whether it's Active Server Pages (ASP), ASP.NET, ColdFusion, PHP: Hypertext Preprocessor (often just called PHP), or JavaServer Pages (JSP)—works essentially the same way [c1-1]:

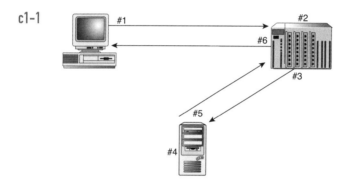

c1-1

1. Someone browsing the Web selects a link. This action sends a request for that particular URL from the server that is hosting the site.
2. When the host server receives the request, if the page has an .htm or .html extension (or other recognized HTML extensions), the page is sent directly to the client.
3. If the page has another file extension—such as .asp or .cfm—the host server forwards the requested page (which is a mix of server-side and HTML code) to the corresponding application server.
4. The application server accepts the page and executes the server-side code, outputting the results as HTML and integrating them into the other code of the page.
5. The page is returned to the host server completely stripped of server-side code and consisting only of HTML.
6. The host server sends the HTML-only page back to the requesting browser.

This process explains why you can never see the server-side source code for an ASP or ColdFusion page you're browsing by simply viewing the source code of the page.

Application Server Technologies Overview

Before we discuss the pros and cons of the various application technologies, let's clarify some terminology. *Application server technology* refers to the overall server-side system for communicating with data sources and other servers, including Web and mail servers. Some examples of application technologies are ASP, ColdFusion, PHP, and JSP. Application server technologies are also referred to as *server models*. An *application server* is a particular piece of software that implements an application server technology; Apache Tomcat, BEA WebLogic, and IBM Websphere are application servers that run JSP.

You can choose from a number of application technologies, but only a few have achieved prominence. In some situations, the choice may have already been made for you if you're working for a client who has an application server in place. Some application server technologies, such as ASP, allow you to write code in more than one language; ASP supports both VBScript and JScript (another name for JavaScript). Because server-side coding is fairly involved, many Web developers specialize in one or two application servers in a specific language.

Dreamweaver offers native support for five server technologies and several language variations: ASP (VBScript and JavaScript), ASP.NET (C# and Visual Basic), ColdFusion, PHP, and JSP.

ASP

ASP is a Microsoft technology supported by a range of Windows systems, including Windows NT, Windows 2000, and Windows XP Professional servers running Internet Information Server/Services (IIS) 4.0 and higher. This application technology is fairly popular partly due to the widespread availability of ASP on development systems through the Personal Web Server (PWS). You'll find PWS capability on Windows 98, Windows NT Workstation, and Windows 2000 Professional. ASP has proven so popular that a non-Microsoft variation is now available from Sun Microsystems; originally called Chili!Soft ASP and now termed Sun ONE Active Server Pages, this application server makes it possible to run ASP pages on Sun Solaris, Linux, HP-UX, and IBM AIX servers.

ASP uses code marked with angle bracket and percent sign combinations, like this:

```
<% Response.Write("Hello World") %>
```

Because the `Response.Write()` function—which outputs whatever is in the parentheses—is so frequently used, you'll also see this shorthand method of coding that uses an equal sign to replace the `Response.Write()` wording:

```
<%= "Hello World" %>
```

As noted earlier, ASP applications can be coded in either VBScript or JavaScript. Although VBScript is more popular, JavaScript is being used increasingly. *Dreamweaver MX 2004 Web Application Recipes* includes code written in both language variations for ASP.

ASP.NET

A fairly recent entry, ASP.NET is the next generation of application server technology from Microsoft. Capable of running on Windows 2000 or Windows XP Professional servers with IIS 5 or later, .NET offers enhanced performance, more robust coding support, and greater scalability over standard ASP.

One major difference between .NET and ASP is that .NET pages are compiled the first time they are executed. The compiled pages are then saved and become available for subsequent client requests. This greatly speeds up server-side processing while reducing the demand on the server. Another key distinction is the number of languages supported; .NET applications can be written in any of more than 25 coding languages, including VB.NET, C#, and JScript.NET.

You can identify ASP.NET pages by their .aspx extension. Although .NET pages—assuming they are using VB.NET—are capable of including ASP `<%...%>` code blocks, the real flexibility and power come from using server controls. A *server control* is an element defined on the server that is called from the application page; server controls use an `<asp:.../>` syntax and contain a `runat="server"` attribute. .NET has replacements for standard HTML form elements, such as text fields:

```
<asp:textbox id="Name" runat="server" />
```

as well as more advanced elements, like a monthly calendar:

```
<asp:Calendar id=Calendar01 onselectionchanged="Date_Selected" runat="server" />
```

Although it looks extremely promising, some developers are maintaining a wait-and-see attitude on .NET; however, it should be noted that Microsoft is no longer working on traditional ASP. For more information on ASP.NET, see `http://asp.net/`.

ColdFusion

ColdFusion lays claim to being both the oldest and the newest of the application technologies covered here. First released by Allaire in 1995, ColdFusion quickly became identified as the easy-to-learn application server because of its HTML-like syntax, known as the ColdFusion Markup Language (CFML). After Macromedia and Allaire merged, ColdFusion underwent a complete restructuring and released a Java-based version, ColdFusion MX, in 2002. ColdFusion pages use either .cfm or .cfml as a filename extension.

The core of ColdFusion is composed of a full complement of proprietary tags, all of which begin with the initials `cf`. For example, to establish a variable, you use the `<cfset>` tag, like this:

```
<cfset greetings="Hello World!">
```

You then output the variable with the `<cfoutput>` tag:

```
<cfoutput>#greetings#</cfoutput>
```

Variables including data source field names are enclosed with the # symbol—variously known as the pound sign, hash mark, or octothorpe. ColdFusion developers can also develop their own custom tags and, with ColdFusion MX, their own Web services with ColdFusion Components. ColdFusion MX—because of the Java foundation—also can incorporate JSP tag libraries and Encapsulated JavaBeans for extended J2EE functionality.

The applications in the Recipes are coded to work with ColdFusion 5 and ColdFusion MX.

PHP

PHP is an open source application technology that is popular on a range of servers, including Apache and IIS.

Other editions of PHP are available for Windows, Linux, Unix, HP-UX, Solaris, and Mac OS X servers. PHP pages have a number of extensions, some of which designate the version of the server; for example `.php`, `.php3`, and `.php4` are all valid filename extensions for PHP applications.

You identify PHP code by using `<?php... ?>` code blocks. In terms of programming, PHP is somewhat of a cross between ASP and C in syntax. For example:

```
<?php echo "Hello World!" ?>
```

A data-driven application engine, PHP is most frequently paired with MySQL, which is an open source database. As a platform-independent and freely available technology, PHP enjoys a widespread user base. For more information on PHP, visit `http://www.php.net/`.

The recipes in this book are designed to work with MySQL and PHP4.

JSP

Developed by Sun Microsystems, JSP is a Java-based technology that compiles server-side scripting and other components such as JavaBeans and servlets. Many application servers are capable of running JSP, including Macromedia JRun, IBM Websphere, BEA WebLogic, and Apache Tomcat.

Because of scalability and robust performance—and its connection to the Java 2 Enterprise Edition (J2EE) protocol—JSP is fairly prominent in the enterprise, as evidenced by the many .jsp pages found on commercial Web sites.

JSP applications use a combination of JSP tags, encapsulated in a `<%... %>` code block similar to ASP, and XML style tags, such as `<jsp:forward page="sales.jsp" />`. Much of the robustness of JSP comes from its ability to work with JavaBeans. After a JavaBean has been created and made available on the server, it is incorporated in the page like this:

```
<jsp:usebean id="hworld" class="com.taglib.wdjsp.fundamentals.HelloWorldBean"/>
```

In addition to working with JavaBeans, JSP developers have access to a library of special customizable functions known collectively as JSP Tag Libraries. You'll find more information about JSP at `http://java.sun.com/products/jsp/`.

Types of Data Sources

Although application servers can do much more than communicate with data sources, that functionality is, by far, most commonly used to create dynamic Web sites. A *data source* is any application or file that stores structured data. It's the structure that's important in a data source; given a known structure, data can be extracted by other applications and processes. Relational databases, XML, spreadsheets, and even text files can serve as data sources.

Most often, however, data-driven Web sites extract their information from the output of a data source application. Data source applications are either *file-based* or *server-based*. File-based data source applica-

You might be more familiar with the term database rather than the more generic term data source. A database is one type of data source.

NOTE

tions, such as Microsoft Access, save their data in computer files that you can copy, transfer, or rename. Server-based data source applications, such as Microsoft SQL Server and MySQL, maintain the data in a dedicated server. Although file-based data sources tend to be easier to develop for, server-based data sources are more robust and better suited for Web work. Some developers work in both worlds by developing in Access and transferring their work to SQL Server through a process called *upsizing*, which is discussed later in this chapter.

Both file-based and server-based data sources use the table as a basic building block. A data source table is composed of a series of rows and columns, much like a spreadsheet. Each column in a table makes up a data source field, and each row is a separate data source record. For example, in the Recipes data source, you'll find an employee table that looks, in part, like this:

EmployeeID	EmployeeFirst	EmployeeLast	EmployeeEmail
1	Hugh	Moultry	hmoultry@leafmedia.com
2	Cody	Cannata	ccannata@leafmedia.com
3	Jamie	Santa	jsanta@leafmedia.com
4	Emilia	Shepley	eshepley@leafmedia.com
5	Lorrie	Nakagawa	lnakagawa@leafmedia.com

This example has five records, each with four columns or fields: `EmployeeID`, `EmployeeFirst`, `EmployeeLast`, and `EmployeeEmail`. Each column is a particular data type; here, all but `EmployeeID` are text fields. `EmployeeID` only accepts numeric data. Making sure that your data field has the proper data type is the first step in designing a data source *schema* or structure; other data types include boolean (yes or no), currency, and date/time.

Because a data source holds data in a structured manner, the data is easy to manipulate. The example table shows records in the order in which they were entered; we can easily sort the table to show it in alphabetical order by the last name field, `EmployeeLast`:

EmployeeID	EmployeeFirst	EmployeeLast	EmployeeEmail
2	Cody	Cannata	ccannata@leafmedia.com
1	Hugh	Moultry	hmoultry@leafmedia.com
5	Lorrie	Nakagawa	lnakagawa@leafmedia.com
3	Jamie	Santa	jsanta@leafmedia.com
4	Emilia	Shepley	eshepley@leafmedia.com

In addition to sorting, another important concept in manipulating data sources is filtering. Data sources are typically filtered to retrieve only the significant records. For example, if you wanted to show only those employees whose last name begins with an *S*, your resulting table would show this:

EmployeeID	EmployeeFirst	EmployeeLast	EmployeeEmail
3	Jamie	Santa	jsanta@leafmedia.com
4	Emilia	Shepley	eshepley@leafmedia.com

A filtered subset of a table is called a *recordset*, and the directions for creating a recordset are referred to as a *query*. Later in this chapter, we'll discuss the syntax for creating queries using SQL.

Structuring Your Data

A data source that is capable of referencing only a single table is called a *flat-file* database and is of limited use. Most modern data sources can address multiple tables and are referred to as *relational* data sources.

Remember the `EmployeeID` field, singled out as the only numeric data type in our example table? Actually, the `EmployeeID` field is more than just a number—it's the *index* or *primary key*, which is a unique field that identifies each record. The field designated as the primary key field is often established as a number field that automatically increments every time another record is added. Although the primary key could just as easily be a text field—as long as the text is unique for every record—best practice dictates that a primary key field has no other function.

Primary key fields are essential to using relational data sources; they are, in effect, the glue that relates one table to another. As an example, let's say that we wanted to track a customer's orders at our online store. Each customer would have a record in the customers table with, of course, a unique identifying number. You'd also need a table of orders that shows the items ordered and the amount paid, among other things. Hopefully, the customer will come back time and again, so the orders table would have multiple orders from the same customer. How do you identify the customer in the orders table without reentering the name and all the record information each time? You do this by using the customer's primary key value. Some database applications, like Access, provide a visual method for seeing how one table connects to another [c1-2].

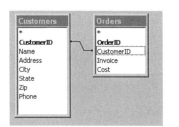

c1-2

In our example, we show how we can track a single customer making multiple transactions; this is referred to as *one-to-many relationship*. One-to-many relationships are by far the most commonly used. Data sources can also include many-to-many relationships. With a *many-to-many relationship*, two tables are generally connected via a third, linking table. The linking table would contain primary keys from the other two tables in addition to any data that pertains to the intersection of the tables. A good example of a many-to-many relationship is the orders and catalog items correlation. A single order might include many catalog items and, hopefully, several orders. To relate the Orders table to the Items table, we need a third table, Sales. The Sales table contains a link to both Orders and Items [c1-3].

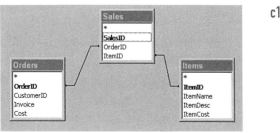

c1-3

Designing the database structure or schema properly is important to the efficient processing of your database queries. Here are some pointers to help you approach the design of your data source:

- Before creating the data source, it's best to decide the nature of the data needed and how items relate to one another. Work out the details on paper well before beginning to create a data source structure. It's often best to examine this issue from a perspective of how the data source will be used.
- Try to break each field down to its component parts; compound fields that combine city, state, and zip into one field, for example, are a major mistake because combined fields make it difficult to sort or search the field based solely on a single element, such as zip code.
- Play close attention to the data types involved; don't, for example, make the mistake of setting a phone number field as a number data type because it is composed mainly of numbers. Set the data type according to how the field will be used, not what's inside it.
- Be careful when naming a data source field. Avoid duplicate names, such as using ID for every primary key. It's also good to steer clear of commonplace words, such as *date*, which are often keywords in an application server or language and can cause errors.
- Whenever possible, use a separate table for information that might be required more than once. Be sure to include primary keys for each table and related keys between tables that are connected.
- Data stored in one table should not be repeated in another. The primary and related keys provide links between tables that allow you to display recurring information many times while only storing it once.

Proper data source design is often a shortcoming in Web applications; developers just don't pay as much attention to it as they should. A properly designed data source is more efficient, secure, and serviceable than one that is just cobbled together.

Connecting to Data Sources

With a well-designed data source at the ready, you're prepared to establish a connection to it from your Web application. You can achieve a connection in several ways, depending on the application server in use. Typically, application servers offer several alternative routes to establishing a connection. One method might be easier to set up but not quite as efficient, whereas the other might be more difficult to create but more robust. It's good to know what the options are so that you can decide which type of connection is best in a given situation.

Making ASP Connections

Although there are some variations, ASP connections occur in one of two ways: either through a Data Source Name (DSN) or through a connection string. Although the DSN connection is easier to set up, it

Because only ASP, PHP and ColdFusion applications are used in the recipes, details on creating connections are covered for only those server models. See Dreamweaver Help for information on creating connections for other application technologies.

NOTE

does have somewhat of an impact on the performance of the application server. Connection strings are, in general, more robust but also require more detailed information, such as a precise path to the data source on the server.

When you create an ASP connection—whether through DSN or connection string—Dreamweaver stores the information in a file saved in the Connections folder of your site. Every time you create a recordset using that connection, the file is incorporated into your pages by using an <include> tag, like this:

```
<!--#include file="../Connections/Recipes.asp" -->
```

Dreamweaver regards this as a dependent file; when you upload your .asp files to the server via FTP, you'll see an option to include dependent files. Selecting OK will automatically transfer the connection file, and you'll be good to go.

DSN Connections

A DSN is similar to a domain name in that it, too, is an alias that represents the file path of the data source. As with domains, the mapping from DSN to file location is handled on the server side. DSN connections contain other vital information, such as the type of data source driver required and any security information, such as username and password.

On a remote testing server, DSNs are established by a system administrator. On a development system, a DSN is defined in a Windows program: the ODBC Data Source Administrator. ODBC stands for Open Database Connectivity; it is a system of drivers that allows the same language, SQL, to communicate with a variety of data sources.

If you intend to follow along with the recipes, be sure to copy the recipes.mdb file from the Web site (www.webassist.com/recipes) to your system. It's best not to place the data source in a defined site so that the file isn't uploaded inadvertently.

NOTE

Here's how a local DSN is established through the ODBC Data Source Administrator:

1. Run the appropriate ODBC management program for your system:
   - Windows 95, Windows 98, and Windows ME: Select **ODBC Data Source** (32 bit) from the Control Panel folder.
   - Windows 2000 and Windows XP Professional: Choose **Data Sources (ODBC)** from the Administrative Tools folder.
2. In the ODBC Data Source Administrator dialog, select the **System DSN** tab.

   All the previously defined DSNs are listed on the System DSN panel.
3. Select Add to open the Create New Data Source dialog.
4. Select the driver that is appropriate for your data source and click Finish when you're done.

   📖 Select **Microsoft Access Driver (*.mdb)**.

   The Setup dialog for the chosen driver is displayed.
5. Enter an appropriate name in the Data Source Name that properly identifies the data source.

   📖 Enter **Recipes**.
6. Choose Select and locate your data source.

   📖 Locate the file `recipes.mdb` copied to your system from the Web site.
7. If a login name and password are necessary, select **Advanced** and enter them there.
8. Verify your choices and, when finished, select OK to close any open dialogs.

Although you can launch the ODBC Data Source Administrator independently of Dreamweaver, you can also open it from within Dreamweaver as you are defining the DSN connection. Here's how it is done:

1. From the Databases panel, choose Add (+) and select **Data Source Name (DSN)**.
2. The Data Source Name (DSN) dialog appears [c1-4].

c1-4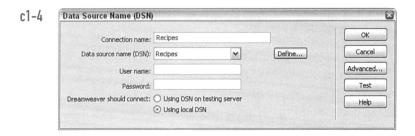

3. For local development connections, choose the **Using Local DSN** option. If the connection you are creating is to a remote DSN, select the **Dreamweaver Should Connect Using DSN On Testing Server** option.

   Macintosh users do not have a local option.

4. Enter an identifying name in the Connection Name field.

   📖 To create a connection to use with the recipes in this book, enter **Recipes**.

5. If the local DSN has been previously defined, you can select its name from the drop-down list.

6. To set up a new local DSN, choose Define.

   The ODBC Data Source Administrator will be displayed. Set up the DSN as described in the previous series of steps. When finished, close the ODBC Data Source Administrator; your new DSN should appear in the drop-down list.

7. To define a remote DSN connection, enter the name in the Data Source Name (DSN) field.

   You also have the option of selecting the DSN button. Dreamweaver will then contact the testing server and gather a list of assigned DSNs that you can select from.

8. Enter your username and password if required.

9. Make sure your connection is working by selecting **Test**. Dreamweaver lets you know if the connection was successful or if it encountered problems. Click OK when you're done.

Your new connection is listed in the Databases panel.

Connection Strings

A connection string, unlike a DSN connection, does not use an alias; rather, it specifies an exact path location—as well as the ODBC driver or OLE DB provider and any other necessary information such as username and password. All this information is put into one rather lengthy text string. Although, as noted, you can include the ODBC driver in a connection string to make what is referred to as a DSN-less connection, it's not as robust as a direct OLE DB connection string. ODBC acts as a translator, facilitating communications from the data source to the underlying engine—and that engine, or *provider*, is OLE DB.

Each data source type has a particular OLE DB provider, which naturally affects the connection string. For example, if you were using an Access database called `thebook.mdb` as your data source, and the file was stored in the `databases` folder on your `d:` drive, the OLE DB connection string would look like this:

```
Provider=Microsoft.Jet.OLEDB.4.0;Data Source=d:\databases\thebook.mdb;
```

If, on the other hand, you were using a SQL Server database called BigBook found on a server called TheShelf, the OLE DB connection string would look like this:

```
Provider=SQLOLEDB;Server=TheShelf;Database=BigBook;UID=jlowery;PWD=starfish
```

Notice that this OLE DB connection string also contains username and password information.

Dreamweaver's Custom Connection Strings feature makes it possible to connect directly to the OLE DB provider. Here's how to do it:

1. From the Databases panel, choose Add (+) and select **Custom Connection String**.
2. In the Custom Connection String dialog [c1-5], enter the label for your connection.

c1-5
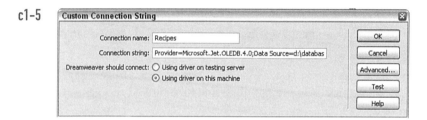

    📖 Enter **Recipes** in the Connection Name field.
3. Enter the full connection string in the Connection String field.
    📖 Enter the following string, substituting the actual path to your copy of the recipes.mdb for the variable yourDriveLetter:\yourPath\:

```
Provider=Microsoft.Jet.OLEDB.4.0;Data
Source=yourDriveLetter:\yourPath\recipes.mdb;
```

4. Select **Test** to make sure that the connection is working properly. If you encounter problems, check your connection string for typos; if you're successful, click OK to exit the dialog.

Setting Up ColdFusion Connections

The best, most flexible way to establish a data source connection in ColdFusion takes three steps:

1. Assign your data source in the ColdFusion Administrator.

2. Create and save an `Application.cfm` file, which includes a variable reference to your data source. The `Application.cfm` file should be stored at the site or application root.

3. In Dreamweaver, add a Data Source Name variable to the Bindings panel.

Although there are other ways to establish a data source that do not require as many steps, the other methods are less modular and far more difficult to adapt if a data source changes.

Declaring a Data Source

The ColdFusion Administrator acts as a central clearinghouse for all data sources, among many other things. The process for setting up a new data source is similar, but slightly different, in ColdFusion MX and ColdFusion 5. Here's how you set up a data source in ColdFusion MX:

1. Run the ColdFusion Administrator by choosing **Administrator** in your Macromedia ColdFusion MX program group.

   You might need to log in, if you haven't done so in the current session.

2. From the main Administrator page, select **Data Sources**, under the Data & Services category.

3. In the Add New Data Source dialog, enter the name for your data source.

   📖 Enter **Recipes** in the Data Source Name field.

4. Select the driver for your particular data source from the list.

   📖 Select **Microsoft Access** from the Drive drop-down list.

5. Choose Add to move to the next screen.

6. Enter the necessary details for your driver and data source. If the data source is file-based, enter the path in the Database File field; otherwise, choose **System Database File**. If necessary, select **Show Advanced Settings** to enter a different ColdFusion username or other security settings.

   📖 Select **Browse Server** next to the Database File field and locate the copy of `recipes.mdb` copied to your system from the Web site.

7. When you've completed all the settings, choose Submit; the new data source should be added to the list.

It is possible at this point to go into Dreamweaver and select this data source to build a recordset. If you do, however, the data source name will be encoded directly into the `<cfquery>` tag. The technique we are following applies a variable to the `<cfquery>` tag rather than a name, which makes the recordset far easier to update across an application.

Setting Up the *Application.cfm* File

The Application.cfm file is a marvelous time- and code-saving aspect of ColdFusion. The code found within an Application.cfm file, if placed at the site root, is automatically included into every ColdFusion page within the site, regardless of where it is located in the file structure. This facility allows us to a variable pointing to the data source name set up in the ColdFusion Administrator, which will, in turn, allow us to declare a Data Source Name variable in Dreamweaver. A site can contain numerous Application.cfm files; additional files are stored in the root folders of one or more applications.

The basic tag to create a variable is the <cfset> tag. If you wanted to assign a variable named theData to a data source you had created called CorporateData, you would use code like this:

```
<cfset theData="CorporateData">
```

Let's build an Application.cfm file together.

1. In Dreamweaver, select File > New to open the New Document dialog.
2. Choose **Dynamic Page** in the first column and **ColdFusion** in the second; click Create when you're ready.

   By selecting a ColdFusion page, Dreamweaver automatically appends the .cfm extension when the page is saved.
3. In the new page, enter into Code view and delete all the standard code inserted.
4. Insert the <cfset> tag that assigns the desired variable name to your defined data source.

   📖 Enter this code:

   ```
   <cfset Recipes="Recipes">
   ```
5. Save the file as Application.cfm at the root of your site.

NOTE | For maximum cross-platform implementation, be sure to save your Application.cfm with an uppercase A. Although application.cfm is acceptable on Windows platforms, it would fail on any Unix system.

Defining the Data Source Name Variable

For our final step in the process, we move into Dreamweaver and use a new feature introduced in Dreamweaver MX: the Data Source Name variable. After declaring a Data Source Name variable, Dreamweaver includes the variable as an option in the appropriate drop-down lists and dialogs. Choosing such a variable while creating a recordset creates code like this:

```
<cfquery name="MyQuery" datasource="#DataSourceName#">
```

Note that the value for the datasource attribute is a ColdFusion variable rather than a direct reference to a data source. Here's how a Data Source Name variable is set up in Dreamweaver:

1. In the Bindings panel, choose Add (+) and select **Data Source Name Variable**.
2. In the Data Source Name Variable dialog, enter the name for the variable.
   - Enter **Recipes** in the Variable Name field.
3. Select the desired data source from the list.
   - Choose **Recipes** from the Data Source list.
4. Verify your choices and click OK to add the variable to the Bindings panel [c1-6].

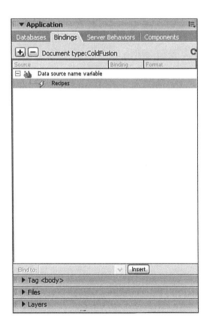

c1-6

Connecting to a MySQL Data Source for PHP

As noted earlier, MySQL is a server-based data source. Dreamweaver provides a direct method for creating a connection to a MySQL data source. Once the connection is established, you'll be able to refer to the connection for all the relevant applications.

The following procedure assumes that you've already installed MySQL on your development system. To learn how to install MySQL, visit www.mysql.org.

NOTE

Inserting a Connection

Connections are created and displayed in the Dreamweaver's Databases panel. Before you can create a connection, MySQL must be running, and you should have a username and password established.

 ☐ To use the data source created for the recipes, follow the instructions in the Introduction of the book for copying the files from the Web site to your system.

To create a connection, follow these steps:

1. From the Databases panel, choose Add (+) and select **MySQL Connection** from the drop-down list.
2. In the MySQL Connections dialog displayed, enter a name for your connection.

 ☐ Enter **Recipes** in the Connection Name field.

3. Insert the server address hosting MySQL.

 The MySQL server address is either an IP address or, if the server is located on your development system, `localhost`.

4. Enter your username and password in their respective fields.
5. Specify the database.

 ☐ Choose Select and click on **Recipes** in the Select Databases dialog. Click OK to confirm your choice and close that dialog [c1-7].

c1-7

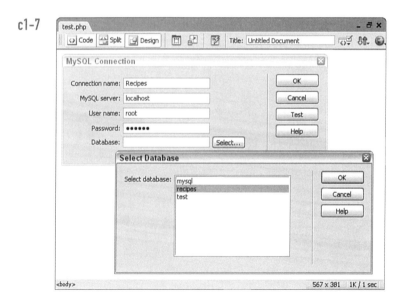

6. Select **Test** to verify that the connection is working.

7. After the connection is confirmed, click OK to close the dialog and create the connection file.

The newly created connection is displayed in the Databases panel. Expand the main connection node to reveal the available tables. The actual connection file is stored in the Connections folder and can be opened and examined in Dreamweaver. Dreamweaver writes a standard PHP file, like this one:

```php
<?php
# FileName="Connection_php_mysql.htm"
# Type="MYSQL"
# HTTP="true"
$hostname_Recipes = "localhost";
$database_Recipes = "recipes";
$username_Recipes = "root";
$password_Recipes = "mypassword";
$Recipes = mysql_pconnect($hostname_Recipes, $username_Recipes,
$password_Recipes) or trigger_error(mysql_error(),E_USER_ERROR);
?>
```

When you create a recordset in Dreamweaver, the connection file is included through the use of a require_once() function. This function is written into your PHP page at the top above the <html> tag, like the following code:

```php
<?php require_once('Connections/Recipes.php'); ?>
```

The connection file is considered a dependent file by Dreamweaver. As such, it can be transferred automatically from the local to remote site with your application page when using Dreamweaver's built-in FTP feature to transfer files. Dreamweaver asks whether you'd like to transfer dependent files as well as the primary file. Answering Yes ensures the connection file is uploaded as well as additional system files necessary for the connection to be completed.

> **NOTE**
>
> If you encounter problems connecting to a MySQL database, make sure the Testing Server information in the Site Definition dialog is correct. Incorrect or incomplete information such as the lack of a needed host directory can prevent Dreamweaver from transferring and executing the necessary connection files.

Preparing SQL Statements

SQL is to databases as HTML is to Web pages. SQL is an amazingly versatile language, as much at home in Microsoft Access as it is in SQL Server or Oracle data sources. SQL can manage records (updating, adding, or deleting), gather subsets, or create tables and even other SQL statements on the fly.

As pointed out in the beginning of this chapter, you don't have to know SQL to build basic applications in Dreamweaver. The key word here is *basic*; when you start to need more than simple recordsets filtered on one field or derived from a single table—and that time will come sooner than later—you'll need to write some SQL. Although advanced SQL statements can become involved and difficult to decipher, the language is quite approachable.

SQL Basics

The most common SQL function in data-driven Web applications is undoubtedly creating recordsets. As the name implies, a *recordset* is merely a subset of all the records. Don't be misled, however; a recordset can also contain all the records. To get all of the records from a data source table, we use two SQL keywords: SELECT and FROM. For example, this SQL statement

```
SELECT * FROM mybooks
```

returns all the records and all the fields from the mybooks table in the current data source. The asterisk is a special wildcard character that signifies to return all the fields. To return only the authors and titles fields, the SQL statement would appear like this:

```
SELECT authors, titles
FROM mybooks
```

Individual fields are entered in a comma-separated list. But what if you wanted to limit not just the fields, but also the records? To limit or *filter* a SQL statement, you use the WHERE clause. For example, let's say you wanted to see only those books written by James Ellroy—or, in other words, where the author was equal to James Ellroy. Here's the SQL statement you would use:

```
SELECT authors, titles
FROM mybooks
WHERE authors="James Ellroy"
```

NOTE

A couple notes on SQL statement formatting before we proceed: Although it is not mandatory to put the different clauses (SELECT, FROM, WHERE) on different lines, whitespace is irrelevant in SQL, and it greatly helps the readability. Also, upper-casing the SQL keywords is convention and not required; it does, however, make the statements easier to follow as they get more complex.

The WHERE clause of a SQL statement is definitely where the action is, and it has the operators to prove it. Within a WHERE clause, you can use a logical AND to return a recordset where two or more conditions are met. For example, if you wanted to find all the hardback editions by James Ellroy in your data source, this SQL statement would give you the answer:

```
SELECT authors, titles, booktype
FROM mybooks
WHERE authors="James Ellroy" AND booktype="hardback"
```

Other SQL logical operators include OR, NOT, and LIKE, among others. Mathematical operators are also supported, including: <, >, <=, >=, =, and <>.

So far, these examples have just output all the requested records in no particular sequence, although in some data sources, such as Access, the records would be returned in the order in which they were entered. To sort the returned records, the ORDER BY key phrase is used. If you're interested in seeing James Ellroy hardbacks in alphabetical order, by title, the SQL would look like this:

```
SELECT authors, titles, booktype
FROM mybooks
WHERE authors="James Ellroy" AND booktype="hardback"
ORDER BY titles ASC
```

The ASC keyword indicates an ascending order; ASC is the default and could be omitted. To see the titles in reverse alphabetical order, use the keyword DESC.

In a table like this one, several of the authors might have written numerous books. Therefore, you have to use another keyword to see a list of the individual authors, without repeating names. That keyword is DISTINCT, and it is paired with SELECT. For example, the following SQL statement

```
SELECT DISTINCT authors
FROM mybooks
WHERE edition="hardback"
ORDER BY authors ASC
```

returns a recordset containing just the unique names of the authors who have hardback books.

Combining Data from Multiple Tables

Modern data sources gain much of their power and flexibility from their ability to provide data that relates to each other. SQL statements make it possible to retrieve information from multiple related tables. In this situation, it takes more than just a SQL keyword to get the desired results—the connection must be embedded in the tables.

Let's look at an example. To truly make the sample data source discussed in the previous topic more useful, you can split the one mybooks table into two: books and authors. Let's say that mybooks contains the following fields:

- title
- author
- edition
- publication_date

Now, the authors table might have these fields:

- name
- website
- genres

How would you relate the two tables? Putting the question another way, what do these two tables have in common? The answer is the author's name; in the books table, it is the author field, and in the authors table, it is name. So, if you wanted to see a list of all the Web sites by authors of paperbacks, your SQL statement might read like this:

```
SELECT authors.websites
FROM books, authors
WHERE edition="paperback" AND books.author=authors.name
```

Immediately you should notice a couple of differences in each clause of the SQL statement. First, in the SELECT clause, we're not just asking for a field, like websites; we're asking for a field name from a specific table, authors.websites. Second, the FROM keyword contains more than one table in a comma-separated list. Third—and most importantly—the WHERE clause contains a segment that joins one table to another, books.author=author.name.

Before we explore the JOIN keyword, it's important to point out a potential problem with our example database design. To successfully match one table to another, the author's names must be identical in both. Although this might work for a while, sooner or later, trouble will arise. Eventually, the author's name might not be entered the same in one table or the other; you could easily enter T. Clancy knowing you meant Tom Clancy. Or, perhaps, a book written by an author using a pseudonym would be entered. It's far better to create a separate field that uses unique numbers as the primary key in the authors table (call it authorID) and then reference that field in the books table, like this:

```
SELECT authors.websites
FROM books, authors
WHERE edition="paperback" AND books.authorID=authors.authorID
```

You can also write this same SQL statement using an INNER JOIN, like this:

```
SELECT authors.websites
FROM (books INNER JOIN authors ON books.authorID=authors.authorID)
WHERE edition="paperback"
```

The two SQL statements are functionally the same, but you're more likely to encounter the second syntax in professionally coded queries.

This is just the start of what's possible with SQL, but it should give you a good foundation for understanding some of the advanced SQL used in the recipes.

Chapter 2

Building Applications in Dreamweaver Workspace

Macromedia Dreamweaver has grown over the years to be quite a substantial program with many features, options, and methods of working. With the introduction of Dreamweaver MX, the two realms of Web design and Web development were brought together in a new interface with enhanced features for both coders and designers.

Whether you're totally new to Dreamweaver or just new to creating dynamic Web applications with Dreamweaver, this chapter will help you find your bearings. The first part of the chapter is an exploration of the Dreamweaver workspace with an emphasis on its application-building capabilities. In addition to providing an overview of the Web authoring environment, you'll also find clear directions on getting started with dynamic pages. The balance of the chapter deals specifically with the basics of Web application tools that are standard in Dreamweaver. Everything from applying server behaviors to working in Live Data view is described.

Working in the Workspace

The Dreamweaver workspace consists primarily of a document representation and a number of panels, both by themselves and collected in panel groups [c2-1]. The document can be viewed in Design view, which approximates how a browser would render the Web page, or Code view, where the underlying source code is revealed. There is also a split window option to see both views at once—a useful tool both for learning about what code Dreamweaver generates and for quickly selecting and modifying an element or tag on the page. Switch from one view to another by selecting your choice under the View menu (Code, Split, or Design) or by choosing one of the view buttons on the Document toolbar.

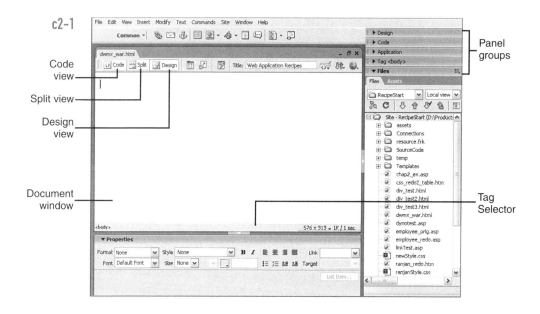

c2-1

Code view

Split view

Design view

Document window

Panel groups

Tag Selector

One of the most useful features in Dreamweaver, the Tag Selector, is displayed at the bottom of the Document window. Select any text or object, and the associated tag will be shown at the far right of the Tag Selector; all previous tags in the code will then be shown to the left. The Tag Selector is often the quickest, surest way to select a specific page element [c2-2].

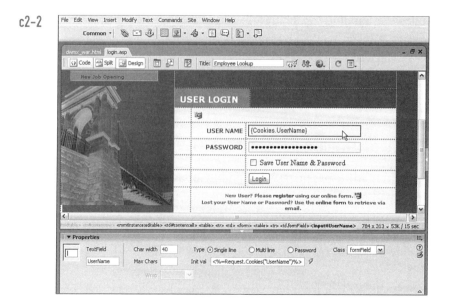

c2-2

Exploring Panels and Panel Groups

The panels and panel groups are quite flexible and can be easily adapted to suit the way you work. As the name implies, panel groups contain individual panels. You can open any panel—whether it is currently onscreen or not—by choosing its entry under the Window menu. You can also display onscreen panels or panel groups by clicking once on the name; clicking the name again closes the panel or panel group.

> **NOTE**
>
> I often find it helpful to concentrate on just one panel group. To maximize a panel group—and simultaneously close all others—double-click the panel group name.

You can rearrange the panel groups, as well as most panels within them, to suit your workflow. To move a panel group outside of the docked area, drag the group by the far left edge of the title bar; this area, which appears to be a series of dots, is called the *gripper*, and you'll know you're in the correct position when your cursor becomes a four-headed arrow [c2-3]. You can drag panel groups or most individual panels so that they are either free-floating or docked. A heavy black border appears when a docking position is available.

Gripper

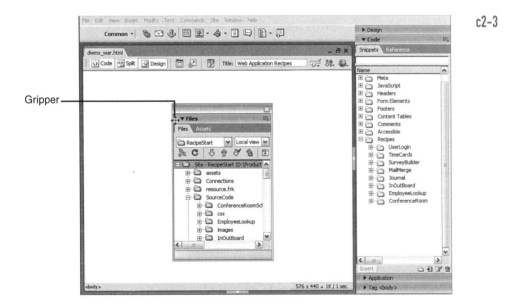

c2-3

You can access any panel in a panel group by selecting its tab. To move a panel from one panel group to another—or to isolate it—you need to use the option menu, available on the right side of the panel group's title bar. From the option menu, choose Group *PanelName* With—where PanelName is the current panel—and then, from the submenu, select the panel group you'd like the current panel to move to. For example, if you wanted to combine the Reference and History panels, select the Options menu from the Reference panel and choose Group Reference With History. You can rename most panel or panel groups—an option also available from the Options menu. To separate a panel from a panel group, select it and, from the Options menu, choose Group *PanelName* With New Panel Group.

In Dreamweaver MX 2004, some panels are an integral part of a panel group and cannot be moved to another group or isolated. The Tag panel group contains three related panels: Attributes, Behaviors, and Relevant CSS. You cannot move or rename any of these individual panels or the panel group. You can, of course, close and reopen the panel group at any time.

Although you'll find yourself using almost every aspect of Dreamweaver, the primary panel group used in building dynamic Web applications is, appropriately enough, labeled Application. In the Application panel group, you'll find four relevant panels:

- **Databases**—The Databases panel lists the connections to data sources that are available throughout the entire site. ColdFusion users will see all the data sources set up through the ColdFusion Administrator, whereas ASP developers are shown those connections explicitly made in Dreamweaver for a given site. Expanding the Databases tree displays the tables, views, and stored procedures of each data source; expanding these elements shows the individual fields used; you can drag these elements onto the page when writing server-side code to avoid typographical errors.

- **Bindings**—The Bindings panel displays any data sources, primarily recordsets and server-side variables, available for use on the current page. You'll frequently need to access recordset fields from the Bindings panel to insert dynamic text on the page. The Bindings panel also controls the server-side formatting of dynamic text.

- **Server Behaviors**—Server behaviors are encapsulated blocks of server-side code. The Server Behaviors panel displays all the server behaviors that have been inserted into the page. Selecting a server behavior in the panel highlights the corresponding code in the Document window.

- **Components**—The Components panel is only active when the document type is one of the ASP.NET options or ColdFusion. Under both ASP.NET and ColdFusion, the Components panel displays available Web Services; with ColdFusion, you'll also see the accessible ColdFusion components.

NOTE

Although ColdFusion components are an exciting technology, they are not backward-compatible with ColdFusion 5. The recipes in this book do not use ColdFusion components so that the applications are ColdFusion 5 compatible.

In all of these Application panels, use Add (+) to insert an element and Remove (-) to delete a selection. You'll notice the Add (+) and Remove (-) controls throughout the Dreamweaver interface.

Modifying Attributes with the Property Inspector

The Property inspector is perhaps the most important of all the panels; it certainly is among the most commonly used. The Property inspector is contextual; that is, it displays the attributes for whatever element is currently selected. A completely different

Property inspector is shown depending on whether a table or a Flash movie is selected, for example. The default state in Design view shows the Text Property inspector with either standard font tag or CSS attributes; toggle between CSS and HTML modes by changing the Use CSS Instead of HTML Tags option found in the General category of Preferences (Edit > Preferences). In addition to numerous list and text fields, the Property inspector has several special function controls [c2-4]:

- **Color swatch**—Select the color swatch to display a palette of available colors to choose from. When the color swatch is open, the eyedropper cursor also permits you to sample a color from anywhere on the screen.
- **Browse for File**—Choose the Browse for File icon when you want to open the Select File dialog, as when assigning a link. The Select File dialog also displays any available data sources, such as data source fields from a recordset.
- **Point to File**—Drag the Point to File icon over any filename in the Site panel to use the path to that file as a value. You can also use the Point to File icon within a page to designate a named anchor.

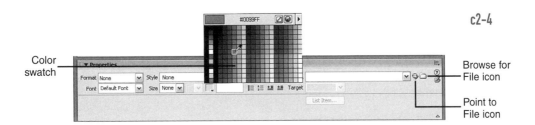

c2-4

Color swatch

Browse for File icon

Point to File icon

One interface control is especially important to building database-driven Web applications: the lightning bolt icon. Selecting the lightning icon gives the user access to the Dynamic Data dialog, which contains a list of recordsets, session variables, and any other data source available to the current page. The lightning bolt icon appears in various Property inspectors, but it is consistently available for any attribute in the Tag panel—which can be used as an alternative to the Property inspector. Unlike the standard Property inspector, the Tag panel displays all the attributes for a selected tag, not just the most commonly used ones [c2-5].

c2-5

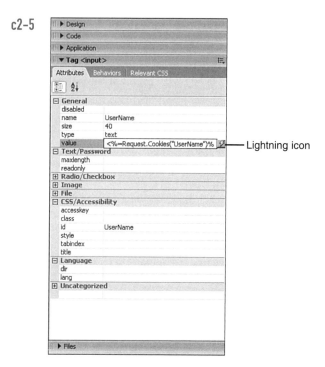

Lightning icon

Adjusting Preferences

The final stop in our brief tour of the Dreamweaver environment is the Dreamweaver Preferences. When you open Preferences by choosing Edit > Preferences (Dreamweaver > Preferences on OS X), a large dialog with many options is displayed [c2-6]. On the left of the dialog is a series of categories; select any category to change related options. There are 20 different categories in Dreamweaver that allow you to control any aspect of the authoring environment and the program's output.

Rather than explain every option in Preferences, I'd like to focus on a few that are especially important to Web application building. For more information on any preference not discussed here, context-sensitive help is available for every category.

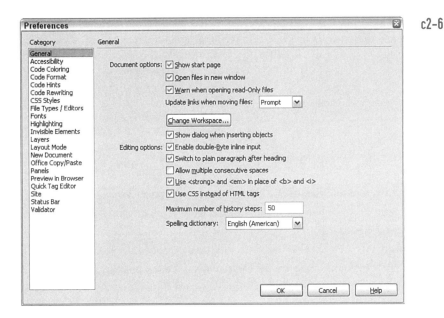

c2-6

Dynamic Web applications are decidedly code-intensive, and I'm sure some would argue that they should, in fact, be code-exclusive. Wherever you stand on the code to design spectrum, you'll greatly appreciate the flexibility and power that Dreamweaver provides in Code view. There are numerous categories in Preferences that deal with code in some way:

- **Code Coloring**—Not only does Dreamweaver provide syntax level code coloring, the color options—both foreground and background—as well as text styles are completely configurable. Moreover, the configuration can vary from one page type to another. For example, in a standard HTML file, the comment tag code could be a medium gray and in an ASP page, the HTML comments could be displayed with a yellow background and blue type. Choose Edit Color Scheme in the Code Coloring category to make modifications.

- **Code Format**—Application developers are very particular when it comes to how their code is formatted, and rightly so. Properly styled code is easier to read and debug. The Code Format category of Preferences controls the general code settings, such as whether tabs or spaces should be used for indenting. You can also shape the output of individual tags and their attributes in the Tag Library Editor, available from the Code Format category or by choosing Edit > Tag Libraries.

- **Code Hints**—No matter how skilled you are as a coder, it's pretty difficult to remember the syntax, tags, and attributes for whatever Web language you're working in. To help developers to code more efficiently, Dreamweaver includes a code hints feature. Just start typing a tag, and a list of available tags appears.

- **Code Rewriting**—Dreamweaver stakes its reputation on respecting valid code. Through the options in the Code Rewriting category, you can affect how Dreamweaver handles documents when opened. For example, by selecting the Fix Invalidly Nested and Unclosed Tags option, Dreamweaver would change this code:

```
Help me <i>help <b>you</i></b>
```

to this:

```
Help me <i>help <b>you</b></i>
```

A number of the categories in the Dreamweaver Preferences will help you develop Web applications in Design view as well as Code view. The Invisible Elements category is a key one that enables you to see representations of unrendered Web page objects, like HTML comments [c2-7]. The Invisible Element symbols allow you to easily copy or cut and paste such tags and code in the Design view. Two Invisible Elements are applicable to dynamic pages: Visual Server Markup Tags and Nonvisual Server Markup Tags. When these options are enabled, server-side code blocks inserted in the <body> of the document are displayed as a symbol. Select the symbol, and you can either quickly find the highlighted code in Code view, or select Edit from the Property inspector to modify the code while in Design view.

c2-7

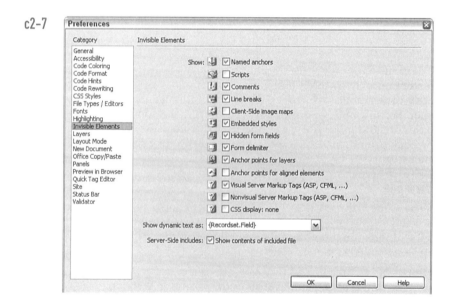

You might also notice another pertinent setting on the Invisible Elements category. Dynamic text—data embedded on the page—is, by default represented in curly braces showing both the recordset and data source field, like this:

I recommend initially selecting all the options in the Invisible Elements category. If necessary, you can remove them all from view on a page at one time by unchecking View > Visual Aids > Invisible Elements. The same option is also available from the toolbar under the View Options button.

NOTE

`{employees.firstname}`

Depending on the design, such representations might make it difficult not to distort the layout; if so, you can change the option so that dynamic text is represented only by a pair of curly braces, without interior text.

Another Preferences category is worth mentioning in this context: Highlighting. To differentiate certain objects or regions at design time, Dreamweaver highlights them, either with a surrounding border or a background color. For example, by default, an editable region in a template is enclosed in a light-blue border, while third-party tags use the same color as their background. All of the color choices used in highlighting are customizable from the Highlights category; you can also decide whether you want to show the highlights.

Two entries in the Highlights category are useful when creating Web applications, both of which are concerned with Live Data view: Untranslated and Translated. When you're in Live Data view, Dreamweaver fetches data according to your recordset and integrates it, temporarily, with the page. Dreamweaver can provide a direct replacement for a single record in an untranslated portion of Live Data view. If your data is within a repeat region, the remainder of the records must be shown in a translated area. I recommend keeping both of these options selected because it differentiates what's really on the page and what's only there during translation. You can turn both of them off by deselecting View > Visual Aids > Invisible Elements.

Setting Up a New Site

Most frequently, the first task when building a Web site in Dreamweaver, whether static or dynamic, is to define a new site. For static sites, the least you need to do for a site definition is to name the site and to designate a folder that acts as the local site root. Many developers also define their remote site initially so that they can transfer the files via FTP or to a networked staging server. The remote site can be defined at any time.

Dynamic sites also require that a *testing server* be declared. In Dreamweaver, a testing server is a particular server model (ASP VBScript, ASP JavaScript, PHP MySQL, or ColdFusion, for example) accessible through a specific folder, which could be located on a local or remote system.

You can define a site in one of two ways, both of which start by choosing Site > Manage Sites. A list of current sites is displayed in the Manage Sites dialog, along with a New button. Selecting New gives you an option of creating a site or defining an FTP or Remote Development Service (RDS) server connection. Choose New Site to display the Site Definition dialog.

WARNING

Dreamweaver MX 2004 makes it possible to work without creating a site by defining a direct server connection. This feature is useful for existing Web sites, but defining a site is critical to developing applications, especially if templates are used as they are throughout this book. Defining a site is highly recommended.

If you're relatively new to Dreamweaver, select the Basic tab of the New Sites dialog to use a wizard-like approach to defining your site. If you're more familiar with Dreamweaver, the Advanced tab uses a series of categories similar to those in the Dreamweaver Preferences.

Let's walk through a basic setup of a site using the Advanced option of the Site Definition dialog. For the purposes of this example, I'm going to assume we're setting up a dynamic site for the Recipes project, using ASP with VBScript on a local system running IIS; in this situation, we'll assume the remote site will be set up later.

1. Select Site > Manage Sites.
2. In the Manage Sites dialog, choose New > Site to open the Site Definition dialog.
3. Select the Advanced tag and choose the first category, **Local Info** [c2-8].

c2-8
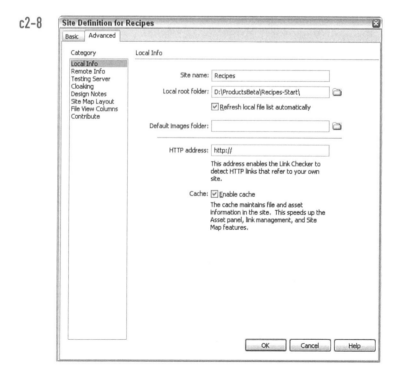

4. In the Local Info category, enter the following information:
   - **Site Name**—Enter the site as it will be known locally within Dreamweaver. For example, I would enter **Recipes**.
   - **Local Root Folder**—Choose the folder that will contain the local site. To avoid typographical errors, it's best to select the folder icon and locate the desired directory through the Choose Local Site Root dialog.
   - **Default Images Folder**—Designate a folder that will serve to hold your images. When you insert images from outside the local site root, Dreamweaver stores a copy of the images in this folder. This information is optional.
   - **HTTP Address**—Enter the URL of the published site so that Dreamweaver can identify external links correctly.

5. Select both the **Refresh Local File List Automatically** and the **Enable Cache** options to enhance productivity.

6. Select the **Testing Server** category [c2-9].

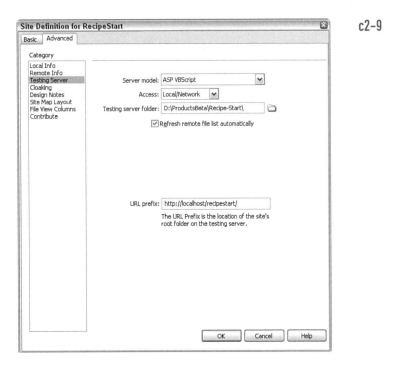

c2-9

7. From the Server Model list, choose the server technology and language for the site.
   For this example, I would choose **ASP VBScript**.

8. From the Access list, choose how the testing server will be accessed: Local/Network or FTP.
   I have ASP running locally on my development system, so I would choose **Local/Network**.

9. Set the properties necessary to access the testing server.

With a Local/Network access, I would select the **Testing Server** folder, which can be the same as the **Local Site Root folder**, and enter a URL prefix for the site. In this case, my URL prefix would be `http://localhost/recipes/` because I have set up a virtual directory named `Recipes` pointing to my testing server folder in IIS.

NOTE

It's a good idea at this point to choose Export from the Manage Sites dialog and store your site definition in a secure location. If you ever need to restore the site, select Import and locate the definition file.

10. Verify your choices on the various categories and click OK to close the dialog.

With the Dreamweaver site set up, you're ready to start creating pages for your Web application.

Creating New Dynamic Pages

Dreamweaver is capable of authoring a wide range of Web-related documents. Anything from HTML, with either standard or XHTML syntax, to dynamic ColdFusion components is feasible in Dreamweaver. To handle this enhanced output capability, Macromedia introduced a new method of creating pages through the New Document dialog. The New Document dialog allows you to create new files of a variety of types as well as documents based on templates. Let's look at how you create blank pages for your Web application first.

1. Choose File > New to open the New Document dialog [c2-10].

c2-10

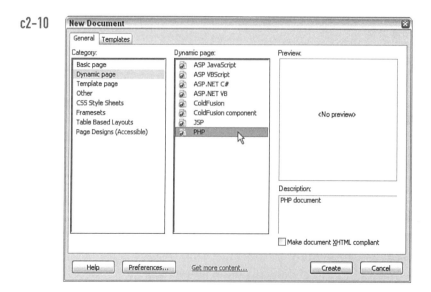

2. Make sure the General tab is selected and choose the **Dynamic Page** category from the first column.

3. Select the server technology for your application from the Dynamic Page column.

    📖 To create example pages in this book, select **ASP JavaScript, ASP VBScript, ColdFusion,** or **PHP**.

4. If desired, choose the **Make Document XHTML Compliant** option and click OK to close the dialog and create the page.

The recipes in this book were developed using standard HTML, conforming to the 4.01 Transitional doctype as established by the W3C.

NOTE

If you're creating several pages for your application, you can set Preferences to use a keyboard shortcut to create a blank page of any file type. In the New Document category, select the desired dynamic page type from the Default Document Type list and then clear the Show New Document Dialog on Ctrl-N (Command-N) option.

NOTE

If you're working with Dreamweaver templates, you can also use the New Document dialog to create new files based on specified templates. Template-derived documents are useful in Web applications because often it's only the dynamic elements that change from one page to the next. Templates give you a solid design on which to build—and, more importantly, any updates to a template are reflected on all the documents derived from that template.

Let's say you've copied the Recipes template files from the Web Site to the `Templates` folder in your local site root. To create a document based on one of those templates, follow these steps:

1. Choose File > New to open the New Document dialog.

2. Select the **Templates** tab.

3. Choose your site from the Templates For category [c2-11].

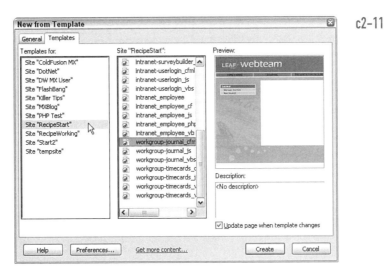

c2-11

NOTE

A complete discussion of templates is beyond the scope of this book. For more information on creating templates, consult Help > Using Dreamweaver or a good reference such as the *Dreamweaver MX Bible* by Joseph Lowery or *Inside Dreamweaver* by Laura Gutman. Advanced template use is also covered in *Joseph Lowery's Beyond Dreamweaver* and *Dreamweaver MX Templates* by Brad Halstead and Murray Summers.

4. Select the desired template from the second column. Previews appear to help you choose the right file.

5. Make sure the Update Page when Template Changes option is selected. If this option is not chosen, the newly created page is automatically detached from the template. When you're done, click OK to close the dialog.

Binding Data to the Page

Your site is defined, and you've created a dynamic page. It's time to add some dynamic content! Most dynamic content comes from a declared *recordset*. As discussed in Chapter 1, "Basic Principles of Data Source Design," recordsets are created by SQL statements and consist of a portion of the data within the connected data source.

NOTE

Make sure you understand how to create a data source connection before continuing. If you're unclear, see the "Connecting to Data Sources" section of Chapter 1.

Dreamweaver provides two alternative dialogs for creating recordsets, in addition to hand-coding: one simple and one advanced. You open both by choosing Add (+) from the Bindings panel or Server Behaviors panel and selecting Recordset (Query) from the menu. As the name implies, the simple view of the Recordset dialog is fairly basic. On the plus side, it allows you to create recordsets without writing SQL; on the other hand, you're restricted to working with a single table or view, one filter, and one level of sorting. Let's walk through the process of creating a simple recordset; the end goal of the example is to get a list of all the first and last names of the employees in the Recipes data source.

NOTE

Before you undertake these next steps, you'll need to have defined at least one connection using the procedure outlined in the previous chapter.

1. From the Bindings panel, choose Add (+) and select **Recordset (Query)**.

2. If the Advanced view of the Recordset dialog is displayed, select **Simple** to switch views.

   The Recordset dialog view is remembered from one use to the next.

3. Enter a name for your example recordset in the Name field.

   📖 Let's call this one **Employees**.

4. Select a connection (or data source as it's called in ColdFusion) from the Connections/Data Source list.

   📖 Choose **Recipes** from the Connection/Data Source list.

   After choosing a data source connection, the Table list is populated.

5. Select a table or view from the Tables drop-down list. Dreamweaver displays all the tables first, followed by the views, if any.

   📖 Choose **Employees** from the Tables list.

6. By default, all of the columns are included in the recordset. To specify certain columns, choose the Selected option and then choose any desired field. Shift+click to select contiguous columns, and Ctrl+click (Command-click) to select columns that are not next to one another.

   📖 Choose **Selected** and highlight `EmployeeFirst` and `EmployeeLast`.

7. Again, by default, all of the records in the selected columns are included. You can limit the recordset by using the four Filter lists to create a SQL WHERE clause with a point-and-click interface.

   📖 We're going to limit our employee list to show only those whose last names begin with the letters **L–Z**. To accomplish this, from the first Filter list, select the column **EmployeeLast**. Next, choose the operator from the second list, >=. From the third list, choose **Entered Value**; this allows us to specify a value. Finally, enter the letter L [c2-12].

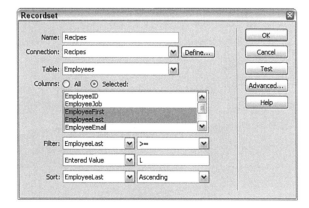

c2-12

8. Order the data by selecting a column from the Sort list and then specifying either **Ascending** or **Descending**.

   📖 Select **EmployeeLast** Ascending from the Sort lists.

9. Choose **Test** to see the data returned from the recordset. When you're done, select OK to close the dialog and insert the recordset code into your page.

After defining a recordset, you'll see all the available data source fields in the Bindings panel by expanding the recordset tree. To add dynamic text to the page, drag a data source field directly onto the page from the Bindings panel. Alternatively, position your cursor where you would like the dynamic text to appear and select Bind from the Bindings panel. With either technique, the dynamic text appears on the page like this:

```
{Employees.EmployeeFirst}
```

After inserting the dynamic text, you can see the data it represents by choosing View > Live Data. In Live Data view, the first data from the first record of your recordset is displayed [c2-13].

c2-13

Live Data view button

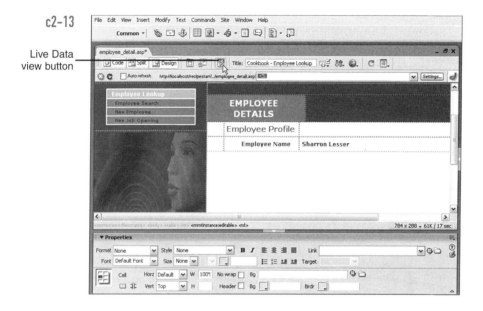

The Bindings panel also controls the server-side formatting of the dynamic text elements. Unlike HTML or CSS formatting, server-side formatting is used to uppercase or lowercase text and show numbers as currency, integers, or percents. To change the format of a dynamic text element, first select the element on the page. Then, in the Bindings panel, select the down-pointing arrow to open the Format list and select an appropriate format from the list.

Stirring in Server Behaviors

Server behaviors are Dreamweaver's powerful mechanism for supplying server-side functionality with point-and-click ease. As with Dreamweaver's client-side JavaScript behaviors, server behaviors allow users to output sophisticated code by choosing their parameters from a series of dialog boxes. Unlike the standard behaviors, server behaviors create different code depending on the current server model.

Many Web applications need to accomplish basic tasks such as inserting, updating, and deleting records. Dreamweaver includes around 30 server behaviors, covering the most common functionality. (The number of server behaviors varies slightly from one server model to another.) All the server behaviors applied to a page appear in a single list in the Server Behaviors panel; to modify an inserted server behavior, double-click its entry in the panel.

To see how server behaviors work, let's look at one of the most commonly used types: Repeat Region. When dynamic text is inserted on the page, it represents a single record from the recordset. To display multiple records, the dynamic text—and whatever elements you also want to repeat, such as a table row or a line break—are enclosed in a Repeat Region. With the Repeat Region server behavior, you can opt to show a specific number of records at a time or all of them. Here's how you apply a Repeat Region:

1. Insert a recordset and place one or more dynamic text elements on the page, as described in the previous section.
2. Select the dynamic text elements and the enclosing HTML.

   The enclosing HTML could be a set of <p> tags, a trailing line break (<br>), or a table row (<tr>). Failing to also include some sort of separator between dynamic elements will result in the data being displayed one after another horizontally, rather than vertically.
3. From the Server Behaviors panel, choose Add (+) and select **Repeat Region**.
4. In the Repeat Region dialog, make sure that recordset chosen in the list is the one you want to work with [c2-14].

   Next, choose how many records should be displayed.

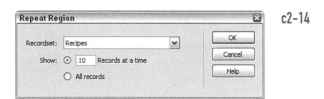 c2-14

5. If you want to show a portion of the recordset, select the **Records at a Time** option and enter the desired number.
6. If you want to display all the records from the recordset, select the **All Records** option.
7. Click OK to close the dialog and insert the code.

NOTE

Although most of the server behaviors are identical in terms of their user interface and usage, several differ from one server model to the next. For example, the Insert Record server behavior is different for ASP and for ColdFusion. Where the procedure for applying a server behavior is different, you'll find the recipe steps presented separately, separated by server model. For similar server behaviors, the steps are given together with individual code clearly marked for each server model.

Dreamweaver places a border around the selected area with a tab to indicate the Repeat Region. One way to see the results is to preview the page in a browser; another way is to use Dreamweaver's Live Data view.

Editing in Live Data View

Incorporating dynamic data into a Web page often requires significant adjustment to the page design. With Dreamweaver's Live Data view, you can continue to modify your design while viewing the actual data from a recordset. Moreover, Dreamweaver includes a number of ways to pass parameters to the recordset for testing purposes.

There are two ways to enter Live Data view. You can either choose View > Live Data or select Live Data View from the Document toolbar. In either case, the Live Data toolbar appears as Dreamweaver sends a request to the testing server and receives, in return, the data from the recordset. You might notice the letter d in the toolbar spinning to indicate that the data retrieval is in process. The first record retrieved is inserted into the corresponding dynamic text fields; if a Repeat Region server behavior is being used, data from the next records are added up to the limit of the Repeat Region. If the Invisible Elements option is enabled, the records will appear to be highlighted [c2-15].

When you're in Live Data view, you can continue to work on the page, adjusting spacing, table cell widths, or whatever. You can also format the dynamic data. Select the data representing the initial dynamic text elements to add formatting; you cannot select the repeated elements in a Repeat Region. To see applied client-side formatting, such as CSS or <strong> tags, in all the repeated data, select Refresh from the Live Data toolbar; server-side formatting, like making the text uppercase, is applied automatically, if the Auto Refresh option on the toolbar is selected.

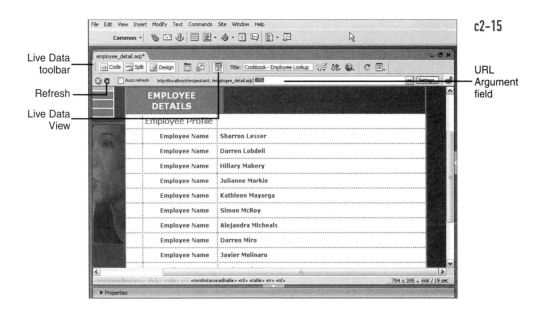

Often a recordset or other elements in a Web application depend on arguments passed to the page. There are two basic ways of passing arguments: attached to the URL in what's known as a *query string* or as entered through a form. Dreamweaver's Live Data view can emulate both methods of argument passing.

A query string is a series of name/value pairs following a question mark at the end of a standard URL. In this example,

```
http://localhost/Recipes/employeelist.asp?ID=34
```

the query string passed to the employeelist.asp page is ID=34, where ID represents the name of a field and 34 is the value. Additional name/value pairs can be added by using an ampersand, like this:

```
http://localhost/Recipes/employeelist.asp?employeeFirst=Joseph&employeeLast=Lowery
```

If a recordset on your page is filtered on a URL parameter, you can use the Live Data toolbar to try different arguments. When you're in Live Data view, enter the name/value pairs, separated by ampersands in the URL Argument field of the Live Data toolbar. After pressing Enter (Return), Dreamweaver retrieves the requested data and integrates it on the page.

The URL Argument field works great for query strings, but you'll have to use the Live Data Settings dialog to enter parameters expected from a form. Open the dialog by choosing View > Live Data Settings or by choosing Settings from the Live Data toolbar. The Live Data Settings dialog also uses name/value pairs; choose Add (+) to add an entry under the Name and Value columns. To emulate form data, enter the name of the form field in the Name column and the value entered under Value. For forms, you'll also need to make sure the Method is set to POST rather than GET. If you'd prefer not to write out the query string, you can use the Live Data Settings dialog in place of the URL Argument field by changing the Method to GET [c2-16].

c2-16

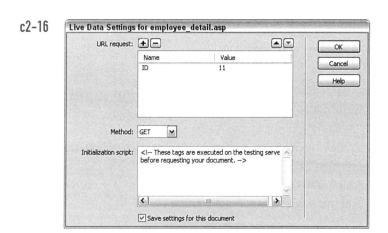

Part II

Main Course:
Intranet Web Applications

Recipe 1

User Login

An intranet is a very different animal than the free-ranging Internet. Whereas designers building for the Web thrive on the number of eyeballs they capture, intranet developers place a premium on their pages being seen by just the right eyeballs. Critical to an intranet is the concept of user authentication. Before anyone can browse an intranet area, he must be authenticated against the company records, and the records, of course, are maintained in a data source by system administrators.

Much—in many cases, all—of a company's intranet is protected against unauthorized viewing. As you'll see in this application, the term "unauthorized" means more than "not registered." For robust authentication applications like the one you're about to build, it means "not cleared to view this particular content," and the content can be anything from an entire site down to an isolated area of a single page.

Macromedia Dreamweaver MX 2004 provides a solid foundation of user authentication tools, which we will use as the base to build our application. In all, there are eight separate pages in our application that fall into either the user or the administrator category. We do, of course, use our own authentication routines to isolate the administrator-oriented applications from those intended for all users.

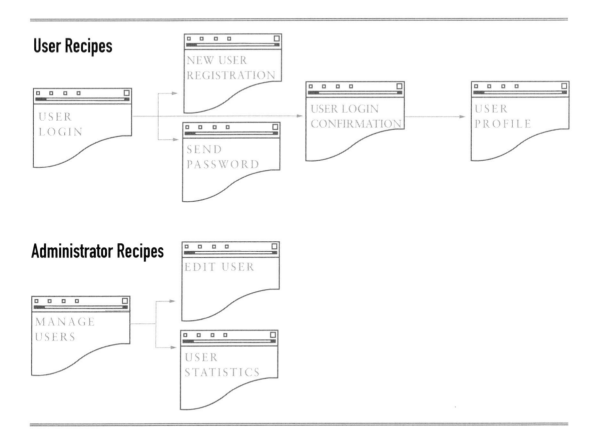

Our application starts with the login page where registered users enter their usernames and passwords. If they had previously specified that it be remembered, the username field is automatically filled. If the login succeeds, users are taken to a confirmation or welcome page where they have an opportunity to update their login info. If the login fails, an error message appears on the login page itself, and they can try again. Users who have forgotten their password can visit a page to request that their password be emailed to them. The login page also provides a link for new users. After completing the registration successfully, the new users are returned to the login page, where their newly registered username is already in place.

All the pages in the application contain links to the administrative functions, but these links can only be seen by administrators, thanks to the conditional logic embedded on the page. The administrator's main page provides both a paged listing of all the users (sorted so that the newest are displayed first) and a form for entering new users. Each of the user listings is linked to a page where the administrator can modify or delete the user's record. On another page, the administrator can get an overview of user registration to see how many users are in the system and how much activity the registration system has seen over various time periods.

Ingredients

8 APPLICATION PAGES:

- 5 User Pages
  - User Login
  - New User Registration
  - User Login Confirmation
  - Send Password
  - User Profile
- 3 Administration Pages
  - Manage Users
  - Edit Users
  - User Statistics

2 DATA SOURCES:

- 1 Database with:
  - 2 Tables

    Users—The registered user records, including first and last name, username, password, and access group level

    AccessGroups—Available access group levels in both numeric (1, 2, 3, and 4) and text (Administrator, Manager, Operator, and User) format
  - 2 Views

    UserView—A virtual table joining the Users and UserGroups tables

    UserRegStats—A calculated recordset with fields for total users and registration statistics by day, week, and month
- 1 Session Variable:
  - **UserID**—Maintains the user's ID to verify authentication

Prep Work

Before you begin to build this application, make sure your prep work has been completed.

1. Create the data source containing the necessary tables.
   - ASP and ColdFusion users should use the **Recipes.mdb** data source found in the downloaded files while PHP users should work with the **Recipes** data source. For assistance in locating and installing these files, choose **Help > Web Application Recipes**.

2. Set up a connection to the data source.

   📖 Name the connection **Recipes**.

3. Create a Dreamweaver site for your application.

4. Build the template to be used for the application.

   📖 Use the template for your server model named **userlogin**.

End User Recipe: User Login

In many intranet applications, the first page a user comes to is the login page. If the user is already registered, a username and password are entered. Selecting the Submit button checks the username and password against the data source and, if found, redirects the users to an application within the intranet. If the username is not found or the password is incorrect, a message appears on the page telling the user of the problem. The user can then try again, register, or ask that the password be emailed.

Our application is somewhat different from Macromedia's standard user login. Rather than sending the user to a different page if the login fails—where he would have to select a link to try again or, worse, to just bring him back to the login page with no additional information—our login page provides a message on the same page to allow for an easier retry.

Our recipe also adds a UserID session variable to the mix. This session variable is used in later application pages to track the logged-in user. In addition, we've added a cookie to sweeten the recipe. With the cookie in place, the application will optionally fill in the UserName text field to allow for a simplified login.

Step 1: Implement User Login Design

First let's build the basic page for the user login. You can build this yourself or have a designer construct the page for you, as it includes no server-side code at this point.

1. Create a basic dynamic page, either by hand or from a template.

   📖 In the **UserLogin** folder, locate the folder for your server model and open the login page found there.

2. Add a table to the content region of your page to contain the interface elements for the application.

   📖 From the Snippets panel, drag the **Recipes > UserLogin > Wireframes > User Login – Wireframe** snippet into the Content editable region.

3. Within the table, insert the form and necessary form elements for the user login. At a minimum, you'll need a text field to hold the username and another for the password, as well as a checkbox for optionally remembering the entries and a submit button.

📖 Place your cursor in the row below the words USER LOGIN in the second cell and insert the **Recipes > UserLogin > Forms > User Login - Form** snippet [r1-1].

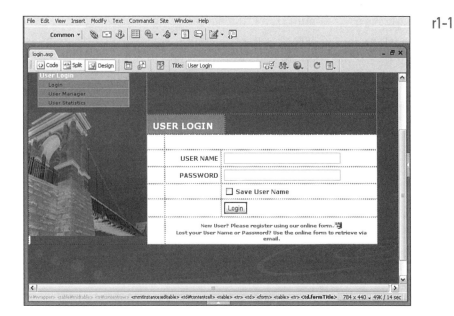

r1-1

4. Save the page. If you created the page from scratch using the template, save the page as `login` with the extension that is appropriate for your platform. For instance, for ASP pages, save the page as `login.asp`.

> **NOTE**
> Although Macromedia's standard login page can be stored as a basic HTML page, our login page includes dynamic elements that require server-side code.

Step 2: Apply Server Behavior for User Authentication

Our first server-side code action is to set up the basic user authentication routines. Dreamweaver includes a standard server behavior that we will use and adapt in our technique. The Log In User server behavior handles the comparison between the user-entered values and entries in the data source. It also redirects the page in both successful (a matching username and password were found) and failed (either the username or its password were not found) scenarios.

NOTE

The following steps use field names from the Recipes database. If you are using your own data source, substitute the equivalent fields.

With the Log In User server behavior, you're offered two degrees of control. The basic option checks only for the username and password; in this situation, everyone registered in the data source can see every page. The second option offers a greater degree of control in which, in addition to the username and password, a group field is also checked. To use the more advanced option, everyone who registers must be assigned to a particular group such as Visitor, Employee, Manager, or Administrator. By incorporating group-level access, you can build one interface that integrates features for both the public and the administrators. The application you are about to build utilizes the group option.

1. From the Server Behaviors panel, choose Add (+) and select **User Authentication > Log In User** [r1-2].

r1-2

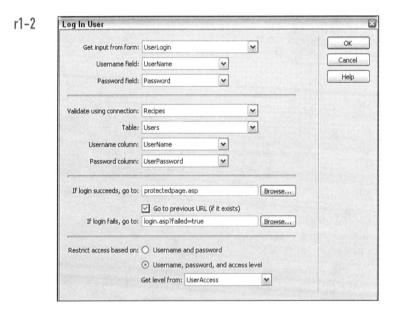

2. Choose the form to work with.

   ⌘ Set the Get Input From Form list to **userLogin**.

3. Choose the form field that holds the username.

   ⌘ Select **UserName** from the Username Field list.

4. Pick the form field that contains the user's password.

    📖 From the Password Field list, choose **Password**.

Now let's make a data source connection.

5. Select the connection that points to your data source with the user table.

    📖 From the Validate Using Connection list, choose **Recipes**.

6. ColdFusion only: Enter the username and password for the data source, if necessary.

7. Select the table from the data source that holds all the user data.

    📖 Set the Table list to **Users** (**users** for PHP).

Dreamweaver will populate the Username Column and Password Column lists after a table is chosen.

8. Declare which column in the table is used to store the username.

    📖 From the Username Column list, choose **UserName**.

9. Select the column to hold the password.

    📖 From the Password Column list, select **UserPassword**.

Now we determine how to react if a login is successful or not.

10. Enter the name of the page you want displayed with a successful login.

    📖 For the If Login Succeeds, Go To field, select Browse and locate the **protectedpage** file for your server model.

11. If you want the user to continue on to his previously entered URL after a successful login, check the Go to Previous URL (if any) option.

12. Enter the page to display if the login is unsuccessful.

    📖 In the If Login Fails, Go To field, enter the following code:

    (VB) `login.asp?failed=true`

    (JS) `login.asp?failed=true`

    (CF) `login.cfm?failed=true`

    (PHP) `login.php?failed=true`

If the login fails, the page submits to itself with an argument identifying the problem. The argument will then be used to trigger a message on the page via additional code added later.

13. Choose whether the access should take the access level into account or not.

    📖 Set the Restrict Access Based On option to **UserName, Password**, and **Access Level**.

14. If you've opted to include the access level, choose the data table column that contains that data.

    📖 From the Get Level From list, choose **UserAccess** and click OK to close the dialog.

15. Save your page.

You won't be able to test your page until the all steps are completed.

Step 3: Insert Error Message

Our next action is to create a custom error message that displays if the login fails. By keeping the error message on the same page, we simplify the user experience.

1. Place the cursor where you'd like the error message to appear.

    📖 Put the cursor in the row above the User Name label.

2. Add the error message code:

    📖 From the Snippets panel, open the **Recipes > UserLogin > Custom Code** folder for your server model and insert the **Login Failure - Display Text** snippet.

    (VB) `<%if (cStr(Request("failed"))<>"") then Response.Write("The Login information you provided is not valid. Please try again.")%>`

    (JS) `<%=(String(Request("Failed"))!="undefined")?"The Login information you provided is not valid. Please try again.":""%>`

    (CF) `<cfif IsDefined("URL.failed")><cfoutput>The Login information you provided is not valid. Please try again </cfoutput></cfif>`

    (PHP) `<?php echo (isset($_GET['failed']))?"The Login information you provided is not valid. Please try again":""; ?>`

3. If you entered the code by hand in Code view, be sure to remove the nonbreaking space character, . (Dragging a snippet into a table in Design view automatically removes the nonbreaking space.)

The ASP-JavaScript and PHP code uses a *conditional operator* (also known as a *trinary* in PHP) instead of a standard If-Then statement. With a conditional or trinary, should the opening statement (the segment before the question mark) be true, the first clause immediately following the question mark is executed. Otherwise, the second clause (found after the colon) is executed.

Step 4: Add Session Objects

Macromedia's Log In User server behavior creates a session variable named MM_Username. In this step, we'll be adding another session variable, UserID, which will be used to filter the recordset on other pages in the application. Our database schema includes the UserID in another related table to keep a record of logins, which will be used later to display the login statistics.

There are three parts to integrating the UserID session object into our code: adding it to the SQL, creating a session variable in the recordset code, and exposing the session variable to Dreamweaver. First we'll add UserID to the SQL statement inserted by the Log In User server behavior.

1. Switch to Code view.
2. Choose Edit > Find and Replace or use the keyboard shortcut Ctrl-F (Command-F) to open the Find and Replace dialog.
3. In the current document, look for the source code SELECT UserName, UserPassword.

   When found, the entire line will be as follows:

   VB `MM_rsUser.Source = "SELECT UserName, UserPassword"`

   JS `MM_rsUser.Source = "SELECT UserName, UserPassword"`

   CF `SELECT UserName,UserPassword,UserGroup FROM Users WHERE UserName='#FORM.UserName#'`

   PHP `$LoginRS__query=sprintf("SELECT UserName, UserPassword, UserAccess FROM users WHERE UserName='%s' AND UserPassword='%s'",`

4. Add a comma after UserPassword (UserGroup in ColdFusion) followed by UserID so that the line now reads:

   VB `MM_rsUser.Source = "SELECT UserName, UserPassword, UserID"`

   JS `MM_rsUser.Source = "SELECT UserName, UserPassword, UserID"`

   CF `SELECT UserName,UserPassword,UserGroup, UserID FROM Users WHERE UserName='#FORM.UserName#'`

   PHP `$LoginRS__query=sprintf("SELECT UserName, UserPassword, UserAccess, UserID FROM users WHERE UserName='%s' AND UserPassword='%s'",`

5. Save your page.

Now that the UserID is part of the recordset, you can create a session object in the code. This new session object will make it easy to reference profile information based on the active user. Once the session variable is created at the login, the UserID can then be accessed from any page in the application.

1. As done previously, use the Find and Replace feature to search for the code Session("MM_Username").

   The entire line reads as follows:

   (VB) `Session("MM_Username") = MM_valUsername`

   (JS) `Session("MM_Username") = MM_valUsername`

   (CF) `<cfset Session.MM_Username=FORM.UserName>`

   (PHP) `$GLOBALS['MM_Username'] = $loginUsername;`

2. Add a paragraph return after the line of code.

3. Insert the following code:

   📖 From the Snippets panel, open the **Recipes > UserLogin > Custom Code** folder for your server model and insert the **Session – User ID** snippet.

   (VB) `Session("MM_UserID") = MM_UserID`

   (JS) `Session("MM_UserID") = String(MM_rsUser.Fields.Item("UserID").Value);`

   (CF)
   ```
   <cfif IsDefined("Form.StoreProfile")>
       <cfset Session.MM_UserID=MM_rsUser.UserID>
   <cfelse>
       <cfset Session.MM_UserID="">
   </cfif>
   ```

   (PHP) `$GLOBALS['MM_UserID'] = mysql_result($LoginRS,0,'UserID');`

4. One additional step is needed for PHP. Just as Dreamweaver registers the `Username` session variable, we must make sure to register the `UserID` session variable. In fact, we'll put our `session_register()` function right after the one inserted by Dreamweaver.

Using Find and Replace in Code view, search for the line `session_register("MM_Username");` and place this code after it:

```
session_register("MM_UserID");
```

Why is the ColdFusion code so much more elaborate than the ASP code here? ColdFusion 5 has a restriction that prevents cookies from being set in a page that is being redirected. In this workaround, the username value is stored in a session variable that will be read in the Confirmation page and then stored in a cookie. This restriction has been removed in ColdFusion MX.

NOTE

The final element in our session object coding is, in all honesty, optional but is a good practice to follow. In this step, we'll create a site-level variable for the session object within Dreamweaver. While not necessary, it makes it possible to insert the `UserID` session object by just dragging and dropping.

1. From the Bindings panel, select Add (+) and choose **Session Variable**.
2. Enter **UserID** in the Name field of the Session Variable dialog and click OK.
3. Expand the Session tree in the Bindings panel to see your new variable [r1-3].

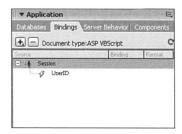 r1-3

Step 5: Add Cookie Logic for the User Login Form

The checkbox on the login form enables the application to remember the username. This makes it far easier for the user to log in while keeping the feature optional for security reasons. The computer remembers each user by storing his information in a cookie on the client's computer. We now need to add the code to create and manage the cookies based on the user-entered values. There are several places to insert additional code: The first code, which creates the cookies, is placed above the recordset, while all the other code is placed within the form elements themselves.

1. In Code view, place your cursor at the top of the source code.

   Because the cookie values are inserted into the form elements when the page loads, the code block needs to be at the top of the page above the recordset declaration.

   For ASP and PHP server models, your cursor should be placed below the tag that includes the connection information.

2. Insert the following code:

   ▫ From the Snippets panel, open the **Recipes > UserLogin > Custom Code** folder for your server model and insert the **Cookie - Object Code** snippet.

   (VB)
```
<%
if (cStr(Request.Form("Login"))<>"")   then
  if (cStr(Request.Form("StoreProfile"))<>"")   then
    Response.Cookies("UserName") = cStr(Request("UserName"))
  else
    Response.Cookies("UserName") = ""
  end if
  today =  DateAdd("d",30, Date())
  Response.Cookies("UserName").Expires = today
end if
%>
```

   (JS)
```
<%
if (String(Request.Form("Login"))!="undefined")  {
  if (String(Request.Form("StoreProfile"))!="undefined")  {
    Response.Cookies("UserName") = String(Request("UserName"));
    } else  {
  Response.Cookies("UserName") = "";
}
  var today = new Date();
  today.setDate(today.getDate()+30);
  ➡Response.Cookies("UserName").Expires =
  ➡(today.getMonth()+1)+"/"+today.getDate()+"/"+
today.getFullYear();
}
%>
```

```
CF   <cflock timeout="20" throwontimeout="No" type="EXCLUSIVE"
    ➥scope="SESSION">
      <cfif IsDefined("Session.MM_UserID")>
            <cfif Session.MM_UserID NEQ "">
                  <cfcookie name="UserName" value="#Session.MM_UserName#"
                  ➥expires="30">
            </cfif>
      </cfif>
    </cflock>
```

```
PHP  <?php
    if (isset($_POST['Login'])) {
          if (isset($_POST['StoreProfile'])) {
                setcookie ("UserName",
                ➥$_POST['UserName'],time()+60*60*24*30);
          } else {
                setcookie ("UserName", "",time()-43200);
          }
    }
    ?>
```

For these code blocks, after verifying that the user form exists and that the StoreProfile checkbox is selected, the cookies are created and are set to expire in 30 days. The PHP code calculates the number of seconds in 30 days as required by the setcookie() function.

When the login page loads, if the username has been previously stored—in other words, if the cookie exists—we want to show the StoreProfile checkbox selected. To do this, we'll have to add some additional code within the <input> tag that describes the checkbox.

> **NOTE**
> You might find it easiest to work in the split Design and Code view for this operation.

1. In Design view, select the **StoreProfile** checkbox.
2. In Code view, place your cursor inside the <input> tag just before the closing angle bracket.
3. Insert the following code:
   - From the Snippets panel, open the **Recipes > UserLogin > Custom Code** folder for your server model and insert the **Cookie - StoreProfile Checkbox** snippet.

```
VB   <%if (cstr(Request.Cookies("UserName"))<>"")then
     Response.Write("checked")%>
```

```
JS   <%=(String(Request.Cookies("UserName"))!="")?"checked":""%
```

CF `<cfif IsDefined("COOKIE.UserName") AND COOKIE.UserName NEQ "">`
`<cfoutput>checked</cfoutput></cfif>`

PHP `<?php echo ($_COOKIE['UserName']!="")?"checked":""; ?>`

Two more modifications, and the login page will be complete. Now we'll tie the UserName and Password text fields to their respective cookies. If a cookie value is defined, it will populate with that value; if the value is empty, the form elements will appear blank.

1. In Design view, select the **UserName** text field.
2. In Code view, move to the end of the input tag, press the spacebar, and then insert the following code:

   📖 From the Snippets panel, open the **Recipes > UserLogin > Custom Code** folder for your server model and insert the **User Name Cookie - Display Text** snippet.

   VB `value="<%=Request.Cookies("UserName")%>"`

   JS `value="<%= Request.Cookies("UserName")%>"`

   CF `value="<cfif isDefined("Cookie.UserName")>`
   `➥<cfoutput>#Cookie.UserName#`
   `</cfoutput></cfif>"`

   PHP `value="<?php echo $_COOKIE['UserName']; ?>"`

3. Save your page.

> **NOTE**
> If the Code Hints pop-up displays when you press space, press Esc to dismiss it.

Test your page by entering usernames and passwords into the appropriate fields. If the application finds a match, you'll be redirected to the protectedpage file. (If you haven't created a placeholder for this page, you'll get a Page Not Found error.) If no match is found, the error message should be shown [r1-4]. Whenever you return to this page, the username should already be filled in after selecting the Save User Name option.

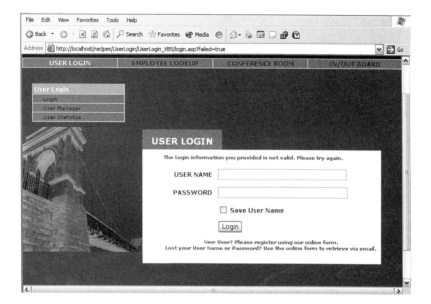

Step 6: Create Links to Other Application Pages

It's important for the developer to cover every situation a user might encounter when interacting with an application page. So far, our page handles both a successful and an unsuccessful registration attempt; but what if the user is not registered at all or has forgotten his password? In this final step, we'll link to pages in the overall application to accommodate these situations.

1. Select the text or image you want to use as a link to a new user registration page.

   📖 Select the word **register** in the text block at the bottom of the form.

2. Link to the appropriate application page.

   📖 Choose the folder icon next to the Link field of the Property inspector. From the Select File dialog, choose the **register_user** page for your server model.

3. Select the text or image to use as a link to the email password page.

   📖 Select the phrase **online form** in the text block at the bottom of the form.

4. Create a link to the desired application page.

   📖 Open the Select File dialog again and choose the **send_password** file for your server model.

5. Save your page when you are done.

In the next recipe, we'll complete the first of our two links: the new user registration page.

End User Recipe: New User Registration

Whether an organization allows new users to register themselves is, of course, a key decision. On the plus side, this policy takes an enormous workload off the administrative staff; however, there are security concerns at work. This application strikes a balance by allowing self-registration but initially restricting those registered to the lowest level of access. A standard Dreamweaver Insert Record server behavior is used to create the record.

Step 1: Build the Application Design

We start with a basic page, inserting all the form elements needed.

1. Create a basic dynamic page either by hand or from a template.
   - In the **UserLogin** folder, locate the folder for your server model and open the register_user page found there.
2. Add a table to the content region of your page to contain the interface elements for the application.
   - From the Snippets panel, drag the **Recipes > UserLogin > Wireframes > Register User - Wireframe** snippet into the Content editable region.
3. Within the table, insert the form and any necessary form elements for the application. You'll need five text fields—one for each of the fields (First Name, Last Name, User Name, Password, and Email Address)—as well as a submit button.
   - Place your cursor in the row below the words REGISTER USER in the second cell and insert the **Recipes > UserLogin > Forms > Register User - Form** snippet [r1-5].

Enhancing Cookie Production

Our recipe just scratches the surface of what you can do with cookies. The real power of cookies lies in personalization. With sufficient planning, you can personalize the Web experience for each and every one of your visitors.

Although you can certainly use the recipe code as a starting point for working with cookies, you might find it more productive to use a dedicated extension. WeAssist has created and extension that greatly simplifies creating, accessing, and deleting cookies. With WA Cookies, you can quickly add functionality to remember users when they come back to your site and easily customize their user experience according to stored cookie data.

For more information, visit
http://www.webassist.com/Products/Recipes/WACookies.asp.

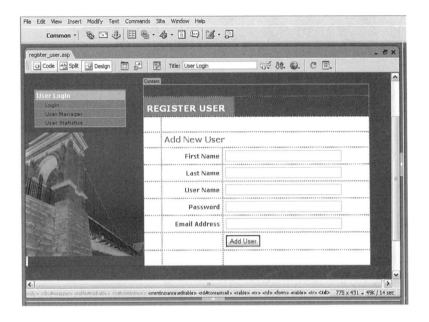

r1-5

Step 2: Add Insert Record Server Behavior

After the framework for the page is in place, we'll apply the first server behavior—Insert Record.

In the process of applying this behavior, you might notice that not all fields have matching form elements. Several columns—UserID, UserAccess, and UserRegDate—are automatically populated by the data source when the new record is created. The UserID is an autonumber field that increments by one for each new user, whereas UserRegDate stores the current date through the use of a special function—Now() in Access, for example—set as the default value. The UserAccess field defaults to the lowest level of access; it's up to the administrator to raise the level if warranted.

For ASP

1. From the Server Behaviors panel, choose Add (+) and select **Insert Record** to display the dialog [r1-6].

To accomodate the different dialogs for the various server models, the steps are presented separately here and when necesary throughout this recipe.

NOTE

r1-6

2. Select the connection to the data source.

   ⌦ Choose **Recipes** from the Connection list.

3. Choose the table in your data source to hold the new records.

   ⌦ From the Insert Into Table list, choose the **Users** table.

4. In the After Inserting, Go To field, enter the page you want the users to see after successfully registering.

   ⌦ Select the Browse button and locate the **login** page for your server model.

5. Declare from which form on the page the data should be taken.

   Set the Get Values From field to the form name, `registerUser`.

6. For the form elements shown in the list, set each one to its equivalent in the data source. All form elements should be submitted as text:

   ⌦ Set form element `FirstName` to field `UserFirstName`.

   　Set form element `Lastname` to field `UserLastName`.

   　Set form element `UserName` to field `UserName`.

   　Set form element `Password` to field `UserPassword`.

   　Set form element `EmailAddress` to field `UserEmail`.

7. When you're done, click OK to close the dialog and insert the behavior.

8. Save your page.

For ColdFusion and PHP

1. From the Server Behaviors panel, choose Add (+) and select **Insert Record**.

2. In the Insert Record dialog, choose the current form.

   ⌦ Select **RegisterUser** from the Submit Values From list.

3. Select your data source from the list.

　　📖 Choose **Recipes** from the Data Source list.

4. ColdFusion users should enter their username and password, if needed.

5. Select the table in the data source to insert into from the list.

　　📖 Choose **Users** (**users** for PHP) from the Insert Into Table list.

6. Set the data source fields to their corresponding form elements.

　　📖 Make sure the UserID data column is set to be an unused Primary Key.

　　　UserAccess should not get a value from the form.

　　　Set UserFirstName to the FORM.FirstName form element and submit as Text type.

　　　Set UserLastName to the FORM.LastName form element and submit as Text type.

　　　Set UserName to the FORM.UserName form element and submit as Text type.

　　　Set UserPassword to the FORM.UserPassword form element and submit as Text type.

　　　Set UserEmail to the FORM.EmailAddress form element and submit as Text type.

　　　UserRegDate should not get a value from the form.

7. In the After Inserting, Go To field, enter **report_projectsummary.cfm** or **report_projectsummary.php** depending on your server model, and click OK to close the dialog.

8. Save the page.

Step 3: Store New User Info in a Cookie

As we did on the login page, we'll now store the just-supplied username in a cookie. The cookie will then be read when the user returns to the login page, automatically filling in the values. This additional bit of code smoothes the user experience.

> **NOTE**
>
> Because of the different requirements for PHP as compared to the other server models, the next steps are presented for ASP and ColdFusion users first before the application of the Check New Username server behavior. The related PHP steps must be applied after the server behavior is added to the page.

For ASP and ColdFusion

1. In Code view, search for a comment that contains the phrase Insert Record: set variables using Dreamweaver's Find and Replace.

　　This comment is the first line in a code block; we want to insert another code block just above this one.

2. Add a paragraph return between the two existing server-side code blocks.

3. Insert the following code:

　　📖 From the Snippets panel, open the **Recipes > UserLogin > Custom Code** folder for your server model and insert the **Register - Save Login in Cookie** snippet.

```
VB  <%
        if (cStr(Request("AddUser"))<>"")   then
          Response.Cookies("UserName") = Request.Form("UserName")
          today = DateAdd("d",30,Date())
          Response.Cookies("UserName").Expires = today
        end if
    %>
```

```
JS  <%
        if (String(Request("AddUser"))!="undefined")   {
          Response.Cookies("UserName") = Request.Form("UserName");
            var today = new Date();
            today.setDate(today.getDate()+30);
            Response.Cookies("UserName").Expires =
          ➥(today.getMonth()+1)+"/"+today.getDate()+"/"+today.
          ➥getFullYear();
        }
    %>
```

```
CF  <cfif IsDefined("FORM.UserName")>
        <cflock scope="Session" timeout="30" type="Exclusive">
          <cfset Session.MM_Username=FORM.UserName>
        </cflock>
      </cfif>
```

4. Save your page.

Step 4: Verify Username Is Unique

One other Dreamweaver server behavior is necessary for the user registration page.
To make sure that the username entered is unique in the data source, we'll employ the
Check New Username server behavior. Should a duplicate username be found, the server
behavior will resubmit to the current page with a query string argument that, in turn,
triggers the display of an error message.

1. From the Server Behaviors panel, select Add (+) and choose **User Authentication >
   Check New Username**.

   The Check New Username dialog displays [r1-7].

r1-7

2. Select the form field containing the username.

 📖 In the Username Field list, choose **UserName**.

3. Choose the page you want the application to present if the username is not unique.

 📖 In the If Already Exists, Go To field, enter the filename for the `register_user` page for your server model followed by the query string `?repeat=true`.

(VB) `register_user.asp?repeat=true`

(JS) `register_user.asp?repeat=true`

(CF) `register_user.cfm?repeat=true.`

(PHP) `register_user.php?repeat=true`

4. Click OK to close the dialog.

The query string variable technique is useful for displaying conditional text without loading another page. Now we'll add the code that controls what effect the query string variable repeat has on the current page.

1. In Design view, place the cursor where you'd like the error message to appear.

 📖 Put the cursor in the row above the Register User label.

2. Add the error message code.

 📖 From the Snippets panel, open the **Recipes > UserLogin > Custom Code** folder for your server model and insert the **Duplicate User Name - Display Text** snippet.

(VB)
```
<%if (cStr(Request("repeat"))<>"") then Response.Write("That
Username is already taken. Please choose a new name and try
again.<br>(Use your browser's back button to update your previous
entry.)")%>
```

(JS)
```
<%=(String(Request("repeat"))!="undefined")?"That Username is
already taken. Please choose a new name and try again.<br>(Use your
browser's back button to update your previous entry.)":""%>
```

(CF) `<cfif IsDefined("URL.repeat_user")><cfoutput> That Username is already taken. Please choose a new name and try again.<br>(Use your browser's back button to update your previous entry.)</cfoutput></cfif>`

(PHP) `<?php echo (isset($_GET['repeat']))?"That Username is already taken. Please choose a new name and try again.<br>(Use your browser's back button to update your previous entry.)":""; ?>`

3. If you entered the code by hand in Code view, be sure to remove the nonbreaking space character, .

4. Save the page.

You can test the Register User page right within Dreamweaver. Select View > Live Data and, in the URL parameter field on the Document toolbar, add the query string repeat=true. Press Tab, and the error message should appear [r1-8].

r1-8

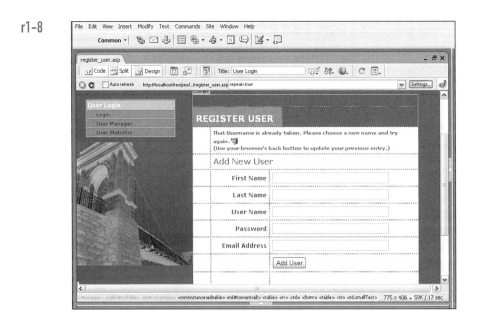

PHP Only

In addition to adding code to set the cookies, PHP also requires that you temporarily store or cache its processing. Without doing so, the act of setting the cookie would supercede the redirection and prevent it from occurring. PHP activity is cached with the code `ob_start()` and restored with `ob_end_flush()`.

It is often necessary to insert code in a particular sequence for everything to work as it should. In this case, we needed to include the caching functions after the Insert Record and Check User Name server behaviors were inserted. Had we made our modifications earlier, the Insert Record server behavior would not have been recognized by Dreamweaver, and therefore the Check Username server behavior could not have been inserted.

NOTE

First, however, we'll add the code to create the cookies.

1. In Code view, use Dreamweaver's Find and Replace to search for `$insertGoTo = "login.php";`.
2. Insert a paragraph return after the found code and enter the following code:

   📖 From the Snippets panel, open the **Recipes > UserLogin > Custom Code_PHP** folder and insert the **Register - Save Login in Cookie** snippet.

   ```
   setcookie ("UserName", $_POST['UserName'],time()+60*60*24*30);
   setcookie ("Password", $_POST['Password'],time()+60*60*24*30);
   ```

   Now let's wrap a slightly larger code block with our caching commands.

3. Again using Find and Replace, search for the code that starts `$insertSQL = sprintf`.
4. Select all the code from the found code line up to and including the code line that begins `header(sprintf`. The entire code block will look like this:

   (PHP)
   ```
   $insertSQL = sprintf("INSERT INTO users (UserFirstName,
   ➥UserLastName, UserName, UserPassword, UserEmail) VALUES (%s, %s,
   ➥%s, %s, %s)",
                  GetSQLValueString($_POST['FirstName'], "text"),
                  GetSQLValueString($_POST['LastName'], "text"),
                  GetSQLValueString($_POST['UserName'], "text"),
                  GetSQLValueString($_POST['Password'], "text"),
                  GetSQLValueString($_POST['EmailAddress'],"text"));

   mysql_select_db($database_Recipes, $Recipes);
   $Result1 = mysql_query($insertSQL, $Recipes) or
   ➥die(mysql_error());

   $insertGoTo = "login.php";
   setcookie ("UserName", $_POST['UserName'],time()+43200);
   setcookie ("Password", $_POST['Password'],time()+43200);
   if (isset($_SERVER['QUERY_STRING'])) {
   ```

   Continues

```
                    $insertGoTo .= (strpos($insertGoTo, '?')) ? "&" : "?";
                    $insertGoTo .= $_SERVER['QUERY_STRING'];
                }
                header(sprintf("Location: %s", $insertGoTo));
```

5. Enter the following code before and after the selected code block:

    📖 From the Snippets panel, open the **Recipes > UserLogin > Custom Code_PHP** folder and insert the **Register – Cache Activity** snippet.

Before:

   (PHP) `ob_start()`

After:

     `ob_end_flush()`

6. Save your page.

Test your new page by entering values you expect to fail as well as those you're sure will work.

End User Recipe: Personalizing and Protecting Pages

It's generally a good idea to provide feedback to a user's action, whether the action succeeds or fails. The feedback can take many forms: A simple thank-you page is often used. However, the more personalized the feedback, the better. By including information the user submitted on the form, you demonstrate that you actually did receive the data. In this recipe, you'll see both how to acknowledge receipt of a form submission in a personal manner and how to protect a page from unregistered users.

Step 1: Implement the Content Design

The first step is to create a page to hold the dynamic content. The Recipes example is rather stark with its title of Protected Page [r1-9], but that's just to keep the concept clear. You are free (and encouraged) to develop your own design.

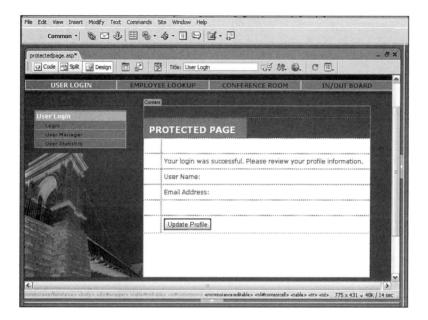

1. Create a basic dynamic page either by hand or from a template.

   📖 In the **UserLogin** folder, locate the folder for your server model and open the `protectedpage` page found there.

2. Add a table to the content region of your page to contain the interface elements for the application.

   📖 From the Snippets panel, drag the **Recipes > UserLogin > Wireframes > Protected Page - Wireframe** snippet into the Content editable region.

3. Within the table, insert a content table with the necessary text and a form button. No form is necessary for this application.

   📖 Place your cursor in the row below the words PROTECTED PAGE in the second cell and insert the **Recipes > UserLogin > ContentTables > Protected Page - Content Table** snippet.

4. Save your page.

Step 2: Add Database Components

To demonstrate to the user that he is properly logged in, this application will pull his data into a recordset and then display a few of the fields on the page. We'll target the recordset by using the session variable created on the login page, `UserID`.

1. From the Bindings panel, select Add (+) and choose **Recordset (Query)**.
2. The Recordset dialog has two views: simple and advanced. Make sure you are in simple mode [r1-10].

r1-10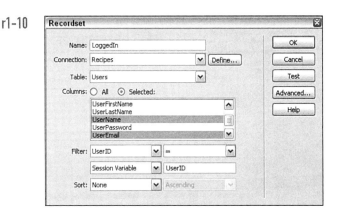

3. In the Name field, enter the label for your recordset.

   ▭ Enter **LoggedIn** as the recordset name.
4. From the Connections list, choose the desired data source connection.

   ▭ Select **Recipes** from the Connections list.
5. Choose the appropriate table containing the users information.

   ▭ Select **Users** from the Table list.
6. Choose the **Selected** option under Columns and select only the necessary columns for this recordset.

   ▭ Choose **UserID**, **UserName**, and **UserEmail** by Ctrl-clicking on each column.

   It's always a good idea to limit the number of columns to the lowest number of usable items.
7. In the Filter area of the Recordset dialog, set the four Filter list elements like this:

| UserID | = (Equals) |
| Session Variable | MM_UserID |

   Effectively, what we are doing is limiting the recordset to the data from just one individual—the one currently logged in—requesting the current page.
8. With just one record, no sorting is necessary. Click OK to confirm your choices and close the dialog.

We now have all we need to output a personalized response.

Step 3: Display Profile Data

In this step, we'll insert the dynamic data from the recordset. Although you could use the Dynamic Text server behavior to make this addition, it's more intuitive—not to mention a bit quicker—to drag the two fields from the Bindings panel.

1. From the Bindings panel expand the recordset, if necessary.
2. Drag the UserName (or corresponding) field onto the page just after the User Name: text.
3. Drag the UserEmail (or similar) field onto the page just after the Email Address: label [r1-11].
4. Save your page before continuing.

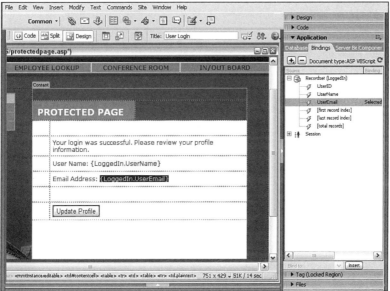

r1-11

You can test your page by entering Live Data view. The first time you preview the page, Dreamweaver will present a dialog asking for a MM_UserID session variable value. Enter **1** or whatever number represents a valid entry in your UserID field.

Step 4: Restrict Access to Pages

Our registration system is in place, and it's time to protect our page from unauthorized viewing. Dreamweaver supplies a very handy server behavior that does the job nicely: Restrict Access to Page. With this server behavior, you can restrict access based on a matching username and password, or you can extend the restriction to check access groups. The Recipes application uses the latter approach for maximum flexibility.

1. From the Server Behaviors panel, choose Add (+) and select **User Authentication > Restrict Access to Page**.
2. Choose the **Restrict Based On Username, Password, and Access Level** option.

   With the Access Level option chosen, the Select Level(s) area becomes active. Before we can select which levels to allow, we need to define them.
3. Choose **Define** to open the Define Access Levels dialog [r1-12].

r1–12

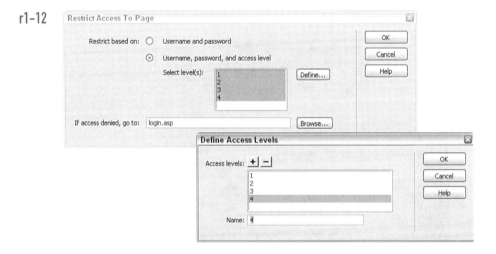

4. Click Add (+) and enter the name of the access level as it appears in your data source.

   📖 The Recipes data source uses a numbering sequence (1 to 4, where 1 is the highest level of access) rather than words to indicate levels. Enter each number on its own line.
5. Repeat step 4 for each level and click OK when you're done to close the Define Access Levels dialog.

6. In the Restrict Access to Page dialog, Shift-select all the access levels to allow all logged-in users to see this page.

    Obviously, when this behavior is applied on different pages, different access levels will be selected.

7. In the If Access Is Denied, Go To field, choose your login page.

8. Click OK to close the dialog box.

Once the Restrict Access to Page server behavior is inserted in a page, visitors cannot go to that page without logging in. If they try, the code redirects them to the user login page.

The Restrict Access to Page server behavior is very powerful, but it has to be inserted on all pages. One way around this chore is to insert the server behavior on the template rather than on individual pages and have Dreamweaver do the installation work for us. It's best to set the server behavior to allow all access levels and then, on a case-by-case basis, restrict the access levels as needed.

> ⌂ To use the template approach, open the **userlogin** template for your server model and apply the steps covered in the last action. Save the template and update all pages. The administrative recipe pages—edit_user, user_manager, and user_statistics—should be opened individually so that the access levels can be reset to 1, the administrative level.

Step 5: Add Link to Update Profile Button

Everyone makes mistakes entering form information sooner or later. Once you press the submit button, the data you entered goes right into the data source, and it's always good to provide a way for the user to amend his entries. In this step, we'll link a button to another page in the application.

1. Select the **Update Profile** form button.

2. From the Behaviors panel, choose Add (+) and select the **Go To URL** behavior.

3. Enter the path to application page for editing user profiles.

    > ⌂ Select the Browse button and choose the **edit_profile** page for your server model.

4. Save the page when you're done.

Obviously, you don't have to use a form button and a JavaScript behavior to get the linking functionality; a text or graphic with a standard link would work as well. On the other hand, the form button provides a certain degree of continuity with the other form elements in our application without having to expend resources to develop suitable graphics.

End User Recipe: Conditional Display

Just as we protected any number of pages from unauthorized viewing, we can protect parts of those pages. With group access levels deployed, any page element can be modified so that it is seen only by members of certain groups. In this recipe, we will allow only those with the highest level of access—administrators—to view particular navigation links.

Make Elements Conditional

WARNING

Although you should exercise care when making changes to any document, you need to be extra careful when applying alterations to templates because of the potential ramifications for numerous files.

Because we want the conditional display to be a part of every page in the application—including those already built—the application template must be modified. Dreamweaver maintains a connection to all files derived from a template, so changes can be propagated automatically to affected documents. If you've already posted some files to your remote server, you'll need to upload them again after the template changes are applied.

In this step, we'll select the page elements—here, two rows of a table used for navigation—prior to applying the code.

1. From the Templates category of the Assets panel, select the template to be used for the login application.

   📖 Choose the **userlogin** template for your server model.

2. Select the Edit button on the bottom of the Assets panel, or double-click the file.

3. In Design view, select the lower two rows of the navigation links on the left side of the page [r1-13].

The links within these rows are associated with administration functions: User Manager and User Statistics.

4. Switch to Code view, where you'll note that only the individual cells have been selected, not the containing rows (the <tr> tags). Adjust the selection so that both rows containing the cells are highlighted.

If you attempt the next step (applying a snippet) with just the cells selected, Dreamweaver will wrap the code around the entire table—which is not the desired effect.

5. Wrap the following code around the selection.

    ▢ From the Snippets panel, open the **Recipes > UserLogin > Custom Code** folder for your server model and insert the **Conditional Display** snippet.

Before:

VB
```
<%
    if (cStr(Session("MM_UserAuthorization"))="1")  {
%>
```

After:

```
    <%
    end if
%>
```

Before:

```
JS  <%
    if (String(Session("MM_UserAuthorization"))=="1")  {
    %>
```

After:

```
    <%
    }
    %>
```

Before:

```
CF  <cfif IsDefined("Session.MM_UserAuthorization") AND
    Session.MM_UserAuthorization EQ "1">
```

After:

```
    </cfif>
```

Before:

```
PHP  <?php if ($_Session["MM_UserGroup"]=="1") { ?>
```

After:

```
    <?php } ?>
```

The code snippet checks to see if the session object MM_UserAuthorization (MM_UserGroup for PHP) is set to 1, the administrator designation as defined in the data source. The resulting effect is that the links to administrative pages are visible only by administrators.

Be sure to save your template and update all derived documents.

End User Recipe: Editing the User Profile

When the user selects Update Profile from the login confirmation page, the application we are about to build is displayed. On this page are all the fields previously seen in the Add User file. The Dreamweaver server behavior Update Record is used here, and we'll also implement a Cancel button to allow the user to back out of the update operation gracefully.

Step 1: Implement Page Design

Let's begin by building the basic page.

1. Open a new dynamic page, either constructing one by hand or deriving one from a template.

   📖 In the **UserLogin** folder, locate the folder for your server model and open the `edit_profile` page found there.

2. Add a table to the content region of your page to contain the interface elements for the application.

   📖 From the Snippets panel, drag the **Recipes > UserLogin > Wireframes > Edit Profile - Wireframe** snippet into the Content editable region.

3. Within the table, insert the form and any necessary form elements for the application. You'll need five text fields—one for each of the fields (`First Name`, `Last Name`, `User Name`, `Password` and `Email Address`)—as well as two buttons, one for submitting the update and another for canceling the action.

   📖 Place your cursor in the row below the words EDIT PROFILE in the second cell and insert the **Recipes > UserLogin > Forms > Edit Profile - Form** snippet [r1-14].

r1-14

4. ColdFusion and PHP Users: These server models require a unique record ID for the Update Record server behavior to work properly. In these situations, a hidden form field is used to convey the needed data.

  ▢ ColdFusion and PHP developers should drag a Hidden Form Field from the Forms category of the Insert bar and name it **UserID**.

Step 2: Add Database Components

To build the recordset for this page, we will again filter the Users table on the session variable previously created, UserID.

1. From the Server Behaviors panel, choose Add (+) and select **Recordset (Query)**.
2. In the simple view of the Recordset panel, give the recordset a meaningful name.
  ▢ Enter **Users** in the Recordset field.
3. Choose the connection for your data source.
  ▢ Select **Recipes** from the Connection list.
4. Choose the desired table.
  ▢ Select **Users** from the Table list.
5. Keep the Columns option set to All.
6. In the Filter area of the Recordset dialog, set the four Filter list elements like this:

UserID	= (Equals)
Session Variable	MM_UserID

Again, this filter limits the recordset to a single record—that of the one currently logged in.
7. Leave the Sort option set to None.
8. Click OK to confirm your choices and close the dialog.
9. Save the page when you're done.

NOTE
PHP and ColdFusion users will also need to populate the Hidden Form field with the session variable.

Step 3: Data Binding Process

With our recordset defined, we're ready to bind the data from the recordset to the individual form elements on the page. Each of the text fields is bound to a separate data column.

1. In the Bindings panel, expand the recordset entry so that all data columns display.
2. Drag each of the following data columns over the corresponding text field:
   - Drag column `UserFirstName` to field `FirstName`.
   - Drag column `UserLastName` to field `LastName`.
   - Drag column `UserName` to field `UserName`.
   - Drag column `Password` to field `Password`.
   - Drag column `UserEmail` to field `Email Address`.
3. Leave the default formatting for all dynamic text fields.

When you're done, all the elements in the form should display a dynamic entry [r1-15].

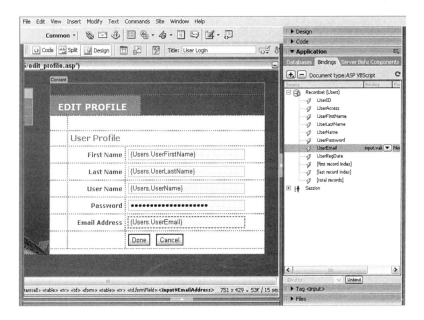

r1-15

This next step is for ColdFusion and PHP users only: Both server models require that a unique ID be used in conjunction with the Update Record server behavior. For this page, this value is contained in the session variable, `UserID`. We'll make it available to the server behavior by embedding the session variable in the hidden form element.

1. Select the desired form element.
   - 📖 Choose the **UserID** hidden form element.

2. Bind the session variable to the element.

📖 Choose the lightning bolt symbol next to the **Value** field in the Property inspector to open the Dynamic Data dialog.

In the Dynamic Data dialog, expand the Session Variable node and choose **UserID**.

Click OK to close the dialog.

3. Save your page.

Step 4: Update User Profile

The essential task of this page—modifying an existing record in a data source—is handled by a Dreamweaver server behavior, Update Record. After the record has been modified, the confirmation page is reloaded.

After the server behavior is applied, make sure the `<form>` tag is selected and take a look at the Property inspector. Notice that the action is set to server-side code: `<%=MM_editAction%>` for ASP, `<cfoutput>#CurrentPage#</cfoutput>` for ColdFusion, and `<?php echo $editFormAction; ?>` for PHP. You'll see the same generic code variable in all of Dreamweaver's server behaviors that modify a data source: Add Record, Update Record, and Delete Record.

For ASP

1. From the Server Behaviors panel, chose Add (+) and select **Update Record** to display the dialog.
2. Select the connection to the data source.

📖 Choose **Recipes** from the Connection list.
3. Choose the table containing the user data.

📖 From the Table To Update list, select **Users**.
4. Select the recordset from which to get data source fields.

📖 Set the Select Record From field to **Users**.
5. Set the primary key for the recordset.

📖 From the Unique Key Column list, choose **UserID** and make sure that the Numeric option is checked.
6. Enter the page you want the users to see after successfully registering.

📖 In the After Inserting, Go To field, select the Browse button and locate the **protected_page** file for your server model.

7. Choose the form on the page from which the values are to be taken.

     Set the Get Values From field to **EditProfile**.

8. For the form elements shown in the list, set each one to its equivalent in the data source. All form elements should be submitted as text:

     Set form element `FirstName` to field `UserFirstName` as Text.

     Set form element `Lastname` to field `UserLastName` as Text.

     Set form element `UserName` to field `UserName` as Text.

     Set form element `Password` to field `UserPassword` as Text.

     Set form element `EmailAddress` to field `UserEmail` as Text.

9. When you're done, click OK to close the dialog and insert the behavior.

10. Save your page.

For ColdFusion and PHP

1. From the Server Behaviors panel, choose Add (+) and select **Update Record**.

2. In the Update Record dialog, choose the current form.

     Select **Users** from the Submit Values From list.

3. Select your data source from the list.

     Choose **Recipes** from the Data Source list.

4. Enter your username and password, if needed.

5. Select the table in the data source to insert into from the list.

     Choose **Users** from the Insert Into Table list.

6. Set the data source fields to their corresponding form elements.

     As the Primary Key, `UserID` selects the record using `FORM.UserID` as a `Numeric` (`Integer` in PHP) type.

     Make sure `UserAccess` does not get a value.

     Set `UserFirstName` to get its value from the `FORM.FirstName` form element as Text.

     Set `UserLastName` to get its value from the `FORM.Lastname` form element as Text.

     Set `UserName` to get its value from the `FORM.UserName` form element as Text.

     Set `UserPassword` to get its value from the `FORM.Password` form element as Text.

     Set `UserEmail` to get its value from the `FORM.EmailAddress` form element as Text.

     Make sure `UserRegDate` does not get a value.

7. In the After Inserting, Go To field, enter the path to the file you want displayed after the record is updated.

     In the After Inserting, Go To field, select the **protectedpage** file for your server model.

8. Check your entries to verify that they are correct; if so, click OK.

9. Save your page.

Step 5: Cancel the Update

Here's a user-friendly addition that takes little effort to implement: a Cancel button. How do you cancel a server-side action that hasn't taken place yet? In this case, a little bit of JavaScript does the trick.

1. Select the Cancel form button.

2. From the Behaviors panel, select Add (+) and choose **Call JavaScript**.

3. In the Call JavaScript dialog, enter the following code:

```
history.back();
```

4. When you're done, click OK to close the dialog.

5. Save the page.

Although it's true that users could just as well click the Back button on their browsers, it's also true that you want to make user experience as clear as possible.

End User Recipe: Emailing Passwords

Forgotten passwords are a fact of life in the modern world, and unless handled dynamically, they're an administrator's nightmare. With the page we are about to build, users enter their mailing address and request their password. The application responds by looking up their mailing address, and if a match is found, the password is emailed to the user.

Setting Up for Server-Side Email

ASP, ColdFusion, and PHP all use different mechanisms to handle email. A separate email component is necessary for ASP, and numerous commercial ones are available. One of the most common is called Microsoft CDONTS (an abbreviation for Collaboration Data Objects for Windows NT Server). The CDONTS component is standard on all Windows servers since IIS 4.0 and up to Windows XP server, which uses a newer version called CDOSYS. Coding for CDOSYS is slightly different from that for CDONTS; examples for both are included in this recipe.

Although the component is included in most Windows servers, it might not be registered with the system. To register CDONTS, make sure cdonts.dll is included in the Windows directory that contains the other DLLs (on Windows 2000, *[system drive letter]*:\WINNT\system32). Then choose Start > Run and enter **regsvr32 cdonts.dll** in the Run dialog. The CDONTS component requires a valid SMTP server to successfully send the email.

ColdFusion, on the other hand, includes the email component right out of the box, and no additional component is required. You do, however, need to specify a valid SMTP server. In ColdFusion MX, this setting is found by entering the Administrator and selecting Server Settings > Mail Server. With ColdFusion 5, it is located at Server Settings > Mail/Mail Logging.

The mail() function is built into PHP, so the only configuration necessary is in the PHP.ini file. If the web space is hosted, the configuration is completed for you. However, if you're testing on your own development server, you'll need to adjust a couple of settings within the [mail function] section of the PHP.ini file. Windows users should set the SMTP setting to your mail server (that is, smtp.myisphost.com), and the sendmail_from variable should be entered as your email address. Macintosh users (connecting through Linux or Unix on OS X) need to set the sendmail_path variable to the location of the sendmail program on your system. You can locate this by opening a terminal window and entering whereis sendmail.

Step 1: Implement Send Password Design

We'll start by building the HTML page:

1. Open a new dynamic page, either constructing one by hand or deriving one from a template.

    📖 In the **UserLogin** folder, locate the folder for your server model and open the send_password page found there.

2. Add a table to the content region of your page to contain the interface elements for the application.

    📖 From the Snippets panel, drag the **Recipes > UserLogin > Wireframes > Send Password - Wireframe** snippet into the Content editable region.

3. Within the table, insert the form and any necessary form elements for the application. For this application, a single text field for entering the user's email address and a submit button are all that are needed.

📖 Place your cursor in the row below the words SEND PASSWORD in the second cell and insert the **Recipes > UserLogin > Forms > Send Password - Form** snippet [r1-16].

r1-16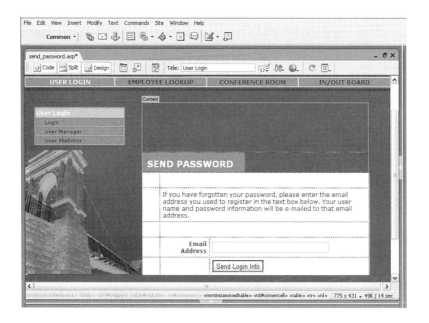

Step 2: Add Database Components

For this application, the initial task is to find a match between the submitted email address and those entered in the database of registered users. If found, a single record—the one that includes the submitted email address—is returned to the recordset. This recordset will later be used to email the password to the user.

For ASP and PHP

1. From the Bindings panel, choose Add (+) and select **Recordset (Query)**.
2. If the simple view is displayed, select Advanced.

   Because we're defining SQL variables, the SQL must be hand-coded.
3. Enter an appropriate name for the recordset.

   📖 Enter **LostPassword** in the Name field.

4. Choose your data source connection from the list.

   📖 Select **Recipes** from the Connections list.

5. Enter the following code in the SQL field:

```
SELECT UserName, UserPassword
FROM Users
WHERE UserEmail = 'EmailParam'
```

6. In the Variables section, select Add (+) and enter **EmailParam** under the Name column.

7. Enter an email address that should be used if the email field is blank, such as Recipesadmin@idest.com in the Default column.

8. In the Run-time Value column, enter code that gathers the data from the form field:

   (VB) `Request.Form("EmailAddress")`

   (JS) `Request.Form("EmailAddress")`

   (PHP) `$_POST['EmailAddress']`

9. Click OK to confirm your choices and insert the recordset. Save your page when the operation is complete.

For ColdFusion

1. From the Bindings panel, choose Add (+) and select **Recordset (Query)**.
2. If the simple view is displayed, select Advanced.

   Because we're defining SQL variables, the SQL must be hand-coded.

3. In the Name field, enter an appropriate name.

   📖 Enter **LostPassword** in the Name field.

4. Choose your data source connection from the list.

   📖 Select **Recipes** from the Data Source list.

5. If necessary, enter the User Name and Password in their respective fields.
6. Enter the following code in the SQL field:

```
SELECT UserName, UserPassword
FROM Users
WHERE UserEmail = '#FORM.EmailAddress#'
```

7. In the Page Parameters section, select Add (+) to display the Add Parameter dialog.

8. In the Add Parameter dialog, make sure `FORM.EmailAddress` in displayed in the Name field.

NOTE | I'm sure the administrator would appreciate it if you substituted his or her email address rather than using mine.

9. In the Default Value fields, enter an email address that should be used if the email field is blank, such as `Recipesadmin@idest.com`, and click OK to close the Add Parameter dialog.

10. When you're done, click OK to close the Recordset dialog.

Step 3: Insert Confirmation Message

Our next action is to create a custom error message that displays if the login fails. By keeping the error message on the same page, we simplify the user experience.

1. Place the cursor where you'd like the error message to appear.

   ▢ Put the cursor in the row above the Email Address form element.

2. Add the following error message code:

   ▢ From the Snippets panel, open the **Recipes > UserLogin > Custom Code** folder for your server model and insert the **Send Email – Confirmation Message** snippet.

   (VB) `<%=ConfirmMessage%>`

   (JS) `<%=ConfirmMessage%>`

   (CF) `<cfoutput>#ConfirmMessage#</cfoutput>`

   (PHP) `<?php echo $ConfirmMessage; ?>`

3. If you entered the code by hand in Code view, be sure to remove the nonbreaking space character, ` `.

ColdFusion users also need to add a `CFParam` to the page that sets the `ConfirmMessage` variable to an empty string.

1. From the Bindings panel, select Add (+) and choose **CFParam**.

2. In the CFParam dialog, enter **ConfirmMessage** in the Name field.

3. Be sure to leave the Default field blank and click OK to close the dialog.

The new `CFParam` is displayed in the Bindings panel.

Step 4: Add Logic to Send Email

With the recordset defined, we're ready to verify it and send the email. The first coding task is to make sure that the recordset is not empty, meaning that a match was found to the submitted email address. After that has been verified, the email will be sent and a confirmation message displayed.

For ASP

1. Select the **LostPassword** recordset from the Server Behaviors panel to highlight the recordset.
2. In Code view, add a line break immediately after the recordset.

   Which of the following two steps you take depends on whether your system uses CDONTS (primarily Windows 2000 servers) or CDOSYS (Windows XP Pro and Windows 2003 servers).
3. Insert the following code for CDONTS-based email:

   📖 From the Snippets panel, open the **Recipes > UserLogin > Custom Code** folder for your server model and insert the **Send Email - CDONTS**.

   (VB)
```
<%
Dim ConfirmMessage
ConfirmMessage = ""
IF (NOT LostPassword.EOF) THEN
   set newMail = Server.CreateObject("CDONTS.NewMail.1")
   newMail.Send "usermanager@yourcompany.com",
   ➥cStr(Request("EmailAddress")), "Re:Your MyCompany Login
   ➥Information", "UserName:
   ➥"&LostPassword.Fields("UserName").value&"\rPassword:
   ➥"&LostPassword.Fields("UserPassword").value
   ConfirmMessage = "Your login information has been sent to: " &
   ➥cStr(Request("EmailAddress"))
END IF
%>
```

   (JS)
```
<%
var ConfirmMessage = "";
if (!LostPassword.EOF)  {
  var newMail = Server.CreateObject("CDONTS.NewMail.1");
   newMail.Send("usermanager@yourcompany.com",String(Request
   ➥("EmailAddress")),"Re:Your MyCompany Login
   ➥Information","UserName:
   ➥"+LostPassword.Fields("UserName").value+"\rPassword:
   ➥"+LostPassword.Fields("UserPassword").value);
```

Continues

```
        ConfirmMessage = "Your login information has been sent to: " +
        ➥String(Request("EmailAddress"));
    }
    %>
```

As you might note, the newMail.send() method takes four arguments: the sender's email address, the destination email address, the subject, and the body of the message. The code block also contains a confirmation message that displays on the user's screen after the email has been sent.

4. Customize the code containing the sender's email address (which now reads "usermanager@yourcompany.com") and the subject line ("Re:Your MyCompany Login Information").

5. Insert the following code for CDOSYS-based email:

   📖 From the Snippets panel, open the **Recipes > UserLogin > Custom Code** folder for your server model and insert the **Send Email – CDOSYS** snippet.

```
VB   <%
     Dim ConfirmMessage
     ConfirmMessage = ""
     IF (NOT LostPassword.EOF) THEN
         set sysMail = Server.CreateObject("CDO.Message")
         sysMail.Configuration.Fields("http://schemas.microsoft.com/cdo/
         ➥configuration/smtpserver") = "smtp.mycompany.com"
         sysMail.Configuration.Fields("http://schemas.microsoft.com/cdo/
         ➥configuration/sendusing") = 2
         sysMail.Configuration.Fields("http://schemas.microsoft.com/cdo/
         ➥configuration/sendusername") = ""
         sysMail.Configuration.Fields("http://schemas.microsoft.com/cdo/
         ➥configuration/sendpassword") = ""
         sysMail.Configuration.Fields.Update
         sysMail.From = "usermanager@yourcompany.com"
         sysMail.To = cStr(Request("EmailAddress"))
         sysMail.Subject = "Re:Your MyCompany Login Information"
         sysMail.TextBody = "UserName: " &
         ➥LostPassword.Fields("UserName").value & vbCrlf & "Password: " &
         ➥LostPassword.Fields("UserPassword").value
         sysMail.Send
         ConfirmMessage = "Your login information has been sent to: " &
         ➥cStr(Request("EmailAddress"))
     END IF
     %>
```

```
JS   <%
     var ConfirmMessage = "";
     if (!LostPassword.EOF)  {
       var sysMail = Server.CreateObject("CDO.Message");
       sysMail.Configuration.Fields("http://schemas.microsoft.com/cdo/
       ➥configuration/smtpserver") = "smtp.mycompany.com";
       sysMail.Configuration.Fields("http://schemas.microsoft.com/cdo/
       ➥configuration/sendusing") = 2;
       sysMail.Configuration.Fields("http://schemas.microsoft.com/cdo/
       ➥configuration/sendusername") = "";
       sysMail.Configuration.Fields("http://schemas.microsoft.com/cdo/
       ➥configuration/sendpassword") = "";
       sysMail.Configuration.Fields.Update();
       sysMail.From = "usermanager@yourcompany.com";
       sysMail.To = String(Request("EmailAddress"));
       sysMail.Subject = "Re:Your MyCompany Login Information";
       sysMail.TextBody = "UserName: " +
       ➥LostPassword.Fields("UserName").value+"\rPassword: " +
       ➥LostPassword.Fields("UserPassword").value;
       sysMail.Send();
       ConfirmMessage = "Your login information has been sent to: " +
       ➥String(Request("EmailAddress"));
     }
     %>
```

6. For CDOSYS, you'll need to customize the smtpserver setting (in the snippet as smtp.mycompany.com) to your own, as well as the sysMail.From email address (in the snippet as usermanager@yourcompany.com).

7. Save the page as send_password.asp.

For ColdFusion

1. In Code view, place a line break above the <html> tag and below the </cfquery> tag.

2. Insert the following code:

    ▢ From the Snippets panel, open the **Recipes > UserLogin > Custom Code** folder for your server model and insert the **Send Email** snippet.

```
CF   <cfif LostPassword.RecordCount NEQ 0>
         <cfmail to="#FORM.EmailAddress#" from="usermanager@yourcompany.
         ➡com" subject="Re:Your MyCompany Login Information">
         UserName: #LostPassword.UserName#
         Password: #LostPassword.UserPassword#
         </cfmail>
           <cfset ConfirmMessage="Your UserName and Password have been sent
           ➡to: #Form.EmailAddress#">
     </cfif>
```

3. Customize the from, subject, and if you like, ConfirmMessage variable values. Be sure not to alter any code containing data source fields.

4. Save your page.

For PHP

1. In Code view, place a line break above the <html> tag.

2. Insert the following code:

       📖 From the Snippets panel, insert the **Recipes > UserLogin > Custom Code_PHP > Send Email** snippet.

```
PHP   <?php
         $ConfirmMessage = "";
         if ($totalRows_LostPassword > 0) {
                 $to = $_POST['EmailAddress'];
                 $from = "From: usermanager@yourcompany.com<usermanager@
                         ➡yourcompany.com>\r\n";
                 $subject = "RE: Your MyCompany Login Information";    $body =
                 ➡"UserName: " . $row_LostPassword['UserName'] . "\rPassword:"
                 ➡. $row_LostPassword['UserPassword'];   @mail($to,
                 ➡$subject,$body,$from);
                 $ConfirmMessage = "Your login information has been sent to: "
                 ➡. $_POST['EmailAddress'];
         }
         ?>
```

3. Customize the from, subject, and if you like, ConfirmMessage variable values. Be sure not to alter any code containing data source fields.

4. Save your page.

Administrator Recipe: Managing Users

With all the user-oriented recipes completed, it's time to build a few pages geared toward the administration. Our first component combines two functions: a master list of registered users and the form for adding new users directly. The add user section is an enhanced version of the register user form we've already built. In addition to the record fields included (`UserFirstName`, `Password`, `UserEmail`, and so on), the administrator also has the capability to set access levels.

Step 1: Implement User Manager Design

The two components of the user manager page require two discrete sections. The top section will display a list of all the users in a Dreamweaver Repeat Region server behavior and will provide a link to a detail record page. The bottom section allows direct entry of new users.

1. Open a new dynamic page, either constructing one by hand or deriving one from a template.

    📖 In the **UserLogin** folder, locate the folder for your server model and open the user_manager page found there.

2. Add a table to the content region of your page to contain the first interface element for the application, its title. This wireframe table should have a minimum of three rows.

    📖 From the Snippets panel, drag the **Recipes > UserLogin > Wireframes > User Manager - Wireframe** snippet into the Content editable region.

3. Within the table, insert the text placeholders for a recordset navigation status object and a recordset navigation bar in the top row. In the second row, add headers for User Name and Access Group. The third row of the table will eventually hold the dynamic data. It's often best to insert a nested table in a situation like this.

    📖 Place your cursor in the row below the words USER MANAGER and insert the **Recipes > UserLogin > Content Tables > View Users - Content Table** snippet [r1-17].

4. In the third row of the wireframe table, add a form with elements for inserting a new user record. These elements include five text fields with their labels (First Name, Last Name, User Name, Password, and Email Address), a drop-down list for assigning group access, and a form button for adding a new record.

    📖 Place your cursor in the last row of the wireframe table and insert the **Recipes > UserLogin > Forms > Add New User - Form** snippet [r1-18].

r1-17

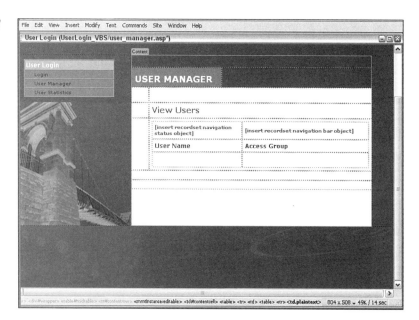

r1-18

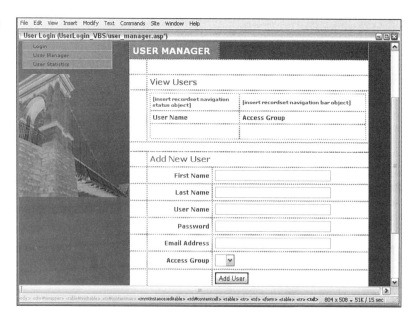

Step 2: Add Database Components

As you might expect with two visual components, this page uses two recordsets. However, what you might not suspect is that one of the recordsets combines two tables in what is known in SQL as an *inner join*. The first recordset gives us the list of access groups set up in the data source and is used to populate the drop-down list. The second recordset uses the inner join and, for the ease of our ASP and ColdFusion Recipes users, is available as an Access view. This recordset returns all the users and their corresponding access levels, which will be integrated into the initial section of the page. Because MySQL does not support views, we'll have to code the SQL directly for PHP.

Let's create the simple recordset first: AccessGroups.

1. From the Bindings panel, choose Add (+) and select **Recordset (Query)**.
2. In the Recordset dialog's simple view, enter the desired name, such as **AccessGroups**.
3. Select your data source connections.

   📖 Choose **Recipes** from the Connections list.
4. Select the table containing the user information.

   📖 Choose **AccessGroups** (**accessgroups** for PHP) from the Table list.
5. Make sure the Columns option is set to All.
6. Leave both Filter and Sort to None and click OK to close the dialog.
7. Save the page.

The second, more complex recordset is handled differently for the different server models.

For ASP and ColdFusion

As previously noted, this recordset requires an Access view that joins two tables, Users and AccessGroups. Here's the SQL behind the view, called UserView, for both version of ASP and ColdFusion:

```
VB  JS  CF  SELECT *
            FROM Users INNER JOIN AccessGroups ON Users.UserAccess =
            ➥AccessGroups.AccessGroupID
            ORDER BY Users.UserID DESC;
```

To implement this SQL statement, we need only use Dreamweaver's simple Recordset dialog for ASP and ColdFusion.

1. From the Bindings panel, choose Add (+) and select **Recordset** (**Query**).
2. In the Recordset dialog's simple view, enter an appropriate name.
   - Enter **Users** in the Recordset field.
3. Select your data source connections.
   - Choose **Recipes** from the Connections list.
4. Select the table or view containing the user information.
   - Select **UserView** from the Tables list.
5. Make sure the Columns option is set to All.
6. Leave both Filter and Sort to None and click OK to close the dialog.
7. Click OK to close the dialog and verify that the recordset is added to the Bindings panel.
8. Save the page.

For PHP

The actual SQL for the PHP version varies slightly from the version used in the other server models, but the major difference is that the SQL statement must be added directly in Dreamweaver because MySQL does not support views.

1. From the Bindings panel, choose Add (+) and select **Recordset** (**Query**).
2. Switch to the advanced view of the Recordset dialog, if necessary.
3. Enter an appropriate name for the recordset.
   - Enter **Users** in the Recordset field.
4. Choose the data source.
   - Select **Recipes** from the Connections list.
5. Enter the following code in the SQL area:

   ```
   SELECT *
   FROM users INNER JOIN accessgroups ON users.UserAccess =
   ➥accessgroups.AccessGroupID ORDER BY users.UserID DESC;
   ```

   Note that the ORDER is set to DESC (descending) rather than ASC (ascending); this displays the last record entered first and makes it easier for administrators to track newly registered users.
6. Click OK to close the dialog and insert the recordset.
7. Save your page.

The Bindings panel should now have two recordsets and one session object.

Step 3: Data Binding Process

Initially, two data fields need to be bound to this page, both from the Users recordset. We'll also create a link to a detail page so that the administrator can easily navigate to a specific user's record for updating.

1. From the Bindings panel, expand the **Users** recordset.
2. Drag the **UserName** field onto the page and into the table cell below the User Name heading.

   Dreamweaver displays this dynamic data as {Users.UserName}.
3. Drag the **AccessGroupName** field onto the page and into the table cell below the Access Group heading.

   Now we're ready to link to our detail page.
4. Select the dynamic data {Users.UserName}.
5. From the Property inspector, select the **Link** folder icon.
6. In the Select File dialog, choose **Parameters**.
7. In the Parameters dialog, enter the variable name.

   📖 In the Name column, enter **ID**.
8. Enter the dynamic value.

   📖 Under the Value column, select the lightning bolt to open the Dynamic Data dialog and select **UserID** from the Users recordset.

   📖 Click OK once to close the Dynamic Data dialog and again to close the Parameters dialog.
9. Select the file you want to pass the parameter to.

   📖 Select Browse and choose the **edit_user** file for your server model.
10. Click OK to close the dialog.

You might notice that a different mechanism is being used for the first time in this application to connect with an associated record. Rather than looking at the session object, UserID, as we did previously, we're passing a URL parameter. This technique will allow us to see records other than those of the user, whose own UserID will be inspected to make sure someone with the proper access level is attempting to adjust a user's record.

One other element on the page needs to be bound to a data field: the Access Groups list. Although it is tempting to hard-code the list options, especially with a limited number of values, it is best not to. Should the data source back-end ever change—adding new access levels, for example—the front-end (this form) would have to be modified as well. By binding the data to the list, any alterations made to the data source are instantly reflected in the application page.

1. Select the **Access Group** list item in the form.
2. From the Property inspector, click the Dynamic button.

    The Dynamic List/Menu dialog appears [r1-19].

r1-19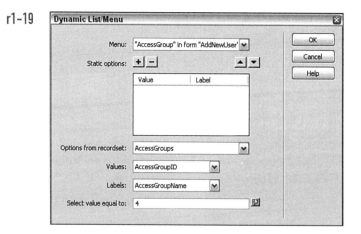

3. Verify that the AccessGroup list element is selected in the Menu list.
4. From the Options From Recordset list choose **AccessGroups.**
5. Set the Values list to **AccessGroupID.**

    These are the values that get inserted into the record. Numbers (1 through 4) are used here rather than words (User, Administrator, and so on) to make comparisons easier.

6. Set the Labels (what the user sees) to **AccessGroupNames.**
7. In the Select Value Equal To field, enter **4** and click OK to close the dialog.

By setting the selected value to 4, the administrator's default choice is the most frequently accessed: User.

Step 4: Create a Repeat Region and Application Objects

If you preview the page now in Dreamweaver by choosing the Live Data View button on the toolbar, you'll see the name and access group for just one record, the last entered. To show multiple records, a Repeat Region server behavior is needed. A Repeat Region can show all the data or just a portion of it. Because we don't want to over-whelm the administrator with too much data, we'll only show a few records at a time. To make all of the records accessible in small groups, we'll also add some recordset navigation and status reports, all easily inserted with Dreamweaver.

Let's start with adding the Repeat Region to the recordset:

1. Place the cursor in either of the table cells containing the dynamic data.
2. From the Tag Selector, select the `<tr>` tag, just to the left of the current `<td>` tag [r1-20].

r1-20

3. From the Server Behaviors panel, choose Add (+) and select **Repeat Region**.

4. In the Repeat Region dialog, select the **Users** recordset.

5. Accepting the default of **Showing 10 Records at a Time**, click OK to close the dialog.

Now, if you go into Live Data view, you'll see the data from the last 10 users to register (r1-21). Of course, if you have fewer than 10 users registered, you'll see all the records. To see the next group of records, we'll now add some recordset navigation tools.

 r1-21

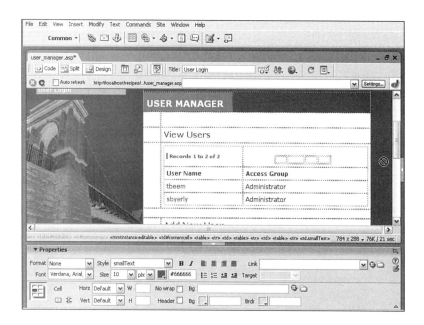

First we'll put in the navigation elements themselves by using one of Dreamweaver's Application Objects, the Recordset Navigation Bar.

1. Place your cursor in the table where you'd like the navigation links to appear.

   Be careful not to place your cursor within the Repeat Region.

   📖 Delete the text that says, "[insert recordset navigation bar object]" and leave your cursor in that cell.

2. Choose **Insert > Application Objects > Recordset Paging > Recordset Navigation Bar**.

   Alternatively, you could select the Recordset Navigation Bar object from the Recordset Paging menu of the Insert bar's Application category.

3. In the Recordset Navigation Bar dialog, select the **Users** recordset.

4. Set the Display Using option to **Text** and click OK.

The Recordset Navigation Bar object is used to display four navigation options: First, Previous, Next, and Last. Each text object contains a hyperlink with functionality to move the cursor to the correct record in the result set.

Additionally, the Recordset Navigation Bar includes built-in server behaviors to show the links only when it is relevant to do so. For example, when the page is first previewed, no Previous link is displayed because there are no prior records to show. Similarly, when the last record is onscreen, the Next link is hidden.

> **NOTE**
> The server behaviors automatically added when inserting the Recordset Navigation Bar can be seen in the Server Behaviors panel.

As you are paging through a recordset, it's helpful to have some feedback stating where you are in the data. Dreamweaver includes another Application Object called Recordset Navigation Status, which provides just such feedback. When added to a page, this object helps the user keep track of the recordset by showing the current records displayed and the total number of records. The Recordset Navigation Status object shows the information like this: `Records 21 to 30 of 55`.

1. Place your cursor in the table where you'd like the navigation status to be displayed.

   Again, be careful not to place your cursor within the Repeat Region.

   📖 Delete the text that says, "[insert recordset navigation status object]" and leave your cursor in that cell.

2. Choose **Insert > Application Objects > Display Recordset Count > Recordset Navigation Status**.

   Alternatively, you could select the Recordset Navigation Status object from the Display Recordset Count menu of the Insert bar's Application category.

3. In the Recordset Navigation Status dialog, select the **Users** recordset and click OK.

To see the initial view, switch to Live Data view [r1-22]. To test the recordset navigation controls, you'll need to preview the page in a browser because Dreamweaver does not support clicking on links.

r1-22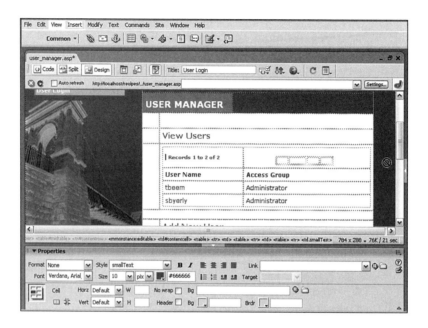

Step 5: Insert New Users

The administrative version of the form to add new users is similar to the user version except for one difference. An additional form element has been added: the Access Group drop-down list, which lets the administrator designate a particular access group for any newly declared user.

For ASP

1. From the Server Behaviors panel, chose Add (+) and select **Insert Record** to display the dialog.
2. Select the connection to the data source.

    📖 Choose **Recipes** from the Connection list.

3. From the Insert Into Table list, choose the **Users** table.

4. Leave the After Inserting, Go To field blank.

   By leaving this field blank, this same page will reload after the record is inserted. Thus, the administrator can enter record after record.

5. Set the Get Values From field to the form name, **AddNewUser**.

6. For the form elements shown in the list, set each one to its equivalent in the data source:

   📖 Set FirstName to UserFirstName as Text.

      Set Lastname to UserLastName as Text.

      Set UserName to UserName as Text.

      Set Password to UserPassword as Text.

      Set EmailAddress to UserEmail as Text.

      Set AccessGroup to UserAccess at Numeric.

7. When you're done, click OK to close the dialog and insert the behavior.

8. Save the page as user_manager using the appropriate extension for your platform.

For ColdFusion and PHP

1. From the Server Behaviors panel, choose Add (+) and select **Insert Record**.

2. In the Insert Record dialog, choose the current form.

   📖 Select **AddNewUser** from the Submit Values From list.

3. Select your data source from the list.

   📖 Choose **Recipes** from the Data Source list.

4. ColdFusion users should enter their username and password, if needed.

5. Select the table in the data source to insert into from the list.

   📖 Choose **Users** (**users** for PHP) from the Insert Into Table list.

6. Set the data source fields to their corresponding form elements.

   📖 Make sure the UserID data column is set to be an unused Primary Key.

      Set UserAccess to the FORM.AccesGroup and submit as Numeric type for ColdFusion and Integer type for PHP.

      Set UserFirstName to the FORM.FirstName form element and submit as Text type.

      Set UserLastName to the FORM.LastName form element and submit as Text type.

      Set UserName to the FORM.UserName form element and submit as Text type.

      Set UserPassword to the FORM.UserPassword form element and submit as Text type.

      Set UserEmail to the FORM.EmailAddress form element and submit as Text type.

      UserRegDate should not get a value from the form.

7. In the After Inserting, Go To field, enter **report_projectsummary.cfm** and click OK to close the dialog.

8. Save the page.

Administrator Recipe: Modifying User Profiles

In the best of all possible worlds, an administrator would never have to see a user's record much less alter it. Very few administrators are lucky enough to live in that world, however, so an administrative-strength edit record application is needed.

In addition to the functionality we've already seen in the user-oriented edit record page, the administrator also requires the capability to alter a user's access group level and to delete the record altogether. Moreover, to maintain security, the SQL statements involved in this page are somewhat more complex than those used in the user version.

Step 1: Implement Login Design

Let's begin by building the basic page.

1. Open a new dynamic page, either constructing one by hand or deriving one from a template.

    📖 In the **UserLogin** folder, locate the folder for your server model and open the edit_user page found there.

2. Add a table to the content region of your page to contain the interface elements for the application.

    📖 From the Snippets panel, drag the **Recipes > UserLogin > Wireframes > Edit User - Wireframe** snippet into the Content editable region.

3. Within the table, insert the form and any necessary form elements for the application. You'll need five text fields—one for each of the fields (First Name, Last Name, User Name, Password, and Email Address)—and a select list to hold the Group Access data. In addition, this application requires three buttons: Update, Delete, and Cancel.

    📖 Place your cursor in the row below the words EDIT USER in the second cell and insert the **Recipes > UserLogin > Forms > Edit User - Form** snippet [r1-23].

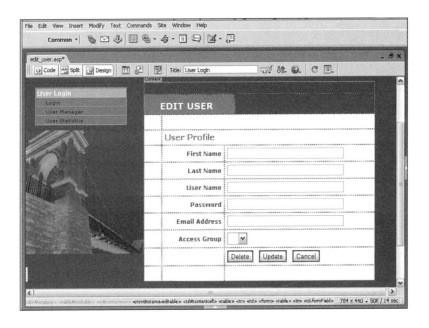

r1-23

4. ColdFusion and PHP Users: Both of these server models require a unique record ID for the Update Record server behavior to work properly. In these situations, a Hidden Form Field is used to convey the needed data.

(CF) (PHP) ColdFusion and PHP developers should drag a Hidden Form Field from the Forms category of the Insert bar and name it UserID.

5. Save the page.

Step 2: Add Database Components

The Edit User page displays when a link is selected in the Manage Users page. The link selected contains a URL parameter, ID, which we will use on this page to filter one of the two recordsets required. The second recordset gets the values necessary to dynamically fill the Access Group list.

1. From the Server Behaviors panel, choose Add (+) and select **Recordset (Query)**.

2. Using the simple view of the Recordset dialog, give the recordset a meaningful name.

   ☐ Enter **Users** in the Recordset field.

3. Choose the connection for your data source.

   📖 Select **Recipes** from the Connection list.

4. Choose the desired table.

   📖 Select **Users** (**users** for PHP) from the Table list.

5. Keep the Columns option set to All.

6. In the Filter area of the Recordset dialog, set the four Filter list elements like this:

UserID	= (Equals)
URL Variable	ID

7. Leave the Sort option set to None and then click OK to confirm your choices and close the dialog.

8. Save the page.

NOTE

The second recordset, AccessGroups, is an exact duplicate of the one built in the Manage User page. If that page has already been developed, you can copy and paste the recordset. To copy a recordset, select it in the Bindings panel and, from the panel Options menu, select Copy. To paste a recordset, switch to the page where the recordset is needed, select the Bindings panel Options menu, and choose Paste. Your recordset should appear in the Bindings panel. Please note that standard Copy and Paste commands will not work with recordsets.

The second recordset, AccessGroups, is just as straightforward.

1. From the Bindings panel, choose Add (+) and select **Recordset (Query)**.

2. In the Recordset dialog's simple view, enter the desired name, such as **AccessGroups**.

3. Select your data source connections.

   📖 Choose **Recipes** from the Connections list.

4. Select the table containing the user information.

   📖 Choose **AccessGroups** from the Table list.

5. Click OK to close the dialog.

Step 3: Data Binding Process

The data-binding procedure for this page is identical to the one followed on the edit profile page with one exception. The Access Group form element—a drop-down list—must be bound to data from the accessgroup table. ColdFusion and PHP users will also need to bind the current record ID to the hidden form field.

1. In the Bindings panel, make sure the **Users** recordset entry is expanded so that all data columns are displayed.

2. Drag each of the following data columns over the corresponding text field:
   - Drag column `UserFirstName` to field `FirstName`.
   - Drag column `UserLastName` to field `LastName`.
   - Drag column `UserName` to field `UserName`.
   - Drag column `Password` to field `Password`.
   - Drag column `UserEmail` to field `EmailAddress`.
3. Leave the default formatting for all dynamic text fields.

   Let's now set up the list element to populate dynamically.
4. Select the **Access Group** list element.
5. In the Property inspector, click the Dynamic button to open the Dynamic List/Menu dialog.
6. Verify that the **AccessGroup** list element is selected in the Menu list.
7. From the Options From Recordset list, choose **AccessGroups**.
8. Set the Values list to **AccessGroupID**.
9. Set the Labels (what the user sees) to **AccessGroupNames**.
10. In the Select Value Equal To field, select the lightning icon to open the Dynamic Data dialog.
11. Expand the `Users` recordset, if necessary, and choose the **UserAccess** (**AccessGroup** for PHP) field.

    Linking the selected value to the UserAccess/AccessGroup field, the record will initially display the current user group level while allowing the administrator to adjust it if necessary.
12. Click OK to close the Dynamic Data dialog. After you've confirmed your selections, click OK in the Dynamic List/Menu dialog to close it.

ColdFusion and PHP users need to complete one additional set of steps in binding dynamic data to the hidden form field previously inserted.

1. Select the desired form element.
   - Choose the **UserID** hidden form element.
2. Bind the current record ID to the element.
   - Choose the lightning bolt symbol next to the Value field in the Property inspector to open the Dynamic Data dialog.
   - In the Dynamic Data dialog, expand the **Users** recordset and choose **UserID**.
   - Click OK to close the dialog.
3. Save your page.

Step 4: Update User Profile

Now we're ready to insert the Update Record server behavior. As part of the procedure, we'll set the behavior to display the Manage User page after the update is complete so that the administrator can continue working.

For ASP

1. From the Server Behaviors panel, choose Add (+) and select **Update Record** to display the dialog.
2. Select the connection to the data source.
   - 📖 Choose **Recipes** from the Connection list.
3. Choose the table containing the user data.
   - 📖 From the Table To Update list, select **Users**.
4. Select the recordset from which to get data source fields.
   - 📖 Set the Select Record From field to **Users**.
5. Set the Primary Key for the recordset.
   - 📖 From the Unique Key Column list, choose **UserID** and make sure that the Numeric option is checked.
6. Enter the page you want the users to see after successfully registering.
   - 📖 In the After Inserting, Go To field, select the Browse button and locate the **user_manager** file for your server model.
7. Choose the form on the page from which the values are to be taken.
   - 📖 Set the Get Values From field to **EditUser**.
8. For the form elements shown in the list, set each one to its equivalent in the data source. All form elements should be submitted as text:
   - 📖 Set form element FirstName to field UserFirstName as Text.

     Set form element Lastname to field UserLastName as Text.

     Set form element UserName to field UserName as Text.

     Set form element Password to field UserPassword as Text.

     Set form element EmailAddress to field UserEmail as Text.

     Set form element AccessGroup to field UserAccess as Numeric.

9. When you're done, click OK to close the dialog and insert the behavior.
10. Save your page.

For ColdFusion and PHP

1. From the Server Behaviors panel, choose Add (+) and select **Update Record**.
2. In the Update Record dialog, choose the current form.

   📖 Select **Users** from the Submit Values From list.
3. Select your data source from the list.

   📖 Choose **Recipes** from the Data Source list.
4. Enter your username and password, if needed.
5. Select the table in the data source to insert into from the list.

   📖 Choose **Users** from the Insert Into Table list.
6. Set the data source fields to their corresponding form elements.

   📖 As the Primary Key, UserID selects the record using FORM.UserID as a Numeric (Integer in PHP) type.

   Set UserAccess to get its value from the FORM.AccessGroup from element as Numeric (Integer in PHP).

   Set UserFirstName to get its value from the FORM.FirstName form element as Text.

   Set UserLastName to get its value from the FORM.Lastname form element as Text.

   Set UserName to get its value from the FORM.UserName form element as Text.

   Set UserPassword to get its value from the FORM.Password form element as Text.

   Set UserEmail to get its value from the FORM.EmailAddress form element as Text.

   Make sure UserRegDate does not get a value.
7. In the After Inserting, Go To field enter the path to the file you want displayed after the record is updated.

   📖 In the After Inserting, Go To field, select the **usermanager** file for your server model.
8. Check your entries to verify that they are correct; if so, click OK.
9. Save your page.

Step 5: Add a Delete Command

If you wanted to add a separate page to delete a record, you could use Dreamweaver's standard Delete Record server behavior. However, if, as this application does, you want to combine a couple of administrative tasks—such as updating and deleting records—you have to take a different approach.

One method is to create a delete command. A *command* is a specialized SQL statement that, among other things, can delete, insert, or update records. Once the command is created using the Dreamweaver interface, the code must be moved above the Update Record behavior. The final step is to wrap the delete code in a conditional block—also called an If statement—so that it executes only when the Delete button is selected.

For ASP

1. From the Bindings panel, choose Add (+) and select **Command**.

    The Command dialog displays [r1-24].

r1-24

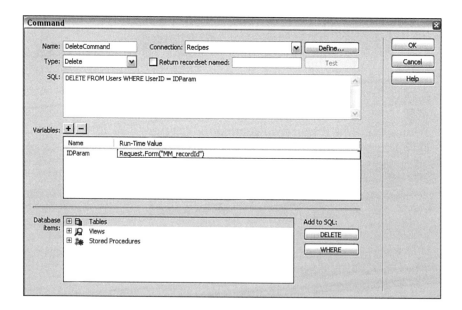

2. Enter an appropriate name for the command.

    📖 Enter **DeleteCommand** in the Name field.

3. Choose your data source connection from the list.

    📖 Select **Recipes** from the Connections list.

4. Choose **Delete** for the Command Type.

5. Enter the following code in the SQL field:

    ```
    DELETE FROM Users WHERE UserID = IDParam
    ```

6. In the Variables section, select Add (+) and enter **IDParam** under the Name column.

7. In the Run-Time Value column, enter **Request.Form("MM_recordId")** and click OK when you're done.

    Inserting the command creates two code blocks. We'll need to move one of them so that the delete command is processed before the update command.

8. In Code view, find the code block for the delete command. It will look like this:

    (VB) <%

    ```
        set DeleteCommand = Server.CreateObject("ADODB.Command")
        DeleteCommand.ActiveConnection = MM_Recipes_VB_STRING
        DeleteCommand.CommandText = "DELETE FROM Users WHERE UserID = " +
        ➥Replace(DeleteCommand__IDParam, "'", "''") + ""
        DeleteCommand.CommandType = 1
        DeleteCommand.CommandTimeout = 0
        DeleteCommand.Prepared = true
        DeleteCommand.Execute()
        %>
    ```

    (JS) <%

    ```
        var DeleteCommand = Server.CreateObject("ADODB.Command");
        DeleteCommand.ActiveConnection = MM_Recipes_STRING;
        DeleteCommand.CommandText = "DELETE FROM Users  WHERE UserID
         "+ DeleteCommand__IDParam.replace(/'/g, "''") + " ";
        DeleteCommand.CommandType = 1;
        DeleteCommand.CommandTimeout = 0;
        DeleteCommand.Prepared = true;
        DeleteCommand.Execute();
        %>
    ```

9. Cut the code block and move it near the top of the page after this related code block:

    (VB) <%

    ```
        if(Request("MM_recordId") <> "") then DeleteCommand__IDParam =
        Request("MM_recordId")
        %>
    ```

    (JS) <%

    ```
        if(String(Request("MM_recordId")) != "undefined")
        { DeleteCommand__IDParam = String(Request("MM_recordId"));}
        %>
    ```

Now all that remains to complete the delete command is to make sure it is only executed when the user selects the Delete button on the form. If this step is not taken, the delete command will run when this page was loaded—not a desirable circumstance. To avoid such a disastrous situation, we'll wrap the two delete command code blocks within an If statement.

1. In Code view, locate the two adjacent delete command code blocks.

   📖 Select the two code blocks to prepare for inserting the snippet.

2. Insert the following code:

   📖 From the Snippets panel, open the **Recipes > UserLogin > Custom Code** folder for your server model and insert the **Delete Button - If Statement** snippet.

   Before:

   (VB)
   ```
   <%
       if (cStr(Request.Form("Delete"))<>"")   then
       %>
   ```

   After:

   ```
       <%
         Response.Redirect("user_manager.asp")
       end if
       %>
   ```

   Before:

   (JS)
   ```
   <%
       if (String(Request("Delete"))!="undefined")   {
       %>
   ```

   After:

   ```
       <%
         Response.Redirect("user_manager.asp");
       }
       %>
   ```

You can, of course, change the page to redirect to after the delete is completed, if your page is named something different than user_manager.asp.

For ColdFusion

1. From the Bindings panel, choose Add (+) and select **Recordset (Query)**.

   Unlike with the ASP server models, there is no separate user interface in ColdFusion for Commands, and the Recordset dialog is used.

2. If the simple view is displayed, select **Advanced**.

3. In the Name field, enter an appropriate name.

   📖 Enter **DeleteOperation** in the Name field.

4. Choose your data source connection from the list.

      📖 Select **Recipes** from the Data Source list.

5. If necessary, enter the User Name and Password in their respective fields.

6. Enter the following code in the SQL field:

```
DELETE FROM Users WHERE UserID = #FORM.UserID#
```

7. In the Page Parameters section, select Add (+) to display the Add Parameter dialog.

8. In the Add Parameter dialog, enter **FORM.UserID** in the Name field.

9. In the Default Value fields, enter **0** and click OK to close the Add Parameter dialog.

10. When you're done, click OK to close the Recordset dialog.

Now all that remains to complete the delete command is to make sure it is only executed when the user selects the Delete button on the form. To do this, we'll wrap the two delete command code blocks within an If statement.

11. In Code view, find the code block for the delete command. It will look like this:

```
<cfquery name="DeleteCommand" datasource="Recipes">
  DELETE FROM Users WHERE USERID = #FORM.UserID#
</cfquery>
```

      📖 Select the two code blocks to prepare for inserting the snippet.

12. Insert the following code:

      📖 From the Snippets panel, insert the **Recipes > UserLogin > Custom Code-CF > Delete Button - If Statement** snippet.

      Before:

  (CF) `<cfif IsDefined("form.DeleteUser")>`

      After:

```
<cflocation url="user_manager.cfm" addtoken="no">
</cfif>
```

You can, of course, change the page to redirect to after the delete is completed, if your page is named something different from `user_manager.cfm`.

For PHP

Adding a Delete button in PHP is simpler than in other server models and requires the addition of a single function.

1. In Code view, position your cursor at the end of the opening line that begins <?php require_once...> and press Enter (Return).
2. Enter the following code:

   📖 Insert the **Recipes > UserLogin > Custom Code-PHP > Edit User – Delete User** snippet.

(PHP)
```php
<?php
if ((isset($_POST['Delete'])) && ($_POST['Delete']=="Delete")) {
  mysql_select_db($database_Recipes_PHP, $Recipes_PHP);
  $deleteSQL = "DELETE FROM users WHERE UserID=".$_POST['UserID'];
  $deleteRS = mysql_query($deleteSQL,$Recipes_PHP);
  header("Location: user_manager.php");
}
?>
```

3. Save the page.

Step 6: Cancel Editing Process

As we did on the Update Record page, we'll use some JavaScript code to implement the Cancel button.

1. Select the Cancel form button.
2. From the Behaviors panel, select Add (+) and choose **Call JavaScript**.
3. In the Call JavaScript dialog, enter the following code:
```
history.back();
```

4. When you're done, click OK to close the dialog.
5. Save the file.

Step 7: Validate the User Name

One final aspect still needs to be addressed. Since this page can potentially alter the username, we must make sure that the new name chosen is unique. Unfortunately, we cannot just apply the Check User Name server behavior as we did in the register_user page because this particular server behavior requires that a variable, MM_flag, be set to MM_insert, and an update page sets MM_flag to MM_update.

The solution is to copy the Macromedia code used on the `register_user` page and adapt it to our needs. In all, three changes will need to be made. While these modifications will give us the functionality we need, it will also prevent further changes to the Update Record server behavior through the dialog. This is indicated by a red exclamation mark next to the server behavior in the Server Behaviors panel.

1. Open the `register_user` page in Code view and copy the following code block:

(VB)
```
<%
' *** Redirect if username exists
MM_flag="MM_insert"
If (CStr(Request(MM_flag)) <> "") Then
  MM_dupKeyRedirect="register_user.asp?repeat=true"
  MM_rsKeyConnection=MM_Recipes_VB_STRING
  MM_dupKeyUsernameValue = CStr(Request.Form("UserName"))
  MM_dupKeySQL="SELECT UserName FROM Users WHERE UserName='" &
  ➥MM_dupKeyUsernameValue & "'"
  MM_adodbRecordset="ADODB.Recordset"
  set MM_rsKey=Server.CreateObject(MM_adodbRecordset)
  MM_rsKey.ActiveConnection=MM_rsKeyConnection
  MM_rsKey.Source=MM_dupKeySQL
  MM_rsKey.CursorType=0
  MM_rsKey.CursorLocation=2
  MM_rsKey.LockType=3
  MM_rsKey.Open
  If Not MM_rsKey.EOF Or Not MM_rsKey.BOF Then
    ' the username was found - can not add the requested username
    MM_qsChar = "?"
    If (InStr(1,MM_dupKeyRedirect,"?") >= 1) Then MM_qsChar = "&"
    MM_dupKeyRedirect = MM_dupKeyRedirect & MM_qsChar &
    ➥"requsername=" & MM_dupKeyUsernameValue
    Response.Redirect(MM_dupKeyRedirect)
  End If
  MM_rsKey.Close
End If
%>
```

(JS)
```
<%
// *** Redirect if username exists
var MM_flag="MM_insert";
if (String(Request(MM_flag)) != "undefined") {
  var MM_dupKeyRedirect="register_user.asp?repeat=true";
  var MM_rsKeyConnection=MM_Recipes_STRING;
  var MM_dupKeyUsernameValue = String(Request.Form("UserName"));
  var MM_dupKeySQL = "SELECT UserName FROM Users WHERE UserName='"
  ➥+ MM_dupKeyUsernameValue + "'"
```

Continues

```
var MM_adodbRecordset = "ADODB.Recordset";
var MM_rsKey = Server.CreateObject(MM_adodbRecordset);
MM_rsKey.ActiveConnection = MM_rsKeyConnection;
MM_rsKey.Source = MM_dupKeySQL;
MM_rsKey.CursorType=0;
MM_rsKey.CursorLocation=2;
MM_rsKey.LockType=3;
MM_rsKey.Open();
if (!MM_rsKey.EOF || !MM_rsKey.BOF) {
  // the username was found - can not add the requested username
  var MM_qsChar = "?";
  if (MM_dupKeyRedirect.indexOf("?") >= 0) MM_qsChar = "&";
  MM_dupKeyRedirect = MM_dupKeyRedirect + MM_qsChar +
  ➥"requsername=" + MM_dupKeyUsernameValue;
  Response.Redirect(MM_dupKeyRedirect);
}
MM_rsKey.Close();
}
%>
```

CF
```
<cfif IsDefined("FORM.UserName")>
  <cfquery name="MM_search" datasource="Recipes">
  SELECT UserName FROM Users WHERE UserName='#FORM.UserName#'
  </cfquery>
  <cfif MM_search.RecordCount GTE 1>
    <cflocation url="register_user.cfm?failed=
    ➥true&requsername=#FORM.UserName#" addtoken="no">
  </cfif>
</cfif>
```

PHP
```
<?php
// *** Redirect if username exists
$MM_flag="MM_insert";
if (isset($_POST[$MM_flag])) {
  $MM_dupKeyRedirect="register_user.php?repeat=true";
  $loginUsername = $_POST['UserName'];
  $LoginRS__query = "SELECT UserName FROM users WHERE UserName='" .
                    ➥$loginUsername . "'";
  mysql_select_db($database_Recipes_PHP, $Recipes_PHP);
  $LoginRS=mysql_query($LoginRS__query, $Recipes_PHP) or
   ➥die(mysql_error());
  $loginFoundUser = mysql_num_rows($LoginRS);
```

```
//if there is a row in the database, the username was found - can
➥not add the requested username
if($loginFoundUser){
   $MM_qsChar = "?";
   //append the username to the redirect page
   if (substr_count($MM_dupKeyRedirect,"?") >=1) $MM_qsChar = "&";
   $MM_dupKeyRedirect = $MM_dupKeyRedirect . $MM_qsChar .
    ➥"requsername=".$loginUsername;
   header ("Location: $MM_dupKeyRedirect");
   exit;
  }
 }
 ?>
```

2. Open the edit_user page and paste the code after the complete delete command sequence.

   Make sure you paste the code after the close of the If statement where the redirection occurs.

3. Near the top of the pasted code block, change the following line from

   ```
   MM_flag=MM_insert
   ```

   to

   ```
   MM_flag=MM_update
   ```

   This change allows the server behavior to work with a record update.

4. Make a second change from

   ```
   MM_dupKeyRedirect="register_user"
   ```

   to

   ```
   MM_dupKeyRedirect="edit_user"
   ```

   This modification specifies the proper page for the redirect operation.

5. Locate the line that starts with the following code:

   (VB) `var MM_dupKeySQL`

   (JS) `var MM_dupKeySQL`

   (CF) `var MM_dupKeySQL`

   (PHP) `$LoginRS__query`

6. Append the following to the end of the code line:

   (VB) `+ Request("MM_recordId")`

   (JS) `+ Request("MM_recordId")`

   (CF) `+ Request("MM_recordId")`

7. PHP users should remove the final three characters on the line (single quote, double quote, and semicolon) and add the following:

   (PHP) *Change:*

   ```
   "'";
   ```

   to:

   ```
   "' AND UserID != ".$_POST['UserID'];
   ```

   With this change, the SQL statement ignores the current record. This action is necessary in case the administrator made other changes to the record other than the username. Without this modification, the SQL statement would identify the current record as the duplicate and the update would not take place.

8. Additionally, PHP users need to locate the code line that ends as follows:

   (PHP) `"requsername=".$loginUsername;`

   Remove the semicolon at the end and append the following:

   (PHP) `."&ID=".$_POST['UserID'];`

9. Save the page when your edits are complete.

Administrator Recipe: Viewing User Statistics

The final page of the User Login application is an administrative function for tracking user registration. With this page, you'll be able to see how many total registered users there are as well as how many registered in the last day, the last week, and the last month.

One special feature of this application is that it makes use of an Access view in a process referred to as *querying the query*, in which a recordset is derived from a rather complex SQL statement within the data source.

Step 1: Implement User Statistics Design

As usual, we'll build the page structure first.

1. Create a basic dynamic page, either by hand or from a template.

   📖 In the **UserLogin** folder, locate the folder for your server model and open the userstatistics page found there.

2. Add a table to the content region of your page to contain the interface elements for the application.

   📖 From the Snippets panel, drag the **Recipes > UserLogin > Wireframes > User Statistics - Wireframe** snippet into the Content editable region.

3. Within the table, insert a content table with the necessary text and a form button. No form is necessary for this application.

   📖 Place your cursor in the row below the words USER STATISTICS in the second cell and insert the **Recipes > UserLogin > ContentTables > User Statistics - Content Table** snippet [r1-25].

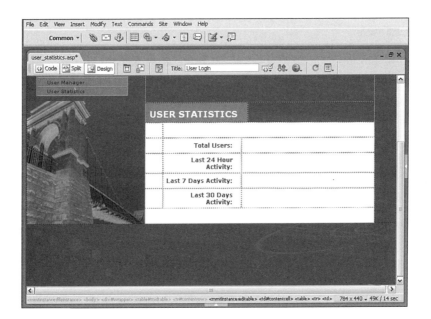

r1-25

Step 2: Add Database Components

Although we're actually adding a very powerful bit of functionality to our application page, Dreamweaver allows us to insert it as a standard recordset. Here's the SQL behind the Access view we'll be using:

```
SELECT (SELECT Count([UserID]) FROM Users WHERE
((([Users].[UserRegDate])>Now()-1))) AS RegToday, (SELECT
Count([UserID]) FROM Users WHERE ((([Users].[UserRegDate])>Now()-7)))
AS RegThisWeek, (SELECT Count([UserID]) FROM Users WHERE
((([Users].[UserRegDate])>Now()-30))) AS RegThisMonth,
Count([UserID]) AS UserCount
FROM Users;
```

Despite the complexity of the view, the implementation of this functionality in Dreamweaver is quite straightforward for ASP and ColdFusion. Because PHP does not support views, the recordset needs to be added directly in the Advanced Recordset dialog.

For ASP and ColdFusion

1. From the Bindings panel, select Add (+) and choose **Recordset**.
2. Make sure you are in Simple mode.
3. In the Name field, enter the label for your recordset.
   - Enter **UserStats** as the recordset name.
4. From the Connections list, choose the desired data source connection.
   - Select **Recipes** from the Connections list.
5. Choose the appropriate table containing the users information.
   - Select **UserRegStats** from the Tables list.
6. Choose the **All** option under Columns.

   No filtering or sorting is necessary; it's all handled in the SQL statement.
7. Click OK to confirm your choices and close the dialog.

For PHP

1. From the Bindings panel, choose Add (+) and select **Recordset (Query)**.
2. Switch to the advanced view of the Recordset dialog, if necessary.
3. Enter an appropriate name for the recordset.
   - Enter **UserStats** in the Recordset field.

4. Select your data source.

   📖 Choose **Recipes** from the Connections list.

5. Enter the following code in the SQL area:

(PHP)
```
SELECT
    SUM(UserRegDate > NOW() - INTERVAL 24 HOUR) AS RegToday,
    SUM(UserRegDate > NOW() - INTERVAL 7 DAY) AS RegThisWeek,
    SUM(UserRegDate > NOW() - INTERVAL 30 DAY) AS RegThisMonth,
    COUNT(UserID) AS UserCount
    FROM
    Users
```

6. Save your page.

Step 3: Display User Statistics

All that's left is to show the results of the recordset. This is simply a matter of dragging dynamic elements into place.

1. From the Bindings panel, expand the **UserStats** recordset.
2. Drag the following dynamic elements onto the page:
   • Drag the `UserCount` field in the cell next to the label Total Users.
   • Drag the `RegToday` field in the cell next to the label Last 24 Hour Activity.
   • Drag the `RegThisWeek` field in the cell next to the label Last 7 Days Activity.
   • Drag the `RegThisMonth` field in the cell next to the label Last 30 Days Activity.

   When completed, the page will resemble the one in Figure r1-26.

3. Save the page as `userstatistics` using the appropriate file extension for your platform.

Your user login application is now complete. Be sure to test all the various pages as both a user and an administrator.

r-26

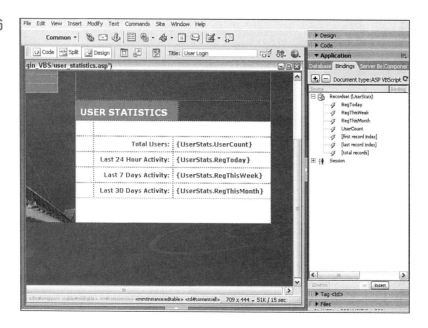

Recipe 2

Employee Lookup

What was the killer app that truly launched the Web? An easy-to-use but powerful search engine named YAHOO!. Adding a search facility to a Web site is one of the most common server-side goals. Similarly, one of an intranet's primary workhorses is often a special-purpose search engine: the employee lookup application. The ability to locate someone quickly and efficiently in an organization is key.

Search engines run the gamut from very straightforward to very advanced, both in features and implementation. The most basic search function—one that checks a single data source field for a word or phrase—is easy to create; you can do it in Macromedia Dreamweaver using nothing more than the simple Recordset dialog. However, any attempts to make the search even a little more powerful, such as adding the ability to search multiple fields or include multiple keywords, significantly ramps up the coding complexity.

The Employee Lookup application includes examples of two kinds of searches: one fairly simple and the other more advanced. Both, however, are a cut above the more basic search routines because the recipe functions allow the user to search for multiple keywords. In addition to the two search pages, this application includes a powerful results page where the real search power is coded. The results page utilizes Dreamweaver's application objects for recordset navigation and provides links to a corresponding detail page.

User Recipes

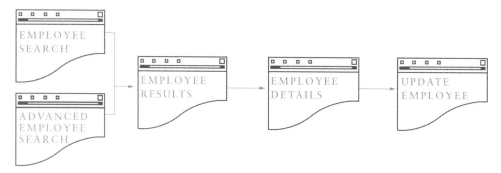

Administrator Recipes

From the detail page, users can choose to update their records; this functionality can easily be limited to an administrator. Two interconnected administrative pages—New Job and New Employee—round out the application. Several of the pages use sophisticated SQL techniques—including run-time WHERE clauses and nested SQL statements—to display meaningful results to the user's search criteria.

Ingredients

7 APPLICATION PAGES:

- 5 User Pages
  - Employee Search
  - Advanced Employee Search
  - Employee Results
  - Employee Details
  - Update Employee

- 2 Administration Pages
    - New Job
    - New Employee

2 DATA SOURCES:

- 1 Database with:
    - 3 Tables
        - **Employees**—The core employee data table with fields for first name, last name, job, email address, phone number, cell phone number, and cubical number.
        - **Departments**—A listing of all the departments in the organization.
        - **Jobs**—Each of the current job titles, with fields to identify the corresponding department and manager; all jobs, whether presently filled or not, are listed here.
    - 3 Views (ASP and ColdFusion)
        - **EmployeeLookup**—A virtual table joining the `Employees`, `Jobs`, and `Departments` tables.
        - **JobsWithDepartments**—A combined listing that shows each job and its matching department, in parentheses.
        - **ManagersByDepartment**—Displays only the managers, sorted by their department.

Prep Work

Before you begin to build this application, make sure your prep work has been completed.

1. Create the data source containing the necessary tables.

    📖 ASP and ColdFusion users should use the **Recipes.mdb** data source found in the downloaded files while PHP users should work with the **Recipes** data source. For assistance in locating and installing these files, choose **Help > Web Application Recipes**.

2. Set up a connection to the data source. If you're unsure how to do this, see the "Connecting to Data Sources" section of Chapter 1.

    📖 Name the connection **Recipes**.

3. Create the template to be used for the application.

    📖 Use the template for your server model named **employeelookup**.

4. ColdFusion users: Make the `Application.cfm` file and store it in the same folder as the application.

End User Recipe: Employee Search

Search applications have two key parts: an entry form and a results page. Typically the entry form uses little or no server-side code; its sole function is to accept the search criteria and pass the values to the results page where the search operation is actually performed. Our first recipe describes how to create just such an entry form page.

Step 1: Implement Employee Search Design

To start, create the basic page with the search criteria form.

1. Create a basic dynamic page, either by hand or derived from a template.

   📖 In the **EmployeeLookup** folder, locate the folder for your server model and open the employee_search page found there.

2. Add a table to the content region of your page to contain the interface elements for the application.

   📖 From the Snippets panel, drag the **Recipes > EmployeeLookup > Wireframes > Employee Search - Wireframe** snippet into the Content editable region.

3. Within the table, insert the form and necessary form elements for the user login. You'll need a single text field to hold the keywords and a Submit button.

   📖 Place your cursor in the row below the words EMPLOYEE SEARCH and insert the **Recipes > EmployeeLookup > Forms > Employee Search - Form** snippet [r2-1].

r2-1

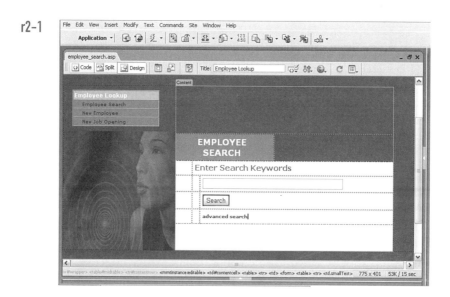

4. Save the page before continuing.

Most examples of single-field search applications target a specific data source field, such as Last Name. Our application is capable of searching across several fields using AND or OR operators; the code that makes this possible is inserted into the search results page. The simple search form also includes a link to an advanced search function.

Step 2: Specify Form Action and Method

The <form> tag on a search page contains both the destination and the means for transmitting the search criteria. Both attributes can be set through Dreamweaver's Property inspector.

1. Place your cursor anywhere within the form in either Design or Code view.
2. From the Tag Selector, select the **<form>** tag.
3. On the Property inspector, enter the path to the search results page.
   - Select Browse and choose the **employee_results** file for your server model.
4. Make sure the Method is set to GET rather than POST or Default.

   Here, we're using GET—which relies on URL arguments to pass parameters—to properly navigate the recordset. The navigation functions, found in other pages of this application, read the passed parameters from the URL and filter the recordset appropriately.
5. Save the page.

You'll note that no data validation is applied here; we're not even making an entry into the required search field. Why? In this situation, we want to allow for a return of all the records, and a blank search field indicates a wide-open filter.

End User Recipe: Employee Advanced Search

The goal of the Advanced Search page is to allow users to search one or more specific data source fields. In addition to standard text fields, the Advanced Search page includes a dynamic list that will be bound to a list of employee locations.

Step 1: Implement Employee Search Design

Let's start by building the page with the search criteria form.

1. Create a basic dynamic page, either by hand or derived from a template.
   - In the **EmployeeLookup** folder, locate the folder for your server model and open the employee_search_advanced page found there.
2. Add a table to the content region of your page to contain the interface elements for the application.
   - From the Snippets panel, drag the **Recipes > EmployeeLookup > Wireframes > Employee Advanced Search - Wireframe** snippet into the Content editable region.

3. Within the table, insert the form and necessary form elements for the user login. For the advanced search, you'll need either a text field or a list for every data source field you want to search as well as a submit button. Use lists for those data sources that have a fixed set of values and text fields for data sources that could contain any text string. In our example, there are five text fields and one list element.

    ☐ Place your cursor in the row below the words ADVANCED SEARCH and insert the **Recipes > EmployeeLookup > Forms > Employee Advanced Search - Form** snippet [r2-2].

r2-2

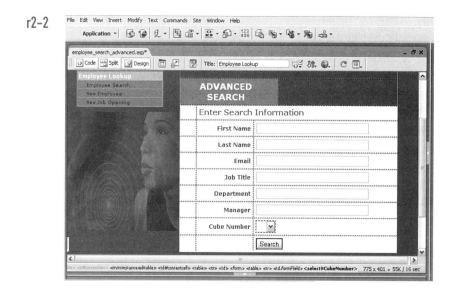

4. Be sure to save the page.

Again, no data validation will be applied to allow for a full-results search.

Step 2: Add Database Components

The list element inserted in the previous step requires a data source to be populated. In this step, we'll add a recordset that contains a list of the cubicles in use. Because it's possible that the cubicle number can be used more than once—in lean times, some of our employees have to share their office space—an advanced SQL statement is used to ensure that each value appears only once.

1. From the Bindings panel, choose Add (+) and select **Recordset**.

2. If necessary, switch to the advanced Recordset dialog [r2-3].

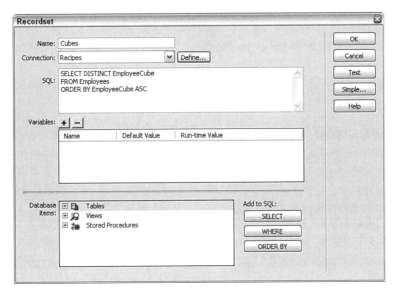

r2-3

3. In the Name field, enter a label associated with the corresponding list.

   📖 Enter **Cubes** in the Name field.

4. Choose your data source connection from the list.

   📖 Select **Recipes** from the Connection or Data Source list.

5. ColdFusion only: If necessary, enter the username and password in their respective fields.

6. In the SQL field, enter the following code, according to your server model:

VB JS CF
```
SELECT DISTINCT EmployeeCube
    FROM Employees
    ORDER BY EmployeeCube ASC
```

PHP
```
SELECT DISTINCT EmployeeCube
    FROM employees
    ORDER BY employeeCube ASC
```

The DISTINCT keyword is a SQL instruction that forces only unique values to be returned.

7. Make sure your settings are correct, and click OK to close the dialog and insert the recordset.

Step 3: Data Binding Process

With the recordset defined, we're ready to use it to primarily populate the dynamic list element on the page. I say *primarily* because Dreamweaver allows us to mix both dynamic and static elements in the list control. We'll use this facility to allow for a wild-card type value.

1. Select the list element you want to assign dynamic values to.

   📖 Choose the **CubeNumber** list element.

2. From the Property inspector, choose **Dynamic**.

   The Dynamic List/Menu dialog appears [r2-4].

r2-4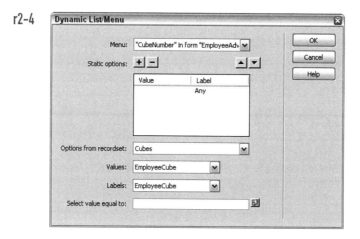

3. Make sure the **CubeNumber** list element is selected in the Menu list.

4. Select Add (+) and, leaving the Value column blank, enter **Any** in the Label column.

   Static values in a dynamic list element appear at the top of the option list. The Value column is left empty so that a choice of Any results in no limiting filter being set.

5. From the Options from Recordset list, choose **Cubes**.

6. Set both the Values and the Labels lists to **EmployeeCube**.

   Because there are no separate identifying labels for the employee cube, the same data source is used for both Values and Labels.

7. Leave the Select Value Equal To field empty and click OK to close the dialog.

   By leaving the Select Value field blank, the item at the top of the list—in this case the static value with the label Any—becomes the default selection.

Step 4: Specify Form Action and Method

As with the simple search form, we need to establish the correct action—the page that will actually process the search request—and the method—how that page receives the data.

1. Place your cursor anywhere within the form in either Design or Code view.
2. From the Tag Selector, select the **<form>** tag.
3. On the Property inspector, enter the path to the search results page.
   -   Select Browse and choose the **employee_results** file for your server model.
4. Make sure the Method is set to GET rather than POST or Default.

Selecting a GET method causes the search criteria and other form-related information to be sent in a query string that is attached to the URL, like this:

```
employee_results.asp?FirstName=&LastName=lowery&Email=&JobTitle=&Department=
&Manager=&CubeNumber=&AdvancedSearch=Search
```

Recordset navigation requires GET rather than POST because POST encodes the form entries in a way that GET does not. Note that in our example only the LastName variable has a value—lowery—and that is what the next page we're going to build would search for.

End User Recipe: Employee Results

The Employee Results page is the heart—and the brains—of this application. Here resides the functionality for accepting the search criteria and returning the matching records in an abbreviated list. Each record in the list is linked to a detail page. This results page is designed to handle input from both simple and advanced with special hand-coded functions.

Step 1: Implement Design

We'll first create the basic page to hold our dynamic content. Although there will be interactive elements for recordset and other navigation, no form is necessary for the results page.

1. Create a basic dynamic page, either by hand or derived from a template.
   -   In the **EmployeeLookup** folder, locate the folder for your server model and open the employee_results page found there.

2. Add a table to the content region of your page to contain the interface elements for the application.

    ▢ From the Snippets panel, drag the **Recipes > EmployeeLookup > Wireframes > Employee Results - Wireframe** snippet into the Content editable region.

3. Within the table, nest another HTML table to display the results from the employee search query. The result list should have a column for each field you want to display; our example table has room for four such fields. The nested table should also contain a row for recordset navigation links and status.

    ▢ Place your cursor in the row below the words EMPLOYEE RESULTS and insert the **Recipes > EmployeeLookup > ContentTables > Employee Results - Content Table** snippet [r2-5].

r2-5

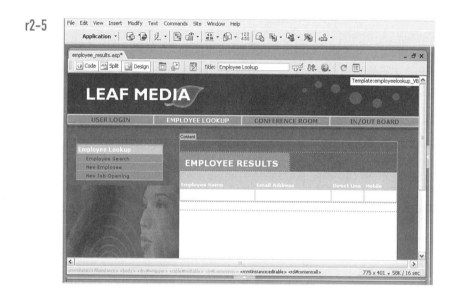

Step 2: Add Database Components

Although there is only one recordset used in this page, it's a powerful one—not so much from what it does by itself, but from the possibilities it engenders. In the recordset, the WHERE clause of the SQL statement is set to a run-time variable termed WhereParam. As you'll see later, the WhereParam variable enables the SQL filter to be dynamically generated, dependent on user input.

For ASP

1. From the Bindings panel, choose Add (+) and select **Recordset** from the list.

2. If necessary, switch to the advanced Recordset dialog [r2-6].

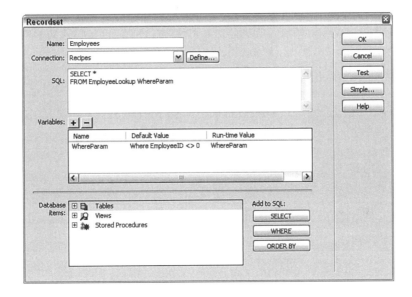

r2-6

3. Enter an appropriate name for the recordset.

   📖 Enter **Employees** in the Name field.

4. Choose a proper connection from the list.

   📖 Select **Recipes** from the Connections list.

5. In the SQL field, insert the following code:

```
SELECT *
FROM EmployeeLookup WhereParam
```

Note that a variable, WhereParam, is substituted for the entire WHERE clause, including the keyword.

6. In the Variables section, choose Add (+) and enter **WhereParam** in the Name column.

7. In the Default Value column, enter this:

```
Where EmployeeID <> 0
```

Because no employee has an ID set to 0, by default—if no search criteria are entered—the recordset will return all the records.

8. In the Run-Time Value column, enter **WhereParam** and click OK to close the dialog and insert the recordset.

9. Save the page.

For ColdFusion

1. From the Bindings panel, choose Add (+) and select **Recordset**.

2. In the advanced Recordset dialog, enter an appropriate name for the recordset.

    ◻ Enter **Employees** in the Name field.

3. Choose your data source from the drop-down list.

    ◻ Select **Recipes** from the Data Source list.

4. If necessary, enter the username and password for the data source in the corresponding fields.

5. In the SQL area, enter the following code:

    ◻
    ```
    Select *
    FROM EmployeeLookup WhereParam
    ```

6. Verify your code and click OK to close the dialog and insert the recordset.

7. Save the page.

For PHP

To compensate for MySQL's lack of support for views, the EmployeeLookup table is temporarily filled with pertinent data. The Employee recordset then retrieves the data from this table at run time. After the Employee recordset has been created, the temporary information is flushed from the EmployeeLookup table and the autonumber controls are reset.

To build the proper application in Dreamweaver, you create the Employee recordset first and then insert the code for the EmployeeLookup table.

1. From the Bindings panel, choose Add (+) and select **Recordset** from the list.

2. If necessary, switch to the advanced Recordset dialog.

3. Enter an appropriate name for the recordset.

    ◻ Enter **Employees** in the Name field.

4. Choose a proper connection from the list.

♪ Select **Recipes** from the Connections list.

5. In the SQL field, insert the following code:

♪
```
Select *
FROM EmployeeLookup WhereParam
```

Note that a variable, WhereParam, is substituted for the entire WHERE clause, including the keyword.

6. In the Variables section, choose Add (+) and enter **WhereParam** in the Name column.

7. In the Default Value column, enter:

♪
```
Where EmployeeID <> 0
```

Because no employee has an ID set to 0, by default—if no search criteria are entered—the recordset returns all the records.

8. In the Run-Time Value column, enter **$WhereParam** and click OK to close the dialog and insert the recordset.

9. Save the page.

Now we're ready to insert the EmployeeLookup code.

10. From the Server Behaviors panel, select the Employees recordset.

11. Switch to Code view, and you'll see the Employees recordset code highlighted.

12. Wrap the following around the selected code:

♪ From the Snippets panel, insert the **EmployeeLookup > CustomCode_PHP > Temporary Query - EmployeeLookup** snippet.

(PHP) *before:*

```php
<?php
mysql_select_db($database_Recipes, $Recipes);
$query_EmployeeLookup = "INSERT INTO employeelookup
➥SELECT employees_1.EmployeeID, jobs.JobID, jobs.JobTitle,
➥employees_1.EmployeeFirst, employees_1.EmployeeLast,
➥departments.DepartmentName, CONCAT(employees.EmployeeFirst,' ',
➥employees.EmployeeLast) AS ManagerName, employees_1.EmployeeEmail,
➥employees_1.EmployeePhone, employees_1.EmployeeMobil,
➥employees_1.EmployeeCube FROM employees, employees employees_1, jobs,
➥jobs jobs_1, departments WHERE ((((jobs.JobTypeID = jobs_1.JobID)
➥AND (jobs.JobDepartment = departments.DepartmentID))
➥AND (employees.EmployeeJob = jobs_1.JobID))
➥AND (employees_1.EmployeeJob = jobs.JobID))";
mysql_query($query_EmployeeLookup,$Recipes);
?>
```

After:

(PHP) ```
<?php
  $query_EmployeeLookup = "DELETE FROM employeelookup";
  mysql_query($query_EmployeeLookup,$Recipes);
?>
```

13. Save your page.

**NOTE**

As you add the dynamic text to the table, the table widens to accommodate the field names. Dreamweaver displays dynamic text with this syntax: {recordset.datasourcefield}. Consequently, the dynamic text names can get quite lengthy and distort the table significantly. This distortion generally disappears, however, after you display the real data. If you would rather not see the full recordset and field name, open Preferences, and in the Invisible Elements category, change the Show Dynamic Text As option to { }.

## Step 3: Data Binding Process

After you've defined the recordset, dynamic text is available to be inserted on the page. In our example, five data source fields will be placed under four table headers: Name, Email, Direct Line, and Mobile. Two of the data sources, EmployeeFirst and EmployeeLast, are combined under the Name heading.

1. From the Bindings panel, expand the **Employees** recordset.

2. Place the desired data source fields onto the page:

   ▢ Drag the EmployeeFirst field under the Name column.

   ▢ Drag the EmployeeLast field after the EmployeeFirst field and add a space between the two dynamic text elements. You might find it easier to place the cursor where you want the last name to go and use the Insert button on the Bindings panel.

   ▢ Drag the EmployeeEmail field under the Email column.

   ▢ Drag the EmployeePhone field under the Direct Line column.

   ▢ Drag the EmployeeMobile field under the Mobile column.

When completed, test the layout by selecting Live Data view from the Document toolbar. The first record's data appears [r2-7]. If necessary, adjust the column spacing on the table by dragging the cell borders.
```

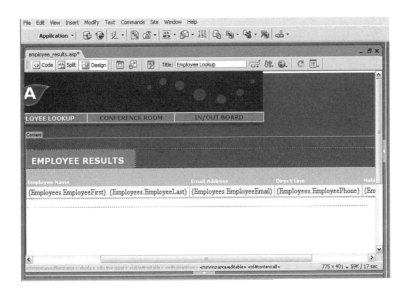

Step 4: Apply Server Behaviors

Although there's no user input on this page, there's a fair degree of interactivity. The recordset returned here could hold anywhere from one to all the employees in a firm, so we must be able to present those results in a manageable fashion. To this end, you can insert Dreamweaver's Repeat Region server behavior to show the results in groups of 10. Next, you can add links to a detail page for each listing.

First, let's add the Repeat Region to show multiple records.

1. Place the cursor in any of the table cells containing the dynamic data.
2. From the Tag Selector, select the **<tr>** tag, located to the left of the current <td> tag.
3. From the Server Behaviors panel, choose Add (+) and select **Repeat Region** from the list.
4. In the Repeat Region dialog, make sure the **Employees** recordset is selected.
5. Accepting the default of Showing 10 Records at a Time, click OK to close the dialog.

Switch to Live Data view to see the information from the first 10 employees in the data source [r2-8]. Because no search criteria has been passed to this page, the default value of the WhereParam variable is used to filter the recordset—which, you'll remember, is set to receive all the employees.

r2-8

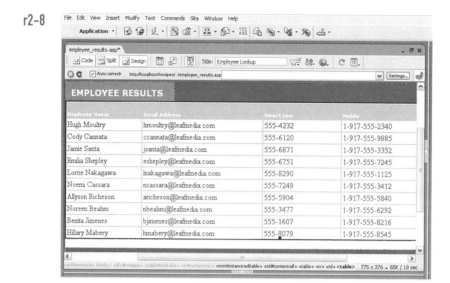

NOTE

After a little testing, you might decide to adjust the table or its cells in some ways, such as choosing the No Wrap option for certain cells or modifying the cell padding. While you're working in Live Data view, any such formatting changes will not ripple through the entire repeat region until the Refresh icon on the Live Data toolbar is selected. Alternatively, you can refresh the display by exiting and re-entering Live Data view.

The final server behavior to be added to this page provides a way for users to see the full details of an employee record.

1. Select the dynamic text elements you want to serve as a link to the detail page.

   📖 Select both **EmployeeFirst** and **EmployeeLast** dynamic text fields. The surest method to do this is to select one (it doesn't matter which one) and then Shift-select the second; this highlights both fields and the space separating them.

2. From the Property inspector, select the folder icon next to the Link field.

3. In the Select File dialog, choose **Parameters**.

4. In the Parameters dialog, enter the variable name.

   📖 In the Name column, enter **ID**.

5. Enter the dynamic value.

   📖 Under the Value column, select the lightning bolt to open the Dynamic Data dialog and select **EmployeeID** from the `Employees` recordset.

   📖 Click OK once to close the Dynamic Data dialog and again to close the Parameters dialog.

6. Select the file you want to pass the parameter to.

   📖 Select Browse and choose the **employee_detail** file for your server model.

7. Save your page.

Step 5: Adding Application Objects

To allow users to page through the records—and see where they are—you'll add record-set navigation tools next. Dreamweaver's Recordset Navigation Bar and Recordset Navigation Status application objects are used to page through and track the records.

1. Place your cursor in the Employee Results table where you would like the navigation links to appear.

   📖 Place the cursor in the row above the Direct Line cell.

2. Choose the **Recordset Navigation Bar** object from the Application category of the Insert bar under the Recordset Paging memo.

   Alternatively, you could select **Insert > Application Objects > Recordset Paging > Recordset Navigation Bar**.

3. In the Recordset Navigation Bar dialog, select the Employees recordset.

4. Leave the Display Using option set to **Text** and click OK.

As you are paging through a recordset, it's helpful to have some feedback stating where you are in the data. Dreamweaver includes another Application object, called Recordset Navigation Status, to provide such feedback.

1. Place your cursor in the Employee Results table where you would like the navigation status to be displayed.

   Again, be careful not to place your cursor within the Repeat Region.

   📖 Place the cursor in the row above the Employee Name cell.

2. Choose the **Recordset Navigation Status** object from the Display Record Count menu in the Insert bar's Application category.

   Alternatively, you could select **Insert > Application Objects > Display Record Count > Recordset Navigation Status**.

3. In the Recordset Navigation Status dialog, select the Employees recordset and click OK.

To get the full effect of the recordset navigation controls, preview the page in a browser [r2-9].

r2-9

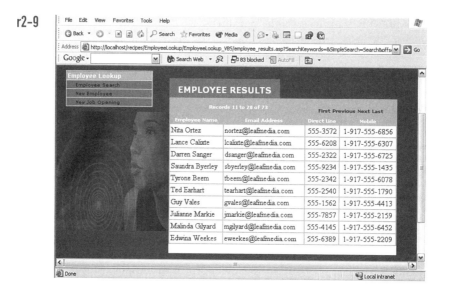

Step 6: Code Search Functions

The infrastructure for the page has been completed, and now it's time to add the core functionality. As you've seen, this page's recordset employs a variable, WhereParam, to represent the entire WHERE clause of the SQL statement. We'll now insert the functions—one for the simple search and one for the advanced search—that are necessary to dynamically construct WhereParam. To simplify the coding, both functions use a third custom function, AddFieldToSearch() which, as the name implies, builds up the search filter one requested field at a time. Finally, to fully integrate the custom code into Dreamweaver's server behavior output, we'll add a couple of function calls.

> **NOTE**
>
> You might want to wrap the entire Recordset Navigation Status object in a conditional region by applying the Show Region If Recordset Is Not Empty server behavior. This technique hides the status text if no records are found to match the search criteria.

> **NOTE**
>
> This step is only necessary for ASP and PHP; for ColdFusion, the functionality is inserted within the recordset.

To make sure our helper function, AddFieldToSearch(), is available, we'll add it first.

1. In Code view, place your cursor at the top of the file, on a new line directly after the <!--#include> statement for ASP and <?php require_once…> for PHP.

2. Insert the following code:

   📖 From the Snippets panel, open the **Recipes > EmployeeLookup > Custom Code** folder for your server model insert the **Add Field to Search** snippet.

VB
```
<%
AddFieldToSearch(CurrentWhere,ColumnName,ValString,Comparison,
➥Separator,OpenEncap,CloseEncap)
   if (ValString <> "") then
      if (CurrentWhere = "") then
         CurrentWhere = "WHERE "
      else
         CurrentWhere = CurrentWhere & " " & Separator & " "
      end if
      CurrentWhere = CurrentWhere & ColumnName & " " & Comparison &
      ➥ " " & OpenEncap & Replace(ValString, "'", "''") &
CloseEncap
   end if
   AddFieldToSearch = CurrentWhere
end function
%>
```

JS
```
<%
function AddFieldToSearch(CurrentWhere,ColumnName,ValString,
➥Comparison,Separator,OpenEncap,CloseEncap) {
   if (ValString!="") {
      if (CurrentWhere == "") {
         CurrentWhere = "WHERE ";
      }
      else {
         CurrentWhere += " " + Separator + " ";
      }
      CurrentWhere += ColumnName + " " + Comparison + " " +
      ➥OpenEncap + ValString.replace(/'/g, "''") + CloseEncap;
   }
   return CurrentWhere;
}
%>
```

PHP
```
<?php
function AddFieldToSearch($CurrentWhere,$ColumnName,$ValString,
➥$Comparison,$Separator,$OpenEncap,$CloseEncap)  {
    if ($ValString!="")  {
        if ($CurrentWhere == "")  {
            $CurrentWhere = "WHERE ";
        } else  {
            $CurrentWhere.= " ".$Separator." ";
        }
```

Continues

```
                    $CurrentWhere.= $ColumnName." ".$Comparison.
                 ➥" ".$OpenEncap.$ValString.$CloseEncap;
                    }

                    return $CurrentWhere;
          }
          ?>
```

Essentially, this function accepts arguments from both the simple and advanced search functions and dynamically constructs a segment of the WHERE clause. The first time this function is called, the WHERE keyword is added; every time after that, the OR operator is appended instead. Next, the new segment is constructed and added to the existing WHERE clause. The ValString argument is either an array of keywords if the simple search is used or the values from specific form fields (Name, Department, and so on) for the advanced search.

Next, we'll add the simple search function. In this function, the query string passed from the simple search page is put into an array so that it can compared—one keyword at a time—to each of the desired fields. The fields used in the comparison are set in the programming loop; you can add additional fields by following the syntax of the AddFieldToSearch() function call and adding the data field names.

1. In Code view, place the cursor in the proper position for your server model.

   (VB) Place the cursor after the AddFieldToSearchFunction() just inserted. The final three lines of that function are as follows:

   ```
   AddFieldToSearch = CurrentWhere
   end function
   %>
   ```

   (JS) Place the cursor after the AddFieldToSearchFunction() just inserted. The final three lines of that function are as follows:

   ```
   return CurrentWhere;
   }
   %>
   ```

   (CF) Place the cursor within the <cfquery> tag that defines the recordset after this line:

   ```
   SELECT * FROM EmployeeLookup
   ```

(PHP) Place the cursor after the `AddFieldToSearchFunction()` just inserted. The final three lines of that function are as follows:

```
return $CurrentWhere;
}
?>
```

2. Insert the following code:

    From the Snippets panel, open the **Recipes > EmployeeLookup > Custom Code** folder for your server model and insert the **Create Simple Keyword Search** snippet.

(VB)
```
<%
dim WhereParam, Keywords, x
if (cStr(Request.QueryString("SimpleSearch"))<>"") then
  WhereParam = ""
  KeyWords = cStr(Request.QueryString("SearchKeywords"))
  if (KeyWords <> "")  then
    KeyWords = Split(Keywords, " ")
      for x=0 to Ubound(KeyWords)
        WhereParam = AddFieldToSearch(WhereParam,"EmployeeFirst",
        ➥KeyWords(x),"LIKE","OR","'%","%'")
        WhereParam = AddFieldToSearch(WhereParam,"EmployeeLast",
        ➥KeyWords(x),"LIKE","OR","'%","%'")
        WhereParam = AddFieldToSearch(WhereParam,"EmployeeEmail",
        ➥KeyWords(x),"LIKE","OR","'%","%'")
        WhereParam = AddFieldToSearch(WhereParam,"JobTitle",
        ➥KeyWords(x),"LIKE","OR","'%","%'")
      next
    end if
  end if
%>
```

(JS)
```
<%
if (String(Request.QueryString("SimpleSearch"))!="undefined")  {
  var WhereParam = "";
  var KeyWords = String(Request.QueryString("SearchKeywords"));
  if (KeyWords != "")  {
    KeyWords = KeyWords.split(" ");
      for (var x=0; x<KeyWords.length; x++)  {
        WhereParam = AddFieldToSearch(WhereParam,"EmployeeFirst",
        ➥KeyWords[x],"LIKE","OR","'%","%'");
        WhereParam = AddFieldToSearch(WhereParam,"EmployeeLast",
        ➥KeyWords[x],"LIKE","OR","'%","%'");
        WhereParam = AddFieldToSearch(WhereParam,"EmployeeEmail",
```

Continues

```
        ➥KeyWords[x],"LIKE","OR","'%","%'");
        WhereParam = AddFieldToSearch(WhereParam,"JobTitle",
        ➥KeyWords[x],"LIKE","OR","'%","%'");
      }
    }
  }
  %>
```

CF
```
<cfif isDefined("URL.SimpleSearch") AND URL.SimpleSearch NEQ "">
  WHERE EmployeeID = 0
  <cfloop index="kWord" list="#URL.SearchKeywords#" delimiters=" ">
    OR EmployeeFirst LIKE '%#kWord#%' OR EmployeeLast
    ➥LIKE '%#kWord#%' OR EmployeeEmail
    LIKE '%#kWord#%' OR JobTitle LIKE '%#kWord#%'
  </cfloop>
</cfif>
```

PHP
```
<?php
  if (isset($_GET['SimpleSearch']))  {
    $WhereParam = "";
    if (isset($_GET['SearchKeywords']))  {
      $KeyWords = explode(" ",$_GET['SearchKeywords']);
      for($x=0; x < count($KeyWords); $x++)  {
        $WhereParam = AddFieldToSearch($WhereParam,
        ➥"EmployeeFirst",$KeyWords[$x],"LIKE",
        ➥"OR","'%","%'");
        $WhereParam = AddFieldToSearch($WhereParam,
        ➥"EmployeeLast",$KeyWords[$x],"LIKE",
        ➥"OR","'%","%'");
        $WhereParam = AddFieldToSearch($WhereParam,
        ➥"EmployeeEmail",$KeyWords[$x],"LIKE",
        ➥"OR","'%","%'");
        $WhereParam = AddFieldToSearch($WhereParam,
        ➥"JobTitle",$KeyWords[$x],"LIKE",
        ➥"OR","'%","%'");
      }
    }
  }
  ?>
```

The simple search function uses a server object (QueryString in ASP, URL in ColdFusion, and $_GET in PHP) to get information from the search page. This is possible because we set the <form> tag method attribute to GET instead of POST. This technique works fine here because the query argument is not likely to be very long. For complex forms, it is better to use the POST method.

This section of code handles the case when the advanced search page is used to find employee results. The SQL variable WhereParam is built out pulling any text entered on the advanced search page into a single query string. The use of the AddFieldToSearch() function provides a simple mechanism to build up the query string.

> **NOTE**
>
> ColdFusion users should note that the insertion of this code block (and the one for the advanced search) within the <cfquery> tag disables Dreamweaver recognition of the recordset in the Bindings panel. Once implemented, you cannot expand the recordset, and a series of errors are reported. To reopen the recordset in the Bindings panel, temporarily cut the code added to the <cfquery> tag. Although this might seem awkward, it is the preferred way to write this function using CFML tags without using <cfscript>.

Next, we'll add the advanced search function. This code also uses the AddFieldToSearch() function to help build up the WHERE clause, but here—unlike in the simple search—you can combine keywords using AND or OR operators in any specified field. For example, the user could look for all Smiths OR Jones in the Sales OR Marketing departments.

1. In Code view, place the cursor after the simple search code block just inserted. The final three lines of that code block are as follows:

VB
```
end if
end if
%>
```

JS
```
}
}
%>
```

CF
```
LIKE '%#kWord#%' OR JobTitle LIKE '%#kWord#%'
   </cfloop>
</cfif>
```

PHP
```
}
}
?>
```

2. Insert the following code:

   📖 From the Snippets panel, open the **Recipes > EmployeeLookup > Custom Code**
   folder for your server model and insert the **Advanced Keyword Search** snippet.

(VB)
```vb
<%
if (cStr(Request.QueryString("AdvancedSearch"))<>"")  then
  WhereParam = ""
  WhereParam = AddFieldToSearch(WhereParam,"EmployeeFirst",
  ➥cStr(Request.QueryString("FirstName")),"LIKE","AND","'","%'")
  WhereParam = AddFieldToSearch(WhereParam,"EmployeeLast",
  ➥cStr(Request.QueryString("LastName")),"LIKE","AND","'","%'")
  WhereParam = AddFieldToSearch(WhereParam,"EmployeeEmail",
  ➥cStr(Request.QueryString("Email")),"LIKE","AND","'%","%'")
  WhereParam = AddFieldToSearch(WhereParam,"JobTitle",
  ➥cStr(Request.QueryString("JobTitle")),"LIKE","AND","'%","%'")
  WhereParam = AddFieldToSearch(WhereParam,"DepartmentName",
  ➥cStr(Request.QueryString("Department")),"LIKE","AND","'","%'")
  WhereParam = AddFieldToSearch(WhereParam,"ManagerName",
  ➥cStr(Request.QueryString("Manager")),"LIKE","AND","'%","%'")
  WhereParam = AddFieldToSearch(WhereParam,"EmployeeCube",
  ➥cStr(Request.QueryString("CubeNumber")),"=","AND","","")
end if
%>
```

(JS)
```js
<%
if (String(Request.QueryString("AdvancedSearch"))!="undefined")  {
  var WhereParam = "";
  WhereParam = AddFieldToSearch(WhereParam,"EmployeeFirst",
  ➥String(Request.QueryString("FirstName")),"LIKE","AND","'","%'");
  WhereParam = AddFieldToSearch(WhereParam,"EmployeeLast",
  ➥String(Request.QueryString("LastName")),"LIKE","AND","'","%'");
  WhereParam = AddFieldToSearch(WhereParam,"EmployeeEmail",
  ➥String(Request.QueryString("Email")),"LIKE","AND","'%","%'");
  WhereParam = AddFieldToSearch(WhereParam,"JobTitle",
  ➥String(Request.QueryString("JobTitle")),"LIKE",
  ➥"AND","'%","%'");
  WhereParam = AddFieldToSearch(WhereParam,"DepartmentName",
  ➥String(Request.QueryString("Department")),"LIKE",
  ➥"AND","'","%'");
  WhereParam = AddFieldToSearch(WhereParam,"ManagerName",
  ➥String(Request.QueryString("Manager")),"LIKE",
  ➥"AND","'%","%'");
  WhereParam = AddFieldToSearch(WhereParam,"EmployeeCube",
  ➥String(Request.QueryString("CubeNumber")),"=",
  ➥"AND","","");
}
%>
```

```
CF   <cfif isDefined("URL.AdvancedSearch")>
       WHERE 1 = 1
       <cfif URL.FirstName NEQ "">
         AND EmployeeFirst LIKE '#URL.FirstName#%'
       </cfif>
       <cfif form.LastName NEQ "">
         AND EmployeeLast LIKE '#URL.LastName#%'
       </cfif>
       <cfif form.Email NEQ "">
         AND EmployeeEmail LIKE '%#URL.Email#%'
       </cfif>
       <cfif form.JobTitle NEQ "">
         AND JobTitle LIKE '%#URL.JobTitle#%'
       </cfif>
       <cfif form.Department NEQ "">
         AND DepartmentName LIKE '#URL.Department#%'
       </cfif>
       <cfif form.Manager NEQ "">
         AND ManagerName LIKE '%#URL.Manager#%'
       </cfif>
       <cfif form.CubeNumber NEQ "">
         AND EmployeeCube = #URL.CubeNumber#
       </cfif>
     </cfif>
```

```
PHP  <?php
     if (isset($_GET['AdvancedSearch'])) {
         $WhereParam = "";
         $WhereParam = AddFieldToSearch($WhereParam,"EmployeeFirst",
         ➡$_GET['FirstName'],"LIKE","AND","'","%'");
           $WhereParam = AddFieldToSearch($WhereParam,"EmployeeLast",
           ➡$_GET['LastName'],"LIKE","AND","'","%'");
           $WhereParam = AddFieldToSearch($WhereParam,"EmployeeEmail",
           ➡$_GET['Email'],"LIKE","AND","'%","%'");
           $WhereParam = AddFieldToSearch($WhereParam,"JobTitle",
           ➡$_GET['JobTitle'],"LIKE","AND","'%","%'");
           $WhereParam = AddFieldToSearch($WhereParam,"DepartmentName",
           ➡$_GET['Department'],"LIKE","AND","'","%'");
           $WhereParam = AddFieldToSearch($WhereParam,"ManagerName",
           ➡$_GET['Manager'],"LIKE","AND","'%","%'");
           $WhereParam = AddFieldToSearch($WhereParam,"EmployeeCube",
           ➡$_GET['CubeNumber'],"=","AND","","");
     }
     ?>
```

The advanced search code block goes through each of the fields possibly used as criteria on the advanced search page. To customize the function, add your own statement following the code syntax and substitute the custom field names. For example, if my search page included a text field for telephone extension, I would add the following code:

```
VB   WhereParam = AddFieldToSearch(WhereParam,"EmployeeExtension",
        cStr(Request.QueryString("Extension")),"LIKE","AND","'","%'")
```

```
JS   WhereParam = AddFieldToSearch(WhereParam,"EmployeeExtension",
        String(Request.QueryString("Extension")),"LIKE","AND","'%","%'");
```

```
CF   <cfif form.Extension NEQ "">
            AND EmployeeExtension = #URL.Extension#
        </cfif>
```

```
PHP  $WhereParam = AddFieldToSearch($WhereParam,"EmployeeExtension",
        $_GET['Extension'],"LIKE","AND","'%","%'");
```

For ASP

The remaining code functions are necessary in ASP only. To handle single quotes in the SQL statements for ASP, Dreamweaver escapes them by replacing each one that has two single quotes with code like this:

```
VB   Replace(Employees__WhereParam, "'", "''")
```

```
JS   Employees__WhereParam.replace(/'/g, "''")
```

For the dynamically generated WhereParam variable to work properly, we need to temporarily replace any single quotes in the search criteria with a character unlikely to be used in data—in our example, an exclamation mark. The replacement takes place before the SQL statement reads the WhereParam and, because all the single quotes have been substituted, there is nothing for Dreamweaver's replace function to do. Then, as a final step, Dreamweaver replaces all exclamation marks with single quotes, thus restoring the correct strings before the SQL statement is evaluated.

Three custom code blocks hold our needed functionality. The first code block contains two functions: RemoveQuotes(), which replaces single quotes with an exclamation mark, and ReturnQuotes(), which does the reverse. Each of the two other codes calls one of these functions. We'll insert the code block with the two functions first.

1. Place your cursor below the advanced search code block.
2. Insert this code:

    ▢ From the Snippets panel, open the **Recipes > EmployeeLookup > Custom Code** folder for your server model and insert the **Quote Handler Function** snippet.

`VB`
```
<%
function RemoveQuotes(theString)
  RemoveQuotes = Replace(theString, "'", "|!|")
end function

function ReturnQuotes(theString)
  ReturnQuotes = Replace(theString, "|!|", "'")
end function
%>
```

`JS`
```
<%
function RemoveQuotes(theString)  {
  return theString.replace(/'/g, "|!|");
}
function ReturnQuotes(theString)  {
  return theString.replace(/\|!\|/g, "'");
}
%>
```

3. To insert the first function caller, place your cursor below the just inserted code block.

4. Insert the following code:

    ▢ From the Snippets panel, open the **Recipes > EmployeeLookup > Custom Code** folder for your server model and insert the **Replace Quotes Function** snippet.

`VB`
```
<%
Employees__WhereParam = RemoveQuotes(Employees__WhereParam)
%>
```

`JS`
```
<%
Employees__WhereParam = RemoveQuotes(Employees__WhereParam)
%>
```

5. To insert the second function caller, place your cursor within the Dreamweaver coded SQL function after the line that starts `Employees.Source = "SELECT...`, and add a paragraph return.

Use Dreamweaver's Find and Replace function to look for this code entry.

6. Insert the following code:

    ▢ From the Snippets panel, open the **Recipes > EmployeeLookup > Custom Code** folder for your server model and insert the **Replace Quotes Function** snippet.

(VB) `Employees.Source = ReturnQuotes(Employees.Source)`

(JS) `Employees.Source = ReturnQuotes(Employees.Source);`

7. Save the file.

The advantage to this subroutine function is that the Dreamweaver visual interface still recognizes and protects the code for the hand-editing recordset definition.

Searching for Users with Multiple Criteria Without Handcoding

As you can see from this recipe, creating complex search functionality is no easy task. Dreamweaver's basic master detail page set is adequate for simple searches, but cannot handle more complex criteria like date ranges or keyword combinations. If you'd prefer not—or don't have time—to delve as deeply into handcoding as needed, but still want more searching power, there is another route you can take.

WebAssist's QueryBuilder creates the SQL necessary for sophisticated searches, much like our recipe but without the handcoding. Moreover, it works hand-in-glove with Dreamweaver's Application Objects to construct basic search, result, and detail pages, all in one operation. WA QueryBuilder helps reduce your implementation time, maintenance costs, and improves the user experience.

To learn more about WA QueryBuilder, visit
`http://www.webassist.com/Products/Recipes/WAQueryBuilder.asp`

End User Recipe: Employee Details

As you've seen, each name displayed in the final Employee Results page is a link to a detail record—the page we are about to build. The Employee Detail page has two functions: to display most of the information stored in the employee record, and to provide a link to a page where that information can be updated.

Step 1: Implement Employee Detail Design

Begin by creating the basic page.

1. Create a basic dynamic page, either by hand or derived from a template.
   - 📖 In the **EmployeeLookup** folder, locate the folder for your server model and open the employee_detail page found there.
2. Add a table to the content region of your page to contain the interface elements for the application.

    📖 From the Snippets panel, drag the **Recipes > EmployeeLookup > Wireframes > Employee Detail - Wireframe** snippet into the Content editable region.

3. Within the table, nest another HTML table to display the detail data and the corresponding labels. This table generally has a row for each field and two columns, with the label in one column and room for the dynamic text in the other.

    📖 Place your cursor in the row below the words EMPLOYEE SEARCH and insert the **Recipes > EmployeeLookup > ContentTables > Employee Detail - Content Table** snippet [r2-10].

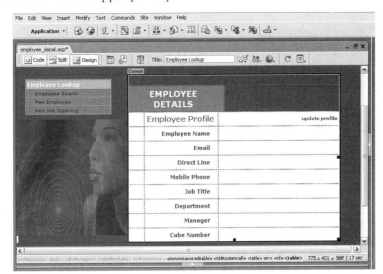

r2-10

Step 2: Add Database Components

The link to this page passes a URL parameter, ID. We'll now use the ID parameter to filter the recordset so that it contains only one record: that of the employee whose name was selected.

The recordset in our example is based on an Access view, EmployeeLookup, which combines data from three tables: Employees, Jobs, and Departments. The SQL used to create this view for ASP and ColdFusion is quite complex and looks like this:

```
SELECT Employees_1.EmployeeID, Jobs.JobID, Jobs.JobTitle,
➥Employees_1.EmployeeFirst, Employees_1.EmployeeLast,
➥Departments.DepartmentName, [Employees].[EmployeeFirst] &
➥' ' & [Employees].[EmployeeLast] AS ManagerName,
➥Employees_1.EmployeeEmail, Employees_1.EmployeePhone,
➥Employees_1.EmployeeMobil, Employees_1.EmployeeCube
FROM (Employees AS Employees_1 LEFT JOIN (Employees
➥RIGHT JOIN (Jobs LEFT JOIN Jobs AS Jobs_1
➥ON Jobs.JobManager = Jobs_1.JobID) ON Employees.EmployeeJob =
➥Jobs_1.JobID) ON Employees_1.EmployeeJob = Jobs.JobID)
➥LEFT JOIN Departments ON Jobs.JobDept = Departments.DepartmentID;
```

In PHP, the equivalent SQL is:

```
SELECT employees_1.EmployeeID, jobs.JobID, jobs.JobTitle,
➥employees_1.EmployeeFirst, employees_1.EmployeeLast,
➥departments.DepartmentName, CONCAT(employees.EmployeeFirst,
➥' ',employees.EmployeeLast) AS ManagerName,
➥employees_1.EmployeeEmail, employees_1.EmployeePhone,
➥employees_1.EmployeeMobil, employees_1.EmployeeCube
➥FROM employees, employees employees_1, jobs, jobs jobs_1,
➥departments WHERE ((((jobs.JobTypeID = jobs_1.JobID)
➥AND (jobs.JobDepartment = departments.DepartmentID))
➥AND (employees.EmployeeJob = jobs_1.JobID))
➥AND (employees_1.EmployeeJob = jobs.JobID))
```

Dreamweaver incorporates available views along with the list of tables in the data-source, and all you need to do is choose the correct one for ASP and ColdFusion. An additional workaround step is required for PHP, similar to the one used in the Employee Results page, which temporarily stores data derived from this SQL statement.

All server models should insert the following recordset.

1. From the Bindings panel, choose Add (+) and select **Recordset**.
2. Make sure the Simple Recordset dialog is displayed, and give the new recordset a meaningful name, such as **Employees** [r2-11].

r2-11

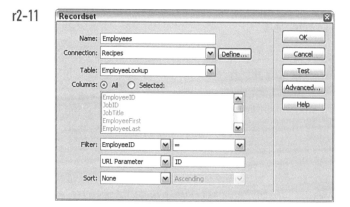

3. Select the connection to your data source.

   📖 Choose **Recipes** from the Connections or Data Source list.
4. Select the table containing the employee record details.

   📖 Choose **EmployeeLookup** (**employeelookup** for PHP) from the Table list.

5. Keep the Columns option set to **All**.

6. In the Filter area of the Recordset dialog, set the four Filter list elements like this:

EmployeeID	= (Equals)
URL Parameter	ID

7. Leave the Sort option set to **None** and click OK to close the dialog.

For PHP

As before, you create the Employees recordset first and then insert the code for the EmployeeLookup table.

> Although the code that surrounds the recordset is the same for both this page and the Employee Results page, the recordset is different; therefore, you cannot copy and paste the code from one page to another.
>
> NOTE

1. From the Server Behaviors panel, select the **Employee** recordset.

2. Switch to Code view, and you'll see the Employee recordset code highlighted.

3. Wrap the following around the selected code:

   ▢ From the Snippets panel, insert the **EmployeeLookup > CustomCode_PHP > Temporary Query - EmployeeLookup** snippet.

   Before:

   ⟮PHP⟯
```php
<?php
mysql_select_db($database_Recipes, $Recipes);
$query_EmployeeLookup = "INSERT INTO employeelookup
➥SELECT employees_1.EmployeeID, jobs.JobID, jobs.JobTitle,
➥employees_1.EmployeeFirst, employees_1.EmployeeLast,
➥departments.DepartmentName, CONCAT(employees.EmployeeFirst,
➥' ',employees.EmployeeLast) AS ManagerName,
➥employees_1.EmployeeEmail, employees_1.EmployeePhone,
➥employees_1.EmployeeMobil, employees_1.EmployeeCube
➥FROM employees, employees employees_1, jobs, jobs jobs_1,
➥departments WHERE ((((jobs.JobTypeID = jobs_1.JobID)
➥AND (jobs.JobDepartment = departments.DepartmentID))
➥AND (employees.EmployeeJob = jobs_1.JobID))
➥AND (employees_1.EmployeeJob = jobs.JobID))";
mysql_query($query_EmployeeLookup,$Recipes);
?>
```

After:

```
<?php
$query_EmployeeLookup = "DELETE FROM employeelookup";
mysql_query($query_EmployeeLookup,$Recipes);
?>
```

Step 3: Data Binding Process

All the data-driven elements on this page are in the form of dynamic text. Dynamic text is for display purposes only and cannot be edited.

1. In the Bindings panel, expand the recordset entry so that all data columns are displayed.
2. Drag each of the following data columns to the table and drop in the column to the right of the labels, in the corresponding row:
   - Drag data column `EmployeeFirst` to the `Employee Name` row.

   As we did on the `Employee Results` page, we're going to concatenate the dynamic text for first and last names.
   - Drag column `EmployeeLast` to the `Employee Name` row, right after the dynamic text element for first name; place your cursor between the two fields and add a space.
   - Drag column `EmployeeEmail` to the `Email` row.
   - Drag column `EmployeePhone` to the `Direct Line` row.
   - Drag column `EmployeeMobil` to the `Mobile` row.
   - Drag column `EmployeeJob` to the `Job Title` row.
   - Drag column `EmployeeDept` (`DepartmentName` in PHP) to the `Department` row.
   - Drag column `EmployeeManager` (`ManagerName` in PHP) to the `Manager` row.
   - Drag column `EmployeeCube` to the `Cube Number` row.
3. Leave the default formatting for all dynamic text fields.

When you're done, every row should have both a label and a matching dynamic text element [r2-12].

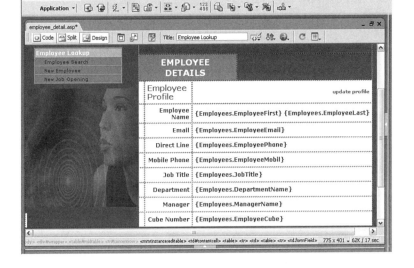

r2-12

Step 4: Link to Employee Update Page

The last task to accomplish on this page is to create a link to an update page. The update page filters the recordset based on the unique employee ID passed via the URL.

1. Select the text or graphic you want to use as a link to the update page.

   ☐ Select the text **update profile**.

2. From the Property inspector, select the Link Folder icon.

3. In the Select File dialog, choose **Parameters**.

4. In the Parameters dialog, enter the variable name.

   ☐ In the Name column, enter **ID**.

5. Enter the dynamic value.

   ☐ Under the Value column, select the lightning bolt to open the Dynamic Data dialog and select **EmployeeID** from the Employees recordset.

   ☐ Click OK once to close the Dynamic Data dialog and again to close the Parameters dialog.

6. Select the file you want to pass the parameter to.

   ☐ Select Browse and choose the **update_employee** file for your server model.

7. Click OK to close the dialog.

8. Save the page.

> **NOTE**
> For ASP users, Dreamweaver includes two server behaviors that could also be used for this purpose: Go to Related Page and Go to Detail Page. The Go to Related Page server behavior automatically passes URL or form parameters it receives from the current page. The Go to Detail Page server behavior allows you to choose which parameters you're going to pass and gives the option of passing existing URL or form arguments.

> **NOTE**
> Whether your organization allows its employees to update their own records is an internal decision. You could hide the Update link conditionally so that it is visible only to registered users who have certain clearances. For more on this technique, see Recipe 1, "User Login."

End User Recipe: Update Employee

The Update Employee page uses the standard Dreamweaver Update Record server behavior and includes a few enhancements. In addition to modifying an employee record, code on this page can also delete the record. Advanced SQL statements are used here to combine data from two related tables in a single drop-down list.

Step 1: Implement Update Employee Design

Build the basic static page before inserting any dynamic elements.

1. Create a basic dynamic page, either by hand or derived from a template.

   📖 In the **EmployeeLookup** folder, locate the folder for your server model and open the update_employee page found there.

2. Add a table to the content region of your page to contain the interface elements for the application.

   📖 From the Snippets panel, drag the **Recipes > EmployeeLookup > Wireframes > Update Employee - Wireframe** snippet into the Content editable region.

3. Within the table, insert the form and necessary form elements for the employee record. For this page, you'll need either a text field or a list for every data source field you want to update as well as submit and delete buttons. As with the Advanced Search page, five text fields and one list element are used in our example [r2-13].

r2-13

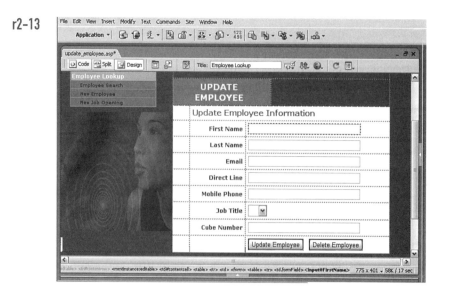

         Place your cursor in the row below the words UPDATE and insert the **Recipes > EmployeeLookup > Forms > Update Employee - Form** snippet.

4. ColdFusion and PHP users: A unique record ID is required for the Update Record server behavior to work properly. A hidden form field conveys the needed data.

         ColdFusion and PHP developers should drag a hidden form field from the Forms category of the Insert bar and name it **EmployeeID**.

5. Save your page.

Step 2: Add Database Components

Two recordsets power the employee update page. As you might expect, one recordset contains the details from the selected employee's record; this recordset uses the familiar technique of filtering on a URL parameter.

1. From the Bindings panel, choose Add (+) and select Recordset.
2. With the Simple Recordset dialog displayed, enter a meaningful name for the recordset, such as **Employees**.
3. Select the connection to your data source.

         Choose **Recipes** from the Connections or Data Source list.

4. Select the table containing the employee record details.

         Choose **Employees** (**employees** for PHP) from the Table list.

5. Keep the Columns option set to **All**.
6. In the Filter area of the Recordset dialog, set the four Filter list elements like this:

EmployeeID	= (Equals)
URL Parameter	ID

7. Leave the Sort option set to **None** and click OK to close the dialog.

The second recordset is somewhat more advanced and concerns the Job Title list element. Job titles can be present in more than one department. (Each department could have a manager and an assistant manager, for example.) Therefore, the Job Title list element needs to show both the name of the job and, parenthetically, the department the employee is in. For ASP and ColdFusion, this is handled through a combination of an Access view and nesting one SQL statement inside another.

The Access view joins fields from the `Jobs` and `Department` tables found in the data source:

```
SELECT [Jobs].[JobTitle] & ' (' & [Departments].[DepartmentName] & ')'
➥AS JobAndDepartment, Jobs.JobID
FROM Jobs INNER JOIN Departments ON Jobs.JobDept =
➥Departments.DepartmentID;
```

PHP does not allow this type of nesting (also called *subselects*). A different SQL statement must be used:

```
SELECT jobswithdepartments.* FROM jobswithdepartments
LEFT JOIN employees ON jobswithdepartments.JobID=
➥employees.EmployeeJob
WHERE employees.EmployeeJob IS NULL OR (employees.EmployeeID =
➥IDParam)
```

For ASP

    📖 Before you begin this step, you'll need to copy the SQL code from the appropriate snippet by right-clicking on **Recipes > EmployeeLookup > SQL > Jobs RS - ASP SQL Statement** snippet and then, from the context menu, choose **Copy Snippet**.

1. From the Bindings panel, choose Add (+) and select **Recordset (Query)**.
2. In the advanced Recordset dialog, enter an appropriate name for the recordset.

    📖 Enter **Jobs** in the Name field.

3. Choose your connection from the drop-down list.

    📖 Select **Recipes** from the Connections list.

4. In the SQL area, enter the following code:

    📖 Paste the copied snippet into the SQL field by pressing Ctrl-V (Command-V).

```
SELECT * FROM JobsWithDepartments WHERE Jobs.JobID
➥NOT IN (SELECT EmployeeJob AS JobID
FROM Employees
WHERE EmployeeID <> IDParam)
```

5. In the Variable area, choose Add (+) and enter **IDParam** in the Name column.
6. In the Default Value column, enter 0.
7. In the Run-Time Value column, enter **Request.QueryString("ID")** and click OK to close the dialog and insert the recordset.
8. Save the page.

For ColdFusion

- ⌨ Before you begin this step, you'll need to copy the SQL code from the appropriate snippet by right-clicking on **Recipes > EmployeeLookup > SQL > Jobs RS - CFML SQL Statement** snippet and then, from the context menu, choose **Copy Snippet**.

1. From the Bindings panel, choose Add (+) and select **Recordset (Query)**.
2. In the advanced Recordset dialog, enter an appropriate name for the recordset.
   - ⌨ Enter **Jobs** in the Name field.
3. Choose your data source from the drop-down list.
   - ⌨ Select **Recipes** from the Data Source list.
4. If necessary, enter the username and password for the data source in the corresponding fields.
5. In the SQL area, enter the following code:
   - ⌨ Paste the copied snippet into the SQL field by pressing Ctrl-V (Command-V).

```
SELECT * FROM JobsWithDepartments WHERE Jobs.JobID NOT IN
(SELECT EmployeeJob AS JobID
FROM Employees
WHERE EmployeeID <> #URL.ID#)
```

6. In the Page Parameters area, choose Add (+) to open the Add Parameter dialog.
7. Make sure that User.ID is selected in the Name list of the Add Parameter dialog and enter 0 as the Default Value. When you're ready, click OK to close the dialog.
8. Verify your code and click OK to close the dialog and insert the recordset.

For PHP

- ⌨ Before you begin this step, you'll need to copy the SQL code from the appropriate snippet by right-clicking on **Recipes > EmployeeLookup > SQL > Jobs RS - PHP SQL Statement** snippet and then, from the context menu, choose **Copy Snippet**.

1. From the Bindings panel, choose Add (+) and select **Recordset (Query)**.
2. In the advanced Recordset dialog, enter an appropriate name for the recordset.
   - ⌨ Enter **Jobs** in the Name field.
3. Choose your connection from the drop-down list.
   - ⌨ Select **Recipes** from the Connections list.

4. In the SQL area, enter the following code:

   📖 Paste the copied snippet into the SQL field by pressing Ctrl-V (Command-V).

```
SELECT jobswithdepartments.* FROM jobswithdepartments
LEFT JOIN employees ON jobswithdepartments.JobID=
↪employees.EmployeeJob
WHERE employees.EmployeeJob IS NULL OR (employees.EmployeeID =
↪IDParam)
```

5. In the Variable area, choose Add (+) and enter **IDParam** in the Name column.
6. In the Default Value column, enter 0.
7. In the Run-Time Value column, enter **$_GET['ID']** and click OK to close the dialog and insert the recordset.
8. Save the page.

Step 3: Update Employee Profile

After defining the recordsets, we're ready to apply Dreamweaver's Update Record server behavior.

For ASP

1. From the Server Behaviors panel, choose Add (+) and select **Update Record**.
2. In the Update Record dialog, select your connection from the list.

   📖 Choose **Recipes** from the Connections list.

3. Select the table in the data source to modify from the list.

   📖 Choose **Employees** from the Table to Update list.

4. Choose the recordset to use.

   📖 Select **Employees** from the Select Record From list.

5. Select the **Unique Key Column** from the list; if the data is a number, make sure the Numeric option is chosen.

   📖 Select **EmployeeID** from the list.

6. Select the path to the file you want the user to visit after the record has been updated.

   📖 Choose Browse and locate the **employee_results.asp** file.

7. With the current form selected in the Get Values From list, set the form elements to their corresponding data source fields.

   📖 Set the `FirstName` form element to the `EmployeeFirst` data column and submit as Text.

   Set the `LastName` form element to the `EmployeeLast` data column and submit as Text.

Set the `Email` form element to the `EmployeeEmail` data column and submit as Text.

Set the `Phone` form element to the `EmployeePhone` data column and submit as Text.

Set the `Phone2` form element to the `EmployeeMobile` data column and submit as Text.

Set the `JobTitle` form element to the `EmployeeJob` data column and submit as Numeric.

Set the `CubeNumber` form element to the `EmployeeCube` data column and submit as Numeric.

8. Verify your choices and click OK to close the dialog.
9. Save the page.

For ColdFusion and PHP

1. From the Server Behaviors panel, choose Add (+) and select **Update Record**.
2. In the Update Record dialog, choose the current form.
   - Select **UpdateEmployee** from the Submit Values From list.
3. Select your data source from the list.
   - Choose **Recipes** from the Data Source list.
4. Enter your username and password, if needed.
5. Select the table in the data source to update from the list.
   - Choose **Employees** (**employees** for PHP) from the Update Table list.
6. Set the data source fields to their corresponding form elements.
   - Make sure the `EmployeeID` data column is set to `FORM.ElementID` as a Numeric type (Integer in PHP) and set as the Primary Key.

     Set `EmployeeFirst` to the `FORM.FirstName` form element and submit as Text.

     Set `EmployeeLast` to the `FORM.LastName` form element and submit as Text.

     Set `EmployeeEmail` to the `FORM.Email` form element and submit as Text.

     Set `EmployeePhone` to the `FORM.Phone` form element and submit as Text.

     Set `EmployeeMobile` to the `FORM.Phone2` form element and submit as Text.

     Set `EmployeeJob` to the `FORM.JobTitle` form element and submit as Numeric for ColdFusion and Integer for PHP.

     Set `EmployeeCube` to the `FORM.CubeNumber` form element and submit as Numeric/Integer.
7. Select the path to the file you want the user to visit after record has been updated.
   - Choose Browse and locate the **employee_results** file for your server model.
8. Verify your choices and click OK to close the dialog.

Step 4: Insert Delete Command

As we did in the User LogIn recipe, we're going to combine code for deleting a record on a page containing an Update Record server behavior. The procedure is basically the same. Again, we're adding a specialized SQL statement (called a command in ASP), which we can do through the Dreamweaver interface. Once inserted, we need to move the command to the top of the page and wrap it in an `If` statement so that it only executes when we select the Delete button.

For ASP

1. From the Bindings panel, choose Add (+) and select **Command**.
2. In the Name field, enter an appropriate name.

    📖 Enter **DeleteCommand** in the Name field.

3. Choose your data source connection from the list.

    📖 Select **Recipes** from the Connections list.

4. Choose a command type.

    📖 Choose **Delete** from the Type drop-down list.

5. Enter the following code in the SQL field:

    ```
    DELETE FROM Employees
    WHERE EmployeeID = IDParam
    ```

6. In the Variables section, select Add (+) and enter **IDParam** under the Name column.
7. In the Run-Time Value column, enter **Request("MM_recordId")** and click OK when you're done.

    Inserting the command creates two code blocks. We'll need to move both of them so that the Delete command is processed before the Update command is. First, we'll move the code block just created. If you haven't selected anything else, it still should be highlighted.

8. In Code view, find the code block for the Delete command, which will look like this:

    VB
    ```
    <%
    set DeleteCommand = Server.CreateObject("ADODB.Command")
    DeleteCommand.ActiveConnection = MM_Recipes_STRING
    DeleteCommand.CommandText = "DELETE FROM Employees
    ➥WHERE EmployeeID = " + Replace(DeleteCommand__IDParam,
    ➥"'", "''") + ""
    DeleteCommand.CommandType = 1
    DeleteCommand.CommandTimeout = 0
    DeleteCommand.Prepared = true
    DeleteCommand.Execute()
    %>
    ```

JS
```
<%
    var DeleteCommand = Server.CreateObject("ADODB.Command");
    DeleteCommand.ActiveConnection = MM_Recipes_STRING;
    DeleteCommand.CommandText = "DELETE FROM Employees
➥WHERE EmployeeID "+ DeleteCommand__IDParam.replace
➥(/'/g, "''") + " ";
    DeleteCommand.CommandType = 1;
    DeleteCommand.CommandTimeout = 0;
    DeleteCommand.Prepared = true;
    DeleteCommand.Execute();
%>
```

9. Cut the selected code block and paste it at the top of the page just under the `<!--include>` statement.

10. Locate and cut this related code block:

VB
```
<%
    if(Request("MM_recordId") <> "") then DeleteCommand__IDParam =
    Request("MM_recordId")
%>
```

JS
```
<%
    if(String(Request("MM_recordId")) != "undefined"){
    DeleteCommand__IDParam = String(Request("MM_recordId"));}
%>
```

11. Paste the just-cut code block after the `<!--include>` tag and before the Delete command.

The last part of this step is to make sure that the Delete command executes only after we select the Delete button on the form.

12. In Code view, locate and select the two adjacent Delete command code blocks moved to the top of the page.

13. Insert the following code:

   📖 From the Snippets panel, open the **Recipes > EmployeeLookup > Custom Code** folder for your server model and insert the **Edit User - Conditional** snippet.

   Before:

VB
```
<%
    if (cStr(Request.Form("Delete"))<>"")   then
%>
```

   After:

```
<%
   Response.Redirect("employee_results.asp")
end if
%>
```

Before:

JS
```
<%
    if (String(Request("Delete"))!="undefined")  {
    %>
```

After:

```
<%
      Response.Redirect("employee_results.asp");
    }
    %>
```

You can, of course, change the page to redirect *after* the delete is completed, if you would prefer to use something other than the employee_results page.

For ColdFusion

1. From the Bindings panel, choose Add (+) and select **Recordset**.

   Unlike the ASP server models, there is no separate user interface in ColdFusion for commands. The Recordset dialog is used.

2. If the Simple view is displayed, select **Advanced**.

3. In the Name field, enter an appropriate name.

   ▢ Enter **DeleteCommand** in the Name field.

4. Choose your data source connection from the list.

   ▢ Select **Recipes** from the Data Source list.

5. If necessary, enter the username and password in their respective fields.

6. Enter the following code in the SQL field:

   ```
   DELETE FROM Users WHERE UserID = #FORM.EmployeeID#
   ```

7. In the Page Parameters section, select Add (+) to display the Add Parameter dialog.

8. In the Add Parameter dialog, enter **FORM.EmployeeID** in the Name field.

9. In the Default Value fields, enter **0** and click OK to close the Add Parameter dialog.

10. When you're done, click OK to close the Recordset dialog.

    Now all that remains to complete the Delete command is to make sure it executes only when the user selects the Delete button on the form. To effect this process, we'll wrap the two Delete command code blocks within an If statement.

11. In Code view, find the code block for the Delete command, which looks like this:

    ```
    <cfquery name="DeleteCommand" datasource="Recipes">
       DELETE FROM Employees WHERE EmployeeID = #FORM.EmployeeID#
    </cfquery>
    ```

    ▢ Select the code block to prepare for inserting the snippet.

12. Insert the following code:

   📖 From the Snippets panel, open the **Recipes > EmployeeLookup > Custom Code-CF** folder and insert the **Edit User - Conditional** snippet.

   Before:

   ```
   CF  <cfif IsDefined("FORM.DeleteEmployee")>
   ```

   After:

   ```
   CF  <cflocation url="employee_results.cfm">
       </cfif>
   ```

13. Save your page.

If you'd prefer to redirect the page to something other than the employee_results page, feel free to adapt the code.

For PHP

PHP does not include direct support for commands, but you can use the Recordset dialog to enter the equivalent SQL. After the recordset has been inserted, we'll need to add some code to make its execution conditional on the pressing of the Delete button.

1. In Code view, place your cursor beneath the connection code at the top of the file that starts <?php require-once… and enter the following code:

   📖 From the Snippets panel, insert the **Recipes > EmployeeLookup > CustomCode-PHP > Delete Employee Record** snippet.

   ```
   PHP  <?php
        // mysql delete command
        if (isset($_GET['MM_recordId'])) {
            mysql_select_db($database_Recipes, $Recipes);
            $query_DeleteOperation = "DELETE FROM employees
            ➥WHERE EmployeeID = '".$_GET['MM_recordId']."'";
            mysql_query($query_EmployeeLookup,$Recipes);
        }
        ?>
   ```

   The next part of this step is to make sure that the Delete command is executed only when someone selects the Delete button on the form.

2. Select the just-inserted code block and enter the following code:

   📖 From the Snippets panel, insert the **Recipes > EmployeeLookup > Custom Code-PHP > Edit User - Conditional** snippet.

Before:

(PHP)
```php
<?php
    if (isset($_GET['DeleteEmployee'])) {
    ?>
```

After:

(PHP)
```php
<?php
        header("Location: employee_results.php");
    }
    ?>
```

3. Save your page.

Naturally, you're free to change the page to redirect to after the delete is completed to something other than employee_results page.

Step 5: Data Binding Process

The final step for this page is to bind the recordset data to the various form elements. All but one of the form elements are text fields and can be bound by dragging the proper item from the Bindings panel. For the list element, you'll need to enter the information through the Dynamic List/Menu dialog, which is accessible either through the Dynamic button on the Property inspector or the Server Behaviors panel.

1. From the Bindings panel, expand the Employees recordset and drag the data source fields over their corresponding text fields.

   📖 Drag the data source field EmployeeFirst to the form field FirstName.

   Drag the data source field EmployeeLast to the form field LastName.

   Drag the data source field EmployeeEmail to the form field Email.

   Drag the data source field EmployeePhone to the form field Phone.

   Drag the data source field EmployeeMobile to the form field Phone2.

   Drag the data source field EmployeeCube to the form field CubeNumber.

2. Select the **JobTitle** list element.
3. From the Property inspector, select **Dynamic**.
4. In the Dynamic List/Menu dialog, select the **Jobs** recordset from the Options From Recordset list.

   📖 Remember that the Jobs recordset is derived from an Access view combining three different tables.

5. In the Values field, choose **JobID**.
6. In the Labels field, select **JobAndDepartment**.

7. In the Select Value Equal To Field, choose the lightning bolt symbol and, from the Dynamic Data dialog, choose **EmployeeJob** from the `Employee` recordset.

8. Click OK once to close the Dynamic Data dialog and then again to close the Dynamic List/Menu dialog.

9. Save your page.

By incorporating data fields from two recordsets in the list form element, we accomplish both of our goals. First, the connection to the EmployeeJob data field assures us that when the update page is opened, the employee's current job will be shown. Second, the list will display all available jobs in the proper department, and we can choose a new job. With all the form fields now attached to data, the `Update Employee` page is complete [r2-14].

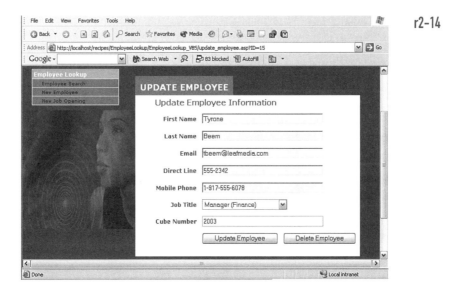

r2-14

Administrator Recipe: New Job

The administrator's role in this application is limited to two interconnected tasks: creating records for new job openings and new employees. Although both are, at their core, insert record routines, the implementations have some notable features. The new job page, for example, includes server-side (with a little JavaScript assist) dynamic lists in which a choice in one list alters the options in another.

Step 1: Implement New Job Design

Let's create our static page first.

1. Create a basic dynamic page, either by hand or derived from a template.

   📖 In the **EmployeeLookup** folder, locate the folder for your server model and open the new_job page found there.

2. Add a table to the content region of your page to contain the interface elements for the application.

   📖 From the Snippets panel, drag the **Recipes > EmployeeLookup > Wireframes > New Job - Wireframe** snippet into the Content editable region.

3. Within the table, insert the form and necessary form elements for the new job. If you follow our example for this page, you'll need two list elements: one for the departments and one for the manager, in addition to a text field for the job and a Submit button.

   📖 Place your cursor in the row below the words NEW JOB and insert the **Recipes > EmployeeLookup > Forms > Enter Job Information - Form** snippet [r2-15].

r2-15

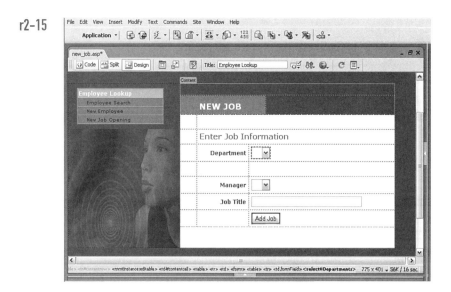

Step 2: Add Database Components

To populate two lists, two recordsets are required, but these two are interconnected. Because each department has its own managers (each of whom could be responsible for a new job), the list of managers depends on which department is chosen. Although the Department recordset is a simple collection of all the available departments, the Manager recordset is filtered by the Department recordset selection. To accomplish this, the SQL keyword TOP is used; TOP limits the number of records in a recordset to a specified value. For example, the SQL statement

```
SELECT TOP 10 FROM EMPLOYEES WHERE EmployeeLast LIKE 'L%'
```

would return the first 10 records from a recordset of all the employees who have a last name that starts with the letter *L*. As you'll see, our SQL statement will be limited to the TOP 1 returned for a specific department—the selection.

Because MySQL does not include view support, we'll again use the method of creating the needed data on-the-fly with later hand-coded functions for the more complex Manager recordset.

Let's start by adding the straightforward Department recordset.

1. From the Bindings panel, choose Add (+) and select **Recordset**.
2. Make sure the Simple Recordset dialog is displayed and give the new recordset a meaningful name.

   ☐ Enter **Departments** in the Recordset field.
3. Select the connection to your data source.

   ☐ Choose **Recipes** from the Connections or Data Source list.
4. Select the table containing the department details.

   ☐ Choose **Departments** (**departments** in PHP) from the Table list.
5. Keep the Columns option set to **All**.
6. Leave both the Filter and Sort option set to **None** and click OK to close the dialog.

With the Department recordset ready to go, we can develop the one for the managers. In addition to employing a SELECT TOP clause, the Manager recordset also uses an Access view, which combines data from the Managers and Departments tables. The SQL for the view is as follows:

```
SELECT [EmployeeID], [EmployeeFirst] & ' ' & [EmployeeLast]
➥AS ManagerName, [Jobs].[JobDept]
FROM Employees INNER JOIN (Jobs INNER JOIN Departments
➥ON [Jobs].[JobDept]=[Departments].[DepartmentID])
➥ON [Employees].[EmployeeJob]=[Jobs].[JobID];
```

Establishing the recordsets is just the first step in linking the two list elements, but it is a critical one.

For ASP

1. From the Bindings panel, choose Add (+) and select **Recordset**.
2. In the advanced Recordset dialog, enter an appropriate name for the recordset.

   📖 Enter **Managers** in the Name field.
3. Choose your connection from the drop-down list.

   📖 Select **Recipes** from the Connections list.
4. In the SQL area, enter the following code:

   ```
   SELECT *
   FROM ManagersByDepartment
   WHERE JobDept = IDParam
   ```

5. In the Variable area, choose Add (+) and enter **IDParam** in the Name column.
6. In the Default Value column, enter this:

   ```
   (SELECT TOP 1 DepartmentID FROM Departments)
   ```

7. In the Run-Time Value column, enter **Request("DeptID")** and click OK to close the dialog and insert the recordset.

For ColdFusion

1. From the Bindings panel, choose Add (+) and select **Recordset**.
2. In the advanced Recordset dialog, enter an appropriate name for the recordset.

   📖 Enter **Managers** in the Name field.
3. Choose your data source from the drop-down list.

   📖 Select **Recipes** from the Data Source list.
4. If necessary, enter the username and password for the data source in the corresponding fields.
5. In the SQL area, enter the following code:

   ```
   SELECT *
   FROM ManagersByDepartment
   WHERE JobDept = #URL.DeptID#
   ```

6. In the Page Parameters section, select Add (+) to display the Add Parameter dialog.
7. In the Add Parameter dialog, enter **URL.DeptID** in the Name field.
8. In the Default Value fields, enter

   ```
   (SELECT TOP 1 DepartmentID FROM Departments)
   ```

9. Click OK once to close the Add Parameter dialog and again to insert the recordset.

For PHP

     ☐ Before you begin this step, you'll need to copy the SQL code from the appropriate snippet by right-clicking on **Recipes > EmployeeLookup > SQL > Managers RS - PHP SQL Statement** snippet and then, from the context menu, choose **Copy Snippet**.

1. From the Bindings panel, choose Add (+) and select **Recordset**.

2. In the advanced Recordset dialog, enter an appropriate name for the recordset.

     ☐ Enter **Managers** in the Name field.

3. Choose your connection from the drop-down list.

     ☐ Select **Recipes** from the Connections list.

4. In the SQL area, enter the following code:

     ☐ Paste the copied snippet into the SQL field by pressing Ctrl-V (Command-V).

```
(PHP) SELECT managersbydepartment.* FROM managersbydepartment,
      ➥departments, jobs WHERE (((managersbydepartment.JobID =
      ➥jobs.JobID) AND (jobs.JobDepartment = departments.DepartmentID))
      ➥AND (departments.DepartmentID = IDParam))
```

5. In the Variable area, choose Add (+) and enter **IDParam** in the Name field of the Add Parameter dialog.

6. In the Default Value field, enter **1**.

7. In the Run-Time Value field, enter **$_GET['DeptID']** and click OK once to close the Add Parameter dialog and again to close the Recordset dialog and to insert the recordset.

Now we'll wrap the just-entered recordset with our routines for creating and removing the temporary queries.

8. From the Server Behavior panel, select the Managers recordset.

9. Switch to Code view, and locate the highlighted code.

10. Wrap the following code around the recordset:

     ☐ From the Snippets panel, insert the **Recipes > EmployeeLookup > CustomCode_PHP > Temporary Query – ManagersByDepartment** snippet.

Before:

```
(PHP) <?php
      mysql_select_db($database_Recipes, $Recipes);
      $query_ManagersByDepartment = "INSERT INTO managersbydepartment
      SELECT CONCAT(employees.EmployeeFirst,' ', employees.EmployeeLast)
      ➥AS ManagerName, jobs.JobID, jobs.JobDepartment AS JobDept
      ➥FROM employees, jobs, departments
      ➥WHERE ((employees.EmployeeJob = jobs.JobID)
      ➥AND (jobs.JobDepartment = departments.DepartmentID))";
      mysql_query($query_ManagersByDepartment,$Recipes);
      ?>
```

After:

(PHP)
```php
<?php
$query_ManagersByDepartment = "DELETE FROM managersbydepartment ";
mysql_query($query_ManagersByDepartment,$Recipes);
?>
```

11. Save the page.

Step 3: Data Binding Process

In addition to the standard procedure of binding the recordset fields to the form elements, we'll also need to add some JavaScript to cement the connection between the two lists. While the server-side coding is completely capable of filling one list based on the selection of another, you have to rely on client-side scripting to detect a new selection and resubmit the page to the server. But before we insert our JavaScript code, let's bind the data to the form elements.

1. Select the **Departments** list element.
2. From the Property inspector, select **Dynamic**.
3. In the Dynamic List/Menu dialog, select the **Departments** recordset from the Options From Recordset list.
4. In the Values field, choose **DepartmentID**.
5. In the Labels field, select **DepartmentName**.
6. In the Select Value Equal To field, choose the lightning symbol and, from the Dynamic Data dialog, choose **JobDept** (**JobID** in PHP) from the Managers recordset.
7. Click OK once to close the Dynamic Data dialog and then again to close the Dynamic List/Menu dialog.

Now that the Department list is completed, let's move on to the Managers list element.

1. Select the **Managers** list element.
2. From the Property inspector, select **Dynamic**.
3. In the Dynamic List/Menu dialog, select the **Managers** recordset from the Options From Recordset list.
4. In the Values field, choose **JobID**.
5. In the Labels field, select **ManagerName**.
6. To avoid presetting the list to any specific value, leave the Select Value Equal To field blank.
7. Click OK to close the Dynamic List/Menu dialog.
8. Save your page.

Now it's time to add that JavaScript we've been talking about. We'll tie execution of the JavaScript code to the onChange event of the Department list. This will ensure that whenever a selection is made, the page will be resubmitted to the server with an argument conveying the selection—which in turn triggers the SQL statement in the Managers recordset and repopulates the list.

    📖 Before you begin this step, you'll need to copy the SQL code from the appropriate snippet by right-clicking on **Recipes > EmployeeLookup > ClientJavaScript > Department Behavior** snippet and then, from the context menu, choose **Copy Snippet**.

1. Select the **Department** list.
2. From the Behaviors panel, choose Add (+) and select Call **JavaScript**.
3. Enter the following code in the Call JavaScript dialog:

(VB) (JS)
```
document.location.href = 'new_job.asp?DeptID=
➥'+document.forms[0].Departments.options[document.forms[0].
➥Departments.selectedIndex].value
```

(CF)
```
document.location.href = 'new_job.cfm?DeptID=
➥'+document.forms[0].Departments.options[document.forms[0].
➥Departments.selectedIndex].value
```

(PHP)
```
document.location.href = 'new_job.php?DeptID=
➥'+document.forms[0].Departments.options[document.forms[0].
➥Departments.selectedIndex].value
```

4. Click OK to close the dialog and insert the JavaScript.
5. Make sure that the event in the Behaviors panel is onChange; if necessary, select the down triangle next to the event and choose **onChange**.

Test the dynamic list functionality in the browser. Choosing a new department should generate a new list of managers [r2-16].

r2-16

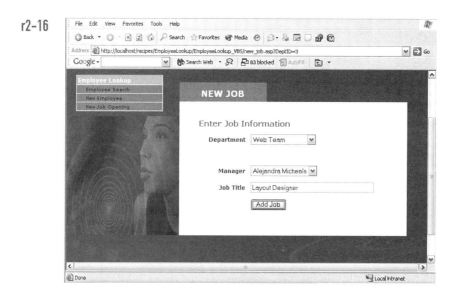

Step 4: Insert Record—New Job

Now we're ready to add the Insert Record server behavior. It's important to keep in mind that both of the list elements in our example will submit their values to the data source as numbers. Why not the text displayed in the lists? Although the lists labels are textual, the underlying values are numeric. It's not unusual for data source schemas to include this dual functionality, which allows greater flexibility and integration with other tables.

For ASP

1. From the Server Behaviors panel, choose Add (+) and select **Insert Record**.
2. In the Insert Record dialog, select your connection from the list.
   - Choose **Recipes** from the Connections list.
3. Select the table in the data source to modify from the list.
   - Choose **Jobs** from the Insert into Table list.
4. Enter the path to the file you want the user to visit after the record has been updated in the After Inserting, Go To field.
   - Choose Browse and locate the **employee_results.asp** file.

5. Choose the form to use.

   □ Select **InsertJob** from the Get Values From list.

6. With the current form selected in the Get Values From list, set the form elements to their corresponding data source fields.

   □ Set the `Department` form element to the `JobDept` data column and submit as Numeric.

   □ Set the `Managers` form element to the `JobManager` data column and submit as Text.

   □ Set the `JobTitle` form element to the `JobTitle` data column and submit as Text.

7. Verify your choices and click OK to close the dialog.

For ColdFusion and PHP

1. From the Server Behaviors panel, choose Add (+) and select **Insert Record**.

2. In the Insert Record dialog, choose the current form.

   □ Select **InsertJob** from the Submit Values From list.

3. Select your data source from the list.

   □ Choose **Recipes** from the Data Source list.

4. Enter your username and password, if needed.

5. Select the table in the data source to insert into from the list.

   □ Choose **Jobs** (**jobs** for PHP) from the Insert Into Table list.

6. Set the data source fields to their corresponding form elements.

   □ Make sure the `JobID` data column is set to be an unused Primary Key.

   Set `JobDept` to the `FORM.Departments` form element and submit as Numeric (Integer for PHP).

   Set `JobTitle` to the `FORM.JobTitle` form element and submit as Text.

   (CF) Set `JobManager` to the `FORM.Managers` form element and submit as Numeric.

   (PHP) Set `ManagerID` to the `FORM.Managers` form element and submit as Integer.

7. Enter the path to the file you want the user to visit after the record has been inserted in the After Inserting, Go To field.

   □ Choose Browse and locate the **employee_results** file for your server model.

8. Verify your choices and click OK to close the dialog.

9. Don't forget to save the page.

Step 5: Error Text: No Job Openings

In the workflow of the overall application, the ability to create a new job opening in the data source is critical. If there are no job openings, you cannot, logically, hire a new employee; an informative error message should alert the user to the problem. In some other recipes—such as user authentication—error messages appeared to point out a problem on the same page. However, in this application, we'll insert an error message that occurs only when an error occurs in another page. This is accomplished by an `If` statement, which is triggered if the query string contains a variable named `empty`.

1. Place the cursor on the page where you would like the error message to appear.

   📖 Put the cursor in the row above the text Enter Job Information.

2. Insert the following code:

   📖 From the Snippets panel, open the **Recipes > EmployeeLookup > Custom Code** folder for your server model and insert the **No Job Openings - Display Text** snippet.

   VB `<%if (cStr(Request("empty"))<>"") then Response.Write("There are no job openings for a new employee. You must add a job before adding an employee.")%>`

   JS `<%=(String(Request("empty")))!="undefined")?"There are no job openings for a new employee. You must add a job before adding an employee.":""%>`

   CF `<cfif IsDefined("URL.empty")><cfoutput>There are no job openings for a new employee. You must add a job before adding an employee.</cfoutput></cfif>`

   PHP `<?php echo (isset($_GET['empty']))?"There are no job openings for a new employee. You must add a job before adding an employee.":""; ?>`

3. Save your page.

To see the error message in action, first enter into Live Data view. The error message should disappear. Now, in the query string field of the Live Data toolbar, enter **empty=true** and, if AutoRefresh is enabled, press Enter (Return); otherwise, select Refresh from the Live Data toolbar. The error message should appear.

Administrator Recipe: New Employee

The goal of the final page in the Employee Lookup application is to add an employee to the data source. But isn't that just a basic insert record operation? Although our implementation does use Dreamweaver's standard Insert Record server behavior, we've also added a bit of intelligence that ties this page into the rest of the application. As we saw in the New Job page, you can't hire an employee unless there is at least one job opening. If you try to add an employee to the data source and no job opening is available, this page redirects you to the New Job page and displays an error message.

Step 1: Implement Design

Building a static page with all the necessary form elements is the first step.

1. Create a basic dynamic page, either by hand or derived from a template.

   📖 In the **EmployeeLookup** folder, locate the folder for your server model and open the new_employee page found there.

2. Add a table to the content region of your page to contain the interface elements for the application.

   📖 From the Snippets panel, drag the **Recipes > EmployeeLookup > Wireframes > New Employee - Wireframe** snippet into the Content editable region.

3. Within the table, insert the form and necessary form elements for the new employee. If you follow our example for this page, you'll need five text fields: first name, last name, email, direct line, cell phone, and cubicle number. You'll also need a list element for the job listings as well as a Submit button.

   📖 Place your cursor in the row below the words NEW EMPLOYEE and insert the **Recipes > EmployeeLookup > Forms > New Employee - Form** snippet [r2-17].

r2-17

Step 2: Add Database Components

A single recordset is needed for this page to populate the Job Title list element. To develop the list of jobs, we'll use an Access view and nested SQL statement. The SQL statement reads as follows:

```
SELECT *
FROM JobsWithDepartments
WHERE JobID NOT IN (SELECT EmployeeJob AS JobID FROM Employees)
```

> **NOTE**
>
> The JobsWithDepartment view was previously used on the Update Employee page and is discussed in that section.

Essentially, with this SQL statement, the recordset displays all the JobID records (that is, all the jobs) that are not assigned to an employee.

- ☐ Before you begin this step, you'll need to copy the SQL code from the appropriate snippet by right-clicking on **Recipes > EmployeeLookup > SQL > New Employee Jobs RS** snippet for your server model and then, from the context menu, choose **Copy Snippet**.

1. From the Bindings panel, choose Add (+) and select **Recordset**.
2. In the advanced Recordset view, enter a meaningful name for the query.
   - ☐ Enter **Jobs** in the Name field.
3. Select your data source connection.
   - ☐ Choose **Recipes** from the Connections (or Data Source) list.

4. ColdFusion users: Enter the username and password for the data source, if necessary.

5. In the SQL area, enter the following code:

   📖 Paste the copied snippet into the SQL field by pressing Ctrl-V (Command-V).

(VB) (JS) (CF)
```
SELECT *
FROM JobsWithDepartments
WHERE JobID NOT IN (SELECT EmployeeJob AS JobID FROM Employees)
```

(PHP)
```
SELECT jobswithdepartments.* FROM jobswithdepartments
LEFT JOIN employees ON jobswithdepartments.JobID=
employees.EmployeeJob
WHERE employees.EmployeeJob IS NULL)
```

6. Verify your code and close the dialog to insert the recordset.

7. Save your page.

Step 3: Data Binding Process

On this page, only one form element—the list—needs to be populated dynamically.

1. Select the **JobTitle** list element.
2. From the Property inspector, select **Dynamic** to open the Dynamic List/Menu dialog.
3. In the Options From Recordset list, choose **Jobs**.
4. In the Values field, select **JobID**.
5. In the Labels field, choose **JobAndDepartment**.
6. Leave the Select Value Equal To field blank and click OK to close the dialog.

By previewing the page in a browser, you can check to see what job titles are currently available [r2-18]. You won't be able to use Live Data Preview because list elements are not populated within Dreamweaver in Preview mode.

r2-18

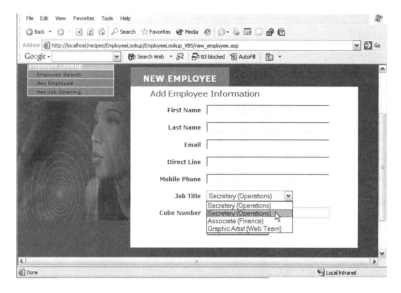

NOTE

As noted before, the Insert Record dialog is different for ASP and ColdFusion server models and easiest understood when presented separately.

Step 4: Insert Record—New Employee

Now it's time to apply the Insert Record server behavior.

For ASP

1. From the Server Behaviors panel, choose Add (+) and select **Insert Record**.

2. In the Insert Record dialog, select your connection from the list.

   📖 Choose **Recipes** from the Connections list.

3. Select the table in the data source to modify from the list.

   📖 Choose **Employees** from the Insert into Table list.

4. Enter the path to the file you want the user to visit after the record has been updated in the After Inserting, Go To field.

   📖 Choose Browse and locate the **employee_results.asp** file.

5. Choose the form to use.

   📖 Select **NewEmployee** from the Get Values From list.

6. With the current form selected in the Get Values From list, set the form elements to their corresponding data source fields.

   📖 Set the `FirstName` form element to the `EmployeeFirst` data column and submit as Text.

  □ Set the `LastName` form element to the `EmployeeLast` data column and submit as Text.

  Set the `Email` form element to the `EmployeeEmail` data column and submit as Text.

  Set the `Phone` form element to the `EmployeePhone` data column and submit as Text.

  Set the `Phone2` form element to the `EmployeeMobile` data column and submit as Text.

  Set the `JobTitle` form element to the `EmployeeJob` data column and submit as Numeric.

  Set the `CubeNumber` form element to the `EmployeeCube` data column and submit as Numeric.

7. Verify your choices and click OK to close the dialog.

For ColdFusion and PHP

1. From the Server Behaviors panel, choose Add (+) and select **Update Record**.
2. In the Update Record dialog, choose the current form.

  □ Select **NewEmployee** from the Submit Values From list.

3. Select your data source from the list.

  □ Choose **Recipes** from the Data Source list.

4. Enter your username and password, if needed.
5. Select the table in the data source to insert into from the list.

  □ Choose **Employees** (**employees** for PHP) from the Insert into Table list.

6. Set the data source fields to their corresponding form elements.

  □ Make sure the `EmployeeID` data column is set to an Unused Primary Key.

  Set `EmployeeFirst` to the `FORM.FirstName` form element and submit as Text.

  Set `EmployeeLast` to the `FORM.LastName` form element and submit as Text.

  Set `EmployeeEmail` to the `FORM.Email` form element and submit as Text.

  Set `EmployeePhone` to the `FORM.Phone` form element and submit as Text.

  Set `EmployeeMobile` to the `FORM.Phone2` form element and submit as Text.

  Set `EmployeeJob` to the `FORM.JobTitle` form element and submit as Numeric for ColdFusion and Integer for PHP.

  Set `EmployeeCube` to the `FORM.CubeNumber` form element and submit as Numeric for ColdFusion and Integer for PHP.

7. Enter the path to the file you want the user to visit after the record has been inserted in the After Inserting, Go To field.

  □ Choose Browse and locate the **employee_results** file for your server model.

8. Verify your choices and click OK to close the dialog.

Step 5: Hand Code—Redirect When No Job Openings

Our final step on this page and the entire application is to insert some custom code to properly react when no jobs are available. Because this redirect relies on the recordset on the page—which returns a list of available jobs—you can place the redirect on the page itself, where you can be sure the recordset code has already been defined. As noted earlier, should no jobs be available, the code redirects the visitor to the New Job page and triggers the error message previously embedded.

1. In Code view, place your cursor just above the opening <html> tag.

   Although you could place this code elsewhere for ASP and ColdFusion, PHP requires that the code appear directly after the recordset definition.

2. Insert the following code:

   ☐ From the Snippets panel, open the **Recipes > EmployeeLookup > Custom Code** folder for your server model and insert the **No Job Openings - Display Text** snippet.

   VB
   ```
   <%
   if (Jobs.EOF) then
     Response.Redirect("new_job.asp?empty=true")
   end if
   %>
   ```

   JS
   ```
   <%
   if (Jobs.EOF)
     Response.Redirect("new_job.asp?empty=true");
   %>
   ```

   CF
   ```
   <cfif Jobs.RecordCount EQ 0>
     <cflocation url="new_job.cfm?empty=true">
   </cfif>
   ```

   PHP
   ```
   <?php
   if ($totalRows_Jobs<=0) {
       $url = "new_job.php?empty=true";
       Header("Location: $url");
   }
   ?>
   ```

3. Save your page.

The only way to test the redirection functionality is to preview the page in a browser when all the available jobs are filled. The recipe data source has a full slate of company employees for you to test your application with.

Recipe 3

Conference Room Scheduler

Although it may seem that you spend all your life online interacting with others digitally through email or perhaps teleconferencing, face-to-face meetings in any organization are still a fact of life. Offices have a limited supply of conference rooms in which to hold these meetings, and thus the need for a conference room scheduling application was born. Any scheduling application must take special notice of time as well as space. When a meeting is scheduled and how long it is to last are just as important as the location and dimensions of the room.

Our Conference Room Scheduler recipe is very user-oriented. The administrator has only two special pages: one for making new rooms available on the system and the other for editing those room descriptions. All other aspects of the application are designed around the user's needs. Typically, the user would begin by attempting to schedule a meeting. If a meeting is already set for the chosen time or place, the user is informed of the conflict and then given an opportunity to try again or search the already-scheduled meetings to look for an available slot. After a meeting has been established, the user is able to update or delete the record.

This recipe focuses largely on date and time functionality. Data sources store time and date values in special formats and, depending on the server model, require special handling to read and save related values. Not only are specific times, such as starting times, incorporated, but durations of meetings are also calculated. Such calculations—included in this recipe—have many uses in various other intranet and workgroup applications.

User Recipes

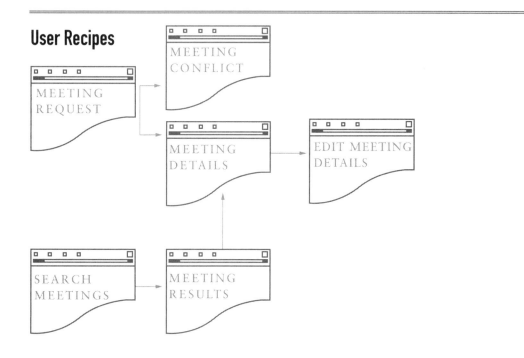

Administrator Recipes

Ingredients

8 APPLICATION PAGES:

- 6 User Pages
  - Meeting Request
  - Meeting Conflict

- Meeting Details
- Edit Meeting Details
- Meeting Search
- Meeting Results

■ 2 Administration Pages

- Add Conference Room
- Update Conference Room

1 DATA SOURCE:

■ 1 database with:

- 2 tables
  - **Conferences**—Includes records for all scheduled meetings including fields for the ID, the meeting name, its owner, the room, the meeting purpose, the start time, and its duration.
  - **Rooms**—Keeps track of which rooms are available and their descriptions.
- 1 view
  - **ConferenceDisplay**—A virtual table joining the Conferences and Rooms tables.

Prep Work

Before you begin to build this application, make sure your prep work has been completed.

1. Create the data source containing the necessary tables.

   📖 ASP and ColdFusion users should use the **Recipes.mdb** data source found in the downloaded files while PHP users should work with the **Recipes** data source. For assistance in locating and installing these files, choose **Help > Web Application Recipes**.

2. Set up a connection to the data source. If you're unsure how to do this, see the "Connecting to Data Sources" section of Chapter 1.

   📖 Name the connection **Recipes**.

3. Create the template to be used for the application.

   📖 Use the template for your server model named **conferenceroom**.

End User Recipe: Meeting Request

The entry point to a conference room scheduling application is the meeting request form. From the user's perspective, the form is fairly straightforward. After entering a few descriptive details—the meeting's name, owner, and description—the when (time, date, and duration) and where are input.

When the request is submitted, however, all pretense of simplicity fades away. The request is first compared to existing meetings to check for a conflicting meeting. Should no conflict be found, the meeting details are added to the data source; but if another meeting is booked for the same room and time, the user is taken to another page where the particulars of the conflicting meeting are displayed.

This application page incorporates three recordsets, including one that gets the just-inserted data for confirmation purposes. You'll also find a somewhat sophisticated method of gathering time and date information and combining the details into a data source-friendly format.

Step 1: Implement Meeting Request Design

The meeting request page requires a fair degree of information, and you'll need to construct the form so that it remains easy to use. A series of text fields (both single line and text areas) are used to gather the basic descriptive information whereas the time and place information is primarily input through drop-down lists.

1. Create a basic dynamic page, either by hand or derived from a template.

   📖 In the **ConferenceRoomScheduler** folder, locate the folder for your server model and open the meeting_request page found there.

2. Add a table to the content region of your page to contain the interface elements for the application.

   📖 From the Snippets panel, drag the **Recipes > ConferenceRoom > Wireframes > Meeting Request - Wireframe** snippet into the Content editable region.

3. Within the table, place another HTML table to hold the form and its elements: three text fields (meeting name, owner, and date), one text area for the description, three drop-down lists (start time, duration, and conference room) and a submit button. You'll also need a hidden field used to combine the date and time entries.

   📖 ASP and ColdFusion users should place your cursor in the row below the words MEETING REQUEST and insert the **Recipes > ConferenceRoom > Forms > Enter Meeting Request Form** snippet; PHP users should use the **Recipes > ConferenceRoom > Forms > Enter Meeting Request Form (PHP)** snippet instead [r3-1].

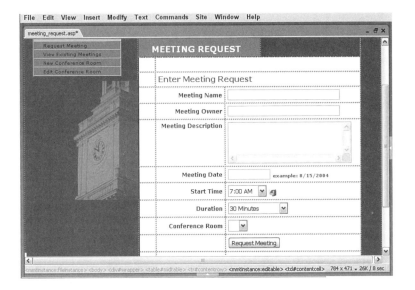

r3-1

4. Make sure the method attribute of the <form> tag is set to **POST** and save the page.

Recipe Variations: User Interface Enhancement

Depending on your organization, you might find it useful to replace the open text field for meeting owner with a dynamic list tied to an employee data source. A similar technique was demonstrated in a number of the pages for the Employee Lookup application covered in Recipe 2.

Step 2: Add Database Components, Part 1

The meeting request page is fairly involved from a recordset perspective. The three recordsets range from straightforward to advanced in terms of their SQL sophistication. The simplest recordset, Rooms, is used to populate the list of conference rooms. A more advanced recordset is used to obtain the ID of the just inserted record that will be passed to create a confirmation page. The final recordset compares the requested meeting time and place to already-scheduled meetings. If a conflict is found, the user is redirected to a page detailing the existing meeting.

Let's work our way up to the more complex recordsets by starting with the easiest one first, Rooms.

1. From the Server Behaviors panel, choose Add (+) and select **Recordset (Query)**.

2. In simple view, enter the name of the recordset.

   📖 Enter **Rooms** in the Name field.

3. Select the data source connection.

   📖 Choose **Recipes** from the Connection (Data Source) list.

4. Choose the table to work with.

   📖 Select **Rooms** (**rooms** in PHP) from the Table list.

5. Limit your data source columns to only those that are needed.

   📖 Choose the **Selected Columns** option and highlight **RoomID** and **RoomName**.

   It's generally considered good practice to limit your data source fields to those that are necessary, and when one of the unnecessary fields is a memo type field such as RoomDescription that could hold a great deal of text, it's especially important.

6. Leave the Filter option set to None.

7. Set the Sort option to present an alphabetical listing of the rooms.

   📖 Choose **RoomName** from the Sort list and accept the Ascending order.

8. Verify your choices and click OK when you're done.

9. Save your page.

The next recordset to add involves a useful technique for getting the ID of a just-inserted record for ASP and ColdFusion users; PHP offers a built-in function that handles this for us and we do not need to create the Inserted recordset. During the normal workflow of an insert record operation for these server models, an ID—an automatically generated unique number—would not be available until the application has successfully inserted the record and moved on to the next page. In this situation, we want to be able to display details of the just-inserted record on that next page, the confirmation page. To accomplish that, we'll need to pass the ID as part of the Insert Record server behavior—which we'll get through the recordset we are about to add. A little later in the application set-up, we'll wrap a conditional statement around this recordset so that it is executed only if the Insert Record server behavior has been called.

NOTE To accommodate the different dialogs for the various server models, the steps are presented separately here and when necessary throughout this recipe. In this instance, only steps for ASP and ColdFusion are included as the Inserted recordset is not necessary in PHP.

For ASP

1. From the Server Behaviors panel, choose Add (+) and select **Recordset (Query)**.

2. Switch to the advanced view of the dialog and enter an appropriate name for the recordset.

   📖 Enter **Inserted** into the Name field.

3. Choose the connection for the recordset.

   ▢ Select **Recipes** from the Connection list.

4. In the SQL area, enter the following code:

```
SELECT TOP 1 ConferenceID
FROM Conferences
WHERE ConferenceName = 'NameParam'
ORDER BY ConferenceID DESC
```

   This SQL statement selects the last entered record of the data that matches the entry in the Meeting Name field. This assures us of retrieving the just inserted ID, even if there are other records with the same meeting name.

5. In the Variable area, choose Add (+) and enter **NameParam** under the Name column.

6. In the Default Value column, enter **test**.

   The test value is merely a placeholder; any other text string could be used.

7. In the Run-time Value column, enter **Request.Form("MeetingName")** and click OK to close the dialog.

8. Save your page.

For ColdFusion

1. From the Server Behaviors panel, choose Add (+) and select **Recordset (Query)**.

2. Switch to the advanced view of the dialog and enter an appropriate name for the recordset.

   ▢ Enter **Inserted** in the Name field.

3. Choose your data source.

   ▢ Select **Recipes** from the Data Source list.

4. Enter a user name and password if necessary.

5. In the SQL area, enter the following code.

```
SELECT TOP 1 ConferenceID
FROM Conferences
WHERE ConferenceName = '#FORM.MeetingName#'
ORDER BY ConferenceID DESC
```

   This SQL statement selects the last entered record of the data that matches the entry in the Meeting Name field. This assures us of retrieving the just-inserted ID, even if there are other records with the same meeting name.

6. In the Page Parameter section, choose Add (+) and, in the Add Parameter dialog, make sure **FORM.MeetingName** is chosen in the Name list.

7. Enter **test** as the Default Value and click OK to close the dialog.

8. Verify your entries in the Recordset dialog and click OK to close that dialog.

9. Save your page.

Step 3: Add Database Components, Part 2

The final recordset needed for this page is required to check for a conflicting meeting. The SQL statement is fairly complex, primarily because a match for the requested place and specified date/time range is being checked; three different variables—DateParam, DurationParam, and RoomParam—must also be added. Like the Inserted recordset, a conditional statement will be wrapped around this recordset code later to ensure that it is executed only when needed.

For ASP

  📖 Because this SQL statement is so complex, we've included it as a snippet. However, you can't insert a snippet into a Dreamweaver dialog directly, but you can copy it before opening the Recordset dialog. To copy the SQL code to the clipboard, right-click (Control-click) the **Recipes > ConferenceRoom > SQL > Conflict RS - ASP SQL Statement** snippet and choose **Copy Snippet** from the context menu. Now, you're ready to return to the application page and insert the recordset.

1. From the Server Behaviors panel, choose Add (+) and select **Recordset (Query)**.

2. Switch to the advanced view of the dialog and enter an appropriate name for the recordset [r3-2].

r3-2

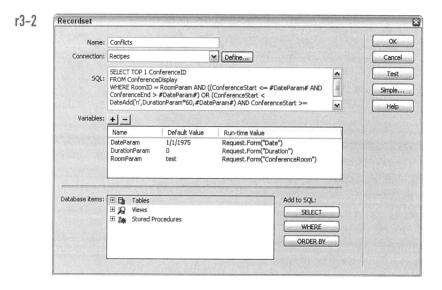

  📖 Enter **Conflicts** into the Name field.

3. Choose the connection for the recordset.

  📖 Select **Recipes** from the Connection list.

4. In the SQL area, enter the following code:

   📖 Press Ctrl-V (Command-V) to paste in the copied snippet.

   ```
   SELECT TOP 1 ConferenceID
   FROM ConferenceDisplay
   WHERE RoomID = RoomParam AND ((ConferenceStart <= #DateParam#
   ➥AND ConferenceEnd > #DateParam#) OR (ConferenceStart < DateAdd
   ➥('n',DurationParam*60,#DateParam#)
   ➥AND ConferenceStart >= #DateParam#))
   ```

The pound signs surrounding the DateParam field indicate that this is an Access date format field.

5. In the Variable area, choose Add (+) and enter **DateParam** under the Name column.
6. In the Default Value column, enter **1/1/1975**.
7. In the Run-time Value column, enter **Request.Form("FullDate")**.
8. Add another variable by choosing Add (+) and enter **DurationParam** under the Name column.
9. In the Default Value column, enter **0**.
10. In the Run-time Value column, enter **Request.Form("Duration")**.
11. Choose Add (+) to insert one more variable and enter **RoomParam** under the Name column.
12. In the Default Value column, enter **0**.
13. In the Run-time Value column, enter **Request.Form("ConferenceRoom")** and click OK to close the dialog.
14. Save your page.

For ColdFusion

Because the SQL statement for this recordset is quite complex, it is included as a snippet. However, you can't insert a snippet into a Dreamweaver dialog directly, but ColdFusion allows us to insert it directly within a `<cfquery>` tag pair. To accomplish this, we'll insert the tag from the Insert bar rather than use the Recordset dialog. To complete this ColdFusion recordset, three `<cfparam>` tags will also have to be added.

1. From Code view, position your cursor on a new line after the existing `<cfparam>` tag.
2. From the CFML category of the Insert bar, choose the **cfquery** object to open the Tag Editor.
3. In the General category of the Tag Editor, name the query appropriately.

   📖 Enter **Conflicts** in the Query Name field.

4. Choose your data source.

   📖 Enter **Recipes** in the Data Source field.

5. Enter a user name and password if necessary and choose OK to close the dialog.

6. Make sure your cursor is positioned within the <cfquery> tag pair and enter the following code:

   📖 From the Snippets panel, insert the **Recipes > ConferenceRoom > SQL > Conflict RS - CFML SQL Statement** snippet.

   ```
   SELECT TOP 1 ConferenceID
   FROM ConferenceDisplay
   WHERE RoomID = #FORM.ConferenceRoom#
   AND ((ConferenceStart <= ###FORM.FullDate###
   AND ((ConferenceStart <= #CreateODBCDateTime(FORM.FullDate)#
   ➥AND ConferenceEnd > #CreateODBCDateTime(FORM.FullDate)#)
   OR (ConferenceStart < DateAdd('n',#FORM.Duration#*60,
   ➥#CreateODBCDateTime(FORM.FullDate)#)
   AND ConferenceStart >= #CreateODBCDateTime(FORM.FullDate)#))
   ```

   The CreateODBCDateTime() functions are used to convert the date values to ODBC driver compatible versions.

7. Switch to Design view and, from the Bindings panel, choose Add (+) and select **CFParam**.

8. In the CFParam dialog, enter **FORM.FullDate** in the Name field.

9. Enter **1/1/1975** as the Default value.

10. Choose **Date** from the Type list and click OK to close the dialog.

11. From the Bindings panel, choose Add (+) and select **CFParam** to add another variable.

12. In the CFParam dialog, enter **FORM.Duration** in the Name list.

13. Enter **0** as the Default value.

14. Choose **Numeric** from the Type list and click OK to close the dialog.

15. From the Bindings panel, choose Add (+) and select **CFParam** to add a final variable.

16. In the CFParam dialog, enter **FORM.ConferenceRoom** in the Name list.

17. Enter **0** as the Default value.

18. Choose **String** from the Type list and click OK to close the dialog.

19. Save your page.

Both the CFParams and the Conflicts recordset should now be visible in the Binding panel.

For PHP

    □ Because this SQL statement is so complex, we've included it as a snippet. However, you can't insert a snippet into a Dreamweaver dialog directly, but you can copy it before opening the Recordset dialog. To copy the SQL code to the clipboard, right-click (Control-click) the **Recipes > ConferenceRoom > SQL > Conflict RS - PHP SQL Statement** snippet and choose **Copy Snippet** from the context menu.

1. From the Server Behaviors panel, choose Add (+) and select **Recordset (Query)**.

2. Switch to the advanced view of the dialog and enter an appropriate name for the recordset.

    □ Enter **Conflicts** into the Name field.

3. Choose the connection for the recordset.

    □ Select **Recipes** from the Connection list.

4. In the SQL area, enter the following code:

    □ Press Ctrl-V (Command-V) to paste in the copied snippet.

```
SELECT ConferenceID
FROM conferences,rooms
WHERE conferences.ConferenceRoom = rooms.RoomID
AND
ConferenceRoom = 'RoomParam'
AND
(UNIX_TIMESTAMP(ConferenceStart) = 'DateParam'
OR
UNIX_TIMESTAMP(ConferenceStart) = UNIX_TIMESTAMP
➥(INTERVAL HOUR('DurationParam')HOUR +
INTERVAL MINUTE('DurationParam') MINUTE +
➥FROM_UNIXTIME('DateParam')))
```

5. In the Variable area, choose Add (+) and in the Add Parameter dialog enter **DateParam** under the Name field.

6. In the Default Value field, enter **157766400**, a UNIX timestamp equivalent to January 1, 1975.

7. In the Run-time Value field, enter **$_POST['FullDate']** and click OK to close the Add Parameter dialog.

8. Add another variable by choosing Add (+) and, in the Add Parameter dialog, enter **DurationParam** in the Name field.

9. In the Default Value field, enter **0**.

10. In the Run-time Value field, enter **$_POST['Duration']** and click OK to close the Add Parameter dialog.

11. Add the final variable by choosing Add (+) and, when the Add Parameter dialog opens, enter **RoomParam** in the Name field.

12. In the Default Value field, enter **0**.

13. In the Run-time Value field, enter **$_POST['ConferenceRoom']** and click OK to close the Add Parameter dialog.

14. Click OK to close the Recordset dialog and save your page after Dreamweaver inserts the recordset.

A function to convert the FullDate value into a MySQL-friendly format is now needed. We'll insert the necessary code near the top of the page so that it will be executed first.

1. In Code view, place your cursor after the code for including the connection that starts `<?php require_once...` and press Enter (Return).

2. Insert the following code:

   From the Snippets panel, insert the **Recipes > ConferenceRoom > CustomCode_PHP > Enter Meeting Request - Convert FullDate** snippet.

   ```php
   <?php
   if ((isset($_POST['FullDate']))||(isset
   ➥($_POST['FullDate']))) {
       $_POST['FullDate'] = strtotime
   ➥($_POST['FullDate']);
       $_POST['FullDate'] = strtotime($_POST['FullDate']);
   }
   ?>
   ```

   Later in the recipe, we'll include a function that will revert the date values into strings so that they may be stored properly in the data source.

3. Save your page.

Step 4: Data Binding Process

Most of the form elements of the request meeting page do not need to be bound to dynamic data at all. Of the three drop-down lists, only one—the Room list—has a dynamic connection; the other two lists are populated with static values. One other form element—the hidden field that contains the full date value—is bound to data, but not in the traditional sense. JavaScript behaviors are used to combine the time and date entries.

Before we add the JavaScript behaviors, let's populate the Rooms list with data. By binding the room data to a form element, we make it easier for the user to choose a location and simultaneously cut down on the error checking.

1. In Design mode, select the **ConferenceRoom** list element.
2. From the Property inspector, click the **Dynamic** button to open the Dynamic List/Menu dialog.
3. In the Options from Recordset list, choose **Rooms.**
4. In the Values list, select **RoomID.**
5. In the Labels list, choose **RoomName.**
6. Leave the Select Value Equal to field blank and click OK to close the dialog.

The two other lists are populated with static values. The Start Time list uses the same entries for both labels and values: half-hour increments starting at 7:00 AM and continuing until 7:00 PM. The Duration list, although also comprised of static values, is a little different. The labels are text descriptions of a variety of time lengths from 30 minutes to 5 hours, also in half-hour increments. The corresponding values, however, are given in decimal notation to allow for calculation in the SQL statements. For example, two and one-half hours is represented as 2.5.

To simplify user entry, this page separates the date and time into two form elements, one a text field and the other a list. However, most data sources combine dates and times into one field type. On this page, custom JavaScript code is used to merge the entries from the date text field and the time list into a hidden form element that later will be inserted into a new meeting record. Two JavaScript custom code statements are applied through the Call JavaScript behavior.

> 📖 Because of the length of the JavaScript involved, the custom code is provided in snippet format. To use the snippet in combination with the Call JavaScript behavior, you need to copy the snippet first by using the Copy Snippet extension installed with the recipe files. The snippet used in both applications of the behavior is found in **Recipes > ConferenceRoom > ClientJavaScript > Meeting Request - Populate FullDate Hidden Form Element.**

1. Select the **MeetingDate** text field.
2. From the Behaviors panel, choose Add (+) and select **Call JavaScript.**
3. In the Call JavaScript dialog, insert the following code:

> 📖 Paste the clipboard by pressing Ctrl-V (Command-V).

```
document.MeetingRequest.FullDate.value =
➥document.MeetingRequest.MeetingDate.value +' '+
➥document.MeetingRequest.StartTime.options
➥[document.MeetingRequest.StartTime.selectedIndex].value
```

4. Click OK to close the dialog and make sure the event is listed as onBlur in the Behaviors panel [r3-3].

r3-3

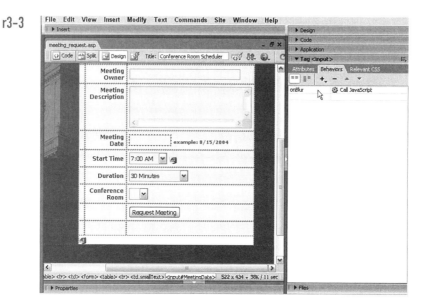

Now, let's apply the same behavior to the StartTime list element.

1. Select the **StartTime** list element.
2. Again, from the Behaviors panel, choose Add (+) and select **Call JavaScript**.
3. In the Call JavaScript dialog, insert the same code again:
    - Paste the clipboard by pressing Ctrl-V (Command-V).

```
document.MeetingRequest.FullDate.value =
➡document.MeetingRequest.MeetingDate.value +' '+
➡document.MeetingRequest.StartTime.options
  ➡[document.MeetingRequest.StartTime.selectedIndex].value
```

4. Click OK to close the dialog and make sure the event is listed as onChange in the Behaviors panel.
5. Save the page.

Sorting Lists with Dynamic Dropdowns

Our recipe uses one drop-down list to display all the available conference rooms. This solution works fine for small to medium organizations, but when faced with numerous rooms in multiple buildings, it may be inadequate. Rather than list all the rooms in a single drop-down list, a better way might be to use multiple lists where a choice in one determines what is displayed in another. For example, one list might contain all the buildings in the organization; choose a particular building, and a second list is populated with the rooms available in just that building.

This technique, referred to as *dynamic dropdowns*, is typically developed with a combination of server- and client-side code. WebAssist offers an extension designed to handle this very situation. WA Dynamic Dropdowns ensures that your customers will find what they're looking for quickly.

For more information, visit
`http://www.webassist.com/Products/WADynamicDropdowns.asp`.

Step 5: Insert Record for Meeting Request

The page is now ready to add the Insert Record server behavior. Although most of the form elements have corresponding data source fields, two are ignored. The values from the MeetingDate text field and StartTime list are combined into the hidden form field, FullDate, and so those two fields are disregarded.

For ASP

1. From the Server Behaviors panel, choose Add (+) and select **Insert Record**.
2. Select the desired data source connection.
   - Choose **Recipes** from the Connection list.
3. Choose the table in the data source that will receive the form values.
   - From the Insert Into Table list, choose **Conferences**.
4. Leave the After Inserting, Go To field empty.

   In this application, the redirection will be hand-coded; the page chosen depends on whether a conflicting meeting is found or not.
5. Choose the form on the page from which to get the values.
   - From the Get Values From list, choose **MeetingRequest**.
6. In the Form Elements area, set the form elements to their corresponding data source fields.
   - Set the `MeetingName` form element to the `ConferenceName` data source field as Text type.

     Set the `MeetingOwner` form element to the `ConferenceBy` data source field as Text type.

     Set the `MeetingDescription` form element to the `ConferenceDescription` data source field as Text type.

     Leave both the `MeetingDate` and `StartTime` form elements set to <ignore>.

     Set the `FullDate` form element to the `ConferenceStart` data source field as Date MS Access type.

  📖 Set the `Duration` form element to the `ConferenceDuration` data source field as Numeric.

   Set the `ConferenceRoom` form element to the `ConferenceRoom` data source field as Numeric.

7. Make sure your entries are correct and then click OK to close.

8. Save the page.

For ColdFusion and PHP

After completing the Insert Record server behavior, PHP users will also need to add the date-to-string conversion function mentioned earlier.

1. From the Server Behaviors panel, choose Add (+) and select **Insert Record**.

2. In the Insert Record dialog, choose the current form.

  📖 Select **MeetingRequest** from the Submit Values From list.

3. Select your data source from the list.

  📖 Choose **Recipes** from the Data Source list.

4. Enter your user name and password, if needed.

5. Select the table in the data source to insert into from the list.

  📖 Choose **Conferences** (**conferences** in PHP) from the Insert Into Table list.

6. Set the data source fields to their corresponding form elements.

  📖 Make sure the `ConferenceID` data column is set to be an unused Primary Key.

   Set `ConferenceRoom` to the `FORM.ConferenceRoom` form element and submit as Numeric type in ColdFusion and Integer type in PHP.

   Set `ConferenceName` to the `FORM.MeetingName` form element and submit as Text type.

   Set `ConferenceDescription` to the `FORM.MeetingDescription` form element and submit as Text type.

   Set `ConferenceStart` to the `FORM.FullDate` form element and submit as Date MS Access type for ColdFusion and Date type for PHP.

   Set `ConferenceDuration` to the `FORM.Duration` form element and submit as Numeric type in ColdFusion and Integer type in PHP.

   Set `ConferenceBy` to the `FORM.MeetingOwner` form element and submit as Text type.

7. Leave the After Inserting, Go to field blank and click OK to close the dialog.

8. Save the page.

The following steps are for PHP users only:

1. From the Server Behaviors panel, select the **Insert Record** server behavior just added.
2. In Code view, you'll see the Insert Record code highlighted; move your cursor above this code block.
3. Insert the following code:

      ☐ From the Snippets panel, insert the **Recipes > ConferenceRoom > CustomCode_PHP > Enter Meeting Request - Reconvert FullDate** snippet.

   ```php
   <?php
   if (($_POST['FullDate']!="")||($_POST['FullDate']!="")) {
       $_POST['FullDate'] = date("YmdHis",$_POST['FullDate']);
   $_POST['FullDate'] = date("YmdHis",$_POST['FullDate']);
   }
   ?>
   ```

4. Save your page.

Step 6: Add Server-Side Date Validation

To make sure the date entered by the user is in the proper format, this page employs server-side date validation. If an improper date is found, an error message appears on the page above the form. This is accomplished by having the page submit to itself with an argument indicating an error. Additional custom code is required to display the error message when such an argument is present.

The server-side date validation then is comprised of two parts: one code block to redirect the page with an argument and another to present a message. We'll insert the redirection code first.

> **NOTE** Both VBScript and CFML include functions for identifying a properly formatted date; however JavaScript and PHP do not. Those developers programming in ASP-JavaScript and PHP will need to include two code blocks—one is a custom function to verify the date format and the other to call the function—while developers using ASP-VBScript or ColdFusion will only require one custom code block.

1. In Code view, place the cursor at the top of the page.

   ASP users should position the cursor after the `<!-- include>` statement.
2. ASP-JavaScript users only: insert the following code:

      ☐ From the Snippets panel, insert the **Recipes > ConferenceRoom CustomCode_JS > IsADate Function** snippet.

   ```
   JS   <%
       function isADate(DateString)  {
         var DateRegex = /^(\d{1,2})\/(\d{1,2})\/(\d{4})$/
         var theMatch = DateString.match(DateRegex);
         var validDate = false;
   ```

Continues

```
        if (theMatch)  {
          var DateObj = new Date(DateString);
        if ((DateObj.getMonth()+1 == parseInt(theMatch[1])) &&
        ➥(DateObj.getDate() == parseInt(theMatch[2])) &&
        ➥(DateObj.getFullYear() == parseInt(theMatch[3])))
            validDate = true;
        }
        return validDate;
      }
      %>
```

3. PHP users only: insert the following code:

    📖 From the Snippets panel, insert the **Recipes > ConferenceRoom > Custom
    Code_PHP > IsADate Function** snippet.

    (PHP) <?php

```
      function isADate($DateString) {
        $validDate = false;
        if (ereg("^[0-9]{1,2}\/[0-9]{1,2}\/[0-9]{4}$",$DateString)) {
          $today = date("Y");
          $submittedDate = explode("/",$DateString);
          $month = $submittedDate[0];
          $day = $submittedDate[1];
          $year = $submittedDate[2];
          if ($year >= $today) {
            $validDate = (checkdate($month,$day,$year))?true:false;
          }
        }
        return $validDate;
      }
      ?>
```

4. For all server models, insert the following code at the current cursor position (after
    the last code inserted for ASP-JS and PHP and at the top of the page for ASP-VB
    and ColdFusion):

    📖 From the Snippets panel, open the **Recipes > ConferenceRoom > Custom Code**
    folder for your server model and insert the **Meeting Request - Date Validation**
    snippet.

    (VB) <%

```
      if (cStr(Request.Form("FullDate")) <> "")  then
        if not (isDate(Request.Form("FullDate"))) then
        ➥Response.Redirect("meeting_request.asp?badDate=true")
      end if
      %>
```

(JS)
```
<%
if (String(Request.Form("MeetingDate"))!="undefined" &&
➥!isADate(String(Request.Form("MeetingDate"))))
  Response.Redirect("meeting_request.asp?badDate=true")
%>
```

(CF)
```
<cfif IsDefined("FORM.MeetingDate")>
  <cfif not IsDate(FORM.MeetingDate)>
    <cflocation url="meeting_request.cfm?badDate=true">
  </cfif>
</cfif>
```

(PHP)
```
<?php
if ((isset($_POST['MeetingDate'])) &&
➥(!isADate($_POST['MeetingDate']))) {
  $url = "meeting_request.php?badDate=true";
  header("Location: $url");
}
?>
```

Now that our validation routine is in place, we need to insert the error message that will be displayed if the URL variable baddate is present.

5. In Design view, place your cursor where you want the error message to appear.

   📖 Position the cursor in the table row above the Enter Meeting Request text.

6. Insert the following code:

   📖 From the Snippets panel, open the **Recipes > ConferenceRoom > Custom Code** folder for your server model and insert the **Date Error - Dynamic Text** snippet.

(VB)
```
<% if (cStr(Request.QueryString("badDate")) <> "") Then
Response.Write("The date you entered was not in the proper
format.  Dates should be in the format mm/dd/yyyy.%>
```

(JS)
```
<%=(String(Request.QueryString("badDate")) != "undefined")?"The date
you entered was not in the proper format.  Dates should be in the
format mm/dd/yyyy.":""%>
```

(CF)
```
<cfif isDefined("URL.badDate")>The date you entered was not in the
proper format.  Dates should be in the format mm/dd/yyyy.</cfif>
```

(PHP)
```
<?php
if (isset($_GET['badDate'])) {
  echo "The date you entered was
  not in the proper format.
  Dates should be in the format
  mm/dd/yyyy.";
}
?>
```

> **NOTE**
> Don't try to test the page at this point. The `Conflicts` recordset needs to be moved above the other recordsets and modified so that it is accessed only at the appropriate time.

Step 7: Hand Code Edits to Handle Meeting Conflicts

To get the `Conflicts` recordset fully operational, we're going to have to perform four operations:

- Move the `Conflicts` recordset and its three parameter declarations above the Insert Record server behavior code.
- Add a redirect statement to the end of the `Conflicts` recordset if a conflict is found.
- Wrap all `Conflicts` recordset-associated code in a conditional statement so that it is executed only if the Insert Record operation is attempted.
- Wrap the code that closes the `Conflicts` recordset in a similar conditional statement.

Let's get started by moving the `Conflicts` recordset code blocks.

1. From the Server Behaviors panel, select the `Conflicts` recordset.

   Selecting the recordset in the Server Behaviors panel highlights a portion of the relevant code.

2. In Code view, select the highlighted recordset and the three SQL parameter code blocks above the recordset code and cut it. The code to select is:

   (VB)
   ```
   <%
   Dim Conflicts__DateParam
   Conflicts__DateParam = "1/1/1975"
   If (Request.Form("FullDate") <> "") Then
     Conflicts__DateParam = Request.Form("FullDate")
   End If
   %>
   <%
   Dim Conflicts__DurationParam
   Conflicts__DurationParam = "0"
   If (Request.Form("Duration") <> "") Then
     Conflicts__DurationParam = Request.Form("Duration")
   End If
   %>
   <%
   Dim Conflicts__RoomParam
   Conflicts__RoomParam = "test"
   If (Request.Form("ConferenceRoom") <> "") Then
     Conflicts__RoomParam = Request.Form("ConferenceRoom")
   End If
   %>
   <%
   Dim Conflicts
   Dim Conflicts_numRows
   ```

```
Set Conflicts = Server.CreateObject("ADODB.Recordset")
Conflicts.ActiveConnection = MM_Recipes_STRING
Conflicts.Source = "SELECT TOP 1 ConferenceID  FROM
➥ConferenceDisplay  WHERE (ConferenceStart <= #" +
➥Replace(Conflicts__DateParam, "'", "''") +
➥"# AND ConferenceEnd > #" + Replace(Conflicts__DateParam,
➥"'", "''") + "#) OR (ConferenceStart < DateAdd('n'," +
➥Replace(Conflicts__DurationParam, "'", "''") + "*60,#" +
➥Replace(Conflicts__DateParam, "'", "''") + "#)
➥AND ConferenceStart >= #" + Replace(Conflicts__DateParam,
➥"'", "''") + "#)"
Conflicts.CursorType = 0
Conflicts.CursorLocation = 2
Conflicts.LockType = 1
Conflicts.Open()

Conflicts_numRows = 0
%>
```

```
<%
var Conflicts__DateParam = "1/1/1975";
if (String(Request.Form("FullDate")) != "undefined" &&
    String(Request.Form("FullDate")) != "") {
  Conflicts__DateParam = String(Request.Form("FullDate"));
}
%>
<%
var Conflicts__DurationParam = "0";
if (String(Request.Form("Duration")) != "undefined" &&
    String(Request.Form("Duration")) != "") {
  Conflicts__DurationParam = String(Request.Form("Duration"));
}
%>
<%
var Conflicts__RoomParam = "0";
if (String(Request.Form("ConferenceRoom")) != "undefined" &&
    String(Request.Form("ConferenceRoom")) != "") {
  Conflicts__RoomParam = String(Request.Form("ConferenceRoom"));
}
%>
<%
var Conflicts = Server.CreateObject("ADODB.Recordset");
Conflicts.ActiveConnection = MM_Recipes_STRING;
Conflicts.Source = "SELECT TOP 1 ConferenceID  FROM
➥ConferenceDisplay  WHERE (ConferenceStart
➥<= #"+ Conflicts__DateParam.replace(/'/g, "''") +
```

Continues

```
➥"# AND ConferenceEnd > #"+ Conflicts__DateParam.replace
➥(/'/g, "''") + "#) OR (ConferenceStart < DateAdd('n',"+
➥Conflicts__DurationParam.replace(/'/g, "''") + "*60,#"+
➥Conflicts__DateParam.replace(/'/g, "''") + "#)
➥AND ConferenceStart >= #"+ Conflicts__DateParam.replace
➥(/'/g, "''") + "#)";
Conflicts.CursorType = 0;
Conflicts.CursorLocation = 2;
Conflicts.LockType = 1;
Conflicts.Open();
var Conflicts_numRows = 0;
%>
```

CF
```
<cfquery name="Conflicts" datasource="Recipes">
SELECT TOP 1 ConferenceID
FROM ConferenceDisplay
WHERE (ConferenceStart <= #CreateODBCDateTime(FORM.FullDate)#
AND ConferenceEnd > #CreateODBCDateTime(FORM.FullDate)#)
➥OR (ConferenceStart < DateAdd('n',#FORM.Duration#*60,
➥#CreateODBCDateTime(FORM.FullDate)#)
➥AND ConferenceStart >= #CreateODBCDateTime(FORM.FullDate)#)
</cfquery>
```

NOTE | Because ColdFusion routinely places the SQL parameters (in the <cfparam> tags) at the top of the page, they do not need to be moved.

PHP
```
$DateParam_Conflicts = "157766400";
if (isset($_POST['FullDate'])) {
  $DateParam_Conflicts = (get_magic_quotes_gpc()) ?
  ➥$_POST['FullDate'] : addslashes($_POST['FullDate']);
}
$DurationParam_Conflicts = "0";
if (isset($_POST['Duration'])) {
  $DurationParam_Conflicts = (get_magic_quotes_gpc()) ?
  ➥$_POST['Duration'] : addslashes($_POST['Duration']);
}
$RoomParam_Conflicts = "0";
if (isset($_POST['ConferenceRoom'])) {
  $RoomParam_Conflicts = (get_magic_quotes_gpc()) ?
  ➥$_POST['ConferenceRoom'] : addslashes($_POST['ConferenceRoom']);
}
mysql_select_db($database_Recipes_PHP, $Recipes_PHP);
$query_Conflicts = sprintf("SELECT ConferenceStart
➥FROM conferences,rooms WHERE conferences.ConferenceRoom =
➥rooms.RoomID  AND  ConferenceRoom = '%s'
```

```
➥AND  (UNIX_TIMESTAMP(ConferenceStart) = '%s'
➥OR  UNIX_TIMESTAMP(ConferenceStart) = UNIX_TIMESTAMP
➥(INTERVAL HOUR('%s')HOUR +  INTERVAL MINUTE('%s') MINUTE +
➥FROM_UNIXTIME('%s')))", $RoomParam_Conflicts,$DateParam_Conflicts,
➥$DurationParam_Conflicts,$DurationParam_Conflicts,
➥$DateParam_Conflicts);
$Conflicts = mysql_query($query_Conflicts, $Recipes_PHP)
➥or die(mysql_error());
$row_Conflicts = mysql_fetch_assoc($Conflicts);
$totalRows_Conflicts = mysql_num_rows($Conflicts);
```

3. Place the cursor on a new line after the date validation code inserted in the previous step near the top of the page and paste in the just-cut `Conflicts` recordset code.

4. PHP Users only: Wrap PHP delimeters around the just-inserted code block.

   Before:

   (PHP) `<?php`

   After:

   `?>`

> **NOTE**
>
> Note that the selection does not include the `<?php ?>` delimiters, nor the Rooms recordset. Dreamweaver merges the code for the `Conflicts` recordset with that of the other recordsets. Therefore, after placing this portion of the `Conflicts` recordset elsewhere on the page, new delimiters must be manually added to it.

Now, we're ready to add a bit of code that checks the `Conflicts` recordset and, if at least one record is found, redirects the user to the `meeting_conflict` page. This redirection code is placed before the Insert Server Behavior to avoid adding conflicting meetings into the data source.

1. In Code view, place your cursor on a new line after the just-moved `Conflicts` recordset.

2. Insert the following code:

   📖 From the Snippets panel, open the **Recipes > ConferenceRoom > Custom Code** folder for your server model and insert the **Meeting Conflict Redirect** snippet.

   (VB)
   ```
   <%
   if (Not Conflicts.EOF) Then Response.Redirect
   ("meeting_conflict.asp?ID="+Conflicts.Fields("ConferenceID").value);
   %>
   ```

   (JS)
   ```
   <%
   if (!Conflicts.EOF) Then Response.Redirect
   ("meeting_conflict.asp?ID="+Conflicts.Fields("ConferenceID").value);
   %>
   ```

(CF)
```
<cfif Conflicts.RecordCount NEQ 0>
    <cflocation url="meeting_conflict.cfm?ID=
    ➥#Conflicts.ConferenceID#">
</cfif>
```

(PHP)
```php
<?php
if ($totalRows_Conflicts > 0){
    $url = "meeting_conflict.php?ID=".$row_Conflicts['ConferenceID'];
    header("Location: $url");
    exit();
}
?>
```

The third phase of adjusting the Conflicts recordset is to make it conditional. To do this, we'll need to wrap the Conflicts recordset and the parameters and redirection code just inserted into an If type statement. With this conditional code in place, the Conflicts-associated code is only executed after the Insert Record server behavior has been called.

1. In Code view, highlight all the contiguous Conflicts-related code.

   (CF) In ColdFusion, you don't need to select the <cfparam> tags, just the <cfquery> and the <cfif> Conflicts code blocks.

2. Wrap the following code around the selection:

   ☐ From the Snippets panel, open the **Recipes > ConferenceRoom > Custom Code** folder for your server model and insert the **If Statement - Only on Insert** snippet.

   Before:

   (VB)
   ```
   <%
   If (CStr(Request("MM_insert")) = "MeetingRequest") Then
   %>
   ```

   After:

   ```
   <%
   end if
   %>
   ```

   Before:

   (JS)
   ```
   <%
   if (String(Request("MM_insert")) == "MeetingRequest") {
   %>
   ```

After:

```
<%
}
%>
```

Before:

CF `<cfif IsDefined("FORM.MM_InsertRecord")>`

After:

```
</cfif>
```

Before:

PHP `<?php if (isset($_POST['MM_insert'])) { ?>`

After:

```
<?php } ?>
```

3. Save the page.

The final action involving the Conflicts recordset is to apply the same conditional statement to the code block that explictly closes the recordset, found at the bottom of the page. This is an ASP and PHP-only step.

For ASP

1. In Code view, move to the bottom of the page and select the code block that closes the Conflicts recordset. The code will look like this:

VB
```
<%
Conflicts.Close()
Set Conflicts = Nothing
%>
```

JS
```
<%
Conflicts.Close();
%>
```

2. Wrap the following code around the selection:

- 📖 From the Snippets panel, open the **Recipes > ConferenceRoom > Custom Code** folder for your server model and insert the **If Statement - Only on Insert** snippet.

Before:

(VB) ```
<%
    If (CStr(Request("MM_insert")) = "MeetingRequest") Then
    %>
```

*After:*

```
    <%
    end if
    %>
```

Before:

(JS) ```
<%
    if (String(Request("MM_insert")) == "MeetingRequest") {
    %>
```

After:

```
    <%
    }
    %>
```

3. Save your page.

For PHP

PHP users first will need to separate two merged code blocks and then make the second of the two conditional.

1. At the bottom of the page, locate the code block that begins `<?php mysql_free_result($Rooms);`. The complete code block looks like this:

(PHP) ```
<?php
    mysql_free_result($Rooms);
    mysql_free_result($Conflicts);
    ?>
```

2. This code block represents the closing of the two recordsets. Because we want to make one of those recordsets, `Conflicts`, conditional, you must separate the single block into two, like this:

(PHP) ```
<?php
    mysql_free_result($Rooms);
    ?>
    <?php
    mysql_free_result($Conflicts);
    ?>
```

3. Select the second of the two blocks.

4. Now wrap conditional code around the second code block, which clears the Conflicts recordset.

      📖 From the Snippets panel, insert the **Recipes > ConferenceRoom > CustomCode_PHP > If Statement – Only on Insert** snippet.

   Before:

   (PHP)
   ```php
   <?php if (isset($_POST['MM_update'])) { ?>
   ```

   After:

   ```php
   <?php } ?>
   ```

5. Save your page.

Step 8: Hand Code *If* Statements for *Inserted* Recordset

The final step to complete this page is to make the Inserted recordset conditional, as we did with the Conflicts recordset. However, the Inserted recordset does not need to be moved. In this instance, the conditional code is combined with redirection code that, after a successful record insertion, redirects the user to a confirmation page. The redirection code passes the ID of the new record through a URL parameter. PHP users will be able to take advantage of some built-in functionality and only need add a single function after the record insert code. Finally, ASP users will also need to make the code section that expressly closes the Inserted recordset conditional.

For ASP and ColdFusion

1. From the Server Behaviors panel, select the **Inserted** recordset.

   Selecting the recordset in the Server Behaviors panel highlights a portion of the relevant code.

   ASP users will also need to select the code block defining the SQL parameter, **NameParam**.

2. In Code view, select the following code:

   (VB)
   ```vb
   <%
       Dim Inserted__NameParam
       Inserted__NameParam = "test"
       If (Request.Form("MeetingName") <> "") Then
         Inserted__NameParam = Request.Form("MeetingName")
       End If
   %>
   <%
   ```

   Continues

```
          Dim Inserted
          Dim Inserted_numRows

          Set Inserted = Server.CreateObject("ADODB.Recordset")
          Inserted.ActiveConnection = MM_Recipes_STRING
          Inserted.Source = "SELECT TOP 1 ConferenceID  FROM Conferences
          ➥WHERE ConferenceName = '" + Replace(Inserted__NameParam,
          ➥"'", "''") + "'  ORDER BY ConferenceID DESC"
          Inserted.CursorType = 0
          Inserted.CursorLocation = 2
          Inserted.LockType = 1
          Inserted.Open()

          Inserted_numRows = 0
          %>
```

(JS)
```
          <%
          var Inserted__NameParam = "test";
          if (String(Request.Form("MeetingName") ) != "undefined" &&
              String(Request.Form("MeetingName") ) != "") {
            Inserted__NameParam = String(Request.Form("MeetingName") );
          }
          %>
          <%
          var Inserted = Server.CreateObject("ADODB.Recordset");
          Inserted.ActiveConnection = MM_Recipes_STRING;
          Inserted.Source = "SELECT TOP 1 ConferenceID  FROM Conferences
          ➥WHERE ConferenceName = '"+ Inserted__NameParam.replace
          ➥(/'/g, "''") + "'  ORDER BY ConferenceID DESC  ";
          Inserted.CursorType = 0;
          Inserted.CursorLocation = 2;
          Inserted.LockType = 1;
          Inserted.Open();
          var Inserted_numRows = 0;
          %>
```

(CF)
```
          <cfquery name="Inserted" datasource="Recipes">
          SELECT TOP 1 ConferenceID FROM Conferences
          ➥WHERE ConferenceName = '#FORM.MeetingName#'
          ORDER BY ConferenceID DESC
          </cfquery>
```

3. Wrap the following code around the selection:

   📖 From the Snippets panel, open the **Recipes > ConferenceRoom > Custom Code**
   folder for your server model and insert the **Redirect after Insert** snippet.

Before:

(VB)
```
<%
If (CStr(Request("MM_insert")) = "MeetingRequest") Then
%>
```

After:

```
<%
if (NOT Inserted.EOF) Then    Response.Redirect
➥("meeting_details.asp?ID=" &
Inserted.Fields("ConferenceID").value)
end if
%>
<%
end if
%>
```

Before:

(JS)
```
<%
if (String(Request("MM_insert")) == "MeetingRequest") {
%>
```

After:

```
<%
Response.Redirect("meeting_details.asp?ID="+Inserted.Fields
➥("ConferenceID").value);
}
%>
```

Before:

(CF)
```
<cfif IsDefined("FORM.MM_InsertRecord") AND FORM.MM_InsertRecord
➥EQ "MeetingRequest">
```

After:

```
<cflocation url="meeting_details.cfm?ID=#Inserted.ConferenceID#">
</cfif>
```

The final action for this page is to apply a conditional statement to the code block that explictly closes the Inserted recordset, found at the bottom of the page, so that it will be executed only if the record is inserted. Please note that this is a ASP-only step.

1. In Code view, move to the bottom of the page and select the code block that closes the Conflicts recordset. The code will look like this:

(VB)
```
<%
Inserted.Close()
Set Inserted = Nothing
%>
```

(JS)
```
<%
Inserted.Close();
%>
```

2. Wrap the following code around the selection:

   📖 From the Snippets panel, open the **Recipes > ConferenceRoom > Custom Code** folder for your server model and insert the **If Statement - Only on Insert** snippet.

   Before:

   (VB)
```
<%
If (CStr(Request("MM_insert")) = "MeetingRequest") Then
%>
```

   After:
```
<%
end if
%>
```

   Before:

   (JS)
```
<%
if (String(Request("MM_insert")) == "MeetingRequest") {
%>
```

   After:
```
<%
}
%>
```

3. Save your page.

To make sure that the date validation is working, enter a partial date such as month or day when testing in a browser. You can test the error message handling in Live Data view by entering **badDate=true** in the URL parameter field of the Live Data toolbar. Note that no question mark is necessary because the form uses the POST method rather than GET [r3-4].

NOTE | ASP–VBScript and ColdFusion developers will notice that the year is optional; this is a result of the Access function that considers any date with just the day and month to be in the current year.

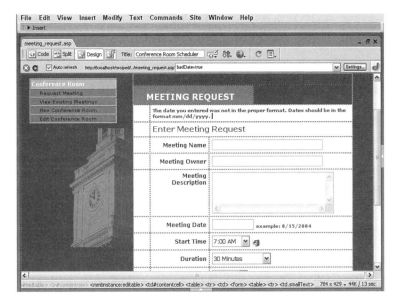

r3-4

For PHP

1. From the Server Behaviors panel, select the **Insert Record** command.
2. In Code view, position your cursor after the selected code block.
3. Insert the following code:

   📖 From the Snippets panel, insert the **Recipes > ConferenceRoomScheduler > CustomCode_PHP > Redirect After Insert** snippet.

   (PHP)
   ```php
   <?php
   if (isset($_POST['MM_insert'])) {
     $url = "meeting_details.php?ID=".mysql_insert_id();
     header("Location: $url");
   }
   ?>
   ```

4. Save your page.

End User Recipe: Meeting Conflict

After the user submits the meeting request, the data source is checked to see if a conflicting meeting is already scheduled. If so, the meeting_conflict page is displayed with an error message and details of the existing meeting. From this page, the user is advised to return to the meeting_request form and modify the request.

All the data-driven elements on the meeting_conflict page come from a single recordset. The recordset's filter is based on a URL parameter passed by the meeting_request page.

Step 1: Implement Meeting Conflict Design

No form is needed for the meeting_conflict page; only a series of dynamic text elements are used.

1. Create a basic dynamic page, either by hand or derived from a template.

   📖 In the **ConferenceRoomScheduler** folder, locate the folder for your server model and open the meeting_conflict page found there.

2. Add a table to the content region of your page to contain the interface elements for the application.

   📖 From the Snippets panel, drag the **Recipes > ConferenceRoom > Wireframes > Meeting Conflict - Wireframe** snippet into the Content editable region.

3. Add the table area to hold the dynamic text for the conflicting record details and an informative error message.

   📖 Place your cursor in the row below the words MEETING CONFLICT and insert the **Recipes > ConferenceRoom > ContentTables > Meeting Conflict - Content Table** snippet [r3-5].

r3-5

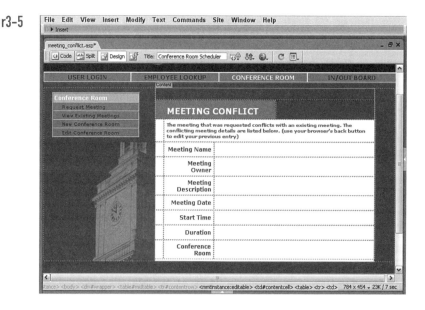

4. Save the file in your site.

> **Recipe Variation: Adding a Return to Form Button**
>
> Although it's perfectly fine to advise the user to select his or her browser's Back button to return to the previous form, some developers might want to provide a dedicated button for this functionality. As described in Recipe 1, a bit of JavaScript—history.back()—added to the onClick event of a form button, either directly in the tag or through the Call Javascript behavior, works quite well.

Step 2: Add Database Components

Only one data source is required for this page: a recordset containing only the conference details of the just-entered record. For ASP and ColdFusion, this recordset uses a view that combines the Conferences and Rooms tables as well as two formatted data source fields, StartDate and StartTime and one calculated one, ConferenceEnd. Here's the SQL statement used to construct the view:

```
SELECT Conferences.ConferenceID, Rooms.RoomName, Rooms.RoomID,
Rooms.RoomDescription, Conferences.ConferenceName,
Conferences.ConferenceDescription, Conferences.ConferenceStart,
Conferences.ConferenceDuration, Conferences.ConferenceBy,
Format([ConferenceStart],'h:nn ampm') AS StartTime,
Format([ConferenceStart],'m/dd/yyyy') AS StartDate,
DateAdd('n',([ConferenceDuration]*60),[ConferenceStart])
AS ConferenceEnd
FROM Conferences INNER JOIN Rooms ON Conferences.ConferenceRoom =
Rooms.RoomID;
```

Because Dreamweaver makes views as accessible as tables, this complex SQL statement can be added through the simple Recordset dialog for ASP and ColdFusion developers.

PHP users must take a different route because views are unsupported in MySQL.

For ASP and ColdFusion

1. From the Bindings panel, choose Add (+) and select **Recordset (Query)**.
2. In the simple Recordset dialog, enter an appropriate name.
   - 📖 Enter **Conferences** in the Name field.
3. Select the desired data source connection.
   - 📖 Choose **Recipes** from the Connection (Data Source) list.

4. Choose the needed view.

    📖 From the Tables list, select **ConferenceDisplay**.

5. Leaving the Columns option set to All, set the four Filter list elements like this:

ConferenceID	= (Equals)
URL Parameter	ID

6. Keep the Sort option set to None and click OK to close the dialog.

For PHP

PHP users have two hurdles to overcome when defining this recordset. First, we'll have to compensate for the lack of view support in MySQL. This is accomplished fairly easily by using a custom SQL statement. Second, Dreamweaver's implementation of PHP code requires a work-around. Unfortunately, the Dreamweaver MX 2004 MySQL engine does not support complex date and time formatting, such as DATE_FORMAT (conferences.ConferenceStart,'%m/%d/%Y'), which converts the string returned by ConferenceStart field to a month/day/year format. To get around this issue, we'll insert a pseudo recordset and then replace the code that Dreamweaver writes a bit later.

    📖 To prepare for this step, right-click (Control-click) on the **Recipes > ConferenceRoom > SQL > Meeting Conflict - Fake PHP SQL Statement** snippet and select the **Copy Snippet** command.

1. From the Bindings panel, choose Add (+) and select **Recordset (Query)** from the list.

2. In the advanced Recordset dialog, enter an appropriate name for the recordset.

    📖 Enter **Conferences** in the Recordset field.

3. Choose the desired data source.

    📖 Select **Recipes** from the Connections list.

4. Enter the proper SQL statement:

    📖 In the SQL area, press Ctrl-V (Command-V) to paste the code copied from the snippet.

    (PHP)
```
SELECT
    conferences.ConferenceID, rooms.RoomName, rooms.RoomID,
    rooms.RoomDescription, conferences.ConferenceName,
    conferences.ConferenceDescription, conferences.ConferenceStart,
    conferences.ConferenceDuration, conferences.ConferenceBy,
    conferences.ConferenceStart AS StartTime,
```

```
conferences.ConferenceStart
AS StartDate, conferences.ConferenceDuration
AS ConferenceEnd
FROM conferences, rooms
WHERE
conferences.ConferenceRoom = rooms.RoomID
AND
conferences.ConferenceID = 'IDParam'
```

5. In the Variables section, choose Add (+) and enter the following details in the Add Parameter dialog:

Name:	IDParam
Default Value:	0
Run-time Value:	$_GET['ID']

6. Click OK to close the dialog and insert the recordset.

7. Save your page.

This temporary recordset will enable us to complete the next step in the recipe—binding the data to the page—after which we will replace the temporary code with the actual code.

Step 3: Data Binding Process

Data binding for the `meeting_conflict` page is very straightforward. After the recordset has been defined, all that remains to complete that operation is to put seven dynamic text elements in place.

> **NOTE** PHP users need to complete one additional action after the data–binding step is done.

1. From the Bindings panel, expand the **Conferences** recordset.
2. Place the data source fields onto the page in their respective areas:
   - Drag **ConferenceName** to the cell next to the Meeting Name label.

   Drag **ConferenceBy** to the cell next to the Meeting Owner label.

   Drag **ConferenceDescription** to the cell next to the Meeting Description label.

   Drag **StartDate** to the cell next to the Meeting Date label.

   Drag **StartTime** to the cell next to the Start Time label.

   Drag **ConferenceDuration** to the cell next to the Duration label.

   Drag **RoomName** to the cell next to the Conference Room label.
3. Save the page when you're done.

To test this page, browse to meeting_request and enter information for a new meeting that conflicts with an existing meeting. Remember, the room as well as the date and time must conflict to display the meeting_conflict page [r3-6].

r3-6

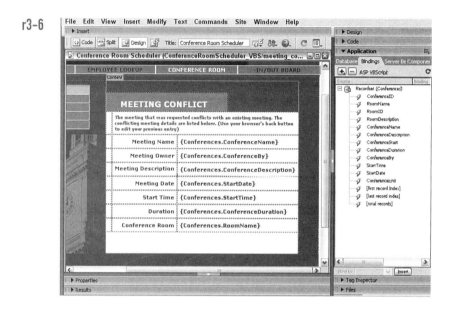

There's one more chore for PHP users before this page is ready. With the data fields properly placed on the page, we can substitute the pseudo-code with the actual code for the Conferences recordset.

1. From the Server Behaviors panel, select the **Conferences** recordset.
2. In Code view, select and cut the unneeded section of the recordset:

```
$query_Conferences = sprintf("SELECT  conferences.ConferenceID,
rooms.RoomName, rooms.RoomID, rooms.RoomDescription,
conferences.ConferenceName, conferences.ConferenceDescription,
conferences.ConferenceStart,  conferences.ConferenceDuration,
conferences.ConferenceBy, conferences.ConferenceStart
AS StartTime, conferences.ConferenceStart AS StartDate,
conferences.ConferenceDuration AS ConferenceEnd FROM conferences,
rooms WHERE  conferences.ConferenceRoom = rooms.RoomID
AND conferences.ConferenceID = '%s'", $IDParam_Conferences);
```

Although the code is quite long, if you have Automatic wrapping turned off in Preferences, it will appear as a single line.

3. Insert the replacement code:

    📖 From the Snippets panel, insert the **Recipes > ConferenceRoom > SQL > Meeting Conflict - Real PHP SQL Statement** snippet.

```
$query_Conferences = "SELECT conferences.ConferenceID,
rooms.RoomName, rooms.RoomID, rooms.RoomDescription,
conferences.ConferenceName, conferences.ConferenceDescription,
conferences.ConferenceStart,
TIME_FORMAT(conferences.ConferenceDuration,'%k:%i')
AS ConferenceDuration, conferences.ConferenceBy,
DATE_FORMAT(conferences.ConferenceStart,'%k:%i %p') AS StartTime,
DATE_FORMAT(conferences.ConferenceStart,'%c/%d/%Y') AS StartDate,
(INTERVAL HOUR(conferences.ConferenceDuration) HOUR +
INTERVAL MINUTE(conferences.ConferenceDuration) MINUTE +
conferences.ConferenceStart) AS ConferenceEnd FROM conferences,
rooms WHERE conferences.ConferenceRoom = rooms.RoomID
AND conferences.ConferenceID = " . $IDParam_Conferences;
```

4. Save your page.

The PHP page is now ready for testing.

End User Recipe: Meeting Details

If a meeting request is successful and no conflicting meetings are found, a confirmation page is displayed. The meeting_details page is almost identical to the meeting_conflict page—even down to the recordset—with two important differences. First, on the meeting_details page, there is no error message to inform the user of a problem, and second, a link is provided so that the record details can be edited.

This page is also available through the search meetings application discussed later in this recipe.

> **NOTE**
>
> For the sake of completeness, all the steps for creating the meeting_details page are presented here. However, you could save a fair amount of work by opening the meeting_conflict page and saving it as meeting_details. Then, all you would need to do is change the text on the page from Meeting Conflict to Meeting Detail, remove the error message, and add the link to the edit_meetingrequest page.

Step 1: Implement Meeting Details Design

The meeting_details page uses only a series of dynamic text elements and a link to an edit page.

1. Create a basic dynamic page, either by hand or derived from a template.

      ⚏ In the **ConferenceRoomScheduler** folder, locate the folder for your server model and open the `meeting_details` page found there.

2. Add a table to the content region of your page to contain the interface elements for the application.

      ⚏ From the Snippets panel, drag the **Recipes > ConferenceRoom > Wireframes > Meeting Details - Wireframe** snippet into the Content editable region.

3. Add the table area to hold the dynamic text for the record details and a link to a page for modifying the record.

      ⚏ Place your cursor in the row below the words MEETING DETAILS and insert the **Recipes > ConferenceRoom > ContentTables > Meeting Details - Content Table** snippet [r3-7].

r3-7

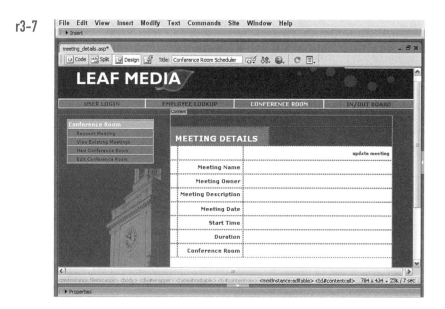

4. Be sure to save the file before proceeding.

Step 2: Add Database Components

As with the `meeting_conflict` page, only one data source is required for this page. In fact, it's the same recordset based on the same view and filtered in the same way. Accordingly, the setup is different for the various server models.

For ASP and ColdFusion

1. From the Bindings panel, choose Add (+) and select **Recordset (Query)**.

2. In the simple Recordset dialog, enter an appropriate name.

   📖 Enter **Conferences** in the Name field.

3. Select the desired data source connection.

   📖 Choose **Recipes** from the Connection (Data Source) list.

4. Choose the needed view.

   📖 From the Tables list, select **ConferenceDisplay**.

5. Leaving the Columns option set to All, set the four Filter list elements like this:

If you've already created the meeting_ conflict page and want to save yourself some work, you can copy the existing recordset and use it on this page. To do this, open the meeting_conflict page and, from the Bindings panel, select the Conferences recordset. Then choose Copy from the panel options menu. Next, switch to the meeting_details page and, again in the Bindings panel, choose Paste from the panel options menu. The Conferences recordset should appear, and you're ready to move on to the next step.

NOTE

ConferenceID	= (Equals)
URL Parameter	ID

6. Keep the Sort option set to None and click OK to close the dialog.

For PHP

Again, PHP users have two obstacles to overcome when defining this recordset: the lack of views in MySQL and the date formatting incompatibilities with the Dreamweaver server model implementation. As with the previous recipe, a temporary recordset is first created to allow placement of the data fields. After that step is accomplished, the proper code is inserted.

📖 To prepare for this step, right-click (Control-click) on the **Recipes > ConferenceRoom > SQL > Meeting Conflict - Fake PHP SQL Statement** snippet and select the **Copy Snippet** command.

1. From the Bindings panel, choose Add (+) and select **Recordset (Query)** from the list.

2. In the advanced Recordset dialog, enter an appropriate name for the recordset.

   📖 Enter **Conferences** in the Recordset field.

3. Choose the desired data source.

   📖 Select **Recipes** from the Connections list.

4. Enter the proper SQL statement:

   📖 In the SQL area, press Ctrl-V (Command-V) to paste the code copied from the snippet.

```
(PHP)  SELECT
         conferences.ConferenceID, rooms.RoomName, rooms.RoomID,
         rooms.RoomDescription, conferences.ConferenceName,
         conferences.ConferenceDescription, conferences.ConferenceStart,
         conferences.ConferenceDuration, conferences.ConferenceBy,
         conferences.ConferenceStart AS StartTime,
         conferences.ConferenceStart AS StartDate,
         conferences.ConferenceDuration AS ConferenceEnd
         FROM conferences, rooms
         WHERE
         conferences.ConferenceRoom = rooms.RoomID
         AND
         conferences.ConferenceID = 'IDParam'
```

5. In the Variables section, choose Add (+) and enter the following details in the Add Parameter dialog:

Name:	IDParam
Default Value:	0
Run-time Value:	$_GET['ID']

6. Click OK to close the dialog and insert the recordset.
7. Save your page.

Step 3: Data Binding Process

With the recordset defined, you're ready to incorporate the seven dynamic text elements.

1. From the Bindings panel, expand the **Conferences** recordset.
2. Place the data source fields onto the page in their respective areas:
   - Drag **ConferenceName** to the cell next to the Meeting Name label.

   Drag **ConferenceBy** to the cell next to the Meeting Owner label.

   Drag **ConferenceDescription** to the cell next to the Meeting Description label.

   Drag **StartDate** to the cell next to the Meeting Date label.

   Drag **StartTime** to the cell next to the Start Time label.

   Drag **ConferenceDuration** to the cell next to the Duration label.

   Drag **Room Name** to the cell next to the Conference Room label.
3. Save your page.

As noted, PHP users have another task to complete before they can move on: the substitution of the temporary code with the actual code for the Conferences recordset.

1. From the Server Behaviors panel, select the **Conferences** recordset.
2. In Code view, select and cut the unneeded section of the recordset:

```
$query_Conferences = sprintf("SELECT  conferences.ConferenceID,
rooms.RoomName, rooms.RoomID, rooms.RoomDescription,
conferences.ConferenceName, conferences.ConferenceDescription,
conferences.ConferenceStart,  conferences.ConferenceDuration,
conferences.ConferenceBy, conferences.ConferenceStart
AS StartTime, conferences.ConferenceStart AS StartDate,
conferences.ConferenceDuration AS ConferenceEnd FROM conferences,
rooms WHERE  conferences.ConferenceRoom = rooms.RoomID
AND conferences.ConferenceID = '%s'", $IDParam_Conferences);
```

Although the code is quite long, if you have Automatic wrapping turned off in Preferences, it will appear as a single line.

3. Insert the replacement code:

   📖 From the Snippets panel, insert the **Recipes > ConferenceRoom > SQL > Meeting Conflict - Real PHP SQL Statement** snippet.

```
$query_Conferences = "SELECT conferences.ConferenceID,
rooms.RoomName, rooms.RoomID, rooms.RoomDescription,
conferences.ConferenceName, conferences.ConferenceDescription,
conferences.ConferenceStart,
TIME_FORMAT(conferences.ConferenceDuration,'%k:%i')
AS ConferenceDuration, conferences.ConferenceBy,
DATE_FORMAT(conferences.ConferenceStart,'%k:%i %p') AS StartTime,
DATE_FORMAT(conferences.ConferenceStart,'%c/%d/%Y') AS StartDate,
(INTERVAL HOUR(conferences.ConferenceDuration) HOUR +
INTERVAL MINUTE(conferences.ConferenceDuration) MINUTE +
conferences.ConferenceStart) AS ConferenceEnd FROM conferences,
rooms WHERE conferences.ConferenceRoom = rooms.RoomID
AND conferences.ConferenceID = " . $IDParam_Conferences;
```

4. Save your page.

PHP developers will notice some out-of-the-norm Dreamweaver behavior at this point: The Conferences recordset will no longer be available from the Bindings panel. This is the unfortunate side effect of replacing the code—which was necessary to get the desired functionality. The current PHP server model implementation uses the sprintf() function to insert values into strings, and the %s pointers that mark the variable values clash with MySQL formatting techniques.

We're now ready for the next step: linking to a record edit page.

Step 4: Link to Update Meeting

The final step for the `meeting_detail` page is to provide a way for users to change the details if they see a problem. To accomplish this, we link to an update page and pass the ID number as a URL argument.

For ASP and ColdFusion

1. Select the text or image you want to use as a link.

   📖 Select the text **update meeting** in the top row of the content table.

2. From the Property inspector, choose **Browse for File**, the folder icon next to the Link field.

3. In the Select File dialog, choose the file you want to handle the update.

   📖 Choose **edit_meetingrequest**.

4. Select **Parameters** from the Select File dialog.

5. In the Parameters dialog, enter **ID** under the Value column.

6. Under the Value column, select the lightning symbol to open the Dynamic Data dialog and choose **ConferenceID** [r3-8].

r3-8

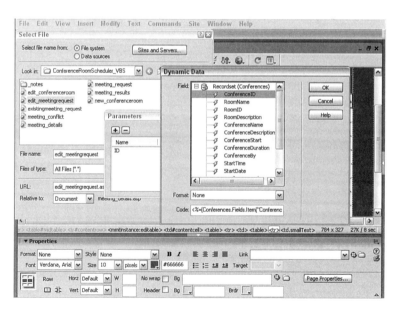

7. Click OK to close the Dynamic Data, Parameters, and Select File dialogs.

8. Save the page.

The meeting_details page is now ready for testing. To test this page, request a new meeting that does not conflict with an existing one. After the meeting request is added to the data source, this page—the meeting details—is presented.

For PHP

Instead of using the Dynamic Data dialog to assign parameters to the link to the meeting_details page, we'll need to hand-code it for PHP.

1. Select the text or image you want to use as a link.

   (PHP) Select the text **update meeting** in the top row of the content table.

2. From the Property inspector, enter the following code in the Link field:

   ```
   (PHP) edit_meetingrequest.php?ID=<?php echo
         ➥$row_Conferences['ConferenceID']; ?>
   ```

3. Save your page.

End User Recipe: Edit Meeting Request

After a meeting has been scheduled, changes are all but inevitable, and users need a way to update an existing meeting. The Edit Meeting Request page offers a familiar layout—identical to that of the Meeting Request page—with similar error checking routines. This page verifies that no meeting has been scheduled that conflicts with the updated time and place and makes sure that the entered date is valid.

Step 1: Implement Edit Meeting Request Design

The meeting edit request page uses a series of form text fields (both single line and text areas) to display the descriptive details of the current record entries and enable them to be edited. The time and place data is handled through drop-down lists that are preset to the record's values.

> **NOTE**
> ColdFusion and PHP users will need to add an additional hidden form field for the update operation as described in the following steps.

1. Create a basic dynamic page, either by hand or derived from a template.

   📖 In the **ConferenceRoomScheduler** folder, locate the folder for your server model and open the edit_meetingrequest page found there.

2. Add a table to the content region of your page to contain the heading and interface elements for the application.

   ☐ From the Snippets panel, drag the **Recipes > ConferenceRoom > Wireframes > Edit Meeting Request - Wireframe** snippet into the Content editable region.

3. Within the table, place another HTML table to hold the form and its elements: three text fields (meeting name, owner, and date), one text area for the description, three drop-down lists (start time, duration, and conference room), and a submit button. You'll also need a hidden field used to combine the date and time entries.

(ASP) (CF) ASP and ColdFusion users: Place your cursor in the row below the words EDIT MEETING REQUEST and insert the **Recipes > ConferenceRoom > Forms > Edit Meeting Request Form** snippet [r3-9].

(PHP) PHP users: Place your cursor in the row below the words EDIT MEETING REQUEST and insert the **Recipes > ConferenceRoom > Forms > Edit Meeting Request Form (PHP)** snippet.

r3-9

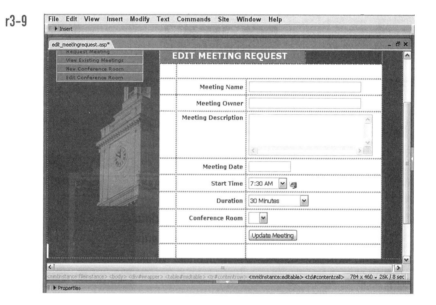

4. If necessary, add a hidden form field to convey a unique record identifier when updating the record.

(CF) (PHP) ColdFusion and PHP Users: From the Forms category of the Insert bar, add a Hidden Field form element to the left of the form button and, in the Property inspector, name the hidden field element **ConferenceID**.

5. Make sure the method attribute of the `<form>` tag is set to **POST** and save the page.

Step 2: Add Database Components, Part 1

As with the meeting request page, three recordsets are used for this page: Rooms, Conflicts, and Conferences. The three recordsets are similar to those used earlier, but with key differences because we are now working with an existing record.

Again, we'll take the simplest recordset first, Rooms.

1. From the Server Behaviors panel, choose Add (+) and select **Recordset (Query)**.
2. In simple view, enter the name of the recordset.
    - Enter **Rooms** in the Name field.
3. Select the data source connection.
    - Choose **Recipes** from the Connection (Data Source) list.
4. Choose the table to work with.
    - Select **Rooms** (**rooms** for PHP) from the Table list.
5. Limit your data source columns to only those that are needed.
    - Choose the Selected Columns option and highlight **RoomID** and **RoomName**.
6. Leave the Filter option set to None.
7. Set the Sort option to present an alphabetical listing of the rooms.
    - Choose **RoomName** from the Sort list and accept the **Ascending** order.
8. Verify your choices and click OK when you're done.

The Conference recordset found here is quite different from the Inserted recordset in the Meeting Request page. First, rather than working with an ID from a just-entered record, the recordset is filtered on the ID passed from the meeting_details page. In addition, the record's date/time field is formatted into two separate fields—one that just holds the date and another for the time. These values will be associated with their corresponding lists later.

For ASP

- Due to the complexity of this SQL statement, it is included as a snippet, **Recipes > ConferenceRoom > SQL > Conference RS - ASP SQL Statement**. Copy the snippet to the clipboard by using the **Copy Snippet** command from the Snippets panel context menu.

1. From the Server Behaviors panel, choose Add (+) and select **Recordset (Query)**.
2. Switch to the advanced view of the dialog and enter an appropriate name for the recordset.
    - Enter **Conference** into the Name field.

3. Choose the connection for the recordset.

    📖 Select **Recipes** from the Connection list.

4. In the SQL area, enter the following code:

    📖 Paste in the copied SQL statement.

```
SELECT *, Format(ConferenceStart,'m/dd/yyyy') AS StartDate,
➥Format(ConferenceStart,'h:nn ampm') AS StartTime
FROM Conferences
WHERE ConferenceID = ColParam
```

5. In the Variable area, choose Add (+) and enter **ColParam** under the Name column.

6. In the Default Value column, enter **1**.

7. In the Run-time Value column, enter **Request.QueryString("ID")** and click OK to close the dialog.

8. Save the page.

For ColdFusion

    📖 Due to the complexity of this SQL statement, it is included as a snippet, **Recipes > ConferenceRoom > SQL > Conference RS - CFML SQL Statement**. Copy the snippet to the clipboard by using the Copy Snippet command from the Snippets panel context menu.

1. From the Server Behaviors panel, choose Add (+) and select **Recordset (Query)**.

2. Switch to the advanced view of the dialog and enter an appropriate name for the recordset.

    📖 Enter **Conference** in the Name field.

3. Choose your data source.

    📖 Select **Recipes** from the Data Source list.

4. Enter a user name and password if necessary.

5. In the SQL area, enter the following code:

    📖 Paste in the copied SQL statement.

```
SELECT *, Format(ConferenceStart,'m/dd/yyyy') AS StartDate,
➥Format(ConferenceStart,'h:nn ampm') AS StartTime
FROM Conferences
WHERE ConferenceID = #URL.ID#
```

6. In the Page Parameter section, choose Add (+) and, in the Add Parameter dialog, make sure **URL.ID** is chosen in the Name list.

7. Enter **0** as the Default Value and click OK to close the dialog.

8. Verify your entries in the Recordset dialog and click OK to close that dialog.

9. Save the page.

For PHP

Integrating the proper MySQL code into Dreamweaver requires several steps. A record-set is first created using custom SQL code, and then an additional date conversion function is added to the top of the page. Later, another function will be incorporated to complete the needed conversions.

  📖 Due to the complexity of this SQL statement, it is included as a snippet, **Recipes > ConferenceRoom > SQL > Conference RS - PHP SQL Statement**. Copy the snippet to the clipboard by using the Copy Snippet command from the Snippets panel context menu.

1. From the Server Behaviors panel, choose Add (+) and select **Recordset (Query)**.

2. Switch to the advanced view of the dialog and enter an appropriate name for the recordset.

  📖 Enter **Conference** into the Name field.

3. Choose the connection for the recordset.

  📖 Select **Recipes** from the Connection list.

4. In the SQL area, enter the following code:

  📖 Paste in the copied SQL statement.

```
SELECT ConferenceID, ConferenceRoom, ConferenceName,
➥ConferenceDescription,ConferenceDuration,ConferenceBy,
➥UNIX_TIMESTAMP(ConferenceStart) AS ConferenceStart,
➥DATE_FORMAT(ConferenceStart,'DateFormatParam') AS StartDate,
➥DATE_FORMAT(ConferenceStart,'TimeFormatParam') AS StartTime
FROM Conferences
WHERE ConferenceID = ColParam
```

Next we'll need to add three variables: **ColParam, DateFormatParam**, and **TimeParam**.

5. In the Variable area, choose Add (+) and enter the following values in the Add Variable dialog:

Name:	ColParam
Default Value:	1
Runtime Value:	$_GET['ID']

6. Close the Add Variable dialog and choose Add (+) again to add the second variable with these values:

Name:	DateFormatParam
Default Value:	%c/%d/%Y
Runtime Value:	$dateFormat

7. Close the Add Variable dialog again and choose Add (+) one last time to add the third variable with these values:

Name:	TimeFormatParam
Default Value:	%H:%i:00
Runtime Value:	$timeFormat

8. Click OK once to close the Add Variable dialog and again to close Recordset dialog.

Before we continue, let's add the first of our support functions for converting the date and time formats properly.

1. In Code view, place your cursor at the top of the page, after the code that begins `<?php require_once`.
2. Insert the following code:

   📖 From the Snippets panel, insert the **Recipes > ConferenceRoom > CustomCode_PHP > Date and Time Formats** snippet.

   ```php
   <?php
   $dateFormat = '%c/%d/%Y';
   $timeFormat = '%H:%i:00';
   ?>
   ```

3. Save the page.

Step 3: Add Database Components, Part 2

The final recordset is used to check for a conflicting meeting. Although similar to the Conflicts recordset developed for the Meeting Request page, this recordset employs an additional parameter to filter out the current record being updated. Because the Macromedia Update Record server behavior is being used on the page, we work with the MM_recordId variable.

For ASP

    📖 The SQL statement for this recordset is available to be copied using the previously described techniques at **Recipes > ConferenceRoom > SQL > Edit Meeting - ASP Conflicts RS SQL Statement**

1. From the Server Behaviors panel, choose Add (+) and select **Recordset (Query).**

2. Switch to the advanced view of the dialog and enter an appropriate name for the recordset.

    📖 Enter **Conflicts** into the Name field.

3. Choose the connection for the recordset.

    📖 Select **Recipes** from the Connection list.

4. In the SQL area, enter the following code:

    📖 Press Ctrl-V (Command-V) to paste in the copied snippet.

```
SELECT TOP 1 ConferenceID
FROM ConferenceDisplay
WHERE RoomID = RoomParam AND ((ConferenceID <> IDParam) AND
➥((ConferenceStart <= #DateParam# AND ConferenceEnd > #DateParam#)
➥OR (ConferenceStart < DateAdd('n',DurationParam*60,#DateParam#)
AND ConferenceStart >= #DateParam#)))
```

5. In the Variable area, choose Add (+) and enter **DateParam** under the Name column.

6. In the Default Value column, enter **1/1/1975**.

7. In the Run-time Value column, enter **Request.Form("FullDate")**.

8. Add another variable by choosing Add (+) and enter **DurationParam** under the name catalog.

9. In the Default Value column, enter **0**.

10. In the Run-time Value column, enter **Request.Form("Duration")**.

11. Add one last variable by choosing Add (+) and enter **IDParam** under the name catalog.

12. In the Default Value column, enter **0**.

13. In the Run-time Value column, enter **Request.Form("MM_recordId")** and click OK to close the dialog.

14. Choose Add (+) to insert one more variable and enter **RoomParam** under the Name column

15. In the Default Value column, enter **0**.

16. In the Run-time Value column, enter **Request.Form("ConferenceRoom")** and click OK to close the dialog.

17. Save the page.

For ColdFusion

Because the SQL statement for this recordset is quite complex, it is included as a snippet. However, you can't insert a snippet into a Dreamweaver dialog directly, but ColdFusion enables us to insert it directly within a <cfquery> tag pair. To accomplish this, we'll insert the tag from the Insert bar rather than use the Recordset dialog. To complete this ColdFusion recordset, several <cfparam> tags will also have to be added.

1. From Code view, position your cursor after the initial <cfparam> tag near the top of the document.
2. From the CFML category of the Insert bar, choose the **cfquery** object to open the Tag Editor.
3. In the General category of the Tag Editor, name the query appropriately.
   - Enter **Conflicts** in the Query Name field.
4. Choose your data source.
   - Enter **Recipes** in the Data Source field.
5. Enter a user name and password if necessary and choose OK to close the dialog.
6. Make sure your cursor is positioned within the <cfquery> tag pair and enter the following code:
   - From the Snippets panel, insert the **Recipes > ConferenceRoom > SQL > Edit Meeting - CFML Conflicts RS SQL Statement** snippet.

```
SELECT TOP 1 ConferenceID
FROM ConferenceDisplay
WHERE RoomID = #FORM.ConferenceRoom#
AND (ConferenceID <> #FORM.ConferenceID# AND ((ConferenceStart <=
➥#CreateODBCDateTime(FORM.FullDate)# AND ConferenceEnd >
➥#CreateODBCDateTime(FORM.FullDate)#) OR (ConferenceStart <
➥DateAdd('n',#FORM.Duration#*60,#CreateODBCDateTime(FORM.FullDate)#)
AND ConferenceStart >= #CreateODBCDateTime(FORM.FullDate)#)))
```

The CreateODBCDateTime() functions are used to convert the date values to ODBC driver compatible versions.

To complete this recordset, we need to create a CFParam for each of the four variables used in the SQL statement. There is no need to declare a type for any of these CFParam statements.

1. From the Bindings panel, choose Add (+) and select **CFParam**.
2. In the CFParam dialog, enter **FORM.FullDate** in the Name list.
3. Enter **1/1/1975** as the Default value and click OK to close the dialog.
4. From the Bindings panel, choose Add (+) and select **CFParam** to add another variable.
5. In the CFParam dialog, enter **FORM.Duration** in the Name list.

6. Enter 0 as the Default value and click OK to close the dialog.

7. From the Bindings panel, choose Add (+) and select **CFParam** to add the third variable.

8. In the CFParam dialog, enter **FORM.ConferenceID** is in the Name list.

   As you might recall, **ConferenceID** is the name of the hidden form element inserted earlier.

9. Enter 0 as the Default value and click OK to close the dialog.

10. From the Bindings panel, choose Add (+) and select **CFParam** to add the final variable.

11. In the CFParam dialog, enter **FORM.ConferenceRoom** in the Name list.

12. Enter 0 as the Default value and click OK to close the dialog.

13. Save the page.

All the CFParams and the Conflicts recordset should now be visible in the Binding panel.

For PHP

📕 The SQL statement for this recordset is available to be copied using the previously described techniques at **Recipes > ConferenceRoom > SQL > Edit Meeting - PHP Conflicts RS SQL Statement.**

1. From the Server Behaviors panel, choose Add (+) and select **Recordset (Query).**

2. Switch to the advanced view of the dialog and enter an appropriate name for the recordset.

   📕 Enter **Conflicts** into the Name field.

3. Choose the connection for the recordset.

   📕 Select **Recipes** from the Connection list.

4. In the SQL area, enter the following code:

   📕 Press Ctrl-V (Command-V) to paste in the copied snippet.

```
SELECT ConferenceID
FROM conferences,rooms
WHERE conferences.ConferenceRoom = rooms.RoomID
AND
ConferenceRoom = RoomParam
AND
ConferenceID != IDParam
AND
(UNIX_TIMESTAMP(ConferenceStart) = 'DateParam'
OR
UNIX_TIMESTAMP(ConferenceStart) = UNIX_TIMESTAMP(INTERVAL HOUR
➥('DurationParam')HOUR + INTERVAL MINUTE('DurationParam')
➥MINUTE + FROM_UNIXTIME('DateParam')))
```

5. In the Variable area, choose Add (+) and enter the following values in the Add
   Variable dialog:

Name:	DateParam
Default Value:	157766400
Runtime Value:	$_POST['FullDate']

Again, a Unix timestamp value is used to represent 1/1/1975.

6. Close the Add Variable dialog and choose Add (+) again to add the second variable with these values:

Name:	DurationParam
Default Value:	0
Runtime Value:	$_POST['Duration']

7. Close the Add Variable dialog again and choose Add (+) to add the third variable
   with these values:

Name:	IDParam
Default Value:	0
Runtime Value:	$_POST['ConferenceID']

8. Close the Add Variable dialog again and choose Add (+) one last time to add the
   fourth variable with these values:

Name:	RoomParam
Default Value:	0
Runtime Value:	$_POST['ConferenceRoom']

9. After closing the Add Variables dialog, click OK to close the Recordset dialog and
   then save the page.

Step 4: Data Binding Process

Time to put the just-created recordsets to work. The data binding for this page runs the gamut—a number of the form elements can be bound with fields dragged from the Bindings panel, one list element needs to have its values and labels data-bound while two others pick up their selected values dynamically, and another form element requires JavaScript behaviors to gather the data.

Let's start by binding the text and hidden fields to dynamic data.

1. From the Bindings panel, expand the **Conference** recordset.
2. Place the data source fields onto the page in their respective areas:

   📖 Drag **ConferenceName** onto the `MeetingName` text field.

   Drag **ConferenceBy** onto the `MeetingOwner` text field.

   Drag **ConferenceDescription** onto the `MeetingDescription` text field.

   Drag **StartDate** onto the `MeetingDate` text field.

   ASP and ColdFusion users: Drag **ConferenceStart** onto the hidden field `FullDate`.

3. PHP users must insert some custom code for the FullDate hidden form field.

   (PHP) Select the hidden form field and switch to Code view.

   Place the cursor inside the `input` tag, add a space, and insert this code:

   From the Snippets panel, insert the **Recipes > ConferenceRoom > CustomCode_PHP > Formatted ConferenceStart Column** snippet, which includes this code:

   (PHP)
   ```
   value="<?php echo date("n/d/Y
       H:i:00",$row_Conference['ConferenceStart']); ?>"
   ```

   This code snippet formats the `ConferenceStart` data properly.

4. Save your page.

When you're done with this part of the page, all the visible text elements should have corresponding data source fields [r3-10].

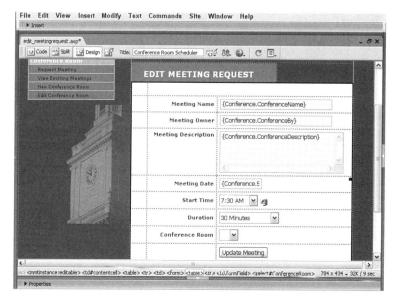

Now let's bind the appropriate data to the three list elements on the page. First we need to assign dynamic data fields to the selected list value so that the record is accurately reflected when the Edit Meeting Request page loads.

1. Select the **StartTime** list menu and click the Dynamic button on the Property inspector.

2. In the Dynamic List/Menu dialog, choose the lightning symbol next to the Set Selected Value To field to open the Dynamic Data dialog.

3. In the Dynamic Data dialog, choose **StartTime** from the Conference recordset and click OK twice to close the two dialogs.

    Now, we'll perform the same operation with the Duration list element.

4. Select the **Duration** list menu and click the Dynamic button on the Property inspector.

5. In the Dynamic List/Menu dialog, choose the lightning symbol next to the Set Selected Value To field to open the Dynamic Data dialog.

6. In the Dynamic Data dialog, choose **ConferenceDuration** from the Conference recordset and click OK twice to close the two dialogs.

    The final list element, Conference Room, is populated dynamically in addition to the selection being assigned dynamically. All these operations are handled in the Dynamic List/Menu dialog.

7. Select the **ConferenceRoom** list menu and click the Dynamic button on the Property inspector.

8. In the Dynamic List/Menu dialog, choose **Rooms** from the Options from Recordset list.

9. Set the `Values` list to **RoomID** and `Labels` to **RoomName**.

10. Choose the lightning symbol next to the Set Selected Value To field to open the Dynamic Data dialog [r3-11].

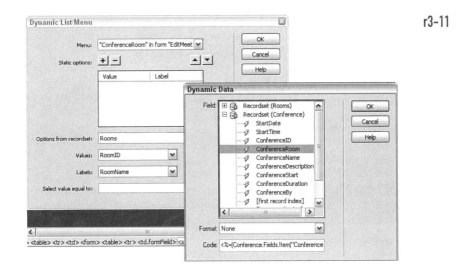

r3-11

11. In the Dynamic Data dialog, choose **ConferenceRoom** from the `Conference` record-set and click OK twice to close the two dialogs.

The final data-binding action for this page requires that a JavaScript behavior be applied to two form elements in order to populate a third. As on the Meeting Request page, the `FullDate` hidden field is populated by a combination of the values found in the `MeetingDate` and `StartTime` elements.

> **NOTE**
>
> The JavaScript function to be applied is fairly complex and is supplied as a snippet: Recipes > ConferenceRoom > Client JavaScript > EditMeeting – Populate FullDate Hidden Form Element. Copy the snippet to the clipboard through the Copy Snippet command. The same snippet is used in both behaviors.

1. Select the **MeetingDate** text field.

2. From the Behaviors panel, choose Add (+) and select **Call JavaScript**.

3. In the Call JavaScript dialog, enter the following code:

   📖 Paste the copied snippet into the JavaScript field.

```
document.EditMeetingRequest.FullDate.value =
➥document.EditMeetingRequest.MeetingDate.value +' '+
➥document.EditMeetingRequest.StartTime.options
➥document.EditMeetingRequest.StartTime.selectedIndex].value
```

4. After closing the Call JavaScript dialog, make sure the onBlur event is listed for the behavior in the Behaviors panel.

5. Select the **StartTime** list form element.

6. From the Behaviors panel, choose Add (+) and select **Call JavaScript**.

7. In the Call JavaScript dialog, enter the following code:

   📖 Paste the copied snippet into the JavaScript field.

   ```
   document.EditMeetingRequest.FullDate.value =
   ➥document.EditMeetingRequest.MeetingDate.value +' '+
   ➥document.EditMeetingRequest.StartTime.options
   ➥document.EditMeetingRequest.StartTime.selectedIndex].value
   ```

8. This time, after closing the Call JavaScript dialog, make sure the onChange event is listed for the behavior in the Behaviors panel.

9. Save the page.

Step 5: Update Record for Meeting Request

The next step is to add the standard Update Record server behavior. As with the Insert Record server behavior used on the Meeting Request page, two of the form fields are ignored on purpose, and the data is instead sent in a combined fashion through a hidden form element.

For ASP

1. From the Server Behaviors panel, choose Add (+) and then select **Update Record**.

2. In the Update Record dialog, select the desired data source connection.

   📖 Choose **Recipes** from the Connection list.

3. Choose the table containg the data you are updating.

   📖 From the Table to Update list, choose **Conferences**.

4. Choose the recordset from which to get data source fields.

   📖 From the Select Record From field, choose **Conference**.

5. Set the primary key for the recordset.

   📖 From the Unique Key Column list, choose **ConferenceID** and make sure the **Numeric** option is selected.

6. Select the file you want to appear when the update is complete.

   📖 For the After Updating, Go To field, select the **meeting_details.asp** page.

7. Choose the form on the page from which to get the values.

   📖 From the Get Values From list, choose **EditMeetingRequest**.

8. In the Form Elements area, set the form elements to their corresponding data source fields.

   📖 Set the `MeetingName` form element to update the `ConferenceName` data source field as Text.

   Set the `MeetingOwner` form element to update the `ConferenceBy` data source field as Text.

   Set the `MeetingDescription` form element to update the `ConferenceDescription` data source field as Text.

   Both `MeetingDate` and `StartTime` form elements are ignored.

   Set the `FullDate` form element to update the `ConferenceStart` data source field as Date MS Access.

   Set the `Duration` form element to update the `ConferenceDuration` data source field as Numeric.

   Set the `ConferenceRoom` form element to update the `ConferenceRoom` data source field as Numeric.

9. Make sure your entries are correct and then click OK to close [r3-12].

r3-12

10. Save the page.

For ColdFusion and PHP

1. From the Server Behaviors panel, choose Add (+) and select **Update Record**.

2. In the Update Record dialog, choose the current form.

   📖 Select **EditMeetingRequest** from the Submit Values From list.

3. Select your data source from the list.

      📖 Choose **Recipes** from the Data Source list.

4. Enter your user name and password, if needed.

5. Select the table in the data source to insert into from the list.

      📖 Choose **Conferences** (**conferences** in PHP) from the Insert Into Table list.

6. Set the data source fields to their corresponding form elements.

      📖 Set `ConferenceID` to the `FORM.ConferenceID` form element as Numeric type for ColdFusion and Integer type for PHP.

      Set `ConferenceRoom` to the `FORM.ConferenceRoom` form element and submit as Numeric type for ColdFusion and Integer type for PHP.

      Set `ConferenceName` to the `FORM.MeetingName` form element and submit as Text type.

      Set `ConferenceDescription` to the `FORM.MeetingDescription` form element and submit as Text type.

      Set `ConferenceStart` to the `FORM.FullDate` form element and submit as Date MS Access type for ColdFusion and Date type for PHP.

      Set `ConferenceDuration` to the `FORM.Duration` form element and submit as Numeric for ColdFusion and Double for PHP.

      Set `ConferenceBy` to the `FORM.MeetingOwner` form element and submit as Text type.

7. In the After Inserting, Go to field, enter the path to the file you want displayed after the record is updated.

      📖 Choose Browse and select the **meeting_details** file for your server model, and then select the **Pass Original Query String** option.

Step 6: Add Server-Side Date Validation

As on the Meeting Request page, we need to ensure that the user enters a date in the proper format. The date validation is handled in the same way with similar routines: one code block to redirect the page with an argument and another to present a message. The redirection code is added first.

NOTE | Again, a custom function is needed for those working with ASP-JavaScript and PHP/MySQL.

1. In Code view, place the cursor on a new line at the top of the page.

ASP users should position the cursor after the `<!-- include>` statement.

2. ASP-JS and PHP users only: insert the following code:

      📖 From the Snippets panel, open the **Custom Code_JS** folder under **Recipes > ConferenceRoom** and insert the **IsADate Function** snippet.

```
JS  <%
    function isADate(DateString)  {
      var DateRegex = /^(\d{1,2})\/(\d{1,2})\/(\d{4})$/
      var theMatch = DateString.match(DateRegex);
      var validDate = false;
      if (theMatch)  {
        var DateObj = new Date(DateString);
      if ((DateObj.getMonth()+1 == parseInt(theMatch[1])) &&
      ➥(DateObj.getDate() == parseInt(theMatch[2])) &&
      ➥(DateObj.getFullYear() == parseInt(theMatch[3])))
          validDate = true;
      }
      return validDate;
    }
    %>
```

```
PHP  <?php
     function isADate($DateString) {
       $validDate = false;
       if (ereg("^[0-9]{1,2}\/[0-9]{1,2}\/[0-9]{4}$",$DateString)) {
         $today = date("Y");
         $submittedDate = explode("/",$DateString);
         $month = $submittedDate[0];
         $day = $submittedDate[1];
         $year = $submittedDate[2];
         if ($year >= $today) {
           $validDate = (checkdate($month,$day,$year))?true:false;
         }
       }
       return $validDate;
     }
     ?>
```

3. Insert the following code:

    📖 From the Snippets panel, open the **Recipes > ConferenceRoom > Custom Code**
    folder for your server model and insert the **Edit Meeting Request - Date**
    Validation snippet.

```
VB  <%
    if (cStr(Request.Form("MeetingDate")) <> "")   then
      if not (isDate(Request.Form("MeetingDate"))) then
    ➥Response.Redirect("edit_meetingrequest.asp?ID=" &
    ➥Request("MM_recordId") & "&badDate=true")
      end if%>
```

```
JS  <%
    if (String(Request.Form("MeetingDate"))!="undefined" &&
    !isADate(String(Request.Form("MeetingDate")))))
    Response.Redirect("edit_meetingrequest.asp?ID=
    ➡"+Request("MM_recordId")+"&badDate=true");
    %>
```

```
CF  <cfif IsDefined("FORM.MeetingDate") AND NOT IsDate
    ➡(FORM.MeetingDate)>
     <cflocation
    url="edit_meetingrequest.cfm?ID=#FORM.ConferenceID#&badDate=true">
    </cfif>
```

```
PHP  <?php
     if ((isset($_POST['MeetingDate'])) && (!isADate
     ➡($_POST['MeetingDate']))) {
       $url = "edit_meetingrequest.php?ID=" .
       ➡$_POST['ConferenceID'] . "&badDate=true";
       header("Location: $url");
     }
     ?>
```

4. Save your page.

The next step is to add the error message that will be displayed should the URL variable badDate be present.

1. In Design view, place your cursor where you want the error message to appear.

   📖 Position the cursor in the table row above the Edit Meeting Request text.

2. Insert the following code:

   📖 From the Snippets panel, open the **Recipes > ConferenceRoom > Custom Code** folder for your server model and insert the **Date Error - Dynamic Text** snippet.

```
VB  <% if (cStr(Request.QueryString("badDate")) <> "") Then
    Response.Write("The date you entered was not in the proper
    format.  Dates should be in the format mm/dd/yyyy.%>
```

```
JS  <%=(String(Request.QueryString("badDate")) != "undefined")?
    "The date you entered was not in the proper format.  Dates should
    be in the format mm/dd/yyyy.":""%>
```

```
CF  <cfif isDefined("URL.badDate")>The date you entered was not in the
    proper format.  Dates should be in the format mm/dd/yyyy. </cfif>
```

```PHP
<?php
if (isset($_GET['badDate'])) {
  echo "The date you entered was not in the proper format.
  Dates should be in the format mm/dd/yyyy.";
}
?>
```

3. Save your page before continuing.

Step 7: Hand Code Edits to Handle Meeting Conflicts

Because we're using the Conflicts recordset as we did in the Meeting Request page, the same code manipulation implemented on that page is necessary on this one. To refresh your memory, there are four phases:

- Move the Conflicts recordset and its three parameter declarations above the Insert Record server behavior code.
- Add a redirect statement to the end of the Conflicts recordset if a conflict is found.
- Wrap all Conflicts recordset-associated code in a conditional statement so that it is executed only if the Insert Record operation is attempted.
- Wrap the code that closes the Conflicts recordset in a similar conditional statement.

The first operation is to move the Conflicts recordset code blocks.

1. From the Server Behaviors panel, select the **Conflicts** recordset.

   Selecting the recordset in the Server Behaviors panel highlights a portion of the relevant code.

2. In Code view, select the highlighted recordset and the four SQL parameter code blocks (for DateParam, DurationParam, IDParam, and RoomParam) above the recordset code and cut the entire selection. The code to select is:

```VB
<%
Dim Conflicts__DateParam
Conflicts__DateParam = "1/1/1975"
If (Request.Form("FullDate") <> "") Then
  Conflicts__DateParam = Request.Form("FullDate")
End If
%>
<%
Dim Conflicts__DurationParam
Conflicts__DurationParam = "0"
If (Request.Form("Duration") <> "") Then
  Conflicts__DurationParam = Request.Form("Duration")
End If
```

Continues

```asp
%>
<%
Dim Conflicts__IDParam
Conflicts__IDParam = "0"
If (Request.Form("MM_recordId") <> "") Then
  Conflicts__IDParam = Request.Form("MM_recordId")
End If
%>
<%
Dim Conflicts__RoomParam
Conflicts__RoomParam = "0"
If (Request.Form("ConferenceRoom") <> "") Then
  Conflicts__RoomParam = Request.Form("ConferenceRoom")
End If
%>
<%
Dim Conflicts
Dim Conflicts_numRows

Set Conflicts = Server.CreateObject("ADODB.Recordset")
Conflicts.ActiveConnection = MM_Recipes_STRING
Conflicts.Source = "SELECT TOP 1 ConferenceID  FROM
➥ConferenceDisplay  WHERE RoomID = " +
➥Replace(Conflicts__RoomParam, "'", "''") + "
➥AND ((ConferenceID <> " +
➥Replace(Conflicts__IDParam, "'", "''") + ")
➥AND ((ConferenceStart <= #" +
➥Replace(Conflicts__DateParam, "'", "''") + "#
➥AND ConferenceEnd > #" +
➥Replace(Conflicts__DateParam, "'", "''") + "#)
➥OR (ConferenceStart < DateAdd('n'," +
➥Replace(Conflicts__DurationParam, "'", "''") + "*60,#" +
➥Replace(Conflicts__DateParam, "'", "''") + "#)
➥AND ConferenceStart >= #" +
➥Replace(Conflicts__DateParam, "'", "''") + "#)))"
Conflicts.CursorType = 0
Conflicts.CursorLocation = 2
Conflicts.LockType = 1
Conflicts.Open()

Conflicts_numRows = 0
%>
```

```js
JS  <%
var Conflicts__DateParam = "1/1/1975";
if (String(Request.Form("FullDate")) != "undefined" &&
    String(Request.Form("FullDate")) != "") {
  Conflicts__DateParam = String(Request.Form("FullDate"));
```

```
}
%>
<%
var Conflicts__DurationParam = "0";
if (String(Request.Form("Duration")) != "undefined" &&
    String(Request.Form("Duration")) != "") {
  Conflicts__DurationParam = String(Request.Form("Duration"));
}
%>
<%
var Conflicts__IDParam = "0";
if (String(Request.Form("MM_recordId")) != "undefined" &&
    String(Request.Form("MM_recordId")) != "") {
  Conflicts__IDParam = String(Request.Form("MM_recordId"));
}
%>
<%
var Conflicts__RoomParam = "0";
if (String(Request.Form("ConferenceRoom")) != "undefined" &&
    String(Request.Form("ConferenceRoom")) != "") {
  Conflicts__RoomParam = String(Request.Form("ConferenceRoom"));
}
%>
<%
var Conflicts = Server.CreateObject("ADODB.Recordset");
Conflicts.ActiveConnection = MM_Recipes_STRING;
Conflicts.Source = "SELECT TOP 1 ConferenceID
➥FROM ConferenceDisplay  WHERE RoomID = "+
Conflicts__RoomParam.replace(/'/g, "''") + "
➥AND ((ConferenceID <> "+ Conflicts__
➥IDParam.replace(/'/g, "''") + ")
➥AND ((ConferenceStart <= #"+ Conflicts__
➥DateParam.replace(/'/g, "''") + "#
➥AND ConferenceEnd > #"+ Conflicts__
➥DateParam.replace(/'/g, "''") + "#)
➥OR (ConferenceStart < DateAdd('n',"+
➥Conflicts__DurationParam.replace(/'/g, "''") +
➥"*60,#"+ Conflicts__DateParam.replace(/'/g, "''") + "#)
➥AND ConferenceStart >= #"+ Conflicts__
➥DateParam.replace(/'/g, "''") + "#)))";
Conflicts.CursorType = 0;
Conflicts.CursorLocation = 2;
Conflicts.LockType = 1;
Conflicts.Open();
var Conflicts_numRows = 0;
%>
```

```
CF  <cfquery name="Conflicts" datasource="Recipes">
    SELECT TOP 1 ConferenceID
    FROM ConferenceDisplay
    WHERE RoomID = #FORM.ConferenceRoom#
    AND ((ConferenceStart <=
    #CreateODBCDateTime(FORM.FullDate)#
    ➥AND ConferenceEnd >
    #CreateODBCDateTime(FORM.FullDate)#)
    OR (ConferenceStart < DateAdd('n',#FORM.Duration#*60,
    ➥#CreateODBCDateTime(FORM.FullDate)#) AND
    ConferenceStart >= #CreateODBCDateTime(FORM.FullDate)#))
PHP </cfquery>
```

> **NOTE**
> You'll remember that in ColdFusion, the SQL parameters, the <cfparam> tags, are automatically inserted at the top of the page and consequently need not be moved.

```
    $RoomParam_Conflicts = "0";
    if (isset($_POST['ConferenceRoom'])) {
      $RoomParam_Conflicts = (get_magic_quotes_gpc()) ?
    $_POST['ConferenceRoom'] : addslashes($_POST['ConferenceRoom']);
    }
    $IDParam_Conflicts = "0";
    if (isset($_POST['ConferenceID'])) {
      $IDParam_Conflicts = (get_magic_quotes_gpc()) ?
      ➥$_POST['ConferenceID'] : addslashes($_POST['ConferenceID']);
    }
    $DateParam_Conflicts = "157766400";
    if (isset($_POST['FullDate'])) {
      $DateParam_Conflicts = (get_magic_quotes_gpc()) ?
      ➥$_POST['FullDate'] : addslashes($_POST['FullDate']);
    }
    $DurationParam_Conflicts = "0";
    if (isset($_POST['Duration'])) {
      $DurationParam_Conflicts = (get_magic_quotes_gpc()) ?
      ➥$_POST['Duration'] : addslashes($_POST['Duration']);
    }
    mysql_select_db($database_Recipes_PHP, $Recipes_PHP);
    $query_Conflicts = sprintf("SELECT ConferenceID FROM
    ➥conferences,rooms WHERE conferences.ConferenceRoom =
    ➥rooms.RoomID  AND  ConferenceRoom = %s AND ConferenceID != %s
    ➥AND  (UNIX_TIMESTAMP(ConferenceStart) = '%s' OR
    ➥UNIX_TIMESTAMP(ConferenceStart) = UNIX_TIMESTAMP
    ➥(INTERVAL HOUR('%s')HOUR +  INTERVAL MINUTE('%s')
    ➥MINUTE + FROM_UNIXTIME('%s')))",
    $RoomParam_Conflicts,$IDParam_Conflicts,$DateParam_Conflicts,
    ➥$DurationParam_Conflicts,$DurationParam_Conflicts,
    ➥$DateParam_Conflicts);
    $Conflicts = mysql_query($query_Conflicts, $Recipes_PHP)
    ➥or die(mysql_error());
    $row_Conflicts = mysql_fetch_assoc($Conflicts);
    $totalRows_Conflicts = mysql_num_rows($Conflicts);
```

Because PHP merges the code blocks, the code to be copied does not have the <?php ?> delimeters, although these should be added manually before the code is pasted into place.

3. Place the cursor on a new line after the date validation code inserted in the previous step near the top of the page and paste in the just-cut Conflicts recordset code. ColdFusion users should put their cursor after the <cfparam> tags and paste in the just-cut query.

As in the meeting_request page, you'll note that the selection does not include the <?php ?> delimiters because of the way Dreamweaver merges the code for the recordsets. Therefore, after placing this portion of the Conflicts recordset elsewhere on the page, new delimiters must be manually added to it.

NOTE

The next code block to insert checks the Conflicts recordset and, should a record be found, redirects the user to the meeting_conflict page. This redirection code is placed before the Update Server Behavior to avoid adding conflicting meetings into the data source.

1. In Code view, place your cursor after the just-moved Conflicts recordset.

   Selecting the recordset in the Server Behaviors panel will highlight it in the Code view.

2. Insert the following code:

   📖 From the Snippets panel, open the **Recipes > ConferenceRoom > Custom Code** folder for your server model and insert the **Meeting Conflict Redirect** snippet.

`VB`
```
<%
if (NOT Conflicts.EOF)
   Response.Redirect("meeting_conflict.asp?ID="&
   ➥Conflicts.Fields("ConferenceID").value)
%>
```

`JS`
```
<%
if (!Conflicts.EOF)
Response.Redirect("meeting_conflict.asp?ID="+Conflicts.Fields
➥("ConferenceID").value);
%>
```

`CF`
```
<cfif Conflicts.RecordCount NEQ 0>
   <cflocation url="meeting_conflict.cfm?ID=
   ➥#Conflicts.ConferenceID#">
</cfif>
```

`PHP`
```
<?php
if ($totalRows_Conflicts > 0) {
   $url = "meeting_conflict.php?ID=".$row_Conflicts['ConferenceID'];
   header("Location: $url");
   exit();
}
?>
```

NOTE

In ColdFusion, you don't need to select the `<cfparam>` tags, just the `<cfquery>` and the `<cfif>` Conflicts code blocks.

Next we need to make all the Conflicts recordset code conditional. This is accomplished by wrapping the Conflicts recordset, the parameters, and the redirection code with an If type statement. After the conditional code has been added, the enclosed code is only executed after the Update Record server behavior has run.

1. In Code view, highlight all the contiguous Conflicts-related code.
2. Wrap the following code around the selection:

    📖 From the Snippets panel, open the **Recipes > ConferenceRoom > Custom Code** folder for your server model and insert the **If Statement - Only on Update** snippet.

Before:

(VB)
```
<%
If (CStr(Request("MM_update")) = "EditMeetingRequest") Then
%>
```

After:
```
<%
end if
%>
```

Before:

(JS)
```
<%
if (String(Request("MM_update")) == "EditMeetingRequest") {
%>
```

After:
```
<%
}
%>
```

Before:

(CF)
```
<cfif IsDefined("FORM.MM_UpdateRecord")>
```

After:
```
</cfif>
```

Before:

(PHP)
```
<?php if (isset($_POST['MM_update'])) { ?>
```

After:
```
<?php } ?>
```

Our final step involving the Conflicts recordset—and for the page—is to apply the same conditional statement to the code block that explictly closes the recordset, found at the bottom of the page. This is an ASP and PHP-only step.

For ASP

1. In Code view, move to the bottom of the page and select the code block that closes the Conflicts recordset. The code will look like this:

   (VB)
   ```
   <%
   Conflicts.Close()
   Set Conflicts = Nothing
   %>
   ```

   (JS)
   ```
   <%
   Conflicts.Close();
   %>
   ```

2. Wrap the following code around the selection:

   📖 From the Snippets panel, open the **Recipes > ConferenceRoom > Custom Code** folder for your server model and insert the **If Statement - Only on Update** snippet.

   Before:

   (VB)
   ```
   <%
   If (CStr(Request("MM_update")) = "EditMeetingRequest") Then
   %>
   ```

   After:
   ```
   <%
   end if
   %>
   ```

   Before:

   (JS)
   ```
   <%
   if (String(Request("MM_update")) == "EditMeetingRequest") {
   %>
   ```

   After:
   ```
   <%
   }
   %>
   ```

For PHP

PHP users first will need to separate two merged code blocks and then make the second of the two conditional. In addition, two special functions that again are concerned with converting the date and time code must be added: one to the top of the page and another after the Insert Record code.

Let's start by making the code conditional.

1. Using Find and Replace, locate the code block that begins `<?php mysql_free_result($Rooms);`. The complete code block looks like this:

   ⒫ʜᵖ
   ```php
   <?php
       mysql_free_result($Rooms);
       mysql_free_result($Conference);
       mysql_free_result($Conflicts);
   ?>
   ```

2. This code block represents the closing of the three recordsets. Because we want to make one of those recordsets, `Conflicts`, conditional, you must separate the single block into two, like this:

   ⒫ʜᵖ
   ```php
   <?php
       mysql_free_result($Rooms);
       mysql_free_result($Conference);
   ?>
   <?php
       mysql_free_result($Conflicts);
   ?>
   ```

3. Select the second of the two blocks.

4. Now wrap conditional code around the second code block; the second code block explicitly clears the `Conflicts` recordset.

   📖 From the Snippets panel, insert the **Recipes > ConferenceRoom > CustomCode_PHP > If Statement – Only on Update** snippet.

   Before:
   ⒫ʜᵖ
   ```php
   <?php if (isset($_POST['MM_update'])) { ?>
   ```

   After:
   ```php
   <?php } ?>
   ```

5. Save your page.

Now, we can add our two remaining functions.

1. In Code view, move to the top of the page and place the cursor after the opening `<?php require_once` code line.

2. Insert the following code function to convert the string entries to date and time format:

   📖 From the Snippets panel, insert the **Recipes > ConferenceRoom > CustomCode_PHP > Enter Meeting Request - Convert FullDate** snippet.

   (PHP)
   ```php
   <?php
   if ((isset($_POST['FullDate']))||(isset
   ➡($_POST['FullDate']))) {
     $_POST['FullDate'] = strtotime($_POST['FullDate']);
     $_POST['FullDate'] = strtotime($_POST['FullDate']);
   }
   ?>
   ```

   The final step is to insert a function that performs the opposite function so that the data can be stored properly.

3. From the Server Behaviors panel, select the **Update Record** server behavior to highlight the code in Code view.

4. Move the cursor to the bottom of the selected code block and enter the following code:

   📖 From the Snippets panel, insert the **Recipes > ConferenceRoom > CustomCode_PHP > Enter Meeting Request - Reconvert FullDate** snippet.

   (PHP)
   ```php
   <?php
   if (($_POST['FullDate']!="")||($_POST['FullDate']!="")) {
     $_POST['FullDate'] = date("YmdHis",$_POST['FullDate']);
     $_POST['FullDate'] = date("YmdHis",$_POST['FullDate']);
   }
   ?>
   ```

5. Save your page.

Now's the time to save and test your page. At this point in the application development, you should be able to add a new meeting, see the confirmation, opt to modify it, make a change, and see the new record confirmed [r3-13].

r3-13

End User Recipe: Search for Existing Meeting

A search page is an important component of a meeting schedule application. Employees trying to schedule a meeting can quickly review if a particular room is open on a certain day and time or see a list of all meetings on a given day. Meeting participants might remember the name and date of the meeting but not where it is to be held.

Like almost all search applications, ours is comprised of a search entry page and a results page. In the search page we are about to construct, you'll be able to search by the meeting name, owner, date, start time, or room, or any combination of these criteria. To see a list of all the meetings in the data source, all the user has to do is select the Find Meeting button without entering any criteria.

Step 1: Implement Search Page Design

The Search Existing Meetings page is comprised of a series of text fields, a list element, and a submit button.

1. Create a basic dynamic page, either by hand or derived from a template.

   📖 In the **ConferenceRoomScheduler** folder, locate the folder for your server model and open the `existingmeeting_request` page found there.

2. Add a table to the content region of your page to contain the interface elements for the application.

   📖 From the Snippets panel, drag the **Recipes > ConferenceRoom > Wireframes > Search Existing Meetings - Wireframe** snippet into the Content editable region.

3. Insert a table and form to hold the various search fields. The example application includes three text fields, a list, and a submit button.

   📖 Place your cursor in the row below the words SEARCH EXISTING MEET-INGS and insert the **Recipes > ConferenceRoom > Forms > Find Meeting - Form** snippet for your server model; to code the <form> tag properly, different snippets are available for ASP, ColdFusion, and PHP.

4. Select the form just inserted and, from the Property inspector, set the Action parameter to your intended results page.

   📖 Select the **Browse for File** icon and choose the meeting_results page for your server model [r3-14].

r3-14

5. Be sure to save the page before continuing.

Step 2: Add Database Components

As with most similar applications, almost all the server-side logic to power the search is located in the results page. The only reason a database component is used is to populate a list element, Rooms.

This is the same recordset used on the Meeting Request and Edit Meeting Request pages. Feel free to copy the Rooms recordset from either of those pages and paste it here as previously described.

NOTE

1. From the Server Behaviors panel, choose Add (+) and select **Recordset (Query)**.

2. In simple view, enter the name of the recordset.

   📖 Enter **Rooms** in the Name field.

3. Select the data source connection.

   📖 Choose **Recipes** from the Connection (Data Source) list.

4. Choose the table to work with.

   📖 Select **Rooms** (**rooms** in PHP) from the Table list.

5. Limit your data source columns to only those that are needed.

   📖 Choose the **Selected Columns** option and highlight **RoomID** and **RoomName**.

   It's generally considered good practice to limit your data source fields to those that are necessary, and when one of the unnecessary fields is a memo type field such as RoomDescription that could hold a great deal of text, it's especially important.

6. Leave the Filter option set to None.

7. Set the Sort option to present an alphabetical listing of the rooms.

   📖 Choose **RoomName** from the Sort list and accept the Ascending order.

8. Verify your choices and click OK when you're done.

Step 3: Data Binding Process

The data binding for this page is simplicity itself. All that is needed is to associate the Room list element with the Room recordset.

1. Select the **ConferenceRoom** list element and click the Dynamic button on the Property inspector.

2. In the Dynamic List/Menu dialog, choose **Rooms** from the Options from Recordset list.

3. Set the Values list to **RoomID** and Labels to **RoomName**.

4. Leave the Select Value Equal To field blank and click OK to close the dialog.

You'll note that the list element already has one static entry where the value is empty and the label is Any. The empty value acts as a wildcard to enable users to search for any available rooms at a given time. Static values always appear first before dynamic values.

Step 4: Add Error Messages

All the actual logic for error checking is handled on the results page. We do, however, need to embed two conditional error messages on the page. The first error message is displayed when an improper date is entered in the Meeting Date field. The other error message is used to indicate that no results were found for the submitted search criteria. By having these messages appear on the current page rather than a result page, the user can immediately try again.

1. In Design view, place the cursor in the row above Search for Meeting Name, Owner, Date and/or Conference Room text.

2. Insert the following code:

   📖 From the Snippets panel, open the **Recipes > ConferenceRoom > Custom Code** folder for your server model and insert the **Date Error - Dynamic Text** snippet.

   (VB)
   ```
   <% if (cStr(Request.QueryString("badDate")) <> "") Then
       Response.Write("The date you entered was not in the proper format.
       Dates should be in the format mm/dd/yyyy.")%>
   ```

   (JS)
   ```
   <%=(String(Request.QueryString("badDate")) != "undefined")?"The date
   you entered was not in the proper format.  Dates should be in the
   format mm/dd/yyyy.":""%>
   ```

   (CF)
   ```
   <cfif isDefined("URL.badDate")>The date you entered was not in the
   proper format.  Dates should be in the format mm/dd/yyyy.</cfif>
   ```

   (PHP)
   ```
   <?php
   if (isset($_GET['badDate'])) {
      echo "The date you entered was not in the proper format.
      Dates should be in the format mm/dd/yyyy.";
   }
   ?>
   ```

   With the date validation message in place, we're ready to insert the "no results" text.

3. With the cursor next to the code just entered, insert the following code:

   📖 From the Snippets panel, open the **Recipes > ConferenceRoom > Custom Code** folder for your server model and insert the **No Results Error - Dynamic Text** snippet.

   (VB)
   ```
   <%=(String(Request.QueryString("noResults")) != "undefined")?"There
   are no meetings scheduled that match your search.":""%>
   ```

   (JS)
   ```
   <%=(String(Request.QueryString("noResults")) != "undefined")?"There
   are no meetings scheduled that match your search.":""%>
   ```

   (CF)
   ```
   <cfif isDefined("URL.noResults")>There are no meetings scheduled
   that match your search.</cfif>
   ```

```php
(PHP)  <?php
       if (isset($_GET['noResults'])) {
         echo "There are no meetings scheduled that match your search.";
       }
       ?>
```

At this point in the process, you can test your error messages in Live Data view by entering arguments in the Live Data toolbar. Try badDate=true to see the date validation message and noResults=true to see what will happen when no matches are found for the search [r3-15].

r3-15

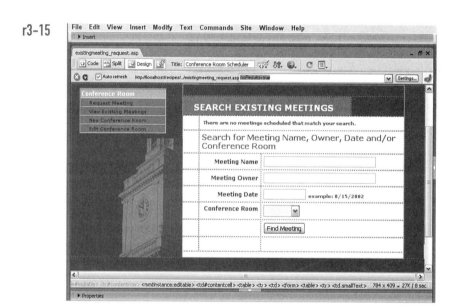

End User Recipe: Meeting Results

After the user has entered the search criteria on the Search Existing Meetings page, selecting the submit button executes the Meeting Results page. If no results are found, the user is redirected back to the search page, and a no-results message is displayed; otherwise, all the results are listed on the the results page. Each of the result entries includes a link to a detail page and, to handle a large number of results being returned, recordset navigation controls are also included.

As noted on the Search Existing Meetings page, the Meeting Results page handles the actual parsing of the submitted search terms as well as the no-results redirection. In addition, this page also makes sure that a valid date was entered. Consequently, there is a fair amount of hand-coding involved, all of which is included in the Recipes snippets.

Step 1: Implement Search Results Design

The results page is basically a table with a repeating region applied with room for recordset navigation controls.

1. Create a basic dynamic page, either by hand or derived from a template.

   📖 In the **ConferenceRoomScheduler** folder, locate the folder for your server model and open the meeting_results page found there.

2. Add a table to the content region of your page to contain the interface elements for the application.

   📖 From the Snippets panel, drag the **Recipes > ConferenceRoom > Wireframes > Meeting Results - Wireframe** snippet into the Content editable region.

3. Add the table area with four columns to display the meeting name, conference room, start time, and duration [r3-16].

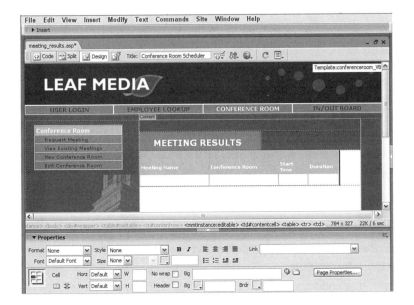

r3-16

   📖 Place your cursor in the row below the words MEETING RESULTS and insert the **Recipes > ConferenceRoom > ContentTables > Meeting Results - Content Table** snippet.

4. Save the page before continuing.

Step 2: Add Database Components

The Meeting Results page uses the same search functions found in Recipe 2, "Employee Lookup." If you've already built that application, you'll recognize the SQL statement's dynamically generated WHERE clause used within this page's recordset. In addition, ASP users will also need to include a statement that initializes the variable, WhereParam.

For ASP

1. From the Bindings panel, choose Add (+) and select **Recordset (Query)**.
2. Switch to advanced view, if necessary, and enter an appropriate name for the recordset.

    📖 Enter **Conferences** in the Name field.
3. Choose the connection for the data source.

    📖 Select **Recipes** from the Connections list.
4. In the SQL area, enter the following code:

```
SELECT *
FROM ConferenceDisplay WhereParam
ORDER BY ConferenceName
```

5. From the Variable area, choose Add (+) to add a new variable.
6. In the Name column, enter **WhereParam**.
7. In the Default Value column, enter **WHERE ConferenceID <> 0.**
8. In the Run-time Value column, enter **WhereParam.**
9. Click OK to close the dialog.

The WhereParam variable is a server-side variable with a default value that returns all records in the Conferences table. When any search criteria are submitted, the WhereParam variable will be built dynamically. To work properly, WhereParam, like all variables in ASP, must be initialized. The following step is necessary for ASP developers only.

1. In Code view, position the cursor near the top of the page on a new line right after the <!--include> tag.
2. Enter the following code:

    📖 From the Snippets panel, open the **Recipes > ConferenceRoom > Custom Code** folder for your server model and insert the **WhereParam Init** snippet.

    (VB)
```
<%
WhereParam = ""
%>
```

```
JS   <%
     var WhereParam = "";
     %>
```

For ColdFusion

The ColdFusion recordset is initially declared without a WHERE clause to enable easy placement of data source fields during the data binding phase. After all the dynamic elements are in place, we'll add code to generate the WHERE clause on the fly.

1. From the Bindings panel, choose Add (+) and select **Recordset (Query)**.
2. In simple view of the Recordset dialog, enter an appropriate name for the recordset.
    Enter **Conferences** in the Name field.
3. Select the desired data source.
    Choose **Recipes** from the Data Source list.
4. Enter the user name and password for the data source, if needed.
5. Select the table or view to use.
    Choose **ConferenceDisplay** from the Table menu.
6. Leave the Columns, Filter, and Sort options at their default settings and click OK to close the dialog.

For PHP

   Prepare for this step by using the Copy Snippet command to copy the **Recipes > ConferenceRoom > SQL > Search Results - PHP SQL Statement** snippet.
1. From the Bindings panel, choose Add (+) and select **Recordset (Query)**.
2. Switch to advanced view, if necessary, and enter an appropriate name for the recordset.
    Enter **Conferences** in the Name field.
3. Choose the connection for the data source.
    Select **Recipes** from the Connections list.
4. In the SQL area, enter the following code:
    Paste the copied snippet in the SQL area by pressing Ctrl-V (Command-V).

```
SELECT ConferenceID, ConferenceRoom, ConferenceName,
➥ConferenceDescription, UNIX_TIMESTAMP(ConferenceStart) AS
➥ConferenceStart, CONCAT(HOUR(ConferenceDuration),':',
➥IF(MINUTE(ConferenceDuration)<10,CONCAT('0',MINUTE
➥(ConferenceDuration)),MINUTE(ConferenceDuration)))
```

Continues

```
➥AS ConferenceDuration, ConferenceBy, RoomID, RoomName,
➥RoomDescription
FROM conferences, rooms
WHERE ConferenceRoom = RoomID WhereParam
```

5. From the Variable area, choose Add (+) to add a new variable.
6. In the Name column, enter **WhereParam**.
7. In the Default Value column, enter **AND ConferenceID != 0**.
8. In the Run-time Value column, enter **$WhereParam** and click OK to close the dialog.
9. Save your page.

Step 3: Data Binding Process

Only four text elements need to be bound to the data source for the Meeting Results page, and all can be dragged directly from the Bindings panel. After the dynamic text elements are in position, we can create a link to a details page.

1. From the Bindings panel, expand the Conferences recordset.
2. Switch to Design mode and place the needed data source fields into position on the page:

   📖 Drag **ConferenceName** to the row under the Meeting Name column.

   Drag **RoomName** to the row under the Conference Room column.

   ASP and ColdFusion users: Drag **ConferenceStart** to the row under the Start Time column.

   (PHP) In PHP, this column requires formatting, so rather than perform this step, click inside this column and then in the Snippets panel, go to **Recipes > ConferenceRoom > CustomCode_PHP** and insert the **Search Results - Display Formatted ConferenceStart** snippet.

   📖 Drag ConferenceDuration to the row under the Duration column.

3. PHP users should enter code specifically to format ConferenceStart properly by inserting the following code in the row under the Start Time column:

   📖 From the Snippets panel, insert the **Recipes > ConferenceRoom > CustomCode_PHP > Formatted ConferenceStart Column** snippet.

   (PHP) `<?php echo date("n/d/Y",$row_Conferences['ConferenceStart']); ?>`

4. Save your page.

Now we're ready to add a link to a details page. In this case, we'll add it to the name of the meeting.

1. Select the dynamic text you want to use as a link to a detail page.

   📖 Choose the **Conferences.ConferenceName** dynamic text element.

2. From the Property inspector, enter the path to the details page.

   📖 Choose the Browse for File icon and select the **meetings_detail** page.

3. Add a parameter to the URL passing the meeting ID.

   📖 From the Select File dialog, click the Parameters button and, in the Parameters dialog, enter **ID** under Value. Then, place the cursor in the Value field, select the lightning icon to open the Dynamic Data dialog, and choose **ConferenceID**. Click OK three times to close all the open dialogs.

When complete, each of the columns should have dynamic text associated with them, and the Meeting name should be linked to the meeting details page [r3-17].

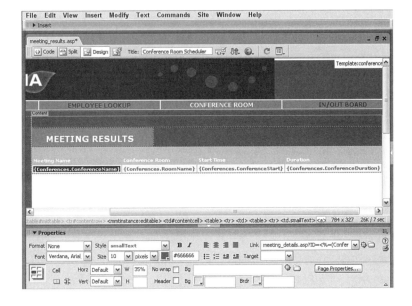

r3-17

Step 4: Add Repeat Region

Enter into Live Data view at this stage, and you'll see just one entry. We'll use the Dreamweaver Repeat Region server behavior to display a number of entries.

1. Select any of the dynamic text elements on the page.
2. From the Tag Selector, select the **<tr>** tag to the left of the current selection.
3. From the Server Behaviors panel, choose Add (+) and select **Repeat Region**.

4. In the Repeat Region dialog, make sure the `Conferences` recordset is displayed.

5. Choose the Show option and enter **10** in the numeric field.

6. Click OK to close the dialog.

Now when you enter into Live Data view (in truth, you didn't really need to exit from it to insert the Repeat Region) you should see the first ten records. Next we'll add record-set navigation to handle larger recordsets [r3-18].

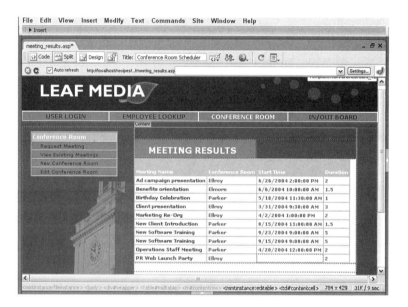

Step 5: Add Application Objects

Dreamweaver includes two standard application objects—Recordset Navigation Bar and Recordset Navigation Status—that are used to navigate through records. Let's add the navigation bar first.

1. Place your cursor in the **Meeting Results** page where you want the navigation links to appear.

   📖 Place the cursor in the row above the `Start Time` label. The `<td>` cell is styled to align text in the center, so the cursor will not appear directly above the label. If you are unsure of your placement, press F6 to enter Expanded Table mode; press F6 again to return to Standard mode.

2. Choose the **Recordset Navigation Bar** object from the Recordset Paging menu button on the Insert bar's Application category.

   Alternatively, you could select **Insert > Application Objects > Recordset Paging > Recordset Navigation Bar**.

3. In the Recordset Navigation Bar dialog, select the **Conferences** recordset.

4. Leave the Display Using option set to Text and click OK.

The other Dreamweaver application object, Recordset Navigation Status, provides feedback about the number of total records and which records are currently being displayed.

1. Place your cursor in the Meeting Results page where you want the navigation status to be displayed.

    📖 Place the cursor in the row above the Meeting Name cell.

2. Choose the **Recordset Navigation Status** object from the Display Record Count menu of the Application category of the Insert bar.

    Alternatively, you could select **Insert > Application Objects > Display Record Count > Recordset Navigation Status**.

3. In the Recordset Navigation Status dialog, select the **Conferences** recordset and click OK.

Preview the page in a browser to get the full effect of the recordset navigation controls [r3-19].

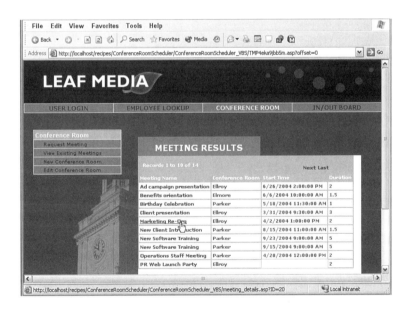

r3-19

Step 6: Add Server-Side Date Validation

Although the date itself was entered on the Search Existing Meeting page, the validation is being handled on this page. Why? Rather than have the search page submit to itself and then, if the date was judged proper, redirect to the results page, all the server-side functions are centralized on one page. If an error is found, the user is redirected to the search page and an error message—already encoded on the search page—is displayed.

> **NOTE**
> A custom function is needed for those working with ASP-JavaScript and PHP, in addition to another code snippet used for all server models.

1. In Code view, place the cursor at the top of the page.

   ASP users should position the cursor after the code block in which the WhereParam variable is initialized. PHP users place the cursor after the <?php require_once statement.

2. ASP-JS and PHP users only: Insert the following code:

   📕 From the Snippets panel, open the **Recipes > ConferenceRoom > Custom Code** folder for your server model and insert the **IsADate Function** snippet.

   `JS`
   ```
   <%
   function isADate(DateString)   {
     var DateRegex = /^(\d{1,2})\/(\d{1,2})\/(\d{4})$/
     var theMatch = DateString.match(DateRegex);
     var validDate = false;
     if (theMatch)   {
       var DateObj = new Date(DateString);
       if ((DateObj.getMonth()+1 == parseInt(theMatch[1])) &&
   ➥(DateObj.getDate() == parseInt(theMatch[2])) &&
   ➥(DateObj.getFullYear() == parseInt(theMatch[3])))
           validDate = true;
     }
     return validDate;
   }
   %>
   ```

   `PHP`
   ```
   <?php
   function isADate($DateString) {
     $validDate = false;
     if (ereg("^[0-9]{1,2}\/[0-9]{1,2}\/[0-9]{4}$",$DateString)) {
       $submittedDate = explode("/",$DateString);
       $month = $submittedDate[0];
       $day = $submittedDate[1];
       $year = $submittedDate[2];
       $validDate = (checkdate($month,$day,$year))?true:false;
   ```

```
        }
        return $validDate;
    }
    ?>
```

3. Users of all server models should insert the following code:

    📖 From the Snippets panel, open the **Recipes > ConferenceRoom > Custom Code** folder for your server model and insert the **Meeting Request - Date Validation** snippet.

(VB)
```
<%
if (cStr(Request.Form("MeetingDate")) <> "")  then
  if not (isDate(Request.Form("MeetingDate"))) then
  ➥Response.Redirect("existingmeeting_request.asp?ID=" &
  ➥Request("MM_recordId") & "&badDate=true")
  end if%>
```

(JS)
```
<%
if (String(Request.Form("MeetingDate"))!="undefined" &&
➥!isADate(String(Request.Form("MeetingDate"))))
Response.Redirect("existingmeeting_request.asp?ID="+Request
➥("MM_recordId")+"&badDate=true");
%>
```

(CF)
```
<cfif IsDefined("FORM.MeetingDate")>
    <cfif not IsDate(FORM.MeetingDate)>
      <cflocation url=" existingmeeting_request.cfm?ID=
      ➥#FORM.ConferenceID#&badDate=true">
    </cfif>
</cfif>
```

(PHP)
```
<?php
if ((isset($_POST['MeetingDate']))
➥&& (!isADate($_POST['MeetingDate']))) {
  $url = "existingmeeting_request.php?badDate=true";
  header("Location: $url");
}
?>
```

You can test this portion of the application by opening Search Existing Meeting in a browser and entering an improper date value. If all goes well, you won't even see the Meeting Results page.

Step 7: Hand Code Search Functionality

The final step to complete on this page is its *raison d'etre*—the search functions. There are three phases to getting the search fully operational.

A custom function, AddFieldToSearch(), that builds the WHERE clause one search criteria field at a time is inserted. This step is not necessary for ColdFusion.

To compensate for the manner in which Dreamweaver deals with single quote characters in its ASP and PHP SQL statements, two quote handler functions are added along with calling code from within the SQL statement. Again, this is not necessary in ColdFusion.

For ASP and PHP

To make sure our helper function, AddFieldToSearch(), is available, we'll add it first.

1. In Code view, place your cursor after the Date Validation code added in the last step.
2. Insert the following code:
   - From the Snippets panel, open the **Recipes > ConferenceRoom > Custom Code** folder for your server model and insert the **Add Field To Search** snippet.

   (VB) <%

```
    AddFieldToSearch(CurrentWhere,ColumnName,ValString,Comparison,
   ↪Separator,OpenEncap,CloseEncap)
       if (ValString <> "") then
          if (CurrentWhere = "") then
             CurrentWhere = "WHERE "
          else
             CurrentWhere = CurrentWhere & " " & Separator & " "
          end if
          CurrentWhere = CurrentWhere & ColumnName & " " &
          ↪Comparison & " " & OpenEncap & Replace
          ↪(ValString, "'", "''") & CloseEncap
       end if
       AddFieldToSearch = CurrentWhere
    end function
    %>
```

```
(JS)  <%
      function AddFieldToSearch(CurrentWhere,ColumnName,ValString,
      ➥Comparison,Separator,OpenEncap,CloseEncap) {
          if (ValString!="") {
              if (CurrentWhere == "") {
                  CurrentWhere = "WHERE ";
              }
              else {
                  CurrentWhere += " " + Separator + " ";
              }
              CurrentWhere += ColumnName + " " + Comparison + " " +
              ➥OpenEncap + ValString.replace(/'/g, "''") + CloseEncap;
          }
          return CurrentWhere;
      }
      %>
```

```
(PHP)  <?php
       function AddFieldToSearch($CurrentWhere,$ColumnName,$ValString,
       ➥$Comparison,$Separator,$OpenEncap,$CloseEncap)  {
         if ($ValString!="")  {
           if ($CurrentWhere == "")  {
             $CurrentWhere = "AND ";
           } else  {
             $CurrentWhere.= " ".$Separator." ";
           }
         $CurrentWhere.= $ColumnName." ".$Comparison." "
         ➥.$OpenEncap.$ValString.$CloseEncap;
         }

         return $CurrentWhere;
       }
       ?>
```

The next code block calls the just-inserted function to build the WhereParam variable. Essentially, the code looks at every form field on the search page and adds its values, if any, to WhereParam so that the variable will eventually be used to filter the recordset.

1. In Code view, place the cursor in the proper position for your server model—after the AddFieldToSearchFunction() just inserted for ASP and PHP and after the Date Validation code added in the previous step for ColdFusion.

2. Insert the following code:

   📖 From the Snippets panel, open the **Recipes > ConferenceRoom > Custom Code**
   folder for your server model and insert the **Find Meeting Search Filter** snippet.

(VB)
```
<%
if (cStr(Request.QueryString("FindMeeting"))<>"") then
WhereParam = AddFieldToSearch(WhereParam,"ConferenceName",cStr
➡(Request.QueryString("MeetingName")),"LIKE","AND","'","%'")
WhereParam = AddFieldToSearch(WhereParam,"ConferenceBy",cStr
➡(Request.QueryString("MeetingOwner")),"LIKE","AND","'","%'")
WhereParam = AddFieldToSearch(WhereParam,"StartDate",cStr
➡(Request.QueryString("MeetingDate")),"=","AND","#","#")
WhereParam = AddFieldToSearch(WhereParam,"RoomID",cStr
➡(Request.QueryString("ConferenceRoom")),"=","AND","","")
end if
%>
```

(JS)
```
<%
if (String(Request.QueryString("FindMeeting"))!="undefined")  {
  WhereParam = AddFieldToSearch(WhereParam,"ConferenceName",String
➡(Request.QueryString("MeetingName")),"LIKE","AND","'","%'");
  WhereParam = AddFieldToSearch(WhereParam,"ConferenceBy",String
➡(Request.QueryString("MeetingOwner")),"LIKE","AND","'","%'");
  WhereParam = AddFieldToSearch(WhereParam,"StartDate",String
➡(Request.QueryString("MeetingDate")),"=","AND","#","#");
  WhereParam = AddFieldToSearch(WhereParam,"RoomID",String
➡(Request.QueryString("ConferenceRoom")),"=","AND","","");
}
%>
```

(PHP)
```
<?php
if(isset($_GET['FindMeeting'])) {
    $WhereParam = AddFieldToSearch($WhereParam,"ConferenceName",
    ➡$_GET['MeetingName'],"LIKE","AND","'","%'");
    $WhereParam = AddFieldToSearch($WhereParam,"ConferenceBy",
    ➡$_GET['MeetingOwner'],"LIKE","AND","'","%'");
    $WhereParam = AddFieldToSearch($WhereParam,"DATE_FORMAT
    ➡(ConferenceStart,'%c/%d/%Y')",$_GET['MeetingDate'],
    ➡"=","AND","'","'");
    $WhereParam = AddFieldToSearch($WhereParam,"RoomID",
    ➡$_GET['ConferenceRoom'],"=","AND","'","%'");
}
?>
```

Next, ASP users will need to insert code to handle Dreamweaver's method of working with single quotes. To do this, we'll need to add two functions, `RemoveQuotes()` and `ReturnQuotes()`, as well as two calls to invoke the functions. The calls to the function will take place before and after the SQL statement for the `Conferences` recordset is actually defined. This step is not needed for PHP.

1. Locate the code block containing the **Conferences** recordset by selecting it from the Server Behaviors panel and switching to Code view. Position the cursor just above that code block and below the code block in which the `WhereParam` variable is initialized.

2. Insert this code:

   ⬜ From the Snippets panel, open the **Recipes > ConferenceRoom > Custom Code** folder for your server model and insert the **Quote Handler Function** snippet.

   (VB)
```
<%
function RemoveQuotes(theString)
  RemoveQuotes = Replace(theString, "'", "|!|")
end function

function ReturnQuotes(theString)
  ReturnQuotes = Replace(theString, "|!|", "'")
end function
%>
```

   (JS)
```
<%
function RemoveQuotes(theString)  {
  return theString.replace(/'/g, "|!|");
}
function ReturnQuotes(theString)  {
  return theString.replace(/\|!\|/g, "'");
}
%>
```

3. To insert the first function call, place your cursor below the quote handler functions just inserted and make a new line.

4. Insert the following code:

   ⬜ From the Snippets panel, open the **Recipes > ConferenceRooms > Custom Code** folder for your server model and insert the **WhereParam - Remove Quotes** snippet.

   (VB)
```
<%
Conferences__WhereParam = RemoveQuotes(Conferences__WhereParam)
%>
```

```
JS  <%
    Conferences__WhereParam = RemoveQuotes(Conferences__WhereParam);
    %>
```

5. To insert the second function call, place your cursor within the Dreamweaver coded SQL function, just after line that starts `Conferences.Source = "SELECT...` and add a new line.

6. On the new line, insert the following code:

   - From the Snippets panel, open the **Recipes > ConferenceRoom > Custom Code** folder for your server model and insert the **Replace Quotes Function** snippet.

```
VB  Employees.Source = ReturnQuotes(Employees.Source)
```

```
JS  Employees.Source = ReturnQuotes(Employees.Source);
```

The advantage to this subroutine function is that the Dreamweaver visual interface still recognizes and protects the code for the hand-editing recordset definition.

WARNING

Although the enhanced code does give a fair degree of power over what Dreamweaver can provide natively, there is a minor downside. After the code is inserted, you cannot examine or change the recordset through the Dreamweaver dialog—doing so causes Dreamweaver to display an error and disrupts the functionality of the Bindings panel. Any additional modifications to the recordset must be made in Code view.

For ColdFusion

ColdFusion doesn't need an external function to incrementally build up the `WhereParam` variable—that can be handled right from within the `<cfquery>` tag.

1. In Code view, position the cursor within the code defining the Conferences recordset, before the closing `</cfquery>` tag.

   You can highlight the recordset in the code by choosing it from the Server Behaviors panel.

2. Insert this code:

   - From the Snippets panel, open the **SQL** folder under **Recipes > ConferenceRoom** and insert the **Conferences RS - CFML SQL Where Statement** snippet.

```
CF  <cfif isDefined("URL.FindMeeting")>
    WHERE 1 = 1
    <cfif URL.MeetingName NEQ "">
      AND ConferenceName LIKE '#URL.MeetingName#%'
    </cfif>
    <cfif URL.MeetingOwner NEQ "">
      AND ConferenceBy LIKE '#URL.MeetingOwner#%'
    </cfif>
    <cfif URL.StartDate NEQ "">
      AND StartDate = ###URL.MeetingDate###
    </cfif>
```

```
<cfif URL.ConferenceRoom NEQ "">
   AND ConferenceRoom = #URL.ConferenceRoom#
</cfif>
</cfif>
```

You may notice that this custom code uses an interesting SQL clause that starts with WHERE 1=1. As this condition will always be true, this clause permits us to establish a series of if statements combined with AND clauses to create search criteria under a range of circumstances. With the WHERE 1=1 clause in place, the SQL statement will execute without error regardless of the fields employed by the user.

Step 8: Handle No Matching Results

The final step for this page is needed to handle situations where no matches to the search criteria are found. A small snippet of code looks to see if the Conferences recordset is empty and, if it is, redirects the application to the Search Existing Meetings page with an error code attached.

1. In Code view, place the cursor after the **Conferences** recordset.
2. Insert the following code:
   - From the Snippets panel, open the **Recipes > ConferenceRooms > Custom Code** folder for your server model and insert the **No Results Redirect** snippet.

VB
```
<%
if (Conferences.BOF AND Conferences.EOF) Then
Response.Redirect("existingmeetings_request.asp?noResults=true")
%>
```

JS
```
<%
if (Conferences.BOF && Conferences.EOF)
Response.Redirect("existingmeetings_request.asp?noResults=true");
%>
```

CF
```
<cfif Conferences.RecordCount EQ 0>
   <cflocation url="existingmeetings_request.cfm?noResults=true">
</cfif>
```

PHP
```
<?php
if ($totalRows_Conferences == 0) {
   $url = "existingmeetings_request.asp?noResults=true";
   header("Location: $url");
   exit();
}
?>
```

3. Be sure to save your page.

The search capabilities of the Conference Room Scheduler are now fully operational. Test your pages by trying a variety of search parameters—ones that you know should return results and ones where you would not expect to see any matches [r3-20].

r3-20

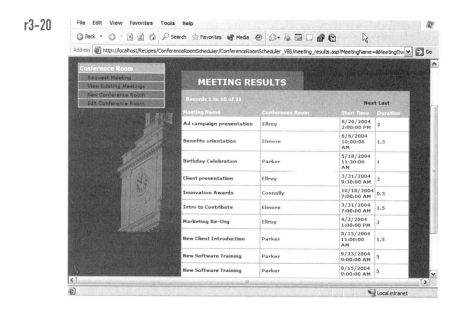

Administrator Recipe: Add Conference Room

One of the elements essential to any meeting is a meeting room; likewise, an important part of a conference scheduling application is the capability to add and edit meeting room details. The Add Conference Room page is the first of two administrative pages concerned with managing meeting rooms. Although some rooms may be set up initially by the data source administrator, being able to bring new rooms into the application is an ongoing need.

The Add Conference Room page is a basic insert record page that utilizes a standard Dreamweaver server behavior, Insert Record.

Step 1: Implement Add Room Design

First, we'll build the framework for the page and add the necessary form elements.

1. Create a basic dynamic page, either by hand or derived from a template.
   - 📖 In the **ConferenceRoomScheduler** folder, locate the folder for your server model and open the new_conferenceroom page found there.

2. Add a table to the content region of your page to contain the interface elements for the application.

   ▢ From the Snippets panel, drag the **Recipes > ConferenceRoom > Wireframes > New Conference Room - Wireframe** snippet into the Content editable region.

3. Within the table, place another another HTML table to hold the form's three elements: one text field, one text area, and a submit button.

   ▢ Place your cursor in the row below the words NEW CONFERENCE ROOM and insert the **Recipes > ConferenceRoom > Forms > New Conference Room - Form** snippet [r3-21].

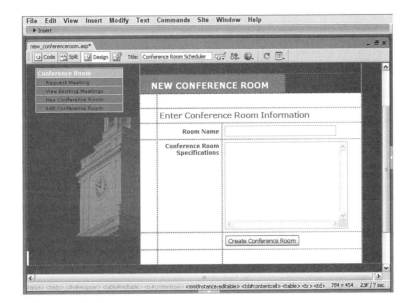

r3-21

Step 2: Insert Record—New Conference Room

There's only one action to perform to complete this page—add the Insert Record server behavior. After the record is inserted, the application presents the Meeting Request page where the new room is automatically incorporated.

For ASP

1. From the Server Behaviors panel, choose Add (+) and then **Insert Record**.
2. Select the desired data source connection.

   ▢ Choose **Recipes** from the Connection list.

3. Choose the table in the data source that will receive the form values.

    📖 From the Insert Into Table list, choose **Rooms**.

4. In the After Inserting, Go To field, enter the page you want the user to visit after the record is inserted.

    📖 Select Browse to locate the **meeting_request** page.

5. Choose the form on the page from which to get the values.

    📖 From the Get Values From list, choose **NewConferenceRoom**.

6. In the Form Elements area, set the form elements to their corresponding data source fields.

    📖 Set the RoomName form element to the RoomName data source field as text type.

      Set the RoomSpecs form element to the RoomDescription data source field as text type.

7. Make sure your entries are correct and then click OK to close.

8. Save the page.

For ColdFusion and PHP

1. From the Server Behaviors panel, choose Add (+) and select **Insert Record**.

2. In the Insert Record dialog, choose the current form.

    📖 Select **NewConferenceRoom** from the Submit Values From list.

3. Select your data source from the list.

    📖 Choose **Recipes** from the Data Source list.

4. Enter your user name and password, if needed.

5. Select the table in the data source to insert into from the list.

    📖 Choose **Rooms** (**rooms** for PHP) from the Insert Into Table list.

6. Set the data source fields to their corresponding form elements.

    📖 Make sure the RoomID data column is set to be an unused Primary Key;

      Set RoomName to the FORM.RoomName form element and submit as Text.

      Set RoomDescription to the FORM.RoomSpecs form element and submit as Text.

7. In the After Inserting, Go to field, enter the path to the file you want the user to visit after the record is inserted.

    📖 Select Browse and choose **meeting_request.cfm** or **meeting_request.php** as appropriate.

NOTE
One enhancement you might apply to this page is client-side validation to make sure that a particular field or fields are required. Dreamweaver's Validate Form behavior is perfect for this.

8. Verify your choices and click OK to close the dialog.

9. Save the page.

Administrator Recipe: Edit Conference Room

Because meeting rooms may vary over time with new features, such as speaker phones or video conferencing facilities, the application needs a way to modify existing room descriptions. The Edit Conference Room page displays the room name and its specifications in a text field for easy modification.

Rather than navigate to the page from a detail page as is common with update type pages, this page uses a drop-down list to change from one room to another. Although this takes a little extra coding, it effectively simplifies the user experience.

Step 1: Implement Design

Let's start by creating the basic page that will require a list, text field, text area, and submit button. ColdFusion users will also need to add a hidden field to be used by the Update Record behavior.

1. Create a basic dynamic page, either by hand or derived from a template.
   - In the **ConferenceRoomScheduler** folder, locate the folder for your server model and open the edit_conferenceroom page found there.
2. Add a table to the content region of your page to contain the interface elements for the application.
   - From the Snippets panel, drag the **Recipes > ConferenceRoom > Wireframes > Edit Conference Room - Wireframe** snippet into the Content editable region.
3. Within the table, place another another HTML table to hold the form's four elements.
   - Place your cursor in the row below the words EDIT CONFERENCE ROOM and insert the **Recipes > ConferenceRoom > Forms > Edit Conference Room - Form** snippet [r3-22].

r3-22

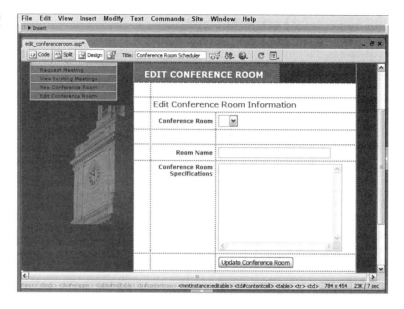

CF **PHP** ColdFusion and PHP users should drag a hidden form element from the Forms category of the Insert bar onto the page next to the submit button and name it **RoomID**.

4. Save your page before continuing.

Step 2: Add Database Components

There are two recordsets used in this page, but they both are based on the same data source table. One recordset is used to display the entries to be modified, while the other recordset serves to populate a list element—which in turn ultimately controls what is in the first recordset.

Let's start with the simple recordset first that eventually will be used to populate the Room drop-down list.

1. From the Server Behaviors panel, choose Add (+) and select **Recordset (Query)**.
2. In simple view, enter the name of the recordset.
    - Enter **RoomList** in the Name field.
3. Select the data source connection.
    - Choose **Recipes** from the Connection (Data Source) list.
4. Choose the table to work with.
    - Select **Rooms** (**rooms** for PHP) from the Table list.

5. Limit your data source columns to only those that are needed.

     📖 Choose the Selected Columns option and highlight **RoomID** and **RoomName**.

6. Leave the Filter and Sort option set to None and click OK when you're done.

The second recordset uses a dynamic variable to create the WHERE clause of the SQL statement.

For ASP

1. From the Server Behaviors panel, choose Add (+) and select **Recordset (Query)**.
2. Switch to the advanced view of the dialog and enter an appropriate name for the recordset.

     📖 Enter **Rooms** into the Name field.

3. Choose the connection for the recordset.

     📖 Select **Recipes** from the Connection list.

4. In the SQL area, enter the following code:

```
SELECT TOP 1 *
FROM Rooms RoomWhere
```

5. In the Variable area, choose Add (+) and enter **RoomWhere** under the Name column.
6. In the Default Value column, enter **WHERE RoomID <> 0**.
7. In the Run-time Value column, enter **RoomWhere** and click OK to close the dialog.

For ColdFusion

1. From the Server Behaviors panel, choose Add (+) and select **Recordset (Query)**.
2. Switch to the advanced view of the dialog and enter an appropriate name for the recordset.

     📖 Enter **Rooms** in the Name field.

3. Choose your data source.

     📖 Select **Recipes** from the Data Source list.

4. Enter a user name and password if necessary.
5. In the SQL area, enter the following code:

```
SELECT TOP 1 *
FROM Rooms #RoomWhere#
```

6. In the Page Parameter section, choose Add (+) and, in the Add Parameter dialog, make sure **RoomWhere** is chosen in the Name list.

7. Enter **WHERE RoomID <> 0** as the Default Value and click OK to close the dialog.

8. Verify your entries in the Recordset dialog and click OK to close that dialog.

For PHP

1. From the Server Behaviors panel, choose Add (+) and select **Recordset (Query)**.

2. Switch to the advanced view of the dialog and enter an appropriate name for the recordset.

   📖 Enter **Rooms** into the Name field.

3. Choose the connection for the recordset.

   📖 Select **Recipes** from the Connection list.

4. In the SQL area, enter the following code:

```
SELECT *
FROM rooms
WHERE RoomWhere LIMIT 1,1
```

5. In the Variable area, choose Add (+) and, in the Add Parameter dialog, enter **RoomWhere** in the Name field.

6. In the Default Value field, enter **RoomID <> 0**.

7. In the Run-time Value field, enter **$RoomWhere** and click OK to close the dialog.

Step 3: Data Binding Process

In addition to the normal binding of data source fields to form elements, this page requires that special attention be paid to the list element for the data binding to be complete. The list element will be populated dynamically and will also use JavaScript to change the currently displayed room.

1. Select the **ConferenceRoom** list element and click the **Dynamic** button on the Property inspector.

2. In the Dynamic List/Menu dialog, choose **RoomList** from the Options from Recordset list.

3. Set the Values list to **RoomID** and Labels to **RoomName**.

4. For the Select Value Equal To field, select the lightning icon to open the Dynamic Data dialog.

5. Choose **RoomsID** from the Rooms recordset and click OK twice to close the dialogs.

Now let's add the JavaScript using Dreamweaver's Call JavaScript behavior.

Make sure you assign the RoomsID field from the Rooms and not the RoomList recordset. Remember that the Rooms recordset is filtered to display the record currently being edited.

NOTE

1. With the ConferenceRoom list selected, from the Behaviors panel, choose Add (+) and select **Call JavaScript**.

2. In the Call JavaScript dialog, enter the following code:

   📖 From the Snippets panel, open the **Client JavaScript** folder under **Recipes > ConferenceRooms** and insert the **Edit Conference Room - Change Room** snippet for your server model.

   (VB)
   ```
   document.location.href = 'edit_conferenceroom.asp?RoomID='
   ➥+document.UpdateConferenceRoom.ConferenceRoom.options
   ➥[document.UpdateConferenceRoom.ConferenceRoom.selectedIndex].value
   ```

   (JS)
   ```
   document.location.href = 'edit_conferenceroom.asp?RoomID='
   ➥+document.UpdateConferenceRoom.ConferenceRoom.options
   ➥[document.UpdateConferenceRoom.ConferenceRoom.selectedIndex].value
   ```

   (CF)
   ```
   document.location.href = 'edit_conferenceroom.cfm?RoomID='
   ➥+document.UpdateConferenceRoom.ConferenceRoom.options
   ➥[document.UpdateConferenceRoom.ConferenceRoom.selectedIndex].value
   ```

   (PHP)
   ```
   document.location.href = 'edit_conferenceroom.php?RoomID='
   ➥+document.UpdateConferenceRoom.ConferenceRoom.options
   ➥[document.UpdateConferenceRoom.ConferenceRoom.selectedIndex].value
   ```

3. Verify the code and click OK to close the dialog.

4. Make sure that the event is set to onChange.

Now we're ready to finish off the data binding by associating the text form elements with their data source equivalents.

1. From the Bindings panel, expand the **Rooms** recordset.

2. Place the needed data source fields into position on the page:

   📖 Drag **RoomName** to the RoomName text field.

   Drag **RoomDescription** to the RoomSpecs text area [r03-25].

   For PHP and Coldfusion: Drag **RoomID** to the RoomID hidden field.

r3-23

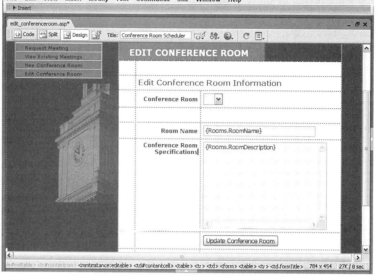

Step 4: Update Record—Conference Room

Let's add the Update Record server behavior.

For ASP

1. From the Server Behaviors panel, choose Add (+) and then **Update Record**.
2. In the Update Record dialog, select the desired data source connection.
    - Choose **Recipes** from the Connection list.
3. Choose the table containg the data you are updating.
    - From the Table to Update list, choose **Rooms**.
4. Choose the recordset from which to get data source fields.
    - From the Select Record From field, choose **Rooms**.
5. Set the primary key for the recordset.
    - From the Unique Key Column list, choose **RoomID** and make sure the Numeric option is selected.
6. Leave the After Updating, Go To field blank.

    By leaving this field blank, the page will resubmit to itself and enable the user to modify another room if desired.
7. Choose the form on the page from which to get the values.
    - From the Get Values From list, choose **UpdateConferenceRoom**.

8. In the Form Elements area, set the form elements to their corresponding data source fields.

   📖 Set the `RoomName` form element to update the `RoomName` data source field as Text.

   Set the `RoomsSpecs` form element to update the `RoomDescription` data source field as Text.

   Set the `ConferenceRoom` form element to be ignored.

9. Make sure your entries are correct and then click OK to close.

For ColdFusion and PHP

1. From the Server Behaviors panel, choose Add (+) and select **Update Record**.
2. In the Update Record dialog, choose the current form.

   📖 Select **UpdateConferenceRoom** from the Submit Values From list.

3. Select your data source from the list.

   📖 Choose **Recipes** from the Data Source list.

4. Enter your user name and password, if needed.
5. Select the table in the data source to insert into from the list.

   📖 Choose **Rooms** (**rooms** in PHP) from the Insert Into Table list.

6. Set the data source fields to their corresponding form elements.

   📖 Set `RoomID` to the `FORM.RoomID` form element as Numeric type in ColdFusion and `FORM.ConferenceRoom` as Integer type in PHP.

   Set `RoomName` to the `FORM.RoomName` form element and submit as Text type.

   Set `RoomDescription` to the `FORM.RoomsSpecs` element and submit as Text type.

7. Choose the page to visit after the update is complete.

   ⒸⒻ Select the **Pass Original Query String option,** which will insert ColdFusion code like this: `#CurrentPage#?#CGI.QUERY_STRING#`.

   ⓅⒽⓅ Leave the After Updating, Go To field blank.

8. Save your page.

Step 5: Hand Code Room Where Clause

The final step for this page (and for the application) is to add custom code to build the WHERE clause of the SQL statement. The code serves to update the variable inserted when the Rooms recordset was defined, RoomWhere.

1. In Code view, locate the **Rooms** recordset and place the cursor before the beginning of that code block.

   In PHP, due to the merging of code blocks, go to the top of the page and place the cursor just after the `<?php require_once` line.

2. Insert the following code:

    📖 From the Snippets panel, open the **Recipes > ConferenceRooms > Custom Code** folder for your server model and insert the **Set RoomWhere for Rooms** snippet.

   (VB)
   ```
   <%
   Dim RoomWhere
   RoomWhere = ""
   if (cStr(Request("RoomID")) <> "") then
     RoomWhere = "WHERE RoomID = " & Request("RoomID")
   end if
   %>
   ```

   (JS)
   ```
   <%
   var RoomWhere = "undefined";
   if (String(Request("RoomID")) != "undefined")
     RoomWhere = "WHERE RoomID = " + Request("RoomID");
   %>
   ```

   (CF)
   ```
   <cfif isDefined("URL.RoomID")>
     <cfset RoomWhere = "WHERE RoomID = #URL.RoomID#">
   </cfif>
   ```

   (PHP)
   ```
   <?php
   if (isset($_GET['RoomID'])) {
     $RoomWhere = "RoomID = " + $_GET['RoomID'];
   }
   ?>
   ```

3. Save the page.

You page is ready for testing. If you're working with a live data source, it's best to modify existing room descriptions and then immediately change them back [r3-24].

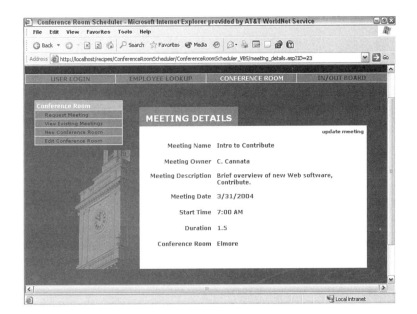

r3-24

Recipe 4

In/Out Dashboard

One of the first rules of business is to keep a close eye on all your assets—and employees are among an organization's primary assets. The In/Out Dashboard application provides a visual representation of the location for all intranet employees. With the Dashboard, you can instantly tell if an employee is in the office, in a meeting, on the road, or wherever. With minor modifications, this application can also serve to keep track of virtually any asset, such as training tapes, laptop computers, or even company cars.

Because the Dashboard is a natural employee-gathering place, it's a good location to display company-wide announcements. Such announcements need to be timely and well managed; corporate messages released before their time can be damaging to business, and those left too long on display lessen the impact of the other notices.

To support the Dashboard and its announcement section, this application uses four pages in all. One page provides the main interface for the in/out board and message section; a bullet character in a particular status column designates an employee's status. A necessary function of any such application is the ability to easily alter an employee's status; in our application, each employee's name on the in/out board is linked to a detail record where the status updates can be made. Two pages are used to administer the announcement section—one to manage the announcements in general, designating which ones should be displayed and which should be deleted; and another page for adding announcements.

User Recipes

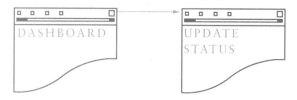

Administrator Recipes

Ingredients

4 APPLICATION PAGES:

- 2 User Pages
  - In/Out Dashboard
  - Update Status
- 2 Administration Pages
  - Manage Announcements
  - Add Announcement

1 DATA SOURCE:

- 1 Database with:
  - 3 Tables
    - **Dashboard**—Dashboard tracks each entry in the Dashboard by employee ID, the current status, and each time the status is changed.
    - **Announcements**—Announcements maintains the announcement text, its active date, and whether or not it should be displayed.
    - **Status**—Status contains each of the available status options, by ID and name. This table is used primarily to populate list elements.
    - **Employees**—Reference is made to this table, so it needs to be included here for clarity.

- 1 View
  - **EmployeeDashboard**—This is a virtual table joining the Announcements, Dashboard, and Status tables.

Prep Work

Before you begin to build this application, make sure your prep work has been completed.

1. Create the data source containing the necessary tables.
   - 📖 ASP and ColdFusion users should use the **Recipes.mdb** data source found in the downloaded files while PHP users should work with the **Recipes** data source. For assistance in locating and installing these files, choose **Help > Web Application Recipes**.
2. Set up a connection to the data source. If you're unsure how to do this, see the "Connecting to Data Sources" section of Chapter 1.
   - 📖 Name the connection **Recipes**.
3. Create the template to be used for the application.
   - 📖 If you're not using the prepared files, use the template for your server model named **inoutboard**.

End User Recipe: Dashboard

Our electronic version of the old In/Out Dashboard gives an immediate visual clue as to the whereabouts of any employee. Instead of pushpins in a chart behind a secretary's desk, we use bullet symbols in a multicolumn table, available from anywhere on the intranet. The example shows seven possible status locations. These columns are, of course, completely customizable. Each employee's name acts as a link to change the status.

An announcement section is included at the bottom of the in/out board. For an announcement to be shown, it must not be dated in the future and it must be cleared for posting by an administrator. The announcements are sorted in descending date order, so the newest are displayed on top.

Step 1: Implement Dashboard Design

The basic Dashboard page consists of two main display areas: one for the Dashboard itself and one for the announcements section.

1. Create a basic dynamic page, either by hand or derived from a template.

   📖 In the **InOutBoard** folder, locate the folder for your server model and open the `dashboard` page found there.

2. Add a table to the Content region of your page to contain the interface elements for the application.

   📖 From the Snippets panel, drag the **Recipes > InOutBoard > Wireframes > InOut Dashboard - Wireframe** snippet into the Content editable region.

3. Within the table, nest another HTML table to display the In/Out Dashboard results. The list should have a column for the employee name as well as one for each status you want to display; our example table has room for seven such fields. Make sure your table has a border of at least 1 pixel to separate the various status fields and employees.

   📖 Place your cursor in the first row below the words IN/OUT DASHBOARD and insert the **Recipes > InOutBoard > ContentTables > InOut Dashboard - Content Table** snippet.

> **NOTE**
> By using the same color for the border as the background color of the header row, you can displays lines where they're vital—in the employee rows—and keep them out of the areas where they would distract, such as the header area.

4. Below the table with the In/Out Dashboard display, add another to hold the current announcements. This table only needs two columns: one for the date and another for the announcement.

   📖 Place your cursor in the bottom row of the wireframe and insert the **Recipes > InOutBoard > ContentTables > Announcements - Content Table** snippet [r4-1].

r4-1
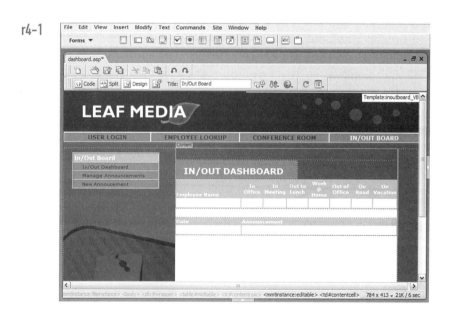

Step 2: Add Database Components (Part 1)

With two different display areas, you might expect that we'd need two different record-sets, and you'd be right. The first recordset contains information that will be used to fill out the In/Out Dashboard area with each employee's name and their status. The second recordset gathers all the data for the announcements area. Each recordset is somewhat involved and worthy of a bit of explanation.

Let's start by adding the recordset for the announcement section because the process is similar for all server models. What distinguishes this recordset is the WHERE clause of the SQL statement. To ensure that an announcement is not displayed before it is supposed to be, a two-part WHERE clause is used. In ASP and ColdFusion, the WHERE clause is as follows:

```
WHERE AnnouncementDate <= Date() AND AnnouncementDisplayed <> 0
```

For PHP/MySQL, the same functionality is achieved like this:

```
WHERE AnnouncementDate <= CURDATE() AND AnnouncementDisplayed!=0
```

The first half of the statement ensures that the announcement date is less than or equal to today (as returned by the Date() or CurDate() function), and the second half checks to see whether the AnnouncementDisplayed field—which is a boolean field controlled on the Manage Announcements page—is not equal to false. You should note that the date functions are related to the databases Access and MySQL; other data sources might require a different syntax.

Here are the steps for building the Announcement recordset:

> To prepare for this step, copy the snippet to the clipboard by first navigating to the **Recipes > InOutBoard > SQL** folder. Then right-click (Control-click) on either the **Dashboard – Announcement RS** or the **Dashboard – Announcement RS PHP** snippet and choose Copy Snippet.

1. From the Bindings panel, choose Add (+) and select **Recordset (Query)**.
2. Switch to the advanced view and enter an appropriate name for the recordset [r4-2].

> Enter **Announcement** in the Name field.

r4-2

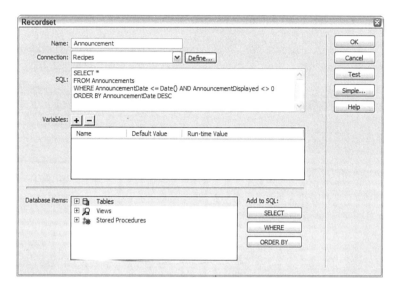

3. Select the connection (data source) for the recordset.

    ▭ Choose **Recipes** from the Connections (Data Source) list.

4. In the SQL area, enter the following code:

    ▭ Press Ctrl-V (Command-V) to paste the copied snippet into the SQL area.

```
SELECT *
FROM Announcements
WHERE AnnouncementDate <= Date() AND AnnouncementDisplayed <> 0
ORDER BY AnnouncementDate DESC
```

(PHP)
```
SELECT *
FROM Announcements
WHERE AnnouncementDate <= CURDATE() AND AnnouncementDisplayed != 0
ORDER BY AnnouncementDate DESC
```

5. Verify your code and click OK to close the dialog.

6. Save the page.

Step 3: Add Database Components (Part 2)

The second recordset required by the Dashboard page is used to populate the main in/out board interface.

For ASP and ColdFusion

At the heart of the `In/Out Dashboard` recordset for ASP and ColdFusion is an Access view that combines three tables: `Employees`, `Dashboard`, and `Status`. To obtain a listing of all the employees—even those who might not have been assigned a status yet—you use particular kinds of SQL `JOIN`s: the `RIGHT JOIN` and the `LEFT JOIN`. You'll remember that an `INNER JOIN` returns only matching results between two tables. A `RIGHT JOIN` returns all the records found in the table on the right side of the SQL clause. (That is, `FROM Dashboard RIGHT JOIN Employees` would return all the Employees records.) Similarly, a `LEFT JOIN` returns all those records in the table to the left of the keywords. To make the SQL statement that comprises the view a bit more readable, I've separated the main clauses:

```
SELECT [Dashboard].[DashboardID], [Employees].[EmployeeFirst],
➥[Employees].[EmployeeLast], [Employees].[EmployeeID],
➥[Status].[StatusID], [Status].[StatusName]

FROM (Dashboard RIGHT JOIN Employees ON
➥[Dashboard].[DashboardEmployee]=[Employees].[EmployeeID])
➥LEFT JOIN Status ON [Dashboard].[DashboardStatus]=
➥[Status].[StatusID]

WHERE Dashboard.DashboardID =  (SELECT TOP 1 DashBoardID
➥FROM Dashboard AS DB2 WHERE DashboardEmployee =
➥Employees.EmployeeID ORDER BY DashboardID DESC)
➥OR  (SELECT TOP 1 DashBoardID FROM Dashboard AS DB2
➥WHERE DashboardEmployee = Employees.EmployeeID
➥ORDER BY DashboardID DESC) IS NULL

ORDER BY [EmployeeLast] & ' ' & [EmployeeFirst];
```

Because the SQL statement is a prebuilt view—and Macromedia Dreamweaver treats views as tables—you can insert all this complexity with point-and-click simplicity.

1. From the Bindings panel, choose Add (+) and select **Recordset**.
2. In the simple view of the Recordset dialog, enter an appropriate name.
   - Enter **Dashboard** in the Name field.
3. Select a connection (data source) to use.
   - Choose **Recipes** from the Connections (Data Source) list.
4. Choose the table or view to work with.
   - Select **EmployeeDashboard** from the Table list.

5. Leave both the Filter and Sort options unchanged, and click OK to close the dialog.

For PHP

PHP users need to take a more circuitous route to build the needed recordset because MySQL does not support views. (If you've built the other applications in this book in order, you've seen a similar technique used before in the EmployeeLookup recipe.) To simulate the use of views, data from a table—employeedashboard—is initially flushed to make sure we start with a clean slate. Then that table is filled with data derived from the employees and dashboard tables, thus creating a view-like structure. The newly filled table is then referenced by this SQL statement:

```
SELECT DISTINCT employeedashboard.*
FROM employeedashboard, employeedashboard employeedashboard2
WHERE employeedashboard.DashboardID > employeedashboard2.DashboardID
➥OR employeedashboard.DashboardID IS NULL
GROUP BY employeedashboard.EmployeeID
ORDER BY employeedashboard.EmployeeLast,
➥employeedashboard.EmployeeFirst
```

Because of the way that Dreamweaver inserts code, we'll first add a new recordset using the preceding SQL and then put in the custom code needed to populate the dashboardemployee table.

    📖 Rather than enter the complex SQL statement by hand, open the Snippets panel and use the Copy Snippet command to copy it from the **Recipes > InOutBoard > SQL > Dashboard - Dashboard RS PHP SQL Statement** snippet.

1. From the Bindings panel, choose Add (+) and select **Recordset** from the list.

2. If necessary, switch to the advanced Recordset dialog.

3. Enter an appropriate name for the recordset.

    📖 Enter **Dashboard** in the Name field.

4. Choose a proper connection from the list.

    📖 Select **Recipes** from the Connections list.

5. In the SQL field, insert the following code:

    📖 Press Ctrl-V (Command-V) to paste the code copied from the snippet into the SQL area:

```
SELECT DISTINCT employeedashboard.*
FROM employeedashboard, employeedashboard employeedashboard2
WHERE employeedashboard.DashboardID >
➥employeedashboard2.DashboardID
➥OR employeedashboard.DashboardID IS NULL
GROUP BY employeedashboard.EmployeeID
ORDER BY employeedashboard.EmployeeLast,
employeedashboard.EmployeeFirst
```

6. Click OK to close the dialog and insert the recordset.

7. Save the page.

Now that Dreamweaver has inserted our recordset code, we're ready to add the custom code that initially clears data from the dashboardemployee table and then refills it with the current values.

1. In Code view, place your cursor after the code that starts <?php require_once near the top of the page and make a new line.

2. Insert the following code:

      📖 From the Snippets panel, insert the **Recipes > InOutBoard > CustomCode_PHP > Dashboard - Temporary Table** snippet.

```php
<?php
// Temporary Table population
mysql_select_db($database_Recipes_PHP, $Recipes);
// Delete current contents of employeedashboards table
$tempSQL = "DELETE FROM employeedashboard";
$tempRES = mysql_query($tempSQL,$Recipes);
$tempSQL = "INSERT INTO employeedashboard
➥SELECT dashboard.DashboardID, employees.EmployeeFirst,
➥employees.EmployeeLast, employees.EmployeeID, status.StatusID,
➥status.StatusName AS StatusName
➥FROM (dashboard RIGHT JOIN employees
➥ON dashboard.DashboardEmployee=employees.EmployeeID)
➥LEFT JOIN status ON dashboard.StatusID=status.StatusID
➥ORDER BY employees.EmployeeLast, employees.EmployeeFirst";
$tempRES = mysql_query($tempSQL,$Recipes);
?>
```

3. Save your page.

Step 4: Data Binding Process for Dashboard

The first aspect of this step should seem fairly familiar as we drag dynamic data for the employee's name into the first column. However, the balance of the step requires a bit of hand-coding to insert values for each of the status columns.

In each column, we'll insert code to display a bullet character if the employee's status ID matches that column. For example, if an employee is in the office—the first column—his status ID is set to 1 and a bullet is displayed in the first column. Anyone in a meeting (the second column) has a status ID of 2, and the bullet is displayed in the second column, and so on. Only one value is changed for each snippet of code placed in a different column.

Let's take care of the dynamic text for the employee name first:

1. From the Bindings panel, expand the **Dashboard** recordset.
2. Drag the **EmployeeFirst** data source field onto the row under the Employee Name column.
3. Press the right arrow key to move away from the selection and add a non-breaking space by pressing Ctrl-Shift spacebar (Command-Shift spacebar).
4. Select the **EmployeeLast** data source field and choose Insert; if you're feeling extremely dexterous, you can try dragging the data source field into position.

Now let's add the code necessary for displaying the bullet character.

1. Place your cursor in the row underneath the first status column and add the following code:

   □ From the Snippets panel, open the **Recipes > InOutBoard > Custom Code** folder for your server model and insert the **In Office Status - Dynamic Text** snippet.

   (VB)
   ```
   <% if (Dashboard.Fields.Item("StatusID").Value = 1) then
   Response.Write("<strong>&#8226;</strong>") else
   Response.Write(" ") end if%>
   ```

   (JS)
   ```
   <%=(Dashboard.Fields.Item("StatusID").Value == 1)?"<strong>&#8226;
   </strong>":" "%>
   ```

   (CF)
   ```
   #IIf(Dashboard.StatusID EQ 1, "'<strong>&bull;</strong>'",
   "' '")#
   ```

   (PHP)
   ```
   <?php echo ($row_Dashboard['StatusID'] == 1)?"<strong>&#8226;
   </strong>":" "; ?>
   ```

2. Repeat step 1 for each status column, incrementing the value in the code by one for each column (snippets are provided for those following the recipe). For example, in the second column, the number 1 would change to 2, like this:

   (VB)
   ```
   <% if (Dashboard.Fields.Item("StatusID").Value = 2) then
   [Response.Write("<strong>&#8226;</strong>") else
   Response.Write(" ") end if%>
   ```

`JS` `<%=(Dashboard.Fields.Item("StatusID").Value == 2)?"<strong>&#8226;`
`</strong>":" "%>`

`CF` `#IIf(Dashboard.StatusID EQ 2, "'<strong>&bull;</strong>'",`
➥ `"' '")#`

`PHP` `<?php echo ($row_Dashboard['StatusID'] == 2)?"<strong>&#8226;`
`</strong>":" "; ?>`

📖 Drag the corresponding snippet into its proper column:

- Drag the **In Meeting Status - Dynamic Text** snippet to the `In Meeting` column.
- Drag the **Out to Lunch Status - Dynamic Text** snippet to the `Out to Lunch` column.
- Drag the **Work at Home Status - Dynamic Text** snippet to the `Work @ Home` column.
- Drag the **Out of Office Status - Dynamic Text** snippet to the `Out of Office` column.
- Drag the **On Road Status - Dynamic Text** snippet to the `On Road` column.
- Drag the **On Vacation Status - Dynamic Text** snippet to the `On Vacation` column.

When you're done, you should see an entire row of symbols for server-side code—that is, if you have Invisible Elements enabled. ColdFusion users see the code or code indicator ({text}) [r4-3].

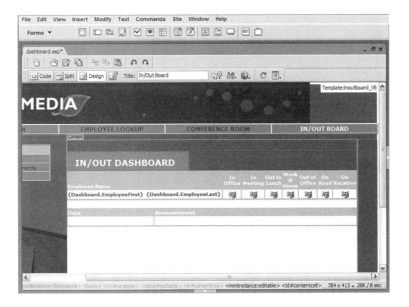

r4-3

3. Make sure all the columns have an incrementing value in the code. If, during testing, two columns show a bullet at the same time, the values are duplicates.

Creating Custom Server Behaviors

Rather than hand-code the display bullet routine seven times, Dreamweaver offers another methodology—custom server behaviors—and a tool for creating them: the Server Behavior Builder. Because this code is used repeatedly with different parameters, it's a prime candidate for a custom server behavior. Let's walk through the process:

1. Copy the code snippet you want to insert into your server behavior.

   📖 To create a server behavior that would show the column bullet, copy the **In Office Status - Dynamic Text** snippet for your server model.

2. From the Server Behaviors panel, choose Add (+) and select **New Server Behavior.**

3. In the New Server Behavior dialog, select your server model and language from the Document Type list and give the custom server behavior a meaningful name unique to other server behaviors, such as `Show Column Bullet`.

   The name you enter appears in the Server Behaviors panel.

4. If this is to be a totally new server behavior, leave the Copy Existing Server Behavior option unchecked. The Copy Existing Server Behavior option allows you to build on other custom server behaviors.

   After you click OK, the main Server Behavior Builder interface appears [r4-4].

r4-4

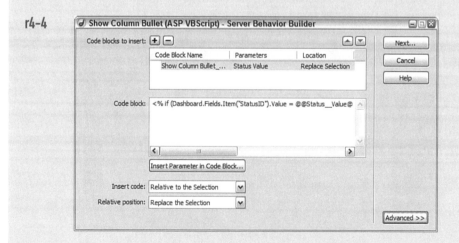

5. In the Server Behavior Builder dialog, select Add (+) to create a new code block.

6. Accept the default name or enter a custom one in the Create a New Code Block dialog, and click OK to close the pop-up dialog.

7. In the Code Block area, select the placeholder text and paste your copied code.

If you were to stop now, the code would just go in as is without parameters and would, in essence, be a code snippet. Let's add a parameter next.

8. In the code you just pasted, select the value you want to turn into a parameter and then choose **Insert Parameter in Code Block**.

  📖 Select the number value (1, 2, 3, and so on) in the code that was previously incremented.

9. Enter a label for the parameter in the Insert Parameter in Code Block dialog and click OK to close the pop-up dialog.

  📖 This label appears in the Custom Server Behavior dialog and should indicate a direction to the user, such as `Status__Value`.

  Note: A double underscore is used in the label name. The underscores maintain the name as a single string in the code, and the Server Behavior Builder displays the double underscores as a space.

10. From the Insert Code list, choose where you want the code to go.

  📖 Because we want the code to go into the current cursor position, select **Relative to the Selection** from the list.

11. From the Relative Position list, choose where the code should go more specifically.

  📖 Select **Replace the Selection** from the list.

12. Make sure all your choices are correct and click Next.

With the code to be inserted complete, all that's left to do is to specify what type of parameters are expected in the Generate Behavior Dialog Box dialog.

Continues

13. In the Generate Behavior Dialog Box dialog, select the parameter, and from the drop-down list under the Display As column, choose the most appropriate form control for that parameter.

    📖 From the Display As list, select **Numeric Text Field**.

14. Click OK to create the custom server behavior.

If you've already inserted the code, you'll see that Dreamweaver identifies that code as a server behavior now and lists all the code blocks in the Server Behaviors panel with the parameters in parentheses.

Step 5: Link to Employee Update Page

Although the code is in place to show the current status of each employee, we need a way to change that status. In this step, we create a link from the employee's name to an update status page.

1. Select the text or graphic you want to use as a link.

    📖 Select **Dashboard.EmployeeFirst** and then Shift-select **Dashboard.EmployeeLast**.

2. From the Property inspector, choose **Browse for File,** which is the folder icon next to the Link field.

3. In the Select File dialog, choose the file you want to handle the update.

    📖 Choose **update_status**.

4. Select **Parameters** from the Select File dialog.

5. In the Parameters dialog, enter **ID** under the Value column.

6. Under the Value column, select the lightning symbol to open the Dynamic Data dialog, and then choose **EmployeeID**.

7. Click OK to close the Dynamic Data, Parameters, and Select File dialogs.

8. Save the page.

Step 6: Data Binding Process for Announcements

Let's flesh out the announcement section a bit. We need to add two dynamic text elements: one for the date and one for the announcement.

1. From the Bindings panel, expand the **Announcements** recordset.

2. Drag the data source fields into their proper positions on the page.

       Drag the data source field **AnnouncementDate** to the row under the Date column.

       Drag the data source field **AnnouncementText** to the row under the Announcement column.

3. Save your page.

Step 7: Add Repeat Regions

The final step on this page is to add two Repeat Region server behaviors, one for each of the dynamic data rows. Let's work with the in/out board section first.

1. Place the cursor in any of the table cells containing the dynamic data in the Dashboard table.

2. From the Tag Selector, select the **<tr>** tag, located to the left of the current <td> tag.

3. From the Server Behaviors panel, choose Add (+) and select **Repeat Region** from the list.

4. In the Repeat Region dialog, make sure the **Dashboard** recordset is selected.

5. Choose the **All Records** option and click OK to close the dialog.

   Now let's do the same thing for the Announcements section.

6. Select either of the dynamic data elements in the second row of the Announcements table.

7. Choose the **<tr>** tag from the Tag Selector.

8. From the Server Behaviors panel, choose Add (+) and select **Repeat Region** from the list.

9. In the Repeat Region dialog, make sure the Announcements recordset is selected.

10. Again, choose the **All Records** option and click OK to close the dialog.

11. Save the page.

Enter into Live Data view to see a list of all the employees, including those with and without a current status [r4-5]. In the next section, we'll create an update status page so that we can modify the status for any employee.

r4-5

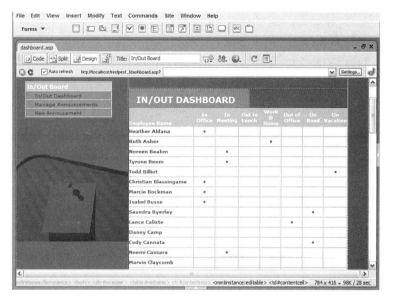

Recipe Variations: Employee Records

As currently designed, the Dashboard page shows all the employees. If your organization is fairly large, you might want to show only a few employees at a time. You can do this by changing the Repeat Region server behavior to anything other than All Records and adding recordset navigation controls as demonstrated in the Employee Results page in Recipe 2, "Employee Lookup."

Another variation would be to limit the employees by department. One way to do this would be to include a list element tied to the department recordset and filter the Dashboard recordset based on the list selection. When a different department is selected, the page is resubmitted to the server and the new filter is applied. A similar technique was used in the New Job page in Recipe 2.

End User Recipe: Update Status

As we've seen in the Dashboard page, a link from the employee's name connects to an update status page, where we can modify the employee status. All the available status options are contained in a dynamically generated drop-down list.

After a new status option has been chosen and the form submitted, the Dashboard table is updated. Because we're keeping track of each update, we're actually inserting a new record.

Not only does this have the expected effect of moving the bullet on the In/Out Dashboard to the proper column, but it also records when the status was altered. This opens the door to a possible enhancement for this application that displays a log of status changes.

Step 1: Implement Update Status Design

The requirements for an update status page are pretty straightforward: a form with a dynamic list element and a submit button.

1. Create a basic dynamic page, either by hand or derived from a template.

   📖 In the **InOutBoard** folder, locate the folder for your server model and open the update_status page found there.

2. Add a table to the Content region of your page to contain the interface elements for the application.

   📖 From the Snippets panel, drag the **Recipes > InOutBoard > Wireframes > Update Status - Wireframe** snippet into the Content editable region.

3. Within the table, place another HTML table to hold the form and its three elements: a dynamic list, a hidden form element to hold the employee's ID, and a submit button. Make sure you leave a labeled space to hold the employee's name, dynamically generated.

   📖 Place your cursor in the row below the words UPDATE STATUS and insert the **Recipes > InOutBoard > Forms > Update Status - Form** snippet [r4-6].

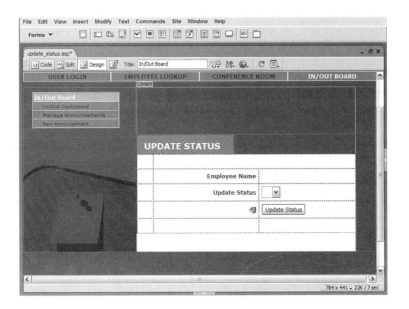

r4-6

Step 2: Add Database Components

Two recordsets are needed for this page: one to hold the employee's name, and one for the status values that will populate the list element. Both are straightforward and can be inserted without going into the Recordset dialog advanced view. We'll extract the employee data first.

1. From the Bindings panel, choose Add (+) and select **Recordset (Query)**.
2. In the dialog's simple view, enter an appropriate name for the recordset.
   - Enter **Employee** in the Name field.
3. Choose a connection (data source) to use.
   - Select **Recipes** from the Connection list.
4. Choose the table in the data source to work with.
   - Select **Employees** (**employees** for PHP) from the Table list.
5. From the Columns option, choose **Selected** and select only those fields you'll need.
   - From the Columns list, choose **EmployeeID**, **EmployeeFirst**, and **EmployeeLast** by selecting one and then holding the Ctrl (Command) key and selecting the others.
6. In the Filter area of the Recordset dialog, set the four Filter list elements like this:

EmployeeID	= (Equals)
URL Parameter	ID

7. Leave the Sort option set to **None** and click OK to close the dialog.

Now let's make a recordset to populate the Status drop-down list.

1. From the Bindings panel, choose Add (+) and select **Recordset**.
2. In the dialog's simple view, enter an appropriate name for the recordset.
   Be careful not to use a reserved word such as Status for your recordset.
   - Enter **rsStatus** in the Name field.
3. Choose a connection (data source) to use.
   - Select **Recipes** from the Connection list.
4. Choose the table in the data source to work with.
   - Select **Status** (**status** for PHP) from the Table list.
5. Leave the Columns, Filter, and Sort options set to their respective defaults and click OK to close the dialog.
6. Save the page.

Step 3: Data Binding Process

It's time to bind the results of our recordsets to elements on the page. Aside from the relatively standard operations of adding dynamic text and populating a list element dynamically, we'll also link our hidden form element to the EmployeeID field of the Employee recordset. As you'll see later, values in hidden form elements can be passed back to the data source just like user-supplied values.

First, we'll bring in the employee name as dynamic text elements:

1. From the Bindings panel, expand the **Employee** recordset.
2. Drag the **EmployeeFirst** data source field onto the row next to the Employee Name label.
3. Press the right-arrow key to move off the selection and add a space.
4. Select the **EmployeeLast** data source field and choose **Insert**.

Now let's apply the Status recordset to populate the list element.

1. Select the **UpdateStatus** list element.
2. From the Property inspector, click the **Dynamic** button.
3. In the Dynamic List/Menu dialog, select the **rsStatus** recordset from the Options From Recordset list.
4. In the Values field, choose **StatusID**.
5. In the Labels field, select **StatusName**.
6. Leave the Select Value Equal To field blank.
7. Click OK to close the Dynamic List/Menu dialog.

Finally, let's associate the hidden form element with a field from one of our recordsets. Make sure you have Invisible Elements enabled so that you can easily locate the hidden form element's icon.

1. Select the hidden form element on the page.
   - Choose the **EmployeeID** hidden form element located in the cell next to the Update Status button.
2. From the Property inspector, select the lightning bolt next to the Value field to open the Dynamic Data dialog.
3. In the Dynamic Data dialog, select **EmployeeID** from the Employee recordset [r4-7] and click OK to close the dialog when you're done.
4. Save the page.

r4-7

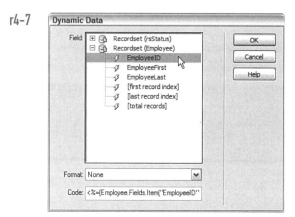

Recipe Variation: Selecting the Current Status

As designed, the Status list element initially always displays the first of the status elements in the list (in our example, In the Office)—regardless of the employee's current status. Some developers might want to bind the selection of the list element to the employee's current status. To do this, you'd need to create another recordset based on the Dashboard table (which contains the DashboardStatus field) and filtered by setting EmployeeID equal to the URL parameter ID. Then, in the Dynamic List/Menu dialog, select the lightning icon next to the Select Value Equal To field and choose **DashboardStatus** from the Dashboard recordset just established.

Step 4: Insert Record to Update Status

All that remains for this page is to store the modified information: the change in the status list. This is handily accomplished with Dreamweaver's standard Insert Record server behavior.

Why are we using Insert Record to modify a value rather than Update Record? By taking this route, we're able to keep track of all the status changes, even when they are made. If you take a close look at the Dashboard table in the Access database, you'll notice that the DashboardUpdate field is formatted as a date/time field and—most importantly—the default value is set to a function, Now(), which returns the current time and date.

For ASP

1. From the Server Behaviors panel, choose Add (+) and select **Insert Record**.
2. In the Insert Record dialog, select your connection from the list.

   📖 Choose **Recipes** from the Connections list.

3. Select the table in the data source to modify from the list.

   📖 Choose **Dashboard** from the Insert into Table list.

4. Enter the path to the file you want the user to visit after the record has been updated in the After Inserting, Go To field.

   📖 Choose Browse and locate the **dashboard.asp** file.

5. Choose the form to use.

   📖 Select **UpdateStatus** from the Get Values From list.

6. With the current form selected in the Get Values From list, set the form elements to their corresponding data source fields.

   📖 Set the `UpdateStatus` form element to the `StatusID` data column and submit it as Numeric.

   📖 Set the `EmployeeID` form element to the `DashboardEmployee` data column and submit it as Numeric.

7. Verify your choices and click OK to close the dialog.
8. Save the page.

For ColdFusion and PHP

1. From the Server Behaviors panel, choose Add (+) and select **Update Record**.
2. In the Update Record dialog, choose the current form.

   📖 Select **UpdateStatus** from the Submit Values From list.

3. Select your data source from the list.

   📖 Choose **Recipes** from the Data Source list.

4. Enter your username and password, if needed.
5. Select the table in the data source to insert into from the list.

   📖 Choose **Dashboard** (**dashboard** for PHP) from the Insert into Table list.

6. Set the data source fields to their corresponding form elements.

   📖 Make sure the `DashboardID` data column is set to be an unused Primary Key.

   Set `DashboardEmployee` to the `FORM.EmployeeID` form element and submit it as Numeric (Integer in PHP).

   Set `StatusID` to the `FORM.updateStatus` form element and submit it as Numeric (Integer in PHP).

   Set `DashboardUpdate` so that it does not get a value.

7. Enter the path to the file you want the user to visit after the record has been inserted in the After Inserting, Go To field.

    📖 Choose Browse and locate the **dashboard** file for your server model.

8. Verify your choices and click OK to close the dialog.

9. Save the page.

Administrator Recipe: Manage Announcements

For an effective announcement system, there needs to be a central page to control the announcements. Ideally, this page would display all the available announcements and give the administrator the option to display the currently applicable ones and delete those that are obsolete. What makes this application different from a standard update record page is that potentially every record could be updated. To accomplish this task, we'll need to set specific parameters for the recordset as well as add custom code to handle the multiple updates and deletions.

Step 1: Implement Manage Announcements Design

The first step in the application is to build the static elements of the page.

1. Create a basic dynamic page, either by hand or derived from a template.

    📖 In the **InOutBoard** folder, locate the folder for your server model and open the `manage_announcements` page found there.

2. Add a table to the Content region of your page to contain the interface elements for the application.

    📖 From the Snippets panel, drag the **Recipes > InOutBoard > Wireframes > Manage Announcements - Wireframe** snippet into the Content editable region.

3. Add a form-wrapped table with four columns. The table should have room for the announcement text, date, and two checkboxes. The only other form element needed is a submit button. It's also a good idea to add some placeholder text that will eventually show the number of announcements.

    📖 Place your cursor in the row below the words Employee Search MANAGE ANNOUNCEMENTS and insert the **Recipes > InOutBoard > Forms > View Announcements - Form** snippet [r4-8].

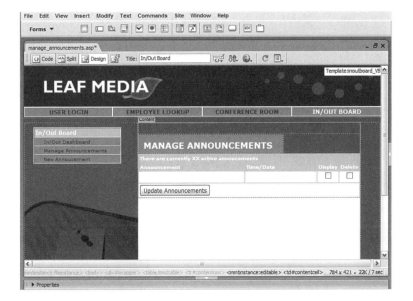

Step 2: Add Database Components

Although there is only one recordset on this page, it has to be handled in a special fashion. Because the page will include multiple updates, in ASP, two default recordset properties need to be adjusted: the *cursor* and the *lock type*. ColdFusion and PHP are capable of handling this degree of manipulation without attributes being altered.

Let's start by creating a simple recordset.

1. From the Bindings panel, choose Add (+) and select **Recordset**.
2. In the simple Recordset dialog, enter an appropriate name.
   - Enter **Announcements** in the Name field.
3. Choose the proper connection or data source.
   - Select **Recipes** from the Connections list.
4. Select the table that contains the announcements data.
   - Choose **Announcements** from the Table list.
5. Leave the Column, Filter, and Sort options at their respective defaults and click OK to close the dialog.

With our recordset set up, ASP users are ready to modify the properties.

The following steps pertains to ASP only.

NOTE

1. From the Server Behaviors panel, select the **Announcements** recordset.

2. On the Property inspector, change the Cursor Type to **Static** and the Lock Type to **Pessimistic**. Make sure that Cursor Location remains at the default setting, **Server**.

A recordset cursor serves the same basic function as a screen cursor: Both indicate position. By default, a recordset cursor moves forward through a recordset and is known as a forward-only cursor. To update and delete multiple records, the SQL operation must be able to move forward and backward through the recordset, and that requires a *static* cursor. By the way, it's called a static cursor not because the recordset navigation is locked, but because a static copy of the recordset from the data source is used.

The lock type controls if or how the records are prevented from being updated by others. The default lock type is read-only. Although the read-only mode prevents changes from being made, it doesn't offer the needed control over the recordset. To accomplish our goal, the lock type should be changed to Pessimistic. With a Pessimistic lock type in place, the records remain locked until an update command is issued.

Step 3: Data Binding Process

In addition to using dynamic text to show the announcement and its associated time and date, we'll add a repeat region to show all the available announcements. To make it easier for the administrator to know how many announcements are in the system, the total number of records is also shown, using slightly different techniques for the various server models.

1. From the Bindings panel, expand the **Announcements** recordset.

2. Drag the **AnnouncementText** data source field onto the row in the Announcement column.

3. Drag the **AnnouncementDate** data source field onto the row in the Time/Date column.

Now let's add the Repeat Region.

1. Select either of the dynamic elements just placed on the page.

2. From the tag selector, choose the **<tr>** tag to the left of the current selection in the tag selector.

3. From the Server Behaviors panel, choose Add (+) and select **Repeat Region**.

4. In the Repeat Region dialog, make sure the Announcements recordset is chosen, and set the option to show All Records. Click OK when you're done.

For ASP

Now we're ready to replace the placeholder with the dynamic record count code.

1. Select the **XX placeholder** text in the top table row.
2. From the Bindings panel, drag the **[total records]** data source item onto the page over the selection.
3. Save the page.

Preview the page in Live Data view to get a count of the number of announcements registered.

For ColdFusion and PHP

Dreamweaver's ColdFusion and PHP server models provide a server behavior for displaying the total number of records easily.

1. Select and delete the **XX placeholder** text.
2. From the Server Behaviors panel, choose Add (+) and then select **Display Record Count > Display Total Records**.
3. In the Display Total Records dialog, choose the **Announcements** recordset and click OK.
4. Save your page.

Preview the page in Live Data view to get a count of the number of announcements registered.

Step 4: Insert Dynamic Checkbox Options

It's time to add in the dynamic checkboxes with our custom code. The custom code is needed to supply two attributes with proper values: name and checked. For ASP and ColdFusion, the name attribute combines the root word Display with the entry's AnnouncementID value, resulting in names such as Display1, Display2, and so on. PHP takes a slightly different tack, where the name indicates an array (Display[]) and the value contains the proper AnnouncementID. These unique names are important because they will be used during the update process to modify or delete the records. The same procedure is applied to both checkboxes found under the Display and Delete columns. To insert the necessary dynamic values, we'll use Dreamweaver's Tag Inspector.

The checked attribute reads the AnnouncementDisplayed value for the record and, if true, includes the attribute; if false, the attribute is left out. The checked state is set with the Dynamic Checkbox server behavior.

Let's start by setting the name (and, for PHP, the value) dynamically for both checkboxes. We'll handle the Display checkbox first:

1. Select the checkbox under the Display column, temporarily named **Display**.
2. Choose **Window > Tag Inspector** to display the Tag Inspector panel; make sure the Attributes category is visible.
3. If necessary, switch to List view by selecting the A–Z icon.

   The two different views for the Tag Inspector (Category and List) were added in Dreamweaver MX 2004; Dreamweaver MX only offers the List view.
4. Select the field next to the name attribute, which currently contains the word "Display."
5. Give the name attribute a dynamic value according to your server model:

   VB JS CF Choose the lightning bolt symbol to open the Dynamic Data dialog and select **AnnouncementID** from the Announcements recordset. Position your cursor at the front of the Code field and add the word **Display** in addition to the code already present. Click OK when you're done to close the dialog.

   PHP Add an opening and closing bracket after the Display name so that the value reads **Display**[].

6. PHP only: Select the field next to the value attribute and choose the lightning bolt symbol to open the Dynamic Data dialog; select **AnnouncementID** from the Announcements recordset. Click OK to close the dialog when you're done.

The same process is now applied to the Delete checkbox to provide unique names for each of those checkboxes.

1. Select the checkbox under the Delete column, temporarily named **Delete**.
2. In the Tag Inspector, select the field next to the name attribute, which currently contains the word "Delete."
3. Give the name attribute a dynamic value according to your server model:

   VB JS CF Choose the lightning bolt symbol to open the Dynamic Data dialog and select **AnnouncementID** from the Announcements recordset. Position your cursor at the front of the Code field and add the word **Delete** in addition to the code already present. Click OK when you're done to close the dialog.

   PHP Add an opening and closing bracket after the Delete name so that the value reads **Delete**[].

4. PHP only: Select the field next to the `value` attribute and choose the lightning bolt symbol to open the Dynamic Data dialog; select **AnnouncementID** from the `Announcements` recordset. Click OK to close the dialog when you're done.

The Display checkbox requires an additional step to toggle the `checked` attribute according to the `AnnouncementDisplayed` value:

1. Select the Display checkbox.
2. From the Property inspector, choose **Dynamic**.
3. In the Dynamic Checkbox dialog, choose the field you want to evaluate.

   📖 Select the lighting bolt in the Check If field and choose **AnnouncementDisplayed** from the `Announcements` recordset.

4. Set the condition that will mark the `form` element with a check.

   📖 In the Equal To field, enter the proper value for your server model:

   (VB) **True**

   (JS) 1

   (CF) 1

   (PHP) 1

5. When you're done, click OK to close the Dynamic Checkbox dialog.
6. Save your page.

After the custom checkboxes are in place, enter Live Data view to see which announcements currently are set to be displayed [r4-9].

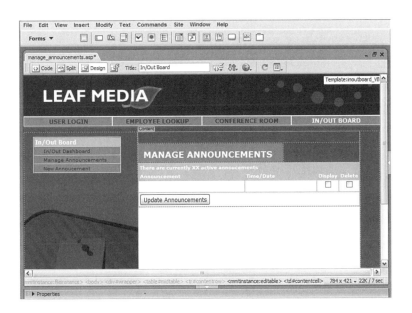

r4-9

Step 5: Update Record

The final step for the Manage Announcements page is to add the supporting logic to update or delete the records as indicated. There are two basic operations here. The first looks for entries in which the Delete checkbox is selected and deletes the record. The second compares the Display checkbox value (whether it is checked or not) to the AnnouncementDisplayed value in the data source. If the two are the same, the user made no changes, and the routine moves to the next record to avoid unnecessary updates. However, if the two differ, the record is updated to reflect the value of the checkbox. The code block needs to be placed beneath the recordset declaration.

1. From the Server Behaviors panel, choose the **Announcements** recordset.
2. Switch to Code view to see the recordset code block highlighted. Create a new line after the recordset code block and before the next code block and place your cursor on that line.
3. Insert the following code:

      📖 From the Snippets panel, open the **Recipes > InOutBoard > Custom Code** folder for your server model and insert the **Update Delete Multiple Announcement Records** snippet.

   `VB`
```
<%
    if (cStr(Request("UpdateAnnouncements"))<>"")  then
      while (NOT Announcements.EOF)
        if (cStr(Request("Delete"&Announcements.Fields
        ➥("AnnouncementID").value))<>"")  then
            Announcements.Delete()
            Announcements.Update()
        else
            Dim Display
            Display = (cStr(Request("Display"&Announcements.Fields
            ➥("AnnouncementID").value))<>"")
            if  (Display <> Announcements.Fields
            ➥("AnnouncementDisplayed").value)  then
              Announcements.Fields("AnnouncementDisplayed").value =
              ➥NOT Announcements.Fields("AnnouncementDisplayed").value
              Announcements.Update()
            end if
        end if
        Announcements.MoveNext()
      wend
      if (Announcements.RecordCount > 0)  then
        Announcements.MoveFirst()
      end if
    end if
%>
```

```
JS  <%
    if (String(Request("UpdateAnnouncements"))!="undefined")  {
      while (!Announcements.EOF)  {
        if (String(Request("Delete"+Announcements.Fields
        ➥("AnnouncementID").value))!="undefined")  {
        Announcements.Delete();
        Announcements.Update();
      }
      else  {
        var Display = (String(Request("Display"+Announcements.Fields
        ➥("AnnouncementID").value))!="undefined")
        if  (Display !=
    Announcements.Fields("AnnouncementDisplayed").value)  {
          Announcements.Fields("AnnouncementDisplayed").value =
          ➥ !Announcements.Fields("AnnouncementDisplayed").value;
          Announcements.Update();
          }
      }
      Announcements.MoveNext();
      }
      if (Announcements.RecordCount > 0)
        Announcements.MoveFirst();
    }
    %>
```

```
CF  <cfif IsDefined("Form.UpdateAnnouncements")>
        <cfloop query="Announcements">
          <cfif isDefined("Form.Delete"&Announcements.AnnouncementID) >
          <cfquery datasource="Recipes">
            DELETE FROM Announcements WHERE AnnouncementID =
            ➥ #Announcements.AnnouncementID#
          </cfquery>
        <cfelse>
          <cfif (isDefined("Form.Display" & Announcements.AnnouncementID)
          ➥NEQ Announcements.AnnouncementDisplayed)>
              <cfquery datasource="Recipes">
              UPDATE Announcements SET AnnouncementDisplayed =
              ➥#isDefined("Form.Display" & Announcements.AnnouncementID)#
              </cfquery>
          </cfif>
        </cfif>
        </cfloop>
        <cfquery name="Announcements" datasource="Recipes">
          SELECT * FROM Announcements
        </cfquery>
      </cfif>
```

```php
PHP  <?php
     mysql_select_db($database_Recipes_PHP, $Recipes_PHP);
     if (isset($_POST['UpdateAnnouncements'])) {
       // First Displays
       if (count($_POST['Display'] > 0)) {
             $bipassArr = array();
             for ($k=0; $k < count($_POST['Display']); $k++) {
                   // First the items to display
                   if ($_POST['Display'][$k]!="") {
                         $sql = "UPDATE announcements
                         ➥SET AnnouncementDisplayed=1
                         ➥WHERE AnnouncementID = " . $_
                         ➥POST['Display'][$k];
                         $bipassArr[] = "AnnouncementID !=
                         ➥ ".$_POST['Display'][$k];
                         mysql_query($sql,$Recipes_PHP);
                   }
             }
             $sql = "UPDATE announcements SET AnnouncementDisplayed=0";
             if (count($bipassArr) > 0) {
                   $sql.= " WHERE " . implode(" AND ",$bipassArr);
             }
             mysql_query($sql,$Recipes_PHP);
       }
       // Now Deletes
       if (count($_POST['Delete']) > 0) {
             for ($k=0; $k < count($_POST['Delete']); $k++) {
                   if ($_POST['Delete'][$k]!="") {
                         $sql = "DELETE FROM announcements
                         ➥WHERE AnnouncementID=".$_POST['Delete'][$k];
                         mysql_query($sql,$Recipes_PHP);
                   }
             }
       }
     }
     ?>
```

4. Save your page.

Your page is now ready for testing, although you might want to wait until the next and final page of the recipe is completed so that you can add dummy announcements for deletion.

Administrator Recipe: Add Announcements

In addition to managing existing announcements, another administrative task is to add new ones. The records for announcements are straightforward and contain only two fields: one for the text and one for the date. The date information is stored in a date/time field in the data source; therefore, it must be properly formatted before it can be inserted. We'll use a bit of server-side validation to make sure our date is in the proper format; if it is not, we include code to trigger an error message.

Step 1: Implement Add Announcement Design

The first step is, of course, to create the basic page to hold the form and its elements.

1. Create a basic dynamic page, either by hand or derived from a template.

   📖 In the **InOutBoard** folder, locate the folder for your server model and open the add_announcement page found there.

2. Add a table to the Content region of your page to contain the interface elements for the application.

   📖 From the Snippets panel, drag the **Recipes > InOutBoard > Wireframes > Add Announcement - Wireframe** snippet into the Content editable region.

3. Within the table, place another HTML table to hold the form and three elements: a text field, a text area, and a submit button. Be sure you leave space to hold a date validation error message.

   📖 Place your cursor in the row below the words ADD ANNOUNCEMENT and insert the **Recipes > InOutBoard > Forms > Add Announcement - Form** snippet [r4-10].

r4-10

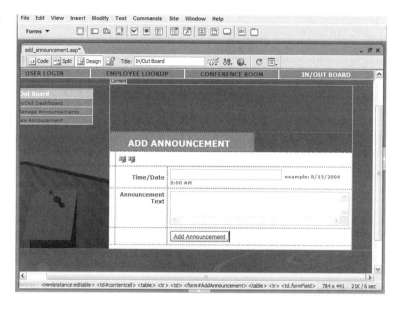

Step 2: Insert Record for Announcement

After the user has entered the new announcement information and pressed the submit button, the Insert Record server behavior logic—which we are about to apply—takes over.

For ASP

1. From the Server Behaviors panel, choose Add (+) and select **Insert Record**.
2. In the Insert Record dialog, select your connection from the list.
   - Choose **Recipes** from the Connections list.
3. Select the table in the data source to modify from the list.
   - Choose **Announcements** from the Insert into Table list.
4. Enter the path to the file you want the user to visit after the record has been updated in the After Inserting, Go To field.
   - Choose Browse and locate the **manage_announcement.asp** file.
5. Choose the form to use.
   - Select **AddAnnouncement** from the Get Values From list.
6. With the current form selected in the Get Values From list, set the form elements to their corresponding data source fields.

     📖 Set the `TimeAndDate` form element to the `AnnouncementDate` data column and submit it as Date.

     📖 Set the `AnnouncementText` form element to the `AnnouncementText` data column and submit it as Text.

7. Verify your choices and click OK to close the dialog.

8. Save the page.

For ColdFusion and PHP

1. From the Server Behaviors panel, choose Add (+) and select **Update Record**.

2. In the Update Record dialog, choose the current form.

     📖 Select **AddAnnouncement** from the Submit Values From list.

3. Select your data source from the list.

     📖 Choose **Recipes** from the Data Source list.

4. Enter your username and password, if needed.

5. Select the table in the data source to insert into from the list.

     📖 Choose **Announcements** (**announcements** for PHP) from the Insert Into Table list.

6. Set the data source fields to their corresponding form elements.

     📖 Make sure the `AnnouncementID` data column is set as an unused Primary Key.

     Set `AnnouncementDate` to the `FORM.TimeAndDate` form element and submit it as Date.

     Set `AnnouncementDisplayed` to not get a value.

     Set `AnnouncementText` to the `FORM.AnnouncementText` form element and submit it as Text.

7. Enter the path to the file you want the user to visit after the record has been inserted in the After Inserting, Go to field.

     📖 Choose Browse and locate the **manage_Announcement** file for your server model.

8. Verify your choices and click OK to close the dialog.

9. Save the page.

> **NOTE**
>
> Although the announcement record will be entered into the data source, it will not immediately appear on the `In/Out Dashboard` page. To ensure that only properly cleared announcements are seen, this application requires that the Display checkbox show as checked on the `Manage Announcements` page—thus, as it is described in Web jargon, pushing the announcement live.

Step 3: Server-Side Form Validation

Two separate code blocks need to be inserted to validate the user-entered date. One code block handles the processing and makes sure a valid date is received, and a second code block outputs an error message if a problem is found. The trick here is to place the error message code block first, so that the page is checked when it is first loaded.

1. Place your cursor in the row below the Add Announcement label and above the Time/Date label and text field.

2. Insert the following code:

   ◻ From the Snippets panel, open the **Recipes > InOutBoard > Custom Code** folder for your server model and insert the **Date Error - Dynamic Text** snippet.

   (VB)
   ```
   <% if (cStr(Request.QueryString("badDate")) <> "") Then
   Response.Write("The date you entered was not in the proper format.
   Dates should be in the format mm/dd/yyyy.  <br>(Use your browser's
   back button to edit your previous entry).")%>
   ```

   (JS)
   ```
   <%=(String(Request.QueryString("badDate")) != "undefined")
   ?"The date you entered was not in the proper format.
   Dates should be in the format mm/dd/yyyy.  <br>
   (Use your browser's back button to edit your previous entry).":""%>
   ```

   (CF)
   ```
   <cfif isDefined("URL.badDate")>The date you entered was not in
   the proper format.  Dates should be in the format mm/dd/yyyy.  <br>
   (Use your browser's back button to edit your previous
   entry).</cfif>
   ```

   (PHP)
   ```
   <?php echo (isset($_GET['badDate']))?"The date you entered was not
   in the proper format.  Dates should be in the format mm/dd/yyyy.
   <br>(Use your browser's back button to edit your previous
   entry).":""; ?>
   ```

   Now, we're ready to add the second code block to perform the date validation.

3. In Code view, place your cursor at the top of the page, just after the connection code, if any.

4. Insert the following code:

   ◻ From the Snippets panel, open the **Recipes > InOutBoard Custom Code** folder for your server model and insert the **Server-side Date Validation** snippet.

   (VB)
   ```
   <%
       if (cStr(Request.Form("AddAnnouncement"))<> "")  then
         dim DateString
         DateString = cStr(Request.Form("TimeAndDate"))
         if not (isDate(DateString)) then
   ```

```
        Response.Redirect("add_announcement.asp?badDate=true;")
      end if
    end if
%>
```

JS
```
<%
function isADate(DateString)  {
  var DateRegex = /^(\d{1,2})\/(\d{1,2})\/(\d{4})$/
  var theMatch = DateString.match(DateRegex);
  var validDate = false;
  if (theMatch)  {
    var DateObj = new Date(DateString);
  if ((DateObj.getMonth()+1 == parseInt(theMatch[1])) &&
➥(DateObj.getDate() == parseInt(theMatch[2])) &&
➥(DateObj.getFullYear() == parseInt(theMatch[3])))
      validDate = true;
  }
  return validDate;
}
%>
<%
if (String(Request.Form("AddAnnouncement"))!="undefined" &&
➥(!isADate(String(Request.Form("TimeAndDate"))) ¦¦
➥String(Request.Form("TimeAndDate"))==""))
  Response.Redirect("add_announcement.asp?badDate=true");%>
```

CF
```
<cfif isDefined("FORM.AddAnnouncement")>
   <cfif NOT IsDate(FORM.TimeAndDate)>
     <cflocation url="add_announcement.cfm?badDate=true">
   </cfif>
</cfif>
```

PHP
```
<?php
function isADate($DateString) {
  $validDate = false;
  if (ereg("^[0-9]{1,2}\/[0-9]{1,2}\/[0-9]{4}$",$DateString)) {
       $today = date("Y");
       $submittedDate = explode("/",$DateString);
       $month = $submittedDate[0];
       $day = $submittedDate[1];
       $year = $submittedDate[2];
       if ($year >= $today) {
            $validDate = (checkdate($month,$day,$year))?true:false;
       }
  }
  return $validDate;
```

Continues

Continued

```php
}
?><?php
if ((isset($_POST['TimeAndDate'])) & (!isADate
➥($_POST['TimeAndDate']))) {
    $url = "add_announcement.php?badDate=true";
    header("Location: $url");
}
?>
```

The server-side data validation is a powerful bit of code that could easily be adapted to different applications. Test your page either by entering into Live Data view and adding the URL parameter badDate=true or by previewing in the browser and entering an improper date format [r4-11].

r4-11
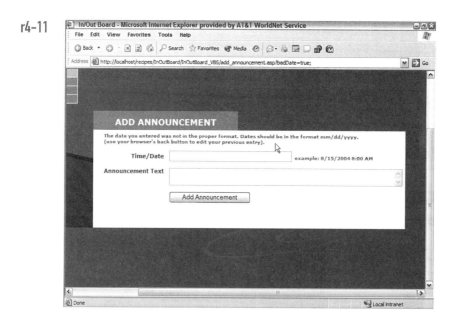

5. Save the page.

The entire application is now ready for testing and deployment.

Part III

Main Course:
Workgroup Web Applications

Recipe 5
Survey Builder

Recipe 6
Time Cards

Recipe 7
Journal

Recipe 8
Mail Merge

Recipe 5

Survey Builder

Surveys aren't just for gauging the political winds. Companies use surveys all the time to test the effectiveness of their marketing campaigns or to evaluate interest in a potential product. Surveys are valuable tools within an intranet or workgroup as well, whether they are intended to determine the direction on a policy option or uncover underlying reactions to a design approach.

There is no one fixed format for a survey; in fact, many surveys mix and match a variety of question formats. The most common survey formats include options for choosing one response from a number of possibilities, such as with a radio button group or a series of checkboxes. A survey builder application must be able to incorporate as many formats as possible, in whatever configuration desired.

The Survey Builder application, described in this chapter, meets that requirement and more. Survey Builder starts by giving you the capabilities to create new surveys and, separately, add questions to them. The Survey Manager page displays an overview of the available surveys, including when they are scheduled to be available and what their current status is—live or offline. Existing surveys and their questions and responses are, of course, editable. The actual survey page, presented to the survey taker, is assembled dynamically and the results stored for later analysis. One of the most useful aspects of the Survey Builder application is the statistics page, which allows you to see the current results at a glance, broken down by percentages.

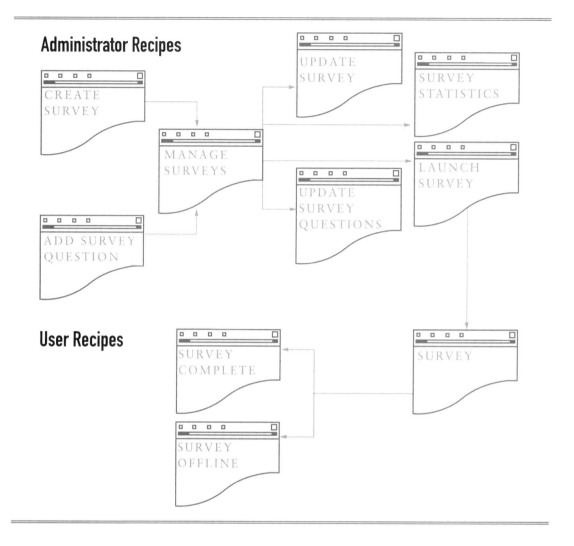

Administrator Recipes

CREATE SURVEY

MANAGE SURVEYS

ADD SURVEY QUESTION

UPDATE SURVEY

UPDATE SURVEY QUESTIONS

SURVEY STATISTICS

LAUNCH SURVEY

User Recipes

SURVEY COMPLETE

SURVEY OFFLINE

SURVEY

Ingredients

10 APPLICATION PAGES:

- 3 User Pages
  - Survey
  - Survey Completed
  - Survey Offline
- 7 Administration Pages
  - Create Survey
  - Add Survey Questions
  - Survey Manager

- Edit Survey
- Edit Survey Questions
- Launch Survey
- Survey Statistics

1 DATA SOURCE:

- 1 Database with:
  - 4 Tables
    - **Surveys**—Includes records for all surveys, such as fields for the ID, the survey name, the start date, the end date, the survey completed message, and the current status (whether the survey is live or not)
    - **SurveyQuestions**—Stores all the questions and possible responses for surveys with fields for the ID, the affiliated survey, the question type, the question, and the responses
    - **SurveyResults**—Keeps track of the survey results by maintaining fields for the ID, the associated survey and question, and the response chosen
    - **QuestionTypes**—Lists and describes the types of questions available, such as multiple choice (radio buttons) and discussion (text area)
  - 3 Views
    - **SurveyLaunchStats**—A virtual table joining the `Surveys` and `SurveyQuestions` tables
    - **SurveyStatistics**—A virtual table joining the `Surveys`, `SurveyQuestions`, and `SurveyResults` tables
    - **SurveyManagerQry**—A virtual table that extracts distinct results from the `Surveys` table
  - 2 Stored Procedures
    - **RemoveOrphanQuestions**—A SQL procedure that deletes questions that no longer have a connected survey; used when deleting surveys
    - **RemoveOrphanResponses**—A SQL procedure that deletes responses that no longer have a connected question; used when deleting surveys or questions

Prep Work

Before you begin to build this application, make sure your prep work has been completed.

1. Create the data source that contains the necessary tables.

   📖 ASP and ColdFusion users should use the **Recipes.mdb** data source found in the downloaded files while PHP users should work with the **Recipes** data source. For assistance in locating and installing these files, choose **Help > Web Application Recipes**.

2. Set up a connection to the data source. If you're unsure how to do this, see the "Connecting to Data Sources" section of Chapter 1.

   ☐ Name the connection **Recipes**.

3. Create the template to be used for the application.

   ☐ Use the template for your server model named **surveybuilder**.

4. Make sure the Copy Snippet extension found in the downloaded files is installed.

Administrator Recipe: Create Survey

The Survey Builder application allows you to create any number of surveys that, in turn, have a varied set of questions. Each survey is, in essence, a record in the Surveys data source. When the user submits the survey information, the new record is created. This record can be modified later. In addition to a straightforward form, a standard Insert Record server behavior is used in this recipe.

Step 1: Implement Create Survey Design

In this recipe, you'll build a form for creating surveys. The form includes fields for specifying a survey title, start date, end date, and brief description. Naturally, a button is also added to the form that will be used to activate the Insert Record server behavior.

1. In the server model of your choice, create a dynamic page.

   ☐ In the **SurveyBuilder** folder, locate the folder for your server model and open the add_survey page from there.

2. Add a table to the Content region of your page to contain the interface elements for the Create Survey application.

   ☐ From the Snippets panel, drag the **Recipes > SurveyBuilder > Wireframes > Create Survey - Wireframe** snippet into the Content editable region.

3. Insert the form and its elements into the table. That includes three text fields (survey title, start date, and end date), one text area for the survey description, and a button.

   ☐ Place your cursor in the row below the words CREATE SURVEY and insert the **Recipes > SurveyBuilder > Forms > Create Survey - Form** snippet [r5-1].

4. Save the file.

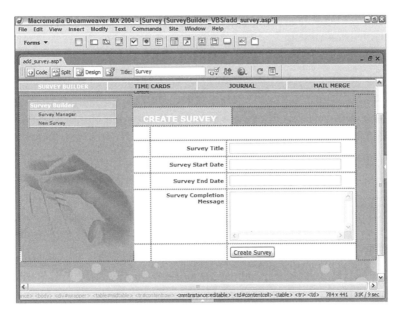

r5-1

Step 2: Insert Record—New Survey

As noted earlier, each new survey is entered as a record in the Surveys data source. To accomplish this, a standard Macromedia Dreamweaver server behavior, Insert Record, is applied. PHP users also need to add a bit of custom code to properly convert the dates for MySQL.

> **NOTE**
> To accommodate the different dialogs for the various server models, the steps are presented separately here and when necessary throughout this recipe.

For ASP

1. From the Server Behaviors panel, choose Add (+) and select **Insert Record** from the list.

2. In the Insert Record dialog, choose your data source.

    📖 Choose **Recipes** from the Connection list.

3. Select the table you want to insert the record into.

    📖 From the Insert into Table list, choose **Surveys**.

4. Set the page you want to appear after the record is inserted.

    📖 Choose the **survey_manager.asp** file from your server model's folder for the After Inserting, Go To field.

5. Select the form on the current page from which to gather the record values.

    📖 From the Get Values From list, make sure **CreateSurvey** is selected.

6. In the Form Elements area, match the form elements on the page to the fields in the data source table.

   📖 Set SurveyTitle to insert into the SurveyName column as the text type.

      Set SurveyStartDate to insert into the SurveyStartDate column as the date type.

      Set SurveyEndDate to insert into the SurveyEndDate column as the date type.

      Set SurveyCompletionMessage to insert into the SurveyCompletedMessage column as the text type.

7. When you're sure your choices are correct, click OK to close the dialog and add the behavior.

For ColdFusion and PHP

1. From the Server Behaviors panel, choose Add (+) and select **Insert Record**.

2. In the Insert Record dialog, choose the current form.

   📖 Select **CreateSurvey** from the Submit Values From list.

3. Select your data source from the list.

   📖 Choose **Recipes** from the Data Source list.

4. Enter your username and password, if needed.

5. Select the table in the data source to insert into from the list.

   📖 Choose **Surveys** from the Insert into Table list.

6. Set the data source fields to their corresponding form elements.

   📖 Make sure the SurveyID data column is set to be an unused Primary Key.

      Set SurveyName to the FORM.SurveyTitle form element and submit it as a Text type.

      Set SurveyStartDate to the FORM.SurveyStartDate form element and submit it as a Date MS Access type.

      Set SurveyEndDate to the FORM.SurveyEndDate form element and submit it as a Date MS Access type.

      Make sure SurveyLive is set not to get a value.

      Set SurveyCompletedMessage to the FORM.SurveyCompletionMessage form element and submit it as a Text type.

7. In the After Inserting, Go To field, enter **survey_manager.cfm** or **survey_manager.php** as appropriate and click OK to close the dialog.

8. Save your page.

PHP developers need to take one additional step to ensure that the date is converted from mm/dd/yyyy format to the more MySQL-friendly yyyy/mm/dd format.

1. In Code view, move your cursor to the top of the page after the line that starts `<?php require_once` and insert the following code:

    (PHP) From the Snippets panel, insert the **Recipes > SurveyBuilder > CustomCode_PHP > Create Survey – Format Date** snippet.

    (PHP)
    ```php
    <?phpif ((isset($_POST['SurveyStartDate']))||(isset($HTTP_POST_VARS
    ➥['SurveyStartDate']))||(isset($_POST['SurveyEndDate']))||
    ➥(isset($HTTP_POST_VARS['SurveyEndDate']))) {
            $_POST['SurveyStartDate'] = substr($_POST['SurveyStartDate']
    ➥,6,4) . substr($_POST['SurveyStartDate'],0,2). substr
    ➥($_POST['SurveyStartDate'],3,2);
            $HTTP_POST_VARS['SurveyStartDate'] = substr
            ➥($HTTP_POST_VARS['SurveyStartDate'],6,4). substr
            ➥($HTTP_POST_VARS['SurveyStartDate'],0,2). substr
            ➥($HTTP_POST_VARS['SurveyStartDate'],3,2);
            $_POST['SurveyEndDate'] = substr($_POST['SurveyEndDate']
    ➥,6,4) . substr($_POST['SurveyEndDate'],0,2).substr
    ➥($_POST['SurveyEndDate'],3,2);
            $HTTP_POST_VARS['SurveyEndDate'] = substr
            ➥($HTTP_POST_VARS['SurveyEndDate'],6,4). substr
            ➥($HTTP_POST_VARS['SurveyEndDate'],0,2). substr
            ➥($HTTP_POST_VARS['SurveyEndDate'],3,2);
    }
    ?>
    ```

2. When you're done, save the page.

Administrator Recipe: Add Survey Questions

Now that we can add surveys, we need a way to add questions for each survey. Survey questions come in many different formats and our survey builder offers six different types: text question and answer, essay, multiple choice with one answer chosen from an option button group, multiple choice with one answer chosen from a drop-down list, multiple choice with multiple answers chosen from checkboxes, and true/false.

Each of these question types is input in the same fashion: The question is entered into a text field and the possible answers are entered into a text area field. When a question type offers multiple options for an answer, each option is placed on a separate line in the text area field. Server-side coding, covered later in this chapter, converts the text area field answer into the proper type—whether drop-down list, radio button group, or whatever—when the survey is presented to the user.

When the question is input completely, the standard Dreamweaver Insert Record behavior is used to add it to the data source and link it to a specific survey. In addition to the onscreen form elements, a hidden form field retains an ID number for the related survey. The survey ID is passed on to the data source record when the record is stored.

Step 1: Implement Add Survey Question Design

Because the formatting of the different types of question is handled by another page in the application, the Add Survey Question requires a limited number of form elements.

1. Create a new page for your server model, either by hand or by using a template.

   📕 In the **SurveyBuilder** folder, locate the folder for your server model and open the add_question page there.

2. Insert a table in the Content region of your page to hold the form elements for the Add Survey Question application.

   📕 From the Snippets panel, drag the **Recipes > SurveyBuilder > Wireframes > Add Survey Question – Wireframe** snippet into the Content editable region.

3. Add the form and the required elements: a drop-down list to choose the question type, a text field for entering the question, a text area field for the answers, two form buttons—one for submitting the question and one for cancelling the operation—and the previously mentioned hidden field.

   📕 Place your cursor in the row below the words ADD SURVEY QUESTION and insert the **Recipes > SurveyBuilder > Forms > Add Survey Question - Form** snippet [r5-2].

r5-2

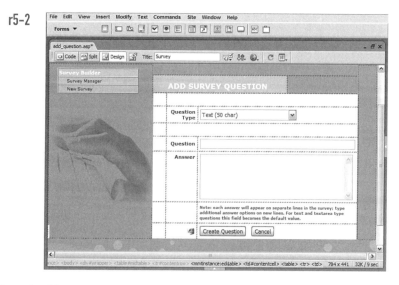

4. Save the file.

Step 2: Add Dynamic Attributes

Two elements require a nominal bit of hand-coding. First, we have to set the hidden element to store the survey ID passed to it by the Edit Survey page. Second, we need to add a bit of JavaScript to effectively abort the operation when the Cancel button is clicked.

Let's enter the code for the hidden element first:

1. Make sure you can see the Hidden Form Field symbol in Design view. If it's not visible, choose **Visual Aids > Invisible Elements** from View Options on the Document toolbar.

   You might also need to enable Hidden Form Fields to display by selecting that option from the Invisible Elements category of Preferences.

2. Select the hidden form element.

3. In the Property inspector, enter the following code into the Value field:

```
VB   <%= Request("ID")%>
```

```
JS   <%= Request("ID")%>
```

```
CF   <cfoutput>#URL.ID#</cfoutput>
```

```
PHP  <?php echo $_GET['ID']; ?>
```

Next, we'll add the JavaScript to effectively cancel the operation:

1. Click the Cancel form button.
2. From the Behaviors panel, choose Add (+) and select **Call JavaScript** from the list.
3. In the Call JavaScript dialog, enter **history.back()**; in the JavaScript field and click OK.

Step 3: Insert Record—New Survey Question

After the user has entered the question and answer, the question is ready to be stored. To store the data, you apply the Insert Record server behavior.

For ASP

1. From the Server Behaviors panel, choose Add (+) and select **Insert Record** from the list.
2. In the Insert Record dialog, choose your data source.

   📖 Choose **Recipes** from the Connection list.

3. Select the table you want to insert the record into.

   📖 From the Insert into Table list, choose **SurveyQuestions**.

4. Set the page you want to appear after the record is inserted.

   📖 Choose the **edit_survey.asp** file from your server model's folder for the After Inserting, Go To field.

5. Select the form on the current page from which to gather the record values.

   📖 From the Get Values From list, make sure **AddSurveyQuestion** is selected.

6. In the Form Elements area, match the form elements on the page to the fields in the `data source` table.

   📖 Set `QuestionType` to insert into the `QuestionType` column as Numeric type.

   Set `QuestionText` to insert into the `QuestionText` column as Text type.

   Set `AnswerText` to insert into the `QuestionAnswers` column as Text type.

   Set `SurveyID` to insert into the `QuestionSurvey` column as Numeric type.

7. When you're sure your choices are correct, click OK to close the dialog and add the behavior.

For ColdFusion and PHP

1. From the Server Behaviors panel, choose Add (+) and select **Insert Record**.

2. In the Insert Record dialog, choose the current form.

   📖 Select **AddSurveyQuestion** from the Submit Values From list.

3. Select your data source from the list.

   📖 Choose **Recipes** from the Data Source list.

4. Enter your username and password, if needed.

5. Select the table in the data source to insert into from the list.

   📖 Choose **SurveyQuestions** (**surveyQuestions** for PHP) from the Insert into Table list.

6. Set the data source fields to their corresponding form elements.

   📖 Make sure the `QuestionID` data column is set to be an unused Primary Key.

   Set `QuestionSurvey` to the `FORM.SurveyID` form element and submit as Numeric type (Integer in PHP).

   Set `QuestionType` to the `FORM.QuestionType` form element and submit as Numeric type (Integer in PHP).

   Set `QuestionText` to the `FORM.QuestionText` form element and submit as Text type.

   Set `QuestionAnswers` to the `FORM.AnswerText` form element and submit as Text type.

7. In the After Inserting, Go To field, enter **edit_survey.cfm** or **edit_survey.php** as appropriate and click OK to close the dialog.

8. Save your page.

Administrator Recipe: Survey Manager

After the surveys and their associated questions are developed, you need a way to interact with them. The Survey Manager recipe shows how to construct a page that provides both an overview of existing surveys and a gateway to altering them. You can even examine results to a particular survey.

The Survey Manager uses a structured table in which each row represents a survey. For any survey, you can tell at a glance if the survey is currently live, what its starting and ending dates are, and how many responses to the survey have been logged. Moreover, any survey entry contains links for modifying the survey itself (and, subsequently, its questions), testing the survey, or launching it. Because this is a fair amount of information to present in a table, icons are used to symbolize survey stats and tasks.

A fairly advanced SQL view—also known as a query of queries—is used to pull together data from several tables and another view. Most of the data is associated with the table through the Bindings panel or through standard links. However, some hand-coding is required to display the proper icon based on the data returned for a particular survey. In addition, we'll add some code to display the total number of surveys available.

Step 1: Implement the Survey Manager Design

To display the data for the existing surveys, you use a multicolumned table structure. The table needs a header row and a data row; before you complete the page, you must apply a Repeat Region server behavior to the data row.

1. Create a page for the Survey Manager recipe, either from a template or from the File > New dialog.

   ☐ In the **SurveyBuilder** folder, locate the folder for your server model and open the `survey_manager` page there.

2. In the Content area of your page, create a header for the page, a placeholder to display the number of surveys, and an area for the structured data.

   ☐ From the Snippets panel, drag the **Recipes > SurveyBuilder > Wireframes > Survey Manager – Wireframe** snippet into the Content editable region.

3. In the structured data area, add a table (2 rows and 7 columns) with the following table headers: Survey Title, Start Date, End Date, Modify, Launch, Test Survey, and View Responses.

   📖 Place your cursor in the row below the words SURVEY MANAGER and insert the **Recipes > SurveyBuilder > ContentTables > Survey Manager - Content Table** snippet [r5-3].

r5-3

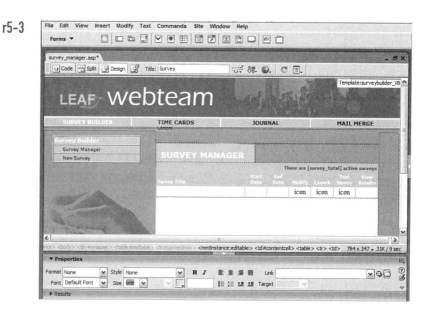

4. Save the page.

Step 2: Add Database Components

The data represented in the Survey Manager is gathered from three data source tables (Surveys, SurveyQuestions, and SurveyResponses) and another view (DistinctResponses) that combines the latter two tables to eliminate repetitive information. Here's the entire SQL statement for ASP and ColdFusion:

```
SELECT Surveys.SurveyID, Surveys.SurveyName,
➥Surveys.SurveyStartDate, Surveys.SurveyEndDate,
➥Count(DistinctResponses.QuestionSurvey)
➥AS CountOfResponseSurvey, Surveys.SurveyLive,
➥([Surveys].[SurveyEndDate]>=Date() And [Surveys].[SurveyLive]
➥And [Surveys].[SurveyStartDate]<=Date()) AS LiveImage,
➥[Surveys].[SurveyEndDate]<=Date() AS EndedImage
```

```
FROM DistinctResponses RIGHT JOIN Surveys ON
➥DistinctResponses.QuestionSurvey = Surveys.SurveyID
GROUP BY Surveys.SurveyID, Surveys.SurveyName,
➥Surveys.SurveyStartDate, Surveys.SurveyEndDate,
Surveys.SurveyLive;
```

The core SQL for PHP is similar. Creating such a SQL statement by hand obviously requires a concerted effort; however, because Dreamweaver exposes data source views as well as data source tables, ASP and ColdFusion developers can apply this to the page through the simple Recordset dialog; PHP users need to use the advanced Recordset dialog as well as a couple of helper functions to build and remove a temporary table.

For ASP and ColdFusion

1. From the Bindings panel, choose Add (+) and select **Recordset (Query)**.

2. In the Recordset dialog, enter an appropriate name.

   📖 Enter **Surveys** into the Name field.

3. Select the desired data source connection.

   📖 Choose **Recipes** from the Connection (Data Source) list.

4. Choose the needed view.

   📖 From the Tables list, select **SurveyManagerQry**.

5. Leave the Columns option set to All.

6. Make sure the Filter is set to None.

7. Keep the Sort option set to None and click OK to close the dialog.

8. Save the page after inserting the recordset.

For PHP

As mentioned earlier, PHP developers need to add their SQL statement by hand due to a limitation in MySQL. After the recordset is inserted, we'll add two functions—one before and one after—to create and remove a necessary temporary table.

Let's start by creating the recordset:

📖 As a preliminary step, from the Snippets panel, use the Copy Snippet command to copy the **Recipes > Survey Builder > SQL > SurveyManager RS - PHP SQL Statement** snippet to the Clipboard.

1. From the Bindings panel, choose Add (+) and select **Recordset**.

2. In the advanced view of the Recordset dialog, enter an appropriate name for your recordset.

   ▢ Enter **Surveys** in the Name field.

3. Pick the data source you want to use.

   ▢ Choose **Recipes** from the Connections list.

4. Enter the following code in the SQL area:

   ▢ From the Snippets panel, press Ctrl-V (Command-V) to paste the copied snippet into the SQL text area.

   (PHP)
```
SELECT surveys.SurveyID, surveys.SurveyName,
➥surveys.SurveyStartDate, surveys.SurveyEndDate,
➥Count(distinctresponses.QuestionSurvey)
➥AS CountOfResponseSurvey, surveys.SurveyLive,
➥(surveys.SurveyEndDate>=CURDATE() AND surveys.SurveyLive
➥AND surveys.SurveyStartDate<=CURDATE()) AS LiveImage,
➥(surveys.SurveyEndDate<=CURDATE()) AS EndedImage
FROM distinctresponses RIGHT JOIN surveys ON distinctresponses
➥.QuestionSurvey = surveys.SurveyID
GROUP BY surveys.SurveyID, surveys.SurveyName, surveys
➥.SurveyStartDate, surveys.SurveyEndDate, surveys.SurveyLive;
```

5. When you're done, click OK to close the dialog and insert the recordset.

To simulate the necessary view, we'll create a temporary table before the recordset is inserted—and then delete it afterward. This requires placing a custom PHP function on either side of the recordset.

1. From the Server Behaviors panel, select the just inserted recordset and switch to Code view.

   Selecting the recordset from the panel highlights it in Code view.

2. Wrap the following code around the selected recordset:

   ▢ From the Snippets panel, insert the **Recipes > Survey Builder > SQL > SurveyManager RS - PHP SQL** snippet.

   Before:

   (PHP)
```
<?php
mysql_select_db($database_Recipes_PHP, $Recipes_PHP);
$tempSQL = "INSERT INTO distinctresponses
➥SELECT DISTINCT surveyresults.ResultSession,
➥surveyquestions.QuestionSurvey FROM surveyresults,surveyquestions
➥WHERE surveyresults.ResultQuestion=surveyquestions.QuestionID;";
$tempRes = @mysql_query($tempSQL,$Recipes_PHP);
?>
```

After:

```php
<?php
$delSQL = "DELETE FROM distinctresponses";
$delRes = mysql_query($delSQL,$Recipes_PHP);
?>
```

3. When you're done, save the page.

Step 3: Data Binding Process

With the recordset in place, we're ready to bind the data to specific table cells. All the binding can be handing by dragging entries from the Bindings panel onto the page. ColdFusion users must apply some additional formatting to the date fields after insert them. PHP uses custom formatting code as well as a conversion function to properly handle the date values.

1. From the Bindings panel, expand the **Surveys** recordset.
2. Place the data fields on the page in their proper places.

   ▢ Drag **SurveyName** into the cell below the Survey Title label.

   (VB) (JS) (CF) ASP and ColdFusion users: Drag **SurveyStartDate** into the cell below the Start Date label.

   (PHP) PHP users: Drag the **Recipes > Survey Builder > CustomCode_PHP > Survey Manager - Reformat SurveyStartDate Column** snippet into the cell below the Start Date Label.

   (VB) (JS) (CF) ASP and ColdFusion users: Drag **SurveyEndDate** into the cell below the End Date label.

   (PHP) PHP users: Drag the **Recipes > Survey Builder > CustomCode_PHP > Survey Manager - Reformat SurveyEndDate Column** snippet into the cell below the End Date Label.

   ▢ Drag **CountOfResponseSurvey** into the cell below the View Results label. This field displays 0 until survey responses have been entered.

3. ColdFusion users should apply date formatting to the two date fields.

   (CF) Select the **Start Date** field inserted on the page and, from the Format column of the selected entry in the Bindings panel, choose **Date/Time > 1/17/00** or whichever date format you would prefer.

   (CF) Select the **End Date** field inserted on the page and, from the Format column of the selected entry in the Bindings panel, choose **Date/Time > 1/17/00** or whichever date format you would prefer.

4. PHP users need to add another function to the page to reconvert the dates to their previous formats:

(PHP) In Code view, position your cursor at the end of the document and, from the Snippets panel, insert the **Recipes > SurveyBuilder > CustomCode_PHP > Survey Manager - Reformat Date** snippet.

(PHP)
```php
<?php
function reformatDate($date) {
    return substr($date,5,2) . "/" . substr($date,8,2)
➥. "/" . substr($date,0,4);
}
?>
```

5. When you're done, save your page [r5-4].

r5-4

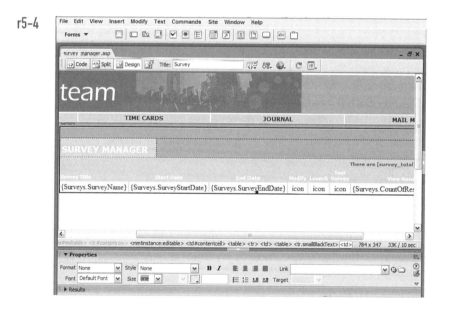

Step 4: Managing Session Data in Hyperlinks

The remaining columns in the on-page table—those that didn't use a data field from the recordset—are all links to other dynamic pages. You can either use image or text as the basis for your links for three out of the four links; the fourth link is assigned to a data field. In each case, the link passes a parameter that identifies the currently selected survey so that the proper data can be inserted into the linked page.

First, let's create the link for editing a survey.

1. Select the text or image you want to link to the edit survey application.

    Choose the word **icon** below the Modify label.

2. Select the **folder** symbol next to the Link field in the Property inspector.

   The Select File dialog opens.

3. Make sure the dialog is set to Select File Name from File System.

4. Choose **Parameters** at the bottom of the dialog.

   Although it might seem counterintuitive, we'll assign the parameter before we select the file. Because many operating systems are set to accept a single mouse click as a selection, if we select the file first, the dialog will choose just the file and close before the parameter can be set.

5. In the Name column of the Parameters dialog, enter the variable name.

    Enter **ID** in the Name column.

6. In the Value column, enter the dynamic value of the current survey's ID.

    Select the lightning bolt next in the Value column and from the Dynamic Data dialog, choose **SurveyID**. When you're done, click OK once to close the Dynamic Data dialog and again to close the Parameters dialog.

7. In the Select File dialog, select the file that will be used to edit the survey information.

    Choose **edit_survey** in the **SurveyBuilder** folder for your server model.

8. When you're done, click OK to insert the link.

Next, let's set the link to launch the survey.

1. Select the text or image you want to link to the launch survey page.

    Choose the word **icon** below the Launch label.

2. Select the **folder** symbol next to the Link field in the Property inspector.

   The Select File dialog opens.

3. Make sure the dialog is set to Select File Name from File System.

4. Choose **Parameters** at the bottom of the dialog.

5. In the Name column of the Parameters dialog, enter the variable name.

    Enter **ID** in the Name column.

6. In the Value column, enter the dynamic value of the current survey's ID.

    Select the lightning bolt next to the Value column, and from the Dynamic Data dialog, choose **SurveyID**. When you're done, click OK once to close the Dynamic Data dialog and again to close the Parameters dialog.

7. In the Select File dialog, select the file that will be used to edit the survey information.

    📖 Choose **launch_survey** in the **SurveyBuilder** folder for your server model.

8. When you're done, click OK to insert the link.

The third link to set is for testing the survey. In this case, we'll link to the same page used to actually run the survey, except that we'll pass an additional parameter that prevents the survey from storing the results.

1. Select the text or image you want to link to the **test the survey** page.

    📖 Choose the word **icon** below the Test Survey label.

2. Select the **folder** symbol next to the Link field in the Property inspector.
   The Select File dialog opens.

3. Make sure the dialog is set to Select File Name from File System.

4. Choose **Parameters** at the bottom of the dialog.

5. In the Name column of the Parameters dialog, enter the variable name.

    📖 Enter **ID** in the Name column.

6. In the Value column, enter the dynamic value of the current survey's ID.

    📖 Select the lightning bolt next to the Value column, and from the Dynamic Data dialog, choose **SurveyID**. When you're done, click OK once to close the Dynamic Data dialog.

7. Choose Add (+) to add another parameter.

8. In the Name column of the Parameters dialog, enter the variable name to set the testmode.

    📖 Enter **Preview** in the Name column.

    In the Value column, enter the boolean value to set the preview mode.

    📖 Enter **true** in the Value column; when you're done, click OK once to close the Dynamic Data dialog and again to close the Parameters dialog.

10. In the Select File dialog, select the file that will be used to edit the survey information.

    📖 Choose **survey** in the **SurveyBuilder** folder for your server model.

11. When you're done, click OK to insert the link.

The final link displays the results for a given survey and is connected to the dynamic value in the View Results column.

1. Select the **CountOfResponseSurvey** data field inserted on the page.

2. Select the **folder** symbol next to the Link field in the Property inspector.
   The Select File dialog opens.

3. Make sure the dialog is set to Select File Name from File System.

4. Choose **Parameters** at the bottom of the dialog.

5. In the Name column of the Parameters dialog, enter the variable name.

   📖 Enter **ID** in the Name column.

6. In the Value column, enter the dynamic value of the current survey's ID.

   📖 Select the lightning bolt next to the Value column and from the Dynamic Data dialog, choose **SurveyID**. When you're done, click OK once to close the Dynamic Data dialog and again to close the Parameters dialog.

7. In the Select File dialog, select the file that will be used to edit the survey information.

   📖 Choose **survey_statistics** in the **SurveyBuilder** folder for your server model.

8. When you're done, click OK to close the dialog and insert the link.

Step 5: Adding Repeat Region

Next, we'll apply a Repeat Region server behavior to display a number of survey entries. The Repeat Region is applied to the table row that contains the dynamic data fields previously inserted.

1. Select any of the dynamic data fields.

2. From the Tag Selector, choose the table row tag.

   📖 Select the **<tr.smallBlackText>** tag from the Tag Selector.

3. From the Server Behaviors panel, choose Add (+) and select **Repeat Region**.

4. In the Repeat Region dialog, choose the desired recordset.

   📖 Choose **Surveys** from the Recordset list.

5. Set the Show option to display the number of records you would like.

   📖 Choose **Show All Records**.

6. Click OK when you're done.

Step 6: Adding Dynamic Status Image

Rather than add another column to show the status of the survey—whether it is ready to go, currently running, or completed—we'll use a simple image. A little hand-coding is required to display the proper image for each survey. The code used is basically a conditional statement that sets a variable, StatusImage, to one of three image files: staged.gif, live.gif, or ended.gif. The variable is then used as the src attribute for the image.

> **NOTE**
>
> If this application is going to have a lot of surveys in the database, it is a good idea to limit the Repeat Region to 10 records and then add recordset navigation to the page. If you use this technique, then all applications that link to this page, such as add_survey, must use GET instead of POST for the <form> tag containing the link.

The LiveImage and EndedImage data fields used to determine which image to display are calculated fields that are constructed in the SQL statement. These fields are based on the starting and ending dates for each survey. If today's date precedes the start date, then neither LiveImage nor EndedImage is set to true. If today's date follows the start date but precedes the completion date, then LiveImage is set to true. Finally, if today's date follows the survey's ending date, then the EndedImage field is set to true.

1. Select the **<tr>** tag used to apply the Repeat Region server behavior.

   📖 Select the **<tr.smallText>** tag from the Tag Selector.

2. Enter Code view.

3. Move your cursor between the start of the Repeat Region code and the beginning of the <tr> tag.

   📖 Press the left arrow key.

4. Insert the following code:

   📖 From the Snippets panel, open the **Recipes > SurveyBuilder > Custom Code** folder for your server model and insert the **Determine Dynamic Image - SurveyStatus** snippet.

   (VB)
   ```
   <%
   StatusImage = "staged.gif"
   if (Surveys.Fields("LiveImage").value)  then
   StatusImage = "live.gif"
   end if
   if (Surveys.Fields("EndedImage").value)  then
   StatusImage = "ended.gif"
   end if
   %>
   ```

   (JS)
   ```
   <%
   var StatusImage = "staged.gif"
   if (Surveys.Fields("LiveImage").value)  {
   StatusImage = "live.gif"
   }
   if (Surveys.Fields("EndedImage").value)  {
   StatusImage = "ended.gif"
   }
   %>
   ```

   (CF)
   ```
   <cfset StatusImage = "staged.gif">
   <cfif (Surveys.LiveImage)>
   <cfset StatusImage = "live.gif">
   </cfif>
   <cfif (Surveys.EndedImage)>
   ```

```
<cfset StatusImage = "ended.gif">
</cfif>
```

```
PHP   <?php
      $StatusImage = "staged.gif";
      if ($row_Surveys['LiveImage']) {
          $StatusImage = "live.gif";
      } else if ($row_Surveys['EndedImage']) {
          $StatusImage = "ended.gif";
      }
      ?>
```

Now that the code is set, let's insert the `<img>` tag with the variable src value.

5. Place your cursor before the `SurveyName` dynamic text element. Add a space to keep a bit of distance between the image and the survey title.

   A nonbreaking space works the most consistently across the browsers and in Dreamweaver Live Data view.

6. Insert the following code:

   From the Snippets panel, open the **Recipes > SurveyBuilder > Custom Code** folder for your server model and insert the **Dynamic Image - SurveyStatus** snippet.

```
VB    <img src="../../images/surveybuilder/<%=StatusImage%>"
      ➥ALT="Survey Status" align="absmiddle">
```

```
JS    <img src="../../images/surveybuilder/<%=StatusImage%>"
      ➥ALT="Survey Status" align="absmiddle">
```

```
CF    <img src="../../images/surveybuilder/#StatusImage#"
      ➥ALT="Survey Status" align="absmiddle">
```

```
PHP   img src="../../images/surveybuilder/<?php echo $StatusImage; ?>"
      ➥ALT="Survey Status" align="absmiddle">
```

This code assumes that `staged.gif`, `live.gif`, and `ended.gif` are stored in the **images/surveybuilder** folder two levels above the current page; if the path to your images is different, alter the code accordingly.

7. Save your page.

> **NOTE**
> Dreamweaver inserts a 32×32 placeholder for the dynamic image. The actual images are 38 pixels wide by 32 pixels high. You can change the size of the placeholder by selecting it and then, in the Property inspector, entering modified values as needed in the Width and Height fields.

After some surveys have been entered, you can test the display of the images in Live Data view. Our example figure illustrates the use of graphics replacing the "icon" text [r5-5].

r5-5

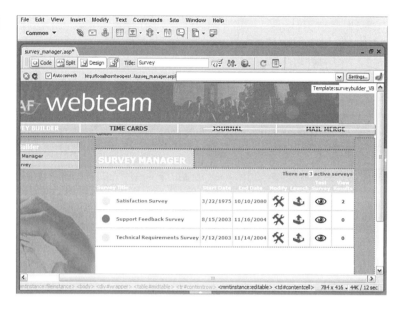

Step 7: Display Total Surveys

The finishing touch to this page is to display the total number of surveys in the system, whether staged, active, or completed. ASP users can drag a data field from the Bindings panel onto the page to accomplish this, whereas ColdFusion and PHP users can take advantage of a Dreamweaver application object.

1. Place your cursor where you would like the number of surveys to appear.

   📖 Select the text [**survey_total**] in the phrase above the header row.

2. ASP users can use the Total Records data element from the Bindings panel:

   (VB) (JS) From the Bindings panel, expand the Surveys recordset and drag the **Total Records** data entry onto the selected text.

3. ColdFusion and PHP users can use the Total Records object:

   (CF) (PHP) Delete the placeholder text and choose **Insert > Application Objects > Display Record Count > Total Records**.

   The same object is available from the Application category of the Insert bar.

4. Save your page.

As noted earlier, after you've added one or more surveys, you can test the page either in Live Data view or on your testing server.

Administrator Recipe: Edit Survey

The `Edit Survey` page serves three main functions: to modify the survey information such as title and start/end dates; to provide an overview of associated questions and a link to modify them; and to take the survey offline, even when in the declared active timeframe. A parameter, passed from the link in Survey Manager, determines the proper survey record to use; our custom code redirects the user to the `Survey Manager` page if the parameter is missing, which is a far better solution than displaying an empty record-set. Because the `Edit Survey` page is also the conduit to modifying the survey's questions, the URL parameter, if found, is put into a session variable and used to filter the survey recordset. In addition to the survey recordset, a second recordset for the questions is created for this page.

When the modifications to the survey record are complete, a standard Update Record server behavior stores the changes. In addition to updating the current survey record, the Edit Survey recipe describes how to delete a record. What makes this delete function different from others included in this book is that it also removes associated records—in this case, orphaned questions.

Step 1: Implement Edit Survey Design

To handle the requirements for the Edit Survey page, the layout must accommodate both a form for displaying the survey fields and a content table for listing the questions.

1. Create a page for the Edit Survey recipe, either from a template or from the File > New dialog.

       In the **SurveyBuilder** folder, locate the folder for your server model and open the `Edit_Survey` page.

2. In the Content area of your page, create a header for the page—a placeholder to hold both the form and the content table.

       From the Snippets panel, drag the **Recipes > SurveyBuilder > Wireframes > Edit Survey – Wireframe** snippet into the Content editable region.

3. In the form area, add a form with the following form elements: three text fields (for the survey title, start date, and end date), one text area (for the completion message), one checkbox to enable or disable the survey, and three buttons (to update or delete the survey or to add a new question).

       Place your cursor in the first row below the words EDIT SURVEY and insert the **Recipes > SurveyBuilder > Forms > Edit Survey - Form** snippet.

4. In the Content area, create a table, 2 rows by 2 columns, to hold the questions.

  📖 Place your cursor in the third row below the words EDIT SURVEY—at the bottom of the content region—and insert the **Recipes > SurveyBuilder > ContentTables > Survey Questions - Content Table** snippet [r5-6].

r5-6

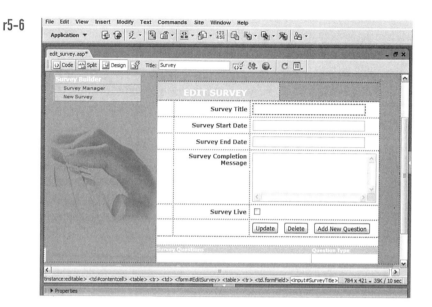

5. Save the page.

Step 2: Adding Database Components

Quite often in this book's recipes when custom code is added, it is inserted after a standard Dreamweaver server behavior has been applied. In this case, however, we need to include the custom code first because the server behavior relies on the code's results.

If you've completed the Survey Manager recipe, you'll remember how a URL parameter (ID) is used to pass the SurveyID to various pages, including this one. Our custom code takes the URL parameter and puts it in a session variable that can be used when editing the associated questions. If the URL parameter is not found, the code redirects the user to the Survey Manager page to select a survey to work on. The user is also redirected to the Survey Manager page if the session has expired.

1. In Code view, place the cursor at the top of the page, just after the DOCTYPE declaration, and press Enter (Return) to make a space.

   Don't worry about the exact placement of this code block; because of the way Dreamweaver inserts recordsets, we'll need to adjust its placement later in the recipe.

2. Insert the following code:

   📖 From the Snippets panel, open the **Recipes > SurveyBuilder > Custom Code** folder for your server model and insert the **Set Session - SurveyID to Request ID** snippet.

   (VB)
   ```
   <%
   if (cStr(Request("ID"))<>"") then
       Session("SurveyID") = cStr(Request("ID"))
   end if
   if (cStr(Session("ID"))="") then
       Response.Redirect("survey_manager.asp")
   end if
   %>
   ```

   (JS)
   ```
   <%
   if (String(Request("ID"))!="undefined")
       Session("SurveyID") = String(Request("ID"));
   if (String(Session("ID"))=="undefined")
       Response.Redirect("survey_manager.asp");
   %>
   ```

   (CF)
   ```
   <cfif isDefined("URL.ID">
       <cfset Session.SurveyID = URL.ID>
   </cfif>
   <cfif not IsDefined("Session.ID")>
       <cflocation url="survey_manager.cfm">
   </cfif>
   ```

   (PHP)
   ```
   <?php
   session_start();
   if (isset($_GET['ID'])) {
       $_SESSION['ID'] = $_GET['ID'];
   } else {
       header("Location: survey_manager.php");
   }
   ?>
   ```

3. When you're done, save the page.

Now we're ready to insert the first of two recordsets, both of which reference the session variable just set.

1. From the Bindings panel, choose Add (+) and select **Recordset (Query)** from the list.
2. In the simple Recordset dialog, give the recordset an appropriate name.

   📖 Enter **Survey** in the Name field.
3. Select the desired data source connection.

   📖 Choose **Recipes** from the Connection (Data Source) list.
4. Choose the needed recordset.

   📖 From the Tables list, select **Surveys** (**surveys** in PHP).

5. Leaving the Columns option set to All, set the four Filter list elements like this:

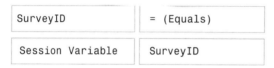

6. Keep the Sort option set to None and click OK to close the dialog.

The second recordset, which displays a list of the survey's questions, is a bit more complex. Records are needed from two data source tables: SurveyQuestions and QuestionTypes. To accomplish this, a SQL statement using an inner join is entered through the Advanced Recordset dialog.

For ASP

📖 As a preliminary step, from the Snippets panel, use the Copy Snippet command to copy the **Recipes > Survey Builder > SQL > Edit Survey RS - ASP SQL Statement** snippet to the Clipboard.

1. From the Bindings panel, choose Add (+) and select **Recordset (Query)** from the list.
2. In the Recordset dialog, choose **Advanced**.
3. Enter an appropriate name for the recordset.

   📖 Enter **Questions** in the Name field.
4. Select the desired data source.

   📖 Choose **Recipes** from the Connections list.

5. In the SQL area, enter the following code:

   📖 Paste the copied snippet into the SQL area by pressing Ctrl-V (Command-V).

   ```
   SELECT *
   FROM SurveyQuestions INNER JOIN QuestionTypes ON
   ➥SurveyQuestions.QuestionType = QuestionTypes.TypeID
   WHERE QuestionSurvey = IDParam
   ```

6. In the Variables section, choose Add (+) to create a new variable.

7. Enter the name for the variable.

   📖 In the Name column, enter **IDParam**.

8. Enter a default value for the variable.

   📖 In the Default Value column, enter **1**.

   Enter a run-time value for the variable.

   In the Run-Time Value column, enter **Session("SurveyID")**.

   📖 Click OK to close the dialog and insert the recordset.

For ColdFusion

   📖 As a preliminary step, from the Snippets panel, use the Copy Snippet command to copy the **Recipes > Survey Builder > SQL > Edit Survey RS - CF SQL Statement** snippet to the Clipboard.

1. From the Bindings panel, choose Add (+) and select **Recordset (Query)**.

2. Switch to the advanced view of the dialog and enter an appropriate name for the recordset.

   📖 Enter **Questions** in the Name field.

3. Choose your data source.

   📖 Select **Recipes** from the Data Source list.

4. Enter a username and password if necessary.

5. In the SQL area, enter the following code:

   📖 Paste the copied snippet into the SQL area by pressing Ctrl-V (Command-V)

   ```
   SELECT *
   FROM SurveyQuestions INNER JOIN QuestionTypes ON
   ➥SurveyQuestions.QuestionType = QuestionTypes.TypeID
   WHERE QuestionSurvey = #Session.SurveyID#
   ```

6. In the Page Parameter section, choose Add (+) and, in the Add Parameter dialog, make sure **Session.SurveyID** is chosen in the Name list.

7. Enter 0 as the Default Value and click OK to close the dialog.

8. Verify your entries in the Recordset dialog and click OK to close that dialog.

For PHP

    📖 As a preliminary step, from the Snippets panel, use the Copy Snippet command to copy the **Recipes > Survey Builder > SQL > Edit Survey RS - PHP SQL Statement** snippet to the Clipboard.

1. From the Bindings panel, choose Add (+) and select **Recordset** from the list.

2. In the Recordset dialog, choose **Advanced**.

3. Enter an appropriate name for the recordset.

    📖 Enter **Questions** in the Name field.

4. Select the desired data source.

    📖 Choose **Recipes** from the Connections list.

5. In the SQL area, enter the following code:

    📖 Press Ctrl-V (Command-V) to paste the copied snippet into the SQL area.

```
SELECT *
FROM surveyquestions INNER JOIN questiontypes
➥ON surveyquestions.QuestionType = questiontypes.TypeID
WHERE questionsurvey = IDParam
```

6. In the Variables section, choose Add (+) to create a new variable.

7. Enter the name for the variable in the Add Variable dialog.

    📖 In the Name field, enter **IDParam**.

8. Enter a default value for the variable.

    📖 In the Default Value field, enter **1**.

9. Enter a run-time value for the variable.

    📖 In the Run-time Value field, enter **$_SESSION['SurveyID']** and click OK to close the Add Variable dialog.

10. Click OK again to close the Recordset dialog and insert the recordset.

Step 3: Data Binding Process

Now that we have our two recordsets ready to go, we'll bind the data to the various form and text elements. First, we'll attach data fields from the Survey recordset to the form elements. As with the Survey Manager page, PHP requires custom formatting code and a function for converting the date values into a usable format.

1. From the Bindings panel, expand the **Survey** recordset.
2. Place the data source fields onto the page in their respective areas:

   📖 Drag **SurveyName** onto the SurveyTitle text field.

   (VB) (JS) (CF) ASP and ColdFusion users: Drag **SurveyStartDate** onto the SurveyStartDate text field.

   (PHP) PHP users: Select the SurveyStartDate text field, switch to Code view, and then insert the **Recipes > Survey Builder > CustomCode_PHP > Survey Manager - Reformat SurveyStartDate Column** snippet into the `value` attribute.

   (VB) (JS) (CF) ASP and ColdFusion users: Drag **SurveyEndDate** onto the SurveyEndDate text field.

   (PHP) PHP users: Select the SurveyEndDate text field, switch to Code view, and then insert the **Recipes > Survey Builder > CustomCode_PHP > Survey Manager - Reformat SurveyEndDate Column** snippet into the `value` attribute.

   📖 Drag **SurveyCompletedMessage** onto the SurveyCompletionMessage text area.

3. ColdFusion users should apply formatting to the two date form fields:

   (CF) Select the `SurveyStartDate` form field and, from the Format column of the selected entry in the Bindings panel, choose **Date/Time > 1/17/00** or whichever date format you would prefer.

   (CF) Select the `SurveyEndDate` form field and, from the Format column of the selected entry in the Bindings panel, choose **Date/Time > 1/17/00** or whichever date format you'd prefer.

4. PHP users need to add another function to the page to reconvert the dates to their previous formats:

   (PHP) In Code view, position your cursor at the end of the document and, from the Snippets panel, insert the **Recipes > SurveyBuilder > CustomCode_PHP > Survey Manager - Reformat Date** snippet.

   (PHP)
   ```php
   <?php
   function reformatDate($date) {
       return substr($date,5,2) . "/" . substr($date,8,2)
   ➥. "/" . substr($date,0,4);
   }
   ?>
   ```

All that's left in the Survey recordset is to link the checkbox to a data field.

1. Select the **SurveyStatus** checkbox next to the Live label.
2. In the Property inspector, choose **Dynamic** to open the Dynamic CheckBox dialog.
3. Select the lightning bolt next to the Check If field to open the Dynamic Data dialog.
4. In the Dynamic Data dialog, select **SurveyLive** from the `Survey` recordset and click OK.

5. In the Equal To field, enter **True** and click OK to close the Dynamic CheckBox dialog [r5-7].

r5-7

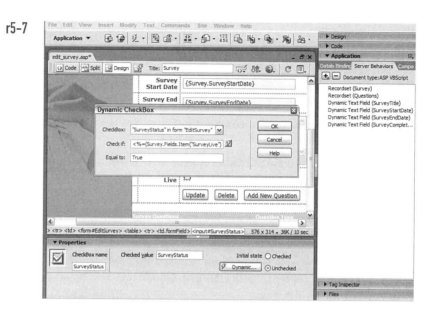

One extra step is required for the ColdFusion and PHP server models for the survey section. A hidden field form element is needed to hold the session variable so that it can be used in the Update Record server behavior applied in the next step of the recipe.

1. From the Forms tab of the Insert bar, choose **Hidden Field**.
2. In the Property inspector, enter **SurveyID** in the Name field on the left side of the inspector.
3. Enter the session variable data field as the hidden element's value:

   In the Property inspector, select the lightning bolt icon next to the Value field to open the Dynamic Data dialog.

   <u>CF</u> In the Dynamic Data dialog, expand the CFParam entry and choose **SESSION.SurveyID**. Click OK when you're done.

   <u>PHP</u> Enter the following code directly into the Init Val field of the Property inspector:

   ```
   <?php echo $_SESSION['SurveyID']; ?>
   ```

4. When you're done, save your page.

Let's move on to binding data in the Survey Questions area. To display a list of questions for a particular form, we'll bind two data fields from the Questions recordset.

1. From the Bindings panel, expand the **Questions** recordset.
2. Place the data fields on the page in the appropriate places.

   📖 Drag **QuestionText** onto the table cell beneath the label Survey Questions.

   📖 Drag **QuestionType** (**TypeName** in PHP) onto the table cell beneath the label Question Type.

Now we'll use one of the fields just inserted as a link for editing a particular question.

1. Select the **Questions.QuestionText** dynamic text entry from the page.
2. In the Property inspector, select the **folder** icon next to the Link field to open the Select File dialog.
3. In the Select File dialog, choose **Parameters**.
4. In the Parameters dialog, enter a variable name.

   📖 Enter **ID** in the Name column.
5. Enter a value for the new variable.

   📖 In the Value column, select the lightning bolt symbol to open the Dynamic Data dialog. From there, choose **QuestionsID** from the Questions recordset and click OK to close the Dynamic Data dialog.
6. Click OK to close the Parameters dialog.
7. Choose a file to pass the parameter to.

   📖 Select the **edit_question** file for your server model.
8. Click OK to close the dialog and add the link.

Finally, we'll apply a Repeat Region server behavior to the entire row.

1. From the Question recordset, select the row that contains the dynamic text elements.

   📖 Choose **<tr>** from the Tag Selector.
2. From the Server Behaviors panel, choose Add (+) and select **Repeat Region** from the list.
3. In the Repeat Region dialog, choose the desired recordset.

   📖 Select **Questions** from the Recordset list.
4. Select the number of records you want to show.

   📖 Choose **Show All Records**.
5. Click OK when you're done.
6. Save the page.

Step 4: Update the Modified Record

The Update Record server behavior stores the modified values in the Survey recordset. After the record has been updated, the user is taken back to the Survey Manager page.

For ASP

1. From the Server Behaviors panel, choose Add (+) and select **Update Record**.
2. In the Update Record dialog, select the desired data source connection. Choose **Recipes** from the Connection list.
3. Choose the table that contains the data you are updating.
   - From the Table to Update list, choose **Surveys**.
4. Choose the recordset from which to get data source fields.
   - From the Select Record From field, choose **Survey**.
5. Set the primary key for the recordset.
   - From the Unique Key Column list, choose **SurveyID** and make sure the Numeric option is selected.
6. Select the file you would like to appear when the update is complete.
   - For the After Updating, Go To field, select the **survey_manager.asp** page.
7. Choose the form on the page from which to obtain the values.
   - From the Get Values From list, choose **EditSurvey**.
8. In the Form Elements area, set the form elements to their corresponding data source fields.
   - Set the SurveyTitle form element to update the SurveyName data source field as Text.
   - Set the SurveyStartDate form element to update the SurveyStartDate data source field as Date MS Access.
   - Set the SurveyEndDate form element to update the SurveyEndDate data source field as Date MS Access.
   - Set the SurveyCompletionMessage form element to update the SurveyCompletedMessage data source field as Text.
   - Set the SurveyStatus form element to update the SurveyLive data source field as Checkbox MS Access.
9. Make sure your entries are correct and then click OK to close.

For ColdFusion and PHP

1. From the Server Behaviors panel, choose Add (+) and select **Update Record**.
2. In the Update Record dialog, choose the current form.

   ☐ Select **EditSurvey** from the Submit Values From list.
3. Select your data source from the list.

   ☐ Choose **Recipes** from the Data Source list.
4. Enter your username and password, if needed.
5. Select the table in the data source to insert into from the list.

   ☐ Choose **Surveys** (**surveys** for PHP) from the Insert into Table list.
6. Set the data source fields to their corresponding form elements.

   ☐ Set `SurveyID` to the `FORM.SurveyID` form element as Numeric, with the Primary Key option selected.

    Set `SurveyName` to the `FORM.SurveyTitle` form element and submit it as Text.

    Set `SurveyStartDate` to the `FORM.SurveyStartDate` form element and submit it as Date MS Access type (Date in PHP).

    Set `SurveyEndDate` to the `FORM.SurveyEndDate` form element and submit it as Date MS Access type (Date in PHP).

    Set `SurveyLive` to the `FORM.SurveyStatus` form element and submit it as Checkbox MS Access type (Checkbox 1.0 in PHP).

    Set `SurveyCompletedMessage` to the `FORM.SurveyCompletionMessage` form element and submit it as Text.
7. In the After Inserting, Go To field, enter the path to the file you want displayed after the record is updated.

   ☐ Choose Browse and select the **survey_manager.cfm** or **survey_manager.php** file, as appropriate.
8. Check your entries to verify they are correct and, if so, click OK.

Step 5: Apply Delete Commands/Queries

So far, we've handled displaying and updating a survey's record. The next step—and it's a fairly involved one—is deleting the survey record. What makes it so involved is that not only must the current survey record be removed, but so must that survey's questions and responses to those surveys. These operations are accomplished through the use of SQL commands (known as queries in ColdFusion) covered in this step.

One command, `RemoveOrphanQuestions`, removes all the fields in the `SurveyQuestions` table that no longer have a corresponding SurveyID in the `Surveys` table:

```
DELETE SurveyQuestions.*
FROM Surveys RIGHT JOIN SurveyQuestions
➥ON [Surveys].[SurveyID]=[SurveyQuestions].[QuestionSurvey]
WHERE ([Surveys].[SurveyID]) Is Null;
```

A second command, `RemoveOrphanResults`, performs a similar function for the results of questions that no longer exist:

```
DELETE SurveyResults.*
FROM SurveyQuestions RIGHT JOIN SurveyResults
➥ON [SurveyQuestions].[QuestionID]=[SurveyResults].[ResultQuestion]
WHERE ((([SurveyQuestions].[QuestionID]) Is Null));
```

As you can see, the sequence of code application is important here. First the survey record is removed, and then the survey's questions, followed by the survey questions' responses.

A bit later in this chapter (Steps 6 and 7), we'll walk through moving the code to its proper location and linking it to the Delete button. It's best to wait to test these commands until all the steps have been completed.

For ASP

First, we'll insert a SQL command to remove the current record. The ID for the current record, `MM_recordId`, is gathered from the Update Server behavior, applied earlier.

NOTE

You'll notice in both instances that a Stored Procedure command type is used. Access does not truly support stored procedures, but this technique allows us to directly execute a database command.

1. From the Bindings panel, choose **Command**.
2. In the Command dialog, enter an appropriate name.

   📖 Enter **DeleteActive** in the Name field.
3. Choose the data source.

   📖 From the Connections list, select **Recipes**.
4. Set the type of command.

   📖 From the Type list, choose **Delete**.
5. Leave the Return Recordset Named options blank.
6. In the SQL area, enter the following code:

```
VB  DELETE FROM Surveys
    WHERE SurveyID = IDParam
```

7. In the Variable area, choose Add (+) to add a new SQL variable.

8. Enter the name of the variable.

  📕 In the Name column, enter **IDParam**.

  Insert the run-time value.

  📕 In the Run-Time value column, enter **Request("MM_recordId")**.

10. Click OK to insert the command.

Next, we'll access a command included in the data source to remove the questions associated with the deleted survey.

1. From the Bindings panel, choose Add (+) and choose **Command**.

2. Enter an appropriate name for the command.

  📕 Enter **RemoveOrphanQuestions** in the Name field.

3. Choose a data source.

  📕 From the Connections list, choose **Recipes**.

4. Select the proper type of command.

  📕 Choose **Stored Procedure** from the Type list.

5. Leave the Return Recordset Named options empty.

6. In the SQL area, enter the following command call:

  `RemoveOrphanQuestions`

7. Click OK to close the dialog and insert the command.

The final command to insert serves to remove any results attached to the previously removed questions.

1. From the Bindings panel, choose Add (+) and choose **Command**.

2. Enter an appropriate name for the command.

  📕 Enter **RemoveOrphanResults** in the Name field.

3. Choose a data source.

  📕 From the Connections list, choose **Recipes**.

4. Select the proper type of command.

  📕 Choose **Stored Procedure** from the Type list.

5. Leave the Return Recordset Named options empty.

6. In the SQL area, enter the following command call:

  `RemoveOrphanResults`

7. Click OK to close the dialog and insert the command.

> **NOTE**
> Again, refrain from testing the delete command until you've completed the remaining steps for this page.

For ColdFusion

The first task is to insert a SQL query to remove the current record. We'll get the ID for the current record from the session variable SurveyID stored earlier.

1. From the Bindings panel, choose **Recordset (Query)**.
2. In the Advanced Recordset dialog, enter an appropriate name.
   - Enter **DeleteActive** in the Name field.
3. Choose the data source.
   - From the Data Source list, select **Recipes**.
4. Enter the username and password, if required.
5. In the SQL area, enter the following code:

   ```
   CF  DELETE FROM Surveys
          WHERE SurveyID = #Session.SurveyID#
   ```

6. Click OK to insert the query.

Next, we'll access a query included in the data source to remove the questions associated with the deleted survey.

1. From the Bindings panel, choose **Recordset (Query)**.
2. In the Advanced Recordset dialog, enter an appropriate name.
   - Enter **RemoveOrphanQuestions** in the Name field.
3. Choose the data source.
   - From the Data Source list, select **Recipes**.
4. Enter the username and password, if required.
5. In the SQL area, enter the following code:

   ```
   PHP  EXECUTE RemoveOrphanQuestions
   ```

6. Click OK to insert the command.

The final command to insert serves to remove any results attached to the previously removed questions.

1. From the Bindings panel, choose **Recordset (Query)**.
2. In the Advanced Recordset dialog, enter an appropriate name.
   - Enter **RemoveOrphanResults** in the Name field.
3. Choose the data source.
   - From the Data Source list, select **Recipes**.

4. Enter the username and password, if required.

5. In the SQL area, enter the following code:

     (CF) `EXECUTE RemoveOrphanResults`

6. Click OK to insert the command.

> **Again, refrain from testing the delete command until you've completed the remaining steps for this page.**
>
> NOTE

For PHP

To handle the delete command in PHP, custom code is added. The code block inserted is conditional and only executes when the Delete button has been encountered. The code block must be placed following the session variable declaration.

1. In Code view, place your cursor after the routine that sets the session variable. You'll find the code block near the top of the page. It looks like this:

(PHP)
```php
<?php
session_start();
if (isset($_GET['ID'])) {
    $_SESSION['ID'] = $_GET['SurveyID'];
} else {
    header("Location: survey_manager.php");
}
?>
```

2. Insert the following code:

     ⌨ From the Snippets panel, insert the **Recipes > SurveyBuilder > CustomCode_PHP > Edit Survey – Delete Command** snippet.

(PHP)
```php
<?php
mysql_select_db($database_Recipes_PHP, $Recipes_PHP);
if ((isset($_POST['Delete'])) && ($_POST['Delete'] == "Delete")) {
    // First delete the selected record
    $deleteSQL = "DELETE FROM surveys WHERE
➥SurveyID = " . $_SESSION['SurveyID'];
    $deleteRes = mysql_query($deleteSQL,$Recipes_PHP);

    // Now clean up orphaned questions
    $deleteSQL = "DELETE surveyquestions.* FROM surveys
➥RIGHT JOIN surveyquestions ON surveys.SurveyID =
➥surveyquestions.QuestionSurvey WHERE surveys.SurveyID
➥IS NULL";
    $deleteRes = mysql_query($deleteSQL,$Recipes_PHP);

    // Now clean up orphaned results
    $deleteSQL = "DELETE surveyresults.* FROM surveyquestions
```

Continues

```
                    ➥RIGHT JOIN surveyresults ON surveyquestions.QuestionID=
                    ➥surveyresults.ResultQuestion WHERE surveyquestions.QuestionID
                    ➥IS NULL";
                    $deleteRes = mysql_query($deleteSQL,$Recipes_PHP);
            }
            ?>
```

3. Save your page.

PHP developers can skip the following two steps because the code is already properly placed and made conditional. Resume the recipe at Step 8.

Step 6: Move Commands to the Top of the Page

For the application to work properly, three groups of code—the delete commands, the delete operation declaration, and the session variable declaration—must be moved before the recordset declarations. As you can see from the Server Behaviors panel, the three delete commands (in ColdFusion, they appear with the prefix CFQUERY) added in

the previous step now follow the two recordsets, Survey and Questions. Unfortunately, the Server Behaviors panel doesn't support drag-and-drop repositioning, so we'll have to move the code manually.

First, let's reposition the code creating the three commands:

1. Switch to Code view.
2. In the Server Behaviors panel, choose the **DeleteActive** command.

    The first of the three commands is selected in the code.
3. Select the current code function as well as the two following it. The selected code should look like this:

    VB <%

    ```
            set DeleteActive = Server.CreateObject("ADODB.Command")
            DeleteActive.ActiveConnection = MM_Recipes_STRING
            DeleteActive.CommandText = "DELETE FROM Surveys WHERE SurveyID =
            ➥" + Replace(DeleteActive__IDParam, "'", "''") + " "
            DeleteActive.CommandType = 1
            DeleteActive.CommandTimeout = 0
            DeleteActive.Prepared = true
            DeleteActive.Execute()

            %>
            <%
```

```
set RemoveOrphanQuestions = Server.CreateObject("ADODB.Command")
RemoveOrphanQuestions.ActiveConnection = MM_Recipes_STRING
RemoveOrphanQuestions.CommandText = "RemoveOrphanQuestions"
RemoveOrphanQuestions.CommandType = 4
RemoveOrphanQuestions.CommandTimeout = 0
RemoveOrphanQuestions.Prepared = true
RemoveOrphanQuestions.Execute()

%>
<%


set RemoveOrphanResults = Server.CreateObject("ADODB.Command")
RemoveOrphanResults.ActiveConnection = MM_Recipes_STRING
RemoveOrphanResults.CommandText = "RemoveOrphanResults"
RemoveOrphanResults.CommandType = 4
RemoveOrphanResults.CommandTimeout = 0
RemoveOrphanResults.Prepared = true
RemoveOrphanResults.Execute()

%>
```

JS `<%`

```
set DeleteActive = Server.CreateObject("ADODB.Command")
DeleteActive.ActiveConnection = MM_Recipes_STRING
DeleteActive.CommandText = "DELETE FROM Surveys WHERE SurveyID = "
➥+ Replace(DeleteActive__IDParam, "'", "''") + " "
DeleteActive.CommandType = 1
DeleteActive.CommandTimeout = 0
DeleteActive.Prepared = true
DeleteActive.Execute()

%>
<%


set RemoveOrphanQuestions = Server.CreateObject("ADODB.Command")
RemoveOrphanQuestions.ActiveConnection = MM_Recipes_STRING
RemoveOrphanQuestions.CommandText = "RemoveOrphanQuestions"
RemoveOrphanQuestions.CommandType = 4
RemoveOrphanQuestions.CommandTimeout = 0
RemoveOrphanQuestions.Prepared = true
RemoveOrphanQuestions.Execute()

%>
<%
```

Continues

```
set RemoveOrphanResults = Server.CreateObject("ADODB.Command")
RemoveOrphanResults.ActiveConnection = MM_Recipes_STRING
RemoveOrphanResults.CommandText = "RemoveOrphanResults"
RemoveOrphanResults.CommandType = 4
RemoveOrphanResults.CommandTimeout = 0
RemoveOrphanResults.Prepared = true
RemoveOrphanResults.Execute()

%>
```

CF
```
<cfquery name="DeleteActive" datasource="Recipes">
DELETE FROM Surveys WHERE SurveyID=#Session.SurveyID#
</cfquery>
<cfquery name="RemoveOrphanQuestions" datasource="Recipes">
EXECUTE RemoveOrphanQuestions
</cfquery>
<cfquery name="RemoveOrphanResults" datasource="Recipes">
EXECUTE RemoveOrphanResults
</cfquery>
```

4. Cut the code by choosing **Edit > Cut** or press Ctrl-X (Command-X).
5. Place the cursor at the top of the page. ASP users should place the cursor just after the Connection Include.
6. Paste the code by choosing **Edit > Paste** or press Ctrl-V (Command-V).
7. Save the page.

Next, we'll need to move the delete operation declaration. (This step is only necessary for the ASP server models.)

1. In Code view, use Find and Replace to locate the first instance of DeleteActive__IDParam.

   Note the double underscore characters in the name.

2. Cut the surrounding function by choosing **Edit > Cut** or press Ctrl-X (Command-X). The code to cut looks like this:

VB
```
<%

if(Request("MM_recordId") <> "") then DeleteActive__IDParam =
➥Request("MM_recordId")

%>
```

(JS) <%

```
    if(String(Request("MM_recordId")) != "undefined")
    ➥{ DeleteActive__IDParam = String(Request("MM_recordId"));}}
```

```
    %>
```

3. Move to the top of the page above the three commands moved previously.

4. Paste the code by choosing **Edit > Paste** or press Ctrl-V (Command-V).

Finally, we'll move the session definition to the top of the page.

1. In Code view, locate the code function above the opening <html> tag. The code should look like this:

(VB) <%

```
    if (cStr(Request("SurveyID"))<>"") then
      Session("SurveyID") = cStr(Request("SurveyID"))
    end if
    if (cStr(Session("SurveyID"))="") then
      Response.Redirect("survey_manager.asp")
    end if
    %>
```

(JS) <%

```
    if (String(Request("SurveyID"))!="undefined")
      Session("SurveyID") = String(Request("SurveyID"));
    if (String(Session("SurveyID"))=="undefined")
      Response.Redirect("survey_manager.asp");
    %>
```

(CF) <cfif isDefined("URL.SurveyID")>

```
        <cfset Session.SurveyID = URL.SurveyID>
    </cfif>
    <cfif not IsDefined("Session.SurveyID")>
        <cflocation url="survey_manager.cfm">
    </cfif>
```

The ColdFusion code is located just above the <cfquery> tags.

> **NOTE**
>
> Don't test the page until we make the delete code conditional! You could inadvertently delete a survey record.

2. Select the code and cut it using **Edit > Cut** or press Ctrl-X (Command-X).

3. Place the cursor at the top of the page under the Connection Include and paste the code by **choosing Edit > Paste** or pressing Ctrl-V (Command-V).

Step 7: Add Conditional Code

As the code now stands, the current survey and all its associated questions and responses would be automatically deleted when this page is executed. Obviously, we want these actions to take place only when the Delete button is selected. To achieve this, we must make certain the code is conditional by wrapping it with an If-then clause so that it executes only when desired.

Our conditional clause is added in two parts. The first sets up the condition and is placed before the DeleteActive declaration and the three commands/queries. The second follows the third command/query and redirects the user to a specific page when the delete action is complete.

1. In Code view, position the cursor after the session variable declaration moved in the previous step and before the delete operation declaration.
2. Insert the following code:
    - From the Snippets panel, open the **Recipes > SurveyBuilder > Custom Code** folder for your server model and insert the **If Statement - Delete Operation** snippet.

    (VB)
    ```
    <%
    if (cStr(Request("Delete"))<>"") then
    %>
    ```

    (JS)
    ```
    <%
    if (String(Request("Delete"))!="undefined") {
    %>
    ```

    (CF)
    ```
    <cfif IsDefined("Session.SurveyID") AND IsDefined("FORM.Delete")>
    ```

    Now let's add the second half of our conditional code.
3. Place the cursor below the third delete command/query, which took care of removing the orphaned survey responses.
4. Insert the following code:
    - From the Snippets panel, open the **Recipes > SurveyBuilder > Custom Code** folder for your server model and insert the **Redirect – Survey Manager** snippet.

    (VB)
    ```
    <%
    Response.Redirect("survey_manager.asp")
    end if
    %>
    ```

```
JS   <%
       Response.Redirect("survey_manager.asp");
       }
     %>
```

```
CF   <cflocation url="survey_manager.cfm">
     </cfif>
```

5. Save the page.

There's one last step to take, but the page can be previewed now if you like.

Step 8: Link to Entering New Questions

The final step is to configure the Add New Question button. We'll use the Go To URL behavior to open the appropriate add_question file while passing the survey ID as a parameter.

1. Select the **Add New Question** form button.
2. From the Behaviors panel, choose Add (+) and select **Go To URL** from the list.
3. In the Go to URL dialog, select **Browse** to open the Select File dialog [r5-8].

r5-8

4. Enter the following code in the File field:

```
VB   add_question.asp?ID=<%=Session("SurveyID")%>
```

```
JS   add_question.asp?ID=<%=Session("SurveyID")%>
```

```
CF   add_question.cfm?ID=<cfoutput>#Session.SurveyID#</cfoutput>
```

```
PHP  add_question.php?ID=<?php echo $_SESSION['SurveyID']; ?>
```

5. Click OK to close the dialog.

6. Save your page.

Administrator Recipe: Edit Survey Questions

Just as the previous recipe allowed editing of the overall survey record, this recipe does the same for individual questions. In fact, the path to this page is through the link on the Edit Survey application. Moreover, many of the same techniques applied in the previous recipe, such as those for deleting a record and all its associated parts, are used here.

Step 1: Implement the Edit Survey Question Design

The layout for the Edit Survey Question design follows that of the Add Survey Question page. There are only two real differences: First, the name of the associated survey is displayed atop the form, and second, a Delete button is added.

1. Create a new dynamic page through the **File > New** dialog or by using a template.

    ☐ In the **SurveyBuilder** folder, locate the folder for your server model and open the edit_question page there.

2. Insert a table in the Content region of your page to hold the form elements for the Add Survey Question application.

    ☐ From the Snippets panel, drag the **Recipes > SurveyBuilder > Wireframes > Edit Survey Questions – Wireframe** snippet into the Content editable region.

3. Add the form and the required elements: a drop-down list to choose the question type, a text field for entering the question, a text area field for the answers, and three form buttons—one for submitting the question, another for deleting it, and one for clearing the form. ColdFusion and PHP users will add a hidden form element later.

    ☐ Place your cursor in the row below the words EDIT SURVEY QUESTION and insert the **Recipes > SurveyBuilder > Forms > Edit Survey Question - Form** snippet [r5-9].

4. Save the file.

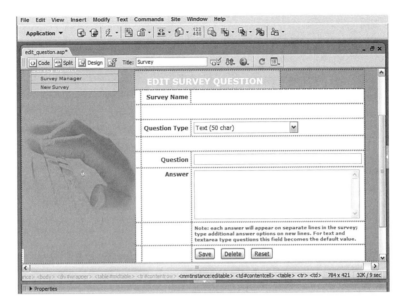

Step 2: Adding Database Components

Although it would appear that only the questions data source would be required here, a second recordset—one for the surveys—is also needed. All the standard question modifications are updated through the Questions recordset, as you would expect. The survey recordset is needed only to supply the survey title; however, an interesting wrinkle is the way this recordset is filtered: through a value contained in the Questions recordset. Because one recordset is dependent on another, the order the recordsets are declared is vital; the Question recordset must execute before the Survey recordset.

1. From the Bindings panel, choose Add (+) and select **Recordset**.
2. In the dialog's simple view, enter an appropriate name for the recordset.
   - Enter **Question** in the Name field.
3. Choose a connection (data source) to use.
   - Select **Recipes** from the Connection list.
4. Choose the table in the data source to work with.
   - Select **SurveyQuestions** from the Table list.
5. Leave the Columns option set to All.
6. In the Filter area of the Recordset dialog, set the four Filter list elements like this [r5-10]:

| QuestionID | = (Equals) |
| URL Parameter | ID |

r5-10

Recordset	☒

Name: Question

Connection: Recipes ▾ [Define...]

Table: SurveyQuestions ▾

Columns: ⦿ All ○ Selected:

QuestionID
QuestionSurvey
QuestionType
QuestionText
QuestionAnswers

Filter: QuestionID ▾ = ▾

URL Parameter ▾ ID

Sort: None ▾ Ascending ▾

[OK] [Cancel] [Test] [Advanced...] [Help]

7. Leave the Sort option set to None and click OK to close the dialog.

Now that the Question recordset is defined, we can use one of its values to filter the Survey recordset.

1. From the Bindings panel, choose Add (+) and select **Recordset**.
2. Switch to the advanced view of the Recordset dialog.
3. Enter an appropriate name for the recordset.
   ⌦ Enter **Survey** in the Name field.
4. Choose a connection (data source) to use.
   ⌦ Select **Recipes** from the Connection list.
5. In the SQL area, enter the following code:

   (VB)
```
SELECT *
FROM Surveys
WHERE QuestionID = IDParam
```

   (JS)
```
SELECT *
FROM Surveys
WHERE QuestionID = IDParam
```

   (CF)
```
SELECT *
FROM Surveys
WHERE QuestionID = #URL.ID#
```

   (PHP)
```
SELECT *
FROM surveys
WHERE
surveys.QuestionID = IDParam
```

The remaining steps are for ASP and PHP users only. ColdFusion users can click OK to close the dialog at this point.

6. In the Variable section, choose Add (+) to add a new variable.
7. In the Name column, enter a name for your variable.

   📖 Enter **IDParam**.

8. Enter a default value.

   📖 Enter 0 in the Default Value column.

9. In the Run-Time Value column, enter the following code:

(VB) (JS) `Question.Fields("QuestionSurvey").`

   (PHP) `$row_Question["QuestionSurvey"]`

10. Click OK to close the dialog and insert the recordset.

Step 3: Data Binding Process

In this step, we'll bind the data made available through the two defined recordsets to various sections and elements on the page. As noted earlier, the Survey recordset is only used for one dynamic element: the related survey's title. The rest of the bound data is drawn from the Question recordset. In addition to the obvious form elements on the page, ColdFusion and PHP users also need to bind a SurveyID to a hidden element to allow the Update Record server behavior, attached later, to work properly

We'll start with the Survey recordset and then continue with the Question recordset.

1. From the Bindings panel, expand the **Survey** recordset, if necessary.
2. Insert the needed dynamic data onto the page.

   📖 Drag the **SurveyName** data field into the table cell to the right of the Survey Name label.

3. In the Bindings panel, expand the **Question** recordset.
4. Select the **QuestionType** drop-down list.
5. From the Property inspector, choose **Dynamic** to open the Dynamic List/Menu dialog.
6. Choose the lightning bolt next to the Select Value Equal To field.
7. In the Dynamic Data dialog, select **QuestionType** from the Question recordset and click OK twice: once to close the Dynamic Data dialog and again to close the Dynamic List/Menu dialog.
8. Add the required dynamic data to the form elements.

   📖 Drag **QuestionText** onto the QuestionText text field.

   📖 Drag **QuestionAnswers** onto the AnswerText text area.

The remaining steps are for ColdFusion and PHP users only.

9. From the Forms tab of the Insert bar, drag a hidden form element onto the table cell next to the explanatory text.

10. Enter **QuestionID** as the name for the hidden element on the Property inspector.

11. Choose the lightning bolt symbol to open the Dynamic Data dialog.

12. From the Question recordset, choose **QuestionID** and click OK to close the dialog.

Step 4: Update Record for Survey Question

The standard Update Record server behavior serves us well on this page.

For ASP

1. From the Server Behaviors panel, choose Add (+) and select **Update Record**.

2. In the Update Record dialog, select the desired data source connection. Choose **Recipes** from the Connection list.

3. Choose the table that contains the data you are updating.

   From the Table to Update list, choose **SurveyQuestions**.

4. Choose the recordset from which to get data source fields.

   From the Select Record From field, choose **Question**.

5. Set the primary key for the recordset.

   From the Unique Key Column list, choose **QuestionID** and make sure the Numeric option is selected.

6. Select the file you would like to appear when the update is complete.

   For the After Updating, Go To field, select the **edit_survey.asp** page.

7. Choose the form on the page from which to obtain the values.

   From the Get Values From list, choose **EditSurveyQuestion**.

8. In the Form Elements area, set the form elements to their corresponding data source fields.

   Set the QuestionType form element to update the QuestionType data source field as Numeric type.

   Set the QuestionText form element to update the QuestionText data source field as Text type.

   Set the AnswerText form element to update the QuestionAnswer data source field as Text type.

9. Make sure your entries are correct and then click OK to close.

For ColdFusion and PHP

1. From the Server Behaviors panel, choose Add (+) and select **Update Record**.

2. In the Update Record dialog, choose the current form.

   📖 Select **EditSurveyQuestion** from the Submit Values From list.

3. Select your data source from the list.

   📖 Choose **Recipes** from the Data Source list.

4. Enter your username and password, if needed.

5. Select the table in the data source to insert into from the list.

   📖 Choose **SurveyQuestions** (**surveyQuestions** for PHP) from the Insert into Table list.

6. Set the data source fields to their corresponding form elements.

   📖 Set `QuestionID` to the `FORM.QuestionID` form element and submit it as Numeric, with the Primary Key option selected.

   Make sure `QuestionSurvey` does not get a value.

   Set `QuestionType` to the `FORM.QuestionType` form element and submit as Numeric (Integer in PHP).

   Set `QuestionText` to the `FORM.QuestionText` form element and submit as Text.

   Set `QuestionAnswers` to the `FORM.AnswerText` form element and submit as Text.

7. In the After Inserting, Go To field, enter the path to the file you want displayed after the record is updated.

   📖 Choose Browse and select the **edit_survey.cfm** or **edit_survey.php** file, as appropriate.

8. Check your entries to verify they are correct and, if so, click OK.

Step 5: Add Delete Command/Query for Survey Question

If you worked through the Edit Survey recipe, these next steps for adding delete functionality should be familiar. These steps are, in fact, a subset of the earlier steps. The basic procedure is the same: Commands (queries in ColdFusion) are added (two instead of three); the commands and other delete-related code are moved to the top of the code; and conditional logic is applied to the adjusted code. We'll start by adding the commands/queries.

One last similarity between the two recipes: Again, you should not test the page until all the delete-associated operations are complete.

For ASP

First, we'll insert a SQL command to remove the current record. The ID for the current record, `MM_recordId`, is gathered from the Update Server behavior, applied earlier.

1. From the Bindings panel, choose **Command**.
2. In the Command dialog, enter an appropriate name.
   - Enter **DeleteQuestion** in the Name field.
3. Choose the data source.
   - From the Connections list, select **Recipes**.
4. Set the type of command.
   - From the Type list, choose **Delete**.
5. Leave the Return Recordset Named options blank.
6. In the SQL area, enter the following code:
   - DELETE FROM SurveyQuestions.

     ```
     WHERE QuestionID = IDParam
     ```
7. In the Variable area, choose Add (+) to add a new SQL variable.
8. Enter the name of the variable.
   - In the Name column, enter **IDParam**.
9. Insert the run-time value.
   - In the Run-Time value column, enter **Request.Form("MM_recordId")** [r5-11].

r5-11

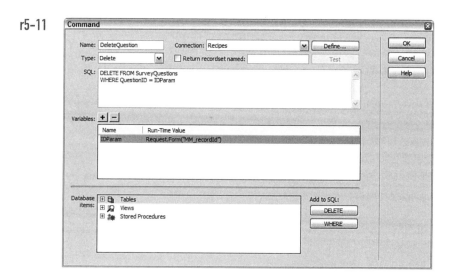

10. Click OK to insert the command.

Next, we'll access a command included in the data source to remove any results that are attached to the previously removed questions.

1. From the Bindings panel, choose Add (+) and choose **Command**.
2. Enter an appropriate name for the command.
   - Enter **RemoveOrphanResults** in the Name field.
3. Choose a data source.
   - From the Connections list, choose **Recipes**.
4. Select the proper type of command.
   - Choose **Stored Procedure** from the Type list.
5. Leave the Return Recordset Named options empty.
6. In the SQL area, enter the following command call:

   ```
   RemoveOrphanResults
   ```

7. Click OK to close the dialog and insert the command.

> **NOTE**
> Again, refrain from testing the delete command until you've completed the remaining steps in this chapter.

For ColdFusion

The first task is to insert a SQL command to remove the current record. We'll get the ID for the current record from the session variable SurveyID stored earlier.

1. From the Bindings panel, choose **Recordset (Query)**.
2. In the Advanced Recordset dialog, enter an appropriate name.
   - Enter **DeleteQuestion** in the Name field.
3. Choose the data source.
   - From the Data Source list, select **Recipes**.
4. Enter the username and password, if required.
5. In the SQL area, enter the following code:

   ```
   CF   DELETE FROM SurveyQuestions
          WHERE QuestionID = #Form.QuestionID#
   ```

6. Click OK to insert the command.

The next command to insert serves to remove any results attached to the previously removed questions.

1. From the Bindings panel, choose **Recordset (Query)**.
2. In the Advanced Recordset dialog, enter an appropriate name.
   - Enter **DeleteQuestion** in the Name field.

3. Choose the data source.

  📖 From the Data Source list, select **Recipes**.

4. Enter the username and password, if required.

5. In the SQL area, enter the following code:

   (CF) `EXECUTE RemoveOrphanResults`

6. Click OK to insert the command.

NOTE   Again, refrain from testing the delete command until you've completed the remaining steps in this chapter.

For PHP

As with the `Edit Survey` page, PHP developers need to use custom code to add delete functionality. The upside of this is that no additional action is necessary for this page.

1. In Code view, place your cursor after the line that begins `<?php require_once` and insert the following code:

  📖 From the Snippets panel, insert the **Recipes > SurveyBuilder > CustomCode_PHP > Edit Question - Delete Record** snippet.

(PHP)
```php
<?php
mysql_select_db($database_Recipes_PHP, $Recipes_PHP);
if ((isset($_POST['Delete'])) && ($_POST['Delete'] == "Delete")) {
    // First delete the selected record
    $deleteSQL = "DELETE FROM surveyquestions WHERE
➥QuestionID = " . $_POST['QuestionID'];
    $deleteRes = mysql_query($deleteSQL,$Recipes_PHP);

    // Now remove orphaned results
    $deleteSQL = "DELETE surveyresults.* FROM surveyquestions
➥RIGHT JOIN surveyresults ON surveyquestions.QuestionID=
➥surveyresults.ResultQuestion WHERE
➥surveyquestions.QuestionID IS NULL";
    $deleteRes = mysql_query($deleteSQL,$Recipes_PHP);
}
?>
```

2. Save your page.

Feel free to test your page completely. When you're ready, you can continue with the next page in the application: Launch Survey.

Step 6: Move Commands' Source Code

Now that the commands/queries are in place, we need to adjust their position in the code. To do this, we'll move both commands and one additional function. Let's start with the commands.

> **The remainder of the steps for this page is for ASP and ColdFusion users only.**
>
> NOTE

1. Switch to Code view.
2. In the Server Behaviors panel, choose the **DeleteQuestion** command/query.

   The first of the two commands is selected in the code.
3. Select the current code function as well as the one following it. The selected code should look like this:

   VB `<%`

```
set DeleteQuestion = Server.CreateObject("ADODB.Command")
DeleteQuestion.ActiveConnection = MM_Recipes_VB_STRING
DeleteQuestion.CommandText = "DELETE FROM SurveyQuestions
➥WHERE QuestionID = " + Replace(DeleteQuestion__IDParam, "'",
➥"''") + ""
DeleteQuestion.CommandType = 1
DeleteQuestion.CommandTimeout = 0
DeleteQuestion.Prepared = true
DeleteQuestion.Execute()

%>
<%

set RemoveOrphanResults = Server.CreateObject("ADODB.Command")
RemoveOrphanResults.ActiveConnection = MM_Recipes_STRING
RemoveOrphanResults.CommandText = "RemoveOrphanResults"
RemoveOrphanResults.CommandType = 4
RemoveOrphanResults.CommandTimeout = 0
RemoveOrphanResults.Prepared = true
RemoveOrphanResults.Execute()

%>
```

   JS `<%`

```
var DeleteQuestion = Server.CreateObject("ADODB.Command");
DeleteQuestion.ActiveConnection = MM_Recipes_STRING;
DeleteQuestion.CommandText = "DELETE FROM SurveyQuestions
➥WHERE QuestionID = "+ DeleteQuestion__IDParam.replace(/'/g,
➥"''") + " ";
```

Continues

```
DeleteQuestion.CommandType = 1;
DeleteQuestion.CommandTimeout = 0;
DeleteQuestion.Prepared = true;
DeleteQuestion.Execute();

%>
<%

set RemoveOrphanResults = Server.CreateObject("ADODB.Command")
RemoveOrphanResults.ActiveConnection = MM_Recipes_STRING
RemoveOrphanResults.CommandText = "RemoveOrphanResults"
RemoveOrphanResults.CommandType = 4
RemoveOrphanResults.CommandTimeout = 0
RemoveOrphanResults.Prepared = true
RemoveOrphanResults.Execute()

%>
```

```
CF   <cfquery name="DeleteQuestion" datasource="Recipes">
     DELETE FROM SurveyQuestions WHERE QuestionID=#FORM.QuestionID#
     </cfquery>
     <cfquery name="RemoveOrphanResults" datasource="Recipes">
     EXECUTE RemoveOrphanResults
     </cfquery>
```

4. Cut the code by choosing **Edit > Cut** or by pressing Ctrl-X (Command-X).

5. Place the cursor at the top of the page. ASP users should place the cursor just after the Connection Include.

6. Paste the code by choosing **Edit > Paste** or by pressing Ctrl-V (Command-V).

7. Save the page.

Next, we'll need to move the delete operation declaration. (This step is only necessary for the ASP server models.)

1. In Code view, use Find and Replace to locate the first instance of **DeleteQuestion__IDParam**. (Note the double-underscore in the phrase.)

2. Cut the surrounding function by choosing **Edit > Cut** or by pressing Ctrl-X (Command-X). The code to cut looks like this:

```
VB   <%

     if(Request("MM_recordId") <> "") then DeleteQuestion__IDParam =
     ➥Request("MM_recordId")

     %>
```

⬭ JS ⬭ `<%`

```
    if(String(Request("MM_recordId")) != "undefined")
 ➡{ DeleteQuestion__IDParam = String(Request("MM_recordId"));}}
```

`%>`

3. Move to the top of the page above the two commands moved previously.
4. Paste the code by choosing **Edit > Paste** or by pressing Ctrl-V (Command-V).

Step 7: Add Conditional Code

To make sure the various delete code functions are executed only when the Delete but-ton is pressed, we need to wrap the functions with conditional statements—one before and one after the functions. The closing statement also serves to redirect the user to the Edit Survey page after the deletion is complete.

1. In Code view, position the cursor before the delete operation declaration just moved.
2. Insert the following code:
   - ▢ From the Snippets panel, open the **Recipes > SurveyBuilder > Custom Code** folder for your server model and insert the **If Statement - Delete Operation** snippet.

   ⬭ VB ⬭ `<%`
   ```
       if (cStr(Request("Delete"))<>"") then
       %>
   ```

   ⬭ JS ⬭ `<%`
   ```
       if (String(Request("Delete"))!="undefined") {
       %>
   ```

   ⬭ CF ⬭ `<cfif IsDefined("Session.SurveyID") AND IsDefined("FORM.Delete")>`

   Now let's add the second half of our conditional code.
3. Place the cursor below the second delete command, which took care of removing the orphaned survey responses.
4. Insert the following code:
   - ▢ From the Snippets panel, open the **Recipes > SurveyBuilder > Custom Code** folder for your server model and insert the **Redirect – Edit Survey** snippet.

   ⬭ VB ⬭ `<%`
   ```
       Response.Redirect("edit_survey.asp")
       end if
       %>
   ```

```
JS   <%
        Response.Redirect("edit_survey.asp");
        }
        %>
```

```
CF   <cflocation url="edit_survey.cfm">
        </cfif>
```

5. Save the page.

Administrator Recipe: Launch Survey

A survey can—and should—go through many iterations before it's ready for public consumption. In our application, when you select the Launch icon from the Survey Manager page, you're provided with a fully formed URL for the survey as well as an opportunity to make additional edits or test the survey. If you're satisfied, a click of the button pushes the survey live—which, in essence, means that the survey is ready to accept and record responses.

Although most of this recipe is straightforward, there are two elements you might not have seen before. The URL for the selected survey is dynamically generated using server variables to gather the domain name as well as the file path. The other concept introduced is a dynamic form button: The final button on the page changes text—and action—based on the state of a particular data field.

Step 1: Implement Launch Survey Design

The Launch Survey layout combines both dynamic text elements and form buttons. Rather than enclose the entire Content area in a form, we'll restrict the form so that it encloses only the button areas. Although there is no real functional difference—the buttons would work in either format—this approach separates basic functionality and allows the page to be designed in stages with no reimplementation or loss of work.

1. Create a page for the Survey Manager recipe, either from a template or from the **File > New** dialog.

   In the **SurveyBuilder** folder, locate the folder for your server model and open the launch_survey page there.

2. In the Content area of your page, create a header for the page—a placeholder to display the dynamic elements and buttons.

   From the Snippets panel, drag the **Recipes > SurveyBuilder > Wireframes > Launch Survey – Wireframe** snippet into the Content editable region.

3. In the structured data area, add labels for the survey URL, title, and number of questions. Below the labels, insert three form buttons (one for Preview, Edit, and Close Survey/Make Live).

   VB Place your cursor in the row below the words LAUNCH SURVEY and insert the **Recipes > SurveyBuilder > Forms > ASP Launch Survey – Form** snippet.

   JS Place your cursor in the row below the words LAUNCH SURVEY and insert the **Recipes > SurveyBuilder > Forms > ASP Launch Survey – Form** snippet.

   CF Place your cursor in the row below the words LAUNCH SURVEY and insert the **Recipes > SurveyBuilder > Forms > CFML Launch Survey – Form** snippet.

   PHP Place your cursor in the row below the words LAUNCH SURVEY and insert the **Recipes > SurveyBuilder > Forms PHP Launch Survey – Form** snippet.

4. Save the page [r5-12].

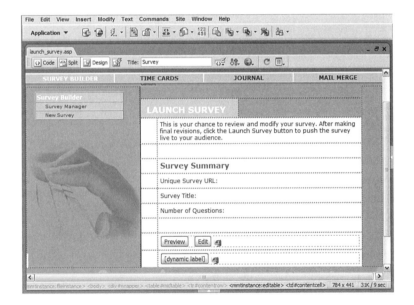

r5-12

Step 2: Adding Database Components

A data view, SurveyStats, is used to make information from two tables, SurveyQuestions and Surveys, available for our page. The view returns standard fields such as SurveyID, SurveyName, and SurveyLive, as well as the total number of questions for a given survey. Because SurveyStats is developed as a view, it's easy to apply it in Dreamweaver for ASP and ColdFusion; it's a little more work in PHP, but it's still quite doable.

For ASP and ColdFusion

1. From the Bindings panel, choose Add (+) and select **Recordset (Query)** from the list.
2. In the simple Recordset dialog, enter an appropriate name for the recordset.

   ◻ Enter **SurveyStats** in the Name field.
3. Choose your data source.

   ◻ From the Connections (Data Source) list, select **Recipes**.
4. Choose the prebuilt view.

   ◻ Select **SurveyLaunchStats** from the Table list.
5. Leave Columns set to All.
6. In the Filter area of the Recordset dialog, set the four Filter list elements like this:

SurveyID	= (Equals)
URL Parameter	ID

7. Leave Sort set to None and click OK to close the dialog.
8. Save the page.

For PHP

◻ As a preliminary step, from the Snippets panel, use the Copy Snippet command to copy the **Recipes > Survey Builder > SQL > Launch Survey RS - PHP SQL Statement** snippet to the Clipboard.

1. From the Bindings panel, choose Add (+) and select **Recordset** from the list.
2. In the Recordset dialog, choose **Advanced**.
3. Enter an appropriate name for the recordset.

   ◻ Enter **SurveyStats** in the Name field.
4. Select the desired data source.

   ◻ Choose **Recipes** from the Connections list.
5. In the SQL area, enter the following code:

   ◻ Press Ctrl-V (Command-V) to paste the copied snippet into the SQL area.

```
SELECT
surveys.SurveyID, Count(surveyquestions.QuestionID)
➥AS CountOfQuestionID,
surveys.SurveyName, surveys.SurveyLive
FROM surveyquestions
RIGHT JOIN surveys ON surveyquestions.QuestionSurvey =
surveys.SurveyID
GROUP BY surveys.SurveyID, surveys.SurveyName, surveys.SurveyLive
HAVING surveys.SurveyID = IDParam
```

6. In the Variables section, choose Add (+) to create a new variable.

7. Enter the name for the variable.

   📖 In the Name column, enter **IDParam**.

8. Enter a default value for the variable.

   📖 In the Default Value column, enter **1**.

9. Enter a run-time value for the variable.

   📖 In the Run-Time Value column, enter **$_GET['ID']**.

10. Click OK to close the dialog and insert the recordset.

Step 3: Creating a Fully Qualified Unique URL

When someone is invited to participate in a survey, whether by e-mail or a section of a Web page, a direct link is generally provided. Because the survey is generated dynamically, the URL must not only reference a particular domain and file path, but it also must pass the proper parameter. Although it's possible to hand-code this URL, it's much better to have your application create it for you. By putting the burden on the application, you'll be sure to get the proper parameter. All that's left for you to do is copy the generated URL and paste it in the appropriate location.

The code required to generate the domain and file path parts of the URL depends on a server-side function generally known as *server variables*; ColdFusion refers to these as CGI variables. Server variables are useful for getting information about the current server, the client, and the file being served. For our purposes, we'll need two server variables: SERVER_NAME and SCRIPT_NAME. The SERVER_NAME variable holds the current domain and SCRIPT_NAME holds the file path. A little string manipulation is necessary to extract just the file path from the SCRIPT_NAME variable.

> **NOTE**
>
> In some situations, this technique of building up the URL string will not work due to a firewall or proxy mask. Should you encounter this problem, the best solution is to hard-code all of the URL except for the query string. Use the final fragment of the code supplied in the following step to generate the query string.

1. Place your cursor where you would like the URL to appear.

   📖 Put the cursor next to the Unique Survey URL label.

2. Enter Code view and insert this code:

   📖 From the Snippets panel, open the **Recipes > SurveyBuilder > Custom Code** folder for your server model and insert the **Fully Qualified - Unique URL** snippet.

```
VB   <a href="http://<%=Request.ServerVariables("SERVER_NAME")%>
     <%=Left(Request.ServerVariables("SCRIPT_NAME"),
     ➥inStrRev(Request.ServerVariables("SCRIPT_NAME"),"/")-1)%>
     ➥/survey.asp?ID=<%=(SurveyStats.Fields.Item("SurveyID").Value)%>"
     ➥>http://<%=Request.ServerVariables("SERVER_NAME")%>
     <%=Left(Request.ServerVariables("SCRIPT_NAME"),inStrRev
     ➥(Request.ServerVariables("SCRIPT_NAME"),"/")-1)%>
     ➥/survey.asp?ID=<%=(SurveyStats.Fields.Item("SurveyID").Value)%>
     </a>
```

```
JS   <a href="http://<%=Request.ServerVariables("SERVER_NAME")%>
     <%=String(Request.ServerVariables("SCRIPT_Name"))
     ➥.substring(0,String(Request.ServerVariables("SCRIPT_Name"))
     ➥.lastIndexOf("/"))%>/survey.asp?ID=<%=(SurveyStats.Fields.Item
     ➥("SurveyID").Value)%>">http://<%=Request.ServerVariables
     ➥("SERVER_NAME")%> <%=String(Request.ServerVariables("SCRIPT_Name"))
     ➥.substring(0,String(Request.ServerVariables("SCRIPT_Namc"))
     ➥.lastIndexOf("/"))%>/survey.asp?ID=
     ➥<%=(SurveyStats.Fields.Item("SurveyID").Value)%>
     </a>
```

```
CF   <a href="http://<cfoutput>#CGI.SERVER_NAME##Left(CGI.SCRIPT_NAME,Len
     ➥(CGI.SCRIPT_NAME)-
     Find("/",Reverse(CGI.SCRIPT_NAME)))#/survey.asp?ID=
     ➥#SurveyStats.SurveyID#/survey.asp?ID=#SurveyStats.SurveyID#">
     http://#CGI.SERVER_NAME##Left(CGI.SCRIPT_NAME,Len(CGI.SCRIPT_NAME)-
     Find("/",Reverse(CGI.SCRIPT_NAME)))#/survey.asp?ID=#SurveyStats
     ➥.SurveyID#</cfoutput>
     </a>
```

```
PHP  <a href="http://<?php echo $_SERVER['SERVER_NAME']
     ➥. dirname($_SERVER['SCRIPT_NAME']); ?>/survey.php?ID=
     ➥<?php echo $SurveyStats['SurveyID']; ?>">http://<?php echo
     ➥$_SERVER['SERVER_NAME'] . dirname($_SERVER['SCRIPT_NAME']); ?>
     ➥/survey.php?ID=<?php echo $SurveyStats['SurveyID']; ?>
     </a>
```

3. Return to Design view [r5-13].

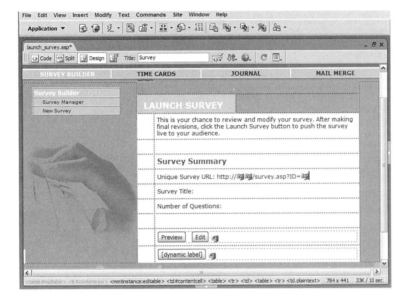

r5-13

Step 4: Data Binding Process

There are only two dynamic text elements included in the Launch Survey page—and both can be dragged into place from the Bindings panel.

1. From the Bindings panel, expand the **SurveyStats** recordset.
2. Place the dynamic text elements in their proper place on the page.

   📖 Drag **SurveyName** next to the Survey Title label.

   📖 Drag **CountOfQuestionID** next to the Number of Questions label [r5-14].

3. Save the page.

r5-14

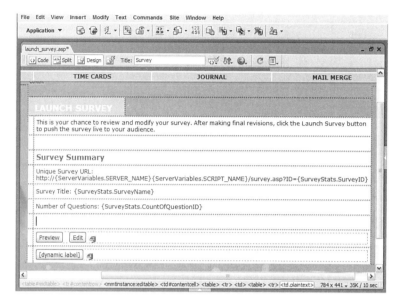

Step 5: Working with the Edit Button

Of the three form buttons on the page, two require additional setup. The first, Preview, triggers the action of the form, which opens the proper survey page in preview mode. The second button, Edit, opens the Edit Survey page. To accomplish this action, a Dreamweaver behavior is used in conjunction with a dynamically generated parameter, as you'll see in this step. The next step in the recipe handles the final button.

There are two parts to this step. First we'll add the JavaScript behavior, and then we'll insert a hidden form field to hold the required value.

1. Select the Edit form button.
2. From the Behaviors panel, choose Add (+) and select **Go to URL** from the list.
3. In the Go to URL dialog, choose **Browse**.
4. In the Select File dialog, choose **Parameters**.
5. In the Parameters dialog, enter a variable name.
   - Enter **ID** in the Name column.
6. Enter a value for the new variable.
   - In the Value column, select the lightning bolt symbol to open the Dynamic Data dialog. From there, choose **SurveyID** from the SurveyStats recordset and click OK to close the Dynamic Data dialog.

7. Click OK to close the Parameters dialog.
8. Choose a file to pass the parameter to.
   - Select the **edit_survey** file for your server model.
9. Click OK to close the dialog and add the link.

Now, let's add a hidden form field to contain the Survey ID value.

1. Select the hidden form element named **ID**.
2. In the Property inspector, select the lightning bolt symbol to open the Dynamic Data dialog.
3. Choose the **Survey Key** field.
   - From the `SurveyStats` recordset, choose **SurveyID**.
4. Click OK to close the Dynamic Data dialog.

Step 6: Working with the Launch Button

The text seen on the Launch button is written dynamically when the page loads. The button label will display either *Close Survey* or *Make Live*, depending on the state of the SurveyLive field for the survey. When the survey is live—and SurveyLive is `true`—the button says *Close Survey*. When the Survey is closed, with SurveyLive set to `false`, the button displays *Make Live*.

The button's action toggles between the two states. The key to this effect is the SurveyLive data field. A hidden form element stores the current value on the page and alters it whenever the Launch button is selected. To keep track of the SurveyLive state properly, an Update Record server behavior is used.

First, let's make the label dynamic.

1. Select the **Launch** button.
   - The Launch button initially displays `[dynamic label]`.
2. Enter Code view and remove the placeholder label text from the value attribute.
   - Change `value = "[dynamic label]"` to `value =` removing the quotation marks as well.
3. Insert the following code:
   - From the Snippets panel, open the **Recipes > SurveyBuilder > Custom Code** folder for your server model and insert the **Launch Button - Dynamic Label** snippet.

```
VB   <%if (SurveyStats.Fields("SurveyLive").value) then
         Response.Write("Close Survey") else Response.Write("Make Live")%>
```

```
JS   <%=(SurveyStats.Fields("SurveyLive").value)
         ?"Close Survey":"Make Live"%>
```

```
CF   <cfoutput><cfif (SurveyStats.SurveyLive NEQ 0)>Close Survey
         <cfelse>Make Live</cfif></cfoutput>
```

```
PHP  <?php echo ($row_SurveyStats['SurveyLive'])
         ?"Close Survey":"Make Live"; ?>
```

4. Switch to Design view [r5-15].

You'll see the inserted code represented as the button label; the unwanted code will, of course, disappear at run-time leaving only a label reading Close Survey or Make Live.

r5-15

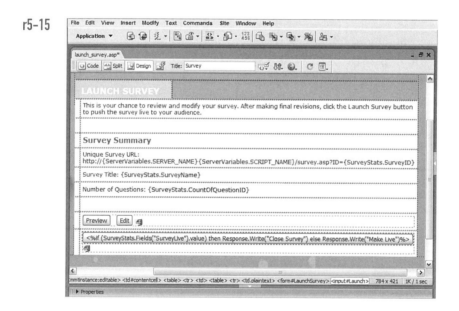

Next, we'll adjust the hidden form element to also contain a dynamic value—one based on the SurveyLive data value.

1. Select the **SurveyLive** hidden form element.

2. In Code view, replace the value (including the quotation marks) with this code:

    📖 From the Snippets panel, open the **Recipes > SurveyBuilder > Custom Code** folder for your server model and insert **the Launch Hidden Element - Dynamic Value** snippet.

```
(VB)  <%if (SurveyStats.Fields("SurveyLive").value)
      ➥then Response.Write("0") else Response.Write("1") end if%>
```

```
(JS)  <%=(SurveyStats.Fields("SurveyLive").value)?0:1%>
```

```
(CF)  <cfoutput><cfif (SurveyStats.SurveyLive NEQ 0)>0
      ➥<cfelse>1</cfif></cfoutput>
```

```
(PHP)  <?php echo ($row_SurveyStats['SurveyLive'])?0:1; ?>
```

3. Return to Design view.

    An additional series of steps is required for ColdFusion and PHP developers.

4. Select the hidden form element, **ID**.

5. From the Property inspector, choose the lightning bolt symbol to open the Dynamic Data dialog.

6. Choose **SurveyID** from the SurveyStats recordset.

The final phase is to insert an Update Record server behavior to record the change in the SurveyLive field.

For ASP

1. From the Server Behaviors panel, choose Add (+) **Update Record**.

2. In the Update Record dialog, select the desired data source connection. Choose **Recipes** from the Connection list.

3. Choose the table that contains the data you are updating.

    📖 From the Table to Update list, choose **Surveys**.

4. Choose the recordset from which to get data source fields.

    📖 From the Select Record From field, choose **SurveyStats**.

5. Set the primary key for the recordset.

    📖 From the Unique Key Column list, choose **SurveyID** and make sure the Numeric option is selected.

6. Select the file you would like to appear when the update is complete.

    📖 For the After Updating, Go To field, select the **survey_manager.asp** page.

7. Choose the form on the page from which to get the values.

    📖 From the Get Values From list, choose **LaunchSurvey**.

8. In the Form Elements area, set the form element to its corresponding data source field.

   ▭ Set the `SurveyLive` form element to update the `SurveyLive` data source field as Numeric.

9. Make sure your entries are correct and then click OK to close.

For ColdFusion and PHP

1. From the Server Behaviors panel, choose Add (+) and select **Update Record**.

2. In the Update Record dialog, choose the current form.

   ▭ Select **LaunchSurvey** from the Submit Values From list.

3. Select your data source from the list.

   ▭ Choose **Recipes** from the Data Source list.

4. Enter your username and password, if needed.

5. Select the table in the data source to insert into from the list.

   ▭ Choose **Surveys** (**surveys** for PHP) from the Insert into Table list.

6. Set the data source field to its corresponding form element.

   ▭ Set `SurveyID` to the `FORM.ID` form element as Numeric, with the Primary Key option selected.

7. In the After Inserting, Go To field, enter the path to the file you want displayed after the record is updated.

   ▭ Choose Browse and select the **survey_manager.cfm** or **survey_manger.php** file, as appropriate.

8. Check your entries to verify they are correct and, if they are, click OK.

Administrator Recipe: Survey Statistics

Analysis of a survey's results is key to its success. The whole point of taking a survey is to find out what people think and, more precisely, what percentage of people surveyed think a particular way. The `Survey Statistics` page described here offers one way to visualize a survey's results. When executed—by selecting the entry in the View Results column of the `Survey Manager` page—the Survey Statistics application displays each of the answers to the questions broken down by percentages. If, for example, 50 out of 200 people surveyed chose yellow as their favorite color, the `Survey Statistics` page would show that yellow was chosen 25% of the time.

Generating the percentage calculations is the major objective of any statistics application and a chore best handled by SQL. We've provided a SQL view that draws data from three primary tables (Surveys, SurveyQuestions, and SurveyResults). After the view is used to create a recordset, implementation in Dreamweaver is a drag-and-drop affair.

Step 1: Implement Survey Statistics Design

The goal of the Survey Statistics page is to show how the responses to each question compare. Therefore, the page uses a structured layout that includes the question, the particular response, and the related percentage—all of which is eventually wrapped in a Repeat Region server behavior.

1. Create a page for the Survey Manager recipe, either from a template or from the **File > New** dialog.

   📖 In the **SurveyBuilder** folder, locate the folder for your server model and open the survey_statistics page there.

2. In the Content area of your page, create a header for the page and an area for the survey response statistics.

   📖 From the Snippets panel, drag the **Recipes > SurveyBuilder > Wireframes > Survey Statistics – Wireframe** snippet into the Content editable region.

3. In the structured data area, add a table with 4 rows and 2 columns; the first row, which holds the questions, should span both columns.

   📖 Place your cursor in the first row below the words SURVEY STATISTICS and insert the **Recipes > SurveyBuilder > ContentTables > Survey Statistics - Content Table** snippet.

   📖 Place your cursor in the bottom row, right-hand cell of the just-added table, and insert the **Recipes > SurveyBuilder > ContentTables > Survey Question Statistics - Content Table** snippet [r5-16].

r5-16

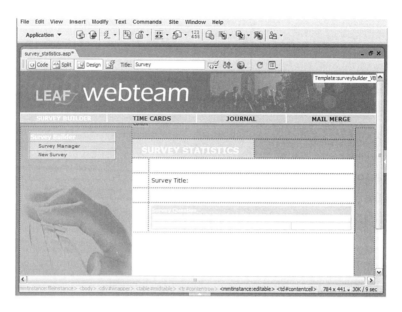

4. Save the page.

Step 2: Adding Database Components

As noted earlier, a SQL view is constructed to extract the survey results and calculate the percentages. The view is quite complex:

```
SELECT Surveys.SurveyID, Surveys.SurveyName,
➥Count(SurveyResults.ResultAnswer) AS TimesAnswered,
➥SurveyQuestions.QuestionSurvey, SurveyQuestions.QuestionAnswers,
➥SurveyResults.ResultAnswer, SurveyQuestions.QuestionID,
➥SurveyResults.ResultQuestion,
➥(SELECT Count(SurveyResults2.ResultQuestion)
➥FROM SurveyResults AS SurveyResults2
WHERE
(((SurveyResults2.ResultQuestion)=SurveyResults.ResultQuestion)))
➥ AS QuestionAnswered, (Count(SurveyResults.ResultAnswer)/
➥(SELECT Count(SurveyResults2.ResultQuestion) FROM SurveyResults
➥AS SurveyResults2 WHERE (((SurveyResults2.ResultQuestion)=
➥SurveyResults.ResultQuestion)))) AS AnswerPercent,
➥SurveyQuestions.QuestionText
FROM (SurveyResults INNER JOIN SurveyQuestions
➥ON SurveyResults.ResultQuestion = SurveyQuestions.QuestionID)
➥INNER JOIN Surveys ON SurveyQuestions.QuestionSurvey =
➥Surveys.SurveyID
GROUP BY Surveys.SurveyID, Surveys.SurveyName,
```

```
➥SurveyQuestions.QuestionSurvey, SurveyQuestions.QuestionAnswers,
➥SurveyResults.ResultAnswer, SurveyQuestions.QuestionID,
➥SurveyResults.ResultQuestion, SurveyQuestions.QuestionText
ORDER BY SurveyQuestions.QuestionID;
```

Because Dreamweaver lists SQL views as just another data source for ASP and
ColdFusion, creating the needed recordset is quite straightforward; PHP developers need
to add some custom code in addition to the recordset.

1. From the Bindings panel, choose Add (+) and select **Recordset (Query)** from the list.
2. In the simple Recordset dialog, enter an appropriate name for the recordset.
   - Enter **Statistics** in the Name field.
3. Choose your data source.
   - From the Connections (Data Source) list, select **Recipes**.
4. Choose the prebuilt view.
   - Select **SurveyStatistics** (**surveystatistics** for PHP) from the Table list.
5. Leave Columns set to All.
6. In the Filter area of the Recordset dialog, set the four Filter list elements like this:

SurveyID	= (Equals)
URL Parameter	ID

7. Leave Sort set to None and click OK to close the dialog.
8. Save the page.

PHP developers must also insert code to build a temporary table, following our often-
used technique for simulating views with MySQL:

1. In Code view, place the cursor after the line near the top of the page that starts
   `<?php require_once` and insert the following code:
   - From the Snippets panel, insert the **Recipes > SurveyBuilder >
     CustomCode_PHP > Survey Statistics – Calculate Temporary Table** snippet.

(PHP)
```php
<?php
// First retrieve the total of questions answered
mysql_select_db($database_Recipes_PHP, $Recipes_PHP);
$query_QuestionAnswered = "SELECT surveyquestions.QuestionID,
➥surveys.SurveyName, surveyquestions.QuestionText,
➥COUNT(surveyresults.ResultQuestion) AS total FROM surveys,
➥surveyquestions, surveyresults, surveyresults surveyresults_1
➥WHERE (((surveyresults.ResultQuestion =
surveyquestions.QuestionID)
➥ AND (surveyquestions.QuestionSurvey = surveys.SurveyID))
```

Continues

```
➥AND (surveyresults_1.ResultID = surveyresults.ResultID))
➥GROUP BY surveys.SurveyName, surveyquestions.QuestionText";
$QuestionAnswered = mysql_query($query_QuestionAnswered,
➥$Recipes_PHP) or die(mysql_error());
$row_QuestionAnswered = mysql_fetch_assoc($QuestionAnswered);
$totalRows_QuestionAnswered = mysql_num_rows($QuestionAnswered);
// empty the statistics table
$cleanupSQL = "DELETE FROM surveystatistics";
$cleanupRS = mysql_query($cleanupSQL,$Recipes_PHP);
// retrieve statistics
$insSQL = "INSERT INTO surveystatistics SELECT NULL,
➥surveys.SurveyID, surveys.SurveyName,
➥Count(surveyresults.ResultAnswer) AS TimesAnswered,
➥surveyquestions.QuestionSurvey, surveyquestions.QuestionAnswers,
➥surveyresults.ResultAnswer, surveyquestions.QuestionID,
➥surveyresults.ResultQuestion, surveyquestions.QuestionText,0,0
➥FROM (surveyresults INNER JOIN surveyquestions
➥ON surveyresults.ResultQuestion = surveyquestions.QuestionID)
➥INNER JOIN surveys ON surveyquestions.QuestionSurvey =
➥surveys.SurveyID GROUP BY surveys.SurveyID, surveys.SurveyName,
➥surveyquestions.QuestionSurvey, surveyquestions.QuestionAnswers,
➥surveyresults.ResultAnswer, surveyquestions.QuestionID,
➥surveyresults.ResultQuestion, surveyquestions.QuestionText
➥ORDER BY surveyquestions.QuestionID";
$insRS = mysql_query($insSQL,$Recipes_PHP);
do {
  $insSQL = "UPDATE surveystatistics SET QuestionAnswered = "
  ➥. $row_QuestionAnswered['total'] . " WHERE QuestionID = "
  ➥. $row_QuestionAnswered['QuestionID'];
  $insRS = mysql_query($insSQL,$Recipes_PHP);
} while ($row_QuestionAnswered =
mysql_fetch_assoc($QuestionAnswered));
// retrieve TotalAnswered and QuestionAnswered columns
$insSQL = "SELECT StatsID, (TimesAnswered/QuestionAnswered)
➥AS AnswerPercent FROM surveystatistics";
$insRS = mysql_query($insSQL,$Recipes_PHP);
$insRow = mysql_fetch_assoc($insRS);
do {
  $updSQL = "UPDATE surveystatistics SET AnswerPercent='"
  ➥.$insRow['AnswerPercent']."' WHERE StatsID=".$insRow['StatsID'];
    $updRes = mysql_query($updSQL,$Recipes_PHP);
} while ($insRow = mysql_fetch_assoc($insRS));
mysql_free_result($insRS);
mysql_free_result($QuestionAnswered);
?>
```

2. When you're done, save the page.

Step 3: Data Binding Process

The steps for completing this page begin with binding four data fields. After applying a format to the percentage field, you'll attach a Repeat Region server behavior.

1. From the Bindings panel, expand the **Statistics** recordset.
2. Place the dynamic text elements in their proper place on the page.

   ☐ Drag **SurveyName** next to the Survey Title label.

   Drag **QuestionText** in the first cell below the Survey Question heading.

   Drag **ResultAnswer** to the second row below the Survey Question heading, in the cell on the left.

   Drag **AnswerPercent** to the same row, below the Survey Question heading, in the cell on the right.

3. Select the **Statistics.AnswerPercent** data field on the page.
4. Format the data field in the following manner:

<u>VB</u> <u>JS</u> In the Bindings panel, select the arrow next to the highlighted entry in the Format column and, from the list, choose **Percent > Default** [r5-17].

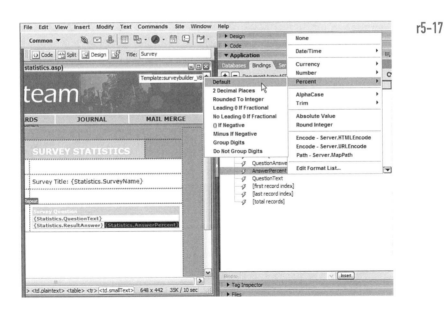

r5-17

The Default setting for the Percent format allows decimals to two places, so 1/3 is shown as 33.33%. You can, of course, choose another percentage format.

Now that we have our dynamic elements on the page, all that remains is to apply a Repeat Region server behavior.

1. Select the area you want to repeat.

   ⌨ From the Tag Selector, choose the **<tr>** tag that encompasses the Survey Question heading and all the dynamic data.

   The easiest way to accomplish this is to first select the nested table that encompasses the heading and the dynamic data and then choose the **<tr>** tag to the left of the selected table in the Tag Selector.

2. From the Server Behaviors panel, choose Add (+) and select **Repeat Region** from the list.

3. In the Repeat Region dialog, choose the desired recordset.

   ⌨ Select **Statistics** from the Recordset list.

4. Select the **Show All Records** option.

5. Click OK to close the dialog [r5-18].

r5-18

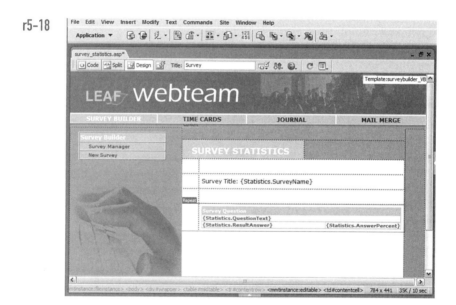

Charting Survey Statistics

The percent values returned in the Survey Statistic page provide an accurate overview of the results—but the representation could be more compelling. Although the statistics are perfectly understandable, the numbers are not as immediately apparent as the same values in a chart would be. A pie chart, for example, showing that over one-half of the survey respondees favored a particular approach is immediately recognizable and very persuasive.

Charting dynamic statistics requires linking real-time graphics engine to data—a task Macromedia Flash is definitely suited for, but difficult to program. WebAssist offers an extension that allows Dreamweaver developers to link their dynamics data to a variety of charts. Combining both the data and the graphics, WA Dynamic Flash Charts lets you visually analyze your data.

To find out more about WA Dynamic Flash Charts, visit
`http://www.webassist.com/Products/Recipes/WADynamicFlashCharts.asp`

End User Recipe: Taking the Survey

So far, we've concentrated on the administrative side of the survey: initial setup of survey and questions and their subsequent managing and editing. It's time to turn our attention to what the user sees—and we'll start with the survey. Because the individual elements of the survey—that is, the questions and possible answers—are stored in a data source, the job of the survey page is twofold. First, the application must reconstruct the survey in a single page and handle each of the different question types as it does so. Second, the application must record all the answers chosen by the survey taker as responses to the survey.

The second requirement—storing the responses—is fairly straightforward and can be handled by the standard Insert Record server behavior. The first requirement—presenting the survey—is more complex and requires a slightly different coding approach for each question type. For those of you following the recipe, all the needed code snippets are provided.

Step 1: Implement Survey Design

The basic layout for the survey page is simple: a survey title; an area for the questions to appear; and two form buttons, one for submitting and one for resetting the survey. Most of the logic for the page—controlling the survey questions and possible answers—is placed in the center Content area of the page later in this recipe. These questions are placed in a Repeat Region server behavior, so your layout should accommodate a flexible area.

1. Create a page for the Survey Manager recipe, either from a template or from the **File > New** dialog.
   - In the **SurveyBuilder** folder, locate the folder for your server model and open the survey page there.

2. In the Content area of your page, create a header for the page—a placeholder to display the dynamic elements and buttons.

   From the Snippets panel, drag the **Recipes > SurveyBuilder > Wireframes > Survey – Wireframe** snippet into the Content editable region.

3. In the structured data area, add a label for the survey title and a section for the questions and responses; a hidden form element is also needed. Below the labels, insert two form buttons: Submit and Reset.

   (**VB**) Place your cursor in the row below the word SURVEY and insert the **Recipes > SurveyBuilder > Forms > ASP Survey – Form** snippet.

   (**JS**) Place your cursor in the row below the word SURVEY and insert the **Recipes > SurveyBuilder > Forms > ASP Survey – Form** snippet.

   (**CF**) Place your cursor in the row below the word SURVEY and insert the **Recipes > SurveyBuilder > Forms > CFML Survey – Form** snippet [r5-19].

   (**PHP**) Place your cursor in the row below the word SURVEY and insert the **Recipes > SurveyBuilder > Forms > PHP Survey – Form** snippet.

r5-19

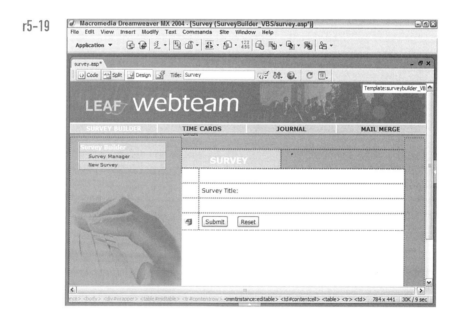

4. Save the page.

Step 2: Add Database Components

The goal of the recordset for the Survey page is to return all the questions and related responses that are associated with a particular survey. A relatively complex SQL statement, which draws from three data tables, is used to define the recordset. The SQL statement is filtered on the URL parameter, ID, which points to a particular survey.

```
SELECT *
FROM (SurveyQuestions INNER JOIN QuestionTypes
➥ON SurveyQuestions.QuestionType = QuestionTypes.TypeID)
➥INNER JOIN Surveys ON SurveyQuestions.QuestionSurvey =
➥Surveys.SurveyID
WHERE SurveyID = IDParam
```

The PHP version is quite similar:

```
SELECT *
FROM (surveyquestions INNER JOIN QuestionTypes
➥ON surveyquestions.QuestionType = QuestionTypes.TypeID)
➥INNER JOIN surveys ON surveyquestions.QuestionSurvey =
➥surveys.SurveyID
WHERE SurveyID = IDParam
```

It's important to realize that the recordset returns all the questions, regardless of their type. Each question and response is later formatted by a series of conditional statements.

For ASP and PHP

    📖 To prepare for the following series of steps, use the Copy Snippet command to copy either the **Recipes > SurveyBuilder > SQL > SurveyQuestions RS - ASP SQL Statement** snippet or the **Recipes > SurveyBuilder > SQL > SurveyQuestions RS - PHP SQL Statement** snippet, according to your server model.

1. From the Bindings panel, choose Add (+) and select **Recordset (Query)** from the list.

2. In the Advanced Recordset dialog, enter a name for the recordset.

    📖 Enter **SurveyQuestions** in the Name field.

3. Choose the data source.

    📖 Select **Recipes** from the Connections list.

4. In the SQL area, enter the following code:

    📖 Paste the copied SQL statement into the SQL text area by pressing Ctrl-V (Command-V).

(VB) (JS)
```
SELECT *
FROM (SurveyQuestions INNER JOIN QuestionTypes
➥ON SurveyQuestions.QuestionType = QuestionTypes.TypeID)
➥INNER JOIN Surveys ON SurveyQuestions.QuestionSurvey =
➥Surveys.SurveyID
WHERE SurveyID = IDParam
```

(PHP)
```
SELECT *
FROM (surveyquestions INNER JOIN QuestionTypes
➥ON surveyquestions.QuestionType = QuestionTypes.TypeID)
➥INNER JOIN surveys ON surveyquestions.QuestionSurvey =
➥surveys.SurveyID
WHERE SurveyID = IDParam
```

5. In the Variable area, choose Add (+) to create a new variable.

   PHP developers should enter their values in the Add Parameter dialog that opens.

6. Add an appropriate name for your variable.

      📖 Enter **IDParam** in the Name column.

7. Enter a default value.

      📖 Enter 0 in the Default Value column.

8. Insert a run-time value.

      📖 Enter the following into the Run-Time Value column:

(VB) (JS) `Request("ID")`

(PHP) `$_GET["ID"]`

   PHP developers can click OK to close the Add Parameters dialog at this time.

9. Click OK to close the dialog and insert the recordset.

For ColdFusion

   📖 To prepare for the following steps, use the Copy Snippet command to copy the **Recipes > SurveyBuilder > SQL > SurveyQuestions RS - CFML SQL Statement** snippet to the Clipboard.

1. From the Bindings panel, choose Add (+) and select **Recordset (Query)**.

2. Switch to the advanced view of the dialog and enter an appropriate name for the recordset.

      📖 Enter **SurveyQuestions** in the Name field.

3. Choose your data source.

      📖 Select **Recipes** from the Data Source list.

4. Enter a username and password if necessary.

5. In the SQL area, enter the following code:

   📖 Paste the copied SQL statement into the SQL text area by pressing Ctrl-V (Command-V).

```
SELECT *
FROM (SurveyQuestions INNER JOIN QuestionTypes
➡ON SurveyQuestions.QuestionType = QuestionTypes.TypeID)
➡INNER JOIN Surveys ON SurveyQuestions.QuestionSurvey =
➡Surveys.SurveyID
WHERE SurveyID = #URL.ID#
```

6. Verify your entries in the Recordset dialog and click OK to close that dialog.

Step 3: Data Binding Process

For this page, we only need to bind two data elements: one dynamic text field for the title and another for the hidden form element. After the data fields are bound, a Repeat Region server behavior is applied to handle the survey's questions and responses.

1. From the Bindings panel, expand the **SurveyQuestions** recordset.
2. Place the needed data fields on the page.

   📖 Drag SurveyName to the right of the Survey Title label.

3. Select the hidden form element.
4. In the Property inspector, enter code to bind the passed ID parameter to the page as the form element's value.

   (VB) In the Value field, enter **<%=Request("ID")%>**.

   (JS) In the Value field, enter **<%=Request("ID")%>**.

   (CF) In the Value field, enter **<cfoutput>#URL.ID#</cfoutput>**.

   (PHP) In the Value field, enter **<?php echo $_REQUEST["ID"]; ?>**.

5. To apply the Repeat Region server behavior, select the table row that will hold the questions and responses. Although the row is currently empty, it will be filled shortly with custom code.

   📖 Place your cursor in the row below the Survey Title label and select the **<tr>** tag from the Tag Selector.

6. From the Server Behaviors panel, choose Add (+) and select **Repeat Region** from the list.
7. Make sure that the **SurveyQuestions** recordset is selected in the Recordset list [r5-20].

r5-20

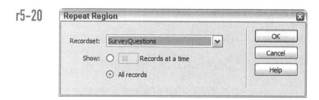

8. Choose the Show All Records option and click OK to close the dialog.

Step 4: Add Conditional Code for Questions and Responses

This step is at the heart of the recipe. Here, we'll insert code to examine the type of question stored and parse the potential responses accordingly. For example, a question stored as one in which only one response can be selected is presented as an option button group. The code needed is a combination of HTML (to create the table rows and form elements) and server-side code (to provide the values).

The Add Question page allows six different types of questions: text, essay (text area), radio button, checkbox, drop-down list (single select), and drop-down list (multiple select). Therefore, six different code formats are required; however, they all follow the same basic structure. Let's look at a pseudo-code example for one type: the radio group:

```
Check to see if question type is #3, a radio group.
  If so, create a table.
    Create the first table row.
      In the table cell, write the question.
    Create the second row.
      In the table cell, write the question description.
      Begin a loop for each of the possible responses, converting
      each response to an array item.
      Create a table row for each response.
        In each table cell, create a radio form element,
        automatically marking the first item as selected.
    End loop of responses
  End table
End of radio group code
```

The particulars of the code, of course, depend on the server model. All the code is placed in the same area within the Repeat Region. Although including all the code for all types of questions will expand the design area significantly, because all the code is conditional, only the code pertinent to the question is executed.

1. Place your cursor in the right cell to which the Repeat Region server behavior has been applied.

2. In Code view, insert the following code snippets, one after another:

   From the Snippets panel, open the **Recipes > SurveyBuilder > Custom Code** folder for your server model and insert the **Survey Question Type - Text** snippet.

   From the Snippets panel, open the **Recipes > SurveyBuilder > Custom Code** folder for your server model and insert the **Survey Question Type - Textarea** snippet.

   From the Snippets panel, open the **Recipes > SurveyBuilder > Custom Code** folder for your server model and insert the **Survey Question Type - Radio** snippet.

   From the Snippets panel, open the **Recipes > SurveyBuilder > Custom Code** folder for your server model and insert the **Survey Question Type – Multi-Select** snippet.

   From the Snippets panel, open the **Recipes > SurveyBuilder > Custom Code** folder for your server model and insert the **Survey Question Type – Drop-Down List** snippet.

   From the Snippets panel, open the **Recipes > SurveyBuilder > Custom Code** folder for your server model and insert the **Survey Question Type - Checkbox** snippet [r5-21].

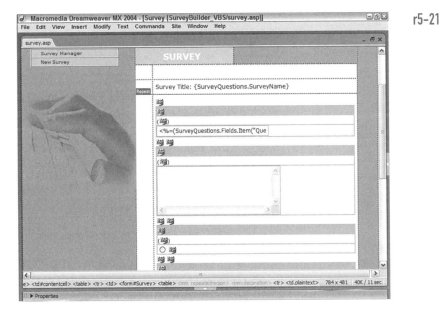

r5-21

3. Return to Design view.

Step 5: Check and Redirect If Survey Offline

We need to make sure that the user cannot take the survey if it is currently offline. At the same time, we want to ensure that a user can access an offline survey in Preview mode. To achieve both of these goals, two different conditional statements are needed. The first conditional statement merely checks the SurveyQuestions recordset; if the recordset is empty, the user is redirected to the Survey Offline page. The second statement, which ensures that the survey can be previewed, verifies that StatusLive is true and that the preview option has been selected—if it hasn't, the user is redirected to the offline page. Because of the values checked in the if-then statements, the code needs to be placed after the SurveyQuestions recordset.

1. From the Server Behaviors panel, select the **SurveyQuestions** recordset.
2. Switch to Code view and locate the selected code.
3. Position your cursor below the SurveyQuestions recordset and insert the following code:

   ☐ From the Snippets panel, open the **Recipes > SurveyBuilder > Custom Code** folder for your server model and insert the **Survey Offline - Redirect** snippet.

   `VB`
   ```
   <%
   if (SurveyQuestions.EOF) then
   Response.Redirect("survey_offline.asp")
   end if
   if (not SurveyQuestions.Fields("SurveyLive").value AND
   ➥cStr(Request("Preview")) = "") then
   Response.Redirect("survey_offline.asp")
   end if
   %>
   ```

   `JS`
   ```
   <%
   if (SurveyQuestions.EOF) {
   Response.Redirect("survey_offline.asp");
   }
   if (!SurveyQuestions.Fields("SurveyLive")
   ➥.value && String(Request("Preview")) == "undefined") {
   Response.Redirect("survey_offline.asp");
   }
   %>
   ```

   `CF`
   ```
   <cfif SurveyQuestions.RecordCount LE 0>
      <cflocation url="survey_offline.cfm">
   </cfif>
   <cfif (NOT SurveyQuestions.SurveyLive AND NOT isDefined
   ➥(URL.Preview))>
   ```

```
        <cflocation url="survey_offline.cfm">
      </cfif>

(PHP)  <?php
      if ($totalRows_SurveyQuestions <= 0) {
        header("Location: survey_offline.php");
      }
      if ((!$row_SurveyQuestions['SurveyLive']) &&
      ➥($_GET['Preview']=="")) {
        header("Location: survey_offline.php");
      }
      ?>
```

4. Save the page.

Step 6: Add Custom Insert Record Code

The final step for this page is an essential one. So far, we've created the page dynamically and redirected the user when needed; now it's time to store all the responses selected by the user in the appropriate data source. Because the page incorporates multiple questions in different formats, a special SQL command is needed to move through all the questions and insert them according to their question type. When the submission is complete, the Survey Completed page is displayed.

The code inserted can be broken down into three key functional parts:

- A custom insert record command/query, called ResultsCommand, is created.
- All the survey questions are examined and their responses placed in the appropriate variables.
- The insert record command is executed and the user is redirected to the Survey_Completed page.

Again, code placement is key. The custom code should be placed after the SurveyQuestions recordset is defined and the offline redirects have been executed.

1. In Code view, place the cursor after the conditional statements inserted in the previous step.
2. Insert the following code:
   - From the Snippets panel, open the **Recipes > SurveyBuilder > Custom Code** folder for your server model and insert the **Survey - Custom Insert** snippet.

VB `<%`

```
if (cStr(Request("SurveyComplete"))<>"")  then
  dim theSession, theQuestionID, theAnswer, theDescription,
  ➥RSFields, RSValues
  set ResultsCommand = Server.CreateObject("ADODB.Command")
  ResultsCommand.ActiveConnection = MM_Recipes_VB_STRING
  ResultsCommand.CommandType = 1
  ResultsCommand.CommandTimeout = 0
  ResultsCommand.Prepared = true

  while (NOT SurveyQuestions.EOF)
    theSession = Session.SessionID
  theQuestionID = SurveyQuestions.Fields("QuestionID").value
    theAnswer = cStr(Request("input" &
SurveyQuestions.Fields("QuestionID").value))
  theDescription = ""
  RSFields = "ResultSession,ResultQuestion,ResultAnswer"
  RSValues = ""

  if (SurveyQuestions.Fields("TypeID").value = 2)  then 'TextArea
    theAnswer = "answered"
    if (cStr(Request("input"&SurveyQuestions.Fields("QuestionID")
    ➥.value)="")) then
      theAnswer = "blank"
    end if
    theDescription = Request("input"&SurveyQuestions
    ➥.Fields("QuestionID").value)
    RSFields = "ResultDescription,"&RSFields
    RSValues = "'" & replace(theDescription,"'","''") & "',"
  else
    if (SurveyQuestions.Fields("TypeID").value = 6)  then
'Checkbox
      theAnswer = "yes"
      if (cStr(Request("input"&SurveyQuestions.Fields("QuestionID")
      ➥.value))="")  then
        tbeAnswer = "no"
      end if
    end if
  end if
  RSValues = RSValues & "'" & Session.SessionID & "',"
  ➥& theQuestionID & ",'" & Replace(theAnswer,"'","''") & "'"
    ResultsCommand.CommandText = "INSERT INTO SurveyResults
    ➥(" &  RSFields & " )  VALUES (" & RSValues & " ) "
  ResultsCommand.Execute()
    SurveyQuestions.MoveNext()
  wend
```

```
    Response.Redirect("survey_completed.asp?ID=" & Request("ID"))
  end if
%>
```

JS
```
<%
  if (String(Request("SurveyComplete"))!="undefined")  {
    var ResultsCommand = Server.CreateObject("ADODB.Command");
    ResultsCommand.ActiveConnection = MM_Recipes_STRING;
    ResultsCommand.CommandType = 1;
    ResultsCommand.CommandTimeout = 0;
    ResultsCommand.Prepared = true;

    while (!SurveyQuestions.EOF)  {
      var theSession = Session.SessionID;
        var theQuestionID =
  SurveyQuestions.Fields("QuestionID").value;
      var theAnswer = String(Request("input"+SurveyQuestions.Fields
      ➥("QuestionID").value));
      var theDescription = "";
      var RSFields = "ResultSession,ResultQuestion,ResultAnswer";
      var RSValues = "";

      if (SurveyQuestions.Fields("TypeID").value == 2)  {
  //TextArea
        theAnswer = ((String(Request("input"+SurveyQuestions.Fields
        ➥("QuestionID").value))!="")?"answered":"blank")
        theDescription =
  String(Request("input"+SurveyQuestions.Fields
        ➥("QuestionID").value));
        RSFields = "ResultDescription,"+RSFields;
        RSValues = "'"+theDescription.replace(/'/g,"''")+"',";
      }
      else if (SurveyQuestions.Fields("TypeID").value == 6)  {
        theAnswer = ((String(Request("input"+SurveyQuestions.Fields
        ➥("QuestionID").value))!="undefined")?"yes":"no");
      }
      RSValues += "'" +Session.SessionID+ "',"+theQuestionID+",
      ➥'"+theAnswer.replace(/'/g,"''")+"'";
      ResultsCommand.CommandText = "INSERT INTO SurveyResults
      ➥("+ RSFields + " )  VALUES ("+ RSValues + " ) ";
      ResultsCommand.Execute();
      SurveyQuestions.MoveNext();
    }
    Response.Redirect("survey_completed.asp?ID=" + Request("ID"));
  }
%>
```

```
CF  <cfif isDefined("Form.SurveyComplete")>
      <cfloop query="SurveyQuestions">
        <cfset theSession = Session.SessionID>
        <cfset theQuestionID = SurveyQuestions.QuestionID>
      <cfparam name="theAnswer" default="">
      <cfif isDefined("Form.input" & SurveyQuestions.QuestionID)>
        <cfset theAnswer = Evaluate("Form.input" &
        ➥SurveyQuestions.QuestionID)>
      </cfif>
        <cfset theDescription = "">
        <cfset RSFields = "ResultSession,ResultQuestion,ResultAnswer">
        <cfset RSValues = "">

        <cfif (SurveyQuestions.TypeID EQ 2)>
          <cfset theAnswer = "answered">
          <cfif isDefined("input" & SurveyQuestions.QuestionID)>
            <cfset theAnswer = "blank">
          </cfif>
          <cfset theDescription = theAnswer>
          <cfset RSFields = "ResultDescription,#RSFields#">
        <cfelse>
          <cfif (SurveyQuestions.TypeID EQ 6)>
            <cfset theAnswer = "yes">
            <cfif isDefined("input" & SurveyQuestions.QuestionID)>
              <cfset tbeAnswer = "no">
            </cfif>
          </cfif>
        </cfif>
        <cfquery datasource="Recipes" name="InsertResults">
        INSERT INTO SurveyResults (#RSFields#) VALUES
        ➥(<cfif (SurveyQuestions.TypeID EQ 2)>'#theDescription#',</cfif>
        ➥'#Session.SessionID#',#theQuestionID# ,'#theAnswer#')
        </cfquery>
      </cfloop>
      <cflocation url="survey_completed.cfm?ID=#Form.ID#">
    </cfif>

PHP <?php
    session_start();
    if ($_POST['SurveyComplete']!="") {
      do {
        $theSession = session_id();
        $theQuestionID = $row_SurveyQuestions['QuestionID'];
        $theAnswer = $_POST['input'.$theQuestionID];
        $theDescription = "";
```

```
$RSFields = "ResultSession,ResultQuestion,ResultAnswer";
$RSValues = "";
if ($row_SurveyQuestions['TypeID']==2) {
    // Text Field
    $theAnswer = ($_POST['input'.$theQuestionID]!="")
    ➥?"answered":"blank";
    $theDescription = $_POST['input'.$theQuestionID];
    $RSFields = "ResultDescription," . $RSFields;
    $RSValues = "'".addslashes($theDescription)."'";
} else if ($row_SurveyQuestions['TypeID']==6) {
    $theAnswer = ($_POST['input'.$theQuestionID]!="")?"yes":"no";
}
$RSValues.= "'" . $theSession .
➥"','".$theQuestionID.",'".addslashes($theAnswer)."'";
$insSQL = "INSERT INTO surveyresults (".$RSFields.")
➥VALUES (".$RSValues.")";
$insRes = mysql_query($insSQL,$Recipes_PHP);
} while ($row_SurveyQuestions = mysql_fetch_assoc
➥($SurveyQuestions));
$url = "survey_completed.php?ID=".$_GET['ID'];
header("Location: $url");
}
?>
```

3. Save the page.

End User Recipe: Survey Completed

When the user has completed and submitted the survey, it's a good idea to acknowledge the user's actions and, in some cases, issue a reward. The Survey Completed page displays just such a message, which was incorporated into the record when the survey was first created. This is a simple page that takes one data field from the Surveys table—filtered to show the current survey record—and binds it on the page. Often, surveys incorporate some sort of incentive to encourage users to take it; the Survey Completed page is an appropriate place for such an incentive.

Step 1: Implement Survey Completed Design

For this page, all you'll need is a heading and an area to hold the message. To allow the most flexibility, the area should be a nested table or some other expandable Web element.

1. Create a page for the Survey Manager recipe, either from a template or from the **File > New** dialog.

   📖 In the **SurveyBuilder** folder, locate the folder for your server model and open the survey_completed page there.

2. In the Content area of your page, create a header for the page and a general area to hold the message.

   📖 From the Snippets panel, drag the **Recipes > SurveyBuilder > Wireframes > Survey Completed – Wireframe** snippet into the Content editable region.

3. In the general area, add a nested table to hold the dynamic text for the completed survey message.

   📖 Place your cursor in the row below the words SURVEY COMPLETED and insert the **Recipes > SurveyBuilder > ContentTables > Survey Completed - Content Table** snippet [r5-22].

r5-22

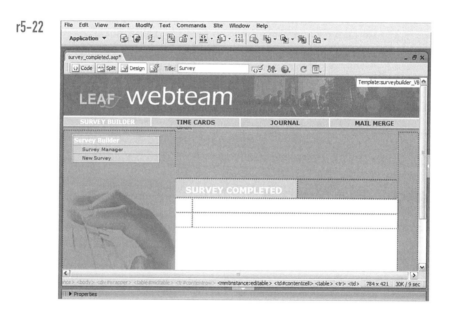

4. Save the page.

Step 2: Add Database Components

As mentioned earlier, this page uses a data field from the Surveys table. The recordset needed is restricted: just one field from one record.

For ASP

1. From the Bindings panel, choose Add (+) and select **Recordset** (**Query**) from the list.
2. In the Advanced Recordset dialog, enter a name for the recordset.

       ▢ Enter **CompletedSurvey** in the Name field.
3. Choose the data source.

       ▢ Select **Recipes** from the Connections list.
4. In the SQL area, enter the following code:

```
SELECT SurveyCompletedMessage
FROM Surveys
WHERE SurveyID = IDParam
```

5. In the Variable area, choose Add (+) to create a new variable.
6. Add an appropriate name for your variable.

       ▢ Enter **IDParam** in the Name column.
7. Enter a default value.

       ▢ Enter 0 in the Default Value column.
8. Insert a run-time value.

       ▢ Enter **Request**("**ID**") into the Run-Time Value column.
9. Click OK to close the dialog and insert the recordset.

For ColdFusion

1. From the Bindings panel, choose Add (+) and select **Recordset** (**Query**).
2. Switch to the advanced view of the dialog and enter an appropriate name for the recordset.

       ▢ Enter **CompletedSurvey** in the Name field.
3. Choose your data source.

       ▢ Select **Recipes** from the Data Source list.
4. Enter a username and password if necessary.
5. In the SQL area, enter the following code:

```
SELECT SurveyCompletedMessage
FROM Surveys
WHERE SurveyID = #URL.ID#
```

6. Verify your entries in the Recordset dialog and click OK to close that dialog.

For PHP

1. From the Bindings panel, choose Add (+) and select **Recordset (Query)** from the list.
2. In the Advanced Recordset dialog, enter a name for the recordset.
   - Enter **CompletedSurvey** in the Name field.
3. Choose the data source.
   - Select **Recipes** from the Connections list.
4. In the SQL area, enter the following code:
   ```
   SELECT SurveyCompletedMessage
   FROM surveys
   WHERE SurveyID = IDParam
   ```

5. In the Variable area, choose Add (+) to create a new variable.
6. Add an appropriate name for your variable.
   - Enter **IDParam** in the Name column.
7. Enter a default value.
   - Enter 0 in the Default Value column.
8. Insert a run-time value.
   - Enter **$_GET["ID"]** into the Run-Time Value column.
9. Click OK to close the dialog and insert the recordset.

Step 3: Adding Dynamic Text

To complete this page, all we need to do is add the dynamic text to the page.

1. From the Bindings panel, expand the **SurveyCompleted** recordset.
2. Place the dynamic text elements in their proper place on the page.
   - Drag **SurveyCompletedMessage** into the bottom row of the content table [r5-23].

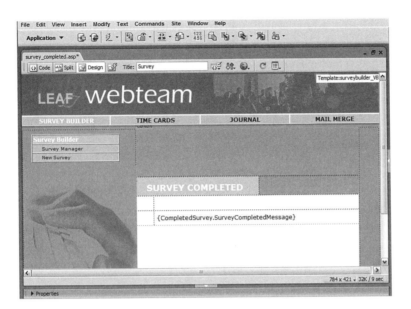

r5-23

3. Save the page.

The Survey Builder application is just one page from completion: Survey Offline.

End User Recipe: Survey Offline

After the survey has been completed, users can still try to access it. In these situations, it's a good idea to offer users a message explaining the status of the survey. The Survey Offline page uses a generic static message for all surveys.

Step 1: Implement Survey Offline Design

As with the Survey Completed page, all you'll need is a heading and an area to hold the message. This page, however, is even simpler because it has no dynamic elements.

1. Create a page for the Survey Manager recipe, either from a template or from the **File > New** dialog.

    ☐ In the **SurveyBuilder** folder, locate the folder for your server model and open the survey_offline page there.

2. In the Content area of your page, create a header for the page and a general area to hold the message.

    ☐ From the Snippets panel, drag the **Recipes > SurveyBuilder > Wireframes > Survey Offline – Wireframe** snippet into the Content editable region.

3. In the general area, add a nested table to hold the offline survey message.

    📖 Place your cursor in the row below the words SURVEY OFFLINE and insert the **Recipes > SurveyBuilder > ContentTables > Survey Offline - Content Table** snippet [r5-24].

r5-24

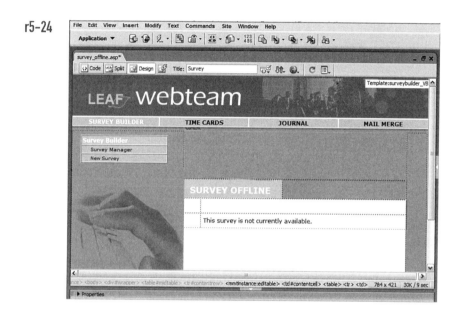

4. Save the page.

Again, feel free to customize the message here. You might also provide a link to the survey coordinator or someone else the user could go to for more information.

Survey Builder is a full-featured application and your implementation should be tested thoroughly before deploying. Try creating sample surveys with mock questions—using one or more of each type—and then having your testers respond to the survey.

Recipe 6

Time Cards

Keeping track of time spent on a client's project is an essential task for any workgroup. Not only does such record keeping enable managers to monitor the project's progress, it also helps to gauge billable hours and to estimate future projects. A time card application can go a long way toward serving these goals.

In a typical workgroup, employees work on a wide range of projects, performing a variety of tasks. For a time card application to be useful, the manager must be able to add new projects and tasks easily. Both the administrators and the employees should be able to log hours for specific projects. The reporting features of a time card application need to be robust and offer a range of views of the data, incorporating summaries of hours entered per project or per employee.

The Time Cards recipe described in this chapter consists of eight separate pages, most of which are geared toward the manager or administrator. Many of the recordsets require rather sophisticated SQL code techniques to extract and summarize the data properly. As described in the recipe overview, the SQL statements are best executed in the data source.

Administrator Recipes

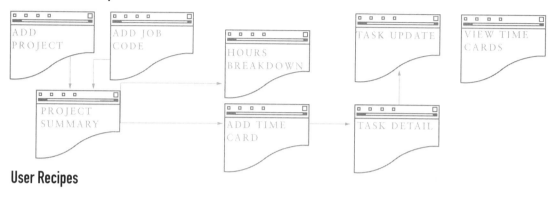

User Recipes

Ingredients

8 APPLICATION PAGES:

- 2 User Pages
  - Add Time Card
  - Project Summary (also accessed by the administrator)
- 6 Administration Pages
  - Add Project
  - Add Job Code
  - Hours Breakdown
  - Task Detail
  - Task Update
  - View Time Cards

1 DATA SOURCE:

- 1 Database with:
  - 4 Tables
    - **TimeCard**—Includes records for all time cards entered in the application with fields for the ID, employee, project, date logged, assigned date, hours, and description.
    - **Projects**—Tracks the available projects, their managers, estimated hours, and actual hours logged.
    - **JobTypes**—A listing of the tasks available to be assigned on a time card; each job type includes a short description, ID, and billing rate.
    - **Employees**—This is the standard employee table used throughout the book, used when a new time card is created.

- 6 SQL Queries
  - **ProjectTimeCards**—A virtual table joining the `TimeCard` and `Projects` tables.
  - **HoursBreakdown**—A SQL statement that combines the `ProjectTimeCards` query and `JobTypes` table.
  - **ProjectSummary**—A SQL statement that extracts data from the `HoursBreakdown` query.
  - **DailyHours, WeeklyHours, and MonthlyHours**—Three separate SQL statements, each of which derives summaries from the `HoursBreakdown` query.

Prep Work

Before you begin to build this application, make sure your prep work has been completed.

1. Create the data source containing the necessary tables.
   - 📖 ASP and ColdFusion users should use the **Recipes.mdb** data source found in the downloaded files while PHP users should work with the **Recipes** data source. For assistance in locating and installing these files, choose **Help > Web Application Recipes.**
2. Set up a connection to the data source. If you're unsure how to do this, see the "Connecting to Data Sources" section of Chapter 1.
   - 📖 Name the connection **Recipes.**
3. Create the template to be used for the application.
   - 📖 Use the template for your server model named **timecards.**

Recipe Overview: Data Source Tables and Queries

The Time Cards recipe is somewhat different from the others in this book. Many of the application pages, especially those displaying time card summaries, are calculation intensive. Although it's possible to include the required complex SQL statements on the Web page, it's far more efficient—and far less error-prone—to construct and execute the SQL within the database itself.

The Time Cards recipe follows the approach of keeping the complex SQL in the data source. Consequently, creating the actual application pages is fairly straightforward with a minimum of hand-coding required. However, to truly understand how the recipe works, we'll need to take a little time to examine the component parts of this application: the data source tables and the queries.

As noted in the "Ingredients" section, this recipe uses four tables: TimeCard, Projects, Employees, and JobTypes. Of these four, only the TimeCard table is specific to this application; the other tables are also used elsewhere in other recipes. The Employees and JobType tables are used to create a new time card, thus ensuring that only current employees and valid job codes are used. The Projects table tracks projects, managers, and hours, both estimated and final.

Much of the power found in the Time Cards recipe is derived from the six interrelated SQL queries used in the application. One query, ProjectTimeCards, creates a virtual table by combining data from two tables, Projects and TimeCard. The ProjectTimeCards query relies on the SQL operation LEFT JOIN. As you might recall from SQL-related discussions in other recipes, a JOIN gathers data from two SQL objects (such as tables or views) to create a new recordset based on some criteria. A LEFT JOIN guarantees that all the records from the first table (the one on the left side of the SQL statement) are included regardless of the criteria. Thus, the ProjectTimeCards query for ASP and ColdFusion is as follows:

```
SELECT Projects.*, TimeCard.*
FROM Projects LEFT JOIN TimeCard ON Projects.ProjectID =
➥TimeCard.CardProject;
```

For MySQL we use the following:

```
SELECT projects.*, timecard.*,jobtypes.JobCode
FROM projects, jobtypes LEFT JOIN timecard
➥ON projects.ProjectID=timecard.CardProject
WHERE timecard.CardJobTypeID = jobtypes.JobTypeID
ORDER BY ProjectID
```

 NOTE You can find a discussion of a similar SQL operation, the RIGHT JOIN, in Recipe 4, "In/Out Dashboard."

These SQL statements will include all the records from the Projects table as well as the records from the TimeCard table where there is a matching project. This is done so that new time cards can be assigned to any project.

The most complex SQL query in the recipe—and the basis for the other four queries used—relies on the ProjectSummary query. The HoursBreakDown SQL statement is referred to as "a query of a query" because it combines the results of the ProjectSummary query and the JobTypes table. Again, a LEFT JOIN is used to get all the records from the ProjectSummary query and only the designated ones from the JobTypes table, as you can see by examining the FROM clause of the SQL statement used in ASP and ColdFusion:

```
SELECT ProjectTimeCards.ProjectID, ProjectTimeCards.ProjectName,
ProjectTimeCards.ProjectManager, ProjectTimeCards.ProjectHours,
Sum([JobTypes].[JobRate]*[ProjectTimeCards].[CardHours]) AS
BillableAmount, ProjectTimeCards.CardDate,
ProjectTimeCards.CardDescription, ProjectTimeCards.CardEmployee,
ProjectTimeCards.CardLogged, JobTypes.JobCode, (SELECT
Sum(TimeCard2.CardHours) FROM TimeCard AS TimeCard2 WHERE
TimeCard2.CardProject = ProjectTimeCards.ProjectID) AS TotalHoursIn,
ProjectTimeCards.CardHours, ProjectTimeCards.CardProject,
ProjectTimeCards.CardID, DateDiff('w',[ProjectDate],[CardDate]) AS
WeeksIn, Sum(ProjectTimeCards.CardHours) AS HoursIn,
JobTypes.JobRate

FROM ProjectTimeCards LEFT JOIN JobTypes ON
ProjectTimeCards.CardJobTypeID = JobTypes.JobTypeID

GROUP BY ProjectTimeCards.ProjectID, ProjectTimeCards.ProjectName,
ProjectTimeCards.ProjectManager, ProjectTimeCards.ProjectHours,
ProjectTimeCards.CardDate, ProjectTimeCards.CardDescription,
ProjectTimeCards.CardEmployee, ProjectTimeCards.CardLogged,
JobTypes.JobCode, ProjectTimeCards.CardHours,
ProjectTimeCards.CardProject, ProjectTimeCards.CardID,
DateDiff('w',[ProjectDate],[CardDate]), JobTypes.JobRate

ORDER BY ProjectTimeCards.CardID DESC;
```

You might note that the SELECT clause is one of the most complex used in this book. In addition to the calculated fields like BillableAmount and WeeksIn, a *nested SQL statement* is also included to create the TotalHoursIn field.

The SQL statements for MySQL are similar but slightly more complex because MySQL has no support for stored queries or views. For this reason, we need to use a custom PHP code block to populate temporary tables that simulate views for our needs. We do this using three SQL statements. The first simulates the ProjectTimeCards query:

```
DELETE FROM projecttimecards;
INSERT INTO projecttimecards
SELECT projects.*, timecard.*,jobtypes.JobCode
FROM projects, jobtypes
LEFT JOIN timecard ON projects.ProjectID=timecard.CardProject
WHERE timecard.CardJobTypeID = jobtypes.JobTypeID
ORDER BY ProjectID
```

Here's the PHP code needed to simulate the HoursBreakDown query:

```
INSERT INTO hoursbreakdown
SELECT
projecttimecards.ProjectID, projecttimecards.ProjectName,
projecttimecards.ProjectManager, projecttimecards.ProjectHours,
Sum(jobtypes.JobRate*projecttimecards.CardHours) AS BillableAmount,
ROUND((TO_DAYS(projecttimecards.ProjectDate) -
TO_DAYS(projecttimecards.CardDate))/7) AS WeeksIn,
projecttimecards.CardDate, projecttimecards.CardDescription,
projecttimecards.CardEmployee,
projecttimecards.CardLogged, jobtypes.JobCode,
SUM(timecard.CardHours) AS TotalHoursIn,
projecttimecards.CardHours, projecttimecards.CardHours AS HoursIn,
projecttimecards.CardProject, CONCAT('$',
➥FORMAT(jobtypes.JobRate,2)) AS JobRate
FROM projecttimecards
LEFT JOIN jobtypes ON projecttimecards.CardJobTypeID =
➥jobtypes.JobTypeID
INNER JOIN timecard ON timecard.CardProject =
➥projecttimecards.ProjectID
GROUP BY projecttimecards.ProjectID, projecttimecards.ProjectName,
projecttimecards.ProjectManager, projecttimecards.ProjectHours,
projecttimecards.CardDate, projecttimecards.CardDescription,
projecttimecards.CardEmployee, projecttimecards.CardLogged,
jobtypes.JobCode, projecttimecards.CardHours,
projecttimecards.CardProject, projecttimecards.CardID,
WeeksIn, jobtypes.JobRate
HAVING BillableAmount IS NOT NULL
ORDER BY
projecttimecards.CardID DESC
```

And finally, to simulate the ProjectSummary view:

```
INSERT INTO projectsummary
SELECT
Sum(HoursBreakdown.CardHours) AS ProjectHoursUsed,
Sum(HoursBreakdown.BillableAmount) AS ProjectDue,
HoursBreakdown.ProjectHours, HoursBreakdown.ProjectManager,
HoursBreakdown.ProjectName, HoursBreakdown.ProjectID
FROM HoursBreakdown

GROUP BY HoursBreakdown.ProjectHours, HoursBreakdown.ProjectManager,
HoursBreakdown.ProjectName, HoursBreakdown.ProjectID

ORDER BY HoursBreakdown.ProjectID;
```

The other four queries referenced in this recipe—ProjectSummary, DailyHours, WeeklyHours, and MonthlyHours—are all based on the HoursBreakdown query. The ProjectSummary query, as the name implies, summarizes data calculated in HoursBreakdown. Similarly, the DailyHours, WeeklyHours, and MonthlyHours queries each extract only the information needed for daily, weekly, and monthly reports, respectively.

Administrator Recipe: Add Job Code

A proper job code is a significant building block for the Time Cards recipe. For an employee's hours to be correctly logged to a specific project, they need to have the right job code. This first application page allows the project administrator to add job codes as needed. The Add Job Code application uses the Insert Record server behavior. The full set of codes is displayed in a list on the Add Time Card page in a list.

Step 1: Implement the Add Job Code Design

The Add Job Code page is basically a simple insert record application. As such, the layout of the page requires a few form elements: three text fields and a submit button. The three fields—Job Name, Job Code, and Rate—are used in other aspects of the application. The Job Name is displayed in a list on the Add Time Card page, while the Job Code and Rate are used in the HoursBreakdown SQL calculations. The Rate field is intended to accept the hourly rate charged to the client for a particular job.

1. In the server model of your choice, create a dynamic page.
    - In the **TimeCards** folder, locate the folder for your server model and open the add_jobcode page from there.
2. Add a table to the content region of your page to contain the form elements for the application.
    - From the Snippets panel, drag the **Recipes > TimeCards > Wireframes > Add Job Code - Wireframe** snippet into the Content editable region.
3. Insert the form and, within it, a two-column table. The table should include form elements and labels for a job name, job code, and rate; the code and rate form fields should be limited to around 10 characters. You'll also need a form button for inserting the new record.
    - Place your cursor in the row below the words ADD JOB CODE and insert the **Recipes > TimeCards > Forms > Add Job Code - Form** snippet.
4. Save the file [r6-1].

r6-1

To accommodate the different dialogs for the various server models, the steps are presented separately here and when necessary throughout this recipe.

Step 2: Insert Record—Add Job Code

The only server-side code required for this page is the standard Insert Record server behavior. The values entered will be stored in the JobTypes table. Once the insertion is completed, the user is taken to the Project Summary page.

For ASP

1. From the Server Behaviors panel, choose Add (+) and select **Insert Record** from the list.

2. In the Insert Record dialog, choose your data source.

   📖 Choose **Recipes** from the Connection list.

3. Select the table into which you want to insert the record.

   📖 From the Insert Into Table list, choose **JobTypes**.

4. Set the page that you want to appear after the record is inserted.

   📖 Choose the **report_projectsummary.asp** file from your server model's folder for the After Inserting, Go To field.

5. Select the form on the current page from which to gather the record values.

   📖 From the Get Values From list, make sure **AddJobCode** is selected.

6. In the Form Elements area, match the form elements on the page to the fields in the data source table.

    📖 Set `JobName` to insert into the `JobType` column as Text type.

    Set `JobCode` to insert into the `JobCode` column as Text type.

    Set `JobRate` to insert into the `JobRate` column as Numeric type.

7. When you're sure your choices are correct, click OK to close the dialog and add the behavior.

8. Save your page before continuing.

For ColdFusion and PHP

1. From the Server Behaviors panel, choose Add (+) and select **Insert Record**.

2. In the Insert Record dialog, choose the current form.

    📖 Select **AddJobCode** from the Submit Values From list.

3. Select your data source from the list.

    📖 Choose **Recipes** from the Data Source list.

4. Enter your username and password, if needed.

5. Select the table in the data source to insert into from the list.

    📖 Choose **JobTypes** (**jobtypes** for PHP) from the Insert Into Table list.

6. Set the data source fields to their corresponding form elements.

    📖 Make sure the `JobTypeID` data column is set to be an unused Primary Key.

    Set `JobType` to the `FORM.JobName` form element and submit as Text type.

    Set `JobCode` to the `FORM.JobCode` form element and submit as Text type.

    Set `JobRate` to the `FORM.JobRate` form element and submit as Numeric type (Double in PHP).

7. In the After Inserting, Go To field, enter **report_projectsummary.cfm** or **report_projectsummary.php** as appropriate and click OK to close the dialog.

8. Save your page.

Administrator Recipe: Add Project

In addition to the ability to add new jobs, the administrator must also be able to add new projects. The Add Project page allows the creation of a new project and the assigning of a manager, an hours budget, and a method to track the timeline. The hours budget is an estimate of how long the project is expected to take. As the time cards related to the project are submitted, the time reported is subtracted from the hours budget. With these figures, actual time spent on the project can be compared to the initial estimate. The final element on the Add Project page is a list that allows the administrator to establish an estimated timeline for the project.

As with the Add Job Code recipe, the Insert Record server behavior is used to implement the server-side logic for this page.

Step 1: Implement Add Project Design

The Add Project layout is only slightly more complex than the preceding recipe. In addition to three text fields (one each for the project name, manager, and hours budget), a drop-down list with static values displaying the number of weeks for a project is used. Our snippet example creates a list element from 1 to 20 weeks as well as an extra option for 1/2 week. You should, of course, create names and values that reflect your own project timelines.

1. Create a dynamic page for your server model.

     📖 In the **TimeCards** folder, locate the folder for your server model and open the add_project page from there.

2. Insert a table into the content region of your page to hold the needed form elements.

     📖 From the Snippets panel, drag the **Recipes > TimeCards > Wireframes > Add Project - Wireframe** snippet into the Content editable region.

3. Insert the form and, within it, a two-column table. The table should include form text fields and labels for a project name, project manager, and hours budget. A select list displaying a number of week options should also be included. Finally, a form button is required to insert the new record.

     📖 Place your cursor in the row below the words ADD PROJECT and insert the **Recipes > TimeCards > Forms > Add Project - Form** snippet.

4. Save the file [r6-2].

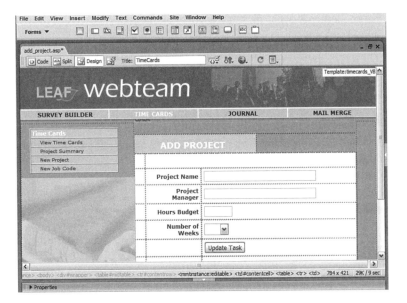

r6-2

Step 2: Insert Record—Add Project

Because we're creating a new record, the Insert Record server behavior is the natural choice for our server-side code. To be consistent with the Add Job Code recipe, we'll set the server behavior to redirect the user to the same page—the Project Summary page—after the insert operation is complete.

> **NOTE**
>
> To enhance this recipe, you might create a drop-down list that displays all the managers in your company. To do this, you'll need to add a recordset of the Employee table filtered to shown only the Manager position and attach that recordset to the values and labels of the list.

For ASP

1. From the Server Behaviors panel, choose Add (+) and select **Insert Record** from the list.

2. In the Insert Record dialog, choose your data source.

   📖 Choose **Recipes** from the Connection list.

3. Select the table you want to insert the record into.

   📖 From the Insert Into Table list, choose **Projects**.

4. Set the page that you want to appear after the record is inserted.

   📖 Choose the **report_projectsummary.asp** file from your server model's folder for the After Inserting, Go To field.

5. Select the form on the current page from which to gather the record values.

   📖 From the Get Values From list, make sure **AddNewProject** is selected.

6. In the Form Elements area, match the form elements on the page to the fields in the data source table.

   📖 Set `ProjectName` to insert into the `ProjectName` column as Text type.

   Set `ProjectManager` to insert into the `ProjectManager` column as Text type.

   Set `TaskHours` to insert into the `ProjectHours` column as Numeric type.

   Set `ProjectWeek` to insert into the `Weeks` column as Numeric type.

7. When you're sure your choices are correct, click OK to close the dialog and add the behavior.

For ColdFusion and PHP

1. From the Server Behaviors panel, choose Add (+) and select **Insert Record**.
2. In the Insert Record dialog, choose the current form.

   📖 Select **AddNewProject** from the Submit Values From list.

3. Select your data source from the list.

   📖 Choose **Recipes** from the Data Source list.

4. Enter your username and password, if needed.
5. Select the table in the data source to insert into from the list.

   📖 Choose **Projects** (**projects** in PHP) from the Insert Into Table list.

6. Set the data source fields to their corresponding form elements.

   📖 Make sure the `ProjectID` data column is set to be an unused Primary Key.

   Set `ProjectName` to the `FORM.ProjectName` form element and submit as Text type.

   Set `ProjectManager` to the `FORM.ProjectManager` form element and submit as Text type.

   Set `TaskHours` to the `FORM.ProjectHours` form element and submit as Numeric type (Double in PHP).

   Set `Weeks` to the `FORM.ProjectWeek` form element and submit as Numeric type (Double in PHP).

7. In the After Inserting, Go To field, enter **report_projectsummary.cfm** or **report_projectsummary.php** as appropriate and click OK to close the dialog.
8. Save your page.

Recipe: Administrator/End–User Recipe: Project Summary

The Project Summary page serves three main purposes. First, as the name indicates, it provides a concise overview of all the various projects. For each project, both the estimated and actual hours logged are shown in addition to the project's manager. Second, this page serves as a gateway to the detail page, where the hours are broken down by employee. Finally, links under each project heading connect to the appropriate Add Time Card page so that new hours can be logged.

Step 1: Implement Project Summary Design

To meet all the needs for this particular page, a compact layout is called for. The summarized information is best displayed in a two-column table along with the associated links; the links should be visually separated from the data. The entire table structure will later be enclosed in a Repeat Region server behavior so that multiple projects can be summarized.

1. In the server model of your choice, create a dynamic page.

   📖 In the **TimeCards** folder, locate the folder for your server model and open the report_projectsummary page from there.

2. Add a table to the content region of your page to contain the form elements for the application.

   📖 From the Snippets panel, drag the **Recipes > TimeCards > Wireframes > Project Summary Report - Wireframe** snippet into the Content editable region.

3. Add a table structure to allow for separation between repeating rows.

   📖 From the Snippets panel, drag the **Recipes > TimeCards > ContentTables > Project Summary Report - Shell** snippet into the row beneath the words PROJECT SUMMARY REPORT.

4. Insert a two-column table with the first column right-justified for labels (for Project Name, Project Manager, Hours Budget, and Hours Used) and the second column left-justified to hold the dynamic text. The header area should include text for the two needed links: View Breakdown and Log Hours.

   📖 Place your cursor in the cell in the right side of the middle row of the just-added snippet and insert the **Recipes > TimeCards > ContentTables > Project Summary Report - Content Table** snippet.

5. Save the file [r6-3].

r6-3

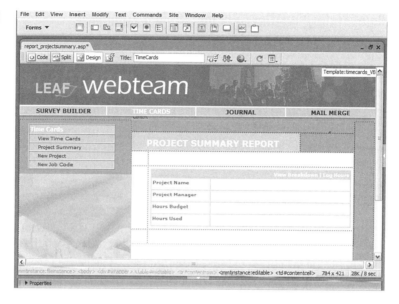

Step 2: Add Database Components

Setting up the page logic for this recipe is very straightforward. Because all of the calculations are handled by the HoursBreakdown query and are presented by the ProjectSummary view, a simple recordset is all that's required for ASP and ColdFusion users. PHP developers will need to add custom code to simulate the queries and views.

1. From the Bindings panel, choose Add (+) and select **Recordset** (**Query**).
2. In the simple view of the Recordset dialog, enter an appropriate name.
     - Enter **ProjectSummary** in the Name field.
3. Select the desired data source connection.
     - Choose **Recipes** from the Connection (Data Source) list.
4. Choose the needed table.
     - From the Tables list, select **ProjectSummary** (**projectsummary** for PHP).
5. Leave the Columns option set to All.
6. Make sure the Filter is set to None.
7. Keep the Sort option set to None and click OK to close the dialog.
8. Save the page after the recordset is inserted.

As previously noted, PHP coders must include some custom code.

1. In Code view, position your cursor near the top of the page after the code that begins `<?php require_once` and insert the following code.

   📖 From the Snippets panel, insert the **Recipes > TimeCards > CustomCode_PHP > Project Summary - Simulate Querys and View** snippet.

```php
(PHP)  <?php
       // ProjectTimeCards Temporary Table
       mysql_select_db($database_Cookbook_PHP, $Recipes);
       $sql = "DELETE FROM projecttimecards";
       @mysql_query($sql,$Recipes);
       $sql = "INSERT INTO projecttimecards SELECT projects.*,
       ➥timecard.*,jobtypes.JobCode FROM projects, jobtypes
       ➥LEFT JOIN timecard ON projects.ProjectID=timecard.CardProject
       ➥GROUP BY ProjectID ORDER BY ProjectID";
       @mysql_query($sql,$Recipes);

       // Hours Breakdown Temporary Table
       $sql = "DELETE FROM hoursbreakdown";
       @mysql_query($sql,$Recipes);
       $sql = "INSERT INTO hoursbreakdown
       ➥SELECT projecttimecards.ProjectID,
       ➥projecttimecards.ProjectName,
       ➥projecttimecards.ProjectManager,
       ➥projecttimecards.ProjectHours,
       ➥jobtypes.JobRate*projecttimecards.CardHours
       ➥AS BillableAmount, ROUND((TO_DAYS(projecttimecards.ProjectDate) -
       ➥TO_DAYS(projecttimecards.CardDate))/7) AS WeeksIn,
       ➥projecttimecards.CardID,projecttimecards.CardDate,
       ➥projecttimecards.CardDescription, projecttimecards.CardEmployee,
       ➥projecttimecards.CardLogged, projecttimecards.CardJobTypeID,
       ➥jobtypes.JobCode, SUM(timecard.CardHours) AS TotalHoursIn,
       ➥projecttimecards.CardHours, projecttimecards.CardHours
       ➥AS HoursIn, projecttimecards.CardProject,
       ➥CONCAT('$',FORMAT(jobtypes.JobRate,2)) AS JobRate FROM
       ➥projecttimecards,jobtypes,timecard WHERE
       ➥(projecttimecards.CardJobTypeID = jobtypes.JobTypeID
       ➥AND timecard.CardProject = projecttimecards.ProjectID) OR
       (projecttimecards.CardJobTypeID = 0) GROUP BY
       ➥projecttimecards.ProjectID
       ➥ORDER BY projecttimecards.CardID DESC";
       @mysql_query($sql,$Recipes);

       // Create the ProjectSummary
       $sql = "DELETE FROM projectsummary";
       @mysql_query($sql,$Recipes);
       $sql = "INSERT INTO projectsummary
       ➥SELECT Sum(HoursBreakdown.CardHours)
```

```
➥AS ProjectHoursUsed, Sum(HoursBreakdown.BillableAmount)
➥AS ProjectDue, HoursBreakdown.ProjectHours,
➥HoursBreakdown.ProjectManager, HoursBreakdown.ProjectName,
➥HoursBreakdown.ProjectID FROM HoursBreakdown
➥GROUP BY HoursBreakdown.ProjectHours,
➥HoursBreakdown.ProjectManager, HoursBreakdown.ProjectName,
➥HoursBreakdown.ProjectID ORDER BY HoursBreakdown.ProjectID";
@mysql_query($sql,$Recipes);
?>
```

2. Save the page.

Step 3: Data Binding Process

In this step, we'll insert dynamic data from the recordset to display the summary information for each project.

1. From the Bindings panel, expand the **ProjectSummary** recordset.
2. Place the data fields on the page in their proper places.

    📖 Drag **ProjectName** into the cell next to the Project Name label.

    Drag **ProjectManager** into the cell next to the Project Manager label.

    Drag **ProjectHours** into the cell next to the Hours Budget label.

    Drag **ProjectHoursUsed** into the cell next to the Hours Used label [r6-4].

r6-4

3. When you're done, save the page.

Step 4: Make Dynamic Links

After the dynamic data is inserted, we're ready to create the links mentioned earlier. The links to the detail and new time card pages both use the ProjectID field—returned in the recordset—to ensure that the proper project is referenced. First let's assemble the link to the detail page, View Breakdown.

1. Select the text or image you want to link to the detail page.

   🕮 Choose the phrase **View Breakdown** at the top of the content table.

2. Select the folder symbol next to the Link field in the Property inspector. The Select File dialog opens.

3. Make sure the dialog is set to **Select File Name From File System**.

4. Choose **Parameters** at the bottom of the dialog.

5. In the Name column of the Parameters dialog, enter the variable name.

   🕮 Enter **ID** in the Name column.

6. In the Value column, enter the dynamic value of the current project's ID.

   🕮 Select the lightning bolt next in the Value column and, from the Dynamic Data dialog, choose **ProjectID**. When you're done, click OK once to close the Dynamic Data dialog and again to close the Parameters dialog.

7. In the Select File dialog, select the file that will be used to display the details of hours logged.

   🕮 Choose **report_hoursbreakdown** in the TimeCards folder for your server model.

8. When you're done, click OK to insert the link.

Next we'll create a link to log hours against a particular project.

1. Select the text or image you want to link to the add timecard application.

   🕮 Choose the phrase **Log Hours** at the top of the content table.

2. Select the folder symbol next to the Link field in the Property inspector. The Select File dialog opens.

3. Make sure the dialog is set to **Select File Name From File System**.

4. Choose **Parameters** at the bottom of the dialog.

5. In the Name column of the Parameters dialog, enter the variable name.

   🕮 Enter **ID** in the Name column.

6. In the Value column, enter the dynamic value of the current project's ID.

   🕮 Select the lightning bolt next in the Value column and, from the Dynamic Data dialog, choose **ProjectID**. When you're done, click OK once to close the Dynamic Data dialog and again to close the Parameters dialog.

7. In the Select File dialog, select the file that will be used to add new hours to a project.

   ◻ Choose **add_timecard** in the TimeCards folder for your server model.

8. When you're done, click OK to insert the link.

Step 5: Add Repeat Region Server Behavior

To show summaries of all the available projects, we'll need to wrap our content table with a Repeat Region server behavior. Depending on how many projects you will be displaying, you could either show them all within the region or show a set number, like 10. If you choose the latter route, you'll also need to add recordset navigation controls.

1. Select any of the dynamic data fields.
2. From the Tag Selector, choose the appropriate table row tag that encompasses the entire table for the summary content.

   ◻ Select the **<tr>** tag to the left of the `<table>` tag in the Tag Selector.
3. From the Server Behaviors panel, choose Add (+) and select **Repeat Region**.
4. In the Repeat Region dialog, choose the desired recordset.

   ◻ Choose **ProjectSummary** from the Recordset list.
5. Set the Show option to display however many records you'd like.

   ◻ Choose **Show All Records**.
6. Click OK when you're done and save your page.

NOTE

There appears to be a bug with the ColdFusion implementation of the Repeat Region server behavior in Dreamweaver MX 2004. If you apply the server behavior to any tag that includes a color attribute—for example, bgcolor="#FFCC00"—Dreamweaver does not escape the # character by adding a second #. This is necessary because ColdFusion uses the # character to mark data fields and variables. If you encounter an error when testing this page, check your code and change any attributes within the `<cfoutput>` tags of the repeated region like bgcolor="#FFCC00" to bgcolor="##FFCC00". This bug is not present in Dreamweaver MX.

After you have a few projects, enter Live Data view to see the summaries in Dreamweaver [r6-5].

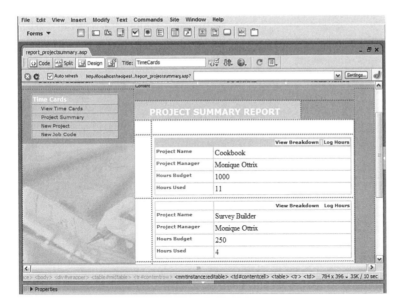

End-User Recipe: Add Time Card

Most likely, the Add Time Card page will be among the most frequently used aspects of the Time Card application. This page enables the employee to attribute a number of hours to a particular project while performing a specific task. The projects are already selected when the Add Time Card link is chosen from the Project Summary page; both the employee name and the type of job are selected from a recordset-filled drop-down list. Once the rest of the information is entered—such as the date, job description, and number of hours—an Insert Record server behavior is used to store the new record.

Step 1: Implement Add Time Card Design

The layout for the Add Time Card design requires a form and various elements. In addition to the two drop-down lists previously noted, the design should include text fields for the date and hours as well as a text area for the task description and a submit button. A hidden form element is also needed to make sure the current project is properly identified when the record is inserted.

1. In the server model of your choice, create a dynamic page.
   - 📖 In the **TimeCards** folder, locate the folder for your server model and open the add_timecard page from there.

2. Add a table to the content region of your page to contain the form elements for the application.

   📖 From the Snippets panel, drag the **Recipes > TimeCards > Wireframes > Add Time Card - Wireframe** snippet into the Content editable region.

3. Insert the form and, within it, a two-column table. The table should include six form elements: two lists (Employee and Job Type), two text fields (Date and Hours), a text area (Task Description), a submit button (Add Task), and a hidden form element (ID).

   📖 Place your cursor in the row below the words ADD TIME CARD and insert the **Recipes > TimeCards > Forms > Add Time Card - Form** snippet.

4. Save the file [r6-6].

r6-6

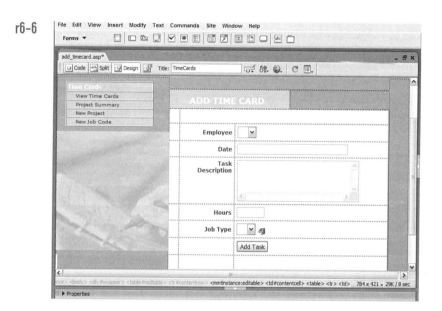

Step 2: Add Database Components

You want to make sure hours are logged quickly and accurately. To help, our recipe calls for two recordsets to populate the drop-down lists, Employees and Job Type. When applied, these recordsets make sure that the time card record includes both an active employee and job type.

Whereas both data components are fairly simple to implement, the Employees recordset has a bit of a twist. Rather than just return the last name from the Employee table, this recordset returns a combination of both the first name and last name fields with the *field alias*, `EmployeeName`. A field alias follows the `AS` keyword in a SQL statement, like this for ASP and ColdFusion:

```
SELECT EmployeeFirst & ' '& EmployeeLast AS EmployeeName
```

In MySQL, the equivalent SQL is as follows:

```
SELECT CONCAT(EmployeeFirst,' ',EmployeeLast) AS EmployeeName
```

This `SELECT` statement concatenates data from the two fields with a space between and stores the result in the alias `EmployeeName`.

Let's start with the simpler of the two recordset declarations:

1. From the Bindings panel, choose Add (+) and select **Recordset (Query)**.
2. In the simple Recordset dialog, enter an appropriate name.
   - 📖 Enter **JobTypes** in the Name field.
3. Select the desired data source connection.
   - 📖 Choose **Recipes** from the Connection (Data Source) list.
4. Choose the needed table.
   - 📖 From the Tables list, select **JobTypes** (**jobtypes** for PHP).
5. Set the Columns option to **Selected** and choose only the necessary fields.
   - 📖 Press Shift and select **JobTypeID** and **JobType** from the Columns list.
6. Make sure the Filter is set to None.
7. Keep the Sort option set to None and click OK to close the dialog.
8. Save the page after the recordset is inserted.

Now we're ready to add the `Employees` recordset to the page.

1. From the Bindings panel, choose Add (+) and choose **Recordset (Query)** from the list.
2. In the Recordset dialog, select **Advanced**.
3. Enter an appropriate name for your recordset.
   - 📖 In the Name field, enter **Employees**.
4. Choose the connection for your data source.
   - 📖 Select **Recipes** from the Connection list.
5. In the SQL area, enter the following code:

VB JS CF
```
SELECT EmployeeFirst & ' '& EmployeeLast AS EmployeeName
    FROM Employees
    ORDER BY Employees.EmployeeLast, Employees.EmployeeFirst
```

In MySQL, use:

```
(PHP) SELECT CONCAT(EmployeeFirst,' ',EmployeeLast) AS EmployeeName
      FROM employees
      ORDER BY employees.EmployeeLast, employees.EmployeeFirst
```

6. Click OK to close the dialog and add the recordset.

Step 3: Data Binding Process

The next task is to bind the two recordsets created in the preceding step to the form list elements on the page; the procedure is the same for both. In addition, we'll also need to give our hidden form element a dynamically assigned value: the project ID passed in from the selecting URL.

We'll work on the Employee list element first.

1. Select the **TaskEmployee** list element.
2. From the Property inspector, select **Dynamic**.
3. In the Dynamic List/Menu dialog, select the **Employee** recordset from the Options From Recordset list.
4. In the Values field, choose **EmployeeName**.
5. In the Labels field, select **EmployeeName**.
   In this case, both the Values and Labels are set to the same data field.
6. Leave the Select Value Equal To Field blank.
7. Click OK once to close the Dynamic Data dialog and then again to close the Dynamic List/Menu dialog.

Next we'll bind the proper dynamic data to complete the Job Code list.

1. Select the **ProjectJobCode** list element.
2. From the Property inspector, select **Dynamic**.
3. In the Dynamic List/Menu dialog, select the **JobTypes** recordset from the Options From Recordset list.
4. In the Values field, choose **JobTypeID**.
5. In the Labels field, select **JobType**.
6. Leave the Select Value Equal To Field blank.
7. Click OK once to close the Dynamic Data dialog and then again to close the Dynamic List/Menu dialog.

The final bit of data binding to add involves the hidden form element. To make sure that, when inserted, the new time card record is associated with the correct project, we'll assign the ID value from the URL to the hidden element's value. This will enable us to pass that value on to the Insert Record server behavior in the next step.

1. Select the hidden form element.

   📖 Choose the hidden form element named **ID** next to the JobType list.

2. In the Property inspector, enter the following code in the Value field [r6-7]:

   (VB) `<%= Request("ID") %>`

   (JS) `<%= Request("ID") %>`

   (CF) `#URL.ID#`

   (PHP) `<?php echo $_GET["ID"]; ?>`

3. Save your page before continuing.

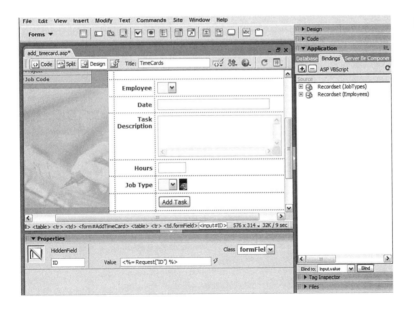

r6-7

Step 4: Apply the Insert Record Server Behavior

One final operation remains to complete this page: adding the Insert Record server behavior. Although the server behavior setup is fairly straightforward, there are a couple minor variations. First, we'll insert the value stored in the hidden field (the Project ID) into the new record. Second, we'll pass that same value to the linking page so that a complete breakdown of the hours—including the just-added ones—is displayed for the current project.

For ASP

1. From the Server Behaviors panel, choose Add (+) and select **Insert Record** from the list.

2. In the Insert Record dialog, choose your data source.

   ☐ Choose **Recipes** from the Connection list.

3. Select the table you want to insert the record into.

   ☐ From the Insert Into Table list, choose **TimeCard**.

4. Set the page that you want to appear after the record is inserted with the ID argument previously passed from the URL.

   ☐ Enter the `report_hoursbreakdown.asp?ID=" + Request("ID") + "` path from your server model's folder for the After Inserting, Go To field.

5. Select the form on the current page from which to gather the record values.

   ☐ From the Get Values From list, make sure **AddTimeCard** is selected.

6. In the Form Elements area, match the form elements on the page to the fields in the data source table.

   ☐ Set `TaskEmployee` to insert into the `CardEmployee` column as Text type.

   Set `TaskDate` to insert into the `CardDate` column as Text type.

   Set `TaskDescription` to insert into the `CardDescription` column as Text type.

   Set `TaskHours` to insert into the `CardHours` column as Numeric type.

   Set `ProjectJobCode` to insert into the `CardJobTypeID` column as Numeric type.

   Set `ID` to insert into the `CardProject` column as Numeric type (Integer type for MySQL).

7. When you're sure your choices are correct, click OK to close the dialog and add the behavior.

For ColdFusion and PHP

1. From the Server Behaviors panel, choose Add (+) and select **Insert Record**.

2. In the Insert Record dialog, choose the current form.

   ☐ Select **AddTimeCard** from the Submit Values From list.

3. Select your data source from the list.

   ☐ Choose **Recipes** from the Data Source list.

4. Enter your username and password, if needed.

5. Select the table in the data source to insert into from the list.

    ☐ Choose **TimeCard** (**timecard** for PHP) from the Insert Into Table list.

6. Set the data source fields to their corresponding form elements.

    ☐ Make sure the `CardID` data column is set to be an unused Primary Key.

    Set `CardEmployee` to insert into the `FORM.TaskEmployee` form element as Text type.

    Set `CardLogged` to not get a value.

    Set `CardDate` to the `FORM.TaskDate` form element as Date MS Access type in ColdFusion and Date type in PHP.

    Set `CardJobTypeID` to the `FORM.ProjectJobCode` form element as Numeric type in ColdFusion and Integer type in PHP

    Set `CardProject` to the `FORM.ID` form element as Numeric type in ColdFusion and Integer type in PHP.

    Set `CardHours` to the `FORM.TaskHours` form element as Numeric type in ColdFusion and Double type in PHP).

    Set `CardDescription` to the `FORM.TaskDescription` form element as Text type.

7. In the After Inserting, Go To field, enter the following code:

    (CF) `report_hoursbreakdown.cfm?ID=#FORM.ID#`

    (PHP) `report_hoursbreakdown.php?ID=" . $_GET["ID"] . "`

8. When you're done, click OK to close the dialog.

9. Save the page.

Administrator Recipe: Hours Breakdown

Although the Project Summary page is great for getting a bird's-eye view of hours spent on all of your projects, it's also helpful to be able to see all the details for a specific one. The Hours Breakdown page displays a table of all the time cards logged for a single project. With this page, just a glance tells you the employee, job code, and number of hours for each time card. Need more detail? Select the employee name link to show the full time card record.

Step 1: Implement Hours Breakdown Design

We want to accomplish two main goals with this layout. First, we want to display a summary of the hours budgeted and those used. Although this information is available in the Project Summary page, it's helpful to have it repeated on this page. Second, we need to show information for all of a project's time cards. The layout handles both requirements by combining a static area for the hours summary and a repeating region for the time card list.

1. In the server model of your choice, create a dynamic page.

      □ In the **TimeCards** folder, locate the folder for your server model and open the report_hoursbreakdown page from there.

2. Add a table to the content region of your page to contain the form elements for the application.

      □ From the Snippets panel, drag the **Recipes > TimeCards > Wireframes > Hours Breakdown Report - Wireframe** snippet into the Content editable region.

3. Add a table structure to allow for separation between repeating rows.

      □ From the Snippets panel, drag the **Recipes > TimeCards > ContentTables > Hours Breakdown Shell - Content Table** snippet into the first row beneath the words HOURS BREAKDOWN REPORT.

4. Insert a three-row-by-three-column table, where the first row is used to title the table (Hours Breakdown), the second row to hold the labels (Employee Name, Job Code, and Hours), and the third to hold the dynamic data.

      □ Place your cursor in the bottom row of the just-added snippet and insert the **Recipes > TimeCards > ContentTables > Hours Breakdown Report - Content Table** snippet.

5. Save the file [r6-8].

r6-8
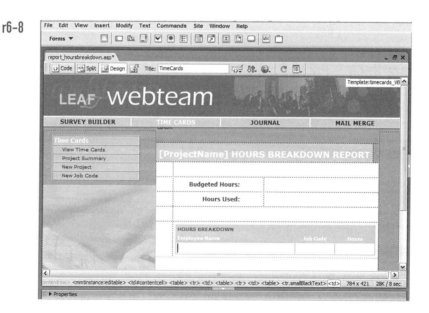

Step 2: Add Database Components

You'll recall from the beginning of this chapter that the HoursBreakdown SQL statement is among the more complex. However, because all of the required calculations are already handled in the database, creating the recordset for this page is very easy.

In addition to the HoursBreakdown recordset, which will be used to populate most of the dynamic text on the page, a second recordset is needed. It's possible for the HoursBreakdown recordset to return no records—if no time cards have been entered for a given project. In that situation, we still want to show the budgeted hours, and we'll get that value from another recordset that relies on the Project table.

As with the Project Summary page, PHP users will need to add some custom code to simulate the views and queries.

Let's start with the HoursBreakdown recordset:

1. From the Bindings panel, choose Add (+) and select **Recordset (Query)**.
2. In the simple Recordset dialog, enter an appropriate name.
   - Enter **HoursBreakdown** in the Name field.
3. Select the desired data source connection.
   - Choose **Recipes** from the Connection (Data Source) list.
4. Choose the needed table.
   - From the Tables list, select **HoursBreakdown** (**hoursbreakdown** for PHP).
5. Leave the Columns option set to All.
6. In the Filter area of the Recordset dialog, set the four Filter list elements like this:

ProjectID	= (Equals)
URL Parameter	ID

7. Set up the recordset to sort according to date, showing the oldest first.
   - In the Sort area, choose **CardDate** from the first list and **Ascending** from the second.
8. Save the page after the recordset is inserted.

Now we'll insert our single entry recordset to get the budgeted hours:

1. From the Bindings panel, choose Add (+) and select **Recordset (Query)**.
2. In the simple Recordset dialog, enter an appropriate name.
   - 📖 Enter **ProjectInfo** in the Name field.
3. Select the desired data source connection.
   - 📖 Choose **Recipes** from the Connection (Data Source) list.
4. Choose the needed table.
   - 📖 From the Tables list, select **Projects** (**projects** for PHP).
5. From the Columns option, choose **Selected** and select only the field you'll need.
   - 📖 From the Columns list, choose **ProjectHours**.
6. In the Filter area of the Recordset dialog, set the four Filter list elements like this:

ProjectID	= (Equals)
URL Parameter	ID

7. Leave the Sort option set to None.
8. Click OK when you're done.
9. Save the page after the recordset is inserted.

The following is for PHP users only:

1. In Code view, place your cursor near the top of the page, after the line that begins `<?php require_once`, and insert the following code.
   - 📖 From the Snippets panel, insert the **Recipes > TimeCards > CustomCode_PHP > Report Hoursbreakdown - Temporary Table** snippet.

(PHP)
```php
<?php
    // ProjectTimeCards Temporary Table
    mysql_select_db($database_Cookbook_PHP, $Recipes);
    $sql = "DELETE FROM projecttimecards";
    @mysql_query($sql,$Recipes);
    $sql = "INSERT INTO projecttimecards SELECT projects.*,
    ➥timecard.*,jobtypes.JobCode FROM projects, jobtypes
    ➥LEFT JOIN timecard
    ➥ON projects.ProjectID=timecard.CardProject
    ➥GROUP BY ProjectID ORDER BY ProjectID";
    @mysql_query($sql,$Recipes);

    // Hours Breakdown Temporary Table
    $sql = "DELETE FROM hoursbreakdown";
```

```
@mysql_query($sql,$Recipes);
$sql = "INSERT INTO hoursbreakdown
➥SELECT projecttimecards.ProjectID,
➥projecttimecards.ProjectName,
➥projecttimecards.ProjectManager,
➥projecttimecards.ProjectHours,
jobtypes.JobRate*projecttimecards.CardHours
➥AS BillableAmount,
➥ROUND((TO_DAYS(projecttimecards.ProjectDate) -
➥TO_DAYS(projecttimecards.CardDate))/7) AS WeeksIn,
➥projecttimecards.CardID,projecttimecards.CardDate,
➥projecttimecards.CardDescription, projecttimecards.CardEmployee,
➥projecttimecards.CardLogged, projecttimecards.CardJobTypeID,
➥jobtypes.JobCode, SUM(timecard.CardHours) AS TotalHoursIn,
➥projecttimecards.CardHours, projecttimecards.CardHours
➥AS HoursIn, projecttimecards.CardProject,
➥CONCAT('$',FORMAT(jobtypes.JobRate,2)) AS JobRate
➥FROM projecttimecards,jobtypes,timecard WHERE
➥(projecttimecards.CardJobTypeID = jobtypes.JobTypeID
➥AND timecard.CardProject = projecttimecards.ProjectID) OR
(projecttimecards.CardJobTypeID = 0) GROUP BY
➥projecttimecards.ProjectID
➥ORDER BY projecttimecards.CardID DESC";
@mysql_query($sql,$Recipes);
?>
```

2. Save your page.

Step 3: Data Binding Process

It's time to make use of the recordsets we created. In addition to putting data in the content table, we'll also bind the project name to the heading at the top of the page to make it absolutely clear which project is being covered.

1. From the Bindings panel, expand the **HoursBreakdown** recordset.
2. Place the data fields on the page in their proper places.

    ⌘ Select the placeholder [**ProjectName**] and drag **ProjectName** over it.

    Skip the Budgeted Hours cell for now; we'll add that in a moment.

    ⌘ Drag **TotalHoursIn** into the cell next to the Hours Used label.

    Drag **CardEmployee** into the cell under the Employee Name label.

    Drag **JobCode** into the cell under the Job Code label.

    Drag **CardHours** into the cell under the Hours label.

3. Expand the **ProjectInfo** recordset.

4. Place the data field from this recordset in the appropriate place.

   📖 Drag **ProjectHours** into the cell next to the Budgeted Hours label.

5. When you're done, save the page [r6-9].

r6-9

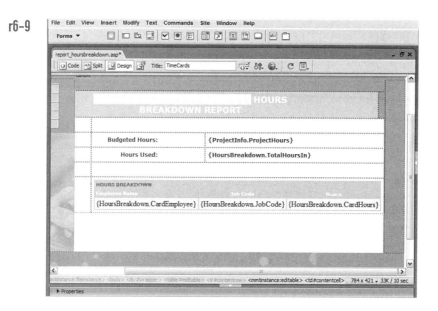

Step 4: Link to Time Card Details Page

This recipe calls for making another level of detail available—the time card record. To reach this information, generated on the task_detail page, we'll add a link to the employee name.

1. Select the text or image you want to link to the detail page.

   📖 Choose **HoursBreakdown.CardEmployee** in the content table.

2. Select the folder symbol next to the Link field in the Property inspector. The Select File dialog opens.

3. Make sure the dialog is set to **Select File Name From File System**.

4. Choose **Parameters** at the bottom of the dialog.

5. In the Name column of the Parameters dialog, enter the variable name.

   📖 Enter **ID** in the Name column.

6. In the Value column, enter the dynamic value of the current project's ID.

    Select the lightning bolt in the Value column and, from the Dynamic Data dialog, expand the **HoursBreakdown** recordset and choose **CardID**. When you're done, click OK once to close the Dynamic Data dialog and again to close the Parameters dialog.

7. In the Select File dialog, select the file that will be used to display the details of hours logged.

   Choose **task_detail** in the `TimeCards` folder for your server model.

8. When you're done, click OK to insert the link.

Step 5: Adding Repeat Region

To complete the Hours Breakdown page, we'll add a Repeat Region server behavior to the content table.

1. Select any of the dynamic data fields in the content table.

   Choose the **CardEmployee** data field from the Hours Breakdown content table.

2. From the Tag Selector, choose the appropriate table row tag that encompasses the entire table.

   Select the **<tr>** tag to the left of the selected tag in the Tag Selector.

3. From the Server Behaviors panel, choose Add (+) and select **Repeat Region**.

4. In the Repeat Region dialog, choose the desired recordset.

   Choose **HoursBreakdown** from the Recordset list.

5. Set the Show option to display however many records you'd like.

   Choose **Show All Records**.

6. Click OK when you're done.

7. Save your page.

Test your page in the browser or in Live Data view in Dreamweaver [r6-10].

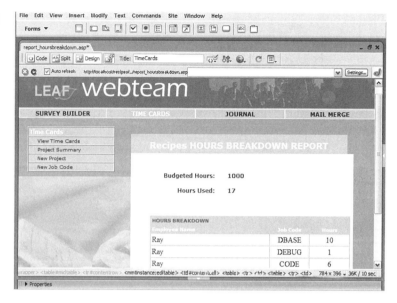

r6-10

Administrator Recipe: Task Detail

Each time card record represents a single job or task undertaken and completed by an employee. (The terms *task detail* and *time card* are used interchangeably in this recipe.) In the previous page, we included a link to a detail page so that the administrator could see all the information on a chosen time card. Now we'll build that page. In addition to the data entered in the original time card—like the employee name, job code, and hours—a calculated field displays the number of weeks into the project. Finally, the Task Detail page will also contain a link to update the information in the record.

Step 1: Implement Task Detail Design

The Task Detail page needs to display basic information about the time card while remaining flexible. Most of the data pulled from the recordset will be displayed on a single line, such as the employee name and job code. However, one field—the task description—could run several sentences or more. The layout design, like the nested table used in the snippet, must be capable of expanding to handle the additional content.

1. In the server model of your choice, create a dynamic page.
   📖 In the **TimeCards** folder, locate the folder for your server model and open the `task_detail` page from there.

2. Add a table to the content region of your page to hold the labels and dynamic elements.

    □ From the Snippets panel, drag the **Recipes > TimeCards > Wireframes > Time Card Details - Wireframe** snippet into the Content editable region.

3. Insert a two-column table in which the right-justified first column is for the labels (Time Card Employee, Time Card Date, Task Description, Hours, Job Code, and Project Week) and the left-justified second column is for the dynamic data.

    □ Place your cursor in the bottom row of the just-added snippet and insert the **Recipes > TimeCards > ContentTables > Time Card Details - Content Table** snippet.

4. Save the file [r6-11].

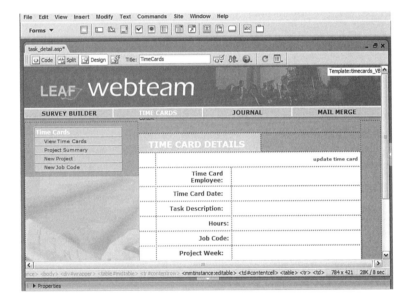

r6-11

Step 2: Add Database Components

The recordset for this page is restricted to details for a single time card—the time card chosen in the Hours Breakdown page. We'll use the value assigned to the URL parameter ID to filter the HoursBreakdown SQL query and thus create the recordset.

As with other pages in the recipe, PHP users will need to add some custom code to the top of the page to simulate the queries and views.

1. From the Bindings panel, choose Add (+) and select **Recordset (Query)**.

2. In the simple Recordset dialog, enter an appropriate name.

    □ Enter **CardDetails** in the Name field.

3. Select the desired data source connection.

    ▢ Choose **Recipes** from the Connection (Data Source) list.

4. Choose the needed table.

    ▢ From the Tables list, select **HoursBreakdown** (**hoursbreakdown** for PHP).

5. Leave the Columns option set to All.

6. In the Filter area of the Recordset dialog, set the four Filter list elements like this:

CardID	= (Equals)
URL Parameter	ID

7. Keep the Sort option set to None and click OK to close the dialog.

8. Save the page when you're done.

PHP users need to take the following step:

1. In Code view, place your cursor near the top of the page, after the line that begins `<?php require_once`, and insert the following code.

    ▢ From the Snippets panel, insert the **Recipes > TimeCards > CustomCode_PHP > Report Hoursbreakdown - Temporary Table** snippet.

(PHP)
```php
<?php
// ProjectTimeCards Temporary Table
mysql_select_db($database_Recipes_PHP, $Recipes);
$sql = "DELETE FROM projecttimecards";
@mysql_query($sql,$Recipes);
$sql = "INSERT INTO projecttimecards SELECT projects.*,
timecard.*,jobtypes.JobCode FROM projects,
➥jobtypes LEFT JOIN timecard
ON projects.ProjectID=timecard.CardProject
➥WHERE timecard.CardJobTypeID
= jobtypes.JobTypeID ORDER BY ProjectID";
@mysql_query($sql,$Recipes);

// Hours Breakdown Temporary Table
$sql = "DELETE FROM hoursbreakdown";
@mysql_query($sql,$Recipes);
$sql = "INSERT INTO hoursbreakdown
➥SELECT projecttimecards.ProjectID,
projecttimecards.ProjectName, projecttimecards.ProjectManager,
projecttimecards.ProjectHours,
jobtypes.JobRate*projecttimecards.CardHours AS BillableAmount,
ROUND((TO_DAYS(projecttimecards.ProjectDate) -
```

```
TO_DAYS(projecttimecards.CardDate))/7) AS WeeksIn,
projecttimecards.CardID,projecttimecards.CardDate,
projecttimecards.CardDescription, projecttimecards.CardEmployee,
projecttimecards.CardLogged, projecttimecards.CardJobTypeID,
jobtypes.JobCode, SUM(timecard.CardHours) AS TotalHoursIn,
projecttimecards.CardHours, projecttimecards.CardHours AS HoursIn,
projecttimecards.CardProject, CONCAT('$',
➥FORMAT(jobtypes.JobRate,2)) AS
JobRate FROM projecttimecards LEFT JOIN jobtypes ON
projecttimecards.CardJobTypeID = jobtypes.JobTypeID
➥INNER JOIN timecard
ON timecard.CardProject = projecttimecards.ProjectID GROUP BY
projecttimecards.ProjectID, projecttimecards.ProjectName,
projecttimecards.ProjectManager, projecttimecards.ProjectHours,
projecttimecards.CardDate, projecttimecards.CardDescription,
projecttimecards.CardEmployee, projecttimecards.CardLogged,
projecttimecards.CardJobTypeID, projecttimecards.CardHours,
projecttimecards.CardProject, projecttimecards.CardID, WeeksIn,
jobtypes.JobRate HAVING BillableAmount IS NOT NULL ORDER BY
projecttimecards.CardID DESC";
@mysql_query($sql,$Recipes);
?>
```

2. Save the page after the code is inserted.

Step 3: Data Binding Process

All six of the dynamic data elements required for this page can be dragged directly from the Bindings panel. While most are entries that were inserted into the record when the time card was created, one of the fields—WeeksIn—is calculated by the HoursBreakdown SQL query to show how many weeks into the project the time card was first entered.

1. From the Bindings panel, expand the **CardDetails** recordset.
2. Place the data fields on the page in their proper places.

       Drag **CardEmployee** into the cell next to the Time Card Employee label.

       Drag **CardDate** into the cell next to the Time Card Date label.

       Drag **CardDescription** into the cell next to the Task Description label.

       Drag **CardHours** into the cell next to the Hours label.

       Drag **JobCode** into the cell next to the Job Code label.

       Drag **WeeksIn** into the cell next to the Project Week label.

3. When you're done, save the page [r6-12].

r6-12

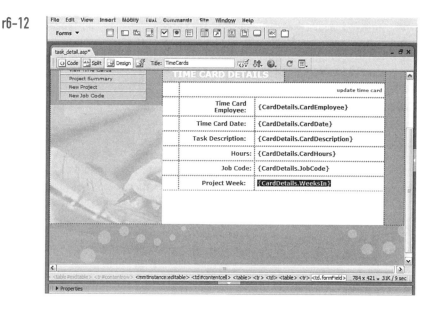

Step 4: Link to Time Card Update Page

The final step for the Task Detail page is to add a link and parameter for modifying the current record. The Task Update page, described in the next recipe, will handle the update, but it needs a parameter—the Card ID—to make sure it's modifying the correct record.

1. Select the text or image you want to link to the detail page.
   - 📖 Choose **update time card** in the heading of the content table.
2. Select the folder symbol next to the Link field in the Property inspector.
   The Select File dialog opens.
3. Make sure the dialog is set to **Select File Name From File System**.
4. Choose **Parameters** at the bottom of the dialog.
5. In the Name column of the Parameters dialog, enter the variable name.
   - 📖 Enter **ID** in the Name column.
6. In the Value column, enter the dynamic value of the current project's ID.
   - 📖 Select the lightning bolt in the Value column and, from the Dynamic Data dialog, expand the **CardDetails** recordset and choose **CardID**. When you're done, click OK once to close the Dynamic Data dialog and again to close the Parameters dialog.

7. In the Select File dialog, select the file that will be used to display the details of hours logged.

   ◻ Choose **task_update** in the `TimeCards` folder for your server model.

8. When you're done, click OK to insert the link.

Administrator Recipe: Task Update

To make sure that the tasks described in every time card are the most accurate they can be, the records must be modifiable. The Task Update page allows any selected record to be changed and resaved. In addition, to avoid cluttering the data source with obsolete records, you can also use the Task Update page to delete the current time card record. Because Dreamweaver does not support multiple record commands, such as update and delete on the same page, a little bit of hand-coding and code manipulation is required.

Step 1: Implement Task Update Design

As with other record update applications, the Task Update layout consists primarily of a series of form elements bound to dynamic data. With this page, you'll be able to modify the time card's date, description, number of hours, and job code. Two form buttons—one to complete the update and one to remove the record—are also needed.

1. In the server model of your choice, create a dynamic page.

   ◻ In the **TimeCards** folder, locate the folder for your server model and open the `task_update` page from there.

2. Add a table to the content region of your page to contain the form elements for the application.

   ◻ From the Snippets panel, drag the **Recipes > TimeCards > Wireframes > Update Time Card - Wireframe** snippet into the Content editable region.

3. Insert the form and, within it, a two-column table. The table should include text fields and labels for a date, a task description, the number of hours, as well as list for job types. In addition, two form buttons are required: one for processing the update and one for deleting the record.

   ◻ Place your cursor in the row below the words UPDATE TIME CARD and insert the **Recipes > TimeCards > Forms > Update Time Card - Form** snippet.

4. Save the file [r6-13].

r6-13

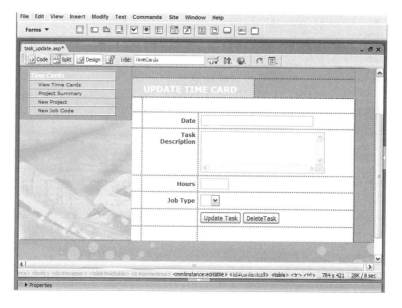

Step 2: Add Database Components

Two recordsets are put to use in the Task Update recipe. One is drawn from the JobTypes table and is used to populate the list of job codes, with the current record's job code initially selected. The other recordset conveys the rest of the time card information and is filtered by the ID parameter contained in the originating link. Both recordsets are straightforward enough to require only the simple recordset dialog.

> **NOTE**
>
> This recordset is the same as the one used in the Add Job Type recipe. Feel free to copy the recordset from that page and paste it into the Bindings panel for this page.

Let's create the recordset to populate the job code list first:

1. From the Bindings panel, choose Add (+) and select **Recordset (Query)**.
2. In the simple Recordset dialog, enter an appropriate name.
   - Enter **JobTypes** in the Name field.
3. Select the desired data source connection.
   - Choose **Recipes** from the Connection (Data Source) list.
4. Choose the needed table.
   - From the Tables list, select **JobTypes** (**jobtypes** for PHP).
5. Set the Columns option to **Selected** and choose only the necessary fields.
   - Press Shift and select **JobTypeID** and **JobType** from the Columns list.

6. Make sure the Filter is set to None.

7. Keep the Sort option set to None and click OK to close the dialog.

8. Save the page after the recordset is inserted.

Next we'll construct the TimeCard recordset:

1. From the Bindings panel, choose Add (+) and select **Recordset (Query)**.

2. In the simple Recordset dialog, enter an appropriate name.

    ⬚ Enter **TimeCard** in the Name field.

3. Select the desired data source connection.

    ⬚ Choose **Recipes** from the Connection (Data Source) list.

4. Choose the needed table.

    ⬚ From the Tables list, select **TimeCard** (**timecard** for PHP).

5. Leave the Columns option set to All.

6. In the Filter area of the Recordset dialog, set the four Filter list elements like this:

CardID	= (Equals)
URL Parameter	ID

7. Keep the Sort option set to None and click OK to close the dialog.

8. Save the page after the recordset is inserted.

Step 3: Data Binding Process

The data from our two recordsets is ready to be applied in two different steps. First we'll drag the data fields from the TimeCard recordset into the appropriate form elements. Next we'll bind data fields from the JobCode recordset to create the JobCode list values and labels.

This page also uses a hidden form element to make sure that the ProjectID is properly passed upon completion of the delete operation. ColdFusion and PHP users will have to add another hidden form element for the update operation.

Let's start by binding the proper data fields to the text fields:

1. From the Bindings panel, expand the **TimeCard** recordset.

2. Place the data fields on the page in their proper places.

  📖 Drag **CardDate** onto the TaskDate text field.

   Drag **CardDescription** onto the TaskDescription text area.

   Drag **CardHours** onto the TaskHours text field.

Now that your fields are in place, let's apply a format to the date element.

3. Select the **TaskDate** text field.

4. ASP and ColdFusion users: In the selected entry of the Bindings panel, select the drop-down list under the Format column and choose **Date/Time > 1/17/00**.

5. When you're done, save the page.

We're now ready to set up the Job Code list:

1. Select the **ProjectJobCode** list element.

2. From the Property inspector, select **Dynamic**.

3. In the Dynamic List/Menu dialog, select the **JobTypes** recordset from the Options From Recordset list.

4. In the Values field, choose **JobTypeID**.

5. In the Labels field, select **JobType**.

6. Leave the Select Value Equal To Field blank.

7. Click OK to close the Dynamic List/Menu dialog.

Now we'll add a hidden form element needed to redirect the page after the update is completed.

1. From the Form category of the Insert bar, drag the **Hidden Form** element next to JobType list.

2. In the Property inspector, give the element a name.

  📖 Enter **ProjectID** in the name field of the Property inspector.

3. Select the lightning bolt symbol to open the Dynamic Data dialog.

4. Expand the TimeCard recordset and choose **CardProject**.

5. Click OK when you're done to close the dialog and insert the code into the Value field.

ColdFusion and PHP users will also need to add another hidden form element for the update server behavior to work properly.

1. From the Form category of the Insert bar, drag the **Hidden Form** element next to newly added hidden element.
2. In the Property inspector, give the element a name.

   ⮡ Enter **ID** in the name field of the Property inspector.
3. In the Property inspector, select the lightning bolt symbol to open the Dynamic Data dialog.
4. Expand the `TimeCard` recordset and choose **CardID**.
5. Click OK when you're done to close the dialog and insert the code into the Value field.

Step 4: Add Update Record Server Behavior

With all the data in its proper place, it's time to add the server-side logic that will store the modified record. The standard Dreamweaver server behavior Update Record is perfect for the job. There is one minor variation to filling out the dialog, however. Rather than specifying just a file to display after the operation is correct, we need to pass an argument as well. The argument consists of the ID parameter for the current record.

For ASP

1. From the Server Behaviors panel, choose Add (+) and select **Update Record**.
2. In the Update Record dialog, select the desired data source connection. Choose **Recipes** from the Connection list.
3. Choose the table containing the data you are updating.

   ⮡ From the Table to Update list, choose **TimeCard**.
4. Choose the recordset from which to get data source fields.

   ⮡ From the Select Record From field, choose **TimeCard**.
5. Set the primary key for the recordset.

   ⮡ From the Unique Key Column list, choose **CardID** and make sure the **Numeric** option is selected.
6. Select the file you'd like to appear when the update is complete.

   ⮡ For the After Updating, Go To field, enter the following path and argument:
   `task_detail.asp?ID=" + (Request("MM_recordID")) + ".`
7. Choose the form on the page from which to get the values.

   ⮡ From the Get Values From list, choose **EditTimeCard**.

8. In the Form Elements area, set the form elements to their corresponding data source fields.

      Set the `TaskDate` form element to update the `CardDate` data source field as Date MS Access.

      Set the `TaskDescription` form element to update the `CardDescription` data source field as Text.

      Set the `TaskHours` form element to update the `CardHours` data source field as Numeric.

      Set the `ProjectJobCode` form element to update the `CardJobTypeID` data source field as Numeric.

      Set the `ProjectID` form element to `<ignore>`.

The ProjectID form element is only used for the Delete operation.

9. Make sure your entries are correct and then click OK to close.

For ColdFusion and PHP

1. From the Server Behaviors panel, choose Add (+) and select **Insert Record**.
2. In the Insert Record dialog, choose the current form.

      Select **EditTimeCard** from the Submit Values From list.

3. Select your data source from the list.

      Choose **Recipes** from the Data Source list.

4. Enter your username and password, if needed.
5. Select the table in the data source to insert into from the list.

      Choose **TimeCard** (**timecard** for PHP) from the Insert Into Table list.

6. Set the data source fields to their corresponding form elements.

      As the Primary Key, `CardID` selects the record using `FORM.ID` as a Numeric type in ColdFusion and Integer in PHP.

      Set `CardDate` to get its value from the `FORM.TaskDate` form element as Date MS Access in ColdFusion and Date in PHP.

      Set `CardDescription` to get its value from the `FORM.TaskDescription` form element as Text.

      Set `CardHours` to get its value from the `FORM.TaskHours` form element as Numeric in ColdFusion and Integer in PHP.

      Set `CardJobTypeID` to get its value from the `FORM.ProjectJobCode` form element as Numeric in ColdFusion and Integer in PHP.

      Set `CardProject` to not get a value.

7. Enter the path to the file you want displayed after the record is updated.

    (CF) In the After Inserting, Go To field, enter the following path and argument:

    ```
    task_detail.cfm?ID=#Form.ID#
    ```

    (PHP) In the After Inserting, Go To field, enter the following path and argument:

    ```
    task_detail.php?ID=".$_POST["ID"]."
    ```

8. Check your entries to verify that they are correct and, if so, click OK.

Step 5: Add Delete Command for Survey Question

Our final phase of operations for this recipe involves adding delete functionality to the page. Three distinct aspects are needed to accomplish this: First, a delete command is added to the page; this procedure will be explained in this step. Next, the code for the delete command must be moved to the top of the page. Finally, the delete command code must be wrapped in additional code that ensures that it only executes when the Delete button is pressed and that the proper page displays after the operation is complete. The code manipulation will be described in the step following this one.

For ASP

1. From the Bindings panel, choose **Command**.
2. In the Command dialog, enter an appropriate name.

    ▭ Enter **DeleteTask** in the Name field.
3. Choose the data source.

    ▭ From the Connections list, select **Recipes**.
4. Set the type of command.

    ▭ From the Type list, choose **Delete**.
5. Leave the Return Recordset Named options blank.
6. In the SQL area, enter the following code:

    ▭ DELETE FROM TimeCard

      WHERE CardID = IDParam
7. In the Variable area, choose Add (+) to add a new SQL variable.
8. Enter the name of the variable.

    ▭ In the Name column, enter **IDParam**.
9. Insert the run-time value.

    ▭ In the Run-Time value column, enter **Request.Form("MM_recordId")**.
10. Click OK to insert the command.
11. Save your page.

> **NOTE**
>
> You should refrain from testing the delete command until the remaining recipe steps are complete.

For ColdFusion

1. From the Bindings panel, choose **Recordset (Query)**.
2. In the Advanced Recordset dialog, enter an appropriate name.
   - 📖 Enter **DeleteTask** in the Name field.
3. Choose the data source.
   - 📖 From the Data Source list, select **Recipes**.
4. Enter the username and password, if required.
5. In the SQL area, enter the following code:

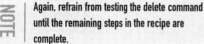

```
CF  DELETE FROM TimeCard
       WHERE CardID = #Form.ID#
```

> **NOTE** Again, refrain from testing the delete command until the remaining steps in the recipe are complete.

6. Click OK to insert the command.

For PHP

To compensate for PHP's lack of support for commands, a custom code block—triggered by a conditional statement—is used. This is the final step needed for this page.

1. In Code view, place your cursor before the opening <html> and insert the following code:
   - 📖 From the Snippets panel, insert the **Recipes > TimeCards > CustomCode_PHP > Task Update – Delete Record** snippet.

```
PHP  <?php
     if ((isset($_POST['Delete'])) && ($_POST['Delete']=="DeleteTask")) {
         mysql_select_db($database_Recipes_PHP, $Recipes);
         $sql = "DELETE FROM timecard WHERE CardID=".$_POST['ID'];
         @mysql_query($sql,$Recipes);
         $url = "report_hoursbreakdown.php?ID=" . $_POST['ProjectID'];
         header("Location: $url");
     }
     ?>
```

2. Save your page.

Your PHP page is now ready for testing.

Step 6: Move and Make Conditional Delete Code

As noted previously, ASP and ColdFusion users now need to move the delete command code and make sure it activates only when it is supposed to. Moving the code is a simple cut-and-paste operation. Making the code conditional involves wrapping it with an if-then statement; the conditional code also handles the redirection of the page after the delete operation.

> **The following step is for ASP and ColdFusion users only.**
>
> NOTE

1. From the Server Behaviors panel, choose the **Delete Task** command.
2. Switch to Code view.

   The following Delete Task command code should be highlighted.

   VB
   ```
   <%
   set DeleteTask = Server.CreateObject("ADODB.Command")
   DeleteTask.ActiveConnection = MM_Recipes_STRING
   DeleteTask.CommandText = "DELETE FROM TimeCard WHERE CardID =
   ➥ " + Replace(DeleteTask__IDParam, "'", "''") + "  "
   DeleteTask.CommandType = 1
   DeleteTask.CommandTimeout = 0
   DeleteTask.Prepared = true
   DeleteTask.Execute()
   %>
   ```

   JS
   ```
   <%
   var DeleteTask = Server.CreateObject("ADODB.Command");
   DeleteTask.ActiveConnection = MM_Recipes_STRING;
   DeleteTask.CommandText = "DELETE FROM TimeCard WHERE CardID =
   ➥ "+ DeleteTask__IDParam.replace(/'/g, "''") + "";
   DeleteTask.CommandType = 1;
   DeleteTask.CommandTimeout = 0;
   DeleteTask.Prepared = true;
   DeleteTask.Execute();
   %>
   ```

   CF
   ```
   <cfquery name="DeleteTask" datasource="Recipes">
   DELETE FROM TimeCard WHERE CardID=#FORM.ID#
   </cfquery>
   ```

3. Cut the code by choosing Ctrl-X (Command-X) or Edit > Cut.
4. Place the cursor at the top of the page. ASP users should place the cursor just after the Connection definition.
5. Paste the code by choosing Ctrl-V (Command-V) or Edit > Paste.

Now we're ready to make the code conditional:

1. Select the just-inserted code.
2. Wrap it with the following code to make it conditional and to add a redirect.

   📖 From the Snippets panel, open the **Recipes > TimeCards > Custom Code** folder for your server model and insert the **If Statement - Delete Operation** snippet.

   Before:

   (VB)
   ```
   <%
   if (cStr(Request("DeleteTask")) <> "") then
   %>
   ```

   After:

   ```
   <%
   Response.Redirect("report_hoursbreakdown.asp?ID=" &
   Request("ProjectID"))
   end if
   %>
   ```

   Before:

   (JS)
   ```
   <%
   if (String(Request("DeleteTask"))!="undefined") {
   %>
   ```

   After:

   ```
   <%
   Response.Redirect("report_hoursbreakdown.asp?ID=" +
   Request("ProjectID"));
   }
   %>
   ```

   Before:

   (CF)
   ```
   <cfif isDefined("FORM.DeleteTask")>
   ```

   After:

   ```
   <cflocation url="report_hoursbreakdown.cfm?ID=#Form.ProjectID#">
   </cfif>
   ```

3. When you're done, save and test the page.

Administrator Recipe: View Time Cards

Up to this point, our application overviews have been project-oriented. With the `report_projectsummary` page, you can get a bird's-eye view of all the available projects. The `report_hoursbreakdown` page offers a more detailed view of the time cards for a specified project. In this recipe, we'll build a page that shows all the time cards logged for all the projects, grouped by employee and displayed in daily, weekly, and monthly views.

Because we are using three different views of the same basic data, the construction of this page will be a bit repetitive. We'll need three recordsets to bind data into three different content tables. When that is done, we'll have to apply three Repeat Region server behaviors. It's important to realize that all the calculations needed for these three different summaries—daily, weekly, and monthly—are all handled through their corresponding SQL queries executed in the data source. Each of the queries are, as noted at the start of this chapter, based on another SQL query, `HoursBreakdown`.

Step 1: Implement View Time Cards Design

Each of the time-based views of data requires its own content area in the layout for this recipe. Although they all have essentially the same information (employee, project, date, amount of time, and billable cost), they need to be contained in separate structures to use the Repeat Region server behavior.

1. In the server model of your choice, create a dynamic page.

   📖 In the **TimeCards** folder, locate the folder for your server model and open the `view_timecards` page from there.

2. Add a table to the content region of your page to hold the content tables and data for the application.

   📖 From the Snippets panel, drag the **Recipes > TimeCards > Wireframes > View Time Cards - Wireframe** snippet into the Content editable region.

3. Add a table structure to allow for separation between the three separate sections.

   📖 From the Snippets panel, drag the **Recipes > TimeCards > ContentTables > View Time Cards - Shell** snippet into the row beneath the words VIEW TIME CARDS.

4. Insert three tables, each consisting of three rows and five columns. The first row is used to designate the focus of the table (Daily, Weekly, or Monthly), and the cells in the second row act as headers for the data: Employee Name, Project, Date, Hours, and Cost. The final row will hold the data itself.

    ◻ Place your cursor in the top row of the shell table and insert the **Recipes > TimeCards > ContentTables > View Time Cards - Daily** snippet.

    Place your cursor in the middle row of the shell table and insert the **Recipes > TimeCards > ContentTables > View Time Cards - Weekly** snippet.

    Place your cursor in the bottom row of the shell table and insert the **Recipes > TimeCards > ContentTables > View Time Cards - Monthly** snippet [r6-14].

r6-14

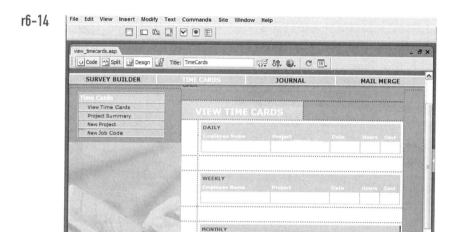

5. Save the file.

Step 2: Add Database Components

The three recordsets used in this recipe are very straightforward to implement. All the hard calculation work has been done within the data source itself. Each recordset relies on a different SQL view of summarized information created in the data source. The three views—DailyHours, WeeklyHours, and MonthlyHours—are all similarly structured. Here's the `DailyHours` SQL statement:

```
SELECT HoursBreakdown.CardEmployee, Sum(HoursBreakdown.CardHours) AS
Hours, Format([HoursBreakdown].[CardDate],'ddd mmm dd') AS [Day],
Sum(HoursBreakdown.BillableAmount) AS BillableAmount,
HoursBreakdown.ProjectName
FROM HoursBreakdown
```

```
WHERE (((HoursBreakdown.CardDate)>Date()-30))
GROUP BY HoursBreakdown.CardEmployee,
Format([HoursBreakdown].[CardDate],'ddd mmm dd'),
HoursBreakdown.ProjectName, DatePart('yyyy',[CardDate]),
DatePart('m',[CardDate]), DatePart('d',[CardDate])
ORDER BY DatePart('yyyy',[CardDate]), DatePart('m',[CardDate]),
DatePart('d',[CardDate]), HoursBreakdown.CardEmployee;
```

The MySQL version is similar:

```
SELECT
hoursbreakdown.CardEmployee,
Sum(hoursbreakdown.CardHours) AS Hours,
DATE_FORMAT(hoursbreakdown.CardDate,"%a %b %d") AS TheDay,
Sum(hoursbreakdown.BillableAmount) AS BillableAmount,
hoursbreakdown.ProjectName
FROM hoursbreakdown
WHERE (((hoursbreakdown.CardDate)>DATE_SUB(CURDATE(), INTERVAL 30
DAY)))
GROUP BY
hoursbreakdown.CardEmployee, TheDay,
hoursbreakdown.ProjectName,
DATE_FORMAT(hoursbreakdown.CardDate,"%Y"),
DATE_FORMAT(hoursbreakdown.CardDate,"%m"),
DATE_FORMAT(hoursbreakdown.CardDate,"%d")
ORDER BY
DATE_FORMAT(hoursbreakdown.CardDate,"%Y"),
DATE_FORMAT(hoursbreakdown.CardDate,"%m"),
DATE_FORMAT(hoursbreakdown.CardDate,"%d"),
hoursbreakdown.CardEmployee
```

All three SQL views are based on the HoursBreakdown query; PHP will again require some custom code to simulate the queries.

Dreamweaver displays recordsets in the order in which they are defined, so let's start with the daily view.

1. From the Bindings panel, choose Add (+) and select **Recordset (Query)**.
2. In the simple Recordset dialog, enter an appropriate name.
   - Enter **DailyHours** in the Name field.
3. Select the desired data source connection.
   - Choose **Recipes** from the Connection (Data Source) list.
4. Choose the needed table.
   - From the Tables list, select **DailyHours**.

5. Leave the Columns option set to All.

6. Make sure the Filter is set to None.

7. Keep the Sort option set to None and click OK to close the dialog.

8. Save the page after the recordset is inserted.

Next we'll create the recordset to hold the weekly data.

1. From the Bindings panel, choose Add (+) and select **Recordset (Query)**.

2. In the simple Recordset dialog, enter an appropriate name.

    ⬚ Enter **WeeklyHours** in the Name field.

3. Select the desired data source connection.

    ⬚ Choose **Recipes** from the Connection (Data Source) list.

4. Choose the needed table.

    ⬚ From the Tables list, select **WeeklyHours**.

5. Leave the Columns option set to All.

6. Make sure the Filter is set to None.

7. Keep the Sort option set to None and click OK to close the dialog.

8. Save the page after the recordset is inserted.

Finally, let's build the monthly hours recordset.

1. From the Bindings panel, choose Add (+) and select **Recordset (Query)**.

2. In the simple Recordset dialog, enter an appropriate name.

    ⬚ Enter **MonthlyHours** in the Name field.

3. Select the desired data source connection.

    ⬚ Choose **Recipes** from the Connection (Data Source) list.

4. Choose the needed table.

    ⬚ From the Tables list, select **MonthlyHours**.

5. Leave the Columns option set to All.

6. Make sure the Filter is set to None.

7. Keep the Sort option set to None and click OK to close the dialog.

8. Save the page after the recordset is inserted.

As with several other pages in this recipe, additional code is required for PHP:

1. In Code view, place your cursor near the top of the page, after the line that begins `<?php require_once`, and insert the following code.

    ⬚ From the Snippets panel, insert the **Recipes > TimeCards > CustomCode_PHP > Report Hoursbreakdown - Temporary Table** snippet.

```
PHP  <?php
     // ProjectTimeCards Temporary Table
     mysql_select_db($database_Cookbook_PHP, $Recipes);
     $sql = "DELETE FROM projecttimecards";
     @mysql_query($sql,$Recipes);
     $sql = "INSERT INTO projecttimecards
     ➡SELECT projects.*, timecard.*,jobtypes.JobCode
     ➡FROM projects, jobtypes LEFT JOIN timecard
     ➡ON projects.ProjectID=timecard.CardProject
     ➡GROUP BY ProjectID ORDER BY ProjectID";
     @mysql_query($sql,$Recipes);

     // Hours Breakdown Temporary Table
     $sql = "DELETE FROM hoursbreakdown";
     @mysql_query($sql,$Recipes);
     $sql = "INSERT INTO hoursbreakdown
     ➡SELECT projecttimecards.ProjectID,
     ➡projecttimecards.ProjectName,
     ➡projecttimecards.ProjectManager,
     ➡projecttimecards.ProjectHours,
     jobtypes.JobRate*projecttimecards.CardHours
     ➡AS BillableAmount,
     ➡ROUND((TO_DAYS(projecttimecards.ProjectDate) -
     ➡TO_DAYS(projecttimecards.CardDate))/7) AS WeeksIn,
     ➡projecttimecards.CardID,projecttimecards.CardDate,
     ➡projecttimecards.CardDescription, projecttimecards.CardEmployee,
     ➡projecttimecards.CardLogged, projecttimecards.CardJobTypeID,
     ➡jobtypes.JobCode, SUM(timecard.CardHours) AS TotalHoursIn,
     ➡projecttimecards.CardHours, projecttimecards.CardHours
     ➡AS HoursIn, projecttimecards.CardProject,
     ➡CONCAT('$',FORMAT(jobtypes.JobRate,2)) AS JobRate FROM
     ➡projecttimecards,jobtypes,timecard WHERE
     ➡(projecttimecards.CardJobTypeID = jobtypes.JobTypeID AND
     ➡timecard.CardProject = projecttimecards.ProjectID) OR
     ➡(projecttimecards.CardJobTypeID = 0) GROUP BY
     ➡projecttimecards.ProjectID
     ➡ORDER BY projecttimecards.CardID DESC";
     @mysql_query($sql,$Recipes);

     // Daily Hours Temporary Table
     $sql = "DELETE FROM dailyhours";
     @mysql_query($sql,$Recipes);
     $sql = 'INSERT INTO dailyhours
     ➡SELECT hoursbreakdown.CardEmployee,
     ➡Sum(hoursbreakdown.CardHours) AS Hours,
     ➡DATE_FORMAT(hoursbreakdown.CardDate,"%a %b %d") AS TheDay,
     ➡Sum(hoursbreakdown.BillableAmount) AS BillableAmount,
```

```
➥hoursbreakdown.ProjectName FROM hoursbreakdown
➥WHERE (((hoursbreakdown.CardDate)>
➥DATE_SUB(CURDATE(), INTERVAL 30 DAY)))
➥GROUP BY hoursbreakdown.CardEmployee, TheDay,
➥hoursbreakdown.ProjectName,
➥DATE_FORMAT(hoursbreakdown.CardDate,"%Y"),
➥DATE_FORMAT(hoursbreakdown.CardDate,"%m"),
➥DATE_FORMAT(hoursbreakdown.CardDate,"%d") ORDER BY
➥DATE_FORMAT(hoursbreakdown.CardDate,"%Y"),
➥DATE_FORMAT(hoursbreakdown.CardDate,"%m"),
➥DATE_FORMAT(hoursbreakdown.CardDate,"%d"),
➥hoursbreakdown.CardEmployee';
@mysql_query($sql,$Recipes);

// Weekly Hours Temporary Table
$sql = "DELETE FROM weeklyhours";
@mysql_query($sql,$Recipes);
$sql = 'INSERT INTO weeklyhours
➥SELECT hoursbreakdown.CardEmployee,
➥Sum(hoursbreakdown.CardHours) AS Hours,
➥CONCAT(DATE_FORMAT(DATE_ADD(hoursbreakdown.CardDate,
➥INTERVAL (-1 * WEEKDAY(NOW())) DAY),"%m/%d-"),
➥DATE_FORMAT(DATE_ADD(hoursbreakdown.CardDate, INTERVAL
➥(7 - WEEKDAY(NOW())) DAY),"%m/%d "),
➥DATE_FORMAT(DATE_ADD(hoursbreakdown.CardDate,
➥INTERVAL (7 - WEEKDAY(NOW())) DAY),"%Y")) AS Week,
➥Sum(hoursbreakdown.BillableAmount) AS BillableAmount,
➥hoursbreakdown.ProjectName FROM hoursbreakdown WHERE
➥(hoursbreakdown.CardDate > DATE_SUB(NOW(),INTERVAL 6 MONTH)
➥&&hoursbreakdown.CardDate < DATE_ADD(NOW(),INTERVAL 6 MONTH))
➥GROUP BY hoursbreakdown.CardEmployee, Week,
➥hoursbreakdown.ProjectName,
➥DATE_FORMAT(hoursbreakdown.CardDate,"%Y"),
➥DATE_FORMAT(hoursbreakdown.CardDate,"%u") ORDER BY Week,
➥hoursbreakdown.CardEmployee';
@mysql_query($sql,$Recipes);

// Monthly Hours Temporary Table
$sql = "DELETE FROM monthlyhours";
@mysql_query($sql,$Recipes);
$sql = 'INSERT INTO monthlyhours
➥SELECT hoursbreakdown.CardEmployee,
➥SUM(hoursbreakdown.CardHours) AS Hours,
➥DATE_FORMAT(hoursbreakdown.CardDate,"%M %Y") AS Month,
```

```
➥SUM(hoursbreakdown.BillableAmount) AS BillableAmount,
➥hoursbreakdown.ProjectName FROM hoursbreakdown WHERE
➥(hoursbreakdown.CardDate > DATE_SUB(NOW(),INTERVAL 6 MONTH)
➥&&hoursbreakdown.CardDate < DATE_ADD(NOW(),INTERVAL 6 MONTH))
➥GROUP BY hoursbreakdown.CardEmployee, Month,
➥hoursbreakdown.ProjectName,
➥DATE_FORMAT(hoursbreakdown.CardDate,"%Y"),
➥DATE_FORMAT(hoursbreakdown.CardDate,"%m")
ORDER BY DATE_FORMAT(hoursbreakdown.CardDate,"%Y"),
➥DATE_FORMAT(hoursbreakdown.CardDate,"%m"),
➥hoursbreakdown.CardEmployee';
@mysql_query($sql,$Recipes);
?>
```

2. After the code is inserted, save your page.

Step 3: Data Binding Process

Applying the dynamic data to the content tables is purely a drag-and-drop affair for this recipe. However, because there are three recordsets, it's important that you be careful and drag the data elements from the proper recordset.

1. From the Bindings panel, expand the **DailyHours** recordset.
2. Place the data fields on the page in their proper places.

   Drag **CardEmployee** into the cell under the Employee Name label.

   Drag **ProjectName** into the cell under the Project label.

   Drag **Day** into the cell next to the Date label.

   Drag **Hours** into the cell next to the Hours label.

   Drag **BillableAmount** into the cell next to the Cost label.

3. From the Bindings panel, expand the **WeeklyHours** recordset.
4. Place the data fields on the page in their proper places.

   Drag **CardEmployee** into the cell under the Employee Name label.

   Drag **ProjectName** into the cell under the Project label.

   Drag **Week** into the cell next to the Date label.

   Drag **Hours** into the cell next to the Hours label.

   Drag **BillableAmount** into the cell next to the Cost label.

5. From the Bindings panel, expand the **MonthlyHours** recordset.

6. Place the data fields on the page in their proper places.

       📖 Drag **CardEmployee** into the cell under the Employee Name label.

       Drag **ProjectName** into the cell under the Project label.

       Drag **Month** into the cell next to the Date label.

       Drag **Hours** into the cell next to the Hours label.

       Drag **BillableAmount** into the cell next to the Cost label.

7. When you're done, save the page [r6-15].

r6-15

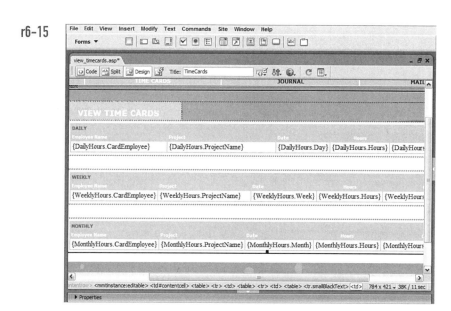

Step 4: Add the Repeat Regions

The final step for the View Time Cards recipe is to apply a Repeat Region server behavior to a row in each of the content tables. The three separate server behaviors will allow all the relevant data to be displayed.

We'll work our way down the page, starting with the Daily view.

1. Select any of the dynamic data fields in the Daily content table.

2. From the Tag Selector, choose the appropriate table row tag.

       📖 Select the **<tr>** tag to the left of the selected tag in the Tag Selector.

3. From the Server Behaviors panel, choose Add (+) and select **Repeat Region**.

4. In the Repeat Region dialog, choose the desired recordset.

   📖 Choose **DailyHours** from the Recordset list.

5. Set the Show option to display however many records you'd like.

   📖 Choose **Show All Records**.

6. Click OK when you're done to close the dialog.

Next, let's apply the server behavior to the Weekly content table.

1. Select any of the dynamic data fields in the Weekly content table.

2. From the Tag Selector, choose the appropriate table row tag.

   📖 Select the **<tr>** tag to the left of the selected tag in the Tag Selector.

3. From the Server Behaviors panel, choose Add (+) and select **Repeat Region**.

4. In the Repeat Region dialog, choose the desired recordset.

   📖 Choose **WeeklyHours** from the Recordset list.

5. Set the Show option to display however many records you'd like.

   📖 Choose **Show All Records**.

6. Click OK when you're done to close the dialog.

Finally, we'll add the server behavior to the Monthly table.

1. Select any of the dynamic data fields in the Monthly content table.

2. From the Tag Selector, choose the appropriate table row tag.

   📖 Select the **<tr>** tag to the left of the selected tag in the Tag Selector.

3. From the Server Behaviors panel, choose Add (+) and select **Repeat Region**.

4. In the Repeat Region dialog, choose the desired recordset.

   📖 Choose **MonthlyHours** from the Recordset list.

5. Set the Show option to display however many records you'd like.

   📖 Choose **Show All Records**.

6. Click OK when you're done to close the dialog.

7. Save the page when you're done [r6-16].

r6-16

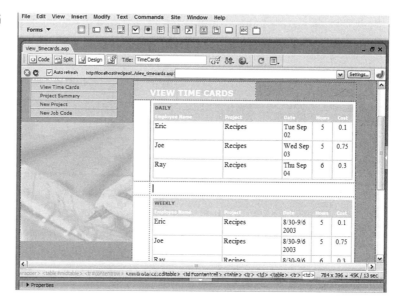

Try out the entire application by entering different time cards for various projects.

Recipe 7

Journal

Workgroups are, by their very nature, collaborative, and collaboration depends on communication. The journal is a terrific tool for facilitating workgroup communication. With a journal, a team member can post his or her thoughts on a particular aspect of a project for all the other team members to see. Responses can come from any other member, and a many-tiered dialog is underway. A journal application not only allows multiple users to enter notes and comments, but it also enables the journal entries to be easily modified and viewed.

The Journal application introduces a new record management concept: *archive*. An archive is a collection of records, typically organized by date. In the Journal application, the user has the option of declaring each journal's archive type: daily, weekly, or monthly. A daily archive contains all the entries made on a particular date, whereas a weekly archive consists of all entries made during a 7-day period, and a monthly archive is comprised of 30 days of entries. The Journal application adapts to show the user different archive periods depending on the journal's archive type.

Administrator Recipes

User Recipes

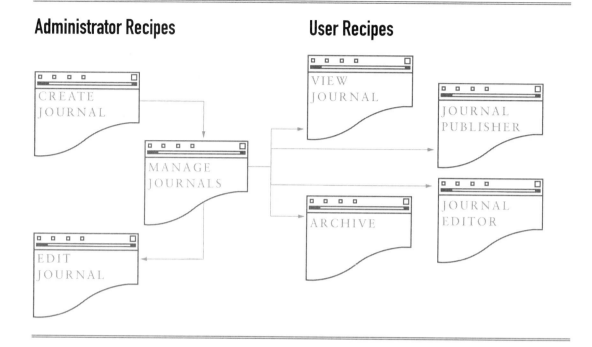

Ingredients

7 APPLICATION PAGES:

- 3 Administration Pages
  - Manage Journals
  - Create Journal
  - Edit Journal
- 4 User Pages
  - View Journal
  - Journal Publisher
  - Journal Editor
  - Archive

1 DATA SOURCE:

- 1 database with:
  - 2 tables
    - **Journals**—Includes records for all journals including fields for the ID, the journal name, its owner, description, archive period, and start date.
    - **JournalEntries**—Stores data concerning individual journal entries with fields for the ID, related journal, author, title, date and time of entry, and the journal text.

- 1 view
    - **JournalArchiveDates**—A virtual table that derives data from the `JournalEntries` table.

Prep Work

Before you begin to build this application, make sure your prep work has been completed.

1. Create the data source containing the necessary tables.
    - ASP and ColdFusion users should use the **Recipes.mdb** data source found in the downloaded files while PHP users should work with the **Recipes** data source. For assistance in locating and installing these files, choose **Help > Web Application Recipes**.
2. Set up a connection to the data source. If you're unsure how to do this, see the "Connecting to Data Sources" section of Chapter 1.
    - Name the connection **Recipes**.
3. Create the template to be used for the application.
    - Use the template for your server model named `journal`.

Administrator Recipe: Manage Journal

As the workgroup shifts from one project to another, the journal becomes an important tool for past as well as ongoing communication. Several journals could evolve out of one project from individuals or subgroups, or a workgroup might want to check how a similar situation was regarded in journals for previous projects. Regardless of the reason, it's undeniably handy to have a central point from which journals can be viewed, new entries can be published, archived journals can be read, and current entries can be removed. The Manage Journal page is designed to fill all those requirements.

> **NOTE**
>
> Although Manage Journal is listed in this chapter as an Administrator Recipe, it could easily fit in the User category. Just as Administrators might want to view and manage the various journals from various individuals, it's entirely likely that individuals could own or participate in multiple journals.

The data source engine behind the Manage Journal page is very straightforward: only a simple recordset connection to a single data table, `Journals`, is needed. Most of the page's features come from connecting to a related page and passing a record identifying parameter. Only aspects of the delete function require hand-coding of any sort. Rather than deleting one journal at a time, this page demonstrates how to mark any number of records for deletion and then remove them all with a single operation.

Step 1: Implement Manage Journals Design

Like most pages where the focus is on managing dynamic applications, the primary design element on the Manage Journals page is a table with a repeating row. In the row, you'll find basic identifiers—the journal name and owner—as well as links to perform related functions, such as viewing or editing the journal entries. We've included a less common option here, the delete checkbox, to make journal clean-up as effortless as possible.

1. In the server model of your choice, create a dynamic page.

   📖 In the **Journal** folder, locate the folder for your server model and open the `man-age_journals` page from there.

2. Add a table to the content region of your page to contain the interface elements for the application.

   📖 From the Snippets panel, drag the **Recipes > Journal > Wireframes > Manage Journals - Wireframe** snippet into the Content editable region.

3. Insert the form and a table with two rows and six columns. The top row should have the following labels: Journal Name, Journal Owner, Journal, Publish, Archive, and Delete. A checkbox form element should be placed under the Delete column, and the form should also include a form button labeled Delete.

   📖 Place your cursor in the row below the words MANAGE JOURNALS and insert the **Recipes > Journal > Forms > Manage Journals - Form** snippet [r7-1].

r7-1

4. Save the file.

Step 2: Add Database Components

The recordset used on this page is one of the simplest varieties. All the data comes from a single data table, Journals, and it is not filtered or sorted in any way. We basically want to get all the journal information on the page so the user can interact with it.

1. From the Bindings panel, choose Add (+) and select **Recordset** (**Query**).
2. In the simple Recordset dialog, enter an appropriate name.
   - Enter **Journal** in the Name field.
3. Select the desired data source connection.
   - Choose **Recipes** from the Connection (Data Source) list.
4. Choose the needed table.
   - From the Tables list, select **Journals** (**journals** for PHP).
5. Leave the Columns option set to All.
6. Make sure the Filter is set to None.
7. Keep the Sort option set to None and click OK to close the dialog.
8. Save the page after the recordset is inserted.

Step 3: Data Binding Process

Only two data fields are needed on the page—the journal name and the journal owner. The journal owner field is added to offset the possibility that journals could have similar names.

1. From the Bindings panel, expand the **Journal** recordset.
2. Place the data fields on the page in their proper places.
   - Drag **JournalTitle** into the cell below the Journal Name label.
   - Drag **JournalOwner** into the cell below the Journal Owner label.
3. When you're done, save the page [r7-2].

r7-2

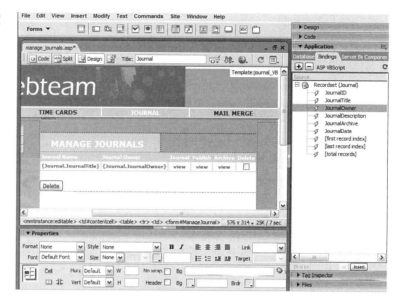

Step 4: Add Links to Manage Journals Page

One of the main purposes of the Manage Journals page is to act as a gateway to associated pages. Through this page, you can edit the journal entry itself, view information on any listed journal, add an entry to that journal, or display the entries of the journal in an archive format. This interaction is all accomplished in the same manner—a page is linked to with an identifying parameter passed in the URL. In each case, the unique data field JournalID is referenced and used to filter the resulting recordset.

Let's start by creating a link to edit the selected journal:

1. Select the text or image you want to link to the journal application.

   📖 Choose the **Journal.JournalTitle** data field below the Journal Name label.

2. Select the folder symbol next to the Link field in the Property inspector.
   The Select File dialog opens.

3. Make sure the dialog is set to **Select File Name From File System**.

4. Choose **Parameters** at the bottom of the dialog.

5. In the Name column of the Parameters dialog, enter the variable name.

   📖 Enter **ID** in the Name column.

6. In the Value column, enter the dynamic value of the current survey's ID.

   📖 Select the lightning bolt next to the Value column and, from the Dynamic Data dialog, choose **JournalID**. When you're done, click OK once to close the Dynamic Data dialog and again to close the Parameters dialog.

7. In the Select File dialog, select the file that will be used to edit the survey information.

   📖 Choose **edit_journal** in the Journal folder for your server model.

8. When you're done, click OK to insert the link.

Now we add a link to view the journal and it's associated entries:

1. Select the text or image you want to link to the journal application.

   📖 Choose the word **view** below the Journal label.

2. Select the folder symbol next to the Link field in the Property inspector.
   The Select File dialog opens.

3. Make sure the dialog is set to **Select File Name From File System.**

4. Choose **Parameters** at the bottom of the dialog.

5. In the Name column of the Parameters dialog, enter the variable name.

   📖 Enter **ID** in the Name column.

6. In the Value column, enter the dynamic value of the current survey's ID.

   📖 Select the lightning bolt next to the Value column and, from the Dynamic Data dialog, choose **JournalID**. When you're done, click OK once to close the Dynamic Data dialog and again to close the Parameters dialog.

7. In the Select File dialog, select the file that will be used to edit the survey information.

   📖 Choose **journal** in the Journal folder for your server model.

8. When you're done, click OK to insert the link.

Next we'll create a link so that new entries can be created for a particular journal.

1. Select the text or image you want to link to the journal application.

   📖 Choose the word **view** below the Publish label.

2. Select the folder symbol next to the Link field in the Property inspector.
   The Select File dialog opens.

3. Make sure the dialog is set to **Select File Name From File System.**

4. Choose **Parameters** at the bottom of the dialog.

5. In the Name column of the Parameters dialog, enter the variable name.

   📖 Enter **ID** in the Name column.

6. In the Value column, enter the dynamic value of the current survey's ID.

   📖 Select the lightning bolt next to the Value column and, from the Dynamic Data dialog, choose **JournalID**. When you're done, click OK once to close the Dynamic Data dialog and again to close the Parameters dialog.

7. In the Select File dialog, select the file that will be used to edit the survey information.

    📖 Choose **journal_publisher** in the Journal folder for your server model.

8. When you're done, click OK to insert the link.

Finally, let's link to the archive page that offers access to the full range of entries for a journal.

1. Select the text or image you want to link to the journal application.

    📖 Choose the word **view** below the Archive label.

2. Select the folder symbol next to the Link field in the Property inspector. The Select File dialog opens.

3. Make sure the dialog is set to **Select File Name From File System**.

4. Choose **Parameters** at the bottom of the dialog.

5. In the Name column of the Parameters dialog, enter the variable name.

    📖 Enter **ID** in the Name column.

6. In the Value column, enter the dynamic value of the current survey's ID.

    📖 Select the lightning bolt next to the Value column and, from the Dynamic Data dialog, choose **JournalID**. When you're done, click OK once to close the Dynamic Data dialog and again to close the Parameters dialog.

7. In the Select File dialog, select the file that will be used to edit the survey information.

    📖 Choose **archive** in the Journal folder for your server model.

8. When you're done, click OK to insert the link.

Step 5: Adding Repeat Region

The Repeat Region server behavior is put to work here to display all the existing journals along with the appropriate links and delete options. You'll notice that the checkbox is included in the Repeat Region; a special technique, discussed in the next step, is needed to identify the individually selected elements.

1. Select any of the dynamic data fields.

2. From the Tag Selector, choose the table row tag.

    📖 Select the **<tr>** tag from the Tag Selector.

3. From the Server Behaviors panel, choose Add (+) and select **Repeat Region**.

4. In the Repeat Region dialog, choose the desired recordset.

    📖 Choose **Journal** from the Recordset list.

5. Set the Show option to display however many records you want.

   📖 Choose **Show All Records**.

6. Click OK when you're done [r7-3].

r7-3

Naturally, if you are working with a great number of journals, you should consider limiting the number of visible records in the Repeat Region and add recordset navigation controls, as was done in Recipe 2, "Employee Lookup."

Step 6: Create the Delete Function

The delete function is the most complex aspect of the Manage Journals page. If we were deleting a single record, the standard Delete Record server behavior could be used, but because we are setting up the page to remove as many journals as selected, some custom steps are required. In all, there are four phases necessary to fulfill this functionality:

- Make each checkbox unique.
- Add a delete record command.
- Adjust the position of the command.
- Make the command conditional on the Delete button being chosen.

We start by setting the checkbox value to a unique number, the JournalID. Because the checkbox is within the Repeat Region, all our checkboxes will have the same name. In such a situation, the values of the checkboxes are combined into a comma-separated list for ASP and ColdFusion; PHP follows the HTTP specifications more closely and uses an array (which will require one small step to name the checkbox properly).

By using the JournalID as the value, our application will later be able to quickly identify which journals have been marked for deletion.

1. Locate the checkbox placed under the Delete column.

2. From the Bindings panel, expand the Journal recordset and drag **JournalID** onto the checkbox.

Dreamweaver places the code for the selected data field into the checkbox's `value` attribute.

PHP developers must alter the name of the checkbox for the array to function properly:

(PHP)   In the Property inspector, change the name from DeleteJournal to DeleteJournal[], appending the opening and closing square brackets that indicate an array to the form element's name.

The second phase of this step is to insert a command to perform the delete operation for all the selected journals. SQL delete commands are applied to a specific recordset. The command added here dynamically builds the recordset to include only those journals with a selected Delete checkbox. This same technique is very flexible and can be applied to many different situations.

 NOTE To accommodate the different dialogs for the various server models, the steps are presented separately here and when necessary throughout this recipe.

For ASP

    📖 Before you begin this step, you'll need to copy the SQL code from the appropriate snippet by opening the **Recipes > Journal > Custom Code** folder for your server model and right-clicking on the **Delete Journal - SQL Parameter** snippet; then, from the context menu, choose **Copy Snippet**.

1. From the Bindings panel, choose **Command**.
2. In the Command dialog, enter an appropriate name.

    📖 Enter **DeleteCheck** in the Name field.

3. Choose the data source.

    📖 From the Connections list, select **Recipes**.

4. Set the type of command.

    📖 From the Type list, choose **Delete**.

5. Leave the Return Recordset Named options blank.
6. In the SQL area, enter the following code:

    📖
```
DELETE FROM Journals
    WHERE JournalID = Delete_IDs
```

7. In the Variable area, choose Add (+) to add a new SQL variable.
8. Enter the name of the variable.

    📖 In the Name column, enter **Delete_IDs**.

9. Insert the following code in the Run-time Value column.

    📖 Paste the copied SQL code into the SQL area by choosing Ctrl-V (Command-V).

(VB) `Replace(Request("DeleteJournal"),", ","OR JournalID = ").`

(JS) `String(Request("DeleteJournal")).replace(/, /g," OR JournalID = ").`

10. Click OK to insert the command.

> **NOTE**
>
> Refrain from testing the delete command until the remaining steps in this section are complete.

For ColdFusion

📖 Before you begin this step, you'll need to copy the SQL code from the appropriate snippet by opening the **Recipes > Journal >Custom Code_CFML** folder, right-clicking the **Delete Journal - SQL Parameter** snippet, and then, from the context menu, choosing **Copy Snippet**.

1. From the Bindings panel, choose **Recordset (Query)**.

2. In the Advanced Recordset dialog, enter an appropriate name.

📖 Enter **DeleteCheck** in the Name field.

3. Choose the data source.

📖 From the Data Source list, select **Recipes**.

4. Enter the user name and password, if required.

5. In the SQL area, enter the following code:

📖 In the SQL area, paste in the copied code snippet by choosing Ctrl-V (Command-V).

(CF)
```
DELETE FROM Journals
    WHERE JournalID = #Deleted_IDs#
```

The `Deleted_IDs` variable will be defined in a later step.

6. Click OK to insert the command.

> **NOTE**
>
> Don't test the delete command until the remaining steps in the recipe are complete.

For PHP

If you've worked on other recipes in this book that delete records, you're probably familiar with the code required by PHP. Additionally, the form must be given an action conforming to the current page to properly execute the delete function. Although the custom code and the form modification are necessary, the good news is that no additional manipulation is needed—after this step is completed, the PHP page is done.

1. From Code view, place the cursor near the top of the page after the line that begins `<?php require_once` and insert the following code:

📖 From the Snippets panel, insert the **Recipes > Journal > CustomCode_PHP > Manage Journals – Delete Records** snippet.

```
(PHP) <?php
      // Delete Journals
      if (isset($_POST['Delete'])) {
        $delArr = $_POST['DeleteJournal'];
        for ($k=0; $k < count($delArr); $k++) {
          $sql = "DELETE FROM journals WHERE JournalID = ".$delArr[$k];
          @mysql_query($sql,$Recipes_PHP);
        }
        header("Location: manage_journals.php");
      }
      ?>
```

2. Switch to Design view and select the form from the Tag Selector.
3. In the Property inspector, choose the folder icon to open Select File dialog and select the current page, **manage_journal.php**.
4. When you're done, save the page.

This page is now complete and can be tested with the sample data included in the book's files by entering into Live Data view. To insert your own data, you'll need to begin work on the next recipe, Add New Journal.

NOTE   The remaining steps for this page are for ASP and ColdFusion only.

Step 7: Complete the Delete Function

The next step in constructing the delete operation is to move the inserted code to the top of the file.

1. Switch to Code view.
2. In the Server Behaviors panel, choose the **DeleteCheck** command.

   The command is selected in the code.
3. The selected code should look like this:

```
(VB) <%

     set DeleteCheck = Server.CreateObject("ADODB.Command")
     DeleteCheck.ActiveConnection = MM_Recipes_VB_STRING
     DeleteCheck.CommandText = "DELETE FROM Journals WHERE JournalID = " +
     ➥ Replace(DeleteCheck__Delete_IDs, "'", "''") + ""
     DeleteCheck.CommandType = 1
     DeleteCheck.CommandTimeout = 0
     DeleteCheck.Prepared = true
     DeleteCheck.Execute()

     %>
```

JS
```
<%

    var DeleteCheck = Server.CreateObject("ADODB.Command");
    DeleteCheck.ActiveConnection = MM_Recipes_STRING;
    DeleteCheck.CommandText = "DELETE FROM Journals WHERE JournalID = "
    ➥+ DeleteCheck__Delete_IDs.replace(/'/g, "''") + "";
    DeleteCheck.CommandType = 1;
    DeleteCheck.CommandTimeout = 0;
    DeleteCheck.Prepared = true;
    DeleteCheck.Execute();

%>
```

CF
```
<cfquery name="DeleteCheck" datasource="Recipes">
DELETE FROM Journals WHERE JournalID = #Deleted_IDs#
</cfquery>
```

4. Cut the code by choosing **Edit > Cut** or by pressing Ctrl-X (Command-X).

5. Place the cursor above the Journal recordset and paste the code by choosing **Edit > Paste** or by pressing Ctrl-V (Command-V).

6. Save the page.

ColdFusion users will need to complete an additional step to define the Deleted_IDs variable.

1. In Code view, place the cursor above the DeleteCheck query.

2. Insert the following code:

   ▢ From the Snippets panel, insert **Recipes > Journal > CustomCode_CFML > DeleteCheck CFQuery - Custom WHERE** clause.

   CF
```
<cfif isDefined("Form.DeleteJournal")>
<cfset Deleted_IDs=ListChangeDelims(Form.DeleteJournal,"
➥OR JournalID = ",", ")>
<cfelse>
<cfset Deleted_IDs=0>
</cfif>
```

3. Save the page.

The final step necessary—only for ASP—to complete the delete function is to make the code conditional. This is done by wrapping the existing delete command with an if-then statement that checks to see if the Delete form button has been selected and, if so, executes the command. After the records are deleted, the current page is redisplayed.

1. In Code view, locate and select the **DeleteIDs** declaration and the **DeleteCheck** command near the top of the page.

2. Insert the following code:

   📖 From the Snippets panel, open the **Recipes > Journal > Custom Code** folder for your server model and insert the **If Statement – Delete Operation** snippet.

   Before:

   (VB)
   ```
   <%
       if (cStr(Request("Delete"))<>"") then
       %>
   ```

   After:

   ```
       <%
       Response.Redirect("manage_journals.asp")
       end if
       %>
   ```

   Before:

   (JS)
   ```
   <%
       if (String(Request("Delete"))!="undefined")  {
       %>
   ```

   After:

   ```
       <%
       Response.Redirect("manage_journals.asp")
       }
       %>
   ```

   Before:

   (CF)
   ```
   <%
       if (String(Request("Delete"))!="undefined")  {
       %>
   ```

   After:

   ```
       <%
       Response.Redirect("manage_journals.asp")
       }
       %>
   ```

3. Save the page.

The page is ready for testing, and the recipe data source includes sample data for viewing.

Administrator Recipe: New Journal

The New Journal page allows the user to define the basic information—journal name, owner, and description—as well as the archive period for each journal created. As noted in the chapter introduction, an archive is a time-based organizational tool. When a specific archive period is chosen from the list element, either daily, weekly, or monthly, a corresponding value (1, 2, and 3, respectively) is entered in the data source. These same values are used later in the other pages of this recipe, including the archive page.

Step 1: Implement New Journal Design

The New Journal layout follows a standard form pattern, with labels on the left and form elements on the right. Text fields are needed to enter the name and owner information, while a text area is used to hold the description. A drop-down list provides the archive options.

1. In the server model of your choice, create a dynamic page.
    - In the **Journal** folder, locate the folder for your server model and open the `new_journal` page from there.
2. Add a table to the content region of your page to contain the form elements for the application.
    - From the Snippets panel, drag the **Recipes > Journal > Wireframes > New Journal - Wireframe** snippet into the Content editable region.
3. Insert the form and, within it, a two columned table. The table should include form elements and labels for a journal name, owner, description, and archive list. You'll also need a form button for inserting the new record.
    - Place your cursor in the row below the words NEW JOURNAL and insert the **Recipes > Journal > Forms > New Journal - Form** snippet.
4. Save the file [r7-4].

r7-4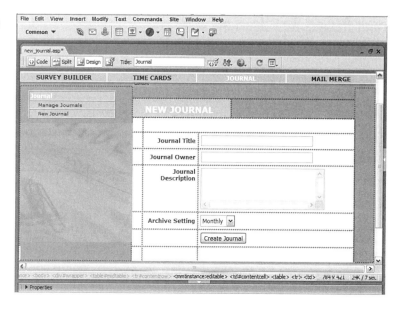

Step 2: Insert Record—New Journal

To store the newly entered values, the Insert Record server behavior is used. Although most of the settings in the dialog are fairly standard, you'll want to be sure to set the archive value type as numeric rather than text.

For ASP

1. From the Server Behaviors panel, choose Add (+) and select **Insert Record** from the list.

2. In the Insert Record dialog, choose your data source.

   📖 Choose **Recipes** from the Connection list.

3. Select the table you want to insert the record into.

   📖 From the Insert Into Table list, choose **Journals**.

4. Set the page you want to appear after the record is inserted.

   📖 Choose the **manage_journals.asp** file from your server model's folder for the After Inserting, Go To field.

5. Select the form on the current page from which to gather the record values.

   📖 From the Get Values From list, make sure **NewJournal** is selected.

6. In the Form Elements area, match the form elements on the page to the fields in the data source table.

  Set JournalName to insert into the JournalTitle column as Text type.

  Set JournalOwner to insert into the JournalOwner column as Text type.

  Set JournalDescription to insert into the JournalDescription column as Text type.

  Set Archive to insert into the JournalArchive column as Numeric type.

7. When you're sure your choices are correct, click OK to close the dialog and add the behavior.

For ColdFusion and PHP

1. From the Server Behaviors panel, choose Add (+) and select **Insert Record**.

2. In the Insert Record dialog, choose the current form.

  Select **NewJournal** from the Submit Values From list.

3. Select your data source from the list.

  Choose **Recipes** from the Data Source list.

4. Enter your user name and password, if needed.

5. Select the table in the data source to insert into from the list.

  Choose **Journals** (**journals** for PHP) from the Insert Into Table list.

6. Set the data source fields to their corresponding form elements.

  Make sure the JournalID data column is set to be an unused Primary Key.

  Set JournalTitle to the FORM.JournalName form element and submit as Text type.

  Set JournalOwner to the FORM.JournalOwner form element and submit as Text type.

  Set JournalDescription to the FORM.JournalDescription form element and submit as Text type.

  Set JournalArchive to the FORM.Archive form element and submit as Numeric type for ColdFusion and Integer for PHP.

  Make sure JournalDate is set not to get a value.

7. In the After Inserting, Go to field, enter **manage_journals.cfm** or **manage_journals.php** as appropriate and click OK to close the dialog.

8. Save your page.

This relatively simple page is now complete. Test the first two pages together by creating a temporary journal with this page and then deleting it through the Manage Journal page.

Administrator Recipe: Edit Journal

To make sure your new journal details aren't written in stone, an Edit Journal page is included in the application. The Edit Journal page enables you to modify all the fields set when the journal was created, including name, owner, description, and archive type. After the modifications are made, the Update Record server behavior is used to store the changes.

Step 1: Implement Edit Journal Design

The layout for the Edit Journal page replicates that of New Journal with the single exception of an Update button being substituted for the Create Journal one.

1. In the server model of your choice, create a dynamic page.

    📖 In the **Journal** folder, locate the folder for your server model and open the edit_journal page from there.

2. Add a table to the content region of your page to contain the form elements for the application.

    📖 From the Snippets panel, drag the **Recipes > Journal > Wireframes > Edit Journal - Wireframe** snippet into the Content editable region.

3. Insert the form and, within it, a two columned table. The table should include form elements and labels for a journal name, owner, description, and archive list to accept the bound data. You'll also need a form button for modifying the new record.

    📖 Place your cursor in the row below the words EDIT JOURNAL and insert the **Recipes > Journal > Forms > Edit Journal - Form** snippet.

4. Save the file [r7-5].

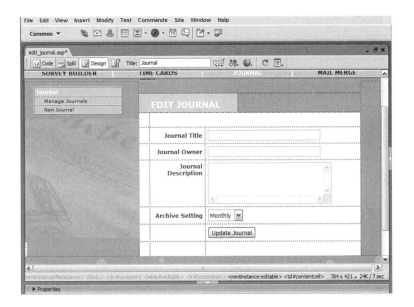

r7-5

Step 2: Add Database Components

The Journals table again serves as the basis for this page's recordset. However, as the page is intended to just display—and modify—a single record, the recordset is filtered by a URL parameter that reflects the desired journal's ID number.

1. From the Bindings panel, choose Add (+) and select **Recordset (Query)**.
2. In the dialog's simple view, enter an appropriate name for the recordset.

   📖 Enter **Journal** in the Name field.
3. Choose a connection (data source) to use.

   📖 Select **Recipes** from the Connection list.
4. Choose the table in the data source to work with.

   📖 Select **Journals** from the Table list.
5. Leave the Columns option set to All.
6. In the Filter area of the Recordset dialog, set the four Filter list elements like this:

JournalID	= (Equals)
URL Parameter	ID

7. Leave the Sort option set to None and click OK to close the dialog.

Step 3: Data Binding Process

Binding most of the elements on the page to the dynamic data of the recordset is a drag-and-drop affair. Only the Archive list element requires additional steps. However, even these can be handled through Dreamweaver's user interface without hand-coding. Because of the requirements of the Update Record server behavior, ColdFusion and PHP users will also need to include a hidden form field with the journal ID embedded in it. When we're through, the Archive list will automatically select the archive type previously
chosen for the journal being modified.

1. From the Bindings panel, expand the **Journal** recordset.
2. Place the data source fields onto the page in their respective areas:
   - Drag **JournalTitle** onto the JournalName text field.

     Drag **JournalOwner** onto the JournalOwner text field.

     Drag **JournalDescription** onto the JournalDescription text area.

   Now, let's bind the JournalArchive value to the Archive list.
3. Select the **Archive** list form element.
4. From the Property inspector, choose **Dynamic**.
5. In the Dynamic List/Menu dialog, select the lightning bolt next to the Set Value Equal To field.
6. In the Dynamic Data dialog, choose **JournalArchive** from the expanded Journals recordset.
7. Click OK once to close the Dynamic Data dialog and again to close the Dynamic List/Menu dialog [r7-6].

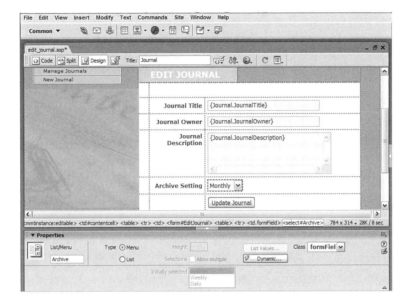

The remaining steps in this section are for ColdFusion and PHP users only.

1. From the Forms tab of the Insert bar, drag a Hidden Form element onto the table cell next to the explanatory text.
2. Enter **JournalID** as the name for the hidden element on the Property inspector.
3. Choose the lightning bolt symbol to open the Dynamic Data dialog.
4. From the Journal recordset, choose **JournalID** and click OK to close the dialog.

Step 4: Update Record—Edit Journal

The standard Update Record server behavior is used to save any changes made through the Edit Journal page. After the record has been modified, the user is redirected to the Manage Journal page to make changes on another record or additions to the current one.

For ASP

1. From the Server Behaviors panel, choose Add (+) and then **Update Record.**
2. In the Update Record dialog, select the desired data source connection.
   - Choose **Recipes** from the Connection list.
3. Choose the table containing the data you are updating.
   - From the Table to Update list, choose **Journals**.

4. Choose the recordset from which to get data source fields.

    □ From the Select Record From field, choose **Journal**.

5. Set the primary key for the recordset.

    □ From the Unique Key Column list, choose **JournalID** and make sure the **Numeric** option is selected.

6. Select the file you want to appear when the update is complete.

    □ For the After Updating, Go To field, select the **manage_journals.asp** page.

7. Choose the form on the page from which to get the values.

    □ From the Get Values From list, choose **EditJournal**.

8. In the Form Elements area, set the form elements to their corresponding data source fields.

    □ Set the `JournalName` form element to update the `JournalTitle` data source field as Text.

      Set the `JournalOwner` form element to update the `JournalOwner` data source field as Text.

      Set the `JournalDescription` form element to update the `JournalDescription` data source field as Text.

      Set the `Archive` form element to update the `JournalArchive` data source field as Numeric.

9. Make sure your entries are correct and then click OK to close.

10. Save your page and begin testing if you want to—this page is complete.

For ColdFusion and PHP

1. From the Server Behaviors panel, choose Add (+) and select **Update Record**.

2. In the Update Record dialog, choose the current form.

    □ Select **EditJournal** from the Submit Values From list.

3. Select your data source from the list.

    □ Choose **Recipes** from the Data Source list.

4. Enter your user name and password, if needed.

5. Select the table in the data source to insert into from the list.

    □ Choose **Journals** (**journals** in PHP) from the Insert Into Table list.

6. Set the data source fields to their corresponding form elements.

    □ As the Primary Key, `JournalID` selects the record using `FORM.JournalID` as Numeric type for ColdFusion and Integer type for PHP.

      Set `JournalTitle` to get its value from the `FORM.JournalName` form element as Text.

Set `JournalOwner` to get its value from the `FORM.JournalOwner` form element as Text.

Set `JournalDescription` to get its value from the `FORM.JournalDescription` form element as Text.

Set `JournalArchive` to get its value from the `FORM.Archive` form element as Numeric for ColdFusion and Integer in PHP.

`JournalDate` should be set not to get a value.

7. In the After Inserting, Go to field enter the path to the file you want displayed after the record is updated.

   📖 Choose Browse and select the **manage_journals.cfm** file (**manage_journals.php** for PHP).

8. Check your entries to verify they are correct and, if so, click OK.

9. Save your page.

You're ready to begin testing—the Edit Journal page is now complete.

User Recipe: View Journal

The View Journal page displays all the entries in a particular journal as well as basic information about the journal itself. The page, in essence, combines information from the `Journal` and `JournalEntries` data tables by using two corresponding recordsets. From here, the user can also look at the journal through an archive view or choose to edit any individual entry.

Step 1: Implement Journal Design

The Journal layout includes two distinct areas: one for basic information on the journal and one displaying all the associated entries. The former is a standard label (dynamic data arrangement) whereas the latter uses a repeating region to display the entries by date.

1. Create a page for the View Journal recipe, either from a template or from the File > New dialog.

   📖 In the **Journal** folder, locate the folder for your server model and open the `journal` page there.

2. In the content area of your page, create a header for the page and an area to hold both the general journal information and the specific entries.

   📖 From the Snippets panel, drag the **Recipes > Journal > Wireframes > Journal – Wireframe** snippet into the Content editable region.

3. Add labels and table cells to hold the journal information (name, owner, and description) and, below that, a two row, two column table for the journal entries.

   📖 Place your cursor in the first row below the words VIEW JOURNAL and insert the **Recipes > Journal > ContentTables > Journal Info - Content Table** snippet.

      Place your cursor in the bottom row of the wireframe and insert the **Recipes > Journal > ContentTables > View Journal - Content Table** snippet [r7-7].

r7-7

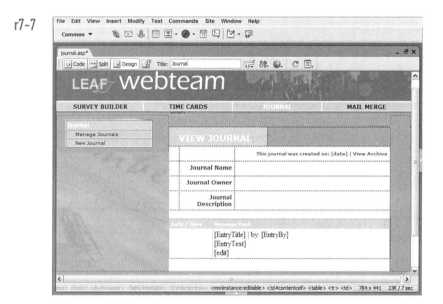

4. Save the page.

Step 2: Add Database Components

For the two layout areas, two separate data sources are needed. As noted earlier, the `Journals` and `JournalEntries` data tables are used to create the recordsets. The `Journals` table is filtered to include information about the currently selected journal while the `JournalEntries` table is filtered—using the same value—to show all the journal's entries.

1. From the Bindings panel, choose Add (+) and select **Recordset**.
2. In the dialog's simple view, enter an appropriate name for the recordset.

   📖 Enter **Journal** in the Name field.

3. Choose a connection (data source) to use.

   📖 Select **Recipes** from the Connection list.

4. Choose the table in the data source to work with.

    📖 Select **Journals** (**journals** for PHP) from the Table list.

5. Leave the Columns option set to All.

6. In the Filter area of the Recordset dialog, set the four Filter list elements like this:

JournalID	= (Equals)
URL Parameter	ID

7. Leave the Sort option set to None and click OK to close the dialog.

Although similar to the Journal recordset, the Entries recordset is filtered differently. Rather than look for a specific entry, this recordset gathers all the entries for the current journal, as represented by the ID parameter in the URL.

1. From the Bindings panel, choose Add (+) and select **Recordset**.

2. In the dialog's simple view, enter an appropriate name for the recordset.

    📖 Enter **Entries** in the Name field.

3. Choose a connection (data source) to use.

    📖 Select **Recipes** from the Connection list.

4. Choose the table in the data source to work with.

    📖 Select **JournalEntries** (**journalentries** for PHP) from the Table list.

5. Leave the Columns option set to All.

6. In the Filter area of the Recordset dialog, set the four Filter list elements like this:

EntryJournal	= (Equals)
URL Parameter	ID

7. Leave the Sort option set to None and click OK to close the dialog.

8. Save your page.

Without sorting the Entries recordset, the journal entries will be presented in the order they were stored—oldest to newest. You could sort on EntryDate Descending if you wanted to put the newest journal entry first.

Step 3: Data Binding Process

Data fields from the two recordsets must be placed in their separate content areas. In all cases for this page, the data fields can be dropped into position from the Bindings panel.

Let's start by binding data fields from the Journal recordset.

1. From the Bindings panel, expand the **Journal** recordset.
2. Place the data source fields onto the page in their respective areas:

   📖 Drag **JournalTitle** in the cell next to the Journal Name label.

   Drag **JournalOwner** in the cell next to the Journal Owner label.

   Drag **JournalDescription** in the cell next to the Journal Description label.

   Select the term [**date**] in the placeholder text at the top of the content area and drag **JournalDate** from the Bindings panel onto the selection.
3. Save the page.

Now, let's add the data fields from the Entries recordset.

1. From the Bindings panel, expand the **Entries** recordset.
2. Place the data source fields onto the page in their respective areas:

   📖 Drag **EntryDate** in the cell below the Date / Time label.

   Select the term [**EntryTitle**] in the placeholder text at the top of the content area and drag EntryTitle from the Bindings panel onto the selection.

   Select the term [**EntryBy**] in the placeholder text at the top of the content area and drag EntryBy from the Bindings panel onto the selection.

   Select the term [**EntryText**] in the placeholder text at the top of the content area and drag EntryText from the Bindings panel onto the selection [r7-8].

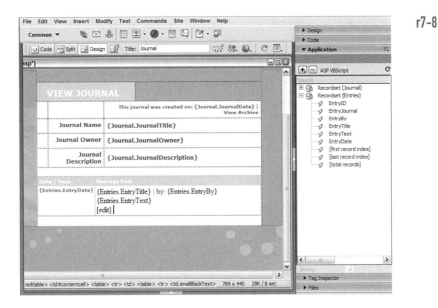

r7-8

3. Save the page.

Step 4: Assigning Dynamic Links

The Journal page is connected to two other pages in the application: Archive and Journal Editor. The Archive page enables you to see all the journal entries organized by their archiving option, whether it is daily, weekly, or monthly. The Journal Editor, as the name implies, allows an entry to be modified.

1. Select the text or image you want to link to the archive page.

   📖 Choose the phrase **View Archive** in the upper-right section of the content area.

2. Select the folder symbol next to the Link field in the Property inspector.

   The Select File dialog opens.

3. Make sure the dialog is set to **Select File Name From File System.**

4. Choose **Parameters** at the bottom of the dialog.

5. In the Name column of the Parameters dialog, enter the variable name.

   📖 Enter **ID** in the Name column.

6. In the Value column, enter the dynamic value of the current survey's ID.

   📖 Select the lightning bolt next to the Value column and, from the Dynamic Data dialog, choose **JournalID** from the Journal recordset. When you're done, click OK once to close the Dynamic Data dialog and again to close the Parameters dialog.

7. In the Select File dialog, select the file that will be used to edit the survey information.

   📖 Choose **archive** in the Journal folder for your server model.

8. When you're done, click OK to insert the link.

To make the link to the edit page functional, we'll need to pass two parameters: one identifying the current journal and another for the selected entry.

1. Select the text or image you want to link to the journal application.

   📖 Choose the word [**edit**] below the Journal label.

2. Select the folder symbol next to the Link field in the Property inspector.

   The Select File dialog opens.

3. Make sure the dialog is set to **Select File Name From File System**.

4. Choose **Parameters** at the bottom of the dialog.

5. In the Name column of the Parameters dialog, enter the variable name.

   📖 Enter **ID** in the Name column.

6. In the Value column, enter the dynamic value of the current survey's ID.

   📖 Select the lightning bolt next to the Value column and, from the Dynamic Data dialog, choose **JournalID** from the Journal recordset. When you're done, click OK once to close the Dynamic Data dialog.

7. Choose Add (+) to insert another parameter.

8. Enter a name for the entry ID variable in the Name column.

   📖 Enter **EditID** in the Name column.

9. Select the dynamic data for the value.

   📖 Select the lightning bolt next to the Value column and, from the Dynamic Data dialog, choose **EntryID** from the Entries recordset. When you're done, click OK once to close the Dynamic Data dialog and again to close the Parameters dialog.

10. In the Select File dialog, select the file that will be used to edit the survey information.

    📖 Choose **journal_editor** in the Journal folder for your server model.

11. When you're done, click OK to insert the link.

Step 5: Adding Repeat Region

The final step on the Journal page is to apply the Repeat Region server behavior. Naturally, the server behavior should only be applied to that area containing multiple records—in this case, dynamic data from the `Entries` recordset.

1. Select any of the dynamic data fields in the entries content area.
2. From the Tag Selector, choose the table row tag.

   📖 Select the **<tr>** tag from the Tag Selector.

3. From the Server Behaviors panel, choose Add (+) and select **Repeat Region**.
4. In the Repeat Region dialog, choose the desired recordset.

   📖 Choose **Entries** from the Recordset list.

5. Set the Show option to display however many records you want.

   📖 Choose **Show All Records.**

6. Click OK when you're done and save your page.

> **NOTE**
>
> If the journals are too numerous, you might consider displaying only a limited number of entries. Of course, if you do limit the records in the Repeat Region server behavior, you'll need to add recordset navigation controls, as we've done in previous recipes such as Employee Lookup.

With this step, the page is now complete, and you can see how it looks in the browser or in Live Data view [r7-9]. If you're testing in Live Data view, make sure you have an active ID ready to go in the Live Data Settings. To set one up, choose View > Live Data Settings and then enter ID in the Name column and the desired ID value in the Value column.

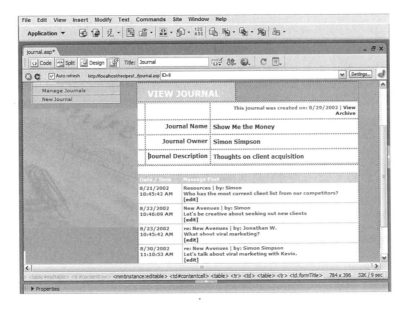

r7-9

User Recipe: Journal Publisher

The Journal Publisher is used to create new entries for a given journal. To help keep new entries on track, all the previously entered ones are also visible. Moreover, any of the older entries can be modified or annotated with the click of a button.

One innovative feature of the Journal Publisher is the capability to store a draft of the current entry prior to publishing it. Our recipe uses JavaScript cookies to store and retrieve the draft. In this recipe, you'll also work with code for formatting date and time functions into a more user-friendly response.

Step 1: Implement Journal Publisher Design

As with the Journal, two separate areas are used in the Journal Publisher layout. The top area is for inserting a new entry and uses standard form elements. The bottom area displays the previous entries, with the entry's date in one column and other information in another.

1. Create a page for the Journal Publisher recipe, either from a template or from the File > New dialog.

   ⌑ In the **Journal** folder, locate the folder for your server model and open the `journal_publisher` page there.

2. In the content area of your page, create a header for the page and an area to hold both the general journal information and the specific entries.

   ⌑ From the Snippets panel, drag the **Recipes > Journal > Wireframes > Journal Publisher – Wireframe** snippet into the Content editable region.

3. Add labels and table cells to hold the journal information (name, owner, and description) and, below that, a two-row, two-column table for the journal entries.

   ⌑ Place your cursor in the first row below the words JOURNAL PUBLISHER and insert the **Recipes > Journal > Forms > Journal Publisher - Message Post** snippet.

   ⌑ Place your cursor in the bottom row of the wireframe and insert the **Recipes > Journal > ContentTables > View Journal - Content Table** snippet [r7-10].

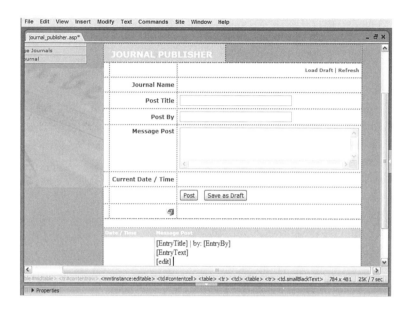

r7-10

4. Save the page.

Step 2: Add Database Components

As in the Journal page, two recordsets are used: one for the journal and the other for the journal entries. They are constructed in exactly the same way as the earlier built page.

Although you're welcome to construct both record-sets following the subsequent steps, you can also copy and paste each of the recordsets used in the Journal page. To copy a recordset, select it in the Bindings panel and, from the panel Options menu, choose Copy. Then switch to the receiving page and, again from the Bindings panel's Options menu, choose Paste.

NOTE

1. From the Bindings panel, choose Add (+) and select **Recordset**.
2. In the dialog's simple view, enter an appropriate name for the recordset.

   ⚏ Enter **Journal** in the Name field.
3. Choose a connection (data source) to use.

   ⚏ Select **Recipes** from the Connection list.
4. Choose the table in the data source to work with.

   ⚏ Select **Journals** (**journals** for PHP) from the Table list.
5. Leave the Columns option set to All.

6. In the Filter area of the Recordset dialog, set the four Filter list elements like this:

JournalID	= (Equals)
URL Parameter	ID

7. Leave the Sort option set to None and click OK to close the dialog.

Although similar to the Journal recordset, the Entries recordset is filtered differently. Rather than look for a specific entry, this recordset gathers all the entries for the current journal, as represented by the ID parameter in the URL.

1. From the Bindings panel, choose Add (+) and select **Recordset**.
2. In the dialog's simple view, enter an appropriate name for the recordset.
   - Enter **Entries** in the Name field.
3. Choose a connection (data source) to use.
   - Select **Recipes** from the Connection list.
4. Choose the table in the data source to work with.
   - Select **JournalEntries** (**journalentries** for PHP) from the Table list.
5. Leave the Columns option set to All.
6. In the Filter area of the Recordset dialog, set the four Filter list elements like this:

EntryJournal	= (Equals)
URL Parameter	ID

7. Leave the Sort option set to None and click OK to close the dialog.

Step 3: Data Binding Process

Only a few data source elements need to be bound to this page: the journal's title, the entry's date, and the entry itself. In addition, we need to set dynamic parameters to allow each entry to be edited.

1. From the Bindings panel, expand the **Journal** recordset.
2. Place the data source fields onto the page in their respective areas:
   - Drag **JournalTitle** in the cell next to the Journal Name label.
3. In the Bindings panel, expand the **Entries** recordset.

4. Place the data fields from `Entries` onto the page.

   📖 Drag **EntryDate** into the cell below the Date/Time label.

     Select the term **[EntryTitle]** in the placeholder text at the top of the content area and drag `EntryTitle` from the Bindings panel onto the selection.

     Select the term **[EntryBy]** in the placeholder text at the top of the content area and drag `EntryBy` from the Bindings panel onto the selection.

     Select the term **[EntryText]** in the placeholder text at the top of the content area and drag `EntryText` from the Bindings panel onto the selection.

5. Save the page.

Let's create a link that will enable us to easily edit any visible journal entry.

1. Select the text or image you want to serve as the link.

   📖 Choose the text **[edit]** below the Journal Description label.

2. Select the folder symbol next to the Link field in the Property inspector.

   The Select File dialog opens.

3. Choose **Parameters** at the bottom of the dialog.

4. In the Name column of the Parameters dialog, enter the variable name.

   📖 Enter **ID** in the Name column.

5. In the Value column, enter the dynamic value of the current journal's ID.

   📖 Select the lightning bolt next to the Value column and, from the Dynamic Data dialog, choose **JournalID** from the `Journal` recordset. When you're done, click OK once to close the Dynamic Data dialog.

6. Choose Add (+) to insert another parameter.

7. Enter a name for the entry ID variable in the Name column.

   📖 Enter **EditID** in the Name column.

8. Select the dynamic data for the value.

   📖 Select the lightning bolt next to the Value column and from the Dynamic Data dialog, choose **EntryID** from the `Entries` recordset. When you're done, click OK once to close the Dynamic Data dialog and again to close the Parameters dialog.

9. In the Select File dialog, select the file that will be used to edit the survey information.

   📖 Choose **journal_editor** in the **Journal** folder for your server model.

10. When you're done, click OK to insert the link [r7-11].

r7-11

Step 4: Adding Repeat Region

To display all the journal entries, a Repeat Region server behavior is attached to the appropriate table row.

1. Select any of the dynamic data fields in the entries content area.
2. From the Tag Selector, choose the table row tag.
   - Select the **<tr>** tag from the Tag Selector.
3. From the Server Behaviors panel, choose Add (+) and select **Repeat Region**.
4. In the Repeat Region dialog, choose the desired recordset.
   - Choose **Entries** from the Recordset list.
5. Set the Show option to display however many records you want.
   - Choose **Show All Records.**
6. Click OK when you're done and save your page.

Step 5: Insert Record—New Journal

After the information for the new journal entry has been entered, the Post button should submit the data to be stored. The standard Dreamweaver Insert Record server behavior is perfectly suited for such a task. However, we'll need to do a little set-up first and make sure the current journal ID value is available for use. We do this by putting the ID value passed in the URL string into a hidden form element.

1. Select the hidden form element.

   📖 Choose the hidden form element named **ID**.

2. In the Property inspector, enter the following code in the Value field:

   (VB) `<%=Request("ID")%>`

   (JS) `<%=Request("ID")%>`

   (CF) `<cfoutput>#URL.ID#</cfoutput>`

   (PHP) `<?php echo $_GET['ID']; ?>`

3. Save your page.

Now that the page is properly set up to handle the Insert Record server behavior, we're ready to add it to the page.

For ASP

1. From the Server Behaviors panel, choose Add (+) and select **Insert Record** from the list.

2. In the Insert Record dialog, choose your data source.

   📖 Choose **Recipes** from the Connection list.

3. Select the table you want to insert the record into.

   📖 From the Insert Into Table list, choose **JournalEntries**.

4. Leave the After Inserting, Go To field blank.

   By leaving this field blank, the user will stay on the same page and be able to add additional entries.

5. Select the form on the current page from which to gather the record values.

   📖 From the Get Values From list, make sure **JournalPublisher** is selected.

6. In the Form Elements area, match the form elements on the page to the fields in the data source table.

   📖 Set `PostTitle` to insert into the `EntryTitle` column as Text type.

   Set `PostBy` to insert into the `EntryBy` column as Text type.

   Set `MessagePost` to insert into the `EntryText` column as Text type.

   Set `ID` to insert into the `EntryJournal` column as Numeric type.

7. When you're sure your choices are correct, click OK to close the dialog and add the behavior.

For ColdFusion and PHP

1. From the Server Behaviors panel, choose Add (+) and select **Insert Record**.
2. In the Insert Record dialog, choose the current form.
   - Select **JournalPublisher** from the Submit Values From list.
3. Select your data source from the list.
   - Choose **Recipes** from the Data Source list.
4. Enter your user name and password, if needed.
5. Select the table in the data source to insert into from the list.
   - Choose **JournalEntries** (**journalentries** for PHP) from the Insert Into Table list.
6. Set the data source fields to their corresponding form elements.
   - Make sure the EntryID data column is set to be an unused Primary Key.

     Set EntryJournal to the FORM.ID form element and submit as Numeric type for ColdFusion and Integer for PHP.

     Set EntryBy to the FORM.PostBy form element and submit as Text type.

     Set EntryTitle to the FORM.PostTitle form element and submit as Text type.

     Set EntryText to the FORM.MessagePost form element and submit as Text type.

     Make sure EntryDate is set not to get a value.
7. Leave the After Inserting, Go to field, blank and click OK to close the dialog.

Step 6: Add Date and Cookie Code

Although "add date and cookie" is an instruction that might be at home in the more traditional form of a recipe, it also goes a long way to adding value in a Web application recipe. Journals, by their very nature, are date-oriented. In the first step of the recipe, we'll add code that displays the current date and time when the new entry page first opens. Another snippet of code, this one in JavaScript, attaches reset functionality to a text link, which will clear the journal form fields and allow the user to start fresh.

The cookies are used to temporarily store and retrieve a draft of the journal. This feature is handy in situations where the journal writer is unable to complete a post and does not want to publish an unfinished draft. The cookies are set to expire in 30 days and will persist from one session to the next. To implement the cookies, we'll need to add four JavaScript functions and the code necessary to call those functions.

Let's start by adding the date functionality. The standard Dreamweaver time formats control either date or time, not both. The code used in this example formats the date and time like this:

```
Tuesday, March 31, 2004 10:12:42 AM
```

Without the specialized formatting, the date and time would be in a less user-friendly format.

1. Place the cursor where you want the date and time to appear.

   ◻ Place the cursor in the cell adjacent to the Current Date / Time label.

2. Insert the following code:

   ◻ From the Snippets panel, open the **Recipes > Journal > Custom Code** folder for your server model and insert the **Current Date & Time - Dynamic Text** snippet.

You can test the date/time code by entering into Live Data view. After you see the date and time string, select Refresh from the Live Data toolbar to verify that it updates properly. Again, you'll need to have an active journal ID available in Live Data Settings for this to work properly.

NOTE

(VB) `<%=FormatDateTime(Now(), 1) & " " & FormatDateTime(Now(), 3)%>`

(JS) `<%=new Date().toLocaleString()%>`

(CF) `<cfoutput>#LSDateFormat(Now(), "ddd, mmmm dd, yyyy")#</cfoutput>`

(PHP) `<?php echo date("l, F j, Y h:i:s A"); ?>`

3. Save the page [r7-12].

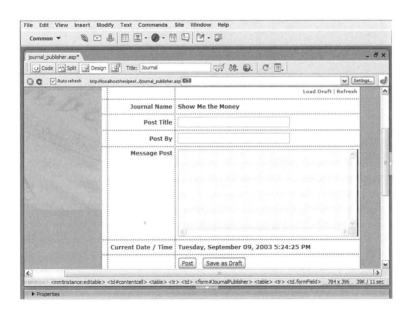

r7-12

The next bit of code applies a JavaScript reset behavior to a standard text link. Although you could use a Reset form button to the same effect, this method provides you with an alternative approach that keeps the number of form buttons to a minimum. After it's added, a click of the reset link clears all the text fields, enabling the user to start over.

1. Select the text you want to apply the reset action to.

   ☐ Choose the text **Refresh** in the upper right of the content area.

2. Add the following as a link in the Property inspector:

   ☐ From the Snippets panel, insert the **Recipes > Journal > ClientJavaScript > Journal Publisher - Refresh** snippet. The snippet includes all the code necessary to create the link and can just be dropped on the selected text.

   ```
   javascript:document.JournalPublisher.reset()
   ```

   This bit of JavaScript tells the form (named JournalPublisher) on the current document to reset its values.

3. Save your page.

Time to add the cookies into the mix. In all, there are four JavaScript functions needed:

- `setDraft()`—Stores the current form entries as a draft in a cookie on the local system.
- `retrieveDraft()`—Reads the stored information from the cookie and repopulates the form.
- `getCookie()`—A helper function that opens a specified cookie.
- `getCV()`—A helper function to get a specific value from an opened cookie.

In addition to adding the four functions to the code, we'll also need to add code to call the two main functions, `setDraft()` and `retrieveDraft()`.

Let's add the four JavaScript functions to the page.

1. Switch to Code view and, if necessary, enter a **<script>** tag pair in the <head> section of the document, just before the closing </head> tag.

   ☐ Place your cursor in the <script></script> tag pair located in the head editable region.

2. Insert the following code:

   ☐ From the Snippets panel, insert the **Recipes > Journal > ClientJavaScript > Journal Publisher - Set Draft** snippet.

   ```
   function setDraft()  {
       var ExpirationDate = new Date()
       ExpirationDate.setMonth(ExpirationDate.getMonth()+1);
       document.cookie = 'PostBy' + "=" +
       ➥escape(document.JournalPublisher.PostBy.value) +
       ➥"; expires=" + ExpirationDate.toGMTString();
       document.cookie = 'PostTitle' + "=" +
       ➥escape(document.JournalPublisher.PostTitle.value) +
       ➥"; expires=" + ExpirationDate.toGMTString();
   ```

```
          document.cookie = 'MessagePost' + "=" +
          escape(document.JournalPublisher.MessagePost.value) +
          "; expires=" + ExpirationDate.toGMTString();
      }
```

Next we'll add the code to retrieve the draft information from the cookie.

3. Place your cursor immediately after the setDraft() function just added.

4. Insert the following code:

 🕮 From the Snippets panel, insert the **Recipes > Journal > ClientJavaScript > Journal Publisher - Retrieve Draft** snippet.

```
      function retrieveDraft()  {
        document.JournalPublisher.PostBy.value = getCookie('PostBy');
        document.JournalPublisher.PostTitle.value =
        getCookie('PostTitle');
        document.JournalPublisher.MessagePost.value =
        getCookie('MessagePost');
      }
```

Now, let's add the two helper functions.

5. Place your cursor below the retrieveDraft() function just added.

6. Insert the following code:

 🕮 From the Snippets panel, insert the **Recipes > Journal > ClientJavaScript > Cookie** snippet. This snippet includes both functions.

```
      function getCookie(name) {
        var arg = name + "=";
        var alen = arg.length;
        var clen = document.cookie.length;
        var i = 0;
        while (i < clen) {
          var j = i + alen;
          if (document.cookie.substring(i, j) == arg)
            return getCV(j);
          i = document.cookie.indexOf(" ", i) + 1;
          if (i == 0) break;
        }
        return "";
      }

      function getCV(offset) {
        var endstr = document.cookie.indexOf(";", offset);
        if (endstr == -1) endstr = document.cookie.length;
        return unescape(document.cookie.substring(offset, endstr));
      }
```

7. Save the page.

NOTE

Because client-side cookies can be disabled by individual browsers, one possible enhancement would be to display the Save as Draft and Load Draft user interface elements only if cookies are available. You can use server-side scripting to detect the user's cookie status.

For the finishing touches, we only need to add the JavaScript function calls. In this recipe, we'll use both a form button and a standard link to show you how it's done in either situation.

Let's start with the form button for saving the draft.

1. Select the form button you want to use to trigger the setDraft() function.

    📖 Choose the form button labeled **Save As Draft**.

2. Switch to Code view and position your cursor within the tag at the very end.

3. Insert the following code:

    ```
    onClick="setDraft()"
    ```

    📖 From the Snippets panel, insert the **Recipes > Journal > ClientJavaScript > Journal Publisher – Save Draft** snippet.

    Now let's add the code to trigger the retrieveDraft() function.

4. From Design view, select the text you want to use to call the retrieveDraft() function.

    📖 Select the phrase **Load Draft** in the upper-right corner of the content area.

5. Add the following as a link in the Property inspector:

    📖 From the Snippets panel, insert the **Recipes > Journal > ClientJavaScript > Journal Publisher – Load Draft** snippet. The snippet includes all the code necessary for creating the link and can just be dropped on the selected text.

    ```
    javascript:retrieveDraft()
    ```

6. Save your page.

As you test this page, be sure to notice that the just-added journal entries are listed at the bottom of the page after the record is inserted. Be sure to check the draft functionality as well by entering in a message and first choosing Save As Draft. Then make a change or two and choose Load Draft—your previous version should be restored.

User Recipe: Journal Editor

The Journal Editor is used to modify existing journal entries. Although this page could be done as a standard update record page with the minimal form elements needed, our recipe takes the concept a step further by including a listing of all the current entries. Journal entries—especially in a workgroup environment—are often reactive to other entries. By including both the balance of the journal and the actual entry being edited, it's easier to reference other thoughts and opinions.

To properly handle all the functionality on the page, three recordsets are needed. In addition to Journals and Entries, we'll also include an UpdateEntries recordset that will hold the values being modified.

Step 1: Implement Journal Editor Design

Like many of the other pages in this application, the layout for the Journal Editor is divided into two sections. The top part of the page displays the currently selected entry and enables it to be edited, while the bottom part displays all the journal entries.

1. Create a page for the Journal Editor recipe, either from a template or from the File > New dialog.

   📖 In the **Journal** folder, locate the folder for your server model and open the journal_editor page there.

2. In the content area of your page, create a header for the page and an area to hold both the general journal information and the specific entries.

   📖 From the Snippets panel, drag the **Recipes > Journal > Wireframes > Journal Editor – Wireframe** snippet into the Content editable region.

3. Add labels and table cells to hold the journal information (name, owner, and description) and, below that, a two-row, two-column table for the journal entries.

   📖 Place your cursor in the first row below the words JOURNAL EDITOR and insert the **Recipes > Journal > Forms > Journal Editor – Edit Message** snippet.

   Place your cursor in the bottom row of the wireframe and insert the **Recipes > Journal > ContentTables > View Journal - Content Table** snippet [r7-13].

4. Save the page.

r7-13

NOTE

As noted in other recipes, where an identical recordset is used on one or more pages, you can copy the recordset from one page and paste it into the other. Be sure to use the Copy and Paste commands from the Bindings panel context menus for these operations.

Step 2: Add Database Components

Two of the recordsets needed for this page have been used before—Journal and Entries. The third one, UpdateEntries, is necessary to complete the primary function of the page—editing the selected entry.

1. From the Bindings panel, choose Add (+) and select **Recordset**.

2. In the dialog's simple view, enter an appropriate name for the recordset.

   📖 Enter **Journal** in the Name field.

3. Choose a connection (data source) to use.

   📖 Select **Recipes** from the Connection list.

4. Choose the table in the data source to work with.

   📖 Select **Journals** (**journals** for PHP) from the Table list.

5. Leave the Columns option set to All.

6. In the Filter area of the Recordset dialog, set the four Filter list elements like this:

JournalID	= (Equals)
URL Parameter	ID

7. Leave the Sort option set to None and click OK to close the dialog.

Now, we'll insert the Entries recordset from which we'll gather the journal entries for display at the bottom of the page.

1. From the Bindings panel, choose Add (+) and select **Recordset**.
2. In the dialog's simple view, enter an appropriate name for the recordset.
   - Enter **Entries** in the Name field.
3. Choose a connection (data source) to use.
   - Select **Recipes** from the Connection list.
4. Choose the table in the data source to work with.
   - Select **JournalEntries** (**journalentries** for PHP) from the Table list.
5. Leave the Columns option set to All.
6. In the Filter area of the Recordset dialog, set the four Filter list elements like this:

| EntryJournal | = (Equals) |
| URL Parameter | ID |

7. Leave the Sort option set to None and click OK to close the dialog.

Our final recordset is called UpdateEntries and consists of the data designed to be modified on the page. The recordset is filtered by applying the URL parameter EditID to its match in the EntryID key field.

ColdFusion and PHP users will also need to add a hidden form field so that the Update Record server behavior, inserted later, will work properly.

1. From the Bindings panel, choose Add (+) and select **Recordset**.
2. In the dialog's simple view, enter an appropriate name for the recordset.
   - Enter **UpdateEntries** in the Name field.
3. Choose a connection (data source) to use.
   - Select **Recipes** from the Connection list.
4. Choose the table in the data source to work with.
   - Select **JournalEntries** (**journalentries** in PHP) from the Table list.
5. Leave the Columns option set to All.
6. In the Filter area of the Recordset dialog, set the four Filter list elements like this:

| EntryID | = (Equals) |
| URL Parameter | EditID |

7. Leave the Sort option set to None and click OK to close the dialog.

The following steps are for ColdFusion and PHP only.

1. From the Forms tab of the Insert bar, drag a Hidden Form element onto the table cell next to the explanatory text.
2. Enter **EditID** as the name for the hidden element on the Property inspector.
3. Choose the lightning bolt symbol to open the Dynamic Data dialog.
4. From the Entries recordset, choose **EntryID** and click OK to close the dialog.

Step 3: Data Binding Process

In this step, we'll bind data from all three recordsets. The Journal recordset is only used once to display the current journal title. All the form elements are pulled from the UpdateEntries recordset. As before, the Entries recordset is the source for the data fields that display the journal's entries. In addition, we'll use that recordset to set up a dynamic link allowing any entry listed to also be edited.

1. From the Bindings panel, expand the **Journal** recordset.
2. Place the data source fields from **Journal** onto the page in their respective areas:

   📖 Drag **JournalTitle** in the cell next to the Journal Name label.

3. In the Bindings panel, expand the **UpdateEntries** recordset.
4. Place the data fields from **UpdateEntries** onto the page.

   📖 Drag **EntryTitle** into the PostTitle text field.

   Drag **EntryBy** into the PostBy text field.

   Drag **EntryText** into the MessagePost text field.

   Now, we'll pull our data fields from the Entries recordset.

5. In the Bindings panel, expand the **Entries** recordset.
6. Place the data fields from **Entries** onto the page.

   📖 Drag **EntryDate** into the cell below the Date/Time label.

   Select the term [**EntryTitle**] in the placeholder text at the top of the content area and drag EntryTitle from the Bindings panel onto the selection.

   Select the term [**EntryBy**] in the placeholder text at the top of the content area and drag EntryBy from the Bindings panel onto the selection.

   Select the term [**EntryText**] in the placeholder text at the top of the content area and drag EntryText from the Bindings panel onto the selection.

   Now let's add in our date and time string.

7. Place the cursor where you want the date and time to appear.

   Place your cursor in the cell next to the Current Date / Time label.

8. Insert the following code:

   📖 From the Snippets panel, open the **Recipes > Journal > Custom Code** folder for your server model and insert the **Current Date & Time - Dynamic Text** snippet.

   (VB) `<%=FormatDateTime(Now(), 1) & " " & FormatDateTime(Now(), 3)%>`

   (JS) `<%=new Date().toLocaleString()%>`

   (CF) `<cfoutput>#LSDateFormat(Now(), "ddd, mmmm dd, yyyy")#</cfoutput>`

   (PHP) `<?php echo date("l, F j, Y h:i:s A"); ?>`

9. Be sure to save your page.

With the rest of our data fields bound, it's time to create a link for editing the separate entries.

1. Select the text or image you want to serve as the link.

   📖 Choose the text **[edit]** below the Journal Description label.

2. Select the folder symbol next to the Link field in the Property inspector.

   The Select File dialog opens.

3. Choose **Parameters** at the bottom of the dialog.

4. In the Name column of the Parameters dialog, enter the variable name.

   📖 Enter **ID** in the Name column.

5. In the Value column, enter the dynamic value of the current survey's ID.

   📖 Select the lightning bolt next to the Value column and, from the Dynamic Data dialog, choose **JournalID** from the `Journal` recordset. When you're done, click OK once to close the Dynamic Data dialog.

6. Choose Add (+) to insert another parameter.

7. Enter a name for the entry ID variable in the Name column.

   📖 Enter **EditID** in the Name column.

8. Select the dynamic data for the value.

   📖 Select the lightning bolt next to the Value column and, from the Dynamic Data dialog, choose **EntryID** from the `Entries` recordset. When you're done, click OK once to close the Dynamic Data dialog and again to close the Parameters dialog.

9. In the Select File dialog, select the file that will be used to edit the survey information.

   📖 Choose **journal_editor** in the Journal folder for your server model.

10. When you're done, click OK to insert the link [r7-14].

r7-14

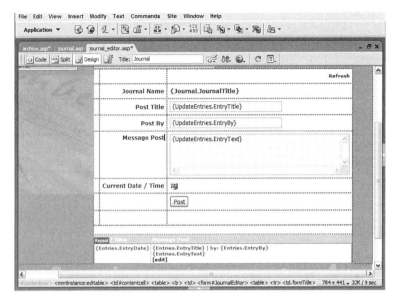

Step 4: Add Repeat Region

To show all the entries of a journal, a Repeat Region server behavior is necessary.

1. Select any of the dynamic data fields in the entries content area.
2. From the Tag Selector, choose the table row tag.
    - Select the **<tr>** tag from the Tag Selector.
3. From the Server Behaviors panel, choose Add (+) and select **Repeat Region.**
4. In the Repeat Region dialog, choose the desired recordset.
    - Choose **Entries** from the Recordset list.
5. Set the Show option to display however many records you want.
    - Choose **Show All Records.**
6. Click OK when you're done and save your page.

Step 5: Update Record—New Journal

The *raison d'etre* of the Journal Editor is to modify an existing entry. After the entry is modified, the Update Record server behavior stores the changes.

For ASP

1. From the Server Behaviors panel, choose Add (+) and select **Update Record.**
2. In the Update Record dialog, select the desired data source connection.
   - Choose **Recipes** from the Connection list.
3. Choose the table containing the data you are updating.
   - From the Table to Update list, choose **JournalEntries.**
4. Choose the recordset from which to get data source fields.
   - From the Select Record From field, choose **UpdateEntries.**
5. Set the primary key for the recordset.
   - From the Unique Key Column list, choose **EntryID** and make sure the **Numeric** option is selected.
6. Select the file you want to appear when the update is complete.
   - For the After Updating, Go To field, select the **journal.asp** page.
7. Choose the form on the page from which to get the values.
   - From the Get Values From list, choose **JournalEditor.**
8. In the Form Elements area, set the form elements to their corresponding data source fields.
   - Set the PostTitle form element to update the EntryTitle data source field as Text.

     Set the PostBy form element to update the EntryBy data source field as Text.

     Set the MessagePost form element to update the MessageText data source field as Text.
9. Make sure your entries are correct and then click OK to close.

For ColdFusion and PHP

1. From the Server Behaviors panel, choose Add (+) and select **Update Record.**
2. In the Update Record dialog, choose the current form.
   - Select **JournalEditor** from the Submit Values From list.
3. Select your data source from the list.
   - Choose **Recipes** from the Data Source list.
4. Enter your user name and password, if needed.
5. Select the table in the data source to insert into from the list.
   - Choose **JournalEntries (journalentries** for PHP) from the Insert Into Table list.

6. Set the data source fields to their corresponding form elements.

   ▢ As the Primary Key, `EntryID` selects the record using `FORM.EditID` as a Numeric type for ColdFusion and Integer for PHP.

   Set `EntryTitle` to get its value from the `FORM.PostTitle` form element as Text.

   Set `EntryBy` to get its value from the `FORM.PostBy` form element as Text.

   Set `MessageText` to get its value from the `FORM.MessagePost` form element as Text.

   `EntryDate` should be set not to get a value.

7. In the After Inserting, Go to field enter the path to the file you want displayed after the record is updated.

   ▢ Choose Browse and select **journal.cfm** or **journal.php** as appropriate.

8. Check your entries to verify they are correct and, if so, click OK.

Step 6: Add Refresh Code

The final task for this page is to set up the Refresh link. When selected, changes to the current record are discarded and the previously stored values inserted for editing.

1. Select the text you want to apply the reset action to.

   ▢ Choose the text **Refresh** in the upper right of the content area.

2. Add the following as a link in the Property inspector:

   ▢ From the Snippets panel, insert the **Recipes > Journal > ClientJavaScript > Journal Editor - Refresh** snippet. The snippet includes all the code necessary for creating the link and can just be dropped on the selected text.

   ```
   javascript:document.JournalEditor.reset()
   ```

3. Save your page.

We're finished with this page. Try it out by choosing Edit for a particular entry from the View Journal or Journal Publisher page; use only test entries, however, as you'll note that if you elect to update the record—even without making changes—the time/date stamp is updated.

There's just one more page to complete for the entire recipe: Journal Archive.

User Recipe: Journal Archive

As you can imagine, an ongoing journal can build up a lot of entries very quickly. The archive feature of our recipe is designed to keep the journal manageable, showing entries from only the most current period initially, but making past periods—whether it's a day, week, or month—accessible.

The Archive page closely resembles the Journal page, with one important difference: A drop-down list displays all the periods in which journal entries have been posted. For example, if a journal is set to archive monthly and entries were posted in July and September but not August, only July and September are listed. When the user chooses a particular period, those entries are retrieved and displayed on the same page in the view journal format used throughout the application.

From a coding perspective, the archive manipulation is by far the most complex and interesting aspect of the page. In addition to the two recordsets previously used (Journal and Entries), a third recordset—TimePeriods—examines the full list of entries and separates them by their different periods. Achieving this functionality will require some custom variables to set the specific periods as well as a bit of client-side JavaScript to trigger the recordset update.

Step 1: Implement Journal Archive Design

As noted, this page closely resembles the Journal page. The layout calls for a top section providing details about the current journal and a bottom section displaying a repeated region filled with the applicable entries. The key—in fact, the only—form element in this page is a list; JavaScript is used to submit the form, thus avoiding the unnecessary addition of a form button.

1. Create a page for the View Journal recipe, either from a template or from the File > New dialog.

    📖 In the **Journal** folder, locate the folder for your server model and open the archive page there.

2. In the content area of your page, create a header for the page and an area to hold both the general journal information and the specific entries.

    📖 From the Snippets panel, drag the **Recipes > Journal > Wireframes > Journal Archive - Wireframe** snippet into the Content editable region.

3. Add labels and table cells to hold the journal information (name, owner, and description) as well as a form element for the time periods and, below that, a two-row, two-column table for the journal entries.

> Place your cursor in the first row below the words VIEW JOURNAL ARCHIVES and insert the **Recipes > Journal > Forms > Journal Archive Info - Form** snippet.

> Place your cursor in the bottom row of the wireframe and insert the **Recipes > Journal > ContentTables > View Journal - Content Table** snippet.

4. Save the page [r7-15].

r7-15

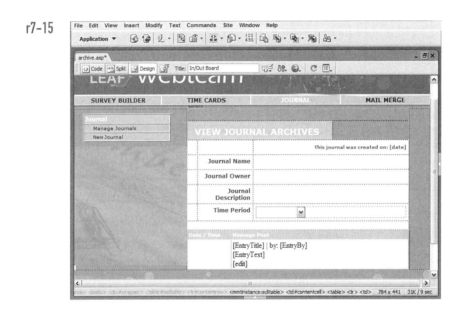

Step 2: Add Database Components: Part 1

Of the recordsets required for the Archive page, ASP and ColdFusion users will recognize the first two as being used in previous pages in this application. PHP coders will find their recordset setup to be a bit more elaborate to better handle the archive date manipulation functionality.

In this step, we'll initially create the Journal and Entries recordsets. A bit later in the recipe, we'll create the TimePeriods recordset to work with the drop-down list as a filter for the Entries recordset.

For ASP and ColdFusion

1. From the Bindings panel, choose Add (+) and select **Recordset**.
2. In the dialog's simple view, enter an appropriate name for the recordset.

   ⌨ Enter **Journal** in the Name field.

3. Choose a connection (data source) to use.

   ⌨ Select **Recipes** from the Connection list.

4. Choose the table in the data source to work with.

   ⌨ Select **Journals** from the Table list.

5. Leave the Columns option set to All.
6. In the Filter area of the Recordset dialog, set the four Filter list elements like this:

JournalID	= (Equals)
URL Parameter	ID

7. Leave the Sort option set to None and click OK to close the dialog.

Now, we'll insert the Entries recordset from which we'll gather the journal entries for display at the bottom of the page.

1. From the Bindings panel, choose Add (+) and select **Recordset**.
2. In the dialog's simple view, enter an appropriate name for the recordset.

   ⌨ Enter **Entries** in the Name field.

3. Choose a connection (data source) to use.

   ⌨ Select **Recipes** from the Connection list.

4. Choose the table in the data source to work with.

   ⌨ Select **JournalEntries** from the Table list.

5. Leave the Columns option set to All.
6. In the Filter area of the Recordset dialog, set the four Filter list elements like this:

EntryJournal	= (Equals)
URL Parameter	ID

7. Leave the Sort option set to None and click OK to close the dialog.

For PHP

> 📖 If you're following our recipe, before you begin this step, copy the SQL code from the provided snippet. Right-click (Control-click) on **Recipes > Journal > SQL > Journal RS SQL - PHP** and select **Copy Snippet** from the context menu.

1. From the Bindings panel, choose Add (+) and select **Recordset (Query)** from the list.
2. In the Recordset dialog, choose **Advanced**.
3. Enter an appropriate name for the recordset.

   > 📖 Enter **Journal** in the Name field.

4. Select the desired data source.

   > 📖 Choose **Recipes** from the Connections list.

5. In the SQL area, enter the following code:

   > 📖 Paste the copied code in the SQL area by pressing Ctrl-V (Command-V).

   ```
   SELECT unix_timestamp(JournalDate) AS JournalTimeStamp, JournalID,
   ➥ JournalTitle, JournalOwner, JournalDescription, JournalArchive
   FROM journals
   WHERE JournalID = IDParam
   ```

The unix_timestamp() function is used to turn the JournalDate field from datetime format so that it can be easily manipulated into different formats using the PHP date() command.

Now we'll add a variable, one for each of the session variables.

1. In the Variables section, choose Add (+) and enter the following details in the Add Parameter dialog:

Name:	IDParam
Default Value:	1
Run-time Value:	$_GET['ID']

2. Click OK to close the dialog and insert the recordset.

Let's follow much the same process to create the Entries recordset:

> 📖 In preparation, you'll need to copy the SQL code from the provided snippet. Right-click (Control-click) on **Recipes > Journal > SQL > Entries RS SQL - PHP** and select **Copy Snippet** from the context menu.

1. From the Bindings panel, choose Add (+) and select **Recordset** (**Query**) from the list.

2. In the Recordset dialog, choose **Advanced**.

3. Enter an appropriate name for the recordset.

   📕 Enter **Entries** in the Name field.

4. Select the desired data source.

   📕 Choose **Recipes** from the Connections list.

5. In the SQL area, enter the following code:

   📕 Paste the copied code in the SQL area by pressing Ctrl-V (Command-V).

   ```
   SELECT EntryID, EntryJournal, EntryBy, EntryTitle, EntryText,
   ➥unix_timestamp(EntryDate) AS EntryDateTimeStamp
   FROM JournalEntries
   WHERE EntryJournal = IDParam ArchiveWhere
   ```

The ArchiveWhere variable will be coded later in the recipe, but we still need to set it up as well as IDParam.

1. In the Variables section, choose Add (+) and enter the following details in the Add Parameter dialog:

Name:	IDParam
Default Value:	1
Run-time Value:	$_GET['ID']

2. Click OK to close the Add Parameter dialog and then choose Add (+) and enter the following details for the second variable:

Name:	ArchiveWhere
Default Value:	;
Run-time Value:	$ArchiveWhere

The semicolon used as the default value for the ArchiveWhere variable ensures that the PHP code will end properly regardless of the variable value.

3. Click OK to close the dialog and insert the recordset.

4. Save your page.

Step 3: Add Database Components: Part 2

The final recordset for the Archive page requires a bit more finesse than the others used here and includes a technique not seen in any of the other applications in this book. The TimePeriods recordset contains a set of periods drawn from a given journal that contain entries. What makes this recordset special is that the period itself (day, week, or month) varies according to the archive period specified for the journal. Thus, one of the actual fields returned by the SQL statement is set up as a variable. Here's the ASP version of the SQL:

```
SELECT DISTINCT (PeriodField) AS Period, ArchPeriod AS IncludeDate
FROM JournalArchiveDates
WHERE EntryJournal = IDParam
ORDER BY ArchPeriod DESC
```

NOTE As noted, this step is only required for ASP and ColdFusion.

Placing (PeriodField) in parentheses designates it as a variable. Later in the recipe, we'll include some custom code for setting the variable properly. Now, we can start by inserting the recordset.

For ASP

    📖 In preparation, you'll need to copy the SQL code from the provided snippet. Right-click (Control-click) on the **Recipes > Journal > SQL > TimePeriods RS – ASP** snippet and select **Copy Snippet** from the context menu.

1. From the Bindings panel, choose Add (+) and select **Recordset (Query)** from the list.

2. In the advanced view of the Recordset dialog, enter an appropriate name for the recordset.

    📖 Enter **TimePeriods** in the Name field.

3. Select the desired data source.

    📖 Choose **Recipes** from the Connections list.

4. In the SQL area, enter the following code:

    📖 Paste the copied code in the SQL area by pressing Ctrl-V (Command-V).

```
SELECT DISTINCT (PeriodField) AS Period, ArchPeriod AS IncludeDate
FROM JournalArchiveDates
WHERE EntryJournal = IDParam
ORDER BY ArchPeriod DESC
```

We'll need to declare three variables seen in the SQL: `IDParam`, `PeriodField`, and `ArchPeriod`.

1. In the Variable area, choose Add (+) to declare the first variable.
2. Enter the name for the variable.

   📖 In the Name column, enter **IDParam**.
3. Enter a default value for the variable.

   📖 In the Default Value column, enter **1**.
4. Enter a run-time value for the variable.

   📖 In the Run-time Value column, enter **Journal.Fields("JournalID").value.**
5. In the Variable area, choose Add (+) again to declare the second variable.
6. Enter the name for the variable.

   📖 In the Name column, enter **PeriodField**.
7. Enter a default value for the variable.

   📖 In the Default Value column, enter **Month**.
8. Enter a run-time value for the variable.

   📖 In the Run-time Value column, enter **PeriodColumn**.
9. In the Variable area, choose Add (+) one more time to declare the last variable.
10. Enter the name for the variable.

    📖 In the Name column, enter **ArchPeriod**.
11. Enter a default value for the variable.

    📖 In the Default Value column, enter **Date3**.
12. Enter a run-time value for the variable.

    📖 In the Run-time Value column, enter **ArchPeriod**.
13. Click OK to close the dialog and then save your page.

For ColdFusion

Unfortunately, the ColdFusion implementation in Dreamweaver MX 2004 isn't properly set up to handle SQL queries with dynamic variables. If you attempt to enter the needed SQL in the recordset dialog, an error is displayed. To work around this issue, we'll drop our recordset code and `<cfparam>` tags in by hand.

The `TimePeriods` recordset must be placed after the `Journal` recordset and before the `Entries` one for all the pieces to work properly together.

1. From the Server Behaviors panel, select the **Entries** recordset.
2. Switch to Code view and move the cursor before the selected recordset.
3. Insert the following code:

   ⎙ From the Snippets panel, insert the **Recipes > Journal > CustomCode_CF > TimePeriods RS** snippet.

   ```
   SELECT DISTINCT (#PeriodColumn#) AS Period, #ArchPeriod#
   ➥AS IncludeDate
   FROM JournalArchiveDates
   WHERE EntryJournal = #IDparam#
   ORDER BY #ArchPeriod# DESC
   ```

4. Place the cursor near the top of the page after the other <cfparam> statements and insert the following code:

   ⎙ From the Snippets panel, insert the **Recipes > Journal > CustomCode_CF > TimePeriods RS - SQL Parameters** snippet.

   ```
   <cfparam name="PeriodColumn" default="Month">
   <cfparam name="ArchPeriod" default="Date1">
   <cfparam name="IDparam" default="#Form.ID#">
   ```

> **NOTE** You'll need to hold off on testing the page until it is complete for the variables to work properly.

5. Save your page.

For PHP

⎙ If you're following our recipe, before you begin this step, copy the SQL code from the provided snippet. Right-click (Control-click) on **Recipes > Journal > SQL > TimePeriods RS - PHP** and select **Copy Snippet** from the context menu.

1. From the Bindings panel, choose Add (+) and select **Recordset (Query)** from the list.
2. In the Recordset dialog, choose **Advanced**.
3. Enter an appropriate name for the recordset.

   ⎙ Enter **TimePeriods** in the Name field.

4. Select the desired data source.

   ⎙ Choose **Recipes** from the Connections list.

5. In the SQL area, enter the following code:

   ⎙ Paste the copied code in the SQL area by pressing Ctrl-V (Command-V).

   ```
   SELECT EntryID, EntryJournal, EntryBy, EntryTitle, EntryText,
   ➥unix_timestamp(EntryDate) AS EntryDateTimeStamp
   FROM JournalEntries
   WHERE EntryJournal = IDParam
   ORDER BY unix_timestamp(EntryDate) ASC
   ```

The unix_timestamp() function is used to turn the JournalDate field from datetime format so that it can be easily manipulated into different formats using the PHP date() command.

Now we'll add a variable for the session variables.

1. In the Variables section, choose Add (+) and enter the following details in the Add Parameter dialog:

Name:	IDParam
Default Value:	1
Run-time Value:	$_GET['ID']

2. Click OK to close the dialog and insert the recordset.
3. Save your page when you're ready.

Step 4: Data Binding Process

Now that our recordsets are defined, we can integrate the data into the page.

1. From the Bindings panel, expand the **Journal** recordset.
2. Place the data source fields onto the page in their respective areas:

     Drag **JournalTitle** in the cell next to the Journal Name label.

     Drag **JournalOwner** in the cell next to the Journal Owner label.

     Drag **JournalDescription** in the cell next to the Journal Description label.

   (VB) (JS) (CF) Select the term [**date**] in the placeholder text at the top of the content area and drag JournalDate from the Bindings panel onto the selection.

   (PHP) Delete the selection and insert the **Recipes > Journal > CustomCode_PHP > Journal Archive – Insert Journal Date** snippet, which contains the following code:

   (PHP)
   ```
   <?php echo date("m/d/Y",$row_Journal['JournalTimeStamp']); ?>
   ```

3. Save the page.

Now, let's add the data fields from the Entries recordset.

1. From the Bindings panel, expand the **Entries** recordset.

2. Place the data source fields onto the page in their respective areas:

   📖 Select the term **[EntryTitle]** in the placeholder text at the top of the content area and drag `EntryTitle` from the Bindings panel onto the selection.

   Select the term **[EntryBy]** in the placeholder text at the top of the content area and drag `EntryBy` from the Bindings panel onto the selection.

   Select the term **[EntryText]** in the placeholder text at the top of the content area and drag `EntryText` from the Bindings panel onto the selection.

(VB) (JS) (CF) Drag EntryDate in the cell below the Date / Time label.

   (PHP) Insert the **Recipes > Journal > CustomCode_PHP > Journal Archive – Insert Entry Date** snippet, which contains the following code:

   (PHP)
```php
<?php echo date("m/d/Y h:i A",$row_Entries['EntryDateTimeStamp']);
?>
```

3. Save the page [r7-16].

r7-16

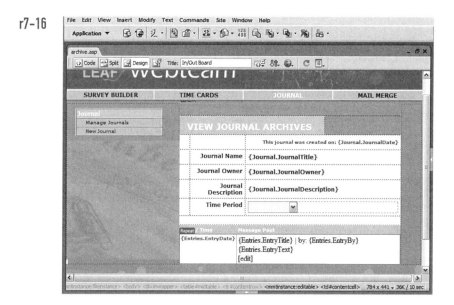

As we've done in other pages in this application, we'll now create a link for editing a listed entry.

1. Select the text or image you want to serve as the link.

   📖 Choose the text **[edit]** below the Journal Description label.

2. Select the folder symbol next to the Link field in the Property inspector.

   The Select File dialog opens.

3. Choose **Parameters** at the bottom of the dialog.

4. In the Name column of the Parameters dialog, enter the variable name.

   📖 Enter **ID** in the Name column.

5. In the Value column, enter the dynamic value of the current survey's ID.

   📖 Select the lightning bolt next to the Value column and, from the Dynamic Data dialog, choose **JournalID** from the `Journal` recordset. When you're done, click OK once to close the Dynamic Data dialog.

6. Choose Add (+) to insert another parameter.

7. Enter a name for the entry ID variable in the Name column.

   📖 Enter **EditID** in the Name column.

8. Insert the following code in the Value column:

   (VB) `<=%Request("ID")%>`

   (JS) `<=%Request("ID")%>`

   (CF) `<cfoutput>#Request.ID#</cfoutput>`

   (PHP) `<?php echo $_GET['ID']; ?>`

9. In the Select File dialog, select the file that will be used to edit the survey information.

   📖 Choose **journal_editor** in the Journal folder for your server model.

10. When you're done, click OK to insert the link.

11. Save your page before continuing.

Step 5: Bind Data to List

The `TimePeriod` list element plays a key role in the Archive page. Initially, the page displays the last period for which a journal's entries are available and that the list element should reflect. Our list uses a static element with the label Current Period in combination with data from the `TimePeriod` recordset, which provides all the other items in the list.

Because of the way PHP is used to work with dates, a slightly different procedure is used in that server model. Much of the functionality of our approach is built into the form element through custom code.

For ASP and ColdFusion

1. Select the **TimePeriod** form element.
2. From the Property inspector, choose **Dynamic**.
3. In the Dynamic List/Menu dialog, choose Add (+) in the Static Options area to add a new list item.
4. Delete the value placeholder and enter **Current Period** in the Label column.

    By entering an empty static value, this ensures that the more recent archive timespan—the current period, in other words—is the first entry available in the list.
5. From the Options from Recordset list, choose **TimePeriods**.
7. Select **IncludeDate** from the Values list.
8. Select **Period** from the Labels list.
9. In the Set Value Equal To field, enter the following code:

    VB `<%= Request("TimePeriod") %>`

    JS `<%= String(new Date(Request("TimePeriod"))) %>`

    CF `<%= String(new Date(Request("TimePeriod"))) %>`

10. Save your page.

For PHP

We'll be replacing the entire list/menu with some custom code to manipulate the dates in PHP in a way not possible with MySQL. To complete this action, we'll need to make sure that the form calls the same page with new parameters when the menu is changed.

1. Select the **TimePeriod** list element and switch to Code view.
2. Insert the following code between the `<select></select>` tag pair:

    PHP From the Snippets panel, insert the **Recipes > Journal > CustomCode_PHP > Journal Archive – Time Period Menu** snippet.

```php
<?php
foreach($dataArray as $temp){
  $tempArray = explode("*",$temp);
  if($tempArray[1] == $_POST['TimePeriod']){
    echo "<option value='" . $tempArray[1] . "' selected>"
    ➥.$tempArray[0] . "</option>";
  } else {
```

```
            echo "<option value='" . $tempArray[1] . "'>"
         ➥.$tempArray[0] . "</option>";
            }
      }
      ?>
```

3. In Design view, select the form tag from the Tag Selector.
4. In the Property inspector, enter the following code in the Action field:

   (PHP) `archive.php?ID=<?php echo $_GET['ID']; ?>`

5. Save your page.

Step 6: Add Repeat Region

The Repeat Region server behavior is used to show all the entries in the selected period of the current journal.

1. Select any of the dynamic data fields in the entries content area.
2. From the Tag Selector, choose the table row tag.

      📖 Select the **<tr>** tag from the Tag Selector.
3. From the Server Behaviors panel, choose Add (+) and select **Repeat Region.**
4. In the Repeat Region dialog, choose the desired recordset.

      📖 Choose **Entries** from the Recordset list.
5. Set the Show option to display however many records you want.

      📖 Choose **Show All Records.**
6. Click OK when you're done and save your page.

Step 7: Move TimePeriods Recordset

The `TimePeriods` recordset relies on values derived from the `Journal` recordset and, in turn, passes other values onto the `Entries` recordset. To fully carry out its functions, the `TimePeriod` recordset needs to be moved from its current location and placed after the `Journal` recordset and before the `Entries` recordset.

1. From the Server Behaviors panel, select the **TimePeriods** recordset.
2. In Code view, extend the selection to include the three associated parameters and cut it.

   📖 The selected code should include:

   `VB`

```
<%
Dim TimePeriods__IDParam
TimePeriods__IDParam = "10"
If (Journal.Fields("JournalID").value <> "") Then
  TimePeriods__IDParam = Journal.Fields("JournalID").value
End If
%>
<%
Dim TimePeriods__PeriodField
TimePeriods__PeriodField = "Month"
If (PeriodColumn <> "") Then
  TimePeriods__PeriodField - PeriodColumn
End If
%>
<%
Dim TimePeriods__ArchPeriod
TimePeriods__ArchPeriod = "Date3"
If (ArchPeriod <> "") Then
  TimePeriods__ArchPeriod = ArchPeriod
End If
%>
<%
Dim TimePeriods
Dim TimePeriods_numRows
Set TimePeriods = Server.CreateObject("ADODB.Recordset")
TimePeriods.ActiveConnection = MM_Recipes_VB_STRING
TimePeriods.Source = "SELECT DISTINCT (" +
➥Replace(TimePeriods__PeriodField, "'", "''") + ")
➥AS Period, " + Replace(TimePeriods__ArchPeriod, "'", "''") +
➥" AS IncludeDate FROM JournalArchiveDates WHERE EntryJournal =
➥ " + Replace(TimePeriods__IDParam, "'", "''") + " ORDER BY " +
➥Replace(TimePeriods__ArchPeriod, "'", "''") + " DESC"
TimePeriods.CursorType = 0
TimePeriods.CursorLocation = 2
TimePeriods.LockType = 1
TimePeriods.Open()
TimePeriods_numRows = 0
%>
```

```
JS  <%
    var TimePeriods__IDParam = "10";
    if (String(Journal.Fields("JournalID").value) != "undefined" &&
    String(Journal.Fields("JournalID").value) != "") {
    TimePeriods__IDParam = String(Journal.Fields("JournalID").value);
    }
    %>
    <%
    var TimePeriods__PeriodField = "Month";
    if (String(PeriodColumn) != "undefined" &&
    String(PeriodColumn) != "") {
    TimePeriods__PeriodField = String(PeriodColumn);
    }
    %>
    <%
    var TimePeriods__ArchPeriod = "Date3";
    if (String(ArchPeriod) != "undefined" &&
    String(ArchPeriod) != "") {
    TimePeriods__ArchPeriod = String(ArchPeriod);
    }
    %>
    <%
    var TimePeriods = Server.CreateObject("ADODB.Recordset");
    TimePeriods.ActiveConnection = MM_Recipes_STRING;
    TimePeriods.Source = "SELECT DISTINCT ("+
    ➥TimePeriods__PeriodField.replace(/'/g, "''") + ")
    ➥AS Period, "+ TimePeriods__ArchPeriod.replace(/'/g, "''") + "
    ➥AS IncludeDate FROM JournalArchiveDates WHERE EntryJournal = "+
    ➥TimePeriods__IDParam.replace(/'/g, "''") + " ORDER BY "+
    ➥TimePeriods__ArchPeriod.replace(/'/g, "''") + " DESC";
    TimePeriods.CursorType = 0;
    TimePeriods.CursorLocation = 2;
    TimePeriods.LockType = 1;
    TimePeriods.Open();
    var TimePeriods_numRows = 0;
    %>
```

```
CF  <cfquery name="TimePeriods" datasource="Recipes">
    SELECT DISTINCT (#PeriodColumn#) AS Period, #ArchPeriod#
    ➥AS IncludeDate FROM JournalArchiveDates
    WHERE EntryJournal = #IDparam# ORDER BY #ArchPeriod# DESC
    </cfquery>
```

```php
(PHP) $IDParam_Archive = "1";
      if (isset($_GET['ID'])) {
        $IDParam_Archive = (get_magic_quotes_gpc()) ?
      ➥$_GET['ID'] : addslashes($_GET['ID']);
      }
      mysql_select_db($database_Recipes, $Recipes);
      $query_Archive = sprintf("SELECT EntryID, EntryJournal, EntryBy,
      ➥EntryTitle, EntryText, unix_timestamp(EntryDate)
      ➥AS EntryDateTimeStamp FROM JournalEntries WHERE EntryJournal = %s
      ➥ORDER BY unix_timestamp(EntryDate) ASC ", $IDParam_Archive);
      $Archive = mysql_query($query_Archive, $Recipes) or
      die(mysql_error());
      $row_Archive = mysql_fetch_assoc($Archive);
      $totalRows_Archive = mysql_num_rows($Archive);
```

3. Place the cursor below the Journal recordset and press Ctrl-V (Command-V) to paste in the cut code.

4. Be sure to save your page before continuing.

Step 8: Establish Variables

With the TimePeriods recordset in the proper location, we can now place the necessary custom code. ASP and ColdFusion need only declare and define two variables (ArchPeriod and PeriodColumn) to be used. PHP, on the other hand, has a bit more to do to enable the date manipulation required.

1. In Code view, place the cursor above the just-moved TimePeriods recordset (and below the Journal recordset) and insert the following code:

   ☐ From the Snippets panel, open the **Recipes > Journal > Custom Code** folder for your server model and insert the **TimePeriod RS - Variable Declarations** snippet.

```vb
(VB)  <%
      Dim ArchPeriod, PeriodColumn
      ArchPeriod = "Date" & Journal.Fields("JournalArchive").value
      PeriodColumn = "Month"
      if (Journal.Fields("JournalArchive").value=1)
      ➥then PeriodColumn = "Day"
      if (Journal.Fields("JournalArchive").value=2)
      ➥then PeriodColumn = "Week"
      %>
```

```
JS  <%
    var ArchPeriod = "Date"+Journal.Fields("JournalArchive").value;
    var PeriodColumn = "Month";
    if (Journal.Fields("JournalArchive").value==1)
    PeriodColumn = "Day";
    if (Journal.Fields("JournalArchive").value==2)
    PeriodColumn = "Week";
    %>
```

```
CF  <cfset ArchPeriod = "Date" & Journal.JournalArchive>
    <cfset PeriodColumn = "Month">
    <cfif (Journal.JournalArchive EQ "1")>
    <cfset PeriodColumn = "Day">
    </cfif>
    <cfif (Journal.JournalArchive EQ "2")>
    <cfset PeriodColumn = "Week">
    </cfif>
```

PHP From the Snippets panel, insert the **Recipes > Journal > Custom Code_PHP >
TimePeriod Code** snippet:

```
$dataArray = "";
for($i=0;$i<$totalRows_Archive - 1;$i++){
  $date = $row_Archive['EntryDateTimeStamp'];
  $day = date("d",$date);
  $month = date("m",$date);
  $year = date("Y",$date);

  if($row_Journal['JournalArchive'] == 1){
    $label = date("D M d Y",$date);
    $startDate = mktime(0,0,0,$month,$day,$year);
    $endDate = mktime(23,59,59,$month,$day,$year);
    $value = "1/" . $startDate . "/" . $endDate;
  }
  if($row_Journal['JournalArchive'] == 2){
    $startDay = date("w",$date);
    $startWeek = mktime(0,0,0,$month,$day - $startDay,$year);
    $endWeek = mktime(0,0,0,$month,$day - $startDay + 7,$year);
    $label = date("d/m",$startWeek) . "-" . date("d/m",$endWeek)
    ➥. " " . date("Y",$endWeek);
    $value = "2/" . $startWeek . "/" . $endWeek;
  }
  if($row_Journal['JournalArchive'] == 3){
    $daysInMonth = date("t",$date);
    $startMonth = mktime(0,0,0,$month,1,$year);
    $endMonth = mktime(0,0,0,$month,$daysInMonth,$year);
```

```
        $label = date("F Y", $startMonth);
        $value = "3/" . $startMonth . "/" . date("Y-m-d",$endMonth);
      }
      $temp = $label . "*" . $value;
      if($i == 0){
        $dataArray[] = $temp;
      } else {
        if(!in_array($temp,$dataArray)){
          $dataArray[] = $temp;
        }
      }
      $row_Archive = mysql_fetch_assoc($Archive);
    }

    if(strlen($_POST['TimePeriod']) > 0){
      $tempArray = explode("/",$_POST['TimePeriod']);
      $ArchiveWhere = " AND unix_timestamp(EntryDate) < " .
    $tempArray[2]
      ➥. " AND unix_timestamp(EntryDate) > " . $tempArray[1];
    }
```

2. Save your page.

PHP users can skip the following step and proceed to the final one, Step 10.

Step 9: Add Custom SQL Clause

It's time to insert the custom WHERE clause, which adds an additional filter to the Entries recordset and effectively displays only the entries of the selected archive period. The

NOTE This step is not necessary for PHP developers as the functionality added here was integrated into the custom code added in the last step.

necessary custom code is applied in two steps: first, a separate code block is added that puts the proper values into the ArchiveWhere variable. Then a code line is inserted into the Entries recordset to integrate the ArchiveWhere filter.

1. In Code view, place the cursor before the SQL parameters associated with the Entries recordset and insert the following code:

   📖 From the Snippets panel, open the **Recipes > Journal > Custom Code** folder for your server model and insert the **Entries RS - ArchiveWhere** snippet.

VB
```
<%
Dim ArchiveWhere
ArchiveWhere = " AND EntryDate >= Date()"
if (Journal.Fields("JournalArchive").value = 2)
➥then ArchiveWhere = " AND EntryDate >= Date()-7
➥AND DatePart('ww',EntryDate) = DatePart('ww',Date())"
if (Journal.Fields("JournalArchive").value = 3)
➥then ArchiveWhere = " AND EntryDate >= Date()-31
➥AND DatePart('m',EntryDate) = DatePart('m',Date())"
%>
<%
if (cStr(Request("TimePeriod"))<>"") then
ArchiveWhere = " AND EntryDate >= #" & cStr(Request("TimePeriod"))
➥& "# AND EntryDate < #" & cStr(Request("TimePeriod")) & "# + 1"
if (Journal.Fields("JournalArchive").value = 2) then ArchiveWhere =
➥" AND EntryDate >= #"+cStr(Request("TimePeriod")) &
➥"# AND EntryDate < #" & cStr(Request("TimePeriod")) & "# + 7"
if (Journal.Fields("JournalArchive").value = 3) then ArchiveWhere =
➥" AND EntryDate >= #"+cStr(Request("TimePeriod")) &
➥"# AND EntryDate < #" & cStr(Request("TimePeriod")) &
➥"# + 31 AND DatePart('m',EntryDate) = DatePart
➥('m',#"+String(Request("TimePeriod"))+"#)"
end if
%>
```

JS
```
<%
var ArchiveWhere = " AND EntryDate >= Date()";
if (Journal.Fields("JournalArchive").value == 2)
ArchiveWhere = " AND EntryDate >= Date()-7
➥AND DatePart('ww',EntryDate) = DatePart('ww',Date())";
if (Journal.Fields("JournalArchive").value == 3)
ArchiveWhere = " AND EntryDate >= Date()-31
➥AND DatePart('m',EntryDate) = DatePart('m',Date())";
%>
<%
if (String(Request("TimePeriod"))!="undefined") {
var ArchiveWhere = " AND EntryDate >= #"+
➥String(Request("TimePeriod"))+"# AND EntryDate < #"+
➥String(Request("TimePeriod"))+"# + 1";
if (Journal.Fields("JournalArchive").value == 2)
ArchiveWhere = " AND EntryDate >= #"+String(Request("TimePeriod"))+
➥"# AND EntryDate < #"+String(Request("TimePeriod"))+"# + 7";
if (Journal.Fields("JournalArchive").value == 3)
ArchiveWhere = " AND EntryDate >= #"+String(Request("TimePeriod"))+
➥"# AND EntryDate < #"+String(Request("TimePeriod"))+"# + 31 AND
```

```
          DatePart('m',EntryDate) = DatePart('m',#"+String(Request
        ➥("TimePeriod"))+"#)";
          }
          %>
```

```
  CF   <cfset ArchiveWhere = " AND EntryDate >= Date()">
       <cfif (Journal.JournalArchive EQ 2)>
       <cfset ArchiveWhere = " AND EntryDate >= Date()-7 AND
       ➥DatePart('ww',EntryDate) = DatePart('ww',Date())">
       </cfif>
       <cfif (Journal.JournalArchive EQ 2)>
       <cfset ArchiveWhere = " AND EntryDate >= Date()-31 AND
       ➥DatePart('m',EntryDate) = DatePart('m',Date())">
       </cfif>
       <cfif isDefined("Form.TimePeriod") >
       <cfset ArchiveWhere = " AND EntryDate >= ##" & Form.TimePeriod &
       ➥"## AND EntryDate < ##" & Form.TimePeriod & "## + 1">
       <cfif (Journal.JournalArchive EQ 2)>
       <cfset ArchiveWhere = " AND EntryDate >= ##" & Form.TimePeriod &
       ➥"## AND EntryDate < ##" & Form.TimePeriod & "## + 7">
       </cfif>
       <cfif (Journal.JournalArchive EQ 3)>
       <cfset ArchiveWhere = " AND EntryDate >= ##" & Form.TimePeriod &
       ➥"## AND EntryDate < ##" & Form.TimePeriod & "## + 31 AND
       DatePart('m',EntryDate) = DatePart('m',##"+Form.TimePeriod+"##)">
       </cfif>
       </cfif>
```

2. Save your page.

The second half of this code adjustment is to append the ArchiveWhere variable, just programmed, to the proper place in the Entries recordset.

1. Locate the **Entries** recordset in Code view and place the cursor in the appropriate place to add the following code.

   📖 From the **Recipes > Journal > CustomCode** folder for your server model, insert the **Entries RS – Append ArchiveWhere** snippet.

   (VB) Place the cursor on a new line after the SQL declaration and add: **Entries.Source = Entries.Source & ArchiveWhere & " ORDER BY EntryID DESC".**

   (JS) Place the cursor on a new line after the SQL declaration and add: **Entries.Source += ArchiveWhere + " ORDER BY EntryID DESC".**

   (CF) Place the cursor at the end of the SQL declaration and add: **#ArchiveWhere# Order By EntryID DESC.**

2. Save your page when you're done.

Step 10: Activate List with JavaScript

The final step on the Archive page is to activate the Time Period drop-down list. With a bit of JavaScript and a standard Dreamweaver behavior, we'll be able to submit the form containing the list whenever the user makes a different selection from the list. After the form is submitted, a new `Entries` recordset is created, and the journal entries for the requested archive period are displayed.

1. In Design view, select the **TimePeriod** list form element.
2. From the Behaviors panel, choose Add (+) and select **Call JavaScript** from the list.
3. In the Call JavaScript dialog field, enter code to submit the current form:
   - In the JavaScript field, enter **document.ChangeTimePeriod.submit**().
4. Click OK to apply the behavior and save your page.

This page, and the entire application, are now complete and ready for testing and deployment. When browsing the Archive page, select the `TimePeriod` list to view different archives. Use the Journal navigation to visit the Journal Manager and then select view under the Archive column to inspect the archives of a different journal [r7-17].

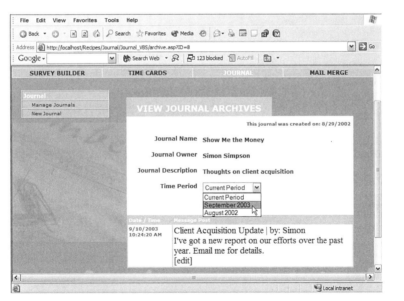

r7-17

Recipe 8

Mail Merge

Email has long been recognized as a true killer app—and it's a vital communication tool for workgroups of any size. Although individuals send email all the time, there are situations in which a mass email capability is advantageous, especially where workgroups are concerned. One advantage of a Web–application-based emailer versus individual email clients is that a history of all emails sent is maintained. Another plus is that emails can be sent to dynamically created groups.

The Mail Merge application allows workgroups to search for a group of recipients or to email a series of individuals. If the user chooses to send to a selected group, his email addresses are listed in the BCC field of the email. The email can either be composed of plain text or HTML. The user can even set the priority of the email. The application includes both a master and a detail page of email information for administrators.

The most difficult part of an email application is actually sending the email—and, with a little custom code, it's not difficult at all. After the custom email function is executed, a standard Insert Record server behavior stores the relevant data for later inspection. Our Mail Merge application includes three user-based pages and two administrator-oriented ones.

User Recipes

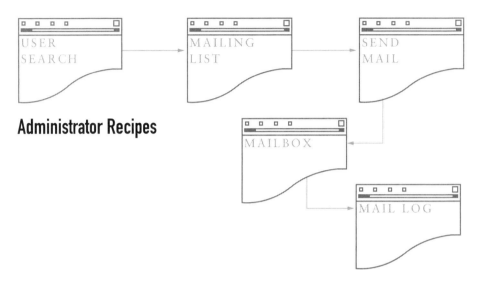

Administrator Recipes

Ingredients

5 APPLICATION PAGES:

- 2 Administration Pages
  - Mailbox
  - Mail Log
- 3 User Pages
  - Search Users
  - Mailing List
  - Send Mail

1 DATA SOURCE:

- 1 Database with:
  - 5 Tables
    - **MailMerge**—Keeps track of all the email sent by the Mail Merge application.
    - **MailPriority**—Lists the names and values for the range of mail priorities (such as Low, Medium, and High).
    - **MailType**—Holds names and values for the different types of email that are available.

- **Users**—Includes the registered user records, such as first and last name, username, password, and access group level.
- **AccessGroups**—Available access group levels in both numeric (that is, 1, 2, 3, and 4) and text format (that is, Administrator, Manager, Operator, and User).

- 1 View
  - **MailBox**—A virtual table that derives data from the three tables: MailMerge, MailPriority, and MailType.

Prep Work

Before you begin to build this application, make sure your prep work has been completed.

1. Create the data source containing the necessary tables.

   📖 ASP and ColdFusion users should use the **Recipes.mdb** data source found in the downloaded files while PHP users should work with the **Recipes** data source. For assistance in locating and installing these files, choose **Help > Web Application Recipes**.

2. Set up a connection to the data source. If you're unsure how to do this, see the "Connecting to Data Sources" section of Chapter 1.

   📖 Name the connection **Recipes**.

3. Create the template to be used for the application.

   📖 Use the template for your server model named **mailmerge**.

End User Recipe: Search Users

Perhaps the most time-consuming—and error-prone—aspect of sending email to a group of people is entering the email addresses. The Search Users page of the Mail Merge application provides an easy way to collect and apply the required addresses. Typically in a workgroup, email is either sent to individuals whose email address is known or to a specific set of people tasked with a particular job, such as managers, whose email address might not be known by the sender. The Search Users page is structured to accommodate either scenario.

You'll find that this search page is different from others in this book in several ways. First, there are two different search forms on the page: one that looks for individuals and another that concentrates on groups. Both forms have their own form buttons, but each button activates the same code—and that's the second major difference. Instead of the form just passing parameters to another page to handle the actual search, the Search Users page first places all the selected search criteria into session variables, which can be referenced throughout the application. This process has the added benefit of ensuring that the currently selected criteria will be present if the user returns to this page either through the Back button or a link. After the variables are stored, the user is redirected to the results page.

A simple recordset is used to gather the available groups for a drop-down list in one of the search forms. By attaching the list dynamically, new groups can be included as a search item as they become available, without additional coding.

Step 1: Implement Search Users Design

The obvious difference between this and most other Web application pages is that this page includes more than one form. When designing the layout for this page, make sure to completely separate the two forms by putting them in two separate table rows or divs. You'll also want to make sure that each form is named differently; the forms contained in our snippet are called SearchUsers and SearchAccessGroups, reflecting their functionality. However, for our purposes, it's important that the Submit buttons in both forms use the same name, such as Search; the identically named buttons will ensure that the same custom code is called regardless of which form is submitted.

1. In the server model of your choice, create a dynamic page.

       📖 In the **MailMerge** folder, locate the folder for your server model and open the search_users page from there.

2. Add a table to the content region of your page to contain the interface elements for the application. You'll need to make sure that the table is suitable to contain two separate forms.

       📖 From the Snippets panel, drag the **Recipes > MailMerge > Wireframes > Search Users - Wireframe** snippet into the Content editable region.

3. Insert the first form and a table with five rows and two columns; name the form SearchUsers or something similar. The left column should include the following labels: First Name, Last Name, and Email. The form should also include a form button labeled and named Search.

       📖 Place your cursor in the row below the words SEARCH USERS and insert the **Recipes > MailMerge > Forms > Search Access Group - Form** snippet.

4. Add the second form (named SearchAccessGroup or something similar) for searching the groups. The table within the form should consist of three rows and two columns. One row should include the label Access Groups and be paired with a list form element. This form should also incorporate a submit button with the name and label Search.

       📖 Place your cursor in the bottom row of the inserted table and insert the **Recipes > MailMerge > Forms > Search Users - Form** snippet [r8-1].

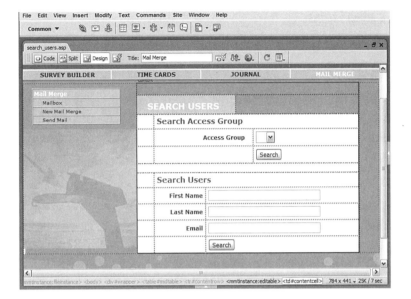

r8-1

5. Save the file.

Step 2: Add Database Components

As mentioned in the introduction to this application page, only one recordset is required. To allow the user to select any of the groups set up for access to the workgroup, we'll create a recordset that includes the names of all the groups. If access groups are not are used in your workplace, you can substitute any other group that is suitable.

> **NOTE**
> If you create this page by hand, be careful if you copy and paste the first Search button to create the second. Dreamweaver automatically adds a number to the name of the second button to distinguish the two. If this happens to you, be sure to rename the second button the same as the first.

> **NOTE**
> For more details on access groups, see the User Log In application in Recipe 1.

1. From the Bindings panel, choose Add (+) and select **Recordset (Query)**.
2. In the simple Recordset dialog, enter an appropriate name.
   - Enter **AccessGroups** in the Name field.
3. Select the desired data source connection.
   - Choose **Recipes** from the Connection (Data Source) list.
4. Choose the needed table.
   - From the Tables list, select **AccessGroups** (**accessgroups** for PHP).
5. Leave the Columns option set to All.
6. Make sure the Filter is set to None.
7. Keep the Sort option set to None and click OK to close the dialog.
8. Save the page after the recordset is inserted.

Step 3: Data Binding Process

We'll put our recordset right to use and apply it to the list element found in the Access Groups form. In addition to making the list dynamic, we'll need to add a hidden form element next to the list. The hidden form element is required for our custom code (added later in this recipe) to work properly.

Let's start by attaching the proper recordset values to the list element.

1. Select the **AccessGroup** list form element.
2. From the Property inspector, choose **Dynamic**.
3. In the Dynamic List/Menu dialog, select the lightning bolt next to the `Set Value Equal To` field.
4. In the Dynamic Data dialog, choose **AccessGroups** from the Recordset list.
5. Select **AccessGroupsID** from the Values list.
6. Select **AccessGroupName** from the Labels list.
7. Leave the `Set Value Equal To` field blank and click OK to close the Dynamic List/Menu dialog [r8-2].

r8-2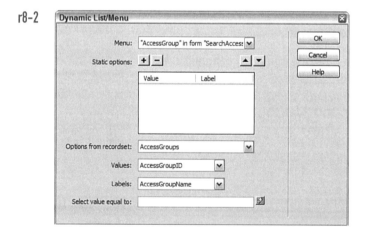

Now we'll add the hidden form element with the needed name and value.

1. Place the cursor to the right of the `AccessGroups` list element.
2. From the Forms tab of the Insert bar, choose the hidden form element.
3. In the Property inspector, enter **Email** in the Name field.
4. Enter **EmptyUsers** in the Value field.

We put this hidden form element in the Access Groups form so that our custom SQL statement (inserted later in the Mailing List page) will not find a match in the Email field when the AccessGroups list is used.

Step 4: Set Form Action

In many other search pages—including those used elsewhere in this book—the form action is set to another dynamic page, which handles the actual search depending on values passed from the initial search page. In this recipe, we're going to demonstrate an alternative approach that sets the action to the calling page—this search page—and uses custom code to redirect the user to the results page after certain session variables have been set. This "same page" method is effective when the search criteria are needed in various other pages in the application.

Because we have two search forms, we'll need to set the actions for both of them, starting with the Search Users form:

1. Place your cursor anywhere in the Search Users form.
2. In the Tag Selector, choose the **<form#SearchUsers>** tag.
3. From the Property inspector, select the folder icon and the current page.

   (VB) Choose **search_users.asp**.

   (JS) Select **search_users.asp**.

   (CF) Choose **search_users.cfm**.

   (PHP) Select **search_users.php**.

Now let's repeat the same procedure for the second form:

1. Place your cursor anywhere in the Search Access Group form.
2. In the Tag Selector, choose the **<form#SearchAccessGroup>** tag.
3. From the Property inspector, select the folder icon and the current page from the Select File dialog.

   (VB) Choose **search_users.asp**.

   (JS) Select **search_users.asp**.

   (CF) Choose **search_users.cfm**.

   (PHP) Select **search_users.php**.

Step 5: Insert Custom Code

We're now ready for the final step in this recipe: inserting the custom code. As noted throughout the recipe, the custom code serves two purposes: to set the search criteria to easily accessible session variables and to send the user to the results page.

The custom code is inserted at the top of the page. What keeps it from being called immediately? An if-then statement surrounds the code and ensures that it will be executed only when the Request string is equal to Search, which happens to be the name assigned to the Submit buttons in both forms. By naming the buttons the same (as we did at the start of this recipe), we're ensured of running the custom code when either is pressed.

1. Switch to Code view and place your cursor at the top of the page.

   ASP and PHP users should place the cursor below the connection statement.

2. Insert the following code:

   ☐ From the Snippets panel, open the **Recipes > MailMerge > CustomCode** folder for your server model and insert the **Search Users Form - Session Variables** snippet.

   VB
   ```
   <%
   if (cStr(Request("Search"))<>"") then
     Session("Search_First") = cStr(Request("FirstName"))
     Session("Search_Last") = cStr(Request("LastName"))
     Session("Search_Email") = cStr(Request("Email"))
     Session("Search_Access") = cStr(Request("AccessGroup"))
     Response.Redirect("mailing_list.asp")
   end if
   %>
   ```

   JS
   ```
   <%
   if (String(Request("Search"))!="undefined")  {
     Session("Search_First") = String(Request("FirstName"));
     Session("Search_Last") = String(Request("LastName"));
     Session("Search_Email") = String(Request("Email"));
     Session("Search_Access") = String(Request("AccessGroup"));
     Response.Redirect("mailing_list.asp");
   }
   %>
   ```

   CF
   ```
   <cfif IsDefined("Form.Search ")>
       <cfparam name="Form.FirstName" default="">
       <cfparam name="Form.LastName" default="">
       <cfparam name="Form.Email" default="">
       <cfparam name="Form.AccessGroup" default="0">
       <cfset Session.Search_First = Form.FirstName>
       <cfset Session.Search_Last = Form.LastName>
       <cfset Session.Search_Email = Form.Email>
       <cfset Session.Search_Access = Form.AccessGroup>
       <cflocation url="mailing_list.cfm">
   </cfif>
   ```

```
PHP   <?php
      session_start();
      if (isset($_POST['Search'])) {
        $_SESSION("Search_First") = $_POST['FirstName'];
        $_SESSION("Search_Last") = $_POST['LastName'];
        $_SESSION("Search_Email") = $_POST['Email'];
        $_SESSION("Search_Access") = $_POST['AccessGroup'];
        header("Location: mailing_list.php");
      }
      ?>
```

You'll note that ColdFusion requires the form elements be initialized through `<cfparam>` tags before the session variables can be set.

3. Save the file.

Your page is now ready for initial testing, but until we complete the next page in the application—Mailing List—you won't be able to see the results of your search.

End User Recipe: Mailing List Results Page

After the user selects his criteria on the search page, a list of resulting names appears on the Mailing List page. The Mailing List page allows the user to confirm the results and, if it is as expected, forward the list to the Send Mail page for emailing. Alternatively, the user can return to the Search Users page to modify the search.

The page is fairly straightforward and consists primarily of a table to hold the recordset data. A Repeat Region server behavior is used to display all the returned records. The recordset is constructed from a somewhat complex SQL statement based on the various session variables constructed in the Search Users page.

> **NOTE**
> This application does not include special handling should the search criteria return no results. You might consider such error handling as described in earlier recipes, such as Recipe 2: Employee Lookup.

Step 1: Implement Mailing List Design

Here's a straightforward page where a table-based layout for holding repeating rows of data is ideal:

1. Create a page for the Mailing List recipe, either from a template or from the **File > New** dialog.

   📖 In the **MailMerge** folder, locate the folder for your server model and open the mailing_list page there.

2. In the content area of your page, create a header for the page and an area to hold both the returned search results.

    From the Snippets panel, drag the **Recipes > MailMerge > Wireframes > Mailing List - Wireframe** snippet into the Content editable region.

3. Add labels and table cells to hold the mailing list information (name, email address, and access group) and links to the pages for sending email and searching again.

    Place your cursor in the row below the words MAILING LIST and insert the **Recipes > MailMerge > ContentTables > Mailing List - Content Table** snippet [r8-3].

r8-3

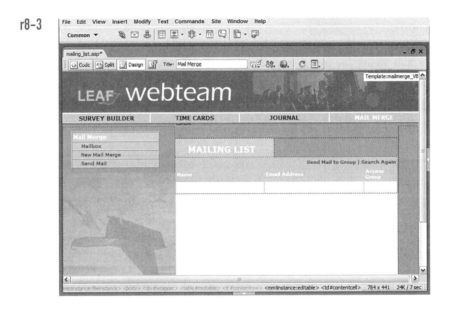

4. Save the page.

Step 2: Add Database Components

You've seen how the search criteria are placed into session variables for easy access in the Search Users page. Now we're ready to use those session variables to build a recordset of search results.

The SQL statement used in the recordset combines two tables—Users and AccessGroups—to accommodate searches either by individual or group. The session variables are incorporated into the SQL statement in different ways, depending on the server model. ASP and PHP users must establish SQL variables for each of the session variables addressed; ColdFusion users can access the session variables directly. However, in all versions, the SQL statement is constructed so that it filters results based on information entered in either of the search forms or both.

For ASP

    ☐ If you're following our recipe, before you begin this step, copy the SQL code from the provided snippet. Right-click (Ctrl-click) on **Recipes > MailMerge > SQL > Search Results – ASP** and select **Copy Snippet** from the context menu.

1. From the Bindings panel, choose Add (+) and select **Recordset (Query)** from the list.

2. In the Recordset dialog, choose **Advanced**.

3. Enter an appropriate name for the recordset.

    ☐ Enter SearchResults in the Name field.

4. Select the desired data source.

    ☐ Choose **Recipes** from the Connections list.

5. In the SQL area, enter the following code:

```
SELECT *
FROM Users Inner Join AccessGroups ON Users.UserAccess =
➥AccessGroups.AccessGroupID
WHERE UserFirstName LIKE 'FirstParam%' AND UserLastName
➥LIKE
'LastParam%' AND UserEmail LIKE 'EmailParam%'
➥OR UserAccess =
AccessParam
```

Paste the copied code in the SQL area by pressing Ctrl-V (Command-V).

Now we'll add four separate variables, one for each of the session variables.

1. In the Variables section, choose Add (+) to create a new variable.

2. Enter the name for the variable.

    ☐ In the Name column, enter **FirstParam**.

3. Enter a default value for the variable.

    ☐ In the Default Value column, enter **%**.

The percent sign acts as a wildcard allowing matches with any value if no other value is available. Wildcards are used for three of the four parameters in this recordset to match the three form fields.

4. Enter a run-time value for the variable.

In the Run-Time Value column, enter **Session("Search_First")**.

    ☐ In the Variables section, choose Add (+) to create a new variable.

5. Enter the name for the variable.

📖 In the Name column, enter **LastParam**.

6. Enter a default value for the variable.

📖 In the Default Value column, enter **%**.

7. Enter a run-time value for the variable.

In the Run-Time Value column, enter **Session("Search_Last")**.

📖 In the Variables section, choose Add (+) to create a new variable.

8. Enter the name for the variable.

📖 In the Name column, enter **EmailParam**.

9. Enter a default value for the variable.

📖 In the Default Value column, enter **%**.

10. Enter a run-time value for the variable.

In the Run-Time Value column, enter **Session("Search_Email)**.

📖 In the Variables section, choose Add (+) to create a new variable.

11. Enter the name for the variable.

📖 In the Name column, enter **AccessParam**.

12. Enter a default value for the variable.

📖 In the Default Value column, enter **0**.

13. Enter a run-time value for the variable.

In the Run-Time Value column, enter **Session("Search_Access")**.

14. Click OK to close the dialog and insert the recordset.

For ColdFusion

📖 If you're following our recipe, before you begin this step, copy the SQL code from the provided snippet. Right-click (Ctrl-click) on **Recipes > MailMerge > SQL > Search Results – CFML** and select **Copy Snippet** from the context menu.

1. From the Bindings panel, choose Add (+) and select **Recordset (Query)**.

2. Switch to the advanced view of the dialog and enter an appropriate name for the recordset.

📖 Enter SearchResults in the Name field.

3. Choose your data source.

📖 Select **Recipes** from the Data Source list.

4. Enter a username and password if necessary.

5. In the SQL area, enter the following code:

```
SELECT *
FROM Users Inner Join AccessGroups ON Users.UserAccess =
AccessGroups.AccessGroupID
```

```
WHERE UserFirstName LIKE '#Session.Search_First#%'
➥AND UserLastName
LIKE '#Session.Search_Last#%'
AND UserEmail LIKE '#Session.Search_Email#%'
OR UserAccess = #Session.Search_Access#
```

   📖 Paste the copied code into the SQL area by pressing Ctrl-V (Command-V).

6. Verify your SQL in the Recordset dialog and click OK to close that dialog.

For PHP

   📖 If you're following our recipe, before you begin this step, copy the SQL code from the provided snippet. Right-click (Ctrl-click) on **Recipes > MailMerge > SQL > Search Results – PHP** and select **Copy Snippet** from the context menu.

1. From the Bindings panel, choose Add (+) and select **Recordset (Query)** from the list.
2. In the Recordset dialog, choose **Advanced**.
3. Enter an appropriate name for the recordset.

   📖 Enter **SearchResults** in the Name field.

4. Select the desired data source.

   📖 Choose **Recipes** from the Connections list.

5. In the SQL area, enter the following code:

```
VB   SELECT *
     FROM users Inner Join accessgroups ON users.UserAccess =
     ➥accessgroups.AccessGroupID
     WHERE UserFirstName LIKE 'FirstParam%' AND UserLastName LIKE
     'LastParam%' AND UserEmail LIKE 'EmailParam%' OR UserAccess =
     AccessParam
```

   📖 Paste the copied code in the SQL area by pressing Ctrl-V (Command-V).

Now we'll add four separate variables, one for each of the session variables.

1. In the Variables section, choose Add (+) and enter the following details in the Add Parameter dialog:

Name:	FirstParam
Default Value:	%
Run-time Value:	$_SESSION['Search_First']

The percent sign acts as a wildcard allowing matches with any value if no other value is available. Wildcards are used for all the parameters in this recordset corresponding to the text fields in the search form.

2. Click OK to close the Add Parameter dialog and then choose Add (+) and enter the following details for the second variable:

Name:	LastParam
Default Value:	%
Run-time Value:	$_SESSION['Search_Last']

3. Click OK to close the Add Parameter dialog and then choose Add (+) and enter the following details for the third variable:

Name:	EmailParam
Default Value:	%
Run-time Value:	$_SESSION['Search_Email']

4. Click OK to close the Add Parameter dialog and then choose Add (+) and enter the following details for the last variable:

Name:	AccessParam
Default Value:	0
Run-time Value:	$_SESSION['Search_Access']

5. Click OK once to close the Add Parameter dialog and then again to close Recordset dialog.

6. Be sure to save your page.

Step 3: Data Binding Process

With our recordset built, we're ready to bind the data fields to specific areas of the page. In this page, four data fields are used, representing the email recipient's first name, last name, email address, and access group.

1. From the Bindings panel, expand the **SearchResults** recordset.
2. Place the desired data source fields onto the page:

   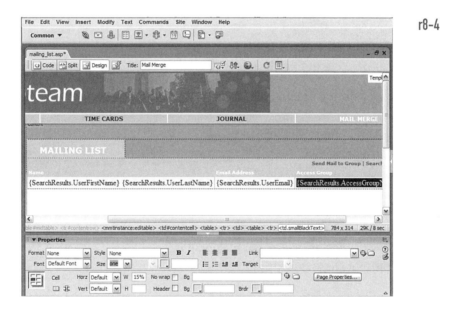 Drag the **UserFirstName** field under the Name column.

   Drag the **UserLastName** field after the UserFirstName field and add a space between the two dynamic text elements.

   Drag the **UserEmail** field under the Email Address column.

   Drag the **AccessGroupName** field under the Access Group column.

3. Save your page [r8-4].

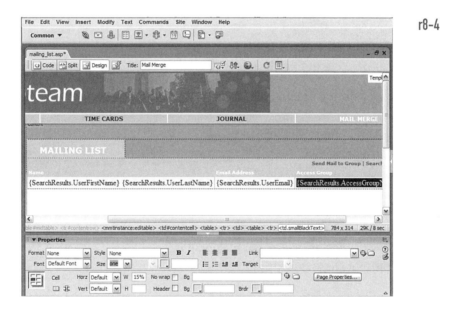

r8-4

Step 4: Add Links

After the user has checked the search results, there are two possible options: Accept the results or perform the search again. The Mailing List page provides links for both possibilities. If the results are accepted, the user would select the link to the Send Mail page to process the email. If the user decides to run the search again, a link to the Search Users page is available.

The link to the Send Mail page requires a bit of special attention. Because we want the link to be available independent of the current page, we need to pass a parameter that indicates that the recordset culled from the search results should be used. Without the parameter, the Send Mail page will open and allow individual email addresses to be entered by hand.

Let's create the link to the Send Mail page first:

1. Select the text or image you want to link to the page that actually sends the email.

    📖 Select the **Send Mail to Group** text.

2. In the Property inspector, select the folder icon next to the Link field to open the Select File dialog.

3. In the Select File dialog, select **Parameters** to begin the process of attaching a name/value pair to the URL.

4. In the Parameters dialog, choose Add (+) and enter the name of the variable you want to pass.

    📖 Enter **UseRS** in the Name column.

5. Insert the value you want to attach to the link.

    📖 Enter **1** in the Value column.

6. Click OK to close the Parameters dialog.

7. Select the file you want to link to.

    (VB) Select **send_mail.asp**.

    (JS) Select **send_mail.asp**.

    (CF) Select **send_mail.cfm**.

    (PHP) Select **send_mail.php**.

8. Click OK to close the Select File dialog.

Now let's create a simple link to the Search Users page. This link effectively replicates the browser's Back button action, but including it indicates the second of the two possible actions the user can choose.

1. Select the text or image you want to serve as a link to the search page.

    📖 Select the **Search Again** text.

2. In the Property inspector, select the folder icon to open the Select File dialog.

3. Choose the search page for your server model.

    (VB) Select **search_users.asp**.

    (JS) Select **search_users.asp**.

    (CF) Select **search_users.cfm**.

    (PHP) Select **search_users.php**.

Step 5: Add Repeat Region

Our final step in the Mailing List recipe is to wrap a Repeat Region server behavior around the embedded data fields.

1. Select any of the dynamic data fields inserted into the mailing list content area.
2. From the Tag Selector, choose the **table row tag**.
   - Select the **<tr>** tag from the Tag Selector.
3. From the Server Behaviors panel, choose Add (+) and select **Repeat Region**.
4. In the Repeat Region dialog, choose the desired recordset.
   - Choose **SearchResults** from the Recordset list.
5. Set the Show option to display the number of records you would like.
   - Choose **Show All Records**.
6. Click OK when you're done and save your page.

End User Recipe: Send Mail

The Send Mail page is the real workhorse of the application and the only page that includes code for sending email. You'll find the Send Mail page to be fairly flexible; you can use it to send email to a group selected via the Search User page or enter one or more email addresses manually—or both. Besides fields for the standard From, To, Subject, and Body text, you can also use the Send Mail page to specify the email's priority, send CCs and BCCs, and even choose between plain and HTML text. There are, however, no HTML formatting tools, so you'll either need to write the code or perform a Copy HTML operation in Dreamweaver and paste in the code.

If you're using the Send Mail page in concert with the Search User and Mailing List pages developed earlier in this recipe, the email addresses will be supplied for you. After you select the Send Mail to Group link on the Mailing List page, the Send Mail page appears with the search results displayed in the BCC field. Using the BCC field ensures that no one except the sender will know all the recipient's addresses.

Constructing the page requires a recordset copied from a previously built page (Mailing List) and several snippets of additional code functions. One function inserts the search results into the BCC field while another handles the actual sending of the email.

There is one important limitation to applying this recipe. The server that is hosting the application must have an SMTP server accessible. With ASP, the CDONTS module

NOTE

Although ColdFusion and PHP include their own mail protocols—CFMAIL and mail(), respectively—there are numerous ways to send email in the ASP world. ASP coders will find that this recipe is designed to work both with CDONTS, a standard module in Windows NT and Windows 2000 servers, and CDOSYS, used if your site is hosted on a Windows 2003 server or you are testing on a Windows XP system.

(used to send the email) only allows email to be sent from the server's own SMTP address to prevent unauthorized use. This means that the SMTP address does not have to be supplied for ASP users. However, it also means that if the user is outside a firewall, he will not be able to run the application unless he is able to utilize a virtual private network (VPN). ColdFusion users will need to supply their own SMTP server address.

Step 1: Implement Send Email Design

Like many application pages, the Send Email layout is based on a form. In the form, you'll need a variety of form elements, mostly text fields, to contain all the email information. Radio buttons are also used to offer a choice between plain text and HTML-formatted email, and a drop-down list provides the priority options. In addition, two hidden form elements are needed to properly track the number of emails sent and to pass along a needed parameter.

1. In the server model of your choice, create a dynamic page.

   ◻ In the **MailMerge** folder, locate the folder for your server model and open the send_mail page from there.

2. Add a table to the content region of your page to contain the interface elements for the application.

   ◻ From the Snippets panel, drag the **Recipes > MailMerge > Wireframes > Send Mail - Wireframe** snippet into the Content editable region.

3. Insert the form and, within it, a table with nine rows and two columns; name the form SendMail or something similar. The left column should include the following labels: Email Type, Email Priority, From, To, CC, BCC, Subject, and Body. Use radio buttons to offer two email type options: Plain Text and HTML. A drop-down list should include three email priorities: High, Normal, and Low. The rest of the form elements should be standard text fields with the exception of the Body, which should be a multiline text field (also known as a textarea). The form should also include a form button named SendMail and two hidden form elements: TotalRecords and UseRS.

   ◻ Place your cursor in the row below the words SEND MAIL and insert the **Recipes > MailMerge > Forms > Send Mail - Form** snippet [r8-5].

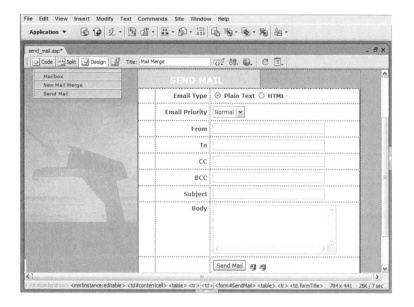

r8-5

4. Save the file.

Step 2: Add Database Components

Here's an example of a time-saving Dreamweaver feature put to good use. The recordset required for this page is a near-duplicate of the one created for the Mailing List page. We can save a great deal of time by copying the recordset on that page and pasting it in this one; if you remember, that SQL statement was fairly complex and required numerous variables. After it's inserted, we can append a small bit of SQL to custom-fit the recordset for the current page.

The code added appends the UseRS URL variable to the SQL statement. Our custom code is designed so that if this value is not equal to 1, then the recordset will not return results. This enables a user to access this page directly and send a single email.

> **You'll need to make sure that you've completed the Mailing List page before proceeding.**
>
> NOTE

First, let's copy the previously built recordset into the current page:

1. Open the **Mailing List** page in Dreamweaver.
2. In the Bindings panel, right-click (Ctrl-click) the SearchResults recordset to display the context menu and choose **Copy**.

3. Switch to the Send Mail page.

4. In the Bindings panel, right-click (Ctrl-click) and choose **Paste** from the context menu.

Now we're ready to customize the recordset by appending a bit of code to the SQL statement and adding a new variable:

1. Double-click the **SearchResults** recordset in the Bindings panel to open the Recordset dialog.

2. Place your cursor at the end of the SQL statement and enter the following code:

   (VB) AND UseRSParam = 1

   (JS) AND UseRSParam = 1

   (CF) AND #URL.UseRS# = 1

   (PHP) AND UseRSParam = 1

3. Add a new variable to the recordset definition:

   (VB) In the Variable area, choose Add (+) and enter **UseRSParam** in the Name column, 0 in the Default Value column, and **Request("UseRS")** in the Run-Time Value column.

   (JS) In the Variable area, choose Add (+) and enter **UseRSParam** in the Name column, 0 in the Default Value column, and **Request("UseRS")** in the Run-Time Value column.

   (CF) In the Variable area, choose Add (+) and select **URL.UseRS** from the Name list, and enter 0 in the Default Value column.

   (PHP) In the Variable area, choose Add (+) and enter **UseRSParam** in the Name column, 0 in the Default Value column, and **$_REQUEST['UseRS']** in the Run-Time Value column.

4. Click OK to close the dialog and insert the amended recordset.

Step 3: Data Binding Process

The data binding process differs from the typical drag-and-drop operation this time around. Instead of dragging data fields from the Bindings panel, we need to enter code using the Property inspector both manually and by using the Dynamic Data dialog. Our first task is to assign a variable to the Init Value property of the BCC text field; this variable is used to contain the search results displayed in the Mailing List page. We'll also need to set the values of the two hidden form fields for our application page to work properly: one to tell us whether or not to use the recordset (UseRS), and another to hold the total number of results returned by the search (TotalSearch).

Let's tackle the initial value of the BCC field first:

1. Select the **BCC** field.
2. In the Property inspector, enter the following code in the Init Value field:

   (VB) `<%=BCCList%>`

   (JS) `<%=BCCList%>`

   (CF) `<cfoutput>#BCCList#</cfoutput>`

   (PHP) `<?php echo $BCCList; ?>`

3. Press Tab to confirm your code entry.

Now let's add dynamic values to the two hidden form elements, starting with the UseRS element.

1. Select the **UseRS** hidden form element.
2. In the Value field of the Property inspector, enter the following code:

   (VB) `<%=Request("UseRS")%>`

   (JS) `<%=Request("UseRS")%>`

   (CF) `<cfoutput>#URL.UseRS#</cfoutput>`

   (PHP) `<?php echo $_REQUEST['UseRS']; ?>`

3. Press Tab to confirm your entry.

Finally, we'll make the TotalSearch hidden form element dynamic.

For ASP

1. Select the **TotalSearch** hidden form element.
2. Choose the lightning bolt symbol next to the Value field to open the Dynamic Data dialog.
3. If necessary, expand the **SearchResults** recordset in the Dynamic Data dialog.
4. Choose the [**total records**] entry and click OK to close the dialog.

For ColdFusion

1. Select the **TotalSearch** hidden form element.
2. Enter the following code in the `Value` field:

   `CF` `<cfoutput>#SearchResults.RecordCount#</cfoutput>`

3. Tab or click anywhere to confirm your code entry.

For PHP

1. Select the **TotalSearch** hidden form element.
2. Enter the following code in the Value field:

   `PHP` `<?php echo $totalRows_SearchResults; ?>`

3. Tab or click anywhere to confirm your code entry.

Step 4: Insert Record: Send Mail

Although it's great to be able to use the Web to send email, it's even better to be able to keep a record of all the email sent. In addition to actually sending the mail, this page uses an Insert Record server behavior to store transaction information in the `MailMerge` table. The remaining pages in this application, `Mailbox` and `Maillog`, display record information from the `MailMerge` table.

For ASP

1. From the Server Behaviors panel, choose Add (+) and select **Insert Record** from the list.
2. In the Insert Record dialog, choose your data source.

   ▭ Choose **Recipes** from the Connection list.
3. Select the table you want to insert the record into.

   ▭ From the Insert Into Table list, choose **MailMerge**.
4. Set the `After Inserting`, `Go To` field to the desired result page.

   ▭ Select Browse and choose **mailbox.asp** from the Select File dialog.
5. Select the form on the current page from which to gather the record values.

   ▭ From the Get Values From list, make sure `SendMail` is selected.
6. In the Form Elements area, match the form elements on the page to the fields in the data source table.

      📖 Set `EmailType` to insert into the `EmailFormat` column as Numeric type.

      Set `EmailPriority` to insert into the `EmailPriority` column as Numeric type.

      Set `From` to insert into the `EmailFrom` column as Text type.

      Set `To` to insert into the `EmailTo` column as Text type.

      Set `CC` to insert into the `EmailCC` column as Text type.

      Set `BCC` to insert into the `EmailBCC` column as Text type.

      Set `Subject` to insert into the `EmailSubject` column as Text type.

      Set `Body` to insert into the `EmailBody` column as Text type.

      Set `TotalSearch` to insert into the `EmailSize` column as Numeric type.

      Set `UseRS` to be ignored.

7. When you're sure your choices are correct, click OK to close the dialog and add the behavior.

For ColdFusion and PHP

1. From the Server Behaviors panel, choose Add (+) and select **Insert Record**.
2. In the Insert Record dialog, choose the current form.

      📖 Select **SearchResults** from the Submit Values From list.

3. Select your data source from the list.

      📖 Choose **Recipes** from the Data Source list.

4. Enter your username and password, if needed.
5. Select the table in the data source to insert into from the list.

      📖 Choose **MailMerge** (**mailmerge** for PHP) from the Insert Into Table list.

6. Set the data source fields to their corresponding form elements.

      📖 Set `EmailFormat` to the `FORM.EmailType` form element and submit as Numeric type for ColdFusion and Integer type for PHP.

      Set `EmailPriority` to the `FORM.EmailPriority` form element and submit as Numeric type for ColdFusion and Integer type for PHP.

      Set `EmailFrom` to the `FORM.From` form element and submit as Text type.

      Set `EmailTo` to the `FORM.To` form element and submit as Text type.

      Set `EmailCC` to the `FORM.CC` form element and submit as Text type.

      Set `EmailBCC` to the `FORM.BCC` form element and submit as Text type.

      Set `EmailSubject` to the `FORM.Subject` form element and submit as Text type.

      Set `EmailBody` to the `FORM.Body` form element and submit as Text type.

      Set `EmailSize` to the `FORM.TotalSearch` form element and submit as Numeric type for ColdFusion and Integer type for PHP.

      Make sure `UseRS` is set not to get a value.

7. Set the After Inserting, Go To field to the appropriate file.

   (CF) Select **mailbox.cfm**.

   (PHP) Select **mailbox.php**.

8. Confirm your entries and click OK to close the dialog and insert the code.

Step 5: Add Custom Code

The two custom functions we'll add in this step of the recipe are key. One populates the BCC field with the prior search results, whereas the other is responsible for actually sending the email.

The BCC-related function is fairly straightforward. For each server model, the function loops through the search results, gets the email address for each record, and concatenates it into one long string. The string is assigned to the BCCList variable which, you'll recall, was attached to the initial value attribute of the BCC text field.

The function to send email is somewhat more complex and specific to the various server models. For ASP, a mail object is created as an instance of the CDONTS or the CDOSYS server object. The email format type is set and mail is sent using the various text fields (To, From, BCC, and so on). CDONTS requires that the mail be sent from an SMTP (Simple Mail Transport Protocol) server found within the current domain so there's no need to specify a SMTP server.

This is not the case for ColdFusion, however, where a valid SMTP server must be declared. The SMTP server is defined within the <cfmail> tag, which also holds all the pertinent information. Additionally a CFParam variable must be defined for proper handling of the MailType field in the database.

Let's add the first of our two functions that are designed to build the BCC list:

1. From the Server Behavior panel, select the **SearchResults** recordset.

2. Switch to Code view and locate the highlighted code.

3. Move your cursor just below the recordset code and insert the following code:

   From the Snippets panel, open the **Recipes > MailMerge > Custom Code** folder for your server model and insert the **Build BCC List** snippet.

   (VB)
   ```
   <%
   Dim BCCList
   BCCList = ""
   While (NOT SearchResults.EOF AND cStr(Request("UseRS")) = "1")
     If (BCCList <> "") then BCCList = BCCList & ";"
   ```

```
        BCCList = BCCList & SearchResults.Fields("UserEmail").value
        SearchResults.MoveNext()
      Wend
      %>
```

(JS)
```
      <%
      var BCCList = "";
      while (!SearchResults.EOF && String(Request("UseRS")) == "1")  {
        if (BCCList !="")
          BCCList += ";";
        BCCList += SearchResults.Fields("UserEmail").value;
        SearchResults.MoveNext();
      }
      %>
```

(CF)
```
      <cfset BCCList = "">
      <cfif URL.UseRS EQ "1">
        <cfloop query="SearchResults">
          <cfif BCCList NEQ "">
            <cfset BCCList = BCCList & ";">
          </cfif>
          <cfset BCCList = BCCList & SearchResults.UserEmail>
        </cfloop>
      </cfif>
```

(PHP)
```
      <?php
      $BCCList = "";
      do {
        if ($BCCList != "") {
          $BCCList .= ";";
        }
        $BCCList .= $row_SearchResults['UserEmail'];
      } while (($row_SearchResults =
      mysql_fetch_assoc($SearchResults))&&($_REQUEST['UseRs']==1));
      $SearchResults = mysql_query($query_SearchResults,
      $Recipes_PHP) or die(mysql_error());
      $row_SearchResults = mysql_fetch_assoc($SearchResults);
      ?>
```

4. Save your page.

Now let's complete the page by adding the custom send mail function:

1. In Code view, position your cursor at the top of the page.

   ASP and PHP users should place their cursor after the connection statement.

2.   Insert the following code:

   ◻ From the Snippets panel, open the **Recipes > MailMerge > Custom Code** folder for your server model and insert the appropriate snippet: **Send Mail - CDONTS** or **Send Mail - CDOSYS** for ASP; **Send Mail - CFMail** for ColdFusion; and **Send Mail - PHP** for PHP.

(VB)
```
<%
    if (cStr(Request("SendMail")) <> "") then
        set mailObject = Server.CreateObject
    ➥("CDONTS.NewMail.1")

    if (cStr(Request("BCC")) <> "") then mailObject.BCC =
    ➥cStr(Request("BCC"))

    if (cStr(Request("CC")) <> "") then mailObject.CC =
    ➥cStr(Request("CC"))

     mailObject.BodyFormat = cInt(Request("EmailType"))
     mailObject.MailFormat = cInt(Request("EmailType"))

     mailObject.Send cStr(Request("From")),cStr(Request("To")),
    ➥cStr(Request("Subject")),cStr(Request("Body")),
    ➥cInt(Request("EmailPriority"))
    end if
%>
```

(JS)
```
<%
  if (String(Request("SendMail"))!="undefined")  {
    var mailObject = Server.CreateObject("CDONTS.NewMail.1");

    if (String(Request("BCC")) != "")
      mailObject.BCC = String(Request("BCC"));

    if (String(Request("CC")) != "")
      mailObject.CC = String(Request("CC"));

     mailObject.BodyFormat = parseInt(Request("EmailType"));
     mailObject.MailFormat = parseInt(Request("EmailType"));
```

```
      mailObject.Send(String(Request("From")),String(Request("To")),
      ➡String(Request("Subject")),String(Request("Body")),
      ➡parseInt(Request("EmailPriority")))
    }
    %>
```

> **NOTE** The next two code snippets are for CDOSYS.

(VB)
```
<%
if (cStr(Request("SendMail")) <> "")  then
  var sysMail = Server.CreateObject("CDO.Message")
  sysMail.Configuration.Fields("http://schemas.microsoft.com/
  ➡cdo/configuration/smtpserver") = "smtp.mycompany.com"
  sysMail.Configuration.Fields("http://schemas.microsoft.com/
  ➡cdo/configuration/sendusing") = 2
  sysMail.Configuration.Fields("http://schemas.microsoft.com/
  ➡cdo/configuration/sendusername") = ""
  sysMail.Configuration.Fields("http://schemas.microsoft.com/
  ➡cdo/configuration/sendpassword") = ""
  sysMail.Configuration.Fields.Update
  sysMail.Fields("urn:schemas:httpmail:importance") =
  ➡cInt(Request("EmailPriority"))
  sysMail.Fields.Update

  if (cStr(Request("BCC")) <> "") then
    sysMail.BCC = cStr(Request("BCC"))
  end if

  if (cStr(Request("CC")) <> "") then
    sysMail.CC = cStr(Request("CC"))
  end if

  sysMail.From = cStr(Request("From"))
  sysMail.To = cStr(Request("To"))
  sysMail.Subject = cStr(Request("Subject"))

  if (cInt(Request("EmailType")) = 0)  then
    sysMail.TextBody = cStr(Request("Body"))
  else
    sysMail.HTMLBody = cStr(Request("Body"))
  end if

  sysMail.Send
end if
%>
```

```
JS   <%
     if (String(Request("SendMail"))!="undefined")  {
       var sysMail = Server.CreateObject("CDO.Message");
       sysMail.Configuration.Fields("http://schemas.microsoft.com/
       ➥cdo/configuration/smtpserver") = "smtp.mycompany.com";
       sysMail.Configuration.Fields("http://schemas.microsoft.com/
       ➥cdo/configuration/sendusing") = 2;
       sysMail.Configuration.Fields("http://schemas.microsoft.com/
       ➥cdo/configuration/sendusername") = "";
       sysMail.Configuration.Fields("http://schemas.microsoft.com/
       ➥cdo/configuration/sendpassword") = "";
       sysMail.Configuration.Fields.Update();
       sysMail.Fields("urn:schemas:httpmail:importance") =
       ➥parseInt(Request("EmailPriority"));
       sysMail.Fields.Update();

       if (String(Request("BCC")) != "")
         sysMail.BCC = String(Request("BCC"));

       if (String(Request("CC")) != "")
         sysMail.CC = String(Request("CC"));

       sysMail.From = String(Request("From"));
       sysMail.To = String(Request("To"));
       sysMail.Subject = String(Request("Subject"));

       if (parseInt(Request("EmailType"))==0)  {
         sysMail.TextBody = String(Request("Body"));
       }
       else {
         sysMail.HTMLBody = String(Request("Body"));
       }

       sysMail.Send();
     }
     %>
```

```
CF   <cfif isDefined("Form.EmailType")>
       <cfif Form.EmailType EQ "0">
         <cfset MailType= "html">
       </cfif>
     </cfif>

     <cfif isDefined("Form.SendMail")>
       <cfmail server="smtp.webassist.com" to="#Form.To#"
```

```
     ➥from="#Form.From#" subject="#Form.Subject#" cc="#Form.CC#"
     ➥bcc="#Form.BCC#" type="#MailType#"><cfmailparam name=
     ➥"X-Priority" value="#Form.EmailPriority#">#Form.Body#</cfmail>
   </cfif>
```

(PHP)
```php
<?php
if (isset($_POST['SendMail'])) {

  if ($_POST['EmailType']==0) {
    // HTML Mail
    $headers  = "MIME-Version: 1.0\r\n";
    $headers .= "Content-type: text/html; charset=iso-8859-1\r\n";
  } else {
    $headers="";
  }
  if ($_POST['CC']!="") {
    $headers.= "Cc: " . $_POST['CC'] . "\r\n";
  }
  if ($_POST['BCC']!="") {
    $headers.= "Bcc: " . $_POST['BCC'] . "\r\n";
  }
  if ($_POST['FROM']!="") {
    $headers.= "From: " . $_POST['FROM'] . "\r\n";
  }
  switch ($_POST['EmailPriority']) {
    case 0:
      // Low Priority
      $headers .= "X-Priority: 4\n";
      break;
    case 2:
      // High Priority
      $headers .= "X-Priority: 1\n";
      break;
  }
  @mail($_POST['TO'],$_POST['Subject'],$_POST['Body'],$headers);
 z
}
?>
```

When coding for CDOSYS, ASP users should be sure to replace the generic smtp.
mycompany.com value included in the snippet with an actual SMTP server address.

3. Save the page.

As mentioned earlier, ColdFusion users require one additional step to insert a CFParam:

1. In Code view, place your cursor at the top of the page.
2. From the Bindings panel, choose Add (+) and select **CFParam** from the list.

3. In the CFParam dialog, enter **MailType** in the Name field.

4. Leaving the Default field blank, click OK to close the dialog.

This CFParam is necessary to properly store the MailType value. The database expects a boolean value (1 or 0), whereas the <cfmail> tag uses either Email or an empty string as its values. The CFParam statement works in conjunction with the custom code to convert the database values into ones the CFML tag understands.

Scaling Up Your Email

Not all organizations run their email on CDONTS, CDOSYS, or CFMAIL. Many third-party vendors—including SoftArtisans SMTPmail, Dimac w3 JMail, Persits AspEmail, and ServerObjects AspMail—offer email components for mass mailing. Each component requires a particular syntax to carry out basic emailing functionality.

For designers who are working with one or more of these systems, WebAssist provides an all-in-one email extension for Dreamweaver. Universal Email works with a full range of email components from a single interface. Designed for quick, simple setup and customization, WA Universal Email is fully loaded with premium features, such as e-commerce support and attachments.

For more information, visit
http://www.webassist.com/Products/Recipes/WA/UniversalEmail.asp

---

Administrator Recipe: Mailbox

Want to see what emails have been sent? Check your Mailbox! The Mailbox page displays a summary of all the messages previously emailed and provides a link for more detail. Summary fields include email subject, number of recipients listed, and email type (HTML or plain text).

As you saw when constructing the Send Mail page in the previous recipe, information about an email is stored in the MailMerge table. The recordset for the Mailbox page is pulled from a view based on this data table and two others (MailPriority and MailType) used to look up values. The Mailbox recordset is designed to display the newest addition first.

Step 1: Implement Mailbox Design

The Mailbox application requirements are straightforward. A basic table to hold the summary items is all that is needed. Navigation to the detail page is handled by attaching a link to one of the data fields.

1. Create a page for this recipe, from the **File > New** dialog or by using a template.

   📖 In the **MailMerge** folder, locate the folder for your server model and open the Mailbox page.

2. In the content area of your page, create a header for the page and an area for the email summary items.

   📖 From the Snippets panel, drag the **Recipes > MailMerge > Wireframes > Mailbox - Wireframe** snippet into the Content editable region.

3. Add labels for three data fields: Sent Items, Recipients, and Email Type.

   📖 Place your cursor in the row below the words MAILBOX and insert the **Recipes > MailMerge > ContentTables > Mailbox Sent Items - Content Table** snippet [r8-6].

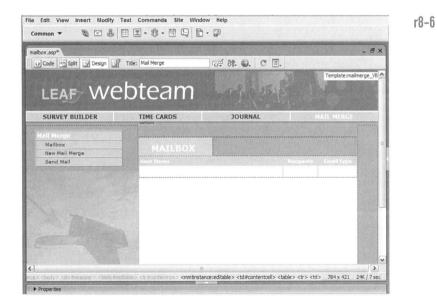

r8-6

Step 2: Add Database Component

The recordset used by the MailBox application is based on a SQL view that combines three tables: MailMerge, MailPriority, and MailType. Although the SQL statement to construct the view might seem somewhat complex, the concept is simple. The basic data is coming from the `MailMerge` table; both `MailPriority` and `MailType` are used to look up text names for numeric values.

```
SELECT MailMerge.*, MailPriority.MailPriorityText,
➥MailType.MailTypeText
FROM (MailMerge INNER JOIN MailPriority
➥ON MailMerge.EmailPriority = MailPriority.MailPriorityPassed)
➥INNER JOIN MailType ON MailMerge.EmailFormat =
MailType.MailTypePassed;
```

As we've seen before, because MySQL does not support views, PHP coders must also add a custom code snippet after creating the recordset that populates the temporary table `MailBox`.

1. From the Bindings panel, choose Add (+) and select **Recordset (Query)**.
2. In the simple Recordset dialog, enter an appropriate name.

   📖 Enter **MailBox** in the Name field.
3. Select the desired data source connection.

   📖 Choose **Recipes** from the Connection (Data Source) list.
4. Choose the needed table.

   📖 From the Tables list, select **MailBox** (**mailbox** for PHP).
5. Leave the Columns option set to All.
6. Make sure the Filter is set to None.
7. Set the Sort option to show the latest record first.

   📖 Choose **EmailID** from the Sort list and select **Descending** from the accompanying field [r8-7].

r8-7

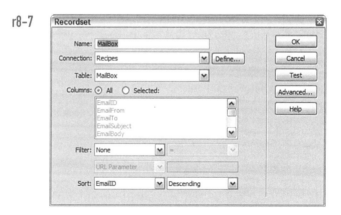

8. Click OK to close the dialog.

9. Save the page after the recordset is inserted.

The following steps are for PHP users only:

1. In Code view, move to the top of the page, place your cursor after the PHP connection line that starts `<?php require_once` and insert the following code:

   📖 From the Snippets panel, insert the **Recipes > MailMerge > CustomCode_PHP > Mailbox - Create Temporary Table** snippet.

   (PHP)
   ```php
   <?php
   mysql_select_db($database_Recipes_PHP, $Recipes_PHP);
   $sql = "DELETE FROM mailbox";
   @mysql_query($sql,$Recipes_PHP);
   $sql = "INSERT INTO mailbox SELECT mailmerge.*,
   ↪mailpriority.MailPriorityText, mailtype.MailTypeText
   FROM (mailmerge INNER JOIN mailpriority
   ↪ON mailmerge.EmailPriority = mailpriority.MailPriorityPassed)
   ↪INNER JOIN mailtype ON mailmerge.EmailFormat =
   ↪mailtype.MailTypePassed";
   @mysql_query($sql,$Recipes_PHP);
   ?>
   ```

   This code simulates an Access view and prepopulates the `Mailbox` table before the recordset information is retrieved.

2. When you're done, save your page.

Step 3: Data Binding Process

In this step, we'll bring the data fields defined in the `MailBox` recordset onto the page.

1. From the Bindings panel, expand the **MailBox** recordset.

2. Place the desired data source fields onto the page:

   📖 Drag the **EmailSubject** field under the Sent Items column.

   Drag the **EmailSize** field under the Recipients column.

   Drag the **MailTypeText** field under the Email Type column.

3. Save your page [r8-8].

r8-8

Step 4: Add Link to Subject Dynamic Text

In concept, this page is referred to as a "master" page because it shows a summary of records. Typically, some element on the master page serves as a link to the detail page, which allows the user to drill down to get more specific information about a given record. On this page, we'll use the email subject data field (inserted in the previous step) as our link; this link will call the final page in our Mail Merge application, Maillog, and pass the record's ID as a parameter.

1. Select the **EmailSubject** data field on the page.
2. In the Property inspector, select the folder icon next to the Link field to open the Select File dialog.
3. In the Select File dialog, select **Parameters** to begin the process of attaching a name/value pair to the URL.
4. In the Parameters dialog, choose Add (+) and enter the name of the variable you want to pass.

   ▢ Enter **ID** in the Name column.
5. Insert the value you want to attach to the link.

   ▢ Choose the lightning bolt symbol to open the Dynamic Data dialog and select **EmailID** from the MailBox recordset. Click OK to close the Dynamic Data dialog.
6. Click OK to close the Parameters dialog.

7. Select the file you want to link to.

    📖 Select the **mail_log** file for your server model.

8. Click OK to close the Select File dialog.

Step 5: Add Repeat Region

We'll finish off the MailBox application by applying a Repeat Region server behavior to the dynamic content.

1. Select any of the dynamic data fields inserted in the MailBox content area.

2. From the Tag Selector, choose the table row tag.

    📖 Select the **<tr>** tag from the Tag Selector.

3. From the Server Behaviors panel, choose Add (+) and select **Repeat Region**.

4. In the Repeat Region dialog, choose the desired recordset.

    📖 Choose **MailBox** from the Recordset list.

5. Set the Show option to display the number of records you'd like.

    📖 Choose **Show All Records**.

6. Click OK when you're done and save your page.

A quick check of Live Data view should give a clear idea of how the page will look [r8-9].

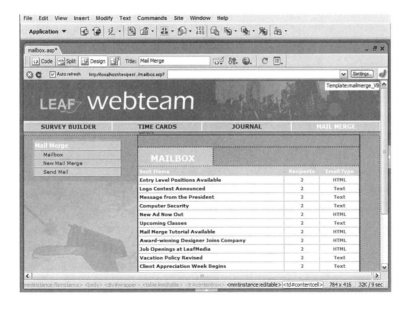

r8-9

Administrator Recipe: Mail Log

The Mail Log page displays details of the summary record selected in the just-completed Mailbox page. All information—including the message and the list of recipients—is included. A recordset is created from the MailMerge table by applying the requested record's ID as a filter.

Step 1: Implement Mail Log Design

A simple layout is all that's needed for this recipe. Here all the data fields are bound to the page as text elements, including the message body and BCC fields.

NOTE

Alternatively, you could use a text area form element to hold the message body. The data is bound to the form field in the same drag-and-drop manner; however, the text would be displayed in a set area where scrollbars are employed as needed.

1. Create a page from the **File > New** dialog or by deriving a page from a template.

      In the **MailMerge** folder, find the folder for your server model and open the maillog page.

2. In the content area of your page, create a header for the page and an area for the email details.

      From the Snippets panel, drag the **Recipes > MailMerge > Wireframes > Mail Log - Wireframe** snippet into the Content editable region.

3. Add labels for the following eight data fields: Email Type, Email Priority, From, To, CC, Subject, Body, and BCC.

      Place your cursor in the row below the words MAIL LOG and insert the **Recipes > MailMerge > ContentTables > Mail Log - Content Table** snippet [r8-10].

r8-10

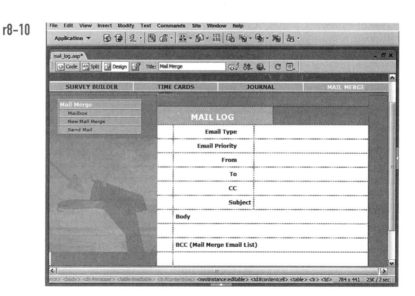

4. Save your page.

Step 2: Add Database Components

In this step, we'll take the EmailID passed as a URL parameter in the previous page and use it to filter our recordset. The MailBox data table serves as the basis for our recordset.

PHP users will need to follow up with some custom code to simulate the view used here.

1. From the Bindings panel, choose Add (+) and select **Recordset (Query)**.
2. In the simple Recordset dialog, enter an appropriate name.

       Enter **Maillog** in the Name field.
3. Select the desired data source connection.

       Choose **Recipes** from the Connection (Data Source) list.
4. Choose the needed table.

       From the Tables list, select **MailBox** (**mailbox** for PHP).
5. Leave the Columns option set to All.
6. In the Filter area of the Recordset dialog, set the four Filter list elements like this:

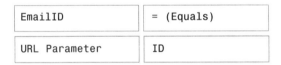

EmailID	= (Equals)
URL Parameter	ID

7. Leave the Sort option blank and click OK to close the dialog.

PHP developers need to insert a little custom code to create the view programatically.

1. In Code view, move to the top of the page, place your cursor after the PHP connection line that starts <?php require_once, and insert the following code:

       From the Snippets panel, insert the **Recipes > MailMerge > CustomCode_PHP > MailMerge - Create Temporary Table** snippet.

    (PHP)
    ```php
    <?php
    mysql_select_db($database_Recipes_PHP, $Recipes_PHP);
    $sql = "DELETE FROM mailbox";
    @mysql_query($sql,$Recipes_PHP);
    $sql = "INSERT INTO mailbox SELECT mailmerge.*,
    ➥mailpriority.MailPriorityText, mailtype.MailTypeText
    FROM (mailmerge INNER JOIN mailpriority
    ➥ON mailmerge.EmailPriority = mailpriority.MailPriorityPassed)
    ➥ INNER JOIN mailtype ON mailmerge.EmailFormat =
    ➥mailtype.MailTypePassed";
    @mysql_query($sql,$Recipes_PHP);
    ?>
    ```

2. Save your page when you're done.

This code simulates an Access view and prepopulates the `Mailbox` table before the recordset information is retrieved.

Step 3: Data Binding Process

Our last step for this recipe and the MailMerge application is a drag-and-drop. With the recordset defined, all we need to do is insert data fields from the Bindings panel onto the page.

1. From the Bindings panel, expand the **Employees** recordset.
2. Place the desired data source fields onto the page:
   - Drag the **MailTypeText** field next to the Email Type label.

     Drag the **MailPriorityText** field next to the Email Priority label.

     Drag the **EmailFrom** field next to the From label.

     Drag the **EmailTo** field next to the To label.

     Drag the **EmailCC** field next to the CC label.

     Drag the **EmailSubject** field next to the Subject label.

     Drag the **EmailBody** field to the line below the Body label.

     Drag the **EmailBCC** field in the line below the BCC (Mail Merge Email List) label.

3. Save your page [r8-11].

r8-11

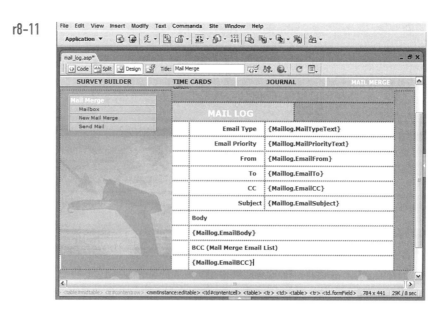

The application is now complete and ready for testing and deployment. Testing a mass emailing application is bit tricky: you want to make sure everything is working properly, but you don't want to annoy your co-workers with too many trial messages. Begin your initial testing by targeting yourself and one or two others on your staff. After you're sure the basic email application is sound, address a larger group, but don't use a mission-critical message. After a few test mailings, check the mail log page and make sure you're getting all the data you need. Remember, these recipes are only a starting point for your own customization and application.

Index

B

VOICES THAT MATTER

VISIT OUR WEB SITE AT WWW.NEWRIDERS.COM

On our web site, you'll find information about our other books, authors, tables of contents, and book errata. You will also find information about book registration and how to purchase our books, both domestically and internationally.

EMAIL US

Contact us at: **nrfeedback@newriders.com**

- If you have comments or questions about this book
- To report errors that you have found in this book
- If you have a book proposal to submit or are interested in writing for New Riders
- If you are an expert in a computer topic or technology and are interested in being a technical editor who reviews manuscripts for technical accuracy

Contact us at: **nreducation@newriders.com**

- If you are an instructor from an educational institution who wants to preview New Riders books for classroom use. Email should include your name, title, school, department, address, phone number, office days/hours, text in use, and enrollment, along with your request for desk/examination copies and/or additional information.

Contact us at: **nrmedia@newriders.com**

- If you are a member of the media who is interested in reviewing copies of New Riders books. Send your name, mailing address, and email address, along with the name of the publication or Web site you work for.

BULK PURCHASES/CORPORATE SALES

The publisher offers discounts on this book when ordered in quantity for bulk purchases and special sales. For sales within the U.S., please contact: Corporate and Government Sales (800) 382-3419 or **corpsales@pearsontechgroup.com**. Outside of the U.S., please contact: International Sales (317) 428-3341 or **international@pearsontechgroup.com**.

WRITE TO US

New Riders Publishing
800 East 96th Street, 3rd Floor
Indianapolis, IN 46240

CALL/FAX US

Toll-free (800) 571-5840
If outside U.S. (317) 428-3000
Ask for New Riders
FAX: (317) 428-3280

New Riders

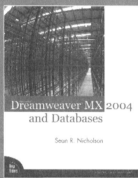